WORLD
COMMUNISM
TODAY

WORLD COMMUNISM TODAY

---★---

BY MARTIN EBON

WHITTLESEY HOUSE

McGRAW-HILL BOOK COMPANY, INC.

NEW YORK : TORONTO

WORLD COMMUNISM TODAY

Copyright, 1948, by MARTIN EBON

*The quality of the materials used in the manufacture
of this book is governed by continued postwar shortages.*

PUBLISHED BY WHITTLESEY HOUSE

A DIVISION OF THE MC GRAW-HILL BOOK COMPANY, INC.

PRINTED IN THE UNITED STATES OF AMERICA

FOREWORD: THE GREAT UNKNOWN

COMMUNISM is the most dynamic political force in the world today. Science has undermined religious faith. Fascism is beaten. Social Democracy is split into rival groups. Monarchy is dead. Parliaments battle outdated procedures. Free enterprise is in retreat.

All over the world there is fear of communism. This is a fear of the unknown. The familiar may be disconcerting. It may even be recognized as dangerous. But it is the vague and shapeless that causes fear or panic. Communism, the great unknown of our time, wears the aura of a supernatural force.

World communism has shrouded itself in secrecy. It seems to work with mysterious and irresistible precision. Secrecy often guards weakness, errors of judgment, internal intrigues, human frailties. By making a fetish of secrecy, communism has made itself look invulnerable. It has also created irrational fear. As a seemingly all-knowing entity, it lends itself to extremes of adherence and opposition.

Communism is hailed as a salvation, or cursed as a menace. Its leaders are called heroes, or criminals. Its organization and plans are presented as the people's will, or as a gigantic conspiracy.

But who are these leaders? What are these plans? What is this organization?

To many of us, communism remains the great unknown, to be fostered or fought, defended or destroyed. But fear is not enough. And uncritical echoing of slogans is not enough. Communism is not something vague and threatening. It is not an enormous entity of supreme evil or supreme good.

Men organize communism. Written words convey its policies. Printing presses produce its propaganda. Artists design its posters. Cables carry

v

its news and instructions. Organizers plan its campaigns. Agitators mount its platforms.

There is agreement within organized communism, and there is conflict. There is obedience, and there is rebellion. Above all, there are men and women who form the leadership and following of communism today. They know hope and frustration, love and hate, revenge and devotion. Human emotions and human experiences have shaped their personalities.

World communism is the sum total of the people who serve it.

World communism is a vast political machine with all the strength and all the weakness of such a construction. It is not abstract. It is not intangible in its dangers or virtues. It is a reality. And a reality, no matter how guarded by secrecy and no matter how elusive, can be observed and recorded.

M. E.

ACKNOWLEDGMENT

THE scope of this book made it imperative for the author to invite the criticism and suggestions of many specialists. Among them were statesmen, scholars, journalists, and other men and women having special regional knowledge and recent first-hand contact with political affairs in the regions under discussion. Much factual data has been obtained from government officials and from functionaries of Communist parties in all parts of the world. Each specialist was consulted on only one country, or one region. Therefore, the author alone is responsible for selection, emphasis and, of course, conclusions. But he desires to acknowledge the generous help of all those who contributed to make this book as comprehensive and accurate as possible.

CONTENTS

I
WORLD - WIDE PATTERN

CHAPTER 1

A Century of Revolution

WHAT ARE the aims of world communism today?

Has it abandoned the idea of global revolution? Is it true that communism and free democracy need not clash, now or later? Will another depression open the way for Communist world domination?

Does Moscow still control Communist parties throughout the world? And just how strong are the Communists? How are they organized; who are their leaders; how do they work? Above all, is Communist use of parliamentary democratic methods only a temporary device, or does it reveal a sincere change of character?

These are questions to which world-conscious men and women seek an answer. Doubts cannot be eliminated by categorical statements, one way or the other. Fears cannot be vanquished by even the most strongly worded pronouncements. Joseph Stalin once described public concern with a Communist world revolution as a "tragic-comical misunderstanding." But Stalin himself has written, in his book *Foundations of Leninism,* "The revolution is spreading beyond the confines of one country; the period of world revolution has begun. The main forces of the revolution are: the dictatorship of the proletariat in one country [the Soviet Union], and the revolutionary movement of the proletariat in all countries."

If these statements seem like contradictions, then what is true and what is false, and who is right and who is wrong? Isn't all this talk about world revolution and the dictatorship of the proletariat dead and forgotten, part of a bygone era? And have we not experienced, during World War II, how courageously Communists fought side by side with the enemies of all dictatorships?

But we cannot look at just one period of Communist development, or at communism in only one region of the world. Like all political concepts, communism has grown. It has been perfected. In our time, with nations

3

interdependent as never before, communism must be viewed as a world-wide factor. Only then can we see it as a whole. Only then can we examine it fully. And we must look beyond our own narrow interests to see clearly what communism is. What, we must ask, is the ultimate aim of communism throughout the world today?

Communist parties everywhere call for social security reforms, for improved housing, for a higher standard of living. These are desirable aims. Can the worker who has made immediate gains through the energetic work of a Communist-led labor union be expected to concern himself with the final goals of communism? Can the member of a minority group, the intellectual who desires a better world, the landless peasant who lives from hand to mouth—can they be expected to look beyond their own immediate interests?

It is only when we examine the principles expressed by distinguished Communist leaders that these questions become pressing. It was V. I. Lenin, the father of modern communism, who wrote that it was desirable "to maneuvre, to utilize the conflicts of interests among one's enemies," and "to temporize and compromise with possible allies." And it was Stalin himself who cited this very statement in *Foundations of Leninism,* to prove that "with revolutionary tactics under the bourgeois regime, reforms are naturally transformed into instruments for disintegrating this regime, into instruments for strengthening the revolution, into a base for the further development of the revolutionary movement." *Foundations of Leninism* is not an old and forgotten Stalin pamphlet. American Communists were urged at their national committee's meeting in July, 1946, to "organize for mass sale" of this book as one of "the chief Marxist classics."

Communist parties today seek leadership in the battle for labor's rights, for improved working conditions, medical care, higher wages, and reasonable prices. These are reforms of great importance to every worker. Communists have been foremost in advocating land reforms in many parts of the world. Was Stalin talking about efforts such as these, when he wrote, "The revolutionary will accept a reform in order to use it as an aid in combining legal work with illegal work, to intensify, under its cover, the illegal work for the revolutionary preparation of the masses for the overthrow of the bourgeoisie."?

We must clarify these contradictions. Truth does not have two heads. This is a time to know.

Communism today is a recognized and powerful political force in all parts of the globe. Veteran Communist leaders are premiers, members of cabinets, outstanding parliamentarians, influential trade-union leaders. As interpreted by Lenin and Stalin, the teachings of Karl Marx form the ideological basis of the Soviet Union and of powerful Communist parties throughout the world.

STRONGER THAN EVER BEFORE

The first century of communism has just ended. One hundred years have passed since the Communist Manifesto was written and published, one hundred years since the European revolutions of 1848 crystallized Communist thought. Wars and economic-political crises were stepping-stones on the century-long road of revolution. The aftermath of war, suffering, and hunger has throughout history kindled the flame of rebellion. World War II has followed this pattern. Today, communism is stronger than ever before.

On May 8, 1945, Premier Stalin hailed the Communist Party of the Soviet Union as the "inspirer and organizer of our victory." Two years earlier, he had announced the dissolution of the Communist International. This action, Stalin said, was directed against the belief that "Communist parties in various countries are allegedly acting, not in the interest of their people, but on orders from outside."

The early postwar years have shown that dissolution of the Communist International strengthened, rather than weakened, the Communist parties of the world. Their devotion to the Soviet Union and its leaders did not suffer, nor did their determination to follow the example of the USSR in working for political and economic changes. National Communist parties have remained loyal to the Soviet Union as the country farthest advanced on the road to communism. Soviet leaders take pride in the progress of their cause throughout the world. Foreign Minister Vyacheslav M. Molotov, who supervised the Communist International in the early 1930's, said on February 6, 1946, that not only "the many millions in the Soviet Union" were following "the leadership of the Communist Party" but that "in other countries, too, it is not a rare thing nowadays to find that the Communists as leaders enjoy the confidence of the broad masses of the people."

Today, at the turn of the first century of communism, the Communist movement is a force conscious of its own strength. What one hundred years ago seemed like the passing thoughts of a few intellectual rebels has grown into a world-wide, eminently successful revolutionary movement.) It was in November, 1847, that the insignificant international Communist League at London asked Karl Marx and Friedrich Engels to draw up a clear-cut, provocative platform. The manuscript was completed two months later. Publication of a French translation coincided with the French Revolution of February 24, 1848, which Engels called "the first great battle between proletariat and bourgeoisie." But the French Revolution of 1848, and simultaneous uprisings in several German states, collapsed. The Manifesto seemed little more than a propaganda pamphlet, composed by just another revolutionary splinter group.

Today, with world communism closer to its goals than ever during the past century, the Communist Manifesto remains the cornerstone of an impressive revolutionary structure. Much more than the highly regarded and rarely read *Das Kapital,* the Manifesto brought basic Communist ideas to the literate masses. In the Manifesto, Marx first expressed the thought that "the history of all hitherto existing society is the history of class struggle" and that "the commercial crises by their periodic return put the existence of the entire bourgeois society on trial, each time more threateningly." And here Marx called "abolition of private property" the main and distinguishing theory of the Communists.

The Manifesto stated, "The proletariat will use its political supremacy to wrest, by degrees, all capital from the bourgeoisie, to centralize all instruments of production in the hands of the state; that is, of the proletariat organized as the ruling class." It is the Manifesto in which Marx gave communism its most rousing slogans: "The Communists disdain to conceal their views and aims. They openly declare that their ends can be attained only by the forcible overthrow of all existing social conditions. Let the ruling classes tremble at a Communist revolution. The proletariat have nothing to lose but their chains. They have a world to win. Workers of the world, unite!"

By a century-long route, modern communism has returned to one of Marx's original concepts, that revolutionary measures "will of course be different in different countries." We can observe today that communism has learned from earlier experiments. It pursues differing national policies in the various nations of the world. For the "most advanced" countries, Marx listed ten points of immediate action:

"(1) Abolition of property in land and application of all rents of land to public purposes; (2) a heavy progressive or graduated income tax; (3) abolition of all rights of inheritance; (4) confiscation of the property of all emigrants and rebels; (5) centralization of credit in the hands of the state, by means of a national bank with state capital and an exclusive monopoly; (6) centralization of the means of communication and transport in the hands of the state; (7) extension of factories and instruments of production owned by the state; the bringing into cultivation of waste lands, and the improvement of the soil generally in accordance with a common plan; (8) equal obligation of all to work; establishment of industrial armies, especially for agriculture; (9) combination of agriculture with manufacturing industries; gradual abolition of the distinction between town and country, by a more equitable distribution of the population over the country; (10) free education for all children in public schools; abolition of child factory labor in its present form; combination of education with industrial production."

The Communist movement today is proud of the heritage of the Communist Manifesto. The Communist Party of Australia stated in February, 1947, in its magazine *Communist Review*, "The fruits of the Communist Manifesto are seen in the Soviet Union, in the mass and in mature Communist parties all over the world, in the advancing tide of struggle by the masses, and in the resultant enormous decline in the power of imperialism. The best way to celebrate the centenary anniversary is to use the Manifesto as never before as a weapon in the final fight against the exploiters."

KARL MARX, IMPATIENT GENIUS

The man who created the basic thoughts to which modern communism confesses allegiance was an impatient genius. He disdained compromise. He was intolerant of those less brilliant than himself. It is fascinating, but hardly rewarding, to speculate how he would view the practices developed by Lenin and Stalin. It is probably best to trace the evolution of revolution, the century of communism up to our present day. Karl Heinrich Marx was European in his background, cosmopolitan in his outlook. Born May 5, 1818, of a middle-class family that had exchanged Judaism for Christianity, he knew the cross winds of French and German culture which swept through his home town of Trier-Trèves. His mother, Henriette Pressburg, had come from the Netherlands.

His father, Heinrich Marx, a not too prosperous lawyer, was a loyal Prussian. To his parents, Karl Marx early became a stranger with a stranger's thoughts. (Henriette Marx wrote once, in her Dutch-tainted German, that "it would have been very much better if Karl had made a lot of capital instead of writing so much about capital.") After leaving the Trier Gymnasium in 1835, Karl spent a riotous student year at Bonn. He moved to Berlin in the fall of 1836. Before leaving to attend the University of Berlin, he became secretly engaged to Jenny von Westphalen, the girl next door. Jenny, a beautiful dark-haired daughter of Prussian nobility, remained deeply attached to Marx throughout the trying years of their later marriage. Their unmarred devotion to each other remained constant during Karl Marx's turbulent career.

The following decade was among the most productive in his whole life. At Berlin, he absorbed—with many misgivings and fits of critical revulsion—the philosophical tenets of George Wilhelm Hegel. Young Hegelians who were Marx's friends shared their idol's belief that the Greek concept of dialectic, viewing life's progress as a battle of opposing contrasts (thesis versus antithesis, which results in synthesis) reveals the root of all development. Karl Marx's later interpretation of the struggle between the classes of society, which must inevitably lead to a classless society, has been regarded as an adaptation of Hegel's dialectic to the realm of materialism.

In Berlin, Marx began to write. Words came in torrents. Not only philosophical essays, or economic theses, but also poetry inspired by his love for Jenny, a humorous novel, and a drama. His poems were rejected by the outstanding German-language poetry magazine of the day, Adalbert von Chamisso's *Deutscher Musen-Almanach*. Soon the torrent found its channel. Marx returned to the Rhineland in 1842. He became editor of the *Rheinische Zeitung* at Cologne. The paper was suppressed by the Prussian authorities when it criticized the Czarist government of Russia. Marx began to read French Socialist literature. In a few months he had completely absorbed French revolutionary thought.

In October, 1843, Karl Marx went to Paris. He became editor of a German-French yearbook. Only one issue of this projected annual was published. It appeared in the spring of 1844 and contained the "Outline of a Criticism of National Economy." The author of this article was Friedrich Engels, a twenty-three-year-old Rhinelander who lived in England. A few months later, he came to Paris. Engels, practical and thorough, and Marx, impractical and brilliant, found much in common. Engels had been born at Barmen on November 28, 1820. He had studied philosophy and gathered practical business experience in Bremen and Berlin. From 1842 on, he had worked in a Manchester textile firm, of which his father was part owner. He was filled with revulsion toward the squalid working conditions he had seen.

Engels's practical experience fused with Marx's theoretical criticism. When the Communist League (originally founded by German exiles as the League of the Just) met in London late in 1847, Engels came from Paris. Marx, forced to leave Paris because of his revolutionary activities for temporary exile in Brussels, also participated. Publication of the Communist Manifesto preceded the French and German uprisings. Marx and Engels rushed back to Cologne. They sought to bolster the German rebellion by republishing the Cologne paper as the *Neue Rheinische Zeitung*. But the German Revolution collapsed. The following years saw the emigration of thousands of freedom-loving Germans from the southwestern provinces, which caused the great wave of German immigration to the United States. Engels had briefly fought with revolutionary troops in the Palatinate. The rebels were driven into Switzerland. Engels returned to England by boat, through the Straits of Gibraltar. Marx, too, found permanent exile in the British Isles.

Years of poverty and overwork followed. *Das Kapital* began to take shape. Marx and his family settled in London. These were decades of tortured existence. Engels, who later became a partner of the Manchester knitting firm of Ermen & Engels, had to help Marx again and again with small sums. On one occasion, Marx (who favored "abolition of all right of inheritance") fell heir to £800. When he wanted to publish a pamphlet on the Cologne trial of Communist leaders, he had to pawn his overcoat to buy paper. At one time, even the shoes and clothes of his children had to be pawned. Marx grew single-minded, egocentric, sometimes morose, and later quite ill. Even Engels almost broke with him when Marx was too absorbed in his own misery to mourn decently the death of Engels's mistress, Mary Burns.

Practically his only steady income came from royalties paid by the *New York Tribune*. Charles A. Dana, the *Tribune*'s editor, asked Marx in August, 1851, for a series of articles on Germany. Engels wrote the series under Marx's name. The articles appeared in the New York paper from October 25, 1851, to October 23, 1852. Later, when Marx grew proficient in writing English, Engels's services as a ghost writer were required less frequently. Marx was paid $5 per article until January, 1853. From then on, he received $10 for each contribution. His dispatches dealt with continental, British, and British Empire affairs. He wrote on one occasion, "The conflict between Russian despotism and Western democracy seems to be everlasting in the Balkans." A few articles later, he said, "From time to time Russia pretends that it has no evil intentions against this or that nation, but merely wishes to protect it. Humanity should be on its guard against claims of protection on the part of Russia." On March 10, 1862, Dana wrote Marx that his articles could no longer be published. News of the American Civil War left no room for the London dispatches of a revolutionary political economist. But Dana did not forget Marx. Ten years later, when Dana was editor of the *New York Sun,* he asked Marx for reports on the Paris Commune.

FIRST INTERNATIONAL: EMOTION AND VANITY

On September 28, 1864, the First International was born. Saint Martin's Hall in London's Soho, Marx wrote, was "filled to suffocation." British and French labor leaders were meeting to discuss joint action. Marx represented German labor. Italian delegates were also present. The meeting agreed that headquarters should be established in London, with subcommittees in all major capitals. Marx was asked to draft a platform acceptable to Socialist labor organizations in Europe and the United States. He could not use the Manifesto for this purpose. It would not appeal to the followers of Pierre Joseph Proudhon in France, Spain, Belgium, and Italy or to the group around the brilliant, egocentric Ferdinand Lassalle in Germany. On October 12, the organization was officially constituted as the International Working Men's Association, and Marx made the inaugural address.

The First International lasted only six years. It was torn between ideological and geographical allegiances. Marx, ailing and impatient, did not tolerate opposition. Other members of the central committee charged him with using autocratic methods. The Latin and Russian Anarchists who followed the emotion-driven, fiery Michael Bakunin accused Marx of Pan-Germanism. Marx, in turn, considered Bakunin a Pan-Slavist.

Bakunin admired Marx as a thinker and a scholar but not as a man. The Russian revolutionary once wrote, "I respected him much for his learning and his passionate and serious devotion—always mixed, however, with personal vanity—to the cause of the proletariat. I sought eagerly his conversation, which was always instructive and clever, when it was not inspired by petty hate which, unfortunately, happened only too often. But there was never any frank intimacy between us. Our temperaments would not permit that. He called me a sentimental idealist, and he was right. And I called him a vain man, faithless and crafty, and I, too, was right." Marx, in turn, denounced Bakunin's program as "a rose-garland of empty motions and insipid improvisation."

Marx was haughty, short-tempered, intolerant. His opponents rallied around Bakunin in their resentment. When the Paris Commune collapsed in 1871, the First International died with it, torn by rivalries and split by factionalism.

Publication of *Das Kapital*'s first volume was a disappointment to Marx. After decades of privation and the exacting labor he had devoted to this book, public reception of so demanding a work was necessarily an anticlimax to its author. After Marx's death, on March 14, 1883, two additional volumes were published by Engels. Modern economic thinking has been profoundly influenced by this work. In our day, when cycles of boom and bust continue to alternate, it calls for restudy and reevaluation. But in current day-to-day Communist activity, *Das Kapital* is almost as dead as Lenin's embalmed body. Communist writers and agitators pay homage to this work but prefer to quote Lenin or Stalin.

Two years before Marx's death, a twenty-seven-year-old man came to London. He was unable to see much of the ailing Marx but had many conversations with Engels. His name was Karl Kautsky. He became the leading theoretician of the Second International. Born in 1854, Kautsky died in obscurity in 1938. In the battle for the heritage of Marxism, he lost to Lenin.

The last decades of the nineteenth century were years of tranquil industrial development. Europe's workers enjoyed relative prosperity. Socialist parties were gaining acceptance as parliamentary groups. In Germany in particular, Chancellor Otto von Bismarck's shrewd, paternalistic policy of social security, old-age benefits, and accident and health insurance took some of the wind out of Socialist sails.

SECOND INTERNATIONAL: EUROPEAN WAR FEVER

On July 14, 1889, one hundred years after the Bastille battle, the Second International was founded during the Paris World's Fair. Its program opposed militarism, favored legal safety for workers, the eight-hour day, and celebration of May Day as a demonstration of labor's strength. The Second International was a very loose organization. Not until 1900 did it manage to set up a permanent secretariat. Delegations represented varying and opposing national interests. It seemed that the workers did have a fatherland after all, or rather quite a number of them. These nationalist trends threatened the delicate cohesion of the Second International. At the same time, a battle between revisionists and ortho-dox Marxists was beginning to reach its peak. The eventual split between the Socialists and the Communists was foreshadowed in the disagreement between Kautsky and Lenin.

Today's international disagreement on an interpretation of democracy has its root in the violent arguments between these two Marxist spokes-men. Communism throughout the world, spear-headed by the Soviet Union on the world's diplomatic scene, adopted Lenin's interpretation. The western, non-Communist world has a conception of democracy akin to that of Kautsky. As early as 1912 Kautsky attacked nondemocratic extremism. In his Stuttgart magazine *Neue Zeit*, he denounced "radical-vulgar Marxism" and "Marxism in its coarsest, most absolute and primitive form." He credited this approach, which he later identified with Lenin's communism as being "so obvious, impressive and popular that it always appears when conditions have made mass instincts ready for it."

World War I put the Second International to its severest test. Would the Socialist parties stand together in an antiwar policy? They did not. Patriotic emotions overruled Marxist principles. The Socialist parties of France, Belgium, and Great Britain backed their nation's policies of national defense. Italy's Socialists, except for an extremist wing originally led by Benito Mussolini, declared themselves neutral. The German and Austrian parties supported a nationalist policy by voting for war credits. As Lenin saw it, the moderate Socialists had betrayed the cause of world revolution. He advocated "immediate transformation of the present imperialist war into civil war." But could Marxist ideals transcend national boundaries? Kautsky wrote later, in his book *Die Internationale*, that the Socialist parties of Germany, Austria, Serbia, and Italy were unable to prevent their governments from entering the war because "the majority of the proletariat had succumbed to the war fever."

THIRD INTERNATIONAL VERSUS "PURE DEMOCRACY"

In September, 1915, at the initiative of the Italian socialists, representatives of eleven nations met in the Swiss village of Zimmerwald. There, at the village inn, Lenin violently attacked the policies of the Second International. He demanded that all Socialist cabinet members of warring nations resign their posts. But the leftist opposition he represented was voted down, 19 to 12. He tried again on Easter, 1916, in the Swiss hamlet of Kienthal, to have his views accepted. His faction was again outvoted. The meetings at Zimmerwald and Kienthal crystallized the split between the moderate Socialists, whom Lenin denounced as "social chauvinists," and the radical advocates of immediate national revolutions.

One year later, Lenin was head of the revolutionary government in Russia. In March, 1919, the Communist Party of Russia called a group of left-wing Socialists together in Moscow. The Third International, the Communist International, was born. Lenin had triumphed. But the voices of accusation would not grow silent. Kautsky opposed the Communist interpretation of democracy. Speaking about the concept of a "dictatorship of the proletariat," he noted that "unfortunately, Marx has refrained from specifying how he imagined such a dictatorship." Kautsky wrote, "Literally, the word means elimination of democracy. But, if we use a literal interpretation, it also means the sole rule of one individual, who is not bound by any law." He accused Lenin of "one-man-rule which differs from despotism because it is regarded not as a permanent state institution but as a temporary emergency rule."

The pedantic Kautsky and his detached vernacular were no match for the violent phamphleteering of Lenin. Where Kautsky pointed an accusing finger, Lenin hurled sticks and stones. In his pamphlet, *The Dictatorship of the Proletariat and the Renegade K. Kautsky*, Lenin called for "a ruthless fight against this renegade-ism, this lack of character, this boot-licking towards opportunism, this unexampled theoretical damnation of Marxism." He wrote that old-fashioned, bourgeois concepts of democracy could not be accepted by determined revolutionaries. "Can there be equality between exploiters and those who are being exploited?" he asked. Lenin's answer was clear-cut:

"The definite basis of dictatorship is suppression *by force* of exploiters as a class, and therefore a *violation* of 'pure democracy.'" The emphasis is Lenin's. The course of the Third International had been charted.

CHAPTER 2

The Seven Strategies

THE END OF World War II opened the seventh phase of international Communist strategy. World communism had outgrown its adolescence. It had become a world-wide force of mature importance. Its leaders were, for the most part, efficient and seasoned organizers, rather than impetuous hotheads. Many of them began where they had left off, years and decades before, when they were forced into prison or exile. The new strategy that they had to translate into action was pliable, subtle, easily adaptable to varying needs.

During the early postwar period, communism was neither on the brink of collapse nor on the threshold of world-wide dominance. It held its ground in eastern Europe, aided by the presence or nearness of Soviet armed forces. It was gaining friends in the Russian-occupied zone of Germany, in Japan, and among colonial peoples. It was fighting a daring battle for lasting power in China and France. It scored scattered successes in Latin America and had entered the battle for the allegiance of peoples in the Near East and Africa. It was trying hard to overcome its limited appeal in the Scandinavian countries, in most parts of the British Commonwealth, and in the United States.

After nearly three decades of organized existence, with many lessons learned and others still to be understood, communism faced the postwar world. And as the armistice documents were signed, as the process of peacemaking began and the nations of the world slowly recovered from the wounds of war, world communism unfolded its Seventh Strategy in a new drive for power and allegiance.

The postwar strategy of communism used wartime gains with revived militancy. The Soviet Union's prestige, the impressive battle performances of the Red Army, and the excellent record of Communist groups in anti-Nazi and anti-Japanese underground warfare—all these positive

15

factors were integrated into the Seventh Strategy of communism. In the clandestine patriot movements, Communists had fought shoulder to shoulder with men who after the war became prominent in the Socialist parties, Catholic parties, and other anti-Nazi and anti-Fascist political organizations. To transform these wartime alliances into peacetime coalitions was the first aim of Communist strategists. To use these coalitions for the execution of Communist-sponsored ideas became their second aim.

NATIONALISM REBORN

After the Nazi-Soviet Pact of 1939 was broken by the German invasion of Russia in June, 1941, Communist parties in Allied countries supported their nations' patriotic efforts. Under the pressure of Nazi occupation and in the general war atmosphere, the nationalist and patriotic spirit of most nations experienced a remarkable renaissance. The Communists adopted this spirit. Deeply rooted in human emotions, patriotism inspired men and women to heroism and persistence of which many had not thought themselves capable. When the war ended, the flame of patriotism continued to blaze with newly found brightness. The peoples of the world, at the end of World War II, were yearning for freedom for their nations as nations, and for themselves as individuals. Democracy had become the keyword of the peace. National consciousness had been reborn. When the Seventh Communist Strategy was formulated, these two concepts were recognized and adapted.

The formal basis for this strategy had been established on May 22, 1943, when Joseph Stalin officially disbanded the Communist International —commonly known by its abbreviation as the Comintern—twenty-four years after its creation in Moscow during the early March days of 1919. Freed of the Comintern framework, Communist parties within the world's nations could adopt a new individuality. By abandoning the Comintern framework, Soviet leaders established a pattern in keeping with basic world-wide trends. Wartime and postwar nationalism left little room for organisms that placed themselves outside and above national allegiances. During the war, Soviet Russia itself had experienced and recognized the immense primitive strength of patriotic sentiment. Speaking to its own people, the Soviet state had emphasized Russian nationalism as threatened by German aggression. By labeling its successful war effort "The Great Patriotic War of the Soviet Union," the Russian government had shown its understanding of the nationalist emotions that World War II had unloosened.

In preparing its Seventh Strategy, communism modified the concept of international class struggle. Instead, it emphasized national class struggles, akin to each other, but nevertheless divided by the frontiers between states. The Seventh Strategy implied that the strata of society do not extend across the globe, boundaryless, like air itself. The new strategy saw proletariat and capitalism as divided into national segments. The class struggle was to continue, but within the environs of each individual nation.

The disbanded Comintern had been tightly organized. Inevitably, it had also been rigid. With the Comintern dissolved, its leaders were nevertheless anxious to preserve international Communist coordination. Otherwise, the use of national Communist parties as an integral part of Soviet foreign policy would have been jeopardized. But coordination remained assured when old-time leaders, many of whom had spent the war years in Moscow, returned to their countries of origin. Among them were functionaries who had stood high in the Comintern hierarchy. Georgi Dimitrov, for eight years Comintern president, became premier of Bulgaria. Palmiro Togliatti, who for many years had lived in exile under the pseudonym of "Ercoli," returned to his Italian homeland. Klement Gottwald accompanied the Czechoslovak government from Moscow to Prague, where he became its premier. Maurice Thorez arrived in Paris to resume his post as secretary-general of the French Communist Party. Wilhelm Pieck returned to the ruins of Berlin. Boleslaw Bierut assumed the leadership of the Polish government. Sanzo Nozaka ended two decades of exile from Japan. Otto Kuusinen became president of the newly created Karelo-Finnish Republic of the Soviet Union. Matyas Rákosi reentered Budapest, where he had been a prisoner for many years. Li Li-san accompanied the Soviet Army into Manchuria. Three energetic women made their way into, or closer to, their homelands: Tsola Dragoitcheva parachuted into Bulgaria; Anna Pauker helped reorganize the Romanian government; and Dolores Ibarruri entered liberated France, thus moving nearer to Spain, the country of her birth.

The return of these expatriates did not lack dramatic pathos. In many cases, these men and women arrived in countries they had not seen in years and decades. These, after all, were their homelands. They returned, free and prominent, to nations where, in many instances, they had been ruthlessly persecuted, where friends and associates had been tortured and killed. The Seventh Strategy of world communism opened new vistas for them. In addition to the cause of social revolution, they were now able to espouse the causes of national strength and grandeur, with their age-old emotional links to blood and soil.

In the Slav nations, the Communists appeared as apostles of Slav unity under the guidance of Russia. In Italy, prominent party members were vocal in pressing their nation's territorial claims against Austria. In France, the cultural and economic renaissance of this leading western European country became a byword of Communist appeals. Throughout Latin America, Communist speakers sided with ultra-nationalist elements in denouncing United States influence.

FROM OPTIMISM TO OPPORTUNISM

The more prominent Communist leaders of each important nation had themselves played a part in formulating this regionally pliable strategy. Nearly all of them could look back on previous tactical changes throughout the history of organized communism. As they installed themselves in government buildings or party offices, these leaders were able to evaluate their peacetime tasks in the light of early experiences. Major fluctuations in policy can be traced, roughly, by listing the following over-all strategies, which were successively adopted during three decades of Communist world activity:

The First Strategy (1918 *to* 1920): *Immediate World Revolution.* After the downfall of the Czarist regime of Russia, the collapse of the Austro-Hungarian Empire, and the German Revolution of 1917, world communism arose with youthful vigor and unbridled ambition. World revolution seemed just around the corner. Gregory Zinoviev, first chairman of the Comintern's executive committee, was the exponent of extreme optimism. On June 12, 1919, he wired Béla Kun, then Communist dictator of Hungary, that "before long the whole of the civilized world will become Communist." Giving itself just a year in which to convert the world, the Comintern's executive committee stated at Petrograd, "The Great Communist International was born in 1919. The Great International Soviet Republic will be born in 1920."

The Comintern was booming. Communist parties in Finland, Switzerland, Sweden, Norway, Bulgaria, Italy, Slovakia, and France affiliated with the Third International. Not only Europe, but America too, seemed ready to adopt the new cause. [The ebullient Zinoviev, welcoming the creation of a Communist Party in the United States, saw in this event an "augury of the fact that the world proletarian revolution will embrace not only old Europe but that it is already stretching out across the ocean and embracing the richest capitalist country: America." Speaking at Petrograd on September 20, he grew lyrical with enthusiasm. "The birth of the American Communist Party and its growth," Zinoviev called out, "is the first swallow which foretells the coming of a world-wide Communist spring."

[To hasten world-wide events so confidently forecast, the Comintern called for concerted mass action. The platform adopted by the First Congress of the Communist International, which met in Moscow from March 2 to 6, 1919, urged "direct collision with the bourgeois state machine in open combat." Pointing to the possibility of more subtle techniques, this document stated that "subject to this aim are all other methods, for instance revolutionary utilization of the bourgeois parliamentary system."

But only one year later, at the time of the Second Congress of the Comintern in July, 1920, a note of caution could be detected. Poland was about to repulse the Red Army. Elsewhere, the world showed itself unready for immediate revolution.

The Second Strategy (1921 *to* 1927): *Agitation Instead of Armed Revolt.* When the Third Comintern Congress met in Moscow in 1921, events dictated a conciliatory line. Zinoviev's flamboyant promises had been premature. Béla Kun had been beaten in Hungary. The German Communists had lost their battles for regional and national power. Fascism, instead of communism, was about to take hold in Italy. Elsewhere, newly created Communist parties were desperately trying to gain strength. They were quite unready to overthrow governments by revolution.

Then, too, the Russian Communists had domestic difficulties. Rash application of orthodox Marxist principles had dislocated the Soviet Union's economy. Lenin had to adopt a moderate New Economic Policy. To succeed in their reconstruction efforts at home, the Russian leaders had to get along with the world they called "capitalist." Foreign experts were needed to aid in the USSR's industrial expansion. Early in 1921, Leonid Kamenev reported to the Tenth Congress of the Russian Communist Party at Petrograd on "The Soviet Republic in a Capitalist

Environment." He tried to give his unorthodox suggestions an orth-
dox Marxist sugar coating. Cooperation with non-Soviet nations woul-
strengthen Soviet Russia, he said. It would thus be "merely a ne-
form of the struggle" for the "consolidation of communism." Lenin an-
Kamenev finally gained acceptance for this new policy of establishin-
economic—and diplomatic—relations with other countries. It was inevitable that these compromise tactics should also be reflected in th-
second over-all strategy of the Comintern.

Lenin had to battle impatient world revolutionaries who assembled in-
Moscow during June and July, 1921. There was trouble at the Third-
Congress. Various non-Russian delegates disagreed with the Moscov-
leadership. Moscow nevertheless imposed its will. Lenin fought untiringly to press for cooperation with the Socialist parties. World conditions, he said, no longer permitted an "elementary and chaotic rush for
ward." History had given the non-Communist world "a fairly long breath-
ing spell," Lenin noted, and the Communist movement was "not yet on-
the threshold of one realization of its ultimate aim: the seizing of power
on a world scale, the world revolution." A period of readjustment
was to begin. Regardless of earlier revolutionary hope, capitalism and
communism might have to share the world for longer than had been
anticipated.

Karl Radek, the brilliant professional revolutionary, translated Lenin's
keynote speech into practical strategic formulas. The party had not yet
reached the masses to the full. But the masses had to be enrolled in the
world-wide struggle. How was that to be done? He wanted revolutionary
agitation, rather than "premature action." Radek called out, "Revolutionary agitation is struggle, revolutionary propaganda is struggle, and
so are underground organizations, the military training of the proletariat,
party schools, demonstrations, uprisings."

The second strategy of communism reflected a lesson learned: only
adequate preparation through international propaganda could open the
way for world revolution.

The Third Strategy (1928 *to* 1934): *Revolutionary Extremism as
Protection for Russia.* Following the Radek formula, world communism
in the mid-twenties passed through a phase of heavy agitation. To the
more impetuous Communist leaders, the results of this technique proved
disappointing. Meanwhile, the Russian Communists were absorbed in
personal internal affairs. Lenin had died. Stalin emerged as the pro-

tagonist of "socialism in a single country." He suggested that the strength and safety of the Soviet Union was the strongest basis for international Communist activity. Stalin and Leon Trotsky clashed. Both were quoting Lenin at each other. They engaged in heated, long-winded, and highly abstract disputes. Their discussions were reflected in the party press throughout the world. Communist literature became almost impenetrable to the uninitiated.

Trotsky, champion of "permanent revolution" as a process leading successively from democracy to socialism and finally to a classless society, ran into a massive barrage of Stalin's ideological guns. The merits of their discussions were overshadowed by the fact that the two men were fighting a personal battle for power. Who was to inherit Lenin's mantle? The answer came when Trotsky went into exile and Stalin emerged as undisputed ruler of the Soviet Union and leader of the Comintern. To be accused of Trotskyism was, from then on, high treason among the followers of the Third International.

The Sixth Comintern Congress of July and August, 1928, fully implemented Stalin's ideas. There had been no Congress since the fifth meeting, in 1924. During these four years, Stalin had consolidated his position. Zinoviev and Kamenev, who had sided with Trotsky, had disappeared. Nikolai Bukharin, who had supported Stalin, was the central figure of the Sixth Congress. The two men collaborated in drafting the official constitution of the Communist International, which was adopted by the Congress.

Stalin's view of the Soviet Union as the main basis of world communism was expressed in the programs and resolution of the Comintern. A large part of this document dealt with the specter of what was called a future capitalist war against the Soviet Union. It said:

"It is essential that attention should be concentrated on the defense of the USSR, which is menaced by the gathering forces of imperialism; we must stimulate coordinated work which can turn a war against the USSR into a war against the imperialist governments, and thus into a war for the defense of the USSR."

Attack being the best form of defense, Communist parties all over the world immediately adopted a new militant revolutionary policy. The Russian Communist Party was no longer a segment, no matter how powerful, of the Communist International. The International itself now was a weapon of the Soviet Union, which could be used for defensive or offensive purposes. The Comintern constitution emphasized that the strength of Russia was paramount. The Communist parties of the world had become foreign outposts of the USSR.

This era of Communist policy, called in this volume the Third Strategy, was labeled by the Soviet leaders themselves as the "third period." It lasted from 1928 to 1934 and divided the Communists more strongly than ever from moderate left-wing and labor groups. Socialists, Social Democrats, and liberal trade unionists were denounced as traitors. Again, world revolution was just around the corner. The right wings of the Communist parties attempted to resist this trend. They recalled the errors of impatience which the First Strategy had brought, and which had been only partly remedied by the Second Strategy. Bukharin, representing the right wing, was forced by Stalin to resign his post as Comintern president. No new president was appointed. Vyacheslav M. Molotov, then president of the Council of People's Commissars, also took over Comintern affairs. In the Soviet Union itself, the first Five-Year Plan became a vast national effort to strengthen Russia's position.

The Fourth Strategy (1935 to 1938): United Front. It took the Comintern more than a year to realize that Adolf Hitler, Germany's ambitious dictator, had to be taken seriously. His regime came to power on January 30, 1933. In January, 1934, the Comintern finally abandoned its Third Strategy of extremist-revolutionary technique. It immediately pressed for a working coalition among the Communists, Socialists, and all other anti-Nazi forces. This was an abrupt change, dictated by the very real fear of Soviet leaders that Hitler's aggressive nationalist regime might translate its rantings against communism into actual military attacks on the USSR. Russia's leaders wanted the rest of the world on their side. This was no time to alienate possible allies. The Socialists, whom the Communists had only a few weeks before denounced as "social fascists," as "imposters," as "knaves of the bourgeoisie," hardly had time to adjust themselves to this sudden change.

The Popular Front government of France was a striking illustration of Communist ability to cooperate when told to do so. There was also a shift in Comintern top leadership. The experienced and colorful Georgi Dimitrov took over as president in 1935. Dimitrov had won world-wide admiration for his courageous defense at the Reichstag trials, staged by the Nazis in 1933.

Then, in the fall of 1936 and throughout 1937, other trials took place in Moscow. Among the defendants were Zinoviev, Kamenev, Bukharin, and Radek, as well as a host of other Russian officials accused of treason. For months, these Moscow trials absorbed world attention. The prosecution charged the defendants with conspiracy, linking them with Nazi Germany and Trotsky. The defendants startled the world with exceedingly frank confessions and were executed or imprisoned.

[Stalin's control and policy remained triumphant. Communist strategy was coordinated with Soviet foreign affairs, then in the hands of the moderate, westernized Maxim Litvinov. Russia joined the League of Nations and concluded alliances with France and Czechoslovakia. Everywhere, Communists cooperated actively with other leftist groups. Civil War in Spain further emphasized the split between fascism and the rest of the world. The Communists were anxious to show that they were on the side of the angels, respectable and democratic.]

[*The Fifth Strategy* (1939 *to* 1940): *"Imperialist War."* The change from extremist-revolutionary protection of Russia to a popular front policy had been rapid. But it could not compare with the propagandistic somersault that followed the Soviet-German Pact of August, 1939. World War II began immediately afterward with the attack on Poland. The blind loyalty of Communist supporters was put to its severest test. Those who had been violently anti-Nazi were suddenly forced to help the Germans by sabotaging the war effort of the Western nations. France, where the Communist Party had enjoyed its highest prestige during the Popular Front period, was particularly affected.

For a year and a half, the Communist press was filled with violent denunciations of British and American leaders. This world-wide spectacle of party discipline and hypocrisy ended, as abruptly as it had begun, with Germany's attack on the Soviet Union, on June 22, 1941.]

[*The Sixth Strategy* (1941 *to* 1945): *United War Effort.* In many respects, the war period marked a return to the "united front" policy. There were, however, important variations. The Comintern had suspended the class struggle. [The charge of imperialism, leveled against the western powers during all previous strategic phases, was dropped. Strikes were no longer regarded as legitimate tools in the hands of the working class. The Communists and Soviet Russia shared with the Allied nations the desire to defeat the Axis quickly and completely.

Communist propaganda stressed United Nations unity. Military effectiveness in the struggle against the Axis powers became paramount.

Communist units played a prominent, and often leading, role in underground movements. This was especially true in France, Italy, Greece, and Yugoslavia.

At the same time, the Communist parties did not fail to press special aims of the Soviet Union. When, in 1943, the western powers believed that establishment of a second front against the German-occupied European continent would be militarily premature, this policy did not coincide with the wishes of the Soviet leaders. Through its diplomatic and military representatives, the USSR pressed for a second front, while Communist groups attempted to create public pressure in the same direction.

As victory approached, the Teheran Conference among President Roosevelt, Prime Minister Churchill, and Premier Stalin was used by the Communists as a symbol of Allied cooperation. Communist emphasis on this pact underlined that it assigned most of eastern Europe and the Balkans, as well as certain Far Eastern areas, to the Soviet Union's sphere of influence.

Throughout the war, Communist strategy played up the role of Soviet-backed military movements throughout the world. The Chinese Communist armies, the Yugoslav Liberation Movement, and the Greek National Liberation Front (EAM) were among the forces held up by the Communist press and defended against all criticism. The most celebrated case was the clash between Marshal Josip Broz-Tito of Yugoslavia and the war minister and guerrilla leader Draja Mikhailovitch, who was later executed by the Tito regime.

Thus, the postwar policy of communism was already perceptible in outline during the war. But it remained for the Seventh Strategy to reveal clearly the aims of communism in a world where the Soviet Union occupies a commanding position.

The Seventh Strategy (1946 *and After*): *National Revolutions.* Stalin's concept of "socialism in one country" was extended during the postwar period. If applicable to Russia, this Stalinist version of Marxism could also be applied outside the Soviet Union, on a country-by-country basis. Thus each Communist party could adapt its policy to regional needs. Communism was even able to champion contradictory nationalist causes, wherever they did not interfere with over-all interests of Soviet foreign policy.

With the Comintern disbanded, there was, of course, no official announcement of a change in strategy. But the world could quickly observe the spectacle of national Communist parties at odds with each other.

Following a nationalist policy, the Communist-dominated government of Poland claimed the Teschen area, which the prewar Warsaw regime had torn away from Czechoslovakia. The Czechoslovak Communist Party, no less patriotic than its Warsaw counterpart, claimed Teschen for the sovereignty of Prague.

Other intra-Communist issues arose, which found their way into the columns of the party press. While Communists all over the world backed Yugoslav claims to the Adriatic port of Trieste, Palmiro Togliatti, chief of the Italian Communists, temporarily favored an all-Italian Trieste. For this, Togliatti was sharply denounced by Jacques Duclos of the French Communist Party. French Communists advocated that the Rhineland and Ruhr regions of Germany be internationalized, with France playing a leading part in their administration. Germany's Communists were equally adamant in claiming these regions as part of an indivisible Reich.

In spite of these striking instances of clashing nationalist interests affecting Communist parties, Soviet policy requirements remained uppermost. Wherever the USSR had a decisive say in territorial arrangements, regional Communist parties denounced nationalist causes. Hungarian Communists, for instance, opposed their country's territorial claims against Romania and Czechoslovakia. German Communists ignored Polish annexation of eastern German territories and the deportation of Germans from Poland and Czechoslovakia. And Polish Communists defended Russia's absorption of eastern Polish regions.

These antagonisms between regional European parties became a danger to the international coordination of Communist policies. In September, 1947, nine Communist parties met in Poland under the guidance of the Communist Party of the Soviet Union to arrange for closer integration of policies which had begun to be overshadowed by nationalist sentiment. Representatives of the Communist parties of the Soviet Union, Yugoslavia, Bulgaria, Romania, Hungary, Poland, France, Czechoslovakia, and Italy signed a resolution denouncing as "incorrect and harmful" any "division between Communist parties." They resolved that an Information Bureau be established at Belgrade. To counteract "disunity of Communist parties," the Belgrade Bureau was to "organize and exchange experience and, in case of necessity, coordinate the activity of Communist parties on foundations of mutual agreement. The Information Bureau also began publication of a new Communist organ as a means of weekly policy guidance.

The new Information Bureau guaranteed that nationalist aspirations such as the latent disagreement between Yugoslavia and Bulgaria regarding the Macedonian region would be subordinated to the interest of the Soviet Union and world communism. But the nationalist aspects of the Seventh Strategy were also expressed at the September conference. The nine parties signed a manifesto stating that Communists "must grasp in their hands the banner of national independence and sovereignty in their own countries." The "united front" facet of the Seventh Strategy was noticeable in the phrase that Communists "place themselves at the head of all forces ready to defend the cause of national honor and independence."

The Seventh Strategy of world communism revived many aspects of the "third phase." Again there was strong emphasis on the security and safety of the Soviet Union. Russian fear of attack by western powers, which had been almost an obsession in the Moscow of 1927, was revived. As a result, the Seventh Strategy was largely designed to weaken the western powers, particularly the United States and Great Britain.

During the immediate postwar period, Communist spokesmen favored the rapid departure of United States troops from Europe, the withdrawal of American units from China, the reduction of British forces in the Near East. Communist papers in various parts of the world prominently displayed news of unsettled conditions in the United States, thus helping to reduce American prestige in other parts of the world. The phrase "American imperialism" entered the Communist vocabulary. The cause of peoples in dependent areas was taken up again. The Soviet Union and the Communist doctrine were pictured as forces of liberation for oppressed nations.

Anti-United States propaganda reached its peak in the manifesto of the nine European Communist parties in the fall of 1947, which compared America with Nazi Germany. "In the same way as the appeasement policy of Munich led to Hitler's aggression," the manifesto stated, "today concessions to the United States of America and the imperialist camp may cause its instigators to grow even more shameless and aggressive."

The Communist parties of the world, now organized on a strictly national basis and using ultra-nationalist appeals, had again become outposts of the Soviet Union. But these parties were no longer the weak minority groups of the prewar era. In country after country, they had achieved prestige, power, and control. And the nation to which they looked with undiminished admiration, the Soviet Union, credited its own rise to world power and influence to the wisdom and persistence of its Communist Party.

II

EASTERN EUROPE

★

CHAPTER 3

USSR: Center of Strength

HERE IN the Soviet Union, in the land of the dictatorship of the proletariat, the fact that not a single important political or organizational question is decided by our Soviet and other mass organizations without directions from the Party must be regarded as the highest expression of the leading role of the Party." Thus, in the current edition of *Problems of Leninism,* does Joseph Stalin outline the functions of the Communist Party of Russia. The overwhelming control position of the party is also recognized in Article 126 of the Soviet Union's constitution of 1936, which specifies:

"The most active and politically conscious citizens in the ranks of the working class and other strata of the toilers are united in the Communist Party of the USSR. It is the vanguard of the toilers in the struggle to strengthen the Socialist system. And it represents the leading core of all organizations, both public and state."

Russia's Communist Party is the center of strength in world communism today. It took the initiative in establishing and later dissolving the Third International. Its experiences during the Bolshevik revolution have influenced Communist parties everywhere. The strength of the Russian party, its access to state resources, and its prestige as the first party to establish a dictatorship of the proletariat assured it decisive influence over Communist parties throughout the world. Communist spokesmen everywhere never tire in their praise of Soviet policy. They consistently view the Communist Party of the Soviet Union as the center of world Communist strength. Among Communist movements, the Russian party is clearly dominant.

How did it achieve this dominance? How did it happen that Marxist theories were applied in a country so much less industrially advanced than the nations of western Europe? What is the strength and role of the Communist Party of the USSR today?

A PARTY OF FANATICAL REBELS

Socialist groups of western Russia, inspired by the development of the Second International, met at Minsk in 1898. They founded the Russian Social Democratic Labor Party. Two years later, Vladimir Ilyitch Ulianov (Lenin) returned from Siberian exile to Europe. Lenin began to publish a Marxist magazine, *Iskra* (Spark) outside Russia. In the summer of 1903, the Social Democrats held their Second Congress in London. Here the exclusive character of the future Communist Party was decided by Lenin. He advocated that the party should accept only members willing to participate actively in revolutionary work. He rejected the idea of dues-paying members who gave merely indirect support.

Lenin wanted a small party of devoted and fanatical rebels. His single-mindedness split the Russian Social Democrats. At London, Lenin received the support of the majority of the delegates. Consequently, his followers were called Bolshevists (derived from *bolshinstvo,* majority) ; and his opponents became known as Menshevists (derived from *menshinstvo,* minority). The split in the Russian party dismayed the Second International. Writing in *Iskra* on May 15, 1904, Kautsky accused the Bolsheviks of stubbornness and said, "the responsibility for this ill-fated discord rests directly with Lenin."

There was much in this split that continues to influence Communist internal party practices to this day. The Mensheviks advocated freedom of criticism and consideration for minority opinion. They accused Lenin of creating minority "serfdom" within the party. Although Lenin then advocated total majority rule, he himself did not submit to party discipline when the Mensheviks gained a majority in 1904. He called a separate Bolshevik Congress and began publication of an anti-Menshevik magazine.

The Russian Revolution of 1905 healed the rift between Bolsheviks and Mensheviks temporarily. Russia's defeat in the war with Japan was followed by strikes, demonstrations, and clashes with police in various parts of western Russia. The revolt was spontaneous. The Marxists called it a "democratic-bourgeois" uprising. The revolution collapsed, but the Czarist government saw itself forced to permit a parliament, the Duma, to be created. The Mensheviks were pleased with this first step toward a parliamentary democracy. The Bolsheviks, according to the current official

History of the Communist Party of the Soviet Union, "regarded the Duma as an impotent appendage of tsardom, as a screen for the evils of tsardom." But a year later, Lenin called boycott of the Duma a "mistake." He noted that "when the Duma assembles, opportunities arise for carrying on useful agitation both from within the Duma and, in connection with it, outside." Consequently, as the official party history puts it, the Bolshevik delegates began "to transform the tsarist body into a platform from which they exposed the annexationist policy of tsardom."

The struggle within the Russian Marxist movement greatly disturbed the Second International. The powerful German Social Democratic Party supported the Russians financially, but there were constant intrigues as to who should get what, and how much. The scholarly Kautsky did not approve of Lenin's all-or-nothing-at-all technique. Lenin, who was then living in Switzerland and dependent on support by the German party, bitterly resented his dependence.

THE REVOLUTION, STEP BY STEP

As we look back on the Russian Revolution of 1917 and the rise of the Soviet Union, events tend to merge with one another. Not only for the sake of historical accuracy, but also as a clarification of present-day Communist political technique, developments leading to Communist victory in Russia need to be disentangled. We shall therefore view them, one by one, in chronological order (all dates correspond to the old style calendar).

February 27, 1917: Workers and soldiers demonstrate against the Czarist government in a spontaneous rebellion against corruption and inefficient administration. A Soviet (Council) of Workers Deputies is formed, in which the Bolshevik, Menshevik, and Social Revolutionary parties participate.

March 2: Yielding to pressure from the populace and his own generals, Czar Nicholas II abdicates in favor of his brother, Grand Duke Michael Romanov.

March 3: Michael Romanov hesitates to accept the throne, deciding to leave the decision up to the forthcoming constituent assembly. This hesitation ends the Czarist rule and places supreme government authority in a provisional government formed under Prince G. Lvov.

March 14: Alexander F. Kerensky, a Social Revolutionary member of the Duma (parliament) and vice-president of the new Soviet, enters the provisional government. The government receives the conditional support of the Soviet. Lenin cables the Bolsheviks from Switzerland: "No confidence or support whatever for the new government. Particularly beware of Kerensky." The Bolshevik members of the Soviet refrain from backing the provisional regime, although it has been recognized by the United States, France, Great Britain, and Italy.

April 3: Lenin arrives on a sealed train at Petrograd's Finland Station, accompanied by Radek, Zinoviev, and Kamenev. He had crossed Germany from Switzerland, traveling with the agreement of the German general staff, which hoped that the Bolshevik propaganda would lead to a separate peace by Russia. (Erich von Ludendorff, German chief of staff, stated later in his memoirs that Lenin's trip "was justified from the military point of view: the fall of Russia was a necessity.")

April 24: First open meeting of the Bolshevik Party since its foundation. Delegates representing some 80,000 party members hear Lenin's demand that power be withdrawn from the government and transferred to the Soviets. The party adopts the slogan: "All power to the Soviets!"

May 6: The revolutionary parties, excluding the Bolsheviks, join the government and issue a policy statement. The government has already decreed full amnesty for political prisoners (which facilitated the return to Petrograd of Lenin, Trotsky, and Stalin); abolished capital punishment; established trial by jury; erased national, religious, and class limitations; and legislated women's suffrage and the eight-hour day. (Lenin wrote at this time, "We must profit by this liberty to establish by force of arms a dictatorship of the proletariat.")

July 3: The collapse of a Russian offensive stirs the antiwar feeling of the masses. The Bolsheviks organize large-scale demonstrations in Petrograd, which coincide with the German counteroffensive. The Bolshevik move is suppressed by the Kerensky government. (The Petrograd law court asserts that Lenin had "formed a group within the Bolshevik Party which, with the object of assisting countries at war with Russia," had "organized propaganda both in the army and the civilian population." Lenin flees to Finland.)

July 24: A second coalition government is formed under Kerensky. At this time, the rapid application of liberal laws has resulted in a critical weakening of government authority in agricultural regions and among the troops.

August 25: The Third Mounted Army Corps, commanded by General Kornilov, moves on Petrograd, ostensibly to halt a planned Bolshevik uprising. Red Guards and sailors meet him outside the city.

August 30: Kerensky, facing the possibility of military coups d'état from the right (Kornilov) and from the left (Lenin), manages to suppress Kornilov's rebellion with the help of the Red Guards mobilized by the Soviet. The Bolsheviks skillfully hold their parts of the Red Guards together, in preparation for a future coup.

October 10: Lenin, who has returned to Petrograd from Finland, tells a meeting of the Bolshevik central committee that "an armed uprising is inevitable." He asks the party organizations to make all necessary preparations for an insurrection. Representatives are sent to various regions to prepare the revolts. Among those who receive such assignments are Vyacheslav M. Molotov, Klementy E. Voroshilov, and Andrei A. Zhdanov.

October 23: The Bolshevik revolutionary military committee sends commissars to military units and to key points in and around Petrograd to agitate in favor of the insurrection. Bolshevik representatives also give instructions to the crews of the warships "Aurora" and "Zarya Svobody."

October 24: Lenin assumes personal direction of the uprising.

October 25: Bolshevik units attack and occupy the railway stations, the post and telegraph offices, the ministries, and the State Bank of Petrograd, the offices of the provisional government and of the preparliament. The cruiser "Aurora" fires on the Winter Palace, the government headquarters. The Bolsheviks break up the preparliament and storm the Winter Palace. The Second All-Russian Congress of Soviets opens at 10:45 P.M. at Petrograd. The Bolsheviks are in command of the city, and particularly of the Smolny Building, where the congress is held. According to the party's official history, the Bolsheviks receive "an overwhelming majority at the congress."

FIXED PENDULUM

This chronology helps to clarify the events leading up to the strikingly successful coup d'état of the Bolsheviks in Petrograd, later appropriately named Leningrad. Lenin, in staging his revolution, had channeled the largely undefined revolutionary sentiment into a Bolshevik revolution. The pendulum of popular rebellion had swung farther and farther to the left extreme ever since the abdication of the Czar. When it reached its farthest point, Lenin seized it and held it there. Russia's Communist Party fixed the pendulum of history at the point it reached on October 24, 1917.

With the capital city in their hands, the Bolsheviks spent the next four months in military action which assured their control throughout the land. The October party congress created the first Soviet government: the Council of People's Commissars. In order to defeat its internal enemies without the strain of an external war, the young Soviet regime signed the Treaty of Brest-Litovsk with Germany, although its conditions were shockingly severe.

The Bolshevik Party Congress of March, 1918, adopted the name Russian Communist Party (Bolsheviks). This was done at Lenin's personal suggestion, and to establish a phraseological bridge between the Communist League of Marx and Engels, and the Russian Bolsheviks—a bridge that spanned three quarters of a century of relatively moderate social democratic activity.

In an attempt to overthrow the Bolshevik government, four of the Allied powers (Great Britain, France, the United States, and Japan) landed troops on various parts of Soviet Russian territory. Lenin called for "war communism," by appealing to the patriotic feelings of his countrymen. The Allied powers were defeated, largely because such obvious foreign intervention aroused the strong nationalist emotions of the Red Army soldiers.

The Eighth Party Congress of 1918 heard Lenin defend his decree on division of land among the "middle peasants" and "poor peasants." Marxists abroad regarded this as a violation of the principles of Marx. Socialization of large estates was considered easier than eventual socialization of small estates. This interpretation suggested that Lenin was retrogressing, rather than progressing, on the road to Marxism. But Lenin was influenced by his desire to gain the peasant's backing. The Red Army was a peasant army. At that time, the Russian Communist Party had 314,000 members. Lenin initiated the first purge of the party. He had not forgotten his principle that the party should be a core of devoted Communist fanatics, rather than an organizational catch-all of dues-paying members.

From then on, the history of the Communist Party of the Soviet Union is identical with the history of the Soviet Union itself. The large literature, representing various views, that exists on this subject permits us to limit attention in this volume to structural-organizational aspects of the party's evolution rather than historical developments. (Trotsky's role and personality are largely ignored in this book, since they have no influence in world communism today. His writings have been consulted as sources and are partly listed in the bibliography.) The principles of Communist Party organization advocated by Lenin have not materially changed to this day. The party is tightly disciplined, efficiently organized, and thoroughly indoctrinated. During World War II, requirements for admission to the party were relaxed. But they were tightened again as soon as the war had ended.

SIX MILLION PARTY MEMBERS

The 8,000 original members of the Bolshevik Party of 1905 had grown to more than half a million early in 1921. The first purge under Lenin removed 175,000 persons from the membership lists. There was an effort to have at least half of the membership composed of workers. A special drive very nearly reached this goal in 1925, when the party had 800,000 members. This figure rose rapidly, from 1,000,000 in 1926, to 1,300,000 in 1928. In 1929, after Leon Trotsky had been eliminated by Stalin, 160,000 persons were expelled from the party. But new admissions more than made up for this loss.

By 1930, the party had 1,852,000 members. Between 1934 and 1939, well over 200,000 persons were expelled from the party's ranks. This period coincided with the large-scale purges that followed the sensational Moscow trials. Party ranks were filled rapidly during World War II. By 1943, membership figures exceeded 4,600,000. In 1947, the number of party members and candidates for party membership reached 6,000,000. Membership requires endorsement by three party members. Thorough knowledge of party literature and theories is required.

Although the Communist Party is described here as a separate entity, it cannot be divorced from the Soviet government. All top government executives are leading party members. A Soviet textbook, *The Soviet Administrative Law*, written in 1946, states that "the Communist Party through its members working in the government agencies, guides their work and directs their activities."

WHO'S WHO IN THE POLITBUREAU?

Party authority begins at the top, in the Politbureau (political bureau) of the party's central committee. In 1947, the members of the Politbureau were:

Joseph V. Stalin, premier and secretary-general of the Communist Party.

Vyacheslav M. Molotov, foreign minister.

Andrei A. Zhdanov, deputy secretary-general of the Communist Party, secretary of the party's Leningrad committee.

Georgi M. Malenkov, secretary of the central committee of the Communist Party.

Klementy E. Voroshilov, marshal of the Soviet Union.

Lazar M. Kaganovitch, minister of the building materials industry, secretary of the Ukrainian Communist Party (reputedly Stalin's brother-in-law).

Nikolai M. Shvernik, president of the supreme council of the USSR.

Lavrenti P. Beria, minister of the interior (previously head of the NKVD, the Soviet secret police).

Nikita S. Khrushchev, chairman of the council of ministers of the Ukrainian Republic.

Anastas I. Mikoyan, minister of foreign trade.

Alexei A. Andreyev, minister of agriculture.

Nikolai A. Voznesensky, minister of production and industry.

Alexei N. Kosygin, premier of the Russian Soviet Socialist Republic.

Nikolai Bulganin, deputy defense minister.

Foreign Minister Molotov should be regarded as Stalin's logical successor to the premiership, and Zhdanov is likely to become secretary-general of the Communist Party in case of Stalin's death. While the Politbureau is a policy-making body, the Orgbureau (organizational bureau) is concerned with questions of internal party administration. The central committee is served by a permanent and anonymous staff of experts. During the period of the purges, in the 1930's, a special revisional commission spoke very highly of the central committee's secretariat. It called the committee a "firm, ideologically galvanized organization, composed of tried and theoretically accomplished Bolsheviks, who have gone through the school of struggle against class enemies and their agents inside the party."

EIGHTEEN MILLION YOUNG COMMUNISTS

Large, and less exclusive in character, is the Communist Youth League, the *Komsomol*. Young men and women from the ages of fifteen to twenty-six may belong to it. Thus the party can count on the services of devoted adolescents and energetic young people throughout the length and breadth of the Soviet Union. Andrei A. Zhdanov served as Komsomol secretary before he became Stalin's deputy in the Communist Party itself. The Komsomol secretary is appointed by the Politbureau. To assure strict adherence of the Youth League to the party itself, one Politbureau member is charged with keeping an eye on Komsomol. The youth organization rose in membership from 22,000 in 1918 to 4 million in 1933 and 9 million in 1939. During the war, its membership doubled. It now exceeds 18 million. Even in a nation of more than 200 million, such as the USSR now represents, Komsomol membership is large enough to be of considerable influence.

When World War II ended, the Communist Party faced the need to assert its control over Soviet soldiers who had come to look to the army staff for leadership. At the same time, the party strove hard to reassert its intellectual control over Russian life. This control had been less rigid during the war years. Emphasis had been put on the war against Nazism, defense of the fatherland, and United Nations unity. As a colonel general, who led Soviet armies against Finland and who later headed the Russian military mission in Helsinki, Zhdanov was well suited to bridge any gap separating army and party. Relations between these two important pillars of the Soviet state have fluctuated considerably. The system of political commissars, directly responsible to the party, was introduced by Stalin on May 10, 1937. It had existed earlier but had been very unpopular. But the announced "Trotskyite infiltration" into the army suggested that commissars might again be required. Early in World War II, the system of commissars was abolished by the decree of August 2, 1940. After the Nazi attack on Russia, the party's control of Army morale was again restored. A decree reinstituting the political commissars was issued on July 16, 1941.

Seesawing between army and party, between political and professional generals, continued. On October 9, 1942, the commissar system was again abolished. The eclipse of Marshal Gregori K. Zhukov and the growing prominence of Colonel General Zhdanov lends itself to the interpretation that the party nevertheless succeeded in impressing its view on the army command. The shifting of Zhukov, who had commanded all Soviet ground forces, to Odessa created speculation that he had taken charge of Soviet military interests in the Balkans and the Near East. His appointment was viewed with particular interest in Turkey. Unsubstantiated reports asserted in the fall of 1946 that Zhukov had conferred with Yugoslav and Bulgarian Communist leaders prior to the flare-up of partisan guerrilla warfare in northern Greece.

NATIONALISM IN THE UKRAINE

Zhukov's shift to Odessa came at a time when Communist Party activity was strongly directed against a nationalist renaissance in the Ukraine, of which Odessa is the leading port city. There can be no question that the Ukraine represents the Soviet Union's most persistent internal problem. The loosening of Communist discipline during the war years and the concentration of the nation's energies on the war permitted a revival of Ukrainian nationalist activity. Throughout the war, informed Allied government officials heard of Ukrainian underground warfare against Russian transports and personnel. There were reports of sabotaged railway lines, assassination of officers, and attacks on isolated army units. United States participants at the Yalta conference have given a particularly interesting reason for Stalin's insistence on separate representation of the Ukrainian Soviet Socialist Republic in the United Nations. Stalin was quoted as telling President Roosevelt that it would help to assure Ukrainian support of the Soviet war effort if that republic received a separate delegate. This would also pacify Ukrainian nationalist aspirations, he is said to have explained. Whether this explanation was put forward merely as a bargaining argument or not, it certainly appears logical in view of Communist Party difficulties in the Ukraine.

On August 23, 1946, Nikita S. Khrushchev, the Ukrainian Politbureau member, revealed during a meeting of the party's central committee at Kiev that 64 per cent of the presidents of regional executive committees had been replaced over an eighteen-month period. In the Sumi district of the northern Ukraine, as many as 91 per cent of such presidents were removed from their posts. In the Nikolaev and Rovno districts, the percentage was 83 per cent.

MANUILSKY, TOP-FLIGHT COORDINATOR

The Politbureau can doubtless well remember that the Communist Party of the Ukraine elected an anti-Russian central committee two years after the Bolsheviks came to power. It has been the specific task of Dmitri Zakharovitch Manuilsky, Ukrainian representative to the United Nations, to reconcile the Ukraine to the centralized Soviet regime. Manuilsky is one of the best informed men in the field of world communism. During the existence of the Comintern, Manuilsky and the Finn Otto Kuusinen were prominent in expressing the views of the Russian central committee to Communist parties abroad.

Manuilsky, born in 1883, the son of a Ukrainian village priest, took part in the 1905 uprisings at Petrograd. Hs was arrested and sentenced to deportation to Siberia. He managed to escape, and, after hiding for a while in the Ukrainian capital city of Kiev, he fled to France. As a Russian revolutionary exile in Paris, Manuilsky first worked as a baggage porter in a railroad station and later did some writing. He returned to Russia during World War I and joined the Mensheviks. His activities as editor of the clandestine magazine *Nashe Slovo* forced him again into exile.

Nationalist Ukrainians created an independent government during the revolutionary period. Manuilsky, on returning to his homeland, persuaded the Ukrainians to accept Moscow's creation of the Ukrainian Soviet Socialist Republics. The Red Army had previously subdued armed Ukrainian resistance. During the interwar years, Manuilsky divided his time between Ukrainian and Comintern affairs. He kept one eye on Kiev, and the other on the rest of the globe. When this proved difficult after the war, Politbureau member Lazar Kaganovitch became secretary of the Ukrainian Communist Party.

Manuilsky achieved international prominence in 1945, when he appeared at the San Francisco meetings as foreign minister of the Ukraine. Since then, he has represented that republic at the various meetings of the United Nations General Assembly. On September 10, 1945, he said in a speech before the United Nations Security Council that it was time to "put an end" to the belief that Communists lack influence in the world.

He said that the war years had given "the masses in all countries" an opportunity "to come to know Communists," and that they have since "expressed their confidence in them." If any one man coordinates the activities of world communism today, that man may well be Manuilsky.

"ALIEN" CULTURAL IDEOLOGIES

Trends in the Ukraine have been paralleled, to a lesser degree, elsewhere in the Soviet Union. Stalin's party deputy, Zhdanov, took charge of tightening the Communist Party's hold on the cultural life of the nation. Apparently, western influence on the artistic life of the Soviet Union had grown during the war years, to the detriment of a Communist approach on the part of artists and writers. On May 21, 1946, a five-year plan for motion-picture production was approved by party authorities. In view of the motion picture's strong influence on the population, even on an illiterate audience, the thirteen-point program thus outlined must be considered as a representative skeleton directive of the Communist Party's agitation program:

1. Advantages of the Soviet system over capitalism.
2. The role of the Communist Party.
3. Solidarity and friendship of the many nationalities composing the Soviet Union.
4. The people's vigilance, patriotism, and duties to the state.
5. Commemoration of outstanding war heroes and heroines.
6. The Soviet way of life.
7. The family.
8. Mother heroines (mothers who have male children).
9. Children and youth.
10. Problems facing the Soviet Union.
11. Documentaries of the Five-Year Plan.
12. Industry, agriculture, and life in the sixteen Soviet republics.
13. Popularization of achievements in science, engineering, and technical progress.

The nationalist-isolationist common denominator of these thirteen points is too striking to require detailed analysis. It is completely in line with the withdrawal of Soviet culture from the international scene, which was later suggested in actions and statements by Andrei A. Zhdanov. *Culture and Life,* organ of the party's central committee Division of Propaganda and Agitation, denounced tendencies in opera, theater, painting, films, and architecture as "soaked through and through with an ideology alien to Soviet society." Speaking on August 21, 1946, at Leningrad, Zhdanov told writers in that city that many of them had "lost the sense of responsibility to their people, State, and party." Zhdanov remarked that "if feudalism and later on, the bourgeoisie in the period of its flourishing, could create art and literature asserting the new systems" then certainly "our new socialist system, embodying all that is best in the history of human civilization and culture, is capable of creating the most advanced literature, which will leave far behind the best creations of olden times."

The most interesting single event of the cultural purge executed by Zhdanov was the partial banning of the motion-picture trilogy *Ivan the Terrible,* produced by the noted Soviet director Serge Eisenstein. In a letter to *Culture and Life,* Eisenstein confessed his shortcomings at having failed to picture the central figure of his film as "Ivan the builder, Ivan the creator of a new, mighty, united Russian power." He agreed that all artists "must master the Lenin-Stalin method of perception of real life and history to such a full and deep extent as to be able to overcome all remnants or survivals of former notions which, although they have been banished from our consciousness a long time, are obstinately and maliciously attempting to infiltrate into our works, as soon as our creative vigilance is weakened ever for only a single moment."

Another internationally known Russian artist, the composer Dmitri Shostakovitch, was sharply criticized by the central committee. His Ninth Symphony was castigated by *Culture and Life* as lacking in appreciation of Soviet ideas and "warm ideological convictions." Shostakovitch followed in Eisenstein's footsteps when he repented his artistic sins by citing "the decision of the central committee of the Communist Party" which "lays upon us the tasks of composing music that expresses many profound and ennobling ideas." He said, "The instructions of the central committee of the Communist Party head a new page in the history of Soviet art; they direct and inspire us."

While the Soviet Union proceeded along the road of its fourth Five-Year Plan, announced in 1946, the Communist Party tightened its hold on the morale of the Soviet population. Its relationship with the Communist parties abroad had been changed by the dissolution of the Comintern. Foreign observers inside the Soviet Union have no opportunity to record the machinery of relations between the Russian Communists and Communist Party headquarters abroad. The last secretary-general, Georgi Dimitrov, is premier of Bulgaria. Molotov performs the duties of foreign minister of the Soviet Union. Kuusinen is head of the Karelo-Finnish Republic of the USSR. Manuilsky, as foreign minister of the Ukraine, has entered the international scene and may continue some of his former Comintern duties.

The extensive secretariat of the central committee of the Soviet Union's Communist Party doubtless observes the activities of Communist parties abroad with continued interest. The all-important question, whether Moscow controls the policies of Communist parties abroad, was answered by Premier Stalin in September, 1946. He answered the Moscow correspondent of the *Sunday Times* of London, Alexander Werth, "I consider this accusation absurd and to be borrowed from the bankrupt arsenal of Hitler and Goebbels." In spite of this authoritative and unequivocal reply, these questions persist in the mind of world-conscious persons: Does a common, over-all policy link the Communist parties of the world? Are their views dictated by their ideological, if not material, allegiance to the Soviet State? Has any Communist Party outside the Soviet Union ever disagreed with Soviet policy on any major point? Is not the Seventh Strategy of world communism designed to foster the interests of the Soviet Union, rather than of other countries in which Communist parties exist?

Only a country-by-country survey of the leadership, policies, and organizations of Communist parties can give the evidence needed to answer these questions without prejudice. Only the sum total of a country-by-country analysis can prove the true allegiance of Communists and their parties throughout the world.

CHAPTER 4

Finland: On Good Behavior

THE CASE OF Finland shows perfectly that world communism today can act with moderation. After the end of World War II, Finland might have become a Soviet Republic, like Estonia, Latvia, and Lithuania. Or it might have been transformed into a "People's Republic," like Bulgaria and Outer Mongolia. Before World War I, Finland had been part of Russia's Czarist Empire. It enjoyed a high degree of autonomy, but it was clearly under Russian sovereignty. Consequently, the Soviet Union could easily have presented a case for the annexation of Finland to the USSR. It chose not to do so. It chose not to set up a Communist-dominated government in Finland, as happened in Poland and elsewhere.

Finland has not lost its sovereignty. It enjoys all basic democratic freedoms, except that its newspaper editors and politicians are careful not to offend the Soviet Union. There has been no extremist purge, such as occurred in Bulgaria. Finns run Finland. Otto Kuusinen, the veteran Communist International official, is president of the Karelo-Finnish Republic, which has been formed as part of the USSR with the inclusion of the former Finnish territory of western Karelia. But he did not become president of Finland. Nor are Communists in control of the Helsinki government. True, Kuusinen's son-in-law, Yrjö Leino, is minister of the interior. This is a post that Communists throughout the world favor greatly, because it can assure effective control of a nation's domestic life through police measures. But Leino has proved himself to be a man of subtlety. Finland has never been a police state. Finns are law-abiding people who generally go about their business in a quiet, matter-of-fact fashion. Leino, as a Finn, has respected this attitude.

Finland's Communist Party is smaller in membership than its three counterparts in the neighboring Scandinavian countries. It claimed 40,000 members in 1947. Communist leadership is a bit of a family affair. Herta

43

Kuusinen-Leino, Otto Kuusinen's daughter and Interior Minister Leino's wife, is probably the most dynamic Communist figure in Finland today. The party itself is led by Secretary-General Ville Pessi, who has spent many years in the Soviet Union and other years in Finnish prisons.

The postwar political picture of Finland was drawn in outline at the elections of March 17 and 18, 1945. These elections were genuinely free. The Parliament that was thus chosen must be considered as a true representation of Finnish political beliefs at that time. All in all, Finland's change from the position of a German ally to that of a defeated nation living in the shadow of the Soviet Union was accomplished with exemplary discretion.

This should not imply that Finland is not aware of its status as a defeated nation. Nor should it suggest that Communist influence on the Helsinki government is slight or that the nation's economic position is not determined by its reparation commitments to Russia. But the contrast of conditions in Finland with those prevailing in other areas where communism has grown powerful is too striking to be ignored.

"RED TERROR"—"WHITE TERROR"

The Communist Party of Finland made a bid for power shortly after the Bolshevik Revolution in Russia. It was defeated in a bloody, if brief, civil war. For fourteen years, from 1930 to 1944, it was illegal. Many of its leaders have been in prisons. It would have been possible for an orgy of revenge to follow the end of World War II. It is to the credit of Finland's Communists and of the Soviet military authorities that this did not occur.

From 1809 until the end of World War I, Finland had been a Grand Duchy within the Czarist Empire. After the turn of the century, Finland's autonomy was more restricted. There were attempts at Russianization, and the foreign policy and military affairs of the nation were strictly in Russian hands. These measures strengthened independence sentiment. When the Czar was overthrown in the spring of 1917, Finland was ready to defy its Russian overlords.

In 1916, the Finnish Social Democrats had achieved a majority in Parliament. They were torn between admiration for the anti-Czarist revolutionaries in Russia and desire to achieve independence for Finland under a Social Democratic regime. Following the Russian example, they

organized Red Guards. But they were defeated in the parliamentary elections of October 17, 1917, and organized a general strike from November
13 to 19. The question was: Should they try to overthrow the conservative government by force? The Social Democratic Party Conference of
November 25 heard Russian Commissar for National Minorities Joseph
Stalin say, "You are experiencing a government crisis similar to the one
we had in Russia on the eve of the October revolution. You, too, have
been threatened with starvation, sabotage, and similar things; but let me
tell you, on the basis of my experiences in the Russian revolution, that
such dangers are not insurmountable if you act with determination and
do not hesitate."

What did Stalin mean? Was he inviting the Finns to follow Lenin's
example of a coup d'état by force?

The Social Democrats were not sure. Meanwhile, the conservative government under Premier Pehr Evind Svinhufvud, who had returned from
Siberian exile, was negotiating with Lenin for a declaration of Finland's
independence. His regime sent a delegation to the Soviet government which
finally managed to obtain the Russian's consent. It was a strange mission
of "bourgeois" parliamentarians to the headquarters of a successful rebel
regime. After the delegates had been assured that Finland's independence
would be granted, they felt that they should thank Lenin. Svinhufvud
later recounted the weird scene. The delegates were standing in Lenin's
civil war headquarters like frightened schoolboys in front of a stern
principal. It was bitter cold, and everyone was sitting around in heavy
overcoats. Lenin glanced pityingly at the uncomfortable Finns and turned
to Trotsky, "What shall I do with these bourgeois? Maybe I should have
them shot after all?"

They got home safely, but the Soviet regime had some second thoughts
on the matter of Finnish independence. After all, it had failed to strengthen
its own sympathizers among the left Social Democrats (who later formed
the Finnish Communist Party) by making the precious gift of independence to the conservative government, rather than to the revolutionaries. Stalin expressed this view a few days later. He said on January
4, 1918, that the Russians had "involuntarily granted liberty not to the
people, not to the Finnish proletariat, but to the bourgeosie of Finland."

But then Moscow had a third thought. While Svinhufvud was trying to
bolster his government's position and neutralize the restless Social Demo-

crats, Trotsky sent a telegram to the Social Democratic Party leaders: "The hour for action has come. Concentrate 15,000 Red Guards in Helsinki and environs. Seize power. Arrest government." He seemed to believe that the Social Democrats might be able to do in Helsinki what the Bolsheviks had done, a few months earlier, in Petrograd. But the military situation in Finland was very different from that in Russia. Not all the Social Democrats favored the use of Bolshevik methods in Finland. Many moderate leaders preferred to use parliamentary techniques. Although Russian troops where then still stationed on Finnish soil—a situation that had worried Svinhufvud a lot—the government was in command of the Civil Guard. In fact, when the left-wing Social Democrats finally tried to carry out Trotsky's instructions, Svinhufvud made himself commander of the Civil Guards on January 16, 1918.

The civil war that followed lasted for three months. An estimated six thousand persons were killed. At first, Baron Carl Gustav Emil Mannerheim turned down Svinhufvud's invitation to lead the Civil Guards. He later accepted on the condition that German troops would not be called in. Finnish volunteers had fought in the German army's so-called "Jägerbatallion" during World War I. Helsinki officials were tempted to call on the Germans for help against the Soviet-supported revolutionaries. Finally, Mannerheim took command over the Civil Guards. However, the Finnish foreign office had negotiated with Germany's General Erich von Ludendorff, and German-commanded troops were on the way to Finland just as Mannerheim managed to crush the revolution.

Both sides appear to have been extremely ruthless. There was much talk of "red terror" during the revolution, and a counterrevolutionary "white terror" was attributed to the Civil Guards after the rebellion had been ended. The Communist view was expressed in a pamphlet published at Amsterdam under the title *The Terror of the Bourgeoisie in Finland*: "When the White Guards of the bourgeoisie took revenge in the first intoxication of their victory over the revolutionaries, they did not even pretend to adhere to any 'formalities of law.' " The pamphlet then forecast that communism would sooner or later triumph and said that "the strong hand of revolution, of the red dictatorship, of red terror, will then destroy the power of Finland's bourgeois robbers and the power of capitalism, thus opening the way for communism." Luckily for the Finnish people, this prophecy did not come true after World War II.

The Communist Party of Finland was founded late in August of 1919. This event, however, took place not in Helsinki but in Moscow. The new party violently denounced the right-wing Social Democrats. At their first Congress, the Communists stated that "the working class must energetically prepare for an armed revolution, and not hang back with the old system with its Parliaments and professional cooperative Socialists." Otto Kuusinen evaluated the experience of the abortive revolution and said, "The idea of the Democratic State with which the People's Commissariat (of the Finnish Social Democrats) deluded itself, was historically false. It wished to build a bridge, to construct a passage from capitalism to socialism, but democracy is unable to bear the burden of such a mission." Kuusinen did not deny that "certain anarchic elements" among the Red Guard had "committed murder and robberies." He stated that this "lack of discipline tended to produce disorder even in the ranks of the revolutionaries."

THE ULTRA-RIGHT RUNS WILD

The Communists pursued the revolutionary activity to which they had committed themselves until, in 1923, the party was accused of a plot against the state and was officially banned. This did not, however, effectively curtail its parliamentary activity. Under one name or another, it managed to submit and elect candidates for Parliament. Its influence grew considerably during the depression. The elections of June 1, 1929, brought the Communists 23 out of 200 parliamentary seats. Under the aggressive, extremist-revolutionary Third Strategy of world communism, the party also made considerable headway in the labor movement.

The Third Strategy proved detrimental to the interests of the Finnish Communists when they announced an antireligious demonstration festival in the strongly Lutheran town of Lapua in November, 1929. Resistance against Communist activity had been mounting for months and years. Vigilantes prevented the Communists from assembling in the town. On December 1, 1929, the anti-Communist Lapua movement—which closely resembled the Nazi Party in Germany and the Italian Fascists—demanded that the government suppress communism completely. The Lapua movement then turned to lawless kidnaping of Communist leaders, or even of attorneys for the defense of persons accused of subversive activities. Finland was struck by an avalanche of chaos created by the ultra-right.

While the Lapua gangs drew most of their support from religious fanatics, another group sought to defeat communism in the economic field. This organization, the Lock movement, appealed to employers not to hire alleged Communists and to fire those whom it considered Communist. The two movements merged in July, 1930, and prepared a "March on Helsinki," a conscious imitation of Mussolini's "March on Rome."

"MARCH ON HELSINKI"

Twelve thousand rightists entered Helsinki, where they were received by high officials, including General Mannerheim. Svinhufvud was entrusted with the formation of a new government. He tried to get three anti-Communist bills passed by the Parliament, but ran into strong opposition from the Social Democrats. He therefore dissolved the Parliament and called for a new election. During the election campaign, from July to October, 1930, the Lapua and Lock movements terrorized not only the Communists, but the Social Democrats as well. Svinhufvud's cabinet banned all "meetings and outdoor celebrations, as well as parades and other manifestations of Communist associations, organizations and individuals." The result was that the Communists, who had polled 128,000 votes in 1929, received only 11,500 in 1930. The new Parliament, in a strict Socialist-against-non-Socialist vote on November 11, 1930, forbade "entrance into Parliament of members of a party working for the overthrow of the state."

From then on the Finnish Communists led a precarious underground existence. Successive Helsinki governments continued to enforce the anti-Communist decrees strongly. Otto Kuusinen, as member of the Comintern secretariat, enjoyed high prestige among Communist parties throughout the world. Together with Karl Radek, and later under Dimitrov, he served as a contact man between the Russian leaders and the Communist parties abroad. Born in 1881, Otto Vilhelm Kuusinen became Comintern secretary in 1926. When the Soviet Union invaded Finland on November 30, 1939, Kuusinen served briefly as head of a Soviet-backed countergovernment, the so-called People's government of Finland. But when the two countries came to a peace agreement in March, 1940, his authority was restricted to the eastern and southeastern territories which Finland ceded to Russia, and which the Soviet government regarded as essential for its security.

When Germany broke the Nazi-Soviet Pact, Finland joined on Germany's side to recover the territories it had ceded. This it succeeded in doing. But on September 4, 1944, Finland signed an armistice with Russia (and with Britain, which had also declared war on Finland). The Allied Control Commission, which had the task of supervising the execution of the armistice terms, was headed by Colonel General Andrei A. Zhdanov, who today is deputy secretary of the Russian Communist Party.

The most important part of the armistice was the payment of 300 million dollars' worth of reparations over an eight-year period ending in 1952. Russia was particularly interested in finished goods, mostly machinery. This was difficult for the Finns, who had no industries for such a purpose. As a result, plants for the production of light engineering products had to be developed. After the reparations are paid off, there will be hardly any markets outside Russia for Finnish-produced machinery.

The elections of 1945 placed the Communist-controlled new Popular Democratic Party in a parliamentary minority. It received only 51 of the 200 seats in Finland's Parliament. The Popular Democratic Party is made up of Communists and the left wing of the Social Democratic Party. The Social Democrats themselves captured 52 seats, the Conservative, Agrarians, Swedish Peoples parties, and the Liberals together obtained a total of 97 seats. Since then Finland has been governed by a coalition intent on meeting the nation's peace-treaty obligations.

JUST A SHOW WINDOW?

The future of communism in Finland depends entirely on the Soviet Union. From Moscow's point of view, a quiet, self-governed, machinery-producing Finland may be preferable to a neighbor whose economy is undergoing sweeping changes and whose political life is in ferment. Russian correctness, the absence of Soviet occupation troops, and the obvious sincerity and competence of most Communist leaders have done much to erase memories of the 1918 civil war and the 1929 indiscretions of the Communists. Nevertheless, as the elections revealed, the majority of Finns do not believe that their nation is ripe for communism. This has been a source of disappointment to the Finnish Communists. Notably Herta Kuusinen-Leino has poured all her energy into agitation for communism, speaking throughout the nation, visiting the Soviet Union from time to time, and warning eloquently against the danger from pro-Nazi remnants among university students and inside non-Communist parties.

Those who find it convenient to see the world in a black-and-white pattern will find little comfort from a study of communism in postwar Finland. Devout Communists will fail to understand why the Finnish people did not draw the final political conclusion from their geographic nearness to the powerful Soviet Union by adopting the Soviet system. Some anti-Communists are likely to write the case of Finland off as a mere Russian trick, as a "show window." But the fact remains that, even in areas where Soviet power is supreme, communism has adopted varying forms. The Seventh Strategy of world communism permits that. As long as a non-Communist government seems more effective to the interest of Russia, such a government will remain in power. Meanwhile, as all Finns know, their country is on its good behavior.

CHAPTER 5

Poland: Out of the Ruins

COMMUNISM CONTROLS Poland. There can be no question about that. But clichés on ruthless Red rule, suppression of popular liberties, and government by terror cannot be blandly applied to Poland today. Opposition sentiment is widespread. It is vocal enough to be audible clearly across the globe. Opposition press and opposition speakers take chances when they criticize the Communist-run regime freely. But it is a credit to their courage, and to the relative moderation of the Warsaw regime, that their words can be read and heard. All this does not distract from the fact that communism rules supreme in Poland.

The Red Army, which pushed the Germans across Poland in 1944, was accompanied by veteran Polish Communists. They organized a government that had its root in Moscow. This government grew from the Polish Union of Patriots at Moscow, and the Polish Committee of National Liberation at Lublin. Finally, at Warsaw, the Liberation Committee constituted itself as the Provisional Polish Government of National Unity. The Big Three, at Yalta, agreed to recognize the Warsaw regime if it were broadened by the inclusion of Polish statesmen from abroad. Stanislaw Mikolajczyk, member of the London Polish government in exile and leader of the Peasant Party, was therefore included in the Warsaw government as vice-premier. At the Potsdam Conference of 1945, the Soviet Union, the United States, and Great Britain specified that "free and unfettered elections" were to be the basis of a permanent Polish government. These elections were held on January 19, 1947. They resulted in a sweeping victory of the Communist-led party bloc, which received 394 out of 444 seats in the single-chamber Parliament. Mikolajczyk's Peasant Party received only 28 seats. The balance of the seats went to three smaller parties.

The pattern of Polish life after World War II had thus been drawn in unmistakable lines. The policy-making posts in the Polish government were placed in the hands of the Polish Workers Party. There can be no doubt that this party is the Communist Party of Poland under a different label. When the *Daily Worker*, organ of the United States Communist Party, reported the preelection merger of the Socialists with the Workers Party, it did so by saying that the "Communist and Socialist parties of Poland, chief support of the present government, joined forces forming a new political combine with some 1,000,000 members." The paper added that the agreement united "500,000 members of Poland's traditional Socialist Party and 400,000 members of the Communist Polish Workers Party." Following the pattern repeated elsewhere (in Bulgaria and Switzerland, for instance), the Communists in Poland have labeled their political organization a Workers, or Labor Party. But this is merely a tag and should not lead to confusion.

Under the leadership of Boleslaw Bierut, Poland's president, the Communists are engaged in a far-reaching program of reconstruction. Nazi administration of Poland during the war, and the movement and countermovement of German and Russian armies, left much of Poland's agricultural land devastated. Horses and cattle are scarce, farm implements are missing or damaged, and much of the farming population itself was dispersed all over Europe and the Soviet Union. On January 1, 1947, the Warsaw government started its ambitious Three-Year Plan for the reconstruction of Poland. Executed by the able Communist economist Hilary Minc, the plan aimed at extensive industrialization. Minc, a veteran member of the Lodz Communist Party, displayed professional knowledge and competence that made him stand out among his colleagues. Through the incorporation of German Silesia, Poland added to its already substantial coal-mining areas. The Three-Year Plan was designed to elevate Poland to the position of an industrial supply center, somewhat similar to that occupied by Germany before the war. Through the nationalization of industrial establishments employing more than fifty persons, the Communist plan assured extensive government control over the nation's economic life. Coal exports strengthened Poland's stand in Europe substantially.

THE EDUCATION OF BOLESLAW BIERUT

President Bierut, under whose supervision Poland's future unfolds, was born at Lublin in 1891 as Boleslaw Krasnodebski. His career as a rebel made it necessary for him to use several aliases. Among them were the names Bienkowski and Rutkowski. He combined the first three letters of both names to arrive at Bierut. When the armies of Marshal Pilsudski defeated Russia's Red Army in 1920 just before it reached Warsaw, all dreams of a legal Communist Party in Poland were shattered. Communist agitation in Poland had to remain underground. But, because of the nearness of Russia, it was relatively successful. Among the Poles who often crossed the Polish-Russian frontier on clandestine missions was the slender, dark-eyed Bierut.

After attending the Lenin School in Moscow, he entered Poland in 1923 for two years of illegal party work. On his return to the Soviet Union, he joined the staff of southeastern agents under the leadership of Georgi Dimitrov, the brilliant Bulgarian revolutionary. Active first in Vienna, and then in Prague, Bierut gathered experience that he is now able to use against the widespread and violent anti-Communist underground movements inside Poland.

Bierut emerged unscathed from the factional strife that shook the Polish Communist Party during the Stalin-Trotsky controversy. He retained the confidence of the Kremlin and of the Comintern and was entrusted with reorganizing the Polish Communist Party. After returning to Poland for this difficult task, he was arrested by the police. Convicted of carrying on subversive activities, he was sentenced to seven years at hard labor. The fact that he had obtained Soviet citizenship during his studies in the USSR helped shorten this sentence. He was exchanged for a Polish national then held by the Soviet government.

Anti-Communist Polish sources assert that Bierut spent a second intensive indoctrination period in the USSR from 1933 to 1936. According to these accounts, he attended special courses first in Leningrad and later in Moscow. Although it is impossible to obtain official Polish or Russian confirmation of these reports, they receive credence from the fact that Bierut was shortly afterward placed in charge of the Polish section of the Soviet secret police. For three years, he served in this responsible position, which provided him with intimate knowledge of personalities and trends inside Poland and within the clandestine groups of Polish Communists and pro-Communist Socialists.

The joint German-Russian invasion of Poland in the fall of 1939 taxed Bierut's knowledge and experience enormously. About 1,500,000 residents of Poland (including hundreds of thousands of Jewish and Ukrainian background) were deported to remote parts of the USSR. The task before Bierut after 1941 was twofold:

(1) He tried to create an active anti-Nazi underground movement in Poland, and to construct a Communist-led coalition of partisans along the lines of the Greek National Liberation Front (EAM); facing the opposition of conservative underground armies, Polish Communists were in the difficult position of fighting against the German occupants and the guerrillas supported by the London Polish exile government at the same time. No reliable figures for casualties resulting from intraguerrilla warfare in Poland are available.

(2) Bierut was instrumental in creating a Polish governing body acceptable to the Soviet Union and the Red Army command. This, too, was difficult, since the number of acceptable Communist and non-Communist leaders was small. Bierut himself is, in fact, a man of much less prestige and capabilities than such experienced Communist leaders as Maurice Thorez of France, Palmiro Togliatti of Italy, or Matyas Rákosi of Hungary.

After working among Polish émigrés inside the Soviet Union (and Soviet-occupied Poland) from 1939 to 1941, he entered the German-controlled areas of Poland clandestinely in the winter of 1942. He parachuted into German-patrolled territory from a Soviet army airplane and began his extensive and dangerous activities of organizing a Communist-led underground movement. Bierut did, in fact, create a resistance movement similar to that led by Marshal Tito in Yugoslavia. Because of his links with the Soviet Union, and the generally fiercely anti-Russian attitude of the Polish population, Bierut's underground organization remained small and little known. It adopted the name National Council of Poland, and Boleslaw Bierut acted as its secretary.

While maintaining contact with the Soviet Union from 1941 to 1943, Bierut organized the Polish Workers Party, which now functions as the party of Communists in Poland. He was also concerned with negotiations between Communists and Socialists, which finally led to a "united front" coalition in which left-wing Socialists participated. Poland's leading Socialist is Joseph Cyrankiewicz, whose prewar anti-totalitarian record is beyond dispute. Pursuing what he believed to be a policy of realism, Cyrankiewicz made his peace with the Communists. Another leading Socialist, Zygmunt Zulawski, refused to follow the Communist lead and founded the opposition party of Independent Socialists.

On December 31, 1944, the Polish Committee of National Liberation was founded by Bierut at Lublin. The foundation for Communist postwar control of the Polish state had been laid. But if it had been difficult to find even relatively prominent non-Communists to cooperate in the Lublin and Warsaw regimes, the task of gaining the support of the Polish nation as a whole offered an even greater challenge. Anti-Communist underground bands created a vast security problem for the Warsaw regime until early in 1947. Terrorist excesses by underground bands have been used extensively to detract from the integrity of all non-Communist Polish groups, whether or not links to guerrillas really existed. The Russian-trained Polish secret police has used its facilities against bands of ultra-nationalist outlaws as well as against the Peasant Party.

The Communist secret police rivaled the underground armies in ruthlessness and determination. It is led by Stanislaw Radkiewicz, who took part in the Union of Polish Patriots, which functioned in Moscow while Poland was occupied by the Germans. Radkiewicz is said to have served in the Russian secret police in capacities similar to those of Bierut. He was minister of security in the Lublin committee, and later of the Warsaw government. Radkiewicz stated in 1946 that he commanded 48,000 security policemen, with an additional 70,000 volunteers. He estimated the number of underground fighters at 15,000. Nongovernment estimates of the strength of the guerrillas have been as high as 30,000.

Born at Kosów in 1903, Radkiewicz served as a Communist agitator in Poland from 1919 on. In 1927, he was condemned at Warsaw to four years' imprisonment. A tall, dark-haired man, Radkiewicz occupies one of the most difficult, thankless, and certainly most unpopular posts in the Warsaw cabinet.

Prior to the 1947 elections, Radkiewicz's secret police was accused by British Foreign Secretary Ernest Bevin of terrorizing leaders of the Polish Peasant Party. Bevin spoke of a number of political murders that had taken place in Poland, "in circumstances that in many cases appeared to point to the complicity of the Polish security police." His charges were countered by Polish officials, who pointed to the murder of Communists and Socialists. Undersecretary of Foreign Affairs Zygmunt Modzelewski declared that terroristic acts were inspired by agents of Lieutenant General Wladyslaw Anders, who headed Polish military units abroad as part of the United Nations armed forces. These statements would suggest that political assassination in Poland has not been the monopoly of any one group. Political murder does, in fact, antedate the existence of organized communism and goes back to anti-Czarist terrorism in the eighteenth and nineteenth centuries.

ELECTIONS IN 1947

When the Communists took power in Poland, they did so under military, economic, and political conditions that could hardly strengthen their popularity. The presence of Soviet army units on Polish soil was repugnant to many Poles. Devastation made orderly administration and transport of food supplies impossible. The elections of 1947 took place at a time when hunger and cold marked the desperate situation of Poland. As the elections approached, the British and United States governments expressed their disapproval of Warsaw's measures against the Polish Peasant Party. A series of notes from Washington and London emphasized the pledges made by the big powers at Yalta and Potsdam that Polish elections be free and unfettered. The Polish view was expressed by Foreign Minister Wincenty Rzymowski, who said that the agreements "did not give any Allied power the right to interfere in Poland's internal affairs." The same view was expressed, on January 15, 1947, in a note sent by Soviet Foreign Minister Molotov to the United States government. Washington had asked both London and Moscow to join in calling to "the attention of the Polish Government in a most friendly but in a most insistent manner the failure of the Polish Government to perform its obligations." Molotov answered that to hinder Polish measures against "criminal elements" would be "unjustifiable, especially on the part of a foreign power."

When the elections finally took place on January 19, 1947, following a wave of arrests, charges, and countercharges, they were relatively calm. It was the first Polish election since 1935. Deputy Premier Wladyslaw Gomolka hailed the results of the election as an expression of mass confidence in the government led by his party. Gomolka, who began his career as a Communist agitator in 1920, when he organized a cell in the Thirty-sixth Polish Infantry Regiment, urging desertion to the Red Army, today is secretary-general of the Polish Communist Party.

Although Gomolka is officially head of the Polish Communist Party, many observers believe that his influence is second to that of Jacob Berman, secretary of the presidium of the council of ministers. Berman was born in 1901 and belonged to the Union of Polish Patriots in Moscow. His official position in the seven-man Political Bureau of the Communist Party is that of chief of agitation and propaganda.

With the disappearance of the Peasant Party from the Warsaw cabinet and from any decisive role in the Polish Parliament, the Socialist Party achieved new importance. Although its outspoken anti-Communist leaders either belong to the Independent Socialists or live abroad, the Socialist Party began to fear for its continued existence as a separate party. Polish Socialists had been able to observe a clear-cut pattern in other eastern European countries: the whittling-down of non-Communist parties, one by one; the emergence of a government using obedient splinters of older parties as a façade of multi-party governments; and finally the concentration of all powers in Communist hands.

The 1947 elections reduced the Peasant Party to ineffectiveness. Shortly afterward, the Socialists had reason to fear that their turn had come. The Communist press campaigned violently against the Socialist-run cooperatives, accusing them of excessive speculation and profits in retail trade. Socialist worries increased when Communist Secretary General Gomolka in his May Day speech urged "organic union of both parties into one." Although the Socialists agreed with the Communists on the need for close cooperation with Russia, they regretted alienation of Poland from the United States and western Europe. This split widened after the breakdown of the Paris conference for European reconstruction in June. Even after Soviet Foreign Minister Molotov rejected the United States offer for a European economic plan, Poland's Socialist premier Cyrankiewicz expressed his country's "positive interest" in the American proposal. But another, more authoritative, voice—Radio Moscow—stated on July 8 that Poland would not participate in preparations for American-aided European recovery.

No realistic evaluation of the Communist position in Poland today can attribute a decisive role to the Socialists, or to any other non-Communist party. Poland's Communists have placed their country on the road to one-part control, no matter how this control may look on the surface. During the interwar years, Polish government often appeared excessively nationalistic, intolerant, and totalitarian. Today, under Communist guidance, Poland has again failed to enter the road of political moderation and free expression of the popular will.

CHAPTER 6

Czechoslovakia: Revolution by Decree

CZECHOSLOVAKIA'S POSTWAR revolution has been ambitious, bloodless, and legal. Today, the Czechoslovak nation stands politically to the left of British Socialism and to the right of Russia's total state rule. The whole country has become the laboratory of socialism by decree. This experiment is powered with Communist impatience, proceeding in accordance with Communist plans, and under the guidance of Communist administrators.

But Czechoslovakia, proud of its young democratic tradition, overthrew its old economic system in good order. Its people voted themselves into a nationalized economy on May 26, 1946. The Communists emerged from this first postwar election as the nation's dominant party. Their success took the world by surprise. They received twice as many votes as any other party. Here, a nation considered the most democratically progressive in east central Europe had cast its votes in free and fair elections, and 30 per cent of its voters chose to ballot in favor of the Communist Party.

True, the people of Czechoslovakia did not give the Czech and Slovak Communist parties an out-and-out majority. Together, these two parties controlled only 114 of 300 parliamentary seats. They needed the 37 representatives of the Czech Social Democrats to achieve as much as a majority of one. To these combined 151 delegates could be added the two parliamentary seats of the Slovak Labor Party. In effect, however, the seven million voters of the Czechoslovak Republic had given a three-year approval to a Communist-sponsored national program that was conceived in Moscow during the war, before it was first published at Košice, temporary seat of the Czechoslovak government, on April 5, 1945.

With the announcement and implementation of the Košice program, the Communist Party came into its own. After more than two decades of

58

relative obscurity, World War II had hurled the party and its leadership into a position of power and responsibility. When Party Chairman Klement Gottwald addressed the newly elected Parliament on July 8, 1946, he did so as Czechoslovakia's first Communist premier. As he outlined his program to the delegates, Gottwald could look back on a lifetime of Marxist endeavor that had finally been crowned by success.

KLEMENT GOTTWALD

When the regions that later formed the Czechoslovak Republic were still part of the Austro-Hungarian Empire, Gottwald was born in the Moravian village of Dediče on November 23, 1896. Czech and Slovak nationalism were already strong within the sprawling, multinational empire. Gottwald's father, who owned a small farm, lived in a region where Czech and German influence met. The elder Gottwald wanted his son to have the benefit of a skilled trade. He sent Klement to Vienna for training when he was twelve years old.

In Vienna, fermenting capital of an overgrown empire, young Gottwald became a carpenter's apprentice. But this did not suffice to absorb his youthful energies. At the age of sixteen, he joined the Social Democratic youth movement, which combined political work with sports activities. When Austria-Hungary joined the Germany of Kaiser Wilhelm II in World War I, Gottwald was drafted into the Imperial Army. He was then twenty-one years old. The rugged peasant youth with the square face and solidly built body advanced quickly. He became a sergeant of the Imperial Artillery and was in command of a unit at the southern Russian front. He was wounded. But, as soon as his wounds had healed, Gottwald was again sent to the front. He fought in the Bessarabian and Italian campaigns, although he had begun to hate the army and the war. While home on leave from the Italian front, he hid and did not return to his unit. Gottwald had deserted a crumbling cause.

The end of the war and the collapse of the Central Powers unloosed forces that were later to crystallize in the Czechoslovak Communist movement. In 1918, Thomas G. Masaryk proclaimed an independent Czechoslovak republic. The struggle for independence split the Marxist party of the young state, the Socialists. The majority of party members and functionaries wholeheartedly supported Masaryk and the cause of self-determination. Only a minority right-wing group, headed by Bohumir

Smeral, continued to favor the old Austro-Hungarian Empire. And then the unimaginable happened. Smeral, a disillusioned politician commanding an insignificant following, broke away from the Socialists. Looking around for a new star to which he might hitch his isolated wagon, he saw the newly bright red star of Moscow and the Comintern. He prepared the ground for a Czechoslovak Communist Party, to be formed around a nucleus of piqued Socialists. Gottwald was not among his immediate supporters. He continued to work with the left-wing Socialists, while making his living as a carpenter in his Moravian home region. But the Socialists, whom he had joined formally in 1919, quickly ran into heavy weather. The new Czechoslovak state they had supported with vigor and enthusiasm was suffering growing pains. The years immediately following the war brought disillusionment to many who had first hailed the new state without reservations. Gottwald was one of these.

CARPENTER INTO JOURNALIST

As the number of disappointed workers mounted, extremism and opposition gained. Riding the tide of disillusionment, Smeral formally founded the Communist Party of Czechoslovakia in 1921. Gottwald joined the new Communist youth movement. Using his Vienna experience, he was instrumental in creating the new Communist sports organization, the "Spartacus," which drilled its members as if they were shock troops. That same year, Klement Gottwald went to Slovakia where the Communists were beginning to take hold. The ex-carpenter edited two party papers in Bratislava. The first was *Hlas Lodu* (People's Voice), the second, *Pravda* (Truth).

Even as an independent body, the Communists under Smeral retained much of the moderate temperament that characterized the Socialist movement. When Comintern policies tightened in the late twenties, there was a predetermined attempt to enforce stronger discipline within the Czechoslovak party. Moscow did not want to perpetuate the existence of a semi-bourgeois movement under the leadership of a man whose background stamped him as nonrevolutionary. Smeral was slowly forced to take a back seat. A central committee was set up, controlled by a strictly left-wing, revolutionary majority. But some of the new central committee members began to consider party funds as a source of personal revenue. They were forced to resign. Gottwald, however, was rising within party ranks. In 1925, he had moved from Bratislava to Prague, where he became a member of the central committee. Smeral's position was shaky. The "Spartacus" sports organization, on which Gottwald continued to keep a watchful eye, meanwhile took on a more militant character. In 1927, Gottwald was elevated from his position as a central committee member to that of secretary-general of the party. Shortly afterward, he made his first appearance in the Czechoslovak Parliament as a Communist delegate.

During the period that followed, probably the most critical of Communist history in Czechoslovakia, Klement Gottwald came fully into his own. His prestige in Moscow seems to have been based on his ability to fit himself into the Comintern apparatus without friction. He was able to coordinate his thinking completely with the ideas of the men in charge of Comintern policy making. Even today, Gottwald lacks the sparkle and vigor that have made other Communist leaders into dynamic orators or militant pamphleteers. He speaks slowly, with deliberation, gesticulating ever so carefully with his long-stemmed pipe.

Gottwald operated the Czechoslovak Communist party during the late 1920's and early 1930's on an even keel and strictly according to Comintern instructions. In 1924, when inflation and economic insecurity hit the existence of Czechoslovak workers, the Communists were able to report a membership roster of about 140,000 names. Official figures for 1929 show that membership went down to about 80,000. The following decade brought no change. Membership hit an all-time low of 70,000 in 1939, just before Nazi Germany's troops crossed the Czechoslovak frontier.

But less than a year after the end of World War II, Klement Gottwald was able to tell the Seventh Convention of the Czech Communist Party in March, 1946, that membership had passed the 1,000,000 mark. And, at the first postwar election, the party received a total of 2,702,452 votes (2,217,711 for the Czech Communists; 484,741 for the Slovak Communists).

THE NO LONGER SILENT GIANT

World War II and its aftermath had given the Communists prestige and support. Behind these membership and ballot figures stood a nation's realization that its fate had been decided by trends beyond its control. When Thomas Masaryk proclaimed the Czechoslovak Republic at Pittsburgh in 1918, he established links of sentiment, democratic ideology, and economic relations between his new state and the United States. Dur-

ing the years that passed between emergence of an independent Czechoslovak state and the Munich agreement, the Soviet Union seemed very
remote from Prague or Brno or Bratislava. The Russian state was a silent
giant of undetermined strength. Prewar Czechoslovakia, child of the western world, looked toward Washington and London and Paris for ideas,
as well as for economic ties.

And then came Munich, in 1938, and the agreement that was to be a
symbol of Czechoslovak disaster. Shortly afterward, Klement Gottwald
left Prague for Moscow. One month later, President Edvard Beneš of
Czechoslovakia arrived in London. Beneš was able to avoid any serious
break within the ranks of Czechoslovaks abroad. There was never a public
suggestion that the London government, directly supported by the British
Foreign Office, disapproved of the activities of Gottwald and other Soviet-
supported Czechoslovak functionaries. Beneš, in fact, paid a cordial visit
to Moscow during the war years. On December 12, 1943, he signed
a Czechoslovak-Soviet treaty of friendship, mutual assistance, and postwar
cooperation. He also inspected the First Czechoslovak Army Corps, which
fought against the Germans in coordination with the Red Army.

It is now known that, during his 1943 visit to Moscow, Beneš had
exhaustive conversations with Gottwald. The Communist leader had been
in close touch with Soviet officials and Comintern functionaries. Gottwald's position in Moscow placed him directly under the experienced
Bulgarian Communist veteran and Comintern chief, Georgi Dimitrov.
The Moscow discussions between Gottwald and Beneš were, to a high
degree, concerned with the postwar existence of Czechoslovakia. But
Beneš did not commit himself to the program that Gottwald, doubtless
with Comintern approval, presented to him. This program called for large-
scale socialization of Czechoslovak economy, as well as for the isolation
and deportation of Czechoslovak nationals of German descent. Although
Beneš's reluctance may not have been completely satisfactory to Moscow
officials, there was no hint that the Soviet Union did anything but approve
of the London exile government.

Beneš did incur a shadow of criticism in one instance. And then he
quickly adjusted his position. While the Soviet government and the London
Polish regime passed through a series of disagreements, Beneš attempted
to play the role of mediator. He even began negotiations with the Poles,
suggesting that an eastern European federation might be a constructive
postwar possibility. This did not go down well in Moscow. Memories of

the prewar concept of an anti-Russian *cordon sanitaire* of eastern European states were awakened. But Beneš quickly broke off his negotiations with the Poles, and the misunderstanding was eliminated.

Well-meaning Poles in London and Washington still took their Czechoslovak colleagues privately aside to tell them that they were guileless fools to trust the Russians. But the Czechoslovaks continued to be realistic. They believed that it was not a question of trust, but a matter of alternatives: to be with Russia, or against Russia. And, though they might have remained aloof from a mute and passive giant, they did not think it wise to take such a course with a giant whose strength and prestige continued to mount.

PRESSURE ON BENES

Nevertheless, there appear to have been moments of doubt in Moscow. Beneš had not committed himself to the Gottwald proposals. Could he and his London government be trusted? Did they, perhaps, play a secret anti-Russian game? And then, in August, 1944, a Slovak National Liberation Movement became active in southeastern Czechoslovakia. Reports of violent and effective anti-Nazi underground warfare emanated from Slovakia and were broadcast by the Moscow radio. The detonation noise of Slovak anti-Nazi sabotage bombs had a distinct political undertone that could be detected in London.

The very name Slovak National Liberation Movement sounded curiously similar to that of the Yugoslav National Liberation Movement and that of the Polish Committee for National Liberation. Both these groups had developed into governments competing with more conservative regimes that had their seats in London. The Beneš government, too, had its offices in London. It, too, had the support of the British Foreign Office.

The sudden appearance of a Slovak underground movement clearly pointed to indirect Soviet pressure on the Beneš government. In effect, the Slovak partisan uprising was a warning flare directed toward the London regime. Beneš and his cabinet members might find themselves out in the cold. What had happened to the government of the Polish Republic and the royal Yugoslav government might just possibly also happen to the London government of the Czechoslovak Republic.

And then, the following spring, the Red Army entered eastern Czechoslovakia. As the communiqués phrased it, the Russian troops "established contact with the Slovak partisans." The members of the Beneš government took an airplane from London to Moscow. Ten days of intensive and secret negotiations began in the Soviet capital. The Gottwald proposals were again discussed. At this time, under the influence of prevailing conditions, they were accepted. A "Government of National Front" was formed. Beneš arrived in Košice, using Red Army facilities. The Czechoslovak government made a detailed statement of policy, based on the Gottwald proposals. The composition and plans of the new regime were announced to the world. And Klement Gottwald became vice-premier.

The official Košice program, an illuminating document, accurately indicated the position of the new government. It noted that "thanks to our great ally, the USSR, it has become possible for the President [Beneš] to return to Czechoslovakia and a new Government to be formed on home soil." The announcement stated that "appreciating the exceptional merits of the Red Army of liberation and in order to secure our future, the Government wants to strengthen even more the fighting cooperation between the Czechoslovak Army and the Red Army, in which the Government sees an example for the building of a new, really democratic anti-Fascist Czechoslovak Army."

There was a new ring to this Czechoslovak statement, the first policy outline to be made from liberated home soil. In London, the Beneš government had been careful to give equal consideration to all the major Allied powers. The Košice program heavily emphasized a new concept of Slav unity. It stressed racial links with Poland, Yugoslavia, and Bulgaria. Expressing the "great gratitude of the Czechoslovak nation to the USSR," the program pledged that "the Government will unwaveringly maintain as the leading line of Czechoslovak foreign policy, the closest alliance with the victorious Slav power of the East." To clarify this policy further, the text continued:

"The Government will, from the beginning, safeguard practical collaboration with the USSR, military, political, economic and cultural. . . . In questions regarding the punishment of Germany, of setting new frontiers, or the organization of future peace, Czechoslovakia shall stand, as closely as possible, at the side of the USSR and in one line with other Slav and democratic countries."

The die, cast at Moscow, had left its impression at Košice. But how far would the Czechoslovak people be willing to go under Communist guidance?

Instrumental in preparing for the Košice program was a man who, more than any other non-Communist official, paved the way toward fulfillment of Czechoslovak Communist aspirations. He is Zdĕnek Fierlinger, who as Czechoslovak ambassador to the Soviet Union, gained the respect and trust of Russian officials. He became premier at Košice, but, after the 1946 elections, he was replaced by Klement Gottwald. Fierlinger had been a stopgap, one-year premier.

When Gottwald addressed the Parliament at Prague, following the 1946 elections, he reiterated the need for a Czechoslovak foreign policy in close collaboration with Soviet Russia and urged delegates to help "destroy the hopes for the return of private enterprise in the fields of finance, mines, natural and energy resources, and our large key industries." He also asked for "constitutional protection for private enterprise in small and middle-sized business and all private property justly gained, especially for farmers, business men, intellectual and manual workers."

Gottwald thus referred to the domestic aspects of the Košice program, which began to take effect shortly after the end of the war. As early as July, 1945, the Ministry of Industry set up a Committee for the Preparation of Nationalization. When President Beneš signed the nationalization decrees on October 25 of that year, he did so after months of lively disputes within the cabinet. Although Beneš, his National Social Party, and other non-Marxist groups had agreed in Moscow to the Gottwald program, they felt that little good could be gained by pressing the plan too rapidly. But the Communists and left-wing Social Democrats were adamant in their demands for immediate and sweeping measures.

THE NATIONALIZATION DECREES

Although it may be said that Czechoslovakia's revolution by decree followed more closely the Soviet pattern than the nationalization efforts of the British Labour government, Gottwald and his cabinet certainly did not completely sovietize their country. The Communists, no matter with what impetuous vigor they railroaded the nationalization decrees through the cabinet, had planned three categories of industrial ownership. The score that the decrees established reads as follows:

"(1) *Nationalized Establishments*. These industries included energy-producing plants, such as electric power and gas; chemical factories; mining; textiles; glass and porcelain, including ceramics; steel production and tool making, including heavy machinery; paper and wood pulp. Each of these industries was placed under the supervision of a government-appointed general manager and a council of managers. Nationalization of commercial banks and insurance companies was easily agreed upon by all political parties. Just as in France, socialization of major basic industries did not encounter public opposition of any importance.

"(2) *Cooperative Establishments.* The cooperative movement, well developed in prewar Czechoslovakia as an elastic economic organization, has been used as a pattern for the administration of the following industries: agricultural processing plants, including sugar refineries and alcohol distilleries; and dairies.

"(3) *Private Industry.* Agriculture, providing a living for some 37 per cent of the Czechoslovak population, remained in private hands. Certainly, Communist experience—going back as far as the Russian food crisis after World War I—did not encourage nationalization of farms. By limiting land ownership to 125 acres of arable land, the government has, however, distributed land to what has been termed 'the landless and almost landless farmers.' "

Potential Soviet imports were an unplayed trump card in the hands of the Communists. The Soviet Union is theoretically very well able to replace all other Czechoslovak export markets. A small industrialized nation with a high raw-material-producing neighbor can hardly ignore the fact of economic-political life.

To serve its own needs and to give whatever help possible to its Soviet neighbor, Czechoslovakia had to produce. It had to produce efficiently in order to supply home demands, to reduce inflationary dangers, build up a favorable trade balance, and eliminate the governmental deficit. Years of economic adjustment are not conducive to quick and efficient production. Czechoslovakia's revolution, no matter how bloodless, posed a problem particularly to Communists in guiding positions.

Here are the factors that Communists in the government, in regional administration and in the management of nationalized establishments, had to face:

(1) German occupation left the country in a chaotic financial condition. Nazi occupation had reoriented the nation's economic life to feed the German war machine. It had also placed a vast part of Czechoslovak key industries under the direct administrative authority of the occupying power.

(2) A large part of the most efficiently functioning enterprises in the Bohemia-Moravia region, as well as in Slovakia, were in the hands of Nazi collaborators. These enemies of the state had to be replaced by management loyal to the Republic.

(3) The nationalization decrees of 1945 placed 75 per cent of Czechoslovakia's industry in the hands of the state. Management had to be taken over by civil servants, working hand in hand with the Communist-controlled nation-wide trade-union body, the Revolutionary Workers Movement (URO).

(4) Deportation of three million Sudeten Germans robbed the Czechoslovak state of 800,000 trained industrial workers. In a nation of fourteen million, the disappearance of three million people was bound to leave a critical vacuum.

Difficulties were inevitable. There was, above all, lack of sufficiently trained managerial personnel. Then, too, there were not enough skilled workers. The war years had reduced the number of men able to produce without retraining. Following the strenuous war period, there was noticeable lethargy. This mood was reflected in reduced production efficiency, which endangered the whole new economic program.

NO STRIKES

The Communists, aided by the Social Democrats, could not simply let the old plant managers stay at their posts. Among workers filled with freshly heightened class-consciousness, a return of old management was likely to be viewed as the reappearance of so many capitalist slave drivers. It is easy to see how these problems might have seriously interfered with the Košice program to which the Communists had committed the government. In April, 1946, when the Revolutionary Workers Movement met in Prague, its delegates heard a straightforward address by Antonin A. Zápotocký, their secretary-general and a leading Communist.

Zápotocký did not mince words. He said that the two million union members had to shoulder the decisive responsibility of reviving the nation's economy. There would be no strikes, he told them, because "Czechoslovak workers have been strong enough to avoid strikes and other work-stoppage activities," by constructing a "cooperative machinery with management, which achieved magnificent results within a very short period of time."

Conscious of impatient rumblings within the sprawling new Czecho-slovak superunion, Zápotocký bluntly told the delegates that there had been too much interference and that "management must be permitted to manage." As far as wages were concerned, there was "a limit as to how high they can go" after starvation levels have been overcome. And, he said, workers would have to realize their new "social responsibility in a system of managed economy, where large industries have been nationalized."

Of all the changes and institutions created by Czechoslovakia's bloodless revolution, the status of union labor is probably most akin to conditions prevailing in the Soviet Union. Russia's organized labor, united in the All-Soviet Council of Trade Unions, also has an important say in the way plants are run. But it does not strike. Where there is a cleavage between union labor and the civil-service management of Soviet plants, grievances are passed through successive arbitration stages. The Czechoslovak 1946 decrees provide for similar conditions. On February 8, 1947, the Prague cabinet approved a labor-mobilization law that gave the government power to remove workers from one job and move them to another. Under this law, permission is required for laborers to change their positions.

When Zápotocký told organized Czechoslovak labor to go easy in its demands, he knew that the Communists had to hold the workers' aspirations down, if they wanted to implement fully the Košice program and their Two-Year Plan. With labor conditions unsettled by general postwar conditions, they made things even tougher for themselves by pushing the vast deportation program, designed to rid Czechoslovakia of three million Sudeten Germans and some 800,000 Hungarians. Premier Gottwald himself told J. Alvárez del Vayo, an editor of the New York weekly *The Nation*, that the expelled workers had left "a gap that must be filled." He added quickly, "But we would do it again, no matter what the consequences to the national economy. We place the security of the state above any consideration of technique and production."

WHOLESALE DEPORTATION

Why were the Communists so adamant in pressing a deportation program that harmed their newly created socialization machinery? Nationalization and deportation were points of the Gottwald proposals and the Košice program. Both were doubtless approved, and possibly inspired, by

Moscow officials. Still, it might have been advantageous to go about the deportation proceedings with less haste and more preparation.

There existed no general objection to the orderly deportation of Germans from the Sudeten area. Germany had made herself as unpopular in Czechoslovakia as anywhere in Europe. The Sudeten Germans, under the leadership of Konrad Henlein, had for the most part been willing pawns in Hitler's hands. They were the pretext for the Nazi annexation of the Sudeten area and the occupation of Prague in 1939. Once and for all, the Communist-inspired program of Košice stated, use of foreign minorities to undermine the Czechoslovak state had to be eliminated. How? By eliminating the minority itself. By expulsion.

President Beneš, while still in London, advocated the transfer of populations as a definitive solution for territorial and minority questions that have puzzled European boundary makers for generations. As Beneš saw it at that time, minority privileges bestowed on foreign groups within another nation had not proved workable. Writing in the American quarterly magazine *Foreign Affairs*, he said that Czechoslovakia would "not deny the right of domicile to anyone who has remained faithful to the Republic" and that "protection of the democratic and human rights of every citizen are guaranteed in Czechoslovakia forever," including "those members of the minority races who may remain within the Republic."

In carrying out the Košice program, however, the Czechoslovak government adopted a much more radical and complete deportation policy. The Communists have been the strongest supporters of the expulsion policy. They needed to be particularly forceful, because the Social Democrats were deeply split on this matter. Among the German-speaking Sudeten residents were a relatively large number of Social Democrats who had opposed Hitler, Henlein, and everything Nazism stood for. In contrast to Dr. Beneš's earlier view, quoted above, these persons and their families were also affected by the deportation proceedings. Just what this speedy, and in many instances ruthless, policy was to accomplish is difficult to see. Certainly, being a sort of racialism in reverse, it did nothing to reeducate the affected Germans to the ideals of democracy and away from exaggerated nationalism.

There was a curious note in these expulsions. Being completely rigid, on a mixed racial-linguistic basis, they affected not only Nazis, but also anti-Nazis such as Jews, Social Democrats, and—Communists. Some of the Communists arrived in Germany, particularly in the Soviet zone, with good credentials. Others merely demonstrated their party discipline by accepting the Communist-espoused doctrine that all Germans were equally guilty of the deeds of Hitlerism and therefore had to share the punishment.

GOTTWALD CALLS FROM MOSCOW

Czechoslovak non-Communists hoped that Gottwald's party would continue its policy of relative moderation. In the summer of 1947, Hungarian Communist leader Matyas Rákosi visited Gottwald in Prague, just after Hungary's Communists had assured themselves lasting control in their country. His visit illustrated the forward march of communism in eastern and central Europe. Anxiety over possible tightening of Communist rule in Czechoslovakia was a result. This feeling was heightened when the Paris conference of Foreign Ministers Molotov, Bevin, and Bidault collapsed a few days later. This conference, which was to have prepared a Europe-wide reconstruction program with American help, might have provided Czechoslovakia with a new opportunity to act as a bridge between East and West. When the Paris talks came to nothing, a wave of pessimism and disappointment hit Czechoslovakia.

On July 7, the Czechoslovak government announced that it planned to send "observers" to the Paris talks on European reconstruction. But two nights later, Premier Gottwald conferred with Premier Stalin in Moscow, and on July 10 he reported on this conversation in a telephone call to the cabinet meeting at Prague. A few hours later, the Czechoslovak government stated that because "other Slav nations were unwilling to join in the Marshall plan," it could not accept the invitation without risking that participation "might be construed as an action against the Soviet Union."

Within three days, and with the help of one long-distance telephone call, the people of Czechoslovakia had been made to realize that communism does not permit wishful wavering.

CHAPTER 7

Austria: Persistent Disappointment

Ever since the downfall of the Habsburg Empire in 1918, Austria's Communist Party has resembled an overexcited puppy caught in a fight between two bulldogs, never quite knowing which one it hated most. The first elections after World War II did not ease this permanent frustration. On November 25, 1945, the Austrian people gave the Social Democrats 76 parliamentary seats and the Catholic People's Party 84. The Communists got 5.

Austria's Communists have suffered persistent disappointment after World War II, just as they did after World War I. That is not said to belittle the courage, or even the political foresight, displayed by Communists in Austria. It merely serves to illustrate a grotesque political situation that has many tragic undertones. During the existence of the Communist International, Moscow officials frequently spoke with contempt of "Austro-Marxism." It was the label that they used for the cautious policy of Vienna's Social Democrats, who were always waiting for a truly democratic mandate from the people. These Austrian Socialists refused all Communist suggestions of a Bolshevik-like coup d'état.

In the end, when the leaders of the Christian Socialists (the prewar counterpart of the Catholic People's Party) crushed the Social Democrats, the Communist could say, "I told you so." In February, 1934, the government of Engelbert Dollfuss did away with democratic parliamentarism and crushed the Social Democrats and Communists by force. This rightist coup came to a climax with a full-scale military siege of Vienna's modern, Socialist-built, workers' apartment houses.

For four years, the Christian Socialists continued their totalitarian rule. Then their government was, in turn, crushed by the invading troops of Nazi Germany. After the Allied victory, the precarious Socialist-Catholic

71

coalition that had lasted from 1918 to 1927 was again taken up. The presence of the Soviet army in eastern Austria relieved somewhat the feeling of permanent frustration that the Communist Party of Austria had experienced during the interwar years. But Austria was divided into zones occupied not only by Russia but by the United States, Great Britain, and France as well. This made it unlikely that the Communists could hope to gain control, as they had managed to do in Romania and Hungary.

In eastern Austria, Hungary, and Romania, Soviet authorities could not rely on a powerful and dominant Communist movement or on a clearly Communist-dominated coalition, such as existed in Bulgaria, Yugoslavia, Albania, and Poland. Consequently, the Soviet military authorities had to do many things themselves. And, while Hungarian Communists could boast experienced and shrewd leadership, Austria presented a very different picture.

ADOLESCENT "PUTSCHISM"

For a brief period, following its foundation on November 1, 1918, the Communist Party of Austria enjoyed relatively high popularity. Its strength lay with Austrian prisoners of war who had returned from Russia, who had seen the men who made the Bolshevik Revolution. Back in impoverished Vienna, they came to look upon the well-entrenched Socialists as traitors to the revolutionary idea. Again and again, the Communists tried to light the torch of rebellion. They failed. Their period of persistent disappointment had begun.

In 1919, Austria found herself briefly between two Soviet governments: Béla Kun's regime in Hungary, and short-lived Soviet government in Bavaria. Russian and Hungarian envoys in Vienna fostered the idea of a Soviet Austria. A special representative, Dr. Ernst Bettelheim, arrived in Vienna in May, 1919, with funds and instructions from Hungary.

The Social Democratic leader Otto Bauer charged later in his book *Austrian Revolution* that Bettelheim and the Austrian Communists had planned an armed insurrection for June 15, 1919. On that date, the Social Democratic domestic army, the Volkswehr, was to be reduced in strength. The Social Democrats asked the Allied powers' permission to retain the army at its full strength, and the revolt was halted.

Earlier, the Communists had tried their hands at a number of unsuccessful embryo rebellions. The Comintern didn't like this toying with the dictatorship of the proletariat and accused its Austrian branch of adolescent "putschism." On one occasion, the Communists attempted to storm the Parliament and a few other government buildings. They were stopped by the Socialists. At another time, Communists occupied the offices of Vienna's leading daily, the *Neue Freie Presse*. They abandoned it after a few hours, not quite knowing what else to do.

This sort of thing did not go down well in Moscow. Dmitri Z. Manuilsky, who today represents the Ukraine before the United Nations, expressed Comintern impatience with overzealous Austrian communism in no uncertain terms. As reported in *Internationale Presse Korrespondenz*, the Communist press service, Manuilsky quoted the Vienna Communist daily *Rote Fahne* as stating that "an immediate revolutionary situation" existed inside Austria. This phrase, according to Manuilsky, should mean that the situation was ripe for "an uprising in Austria." However, he wrote, "the Austrian comrades are not even able to bring 2,000 to 3,000 people into the streets." Manuilsky concluded scornfully that "such an interpretation of 'an immediate revolutionary situation' means to compromise this conception, and to regard this earnest revolutionary task with lack of seriousness and through sectarian eyes."

The *Rote Fahne*, in turn, wrote shortly afterward, on November 21, 1919, "The workers do not exist to satisfy somebody's leader ego, and it isn't their task to try their hands, now and then, at a little coup d'état." Only five months earlier, the Communists had demanded of the Social Democrats that they help them to create a Soviet Austria. One of the most fiery Communist spokesmen was a petite, dark-eyed young woman, Mrs. Elfriede Friedländer, née Eisler, who later came to the United States and testified against her brother, the Comintern's American agent Gerhart Eisler. "What can threaten us," she said in Vienna, "if in this hour of decision and danger, and in defiance of foreign capitalism, we overthrow our domestic capitalism?"

The Social Democrats felt that foreign intervention would soon put an end to Viennese Bolshevik dreams. Nothing much happened to Austrian communism during the decade that followed. The party's popular support dwindled. During the 1919 election, it polled 27,000 votes; in 1923, 21,000; in 1927, 18,000. The rightist opposition representing the Austrian party at the Comintern Congress of 1928 reported that "the Communist Party of Austria has no tangible influence with the workers, and it has no organizational foundation within the decisive strata of the working people." The extremist-revolutionary Third Strategy of the Comintern did not go down well with the easygoing Viennese. And, when the "united front" policy came along, it was too late. The Christian Socialists had established their tight totalitarian regime a year earlier.

THE CONVERSION OF ERNST FISCHER

During the underground period that followed the 1934 coup, a number of Socialists joined the Communist ranks. They felt that it had been useless to work with the Christian Socialists, only to be crushed by them. The Christian Socialists argued, of course, that they had done it all simply to avoid Nazi German intervention. It was a sort of appeasement, which did away with democratic procedure. Among the few prominent Socialist converts to the cause of communism was Ernst Fischer, today the brains of the Austrian Communist Party. Johann Koplenig is the party's secretary-general, but Fischer is the more able of the two.

Born July 3, 1898, in Graz, Fischer fought at the Russian front and was elected to the soldiers' Soviet in 1918. While studying philosophy at Graz University, he worked in a coke-processing plant. He joined the Social Democratic Party in 1920 and became editor of its Graz paper, *Arbeiter-Wille*. His journalistic and political-analytical abilities were recognized, and in 1927 he went to Vienna, where he joined the staff of the Socialist Party's central organ, the *Arbeiterzeitung*. In 1933, he became active in the left-wing opposition within the Social Democratic Party. When the Christian Socialists crushed the Left, Fischer fled to Prague. Austrian Communist activity was centered in Prague from 1934 to 1938, the year of the Munich Pact and the Nazi invasion of Czechoslovakia. As a member of the Austrian Communist central committee, Ernst Fischer contributed qualities that the party had lacked.

Fischer immediately went to Moscow, where he was active in propaganda work. He broadcast over the Russian radio, wrote pamphlets, and contributed to Communist publications in all parts of the world. During the period of the Nazi-Soviet Pact, Fischer wrote a pamphlet entitled, *Is This a War for Freedom?*, in which he said, "This war is an imperialist war, an unjust war, a war that is destroying Europe and threatening to plunge all the nations of the capitalist world into an abyss of blood and misery." About his ardent desire to bring about a Communist society, there can be no doubt. In a pamphlet, *What Is Socialism?*, Fischer clarified his views in colorful terms as follows:

"As mankind rose up from its animal state to fight its way to reason and freedom, so it will rise out of the blood and filth of dying capitalism to make its entry into the realm where reason and freedom hold sway. And from this realm of reason and freedom, from Communist Society, it will look back on the crippled and cramped human beings of capitalism as the man of today on the troglodyte of Neanderthal, the cave dweller, still half a beast and only half a man."

If he today seeks a fusion of Communists and Social Democrats, that has probably not lessened his disdain for the party to which he once belonged. In the *Communist International* of August 5, 1943, Fischer accused the Socialists of "having attached themselves like leeches to capitalism." When the victorious Red Army entered Vienna, a cabinet was created in which Ernst Fischer became minister of education. The 1945 election was highlighted by persistent Communist efforts to persuade the Social Democrats that fusion of the two parties would be a very good thing. Karl Renner, the veteran Socialist who later became Austria's president, argued against such fusion because "the assurances that the men who run the other working class party have suddenly also become democratic, are rather recent and almost, let us say, too obvious." When the election results proved the continued weakness of the Communists, Fischer did not continue as a cabinet member. Instead, he devoted all his time to Communist Party work.

"THE ONLY WAY"

At the time of the 1945 elections, the Communist Party of Austria had 25,000 members. Membership figures climbed quickly during the next six months, but became relatively static afterward. On April 20, 1946, the party held its Thirteenth Conference, and delegates heard that it had enlisted 132,000 members. Ernst Fischer delivered a report, which called for Socialist-Communist "unity of action." Johann Koplenig outlined a six-point program of Communist postwar activities, which climaxed in the appeal that "every Communist must spread the conviction that the only way in which Austria can advance is the way we Communists propose."

In the fall of 1946, the Communists took the initiative in organizing demonstrations and strikes in the United States, British, and French zones of occupation. No strikes occurred in Soviet-occupied eastern Austria. In the month of September alone, the party took credit for thirty-five strikes. In October, the Communists asked the Social Democrats to join them in a thirty-six-hour general strike in protest against the low food supplies, which had then forced the occupation authorities to limit daily rations to 1,200 calories per person.

Although Austria's Communists did not gain control of the interior ministry, they were able to place Heinrich Duermayer at the head of Vienna's political police. On March 20, 1947, Colonel Ilyechev, a Russian member of the Allied Council for Austria, demanded that the interior ministry appoint several Communists to high policy posts. This demand was rejected and was followed by sharp cuts in oil deliveries from the Russian zone to Vienna.

A brief government crisis developed early in June when Ernst Fischer stated at a private party that the Soviet Union would never sign a peace treaty with Austria unless Communist representation in the government were enlarged. On June 9, Fischer alleged that Chancellor Leopold Figl was preparing to resign. The People's Party immediately denied that Figl had made such a statement and assured the public that the Chancellor "does not let himself be led astray by Communist wish dreams."

HALF A CHANCE

Compared with their insignificant rise during the 1920's and early 1930's, Austria's Communists have made enormous gains. But their strength in relation to the dominant Christian Socialist and Social Democratic parties remains inconsequential. The presence of Soviet troops in eastern Austria has not been an unmixed blessing for the cause of communism. Neither the Communist nor, for that matter, the Social Democrats have been happy about the way in which Russian troops tended to confirm some of the Nazi propaganda directed against the Soviet Union. Economic exploitation by Soviet authorities in eastern Austria has weakened the hand of the Socialists, too, because the People's Party has been in the habit of lumping "the two Marxist parties" together, in a somewhat primitive political fashion. The People's Party's right wing is relatively strong. Consequently, it has been retarded in its democratic development. It is far behind such resistance-born Catholic parties as the MRP of France and Italy's Christian Democrats.

The future of communism in Austria depends on the development of the Social Democrats. Austria's Socialists have developed along the road chosen by Britain's Labour Party and the Socialist movements in the Lowlands and Scandinavia. There is little likelihood that, under conditions of political freedom, Austrian Socialism will link its destiny with communism, as has happened in Hungary, Poland, and Italy. It is a truism that communism progresses where hunger and need are rampant. Austria, a small country that has been burdened with quadruple occupation, will have a difficult time recovering from the war and its aftermath. Given half a chance, it is not likely to accept doctrines offered by the extreme left or by the remaining pro-Nazi extreme right.

CHAPTER 8

Hungary: A Lesson Learned

WHEN COMMUNISM returned to Hungary in 1945, it had learned a basic lesson. Twenty-six years earlier, it had tried to impose a revolution from without. The Bolshevik regime of 1919 had been built on blood, and after 133 days it was drowned in blood. One of the men who led the Communist government following World War I is today deputy premier of Hungary and secretary-general of the Communist Party. He is Matyas Rákosi, easily the most important political figure in his country. Five years of illegal activity, fourteen years in a Budapest prison, and five war years in Moscow taught him that revolutions are made from within. He knows that political change takes time and careful preparation—particularly in Hungary.

Nationalist Hungary still dreams of lost grandeur. The Treaty of Trianon destroyed its empire, following World War I. The end of World War II saw Hungary again on the losing side. Revisionism was hopeless but not dead. Hungary has a large conservative peasant population. Its urban self-styled elite has a reputation for cosmopolitan charm and stubborn nationalist pride. Neither Hungary's corn-growing *puszta* nor Budapest's metropolitan asphalt provides a soil on which communism can flourish easily.

The Seventh Strategy of communism has been successful in Hungary. Béla Kun, who engineered the 1919 regime, believed that the shortest way from a non-Communist society to Bolshevik rule is the straight line of dictatorship. Rákosi, who was one of Kun's people's commissars, knows better. Instead of attempting to communize Hungary in one sweeping move, his party entered a coalition in which it presented a minority. A free and fair election was held, in which non-Communist parties received a clear majority.

With the help of Communists in police posts, the influence of non-

78

Communists and anti-Communists was gradually whittled down. Rákosi also pressed actions that were favored by genuinely liberal Hungarians. The number of pro-Nazi collaborators in Hungarian life was reduced, largely because of Communist pressure. For these reasons, and by linking the country's economy ever more tightly to the Soviet Union, Communist influence in Hungary rose steadily. This was largely accomplished by bloodless and nonviolent means, much in contrast to the activity of Communist governments elsewhere in southeastern Europe. In 1947, the Hungarian Communist Party claimed 650,000 members.

Conservative Hungarians who recalled the 1919 regime, or colorful accounts of that period, had noted Rákosi's arrival with misgivings. They were pleasantly surprised. The bald, muscle-packed Communist leader put great emphasis on his love for Hungary's past and future. He was successful in adapting his policies to nationalist grievances. In October, 1945, the Hungarian Communist Party announced that it was "firmly opposed to the oppression of the Hungarian population in Slovakia." The Communists thus took a nationalist stand on a subject on which most of their fellow countrymen felt very strongly. This put Communist Deputy Premier Rákosi in opposition to the policies of Communist Premier Gottwald of Czechoslovakia, who favored deportation of Hungarians from Slovakia.

SOVIET HUNGARY

By displaying none of the more violent characteristics associated with the Kun regime, Rákosi was able to gain a reputation of relative moderation. This was particularly remarkable, since his career might have embittered him against many of the groups which had remained prominent in Hungarian national life. Born on March 9, 1892, in the village of Ada, near Szeged, Hungary's second city, Rákosi had become a radical Marxist in adolescence. He went to the Szeged high school and earned pocket money through tutoring. While still a student, he participated in labor demonstrations and read the Communist Manifesto. Rákosi visited Germany and England in 1912 and 1913. A year later he was at the Russian front as a Hungarian soldier.

While a Russian prisoner in the Chita and Dauria camps, his Marxist thoughts crystallized, and he agitated actively among his fellow prisoners. He secretly made his way to Petrograd (Leningrad), which was in Soviet hands, observed the October revolution, and returned to Hungary in 1918.

Back in Budapest, he was attracted to a political circle around a certain Dr. Eugen Sebestyén, a man of about thirty-five who claimed to have been a military physician. His name was not Dr. Eugen Sebestyén. He was not a former military physician. But he had been in Russia, had organized a Hungarian Red Legion, and was the only Hungarian to enjoy Lenin's confidence. His name, Béla Kun, was to go down in history as that of Hungary's Communist dictator.

Béla Kun's chance to take power came after stringent demands of the Entente powers on the Hungarian liberal-revolutionary government headed by Count Michael Karolyi. Faced with Allied requests that Hungary withdraw from certain regions bordering on Czechoslovakia, Yugoslavia, and Romania, Count Karolyi turned the government over to a Communist-Social Democrat coalition. On March 21, 1919, the two Marxist parties agreed to "take power together under the name of Hungarian Socialist Party."

During the 133 days of the Soviet regime several hundred people were killed. Hungarian anti-Communists have described this "red terror" extensively. The Kun regime does not compare in ruthlessness with the Bulgarian Communist regime that followed World War II, and it is of course completely dwarfed by the slaughtering of millions under the Nazi rule over Europe. After the fall of Béla Kun, Hungary was struck by an anti-Communist "white terror." Viewed through the telescope of history, neither side revealed any particular scruples during these successive waves of violence.

When Kun fled Hungary on August 2, 1919, Rákosi soon followed. At twenty-seven, he had been one of the youngest commissars in the Hungarian Soviet regime. Before the coup d'état, he had established branches of the Communist Party in Szeged and other cities. During the Soviet regime, Rákosi was peoples commissar of supplies, plenipotentiary on the southern and northern fronts, organizer of grain collections, and commander of the Red Militia in Budapest. Rákosi fled to Austria, was interned, and left for the Soviet Union in 1920, in time to attend the Second Comintern Congress.

"I HAVE NO CAUSE WHATEVER TO RELENT"

Like most Comintern officials who were linguistically adept, Rákosi did illegal underground work in a number of European countries. He returned to Hungary in 1924. Two years later his activity was uncovered and he was condemned to eight and a half years in the Vácz prison. His second trial, late in 1935 and early in 1936, attracted international attention because of Rákosi's remarkable courage and poise. He stood accused of treason, mutiny, twenty-five cases of murder, and seventeen cases of inciting to murder and of counterfeiting. Knowing full well that the crimes of which he had been accused might result in a death sentence, he said:

"Wherever I was sent, I honestly pursued my Communist convictions. With a clear conscience I take upon myself full responsibility for every one of my actions during the proletarian dictatorship, and have no intention of belittling the role I played. All I did, I did by conviction. I do not intend to justify my actions. I want only to say that to this day I still hold the convictions I held then. I have no cause whatever to relent, although I have been in prison for ten years."

On February 8, 1936, Rákosi was sentenced to life imprisonment. During the period of the Nazi-Soviet pact, the Russian government negotiated the exchange of Rákosi for Hungarians who were being held inside the Soviet Union. On November 6, 1940, Matyas Rákosi arrived in Moscow. During the war years, he prepared Soviet propaganda aimed at overthrowing the pro-Nazi regime of Admiral Nicholas Horthy, who has been held responsible for much of the "white terror" of 1919 and later repression measures. Rákosi visited prisoner of war camps in the Soviet Union, indoctrinating Hungarian soldiers, just as he had done after the October Revolution.

When Matyas Rákosi reentered Hungary, he was backed by the prestige of the victorious Red Army. His knowledge of English had been extended through reading of British and American literature during his years of imprisonment. The war years, spent in Moscow, had helped him to catch up with ideological-strategic changes caused by the ousting of Trotsky, the purges, and official dissolution of the Comintern. As an old-time critic of Béla Kun's impetuous revolutionary methods, Rákosi doubtless found himself in line with the postwar strategy of world communism.

In trying to rid Hungarians of their anti-Communist anxieties, Rákosi was not immediately aided by the soldiers of the Red Army. Russian troops in Budapest and the provinces showed extreme lack of discipline. Hungary's Communists also encountered the accusation that Soviet removal of national wealth was pushing Hungary to the brink of economic ruin.

ONLY SEVENTEEN PER CENT

Another factor working against popular acceptance of the Communist credo was the attitude of the country's peasant population. Hungary's first postwar elections on November 4, 1945, gave the moderately Socialistic Small Landholders Party 57 per cent of the popular vote. The Communists received only 17 per cent, or 800,000, of the votes. Following American and British protests, the Red Army command had not realized its plan for a combined ticket of all parties. Instead, the elections revealed the true sentiment of the Hungarian voting population. When the Red Army command agreed to separate party lists, it was specified that the Communists would receive the ministry of the interior.

The elections showed that the Small Landholders had taken the wind out of the Communist sails by advocating division of large estates into small homesteads. The Communists, who had hoped to reap the political fruits of the long overdue defeudalization of estates, thus lost much of their appeal among the peasants. But Rákosi took the election's outcome in his stride. Hungary's chaotic inflationary economy would have been a grave liability for an out-and-out Communist regime. With the Social Democratic Party under Arpád Szakasit following Communist leadership, the Hungarian government was split into a rightist (Small Landholder) and a leftist (Communist-led) faction. László Rajk, the Communist interior minister was aided by the former Soviet citizen Peter Gábor, head of the political police. Zoltan Vas, a Hungarian as well as a Soviet citizen, became commissioner of supply and mayor of Budapest.

Following instructions from the Soviet military command, Gábor's police announced in the summer of 1946 that assassination plans against Rákosi and other leftist leaders had been uncovered. A large number of Hungarian organizations were dissolved. Shortly afterward, Communist-Soviet pressure forced the Small Landholders to expel twenty of its parliamentary deputies. Those expelled included a number of people who had opposed the Horthy government or had been known as genuine anti-Nazis. They had, however, objected to growing Communist domination of the government's affairs. The Small Landholders attempted to limit the number of key police posts held by Communists to 50 per cent, but they did not succeed. More and more non-Communist deputies were forced to resign.

Early in 1947, the Communists appeared to have won the battle for control in Hungary, although the elections had gone clearly against them. The efforts to reduce the Small Landholders' powers came to a climax when László Rajk's interior ministry announced that nearly one hundred Smallholders had been implicated in a conspiracy to overthrow the government. The announcement was made on December 31, 1946, and caused widespread confusion and consternation.

In an atmosphere of utmost secrecy, the ministry of the interior carried out a series of arrests. If rightist Hungarians had indeed planned a coup while Soviet troops continued to occupy the country, they were certainly guilty of romanticism and revolutionary naïveté. However, the people whom the Communist-controlled interior ministry accused of plotting were generally regarded as sober men, not given to adventuring. Anti-Communist Hungarians were inclined to think that the Communist Party was merely preparing the ground for governmental control. The Communists, it was assumed, were seeking to establish themselves so securely that they would in effect control the government even after the Soviet Army had left.

WHO INTERFERED?

Pressure against the Smallholders and their premier Ferenc Nagy bore fruit. Nagy agreed to a change in the cabinet, and to the expulsion of yet another group of Smallholder representatives from the Parliament. A United States note addressed to the Soviet Union on March 6, 1947, clarified the American view of the whole matter but did not succeed in stiffening the attitude taken by Premier Nagy. The United States note was an exceedingly plain-spoken document. It accused the Soviet government of "interference in the domestic affairs of Hungary in support of repeated aggressive attempts by Hungarian minority elements to coerce the popularly elected majority." The note said, "Unable to achieve their political ends through normal constitutional processes, the Hungarian Communists, together with other members of the Leftist bloc, have endeavored to implicate a number of representatives of the majority Smallholders party in a recently revealed plot against the Republic, and, by demanding the withdrawal of Parliamentary immunity from Smallholders Deputies, to weaken the Parliamentary position to which that party was duly elected by the Hungarian people. Simultaneously, police and administrative authorities responsive to the dictates of these minority elements have utilized their powers of investigation of the conspiracy not toward the expeditious judicial resolution of a threat against the state, but to conduct a general campaign against their political opponents."

Washington was particularly aroused by the arrest of Béla Kovacs, secretary-general of the Smallholders, by the Soviet occupation army itself. Kovacs had been arrested by the Soviet High Command, the United States note stated, "without prior discussion with the United States and United Kingdom representatives on the Allied Control Commission." What had happened was that Premier Nagy had refused to remove parliamentary immunity from Kovacs, whose anti-Communist sentiments had become well known. Thus the interior ministry could not arrest Kovacs. But the Soviet Army could, after he had been accused of participating in "subversive and anti-Soviet terror groups" and in "organizing espionage directed against the Soviet Union." The United States note described these charges as "unwarranted." Two days later the Soviet High Command in Hungary rejected the American note. There was no need for the Allied powers to investigate the alleged plot, the Soviet answer said, for that would be "a rude violation of the legal rights of Hungary's Peoples Court." As for Kovacs, the Russians regarded the American note as "an attempt to infringe on the legal rights of the Soviet occupation authorities."

It was Béla Kovacs's fate that apparently convinced Premier Ferenc Nagy that it was advisable to bow to Communist demands. Further expulsions of Smallholders delegates brought the number of that party's parliamentary delegates down to 211. In one way or another, thirty-five Smallholders representatives had been expelled from the Parliament, and the party had lost its absolute majority (246 out of 426 seats), which it had achieved through the 1945 national elections. Hungary was slowly but surely moving along the course that the shrewd and patient Matyas Rákosi had charted.

For several months nothing was heard from Béla Kovacs. Suddenly, early in June, 1947, this silence was broken. Kovacs had made a confession to the Russian authorities which implicated Ferenc Nagy and other Small Landholder leaders in an alleged plot. This confession was issued over Kovacs's signature after having been transmitted by Russian authorities to Rákosi. The document recalled the remarkably frank confessions that high Soviet officials made at the Moscow treason trials in the 1930's.

Ferenc Nagy, who was in Switzerland at the time of the crisis, resigned and came to the United States. He denied any part in the alleged conspiracy to which the Kovacs confession referred. Nagy was replaced by Lajos Dinnyes, a Small Landholder representative acceptable to the Soviet authorities and the Communists. Several Hungarian diplomatic representatives abroad resigned their posts. On June 11 the United States published a notice which recalled that the Russians had earlier rejected joint investigation by the three occupation powers of the charges against Kovacs and stated, "It now develops, however, that his offense was the same conspiracy which could not be investigated by three powers but which has in fact been investigated by one, and which has led to a most flagrant interference in Hungarian affairs."

The note stated that "this action has resulted in the realignment of political authority in Hungary so that a minority which obtained 17 per cent of popular support in the last free election has nullified the expressed will of the majority of the Hungarian people, a situation which has apparently been admitted by the leader of the Communist minority, Rákosi, who is reported to have taken public satisfaction that his 'iron-fisted' party, 'conscious of its aims' has thus been able to take over control of Hungary."

Rákosi could indeed look back on two years of patient and effective political maneuvering. The Communists emerged from the second postwar election, held on August 31, 1947, as Hungary's largest party; they polled 1,112,000 votes.

CHAPTER 9

Romania: Without History

ROMANIAN POLITICAL life during the past quarter of a century resembled a repertory theater: frequent changes in the bill, different settings, but always the same actors. From time to time hero and villain had to change places. There was drama, comedy, and opéra bouffe. But the supporting cast hardly changed. And everybody knew that the rivalries among the stars were the most real thing on the whole stage.

Today, the Romanian repertory is under Communist management. New directors have taken over. Some of the former supporting players have been cast in prominent roles, carrying out the directors' instructions. But most of the actors are still the same. They are seasoned troopers now, able to speak the new lines with vigor and seeming conviction. The audience knows better.

Although the postwar change in Romania's government seems staged, there is nothing unreal about the country's need for a genuine economic reform. A peasantry handicapped by debts and backward agricultural methods forms the main body of the Romanian nation. A notoriously corrupt bureaucracy stands between the peasant masses and a glittering urban society that has ruled the country in the past and now follows a policy of watchful opportunist collaboration.

Romania's leading man during the immediate postwar period was Petre Groza. The Communist Party, resurrected after twenty-five years of illegality, divided the job of organizing Romania's workers with Groza's Plowmen's Front. The Communists sought the support of the urban laborers. The Plowmen's Front concentrated on the agricultural masses, trying to reduce the influence of the National Peasant Party.

This arrangement was confirmed on June 23, 1945, by Premier Groza himself. He told a correspondent of the Moscow radio that "the political line of the Plowmen's Front has run parallel with that of the Romanian

Communist Party." Groza said that the "Communist Party defends the interests of the proletariat, while the Plowmen's Front defends the interest of the peasants."

The National Peasant Party and its leader, the septuagenary Iuliu Maniu, became the strongest opponents of the Communists. The Peasant Party and the National Liberal Party had dominated the political life of Romania during the interwar years. The name Liberal Party should not be taken too literally. Although it was founded during the latter half of the nineteenth century for the purpose of promoting liberal ideas, the party later became more and more the tool of the Romanian governing minority. A nonmonarchic dynasty, the Bratianu family, has run the Liberal Party from its conception until the end of World War II. Discredited by its past record, it became an easy target for the Communist pressure. Its leader, Dinu Bratianu, was attacked by Gheorghe Tatarescu, who favored a policy of close collaboration with the Communists and their allies, the Plowmen's Front. Tatarescu split the Liberal Party and joined Groza's Communist-dominated cabinet.

Tatarescu, who emerged in 1945 as deputy premier and foreign minister, personifies the opportunism of both the Communists and some of their erstwhile opponents in Romania. Tatarescu's record, which includes premiership in a totalitarian cabinet in 1940, could easily be used to label him as a "war criminal" in Communist terms. During the years when his governmental power was supreme, Tatarescu suppressed the Communist Party as rigorously as the premiers who preceded and followed him. In a country like Bulgaria, the Communist-run regime would have executed a man with this record. But Romania is different.

Lucretiu Patrascanu, Romania's Communist minister of justice, has been quoted as stating that political conditions in his country demanded that a "more liberal definition of the phrase 'war criminal' must be applied to Romania than in other countries." This policy may account for the number of men with dubious political pasts who have served the postwar Bucharest regime.

Hal Lehrman, Bucharest correspondent for the newspaper *PM* and the weekly *The Nation* (both publications that cannot be accused of wild red baiting) reported in April, 1946, that Giorgiu Macovescu, second-in-command in the propaganda ministry and "an eloquent, indignant Communist," had formerly served the Nazis, when, under the profascist

(Ion) Antonescu regime, he "saw to it that the newspapers went on fighting Bolshevism every day in every way."

Another liberal United States correspondent, Leigh White of the *Chicago Daily News*, reported after a stay in Bucharest, "Whatever the reason, a surprising number of former Fascists appear to have been successful in switching their allegiance to the Communist party. Romanian liberals, whose word I trust, assure me that under the Communists they are being pushed around by many of the self-same persons who pushed them around when the Fascists were in power."

But neither Groza nor Tatarescu is the driving force of the Bucharest regime. The power behind the Romanian government is Anna Pauker, a plump woman past middle age, who sits at Groza's side at public functions. In many ways, her earlier career is similar to that of Matyas Rákosi of Hungary. Born in a small provincial town, Anna Pauker tutored other children when she was only thirteen years old. She began a teacher's career at a Budapest high school at the age of seventeen, while becoming active in the Socialist Party. She went to workers' clubs and distributed the party paper, the *Romanian Worker*.

ANNA PAUKER, MASS AGITATOR

When Romania seized Bessarabia from the Soviet Union after World War I, it also grabbed a hornet's nest of agitation and unrest. There was little Communist activity elsewhere in Romania. But the October revolution had echoed in Bessarabia. In 1918, illegal Communist groups were formed within the Romanian Socialist Party. On November 20, 1918, the Romanian cabinet dissolved the Communist Party and arrested left-wing Socialists who had endorsed the aims of the Third International.

In 1921, another wave of anti-Communist activity began. A great number of agitators were arrested. An account in the *Communist International* (March, 1937) states that Anna Pauker worked "as an organizer, a propagandist and a mass agitator" during this period. She was arrested early in January, 1923, by government police, together with several hundred others, and taken to Bucharest's Vacaresti prison. She was held there, together with other women accused of revolutionary activities, many of whom were beaten. Mrs. Pauker later wrote in a pamphlet published by the Romanian League for Human Rights that she participated in a hunger strike from January 9 to 17 and that she witnessed the torturing of fellow inmates. It appears, however, that she managed to avoid mistreatment. After being released by Romanian authorities, Anna Pauker went abroad, presumably to the Soviet Union. She now speaks Russian and French fluently. She returned to Romania illegally—again following the general pattern of Communist underground workers—and was able to do underground work for some time. She was arrested and condemned to prison but managed to escape to the Soviet Union.

When Romania was liberated, neither Anna Pauker nor any other Romanian Communist could qualify for the position of premier. Following the standard pattern, Communists immediately took over the ministries of the interior and of justice. Lucretiu Patrascanu, minister of justice, was aided by Techari Georgescu, minister of interior, and Gheorghe Gheorghiu-Dej, minister of public works and communications.

A cabinet was formed on August 23, 1944, under the premiership of Constantin Sanatescu. Communist and Communist-inspired political aspirations brought a reshuffle on November 4. A month later, Sanatescu resigned and was succeeded by General Nicolas Radescu. Both Sanatescu and Radescu were army men at the head of the practically identical coalition governments composed of the National Peasant Party, the National Liberal Party, and parties of the National Democratic Front (which included the Communists, Social Democrats, and Plowmen's Front). The National Democratic Front heaped accusations on Radescu, charging him with laxness in fulfilling the armistice terms, particularly in the prosecution of collaborationists, and with failing to "fully democratize" Romania's political institutions.

The anti-Radescu campaign was spear-headed by the Moscow radio, which quoted freely from the Soviet and Romanian Communist press. *Pravda,* as cited by the Moscow radio, said on February 22 that Radescu was "incapable of establishing stability and order in Romania with democratic means." The editorial added, "Soviet public opinion cannot remain indifferent to this internal struggle of the democratic elements against the Fascist elements in Romania." Another broadcast "exposed" the "pro-fascist activity of Radescu and his clique, the retention of war criminals in the Romanian army, the maintenance of secret arms and caches in Bucharest, and the transport of Hitlerite saboteurs to Germany."

Inside Romania, Communist-inspired pressure against Radescu took the form of demonstrations that led to some violence. On February 24, General Radescu appeared before the microphone of the Bucharest radio, charging that "the nationless and the godless" had "begun to set fire to the country and to bathe it in blood." In a voice that shook with emotion and anger, he added, "Under the mask of democracy, a democracy which they trample underfoot at each step, these frightful hyenas hope to obtain control of the country." Radescu told his listeners that two bullets had entered the Royal Palace, and "they fired shots into the prefecture and attacked the Ministry of the Interior where I was, with a bullet falling near my writing desk."

VISHINSKY GETS TOUGH

Open civil war had become a strong possibility. Three days later, Soviet Vice Commissar for Foreign Affairs Andrei Y. Vishinsky arrived in Bucharest by air. He immediately went to see King Michael and told him he was acting on written orders from Premier Stalin. He requested the immediate resignation of Radescu and appointment of a new premier. After consulting party leaders, Michael selected Prince Barbu Stirbey to be the new premier. He sent an announcement of this decision to the Bucharest radio, but the Soviet occupation authorities prevented it from being broadcast. King Michael was advised that Petre Groza would make a more desirable premier. Michael again consulted with the party leaders. Impatient at this delay, Vishinsky told the king that Groza would have to be nominated. Government officials to whom King Michael gave an account of this conversation later stated that Vishinsky said further delays would endanger the "continued independence of Romania." The king relented and proposed a cabinet divided equally between the so-called "historical parties" (Peasants and Liberals), and the parties making up the Communist-led National Democratic Front. Vishinsky went to see Michael for a third time, asking for a cabinet "willing to ignore party lines and to prosecute the NDF program without hesitation."

Groza became premier on March 6, 1945. Radescu found refuge in the British Legation at Bucharest and later went into exile. Moscow radio expressed amazement at the fact that Radescu had gone into hiding, "although he was not persecuted, and that the British representatives found it possible to accord him asylum." British Foreign Secretary Anthony Eden told the House of Commons on March 14 that "Radescu sought sanctuary because he feared for his life from his opponents." Eden added, "As His Majesty's government had no evidence that General

Radescu has been guilty of any activity against the Allies, British representatives in Bucharest were authorized to give him sanctuary."

With Radescu disposed of, the Communist Party accelerated its campaign against Dr. Iuliu Maniu, leader of the Peasant Party, and Titel Petrescu, head of the Social Democratic Party. As a group that had consistently advocated agricultural reform and the abolishment of totalitarian ruling methods, the Peasants represented the most formidable opposition. Petrescu was disposed of in the spring of 1946, when his party split on the issue of forming a combined ticket with the Communists and the other groups of the government bloc. Lotar Radaceanu, labor minister of the Groza government, led the pro-Communist, anti-Petrescu wing into the ruling coalition. Petrescu later found himself unable to publish a newspaper or otherwise engage in effective opposition activity.

Attempts were made to force Maniu's resignation as head of the powerful Peasant Party. On April 8, 1945, the Moscow radio even broadcast a Bucharest report which asserted that "Maniu confirmed his decision to resign the post of National Peasant Party leader, owing to poor health." But the health of the aged Maniu apparently proved more rugged than had been anticipated, and he led his party during the election campaign that was climaxed by the voting on November 19, 1946. There was a general feeling in Bucharest opposition circles, in the London Foreign Office, and in the Washington State Department prior to the election that the Communist-led government coalition would emerge victorious from the elections. In fact, so high was the skepticism of American and British government officials that a series of notes were dispatched to Bucharest, protesting against the government's election tactics. Foreign Minister Tatarescu, however, rejected the British and American protest notes by saying that "the democratic principles of freedom and justice" would "remain the constant guidance of this government's actions in the general elections, as well as in the achievement of the great reforms destined to reorganize the basic establishments of the Romanian state."

Leaders of the opposition charged, however, that the government coalition had prepared duplicate ballot boxes that would be substituted for those containing ballots actually deposited by voters. Maniu therefore urged his followers to remain at balloting places, in order to prevent such tactics. The Peasant Party also charged that the percentage of opposition votes had been fixed in advance by the government coalition. How accurate these accusations were, remained difficult to ascertain. Final results showed, however, that opposition predictions had been remarkably accurate. About 5,000 Romanian citizens appeared at the building of the United States government mission in Bucharest to state that they had not been permitted to cast their votes. In turn, government supporters picketed the mission building. This resulted in a protest by Brigadier General Courtland Van Rensselaer Schuyler, head of the American mission, to the Groza government.

"UNFAIR AND IRREGULAR" ELECTIONS

Of the more than 7,800,000 votes cast, 4,766,360 were said to have endorsed the government coalition, with another 569,651 for a Communist-endorsed Hungarian Popular Union. Maniu's Peasants received 879,927, Bratianu's Liberals 259,306, and Petrescu's Independent Social Democrats 65,528 votes. Another 156,755 votes were said to have been cast for the National Peasant Democrats. As a result, 348 of the 414 seats of the single-chamber Parliament went to the government coalition, with another 29 to the Hungarian Party. (Within the Communist-led National Democratic Front, Radaceanu's dissident Social Democrats gained 78 seats, Tatarescu's dissident Liberals 72, Groza's Plowmen's Front 71, the Communists 70, the government-sponsored National Popular Party 26, and the dissident National Peasants 21. Maniu's Peasants received only 32 seats, Bratianu's Liberals 3, and the Democratic Peasants 2. Petrescu's Social Democrats did not receive any parliamentary representation.)

The British Foreign Office characterized the elections "at least as unfair and irregular as had been feared," and United States Acting Secretary of State Dean Acheson said that they had not been free and unfettered. The way was open for a clearly Communist administration of Romania. But it did not come right away. What had caused the delay?

The answer became clear early in 1947: Romania was going through its worst economic crisis in decades. It was suffering a famine more critical than in any other country on the hungry European continent. This was no time for a Communist government to take power openly. How did it happen that Romania, a nation that formerly had been a food exporter, should suddenly suffer a serious famine?

Many Romanians were inclined to blame the Communists and their Russian friends. Had not the Communists forced a reform of one-tenth of Romania's arable land in 1945? Had they not broken up every farm of more than 125 acres? And had they not done so in a haphazard, inefficient manner? Conservative Romanians were inclined to blame Groza's Communist-minded Plowmen's Front for redistribution of land in accordance with political rather than with sound economic principles.

In the confusion that resulted from the hasty and excited redistribution of land, much of it was not sown, and some of it was sown too late. As a result, the harvest yield hit a record low. The United States, after it had convinced itself of the seriousness of Romania's 1947 famine, sent American army food for half a million persons to Romania. In Washington, where this decision was made, it was noted that American reserves were being used, because Romania did not have any stocks of food left. What had happened to them?

American specialists estimated that Russia had removed from $1,000,000,000 to $2,000,000,000 worth of goods from Romania. In view of this, the $300,000,000 of reparations which the Soviet Union assured itself at the 1946 Paris Peace Conference was a mere trifle. About one million Soviet troops had lived off Romania's land for two and a half years. They had removed not only foodstuffs, but also tractors, cattle, horses, and other farm animals. Even after the bulk of Soviet troops had left, 300,000 remained.

Communists entered the government openly in November, 1947, after Iuliu Maniu had been sentenced to life imprisonment for alleged treason. Anna Pauker replaced Tatarescu as foreign minister, Vasile Luca became finance minister.

CHAPTER 10

Bulgaria: Time of Revenge

No COUNTRY OUTSIDE the Soviet Union is more firmly in Communist hands than Bulgaria. Between the two world wars, Communists in Bulgaria were often ruthlessly suppressed. For decades, the Communist Party had to work underground. Its members were hunted down, sometimes tortured, often imprisoned, frequently executed. It took courage to be a Communist in Bulgaria. And it sometimes twisted the soul with fear and hate. Communists, who received little mercy when they were in the opposition, repaid this ruthlessness in kind when they gained control of Bulgaria after the Red Army's entry into Sofia. The Bulgarian national anthem begins with the words, "Roar Maritza River, red with blood; cry widow, deeply struck." The national anthem was not changed after the end of World War II. It remained as valid as it had ever been. Again, the Maritza River was red with blood. The time of revenge had come. Suppression and persecution had remained unforgotten and unforgiven.

Bulgaria's Communists are not a small minority. Historical, racial, and linguistic relationships link Bulgaria with the people of Russia. It was Russia that helped the Bulgars, at the end of the nineteenth century, to free themselves from Turkish rule. Russia received full credit, in the minds of many Bulgars, for this benevolent attitude. The early growth of Communism in Bulgaria largely paralleled that of the Bolshevist movement inside Russia. So, when the pro-Nazi government at Sofia collapsed in 1944, Russia enjoyed the prestige of a traditionally paternal neighbor state; the Communists basked in the reflected glory of Russia. The stage was set for a government in which the Communists might have gained a decisive or even a dominant role by genuine democratic means.

But they were apparently unable to curb a long-frustrated desire for instant and sweeping revenge. Instead of ruling the nation in true coalition with other parties, the Communists disregarded the existing basis for

94

wide and genuine popular support. A fearful historical pattern repeated itself, bringing imprisonment, torture, and death to thousands. Anti-Communists were intimidated, arrested, or sent to special camps. Opposition parties were strangled, their papers suppressed. The initial, 1944 to 1945, period of violence was followed by a less ruthless but equally definite campaign of domestic political coercion. The aim of both methods was the same: to concentrate all real power in Communist hands, with non-Communist representation only for the sake of outward appearance.

The entry of Soviet troops into Bulgaria was preceded by the attempt of the moderate government of Premier Konstantin Muraviev to place the country on the side of the Allied powers. Bulgaria, although technically at war with Great Britain and the United States, had been neutral in the Nazi-Soviet war. After Muraviev denounced Bulgaria's alliance with Germany, declaring war on the Berlin regime, the Soviet Union declared war on Bulgaria. For twenty-four hours, Sofia was at war with both Russia and Germany. Why had Moscow declared war on a government that had already decided to desert the crumbling Nazi cause? Subsequent events furnish the answer: So that the armistice could be signed in Moscow (not at Cairo, where a Bulgarian delegation was already negotiating with British and American representatives), followed by Red Army occupation of Bulgaria; and so that Moscow-backed Communists could have armed Soviet support in gaining control of the government. Britain and America, embarrassed by the whole maneuver, were unwilling to give the Axis a performance of Allied disunity. British and American signatures were duly and quickly affixed to the Soviet-proposed armistice terms. The Red Army was inside Bulgaria, and so was Mrs. Tsola Dragoitcheva.

The Muraviev cabinet was immediately replaced by a government formed under the guidance of Mrs. Dragoitcheva, the first top-flight Communist to enter Bulgaria in preparation for a postwar regime. A Russian airplane had carried Dragoitcheva across the Bulgarian frontier sometime earlier. She entered her homeland by parachute to organize an anti-Nazi party coalition, the Fatherland Front. This coalition is said to have been founded as early as 1942, but it appears to have taken definite shape shortly before Mrs. Dragoitcheva's arrival. The actual date of her dramatic descent on Bulgarian soil is not known but is believed to have been early in 1944.

The Fatherland Front government, which took office on September 9 of that year, was made up of Communists, Peasants, Social Democrats, and representatives of the "Zveno" group. Two names should be remembered: Dr. G. M. Dimitrov, who headed the Peasant Party, and Nikola Petkov, his second-in-command. The Social Democrats were represented by Grigor Cheshmedjiev; the "Zveno" party—a relatively conservative group of officers, businessmen, and professional men—was represented by General Damian Veltchev. Following an international pattern of Communist-led regimes, the justice and interior portfolios were placed in the hands of Communists. Minister of Interior Anton Yugov, a fiery Communist underground worker, came out of hiding to organize a militia corps. While Yugov formed youthful partisans into armed quasi-police forces, Tsola Dragoitcheva prepared the trials of so-called "war criminals." Official Bulgarian documents show that only a relatively small part of the 11,000 accused men and women fell into the category of "war criminals," as it was generally accepted by the United Nations. Among those sentenced and executed were regents, cabinet ministers, and members of the National Assembly. Some of them doubtless were pro-Nazi collaborators. But there appeared to be a great many others whose only offense was the possibility that they might become rallying points of an anti-Communist opposition.

TSOLA DRAGOITCHEVA: 2,000 DIED

Tsola Dragoitcheva, who was largely responsible for the official trials and the accompanying unofficial reign of terror, is the feminine revolutionary par excellence. Cartoonists' impressions of Communists are usually quite unrealistic. The unshaven fellow with the bomb and the generally unappetizing appearance is hardly the prototype of the modern Communist. But the personality of Miss Dragoitcheva lends itself to standardized caricaturist interpretations: there are the rimmed glasses, the sharply drawn features, the shrillness of voice, and the air of embarrassing masculinity.

Dragoitcheva avoids the subject of her career. It is a story of fanatical devotion to the cause of world communism. Born in 1901, she joined the Communists when they were a hunted group. Her work as a schoolteacher served as a blind, while she attended clandestine meetings and spread underground propaganda. Dragoitcheva became a member of the Bulgarian Communist central committee sometime before World War II. A government investigation blew the Communist committee wide open.

She spent eight and a half years in Bulgarian prisons and was twice sentenced to death. She avoided execution of the first death sentence by becoming pregnant in prison. Another time she escaped death by a daring break from the Sofia prison and by flight to the Soviet Union.

Tsola Dragoitcheva is taciturn even regarding the most dramatic event of her career: her daring escape from a Sofia prison to the Soviet Union. Doubtless, her seemingly psychopathic hatred of anti-Communists dates back to this period of arrest, probable torture, trial, imprisonment, and final flight. Although hardly an excuse for the excesses for which Dragoitcheva is considered responsible, this background serves to explain some of the sadistic aspects of Communist rule in Bulgaria, following the armistice.

There are three clearly discernible layers in Dragoitcheva's personality. To the casual observer, she may appear as a staid middle-aged woman (she is only in her late forties, but years of illegal work have made her look older than she really is), with a liking for such bourgeois pleasures as chocolate bars and drinks of crème de menthe. In party councils and interviews, she is shrewd and cool. In such a setting, she is the experienced, brilliant agitator, propagandist, and strategist. Her red hair and green eyes suggest that, as a young schoolteacher, she may have been attractive in a severe way. But it is on a speaker's platform that her personality suggests something out of the ordinary. Even before a most sympathetic audience (she spoke at New York's Manhattan Center in September, 1946, on the occasion of the American Slav Congress), she works herself into near hysteria. On such occasions, emotional barriers are down. And a sensitive audience either is carried away by her appeal to basic human instincts or is repulsed by the discernible undertone of revengeful sadism. At some time in her life, Tsola Dragoitcheva may have had an experience that twisted her soul. It is a subject on which she remains silent.

Tsola Dragoitcheva has admitted that 2,000 persons were sentenced to death while she ruled Bulgaria indirectly as secretary of the Fatherland Front. While the Allied world was intent on defeating Nazi Germany, the winter months of 1945 were a period of Communist-initiated purges and political maneuvers inside Bulgaria. The original Fatherland Front coalition was falling apart. Mrs. Dragoitcheva, noting that Peasant leader Dr. G. M. Dimitrov sought actual influence within the coalition government, forced his resignation as head of his party. He was succeeded by

Nikola Petkov, who continued to fight Communist domination outside the cabinet. Kimon Georgiev, a Zveno representative, continued to head the government as premier, as he had done since the September coup d'état.

After Germany's surrender, political activity in Bulgaria was accelerated. Anton Yugov's interior ministry drafted rules for the election of a legislative assembly. Preelection talks fixed in advance the percentage of seats that each party could achieve. The election law, as published June 6, 1945, provided that each voter receive one ballot on entering a polling place. Only the names of the Fatherland Front candidates were listed on this ballot. But the voter could not mark it, add other names, or change it in any way. Additions or changes would have made it invalid. Theoretically, a voter could ask for an opposition ballot, but this would have exposed his political views to the militia guard at the polling place.

The British and American governments became convinced that Mrs. Dragoitcheva's Fatherland Front wanted to perpetuate, tighten, and legalize its rule by means of predetermined elections. On August 18, United States Secretary of State James F. Byrnes stated that the Sofia government evidently had not arranged for all democratic elements to participate in the elections "free from the fear of force or intimidation." Three days later, the British government said that it "would welcome elections which gave full and free opportunity for the expression of the opinion of the Bulgarian people." But the London Foreign Office declared itself "unable to believe that such an opportunity will result from elections held under present electoral law and under conditions now obtaining in Bulgaria."

Anglo-American pressure was strong. The Sofia regime bowed to this intercession and announced postponement of the elections on August 25, practically on the eve of the originally announced voting date. The notes of disapproval, sent by Washington and London, coincided with the resignation of four Bulgarian cabinet ministers. The ministers protested against the overwhelming number of Communists in the militia. They called for reduction of the militia from 120,000 to 10,000 members.

The whole construction of the Fatherland Front had changed from a genuine coalition to a group of Communists allied with pro-Communist wings of the original coalition parties. Using a technique previously perfected in Poland, the Communists fostered dissident parties with names similar to those of non-Communist opposition groups. Early in September, Nikola Petkov and eight other top members of the Peasant Party said in a protest to Premier Georgiev that "restrictions of freedom and repression of Bulgarian citizens in towns and villages are increasing." The attitude of the Fatherland Front stiffened, rather than relaxed. Late in October, the Peasants, Social Democrats, and Democrats called on their followers and the independent voters to boycott the elections. This action ruled out any opposition demonstration at the polls.

The Fatherland Front government had retained control of the election machinery through the ministries of justice and the interior. The electoral law remained unmodified. It provided no effective control of vote counting. The militia was in complete control of the country, with power to arrest and imprison. The population lived under a constant threat of arrest and mistreatment. All radio facilities remained in government hands. Reuben H. Markham, Balkan correspondent of the *Christian Science Monitor*, reported from Sofia during this period that the opposition merely wanted the Communists "to assume their proper share in the government, without dominating it through the use of force." Mr. Markham, who knows Bulgaria intimately through some three decades of residence, added that "the whole sad struggle is caused by the determination of one party to impose a coercive regime on the majority of the nation."

The election, postponed to November 19, 1945, approached without any basic revisions in the activities of the Fatherland Front regime. The British and American governments became more and more disturbed over the Bulgarian situation. Mark Ethridge, editor of the *Louisville Courier-Journal*, visited Sofia as a special representative of the United States Department of State. His findings prompted the United States government to advise the Sofia administration three days before the scheduled elections that "no steps have been taken since August to reorganize the present Bulgarian government to make it truly representative of democratic opinions."

But the Bulgarian elections were held on November 19, in spite of the United States protest. Under the watchful eyes of militiamen, who guarded many polling places with fixed bayonets, the Bulgarian populace gave its votes overwhelmingly to the candidates of the Fatherland Front.

THE RETURN OF DIMITROV

Four days before the elections, a man in his late sixties arrived in Bulgaria from Moscow. Behind shell-rimmed glasses, his bushy eyebrows were still a youthful black, as was his full mustache. Georgi Dimitrov, one-time president of the Comintern and hero of the Reichstag trial, had returned to the land where he had begun a revolutionary career at the age of fifteen, had twice been condemned to death, and where people of every town and village knew his name as that of a legendary Communist agitator and strategist.

Dimitrov took up secluded residence at Sofia, not many miles northeast of Radomir, where he had been born on June 28, 1882, and where his father had owned a small hat shop. At the age of twelve, Georgi Dimitrov had left school to become a printer's apprentice. Precocious and studious, the excitable, dark-eyed boy read avidly. His mother, Paraskeva Dimitrova, said many years later that Georgi had always been an exceedingly active and somewhat troublesome boy, who was rarely punished, because "he never lied."

Socialism and unionism were sprouting in the Bulgarian capital in the late nineteenth century. In 1890, a Socialist Party had been founded. But left and right wings were already threatening to break it in two. Dimitrov became a functionary of Sofia's Printers' Union at the age of sixteen. Several years later, when Dimitrov heckled Minister Vassil Radoslavov during a parliamentary session, the minister called back, good-naturedly, "I remember you. When you were a sixteen-year-old brat, monkeying around with my articles, you used to be just as fresh as you are now!" This is one of Dimitrov's favorite anecdotes. He recalls that, shortly before May Day in 1899, Radoslavov had prepared a newspaper article containing some passages critical of trade unionism. Dimitrov, one of the few people who could read Radoslavov's intricate handwriting, was charged with setting it in type. In doing so, he dropped all remarks he did not like, cutting whole paragraphs out of Radoslavov's article.

Georgi Dimitrov became secretary of Sofia's Printers' Union when he was eighteen. Upon joining the Socialist Party, he quickly identified himself with its left-wing group. When, in 1903, the "Broad Socialists" (Social Democrats) and the "Narrow Socialists" (Communists) split the Socialist Party, Dimitrov was instrumental in engineering this break. A year later, the good-looking, fiery, energetic young revolutionary became secretary of the General Workers' Union of Bulgaria. When he reached the required minimum age of thirty in 1913, he entered the Bulgarian Parliament, as well as the city and county councils of Sofia.

The Balkan wars and World War I created the political atmosphere of the 1912 to 1919 period. The appeal of the "Narrow Socialists" was largely limited to urban labor. The peasantry, which even today forms 82 per cent of the population, was instinctively opposed to Communist aims. The unrest and dissatisfaction of the war years helped develop Dimitrov into an extremely active agitator. There were more than six hundred strikes in Bulgaria between 1908 and 1912. Dimitrov played an important part in many of them.

The war years also brought the beginning of Dimitrov's career of secret agitation, court trials, and imprisonment. His first jail term resulted from a libel trial. He spent his prison term in the so-called "Black Minaret," which dated back to the period of Turkish rule. Later, he used his position as parliamentary delegate to visit the front and agitate among the soldiers. Stella D. Blagoyeva, writing in an official Communist Party biography of Dimitrov, admitted that he visited the front "under the pretext of studying the situation of the tobacco workers."

He went to prison again in 1916, having been convicted of insulting a high military officer. Amnesty released Dimitrov from jail after a year and a half, during which he had studied German intensively. Kosta Todorov, a Peasant Party official with an impressive career as a rebel and statesman, said in his book *Balkan Firebrand* that he met Dimitrov in the Sofia prison as a fellow inmate. Todorov reports that Dimitrov was suffering from tuberculosis and that his education had apparently "come entirely from newspapers and orthodox Marxist texts which he seemed to know by heart." Shortly after his release, his party joined the Comintern in 1919. This marked a turning point in Bulgarian Communist history. Vassil Kolarov, who worked with Dimitrov at that time and who was made president of the Bulgarian Assembly in 1945, traced the early development of the party in the *Communist International* of January, 1924. He wrote that the party had only 3,000 members during the early war years, but 20,000 early in 1919, and 40,000 in 1922. Kolarov stated that during this period the party displayed "lack of organizational connection with the masses, which was necessary for control of mass action; inability to take advantage of the antagonism and strife among the various bourgeois parties, and a lack of experience in the handling of large masses."

The fact that the Communists were not doing so well, in spite of wartime growth, was due to the influence of the Peasant Party. The Peasants, under the leadership of Alexander Stambulisky, had vigorously opposed Bulgaria's alliance with Germany and the other central powers. Stambulisky became premier after representing Bulgaria at the Paris Peace Conference. His attitude was anti-intellectual and violently pro-peasant. He tolerated the Communists, although they had little love for him, and he kept the conservative elements in temporary submission. Bulgaria's Communists were dreaming great dreams. They wrote and talked of a Balkan Communist federation. They out-Zinovieved Zinoviev in their hopes that the Marxist millennium was just around the corner. As Kolarov put it, in his 1924 article, they thought "the country had entered into a stage of the revolutionary struggle which was bound to terminate in the establishment of a Soviet régime." The Communists were going too fast. The Peasants had a much better understanding of rural psychology. Nevertheless, the 1919 elections brought the Communists 118,000 votes, the 1920 elections 182,000.

REVOLUTIONARY DRAMA

Dimitrov meanwhile had lost his parliamentary immunity, because of his role in a number of violent strikes. He went underground. The life of a revolutionary became ever more dangerous, dramatic, and exciting. When the Second Comintern Congress was about to be held in Moscow, Dimitrov had no legal way of traveling to the Soviet Union. He set out in a sailboat, disguised as a fisherman, and attempted to make his way through the Black Sea. But the boat ran into heavy weather. It was forced to seek shelter on the Romanian coast. Romanian frontier guards arrested the delegation, charged its members with espionage, and locked them up. The Soviet Foreign Commissariat promptly protested on July 17, 1920. Three days later, Dimitrov was freed. But it was too late for participation in the Second Congress. He did, however, attend the Third Comintern Congress, where he became a member of the Communist International's executive committee.

Dimitrov continued to work inside Bulgaria. He had to remain underground. The Communists, at that time, loved stunts of all sorts. At one time, while he was sought by the police, Dimitrov walked into a session of the Sofia city council. He created a furore. The councilmen were upset when the Communist outlaw began to talk. There was an attempt to have him arrested. But it proved impossible to notify the police. Telephone wires had been cut. Bulky Communists were blocking exits. Dimitrov had his say. He got away during the confusion.

The Communists continued their violent opposition to the Stambulisky regime. They resolved at their 1922 conference that "the party will continue, with ever-increasing vigor, its campaign against the peasant government, which has shown itself merely as the government of the rural bourgeoisie and of political and social reaction." Instead, the Communists hoped to undermine the Peasants locally. Moscow was worried. It seemed to the Comintern that the Bulgarian Communists lacked adaptability. They seemed to ignore the fact that there were other forces in Bulgaria, aside from Stambulisky's party. What about the Macedonian nationalists, the IMRO group of trigger-happy mountain outlaws? The Comintern sent a carefully phrased memorandum to Sofia. But the Bulgarian Communists paid little attention to such suggestions. After all, what did Moscow know about local conditions!

On June 9, 1923, the people of Bulgaria awoke to find a brand-new government in office. It was a coalition under the premiership of Alexander Tsankov, which contained nearly all groups except the Peasants and the Communists. Stambulisky attempted to halt this coup d'état. He was killed. Fighting continued in various parts of the country. The Communist Party of Bulgaria declared itself neutral in this conflict. In doing so, it dug its own grave, and did not know it. Dimitrov went along with the decisions of the central committee in Sofia. On the very day of the coup d'état, the party's publication, *Rabotnicheski Vestnik,* stated that the Communists would "not take part in the armed fight between the urban and the rural bourgeoisie." "Rural bourgeoisie" meant the Peasant Party, and "urban bourgeoisie" was the Communist label for the groups backing Tsankov.

The Comintern was furious. Within a few days, Karl Radek told a session of the enlarged Comintern executive that the Bulgarian coup d'état represented "the most serious defeat ever experienced by any Communist Party" and "a positive defeat" of Communist tactics generally. The Communist Party of Bulgaria, he said, proved "unable to accomplish the transition from agitation and opposition to deeds and action."

Radek indicated, in scathing words, that Sofia had resented Moscow interference. The Comintern, he recalled, had warned the Bulgarian party ahead of time. Radek then blamed the Comintern for "having paid too much heed to the noise made about 'ukases from Moscow.'" Christo Kabaktchiev issued a detailed reply for the Bulgarian Communist Party, saying in effect that the June fracas might have wiped out the party in

Bulgaria. Zinoviev entered the heated discussion, citing Kabaktchiev as having written that Bulgarian "working masses in the towns met the coup d'état with indifference and with a certain feeling of relief." Zinoviev sneered that "the masses, as everybody knows, have a broad back; everything can be loaded on to it. . . . The Bulgarian Central Committee wanted a revolution 'with guarantees.' "

Dimitrov weathered this storm. In September, 1923, the Communists tried an armed uprising inside Bulgaria, hoping to wrest control from Tsankov. It was a belated, in many respects foolhardy, attempt, which probably resulted from Moscow's continued goading. Some otherwise well-informed non-Communist observers have since asserted that the September uprising was not a Communist revolt but merely a trick on Tsankov's part. But Mrs. Blagoyev's official Communist biography admits that Dimitrov and Kolarov left Sofia for the "nearby border regions of Bulgaria, to lead an armed uprising there." The Communist revolt was quelled quickly and ruthlessly. Peasants and Communists were hunted by government-backed mobs. Dimitrov, together with 1,000 to 2,000 other Communists, crossed into Yugoslavia.

TERROR

General Ivan Volkov, who had helped Tsankov to power, tolerated anti-Comunist and anti-Peasant Party excesses that horrified other members of the Tsankov cabinet. The period that followed is one of the blackest in Bulgaria's recent history. Volkov appears to have followed a very definite plan in suppressing Communist and Peasant Party opposition with utmost ruthlessness. The Italians were interested in preventing a rapprochement between Bulgaria and Yugoslavia. They wanted to see Yugoslavia isolated, so as to press their territorial demands for the Dalmatian coast with a greater chance of success. Volkov and the IMRO were Mussolini's tools in the Balkans. Volkov suppressed all opposition groups that favored closer cooperation with the Yugoslavs, and these included both Communists and Peasants.

Communists and Peasants for a time cooperated in their plans for a large-scale armed uprising inside Bulgaria. Dimitrov had gone to Austria from Yugoslavia. He conferred with Kosta Todorov at the Park Hotel in Schoenbrunn in January, 1924. Todorov reported later that Dimitrov, who had shaved his beard, had become "perfumed and elegant." Dimitrov suggested that the Communists and Peasants establish a "Workers' and Peasants' Government," in which the Communists would hold the ministries of war, interior, and communications. It is interesting to note the parallel between this proposal and Bulgaria's regime after World War II, or any other government in which Communist influence is paramount: the ministry of interior is always considered of decisive importance and therefore placed into Communist hands. Later, Todorov met Dimitrov in Moscow. But again the negotiations came to nothing.

After his stay in Moscow, Dimitrov returned to Vienna in 1925. He coordinated Communist propaganda and underground work in the Balkan nations. Even Hollywood could not have created an atmosphere more pregnant with intrigue and danger than Dimitrov's years in Vienna. He changed apartments frequently and met representatives of Communist parties who had smuggled themselves across borders and were to return in the same fashion. The Communist Vienna headquarters published newspapers and clandestine leaflets and bought arms, which were sent into Balkan countries, including Bulgaria. Dimitrov commuted to Moscow whenever that seemed necessary and occasionally made daring trips into countries where the Communist Party was banned.

Dimitrov continued to run clandestine Communist activities inside Bulgaria from Vienna or Moscow. The party remained underground but was able to masquerade briefly under different names. In April, 1925, General Konstantin Gheorgiev, chief of military justice of Bulgaria, was assassinated. Two days after the assassination, on April 16, Tsankov, Volkov, the entire cabinet, and many government officials assembled in Sofia's Sveti Nedelia Cathedral for funeral services. A time bomb in the cathedral tower exploded during the ceremonies. The roof collapsed. Hundreds were wounded, 128 persons killed.

The Communists were immediately blamed for this explosion (which did not kill either Tsankov or Volkov). But Communist spokesmen have always vigorously denied that they had any part in it. They assert consistently that Communists do not resort to single actions of this sort, but prefer mass action. Anti-Communist sources, however, give the following explanation:

The Communists did, indeed, plan mass action inside Bulgaria in the spring of 1925. The cathedral explosion was supposed to kill all key government officials. It was to serve as a signal for a nation-wide uprising. Gavril Genov, Dimitrov's Belgrade representative in charge of contacts with the Communist underground inside Bulgaria, had purchased several hundred kilograms of ecrasite in Yugoslavia, about a month before the Sofia explosion. The cathedral explosion was caused by about fifty kilograms of ecrasite. The sexton of the cathedral had been bribed into planting the explosive.

AND MORE TERROR

Genov left Belgrade for Moscow shortly after the explosion. He died of tuberculosis in the Soviet capital. Possibly he was the only person who knew all the details of the Sofia explosion. Neither Dimitrov nor Kolarov may have been informed of Genov's plan. But the Tsankov government paid no attention to such niceties of intra-Comintern division of responsibility. It banned the Communist Party and expelled its deputies from the Assembly. Two reserve officers, accused of having placed the bomb, were "killed while resisting arrest."

Dimitrov was condemned to death in absentia. Three other alleged conspirators were hanged before 40,000 onlookers. Another wave of atrocities and high-pressure trials began. During a four-month period, 3,557 people were tried. Three hundred were executed officially. The number of those who were killed unofficially may have reached several thousands. Forty-seven Communist and Peasant Party delegates were killed between June, 1923, and April, 1925.

Things grew calmer after that. But only relatively so. Early in 1926, King Boris replaced Tsankov with Andre Liaptchev. The Liaptchev administration was chaotic and corrupt. It was less violent than its predecessors, but it seemed powerless to restrain the various IMRO factions, whose members sometimes engaged in gun duels outside Sofia cafés. Nikola Mushanov succeeded Liaptchev in 1931. Dimitrov, working from Vienna, attempted from time to time to resurrect the Bulgarian Communist Party under various other names. A Bulgarian "Labor Party" was dissolved by the Supreme Court, which charged that it had been "financed by Moscow." Later, an "Independent Labor Party" developed, which may or may not have been based on Communist support, but which certainly attracted the politically homeless Communist voters.

Dr. G. M. Dimitrov followed Alexander Stambulisky's examples in his leadership of the Peasant Party. Meanwhile, a group of autocratic officers and intellectuals founded the *Zveno* (Link) organization. Kimon Georgiev, later premier of the Communist-controlled Sofia government from

1944 to 1946, was head of Zveno. During the eight months which Georgiev served as Bulgaria's premier in 1934, he liquidated the IMRO and recognized the government of the Soviet Union. King Boris replaced Georgiev in 1935.

Meanwhile, Georgi Dimitrov had become a figure that commanded international respect. He entered the world limelight in 1933 during the Reichstag trial, which will be discussed in our chapter dealing with the Communist Party of Germany. Dimitrov's mother, Paraskeva Dimitrova, left Bulgaria for the first time in her life. She visited Berlin and Leipzig to plead the innocence of her son, and she spoke at a mass meeting in Paris. Dimitrov's wife, Luba Ivoshevitch, died in Moscow the same year, after twenty-five years of marriage.

Dimitrov has been credited with effecting the change of the Communist line which took place in 1935. Until then, the Comintern's Third Strategy of revolutionary extremism had ruled out any cooperation with anti-Nazi and anti-Fascist parties. Georgi Dimitrov's political report to the Seventh Congress of the Communist International, held in August, 1935, revealed that the Bulgarian rebel had learned to think in terms of a world struggle. Such a struggle, he realized, could not be won by the Soviet Union and the Communists alone. The "united front" strategy had taken effect.

During World War II, Dimitrov remained in Moscow, planning clandestine resistance and preparing for the day of his return to Bulgaria. At the time of the Reichstag trial, Premier Stalin made him a Soviet citizen. He was exchanged for one or several German spies whom the Russians had arrested. Four days before the 1945 elections in Bulgaria, the Moscow radio announced that Dimitrov had been "permitted" to give up his Soviet citizenship. Shortly afterward, he returned to his homeland. The prodigal son was again a Bulgarian citizen. The 1945 elections made him a deputy from the Sofia district, as he had been from 1912 to 1923. His skill as a parliamentarian and orator had remained undiminished. Although his vernacular fully reflected the militant line of the party, his delivery was more mellow than Bulgarians remembered. During his early stay in Sofia, after returning from Moscow, he hardly left his residence. He had moved into a house close to the quarters of Maynard Barnes, the United States representative in Bulgaria. With his second wife, who bore him a son in 1937, Georgi Dimitrov lived surrounded by a high board fence, with searchlights illuminating all pathways at night.

In December, 1945, the foreign ministers of the United States, the

Soviet Union, and Great Britain met in Moscow. They agreed on a broadening of the Sofia government through the inclusion of opposition representatives. These decisions created temporary optimism. But there was no change in Sofia. Nikola Petkov, foreign minister and vice-premier, asserted that he had been a witness when Premier Stalin told Vice Foreign Commissar Andrei Y. Vishinsky to clarify the Moscow decision to the Bulgarian opposition. According to Petkov, the Soviet premier called Vishinsky in Bucharest by telephone and told him to go to Sofia. He advised Vishinsky that there was no question of real governmental reconstruction but merely a formal inclusion of opposition representatives.

VISHINSKY INTERVENES

Petkov related to American correspondents in Sofia that he had told Vishinsky that opposition members would not enter the cabinet unless there were "new free elections, withdrawal of the ministries of the Interior and Justice from the domination of the Communist party and the withdrawal of political influences within the army." Vishinsky's answer, as quoted by Petkov, was brief: "You must accept the Moscow conclusions and put two men in the government. You either enter, or you don't. If you don't understand the Moscow advice the way we understand it, you are going against the decisions."

However, the American and British governments clarified their views on this matter early in 1946. The United States Department of State noted in an aide-mémoire to the Sofia regime on February 22 that "it was never the understanding of the United States Government that pressure was to be exerted on the Opposition to nominate two candidates for pro forma inclusion into the government without regard to the conditions of their participation." On the contrary, the document stated, Washington had assumed that "participation of these representatives would be on the basis of conditions mutually agreeable to both the Bulgarian Government and the Opposition."

Promptly, on March 9, the Soviet Foreign Commissariat published an answer that flatly contradicted the State Department's interpretation. There had been no agreement on conditions in the Moscow agreement, the reply stated, so there were not going to be any conditions. "Actually," the Soviet answer asserted, the conference had "stipulated only two conditions," namely, that the additional Cabinet members were "really representative of parties not participating in the government" and that they "be really suitable and work loyally with the government." Furthermore, Moscow said, the State Department's interpretation had "infringed" on the foreign ministers' decisions.

But the wrangling had only begun. The British Foreign Office declared itself in agreement with the United States position. Secretary Byrnes confessed on March 10 that "it did not occur to the government of the United States" that opposition participation was "to be pro forma or created by pressure."

The result of this diplomatic eyebrow raising was a new dressing of Sofia's governmental windows. The Georgiev cabinet resigned. Vassil Kolarov, in his newly won dignity as president of the Assembly, asked Kimon Georgiev to form a new government. But when a new cabinet took office on March 31, neither the United States nor Great Britain felt that much of anything had happened. The Bulgarian government explained that opposition representatives had not been included, because Russia considered their terms for participation as contrary to the foreign ministers' Moscow decisions. The Sofia government remained as it had been, and Dimitrov proceeded with his plans for change-over of Bulgaria from a monarchy to a "People's Republic." After King Boris's death during the war years, the boy King Simeon II had nominally been ruler, while successive sets of regents held the real power. Theoretically, the nine-year-old King had retained the power to act as a brake on the cabinet or to dissolve the regime in control. By abolishing the monarchy, the Communist-controlled government eliminated something like a shadow's shadow of potential danger to themselves.

EXIT: A LITTLE BOY

On September 8, the people of Bulgaria voted 92 per cent in favor of a republic. The Coburg dynasty was dead. The campaign for abolition of the monarchy had come to a climax in a mammoth rally of the Communist Party. Vulko Chervenkov, the party's secretary, branded the monarchy as "a tool in foreign hands" which had tried to "oppose the Bulgarian people to other Slav people." Little Simeon, the potential monarchic power, was specifically exempted from these accusations. Chervenkov said that the Communist Party had nothing against the little boy; it just didn't like the Coburgs. Neither did many other Bulgarians. The memory of King

Boris's dealings with Nazi Germany and King Ferdinand's World War I alliance with the Reich was still strong.

More important than the question of the monarchy, however, were Communist plans for the future of the Bulgarian nation. Georgi Dimitrov outlined the party's program for the development of a new state on the eve of the referendum for the abolition of the monarchy:

"1. Bulgaria will not be a Soviet Republic; she will be a People's Republic, in which the directing power will be wielded by the majority of the nation: workers, peasants, artisans and intellectuals. There will be no dictatorship, but in a People's Republic the decisive factor rests basically with the working majority of the nation, with the people whose labor is socially useful, and not with the big speculative capital and a small bourgeois minority that is politically and morally decayed and bankrupt.

"2. Bulgaria will be a People's Republic where private property, acquired by toil and thrift, will have real state protection against brigand speculators, and where the big speculative capitalists will not be allowed to condemn the working people to hunger and misery.

"3. Bulgaria will be a People's Republic which will not leave a single door open for the restoration of the shameful past of the Monarchy, of Fascism and of Bulgarian chauvinism, and which will give all the constitutional guarantees that are indispensable for the development of our country along the lines of progress and the well-being of our people until all exploitation of man by man has been suppressed.

"4. Bulgaria will be a People's Republic, a free and independent state with national sovereignty and she will not dance to the tune of capitalist trusts desirous of subjugating the small nations politically and economically.

"5. Bulgaria will be a People's Republic that will be a factor of unity and Slav brotherhood against any possible aggression. She will never take part in any anti-Slav or anti-Soviet policies that lead towards hatred among nations.

"6. Bulgaria will be a People's Republic which, together with other democratic nations that have regained their liberty, will represent an element of peace and democracy in the Balkans and in Europe, and not an instrument of military adventures and of aggressive wars."

In preparing Bulgaria for its new status of a "People's Republic," Dimitrov used 1946 to consolidate the position of the Communist Party within the Fatherland Front coalition. With the dissident Peasants and Social Democrats completely in line with Communist policy, the Zveno group remained the only undivided non-Communist Party inside the government. Communist pressure against non-Communist or anti-Communist circles within the Zveno was revealed on June 23, at the Zveno's Party Conference in Sofia. Peter Popzlatev, the Zveno's political secretary, spoke of "people who cannot understand that there is a need for Zveno participation in building up the FF (Fatherland Front)." All through the summer months, a purge took place within the army. Some 1,800 officers were removed from their posts up to the month of August. When the Belgrade trial against Draja Mikhailovitch linked Sofia's War Minister Damian Veltchev, a Zveno official, with Mikhailovitch, the Bulgar Communist press began to attack Veltchev. On September 26, Veltchev resigned his cabinet post and became Bulgarian minister plenipotentiary to Switzerland.

Pressure on Premier Georgiev increased. A *New York Times* dispatch from the Paris Peace Conference attributed these moves directly to Dimitrov. Quoting "a well-informed American source," the report said that "the army was purged with the reluctant consent of Premier Georgiev, who was warned that if he refused to go all the way with the Communists he would be liquidated and the Communist Party would take over without the formality of associating itself with the Georgiev party (Zveno) and the factions of the Agrarian (Peasant) party and Social democratic party in the so-called Fatherland Front." Private reports from Sofia indicated that Veltchev had resisted the inclusion of political commissars in the lower ranks of the Bulgarian army.

Another illustration of a tightening Communist hold on the government came with the trial of Dr. G. M. Dimitrov, who had previously been forced to resign his cabinet post and the leadership of the Peasant Party. Dr. Dimitrov (who should not be confused with Georgi Dimitrov, although their first names are also identical), had found refuge at the residence of United States representative Maynard Barnes in the summer of 1945. The American representative was convinced that Dr. Dimitrov was in danger of being assassinated. The deposed Peasant leader was finally evacuated from Bulgaria in an American airplane. He went to Italy, and subsequently to the United States. In the spring of 1946, the Sofia government proceeded to try Dr. Dimitrov in absentia. The prosecution charged him with collaboration with Draja Mikhailovitch, considering these contacts as "proof of the infamous and treacherous role played by Dr. Dimitrov and his gang, and by the defenders of the Opposition." It is well to add, at this point, that Dr. Dimitrov's contacts with other Balkan resistance leaders were doubtless made with the consent of the United States and British governments. The Peasant leader worked closely with these Allied powers during the war, first in Jerusalem and later in London, to foster anti-Nazi resistance inside Bulgaria. Dr. G. M. Dimitrov was sentenced to death in absentia on July 12, 1946. Four months later, Georgi Dimitrov became premier of the Bulgarian People's Republic. Since then he has governed Bulgaria from the Vranya Palace outside Sofia, which was once the residence of the Coburg Dynasty.

Nikola Petkov, who had taken over the leadership of the Peasant Party after Dr. G. M. Dimitrov's resignation, experienced the full wrath of the Communist government early in June of 1947. He was charged with conspiring against the regime and was seized as he left the Parliament building. The government prosecutor charged that Petkov had plotted with a Bulgarian army officer since July, 1945. On August 16, 1947, Petkov was sentenced to death. The only remaining major anti-Communist political leader was thus eliminated. Firmly entrenched, and able to utilize the traditionally large support that communism has been able to muster in Bulgaria in the past, the Communist Party can now transform the nation in accordance with its long-laid plans.

CHAPTER 11

Yugoslavia: "We Cannot Stop Halfway"

THE COMMUNIST PARTY of Yugoslavia is an unknown entity. It governs with absolute and unquestioned power. But it has never revealed the identity of its secretary-general, the details of its organization, or the extent of its membership. Yugoslavia's Communists worked in secrecy for a quarter of a century. They retained their clandestine habits even after gaining governmental control. Not even in Russia has Lenin's original concept of the Communist Party as a secret, disciplined group of fanatically devoted men and women been more rigidly applied than in Yugoslavia. Its parliamentary delegates do not identify themselves as Communists, but only as members of the Communist-ruled "People's Front" coalition. Whether Yugoslavia's Premier Josip Broz, better known as Marshal Tito, is the real head of his nation's estimated 100,000 to 150,000 Communists cannot be determined. He may be more a façade than a real center of power.

Anti-Communist Bulgars, Yugoslavs, and Albanians rival each other in claiming the greatest degree of harshness for the regimes under which they live. It is difficult to measure the intensity of Communist coercion on a comparative basis. One fact, however, cannot be disputed: those nations which suppressed communism most ruthlessly in the past today have the most dictatorial Communist governments. Yugoslavia is one of these. Its Communist Party was established after World War I, when Serbia, Croatia, and Slovenia gained independence together as the Yugoslav state. In the 1920 elections, the Communist Party received 58 of 419 parliamentary seats. It was banned shortly afterward. Stepan Raditch, the Croatian nationalist and peasant leader, temporarily attached his movement to Moscow's Red Peasant International. But he soon abandoned all ideas of cooperation with the Communists. In 1929, Raditch was assassinated during a session of Parliament. He was succeeded by Vladimir

113

Matchek, who remained inside Croatia during World War II. (Matchek rejected all Nazi efforts of collaboration in the Croatian puppet regime. He fled to Paris in May, 1945, while Tito's partisans approached the Croatian capital, Zagreb. Shortly afterward, Matchek asserted that the "so-called liberation of Yugoslavia has merely resulted in the exchange of a totalitarian Nazi regime for a totalitarian Communist regime." When Raditch's widow attempted to publish an anti-Communist opposition paper, her print shop was bombed. The paper had to cease publication.)

King Alexander of the Karageorgevitch dynasty ruled the "Kingdom of Serbs, Croats and Slovenes" (which was founded under this name in 1918 and became the "Kingdom of Yugoslavia" only in 1929) until his assassination at Marseilles in 1934. The Italian-supported Croat terrorist Ustasha organization, headed by Ante Pavelitch, was found responsible for this political murder. Alexander and his successor, the regent Prince Paul, were accused of governing through a Serb nationalist royal dictatorship. That may be an oversimplification. But it is certain that they governed from Belgrade in accordance with principles of pro-Serbian centralization. The Croats, under Matchek's leadership, fought bitterly against Serb control.

The Macedonian nationalist organization IMRO (Internal Macedonian Revolutionary Organization) was more active inside Yugoslavia than in either Bulgaria or Greece, the two other nations that contain Macedonian areas. Italian pressure was the most important factor in Yugoslav foreign relations during the interwar years. The Italian Fascist regime backed the Ustasha in Croatia, the IMRO in Macedonia, and smaller groups of free-lance cutthroats elsewhere. This crazy quilt of nationalist ambitions was further complicated by regional aspirations in the Bosnia-Hercegovina and Montenegro regions. When Nazism came to power in Germany, it began to exercise an influence of its own in Yugoslavia, mainly through economic infiltration and barter trade.

Yugoslavia's population is about 55 per cent Serb Orthodox by religion, approximately 40 per cent Roman Catholic and 5 per cent Moslem. Illiteracy varies, but is about 50 per cent on a nation-wide average. Infant mortality in 1938 was 144 per thousand, and for many years Yugoslavs had the lowest average income in southeastern Europe. This background illustrates the conditions that made the emergence of a powerful Communist government in Yugoslavia possible.

The most outstanding accomplishment of the Communist regime of

Marshal Broz-Tito was Yugoslavia's continued existence as an integrated state. When the Axis powers controlled that nation, everything was done to set Serb against Croat, Catholic against Orthodox. Persecution and massacres were instigated, which left enormous emotional cleavages among the various population groups. The Germans emphasized regional differences. They established Serbian and Croatian puppet states.

The Tito regime solved the intricate administrative question by applying the Soviet system of autonomous republics. The Communist government faced its strongest opposition inside Serbia. This region was subdivided and consequently weakened in its influence on national affairs. The "Federative People's Republic of Yugoslavia" now contains the republics of Serbia, Croatia, Slovenia, Montenegro, Bosnia-Hercegovina, and Macedonia. Trusted Communists were placed in control of regional governments. Disciplined adherence to the policies of the Belgrade regime was assured.

"EMBRYO PEOPLE'S FRONT"

This federal system runs parallel to the subdivisions within the Communist Party of Yugoslavia. The party's Fourth Congress, held in the early 1930's, had agreed on the establishment of regional parties, adapted to nationalist aspirations of the areas in which they functioned. The progress of this policy proved slow. The Slovenian Communist Party, for instance, was not established until December, 1934. Its clandestine existence had little effect. The Slovenian party reported later with modesty that it had been able to establish "an embryo People's Front" during the 1935 municipal elections, in accordance with the "united front" policy adopted at the Comintern's Seventh Congress.

The Catholic populations of Croatia and Slovenia were particularly hostile toward Communist efforts. The Slovenian party tried to ease Catholic apprehensions. It even issued a manifesto that asserted that "every fighter for the freedom of the Slovenian people and, in the first place, every Communist, respects the religious belief of every comrade in the struggle, for the existence of the Slovenian people and the Slovenian national interests are at stake." In spite of its ostensibly autonomous character, the Slovenian party was decidedly only a branch of the Yugoslav Communist Party, which had its secret headquarters in Belgrade. This was confirmed in a message that the central committee of the Slovenian party addressed to Comintern chief Georgi Dimitrov: "We Communists of Slovenia, as part of the Communist Party of Yugoslavia, stand fast under the banner of the Communist International."

The embryonic success of the Slovene party shows how strong anti-Communist sentiment was throughout Yugoslavia. Successive Belgrade governments, and in particular the administration of Premier Milan Stoyadinovitch, ruthlessly suppressed all outspoken opposition to the regime's dictatorial practices. Winifred N. Hadsel, European expert of the Foreign Policy Association, has stated that "although the Yugoslav dictatorship was much milder than Nazism, it came to display some of the same characteristics, such as concentration camps for political opponents." Louis Adamic, the American writer of Yugoslav birth, has reported the experiences of a Communist underground worker in Belgrade's police prison. The anonymous Communist described tortures inside that prison as follows: "I believe no one in human history ever went through such tortures as Bracanovitch. He was nearly seven feet tall, and built in proportion: a veritable giant of a Serb. . . . He was guilty of the worst crimes. He was a member of the Comintern for the Balkans, had been to Russia, was a member of the CPY (the Communist youth organization)." The report states that Bracanovitch was tortured in many ways. His soles were pounded into a bloody mess; live coals were pressed under his armpits, needles stuck under his nails; his genitals were crushed, all the joints of his fingers broken. The Comintern agent, according to the report, refused to reveal the secrets of clandestine Communist activities. Instead, he "taunted the torturers by laughing when they beat him, and while the coals sizzled under his armpits. He told them what would happen to them and their masters when the Balkans went Bolshevik."

Since then, the Balkans have gone Bolshevik. Men like Bracanovitch have been avenged. The Tito government established the Uzunada jail on an island in the Sava River, near Belgrade. Other prisons in the capital city exist at No. 6 Obilicha Venatch and at No. 40 Deligradska. Tortures in the jails of the OZNA, Yugoslavia's secret police, are reported to include electric shocks. Speaking at Tuzla, late in September, 1946, Premier Broz-Tito told his listeners, "Those who will persist in hindering the creation of a better future, the reconstruction of our country, the creation of something better and new, will have to disappear from the face of this earth. We will have no pity toward them and will act toward them as against our worst enemies. We cannot stop halfway. Our road is already marked."

That was a candid appraisal of Communist policy in Yugoslavia. It is worth noting, however, that a number of concentration camps that were established by the Tito regime immediately after it came to power were later closed. Arrests became fewer. The population began to adapt itself to an atmosphere of constantly threatening imprisonment. It became more tractable. Bogdan Raditsa, who in 1945 served as chief of the foreign press department in Tito's ministry of information, believes that half a million persons were imprisoned or executed by the Yugoslav regime.

KARDELJ AND TITO

The secrecy that characterizes the Communist Party of Yugoslavia makes it necessary to speculate on its real leadership and on the distribution of authority and power within its central committee. Premier Broz-Tito is a member of this committee, but not necessarily its most decisive personality. Three men are close to him in status: Edvard Kardelj, the deputy premier who represented his nation at the Paris Peace Conference of 1946; Major General Alexander Rankovitch, minister of the interior and head of the secret police (OZNA); General Milovan Djilas, chairman of the Communist Party.

Kardelj, who was born in 1910, the son of a railway worker, is Yugoslavia's top Communist "brain truster." This well-educated man, who writes and speaks with persuasive fluency, is the main author of Yugoslavia's idealistically worded constitution. Although Edvard Kardelj graduated from the Teachers College at Ljubljana, his Communist leanings and activities ruined his chances of obtaining a teaching position. In 1930, he was sentenced to two years in prison, because of agitation among students. After serving his prison term, he reentered underground work, acted as a Comintern agent, and finally went to Moscow. Kardelj appears to have done illegal party work in several countries. He speaks Serbo-Croatian, Slovenian, Russian, French, German, and a bit of English.

In 1939, he returned openly to Yugoslavia and published a book on *The National Problem of Slovenia*. Because of its criticism of the Belgrade government and its Communist undertone, the book was banned. During the partisan resistance of World War II, Kardelj served as head of underground warfare in Slovenia. Later, when political considerations overshadowed military needs, he joined Tito at his headquarters and prepared Yugoslavia's postwar Communist administration.

Kardelj is a rather short man, with a full shock of hair and a neat mustache. He speaks sharply, almost impatiently, and without hesitation. As a Marxist theoretician, he ranks high among living Communist spokesmen. His general outlook is uncompromising and dogmatic. Bogdan Raditsa reported that Kardelj told him, "Between us and America there is an unbridgeable chasm. We are two worlds. They cannot be united. When we are victorious over the American world, the world will be one." Writing in the *Reader's Digest* for October, 1946, Raditsa quoted confidential instructions by Kardelj to Young Communist Party leaders as follows:

"We have made certain concessions to the capitalist world, in order to gain time. But when the hour strikes we must be ready to pass to the offensive. The Proletarian revolution is on the march. It is linked to the Soviet Union through agreements of mutual political and economic assistance. It is creating, as Stalin has said, a union of all the many parts of the Revolution—in Poland, in Romania, in Bulgaria, perhaps in Italy —into one System. That Revolutionary System will go into a front attack against the Imperialist System."

General Milovan Djilas, chairman of Yugoslavia's Communist Party, has been described as his country's real ruler. This view may have grown from the belief that Djilas has been, or is, a personal friend of Premier Stalin. Djilas has ghostwritten many of Tito's speeches. He is considered responsible for Yugoslavia's often very pronounced anti-British and anti-American actions. According to private British accounts, Djilas had a run-in with the British parachute unit that landed in partisan territory in 1941. When the United States and Yugoslavia exchanged bitter notes in August, 1946, after an American airplane had been shot down over Yugoslav territory, Djilas was believed responsible for the tough line taken by the Belgrade government. The Montenegro-born chairman of the Yugoslav party may even have drafted the sharp notes that his government sent to the United States Department of State.

The personality of Josip Broz-Tito stands in contrast to that of the needle-tongued Kardelj and the gruff Djilas. Tito can smile. He is a charmer who has many of the characteristics that made Hermann Göring Germany's best liked Nazi leader. His life as a Comintern agent, guerrilla leader, and premier of the world's most minority-pocked nation has not lessened his appreciation of wine, women, and song. Although he is one of the best known Communist leaders, his career remains partly shrouded in the secrecy that Yugoslav Communists love so much.

Tito was born on May 25, in either 1892 or 1893, the son of a Croat blacksmith Franjo Broz, and his wife Maria. Both parents are believed to have been illiterate. Their son was christened Givenas Josip Broz at the Catholic Church of the Kmrovec village, Klanjec County, in the Croatian Zagorje hills. Josip Broz was thus nominally a Catholic, until his excommunication in 1946, when his government tried Archbishop Stepinac of Zagreb on charges of alleged collaboration.

In 1915, Josip Broz was drafted into the Austro-Hungarian Army and sent to the Russian front. He was captured, or deserted, during the Galician campaign. The Czarist government sent him to east-central Russia, where he lived as a prisoner of war. He still has some knowledge of the Khirghizean dialect, which he picked up during these years of imprisonment. Following the October Revolution, he fought in the Red Army during the Russian civil war and later received instructions in Marxist theories and revolutionary techniques in either Moscow or Leningrad. He married a Russian woman, who bore him a son, Zharko.

Broz returned to Yugoslavia in 1924. Before World War I, he had worked briefly as a blacksmith's apprentice. When he went back to his homeland, he specialized in agitation among metalworkers at Zagreb and Kraljevica. He continued his organizing activities until he was arrested in 1929. He spent five years in the Mitrovica jail. When his term was up, Josip Broz left Yugoslavia for the Soviet Union.

In the careers of most Communist leaders and agents, clandestine assignments rarely become public knowledge. Tito is no exception. According to his own admission, the nickname "Tito" goes back to the time when he was doing illegal work inside Yugoslavia. He told *New York Times* correspondent C. L. Sulzberger on October 14, 1946, "This is not a nom de guerre. I assumed it before the war as my illegal name in party work. It is just an ordinary Croatian name, like Rude or Georgi, both of which I have used."

Tito speaks German with a pronounced Viennese accent. He once told M. W. Fodor of the *Chicago Sun* that he had picked it up during his years as a student in the Austrian capital. But he may also have served on Georgi Dimitrov's staff of Balkan agents at the Viennese headquarters of Communist underground activities. During the Spanish civil war, Tito recruited soldiers for the International Brigade among Balkan nationalities. He speaks Russian, and, of course, Serbo-Croatian, and some Czech, and he knows a few bits of other Slavic languages. He has a reading knowledge of French and Italian and understands English fairly well.

Tito lived in Zagreb at the time of the German attack on Yugoslavia. He was using the name Josip Tomanek and claimed to be a Czech engineer. He made his way into Serbia and there began to organize a partisan army in 1941, following the German attack on Russia. As his clandestine forces extended their striking power, Tito began to compete with the guerrillas of General Draja Mikhailovitch for support and recognition by the Allied powers.

Much has been written about the rivalry between Tito and Mikhailovitch, then minister of war of the exiled royal Yugoslav government. The royal government had replaced Prince Paul and opposed Nazi German demands. It left Belgrade together with young King Peter II in 1941. Allied interrogation of Nazi leaders indicated later that Yugoslav opposition to Berlin, which resulted in Nazi Germany's furious attack on Belgrade, so delayed the German attack on Russia that the critical advance on Moscow was moved from summer to winter. This, interrogated officers have stated, may have helped considerably in saving the Soviet capital from falling to the Nazis.

Mikhailovitch represented the royal government inside Yugoslavia. He wanted to maintain the authority and strength of that government. Considering the violently anti-Communist policy of earlier Belgrade regimes, it is easy to suppose that General Mikhailovitch saw his country endangered by two forces: Nazism and communism. Which of these two, in Mikhailovitch's eyes, was the greater evil? We do not know the answer to this question, because General Mikhailovitch never provided it. He might have made common cause with Tito against the Nazis, or common cause with the Nazis against Tito. The Nazis were interested in keeping Yugoslavia divided. Tito was interested in fighting the Nazis and in building up his own power.

A tragic and confusing situation developed. Tito's partisans and Mikhailovitch's Chetniks began to fight each other in 1941. Attempts to settle their differences failed. In 1942, Tito established his Yugoslav Army of Liberation in Slovenia, Croatia, western Bosnia, and the Dalmatian region. Mikhailovitch remained strong in Serbia. When the Germans drove Tito's forces into Mikhailovitch's territory during their 1943 campaign, the two guerrilla forces clashed again. From this time dates Tito's charge that Mikhailovitch collaborated with the Germans in battling the Communist-led partisans. Robert Lee Wolff, wartime chief of the Balkan Section of the Research and Analysis Branch in the United States Office of Strategic Services, believes that Mikhailovitch had German help. He has stated that "collaboration was probably always grudging in Mikhailovitch's case, but it involved the acceptance of arms and supplies, the execution of concerted attacks on the Partisans, agreements whereby the Chetniks were allowed the unmolested use of certain roads during certain hours, and the like."

Writing in the *Atlantic Monthly* for October, 1946, Wolff concludes that "in a cut-throat game, Mikhailovitch guessed wrong; his wrong guess led him to what he regarded as justified collaboration with the Germans in defense of causes which turned out to be lost." Two months later, the same American magazine carried a reply by Constantin Fotitch, former Yugoslav ambassador to the United States, who quoted two other officers, Captain Walter Mansfield of the United States and Major Temple Fielding of Great Britain, as contradicting the contention that Mikhailovitch had been guilty of collaboration.

Robert Lee Wolff, who took the view that "the Tito regime had all the evidence it needed to condemn Mikhailovitch in a fair trial," nevertheless accused the Belgrade government of muzzling the defense counsel for Mikhailovitch in the 1946 treason trial at Belgrade. He wrote that "the courtroom was deliberately turned into a claque, with tickets given out to carefully selected supporters of the regime, who frequently demonstrated more or less noisily against the defendants," while "the judges appeared to play into the hands of the claque in remarks from the bench." Although stating that Mikhailovitch was "not a martyr to the cause of democracy," Wolff added, "The Tito regime which could well have afforded to give him a scrupulously fair trial—and even have displayed a little magnanimity by commuting his death sentence to life imprisonment after conclusive demonstration of his guilt—lost an opportunity to improve its reputation in the eyes of a world already disappointed by its failure to keep its wartime promises and by its totalitarian record of suppression of liberty."

TOWARD 88.6 PER CENT

While Mikhailovitch and Tito were still battling with each other in underground warfare, the British Foreign Office exerted pressure on the royal Yugoslav government to come to an arrangement with Tito. Dr. Ivan Subasitch, then Yugoslav premier, left London for Belgrade in 1945 and signed a pact with Tito. The Subasitch-Tito agreement called for a coalition cabinet, which was quickly formed. Tito became premier and defense minister; Dr. Milan Grol and Edvard Kardelj received posts as deputy premiers; Subasitch himself headed the foreign ministry. The subsequent careers of Subasitch and Grol are worth studying.

In September, 1945, Dr. Subasitch was expected to attend the London Conference of Foreign Ministers. He caught a cold while getting ready for this trip. The Soviet Embassy in Belgrade quickly sent a Russian physician to Subasitch's villa. Accompanied by two Yugoslav medical men, the physician examined the foreign minister and proclaimed that he was suffering from a cerebral hemorrhage and would have to remain incommunicado. Forty armed Yugoslav guards surrounded Dr. Subasitch's residence. Ralph S. C. Stevenson, British ambassador to Belgrade, attempted to see Subasitch; he was not admitted.

Subasitch was well enough to be able to take a hint. He resigned his post in a detailed letter to Premier Broz-Tito. The premier answered in a speech, saying that Subasitch's resignation was a political trick, coming on the eve of Yugoslavia's first postwar national elections, and "while the entire home reaction and enemies abroad are using all possible slander and lies in order to harm consolidation of our country." Subasitch retired from public life.

Dr. Milan Grol experienced difficulties similar to those encountered by Subasitch. He attempted to organize an opposition party during the election, after resigning in August, 1945. He even published an opposition paper, *Demokratiya*, but the government-controlled compositors' union refused to produce more than a few issues. The paper ceased publication, the party never developed, and Grol went into retirement. (He took the witness stand briefly during the Mikhailovitch trial, a year later, while the courtroom claque shouted, "Death to Grol!")

Yugoslavia's national elections of November 11, 1945, brought Tito's government the de jure support it desired. Of the 7,432,469 votes cast by

88.6 per cent of the electorate, 6,725,047 went to the government's "People's Front." This coalition ostensibly contained representatives of the Democratic Party, the Serbian Republican Party, the Croatian Republican Party, the Independent Democratic Party, the Communist Party, and the Slovenian Christian Party. The use of nonrepresentative splinter groups of genuine parties, which we have noted in previous chapters, had been perfected in Yugoslavia to such a degree that the coalition façade was pretty well ignored by everyone, inside and outside the government. The elections showed that genuine opposition had been outterrorized and outmaneuvered. In the backward regions of Montenegro, Bosnia-Hercegovina, and Macedonia, electoral support for the Communist "People's Front" reached 95 to 98 per cent. Richard C. Patterson, United States ambassador to Belgrade, stated that "it cannot be said" that "the elections of November 11 provided opportunity for a free choice of the people's representatives."

Five weeks after the election, the Tito government announced the establishment of Yugoslavia as a republic and denounced King Peter II. The Belgrade Constituent Assembly issued a proclamation on November 29, 1945, which stated:

"1. The democratic federal Yugoslavia is proclaimed a people's republic under the name of the Federative People's Republic of Yugoslavia. The Federative People's Republic of Yugoslavia is a united people's state with a republican form of government, a community of equal peoples who have freely expressed their will to remain united within the Yugoslav state.

"2. By this decision, the monarchy has been finally abolished and Peter Karageorgevitch, together with the entire Karageorgevitch dynasty, is deprived of all rights previously vested in him and his dynasty."

The Tito government thus considered the results of the November elections as identical with a plebiscite on the monarchy. The voters had not known this when they cast their ballots. The Belgrade proclamation accused King Peter of having displayed "neither the ability nor the necessary will to organize the people's resistance to the invader." Referring to the royal government's backing of General Mikhailovitch, the proclamation charged that the king had assisted "the traitors who since 1941 fought against the Liberation Army and against the People's Liberation movement and who collaborated with the enemy."

King Peter answered in a statement issued at London on the same date. He called the Belgrade announcement a violation of the Subasitch-Tito agreement, in that it removed the decision on the monarchy "from the hands of the people themselves." Peter noted, incidentally, that the Subasitch-Tito agreement had been signed on the "explicit wish and advice" of the Allied governments. He added, "The Tito Government simply trampled down all their obligations, destroyed the agreement and organized a totalitarian form of government, in most striking contrast to the ideals of the United Nations, the Yalta resolutions, and the promises they themselves had made." Both documents were charged with emotion. They revealed the strong feelings paramount on both sides. While the Belgrade announcement accused the monarchy of bearing "the guilt for the activities of the anti-popular regimes before the war and for all they [the people of Yugoslavia] have suffered at the hands of traitors," King Peter stated, "I did not take upon me, following the summons of the major Allies, the huge responsibility on March 27, 1941, to call the Yugoslav people to arms against Nazi-Fascist totalitarianism, in order that my freedom-loving people should fall, after heavy struggles and ultimate victory, into another and similar slavery, namely that of Josip Broz (Tito)."

Tito's Communist regime speedily consolidated its political position. On January 31, 1946, the Constituent Assembly adopted the new constitution, which contained many excellent articles pertaining to free and democratic activities among the people of the Yugoslav nation. The constitution symbolized the victory that the government had achieved over its political opponents. The following months brought the conflict between the regime and Yugoslavia's religious forces into the foreground.

This clash was most strikingly illustrated by the trial at Zagreb of Archbishop Aloysius Stepinac, head of the Roman Catholic Church of Yugoslavia. Stepinac was accused of collaboration with the puppet government of Croatia and of subversive activities against the Tito regime. On October 10, 1946, Stepinac was judged guilty and sentenced to sixteen years at hard labor. The Vatican's official newspaper, *Osservatore Romano,* charged that the trial had been directed against the Catholic church in general, rather than against one of its dignitaries. Vatican sources also reported that from April, 1944, to May, 1946, 230 priests had been killed in Yugoslavia, 198 of them without trial. The Yugoslav ministry of information replied that this accusation was "a figment of the imagination" and explained that priests who had been executed "were tried as war criminals, not as priests."

The Serbian Orthodox church, which in the past had often been close to nationalist Serbian elements, watched the government's actions against representatives of the Roman Catholic church with concern. Shortly after the sentencing of Archbishop Stepinac, Patriarch Gavrilo, head of the Orthodox church, received a delegation of orthodox priests who were members of the Serbian Constituent Assembly. He expressed his desire to see "closest and sincerest relations" with the Tito regime.

Although the Tito government came close to achieving complete dominance of the political and religious life of the Yugoslav nation, it suffered some critical shortcomings. Above all, it lacked skilled, or even properly educated, personnel. Much of the civil service was discredited by the pro-Nazi government of Premier Milan Stoyadinovitch or by later collaboration with the occupation forces. Non-Communists were permitted to enter or remain in the Tito government's services only if they submerged their views completely to those of the dominant Communist minority. On the other hand, trusted Communists from the underprivileged regions, such as Montenegro, entered the administration and received vast powers. Seeking to make up for a life of privation and for the sufferings of the war years, many Communist leaders reached a very high standard of living.

Marshal Tito himself established residence in the fashionable, hilly Dedinje suburb of Belgrade and placed his office in the White Palace, previously used by the royal family. Other members of the seven-man central committee of the Communist Party have been equally successful in their choice of residences, servants, entertainment, and supplies. Aside from Tito, Kardelj, and Rankovitch, the central committee also contains Sreten Zhujevitch, the party's financial specialist, and Andrija Hebrang, economic specialist. Of the top Communist leaders, only the much-imprisoned Moshe Pijade has continued the frugal existence of a revolutionary.

MACEDONIAN ASPIRATIONS

We noted, in the preceding chapter, how Macedonian nationalism influenced the internal and external affairs of Bulgaria. The stubborn Macedonians have resisted both Bulgar and Serb efforts to absorb them.

Under Soviet guidance, the Tito government seems to have come nearer to satisfying Macedonian aspirations than any government since Alexander the Great of Macedon.

The nationalist IMRO, founded in 1893 to achieve liberation from Turkish rule, went through various stages of development. During the interwar years, it developed terroristic aspects that served Italian Fascist interests more than genuine Macedonian aims. Pro-Yugoslav factions within the IMRO (the so-called Federalists, who desired a free Macedonia within a Balkan federation) and the pro-Bulgar faction (known as Supremists) were too dogmatic for backing by the Comintern and the Soviet Union. A rival organization, the OIMRO (United IMRO) was founded in 1925 in Vienna by Dmitri Vlakhov, a member of the IMRO's original central committee. Vlakhov, who had advocated constitutional autonomy for Macedonia, later entered the Bulgarian consular service. He worked in Vienna and Odessa, where he came into close contact with Soviet officials. From 1934 to 1943, Vlakhov is believed to have been in Moscow. As World War II drew to a close, he returned to Skoplje, the Macedonian capital, as chairman of the Macedonian National Front.

Recalling Serb efforts to halt their separatist aspirations, many Macedonians welcomed Bulgarian occupation, backed by Nazi Germany, which began in 1941. But the Bulgars proved no less intolerant than the Serbs. Macedonian guerrillas soon began to flourish. Communist-led partisans were organized under the command of General "Tempo," whose identity was later revealed as that of General Svetozar Vikmanovitch.

On April 17, 1945, the Tito government sponsored a Macedonian Republic within the Yugoslav Federation. This Macedonian government is headed by two young Communists, Lazar Kulishevski as premier, and Ljubcho Arsov, his deputy. These two men have the difficult job of combining Belgrade's general Communist directives with the exuberant provincial nationalism of their fellow Macedonians. Fiery, unsophisticated Macedonian nationalists desire to march right into Bulgaria or Greece to satisfy their territorial appetites. Such Communist niceties as concern for the prestige of Georgi Dimitrov's Bulgarian regime are beyond the ken of many dyed-in-the-wool Macedonian expansionists.

In August, 1944, the Macedonian National Front expressed its immediate aims concerning Bulgaria with the proper Communist vernacular as follows: "The strengthening of cultural links with Pirin [Bulgarian]

Macedonia and the promotion of the national development of our people in that area will make possible the ardent desire of the people of Pirin and Yugoslav Macedonia that, through fraternal understanding of Fatherland Front Bulgaria and the Federative People's Republic of Yugoslavia, Pirin should be united with the Macedonian Republic." The Communist-led government of Bulgaria was silent, although there were rumors that Dimitrov and Tito had already negotiated the future status of an extended Macedonian Republic.

Regarding Greek Macedonia, also known as Aegean Macedonia, the Macedonian National Front appealed to the Paris Peace Conference in 1946. It referred to "the terror that prevails in that other part of our country." It is exactly this sort of statement which makes it difficult for the Communist Party of Greece, and the Communist-led EAM (National Liberation Front), to convince their fellow Greeks that Communist policy does not plan to sacrifice Greek sovereignty over its Macedonian province.

Shortly after the withdrawal of German troops from the Balkans, members of the Slavic minority in Greek Macedonia joined the EAM. They understood that it would be possible to form a Slav unit within EAM and they would be able to agitate for secession of the Aegean Macedonia from Greece. But EAM apparently did not see eye to eye with these Slavic Macedonians, who finally crossed into Yugoslavia to become part of the newly founded Greek Macedonian Brigade. This brigade, a very "hush-hush" outfit whose existence was later denied, seems to have made its headquarters at Bitolj under Yugoslav Communist guidance. The political division of this brigade has been credited with the statement, made in December, 1944, that a commission had been set up to "direct the struggle of the Macedonians inside Greece."

TITO LOOKS ABROAD

The Communist regime has completely altered the standing of Yugoslavia in world affairs. And yet, even a dictatorial Communist government cannot escape the historical patterns of Balkan politics. The central committee of the Communist Party of Yugoslavia, which is de facto the government of the new Yugoslav state, has emerged from many decades of underground existence. It now faces problems of statesmanship. Its thoroughness in suppressing opposition has provided a relatively solid base for expansion abroad. These are the five key factors in the future international status of Yugoslavia's Communist regime:

1. *The Soviet Union.* The ideological link between Communist Yugoslavia and Communist Russia is real and indisputable. The Tito regime has shown remarkable efficiency in its reconstruction program. Yugoslavia may well become a very important economic factor in achieving the Soviet Union's Five-Year Plan. Premier Broz-Tito announced the drafting of a Yugoslav Five-Year Plan in the fall of 1946. The military relationship between Yugoslavia and Russia goes back to the war period. Russian arms aided the partisans in achieving their aims. Russian troops entered Belgrade to ensure the establishment of the Tito government. Emphasis on vastly increased iron production and on heavy industry are the outstanding features of the Yugoslav Five-Year Plan. Perhaps Yugoslavia will be able to manufacture arms not only for itself and for such friendly neighbors as Albania, but also for the Soviet Union. Thus Tito may be able to pay back some of the debt he owes the Soviet army. In the field of education and culture, Slavic unity remains the key concept. The importance that the Yugoslav state is likely to have in the future of a Slavic world that is conscious of its heritage and potentialities became clear when the Pan-Slav Congress was held in Belgrade in December, 1946.

2. *Balkan Federation.* The narrow, emotion-laden, provincial nationalism of the Balkan peoples has delayed the political and economic maturity of southeastern Europe for centuries. Federation must legitimately be considered as the best way toward solution of this problem. Communism may be able to succeed, at least superficially, by coercion, where other systems of government were unable to make lasting progress. Consultations among the governments of Yugoslavia, Bulgaria, and Albania, aimed at federation, began even before the final surrender of Germany. But two major reasons appear to have delayed the economic and later political unification of these three states. Not only did nationalistic considerations, particularly the loss of prestige that the Sofia government would experience in a Belgrade-led federation, play a part. There was also the desire to have numerous Slav nations represented in the United Nations. Albania's continuous efforts to be admitted into the United Nations as a sovereign state could not be justified with vigor if that nation sacrificed its sovereignty for the purposes of a Balkan federation. On

the other hand, United Nations membership of the Soviet Republics of the Ukraine and White Russia opened the possibility of membership applications by such ostensibly autonomous republics as Serbia, Croatia, Slovenia, Bosnia-Hercegovina, Montenegro, and Macedonia. Statesmen who accepted the autonomous character of the two Soviet Republics might find it difficult to argue convincingly against the admission of the republics forming the Yugoslav Federation, or forming a Balkan federation. Bulgar-Serb rivalry regarding Macedonia remains one of the highest barriers on the road toward such a federation. Possibly several years of indoctrination will be needed before the Yugoslav and Bulgarian masses are conditioned to find other outlets for their nationalist frustrations.

3. *Italy*. Yugoslav relations with Italy are dominated by the Trieste issue, which we shall discuss in the chapter on the Communist Party of Italy. There can be no doubt that the Tito regime has found almost solid domestic backing for its claims to Trieste. Although the virtue of using nationalist claims to strengthen internal prestige is debatable, the Trieste issue has definitely helped to unify Yugoslavs from all walks of life and all parts of the country behind the Belgrade Communist government.

4. *Austria*. During the first two postwar years, the Trieste problem overshadowed Yugoslavia's consistent claims for territories that are part of Austria. But Marshal Tito, in a speech before the National Assembly in April, 1946, gave "the Slovene part of Carinthia" importance equal to that of Trieste. As long as Austria remains on the periphery of rival east-western power interests, Yugoslav claims are likely to be kept alive. They might be dropped, should Austria slip into the Soviet sphere of interest. Or, again, they may be pressed with utmost vigor, should Austria link its destinies clearly with those of western Europe, Great Britain, and the United States. In the summer of 1947, the Austrian government reported border violations by Yugoslav units in Carinthia and appealed to British occupation authorities for military support.

5. *Greece*. The issue of Macedonia may yet lead to war between the Communist government of Yugoslavia and the monarchist government of Greece. Yugoslav-Greek relations are the concern of every world-conscious person. Those who speak of a possible World War III usually envisage a sudden global conflagration. World danger spots, however, are much more likely to develop in isolated areas. They may merge later. Mace-

donia is such a danger spot, because communism and ultra-nationalist monarchism face each other across this politically inflammable territory.

ALTAR LAMP OF TERROR

The Communist government of Yugoslavia is well entrenched. It has superimposed its high-pressure ideology on a half dozen nationalisms of the I-don't-like-anybody-but-myself variety. To drown out the noisy provincialisms inside their country, the Communists had to shout louder than all the regional nationalists combined. That's why there has been so much noise coming out of Belgrade, during the postwar years: violent clamoring for territorial concessions abroad, and oratorical abuse against opponents at home.

Life inside postwar Yugoslavia began to look normal rather quickly, at least on the surface. Prisoners were used to clearing away rubble, to reconstruct the country. Labor battalions, formed by so-called "volunteers," helped put the nation on its feet. Communist Yugoslavia controls its labor unions. There were no strikes to hamper reconstruction. Excess political-economic interest was siphoned off into demonstrations against foreign and domestic wrongdoers. Yugoslavia's Communist Party and the regime it controls have benefited from two factors: their rough-and-ready foreign policy, and the personal prestige of Premier Broz-Tito. And yet they have wasted much of the good will they enjoyed at the end of the war.

The Communists had experienced ruthless suppression. Later they organized and led a successful patriot resistance force. There was around them the aura of magnificent rebellion. They enjoyed the reflected glory of Russia's victory. Tito's name had become a synonym for national courage. Yugoslavia's young generation had been swept into the partisan's camp. There was new hope for those who remembered the harshness of prewar Yugoslav regimes.

But the postwar years drained this reservoir of good will. Victors should be magnanimous rather than vindictive. Tito was popular enough to permit a fairly free expression of the people's will. His government prepared a constitution that gives genuinely democratic government its due. All that was needed was proper application of the letter and spirit of this constitution. Popular support might have become more genuine, although the electoral victory would have been less sweeping. Instead, emerging from the pit of more than two decades of suppression, Yugoslavia's Communists could not tear themselves away from the tenets of their own earlier illegal existence. They remembered only too clearly that one member of their central committee, Pijade, had said, "The altar lamp of terror must never be extinguished. The people must have fear."

CHAPTER 12

Albania: Precocious Miniature

ALBANIA IS Communist, Balkan, nationalist, and small. That combination makes for impetuous action at home, and bumptious behavior abroad. Communist Albania is a shaggy puppy that tries to walk with the swagger of the Russian bear. It has taken tough bites at the flanks of the British lion, and it has ruffled some of the American eagle's feathers. In spite of such self-assurance, Albania might run a race with the Mongolian People's Republic to see which is the least sovereign nation. And win.

Albania today is, in effect, no more sovereign than the Macedonian Republic. If Yugoslavia is a Soviet satellite, then Albania has the distinction of being a subsatellite. Colonel General Enver Hoxha, Albania's premier, had the support of Tito's partisans in gaining power inside Albania. With the eagerness of a precocious pupil, the Albanian regime has followed the Yugoslav example in external and internal affairs. Yugoslav Communist propagandists label the Greek government a "monarcho-fascist clique"; Hoxha himself has referred to the Athens regime as "those howling jackals to the south." Yugoslavia has shot down several American airmen; Albania has caused the death of forty British sailors by mining the Corfu Straits. Yugoslavia has turned its partisans into a peacetime army; Albania's 1945-1946 budget of 1,016,000,000 Albanian francs set 600,000,000 francs aside for military expenditures.

HOXHA: NO COMINTERN VETERAN

The tall, handsome, trumpet-throated Premier Hoxha is an eager amateur in the business of Communist government. He is no old-time Comintern agent, no survivor of purges or changes in command. He is an intelligent ex-teacher who seems to have swallowed a whole dictionary of Marxist terms. Hoxha did not have the revolutionary experience of

Klement Gottwald, Georgi Dimitrov, or even Tito. Perhaps he pictures himself as an Albanian Lenin, and so has repeated some of the mistakes of another Lenin imitator, Béla Kun.

Hoxha was born in 1908 and became interested in Communist ideas when he was studying in Paris on a scholarship. In 1931, he continued his studies in Brussels, while working as secretary of the Albanian consulate in the Belgian capital. He returned to his homeland as a confirmed Communist in 1936 and received a teaching post. But his ideological leanings brought him into early opposition to the government of self-crowned King Zog I. Hoxha lost his teaching position and established himself as a tobacconist in Tirana, the Albanian capital. He continued his revolutionary work into the period of Italian occupation. In 1941, he was incautious enough to lead an anti-Italian demonstration. The police of the Italian-installed puppet government set out to arrest Hoxha, who fled into the mountains, the traditional refuge of Albanian revolutionaries, outlaws, and freedom fighters.

Enver Hoxha joined the guerrillas. There were six underground resistance movements inside Albania. They gained or lost importance as the war went on. King Zog, in exile at London, was represented by the underground units of Major Abas Kupi. Kupi was finally hunted down and captured by Hoxha followers. Zog, who now lives in Egypt, did not retain the support of Colonel Muharrem Bajraktari's guerrillas. Bajraktari operated in the north, while Muslem Peza's units were active in central Albania, near Tirana. In southern Albania, guerrillas were led by Colonel Bilal Nivica.

The Albanian Communist Party was officially formed in 1929, during the extreme-revolutionary Third Strategy of the Comintern. But it was suppressed by Zog and had to be reestablished in the fall of 1941. Its secretary-general is said to be Lieutenant General Koci Xoxe, minister of the interior and chief of the People's Guard, or Communist security police. The decision to form the underground People's Army was taken in 1943, and the Committee of National Liberation was organized in May, 1944. At that time, conditions inside Albania resembled in miniature the internal rivalries of Yugoslavia. Hoxha found himself opposed by a nationalist group, the "Balli Kombetar," which played somewhat the role of Mikhailovitch in Yugoslavia. Hoxha, with Tito's support, was able to seize Tirana from the Germans after considerable fighting in October, 1944.

REFORMS OVERDUE

Albania offered ample opportunities for intelligent governmental and agricultural reform. Its economic life had retained the feudal traditions of Turkish rule. Its beys ran the government as they ran their own vast properties. Hoxha had been disgusted by the pro-Italian, economically stagnant Zog administration. Now his turn had come. Land reform put a maximum ceiling of 75 acres on agrarian property. Nationalization was decreed overnight. Not only industry, banking, and trade fell under the sweeping nationalization decrees, but also stores, motion-picture houses, publications, and restaurants.

Albania also had an "election." It was held on December 2, 1945. According to the election law, it was to be "free, with universal suffrage and the secret ballot" and "designed to protect the interests of the majority and the minority." The Hoxha government won a strikingly sweeping victory. It gained 82 out of 82 seats in the National Assembly. Shortly afterward, it denounced King Zog and declared Albania a republic.

In spite of this overwhelming victory at the polls, the government continued to tighten its grip on the nation. Camille M. Cianfarra, a Rome correspondent of the *New York Times,* reported that from ten to fifteen thousand persons were imprisoned in Albania from the end of 1944 to June, 1946. The dispatch asserted that 3,000 persons were either killed or missing in that nation of about one million inhabitants. Mr. Cianfarra also reported that "the end of 1945 saw seventeen books published, of which four contained a systematic presentation of Communist theory, ten exalted the present regime, its works and achievements, and three were on nonpolitical subjects."

Communist and Communist-led governments often favor a pattern of angry defiance in their relations with states that they regard as bourgeois. Albania has been outstanding in this respect. On April 4, 1946, the British government charged Tirana with having displayed an unfriendly and uncooperative attitude, and stated that it would not send a diplomatic representative to the Albanian capital. Seven months later, on November 8, the United States withdrew its temporary mission and accused the Tirana regime of "continued unwillingness" to adhere to established United States-Albanian treaty relations. Hoxha answered a few days later that the United States government had "made use of the question of the treaties as an argument for opposition to all our legitimate rights."

More serious were British charges that Albanian shore batteries had fired on British warships on May 15, 1946, and that on October 22 freshly laid mines in the Corfu Channel had damaged two British destroyers, causing eighty casualties, including forty dead. London, in an exceedingly angry note, stated on December 9 that Hoxha had committed a "flagrant breach of international law" and submitted the case to the United Nations. The United Nations Security Council, voting seven to two, found Albania guilty. Russia and Poland voted against this resolution, and a Soviet veto blocked action on the matter. Great Britain then turned the matter over to the International Court of Justice.

EMOTIONALISM INSTEAD OF MARXISM

The majority of Albania's population accepted Communist reform on a purely emotional basis. Anti-bey sentiment, rather than understanding of Marxist doctrines and class struggle, brought Hoxha mass support. Albania's overwhelmingly agricultural population had hoped that nationalization of large estates would quickly result in economic betterment. Judging the success or failure of the Tirana regime on the basis of their individual experience, Albanian peasants could hardly be satisfied with their new rulers. Although it was generally agreed that land reforms in feudal Albania had been long overdue, there was criticism of the way in which nationalization and the parceling out of land were undertaken. Strong supporters of the regime received choice strips of land. Government officials took over many of the modern villas in "New Tirana," which was developed during the Italian occupation.

Even Hoxha's followers have grown at least somewhat disillusioned. His summary executions and half-completed, overquick reforms have even been called "Trotskyite" by some of Hoxha's Communist critics. This accusation can, however, hardly be leveled against a Communist-trained leader, who has leaned heavily on the support of Marshal Tito and who has followed the suggestions or orders of Soviet Russian advisers. Dissatisfaction with the Hoxha regime has fundamental economic reasons, which in turn stem from Albania's strategic political role. Military expenditures have been so enormous as to rule out early economic recovery.

On May 20, 1947, the Tirana Radio announced that the government had discovered an "anti-Communist" conspiracy. The regime purged the Albanian Communist movement and even removed Professor Sejfullan Maleshova, who resided in the Soviet Union from 1925 to 1940 and helped reorganize the Communist Party of Albania during World War II. Among nine deputies arrested as involved in the conspiracy was Constantin Boshnjeku, who helped establish the original Communist Party in 1929 and who was director general of the Bank of Albania at the time of his arrest. It was understood that nationalist sentiment and opposition to decisive Russian influence had caused the accused conspirators to oppose Hoxha's policies.

Albania's religious groups constitute a strong barrier to the spreading of Communist doctrines. Two thirds of the population are Moslems who find it difficult to reconcile their faith with the materialistic credo of their new government and political leaders. Neither the Roman Catholics nor the followers of the Greek Orthodox church, who make up the balance of Albania's population, are easily attracted to the views of their new regime. Action against Catholic priests and nuns has followed the pattern adopted in Yugoslavia. A relatively large number of priests were tried in Albania as alleged collaborators or war criminals.

In spite of these difficulties, the Hoxha government exercises undisputed control over the Albanian nation. It appears to have been more successful in suppressing organized opposition than were the Italian occupation forces during the war years. Hoxha has not only maintained closest relations with the Belgrade government but is even believed to have spent part of the war years in the Soviet Union. There, it is said, he received military and ideological indoctrination. This belief, whether based on fact or not, has tended to strengthen his prestige inside Albania, where he is regarded as enjoying the confidence of Premier Stalin. The commanding position that the Soviet Union maintains in the Balkans works strongly in favor of Albania's Communist regime.

CHAPTER 13

Greece: America's Problem Child

FEAR OF Communist control in Greece prompted the United States in 1947 to extend its political-economic influence to the Balkan area. On March 12, President Harry S. Truman told the American people that "the very existence of the Greek state is today threatened by the terrorist activities of several thousand armed men, led by Communists, who defy the government's authority." America made the decision of intervention in Greece with a heavy heart. Greece was a bad place in which to test a new United States foreign policy. Truman admitted that the Greek government had "made mistakes" while it was "operating in an atmosphere of chaos and extremism."

There were a number of people in the United States, including former cabinet member Henry A. Wallace, who blamed the Greek government itself for the growth and influence of communism in Greece. It is a fact that right and left extremism unwittingly helped each other. Fear of communism had given Greek Royalists mass support. Communism thus aided King George II on his return to the throne. That is why the Communist Party of Greece has jestingly been called "the King's Party." In turn, rightist extremism prompted non-Communists to turn to the ultra-left.

When the United States decided to back the Athens government, communism was approaching Greece from four directions: through the three Communist-governed nations to the north, and through the Communist Party inside Greece itself. The Bulgarian government of Premier Georgi Dimitrov sought an outlet to the Mediterranean. It claimed the Greek territory of western Thrace, which Bulgaria occupied temporarily during Nazi rule of the Balkans. The Yugoslav government of Premier Josip Broz-Tito had developed a Macedonian Republic that aspired to incorporate Greek Macedonia. The Albanian regime of Premier Enver Hoxha fiercely

137

opposed the Athens government, and clashes on the Greek-Albanian frontier were frequent. Inside Greece, the Communist Party, under its secretary-general, Nicholas Zachariadis, was engaged in violent conflict with the rightist government at Athens.

FEAR AND HATE

Greece lies on the periphery of clashing power interests. The Teheran Conference of 1943 placed the occupation of Greece in British hands. The rest of the Balkans was placed within the Russian sphere of influence. Greece thus became the only western outpost on the Balkan peninsula. It prevented the Soviet Union from pushing Communist influence to the Mediterranean, from outflanking Turkey and overshadowing the Near East. The battle for Greece, which began with the bloody civil war of December, 1944, revealed the postwar struggle of rival power interests even while World War II was still in progress.

The people of Greece failed to close their ranks against outside power aspirations. Instead, they sharpened the conflict of political emotions that has impaired their well-being since their liberation from the Turks in 1832. Communist extremism of the left and monarchist extremism of the right have cut Greece in two. Like two powerful magnets, Royalists and Communists were able to attract the support of Greek masses. Political extremism followed World War II in every part of the globe. But nowhere did the lines stand out more sharply than in Greece. Moderate political groups were all but eliminated in the Communist-Royalist fight for power. Greece's great republican Liberal Party had fought the royalist Popular Party for decades. But the Liberal house was destroyed in the war's aftermath, and its bricks served to strengthen the opposing bastions of communism and monarchism.

Extremism is the fruit of fear and hate. Greeks have good reason for both. Ancient tribal vendetta traditions form the pattern of open Communist-Royalist conflict. Opponents give and receive no quarter. Since the liberation of Greece, extreme leftist and extreme rightist bands have roamed the countryside. They have killed and tortured and robbed. Each side has avenged the misdeeds of the other in an endless circle of fratricide. Communists and other antimonarchists fear and hate the rightist bands that owe their allegiance to the government. The Populists and their anti-Communist adherents fear and hate the Communist-led units whose record during the 1944 disturbances remains unforgotten. Strengthened by the disintegration of moderate political forces, the two extremes became ever more uncompromising. No one can say with certainty which side has been more guilty of cruelty, of killings, of persecutions. The violence of Greek emotions has erased reliable records of fact.

Both extremes gained support through negative rather than positive aims. The Royalists sought the backing of the west and of moderate Greeks by uncompromising opposition to the Communists. The Communist-led EAM (National Liberation Front) attracted those who sought equally uncompromising opposition to former Nazi-Fascist collaborators, to ultra-rightists, and to the monarchy. Fear of communism added many promonarchist votes to the plebiscite of September 1, 1946, which brought the return of King George II from London, after five years of exile. Many Greeks cast their votes for a symbol of stability rather than for a political system. Earlier, the national elections of March 1, 1946, had brought overwhelming success to the Populists, who subsequently used their newly gained parliamentary majority to push and enforce rigorous emergency measures. Whenever voices arose that these emergency actions were destroying essential freedoms, the answer was that the battle against communism was paramount.

ROYAL SEESAW

Until 1935, the development of the Greek Communist Party was overshadowed by more momentous trends and events. Liberation from the Turks had brought Greece a monarchy that resembled a jack-in-the-box more than an orderly system of government. Otto of Wittelsbach governed for three decades. Prince William of Schleswig-Holstein became Greece's King George I in 1863, and was assassinated in 1913. His son, the pro-German King Constantine I, fled Greece in 1917, when his country sided with the Allies. His son, Alexandros, succeeded him, but died three years later. Constantine returned in 1920, was forced out two years later. George II became his successor but remained on the throne for only eighteen months. A republic was proclaimed, and the nation voted two to one against him.

George remained in exile for eleven years, while Greece was rocked by Republican-Royalist antagonism. Only the government of Eleutherious Venizelos, head of the Liberal Party, brought a period of relative tranquillity from 1928 to 1930. The seesawing between the royalists and the republicans which followed the Venizelos regime prevented the country from regaining its balance. Venizelos tried to return to power through a coup d'état. The revolt was quelled within ten days. The Royalists then held one of the most flagrantly corrupt plebiscites in the history of the Balkans. The king received 97 per cent of the vote and returned in 1935.

Following the king's return, nearly all top-ranking political leaders died in quick succession. General John Metaxas became premier by default. He governed briefly on a parliamentary basis. The early months of 1936 brought a series of strikes among tobacco workers and other laborers. On May 10, nine workers who had been killed in clashes with the police were buried at Salonika. Communists and labor leaders made speeches at the mass grave and later led a crowd of many thousands to the center of the city. This demonstration resulted in sympathy strikes at Kavalla, Larissa, Agris, and several smaller towns. Three days later, the central committee of the Communist Party and the Communist-led "People's Front" (an outgrowth of the "united front" strategy) signed a manifesto that concluded, "Down with the monarchist government of murderers! Down with fascism! Bread, work, and peace and well-being! All for the strike, all out on the streets!" A wave of strikes followed. According to a commentary in the *Communist International* of August, 1936, "that which the Communist Party of Greece had, for day after day, been striving for during recent years and months, by carrying out with persistence and consistency the tactics of a united People's Front, was achieved in action in the days of the battle of May."

METAXAS AND ZACHARIADIS

The Communist-led strikes might have led to widespread and successful revolt. Troops in the main cities showed marked opposition to the Metaxas government. But General Metaxas brought reliable forces from the Peloponese, Larissa, and western Macedonia before the Communists had time to seize the opportunity that had arisen. Communist Secretary-General Nicholas Zachariadis told a session of the party's central committee on May 14 that it would have been possible to overthrow Metaxas. However, he admitted, the Communists had lacked "mobility and at the same time unfailing determination in carrying out the decisions adopted." In other words, Metaxas had been quicker than the Communists.

Three months later, Metaxas convinced George II that the country's parliamentary machinery had hit a deadlock. Republicans and Royalists balanced each other almost evenly, with fifteen Communist parliamentary delegates controlling the balance. (The Liberal Party had 126 seats. The Populists were split into a basic group that controlled 72 seats and a "Radical Union" that had elected 60 delegates.) Metaxas also asserted that the Communists planned to recapture the advantage they had lost in May and were preparing a general strike. He advocated unchecked executive action. On August 6, 1936, Metaxas began a dictatorship that ended only with the fall of Greece in 1941. After installing himself as supreme dictator, Metaxas arrested several thousand of his opponents. These included Communists, Socialists, peasant leaders, and liberal intellectuals. In September, Zachariadis was also arrested. A month later, he was sentenced to four and one-half years in prison. But it wasn't the first time that Zachariadis had entered a prison cell.

Born in 1903, the son of a tobacco worker, Nicholas Zachariadis finished high school at the age of fourteen and went to work in the same factory as his father. Later he became a tailor's helper and a sailor. The Communist Party had been founded in 1918, and Zachariadis had joined its youth movement when he was eighteen. In 1923, he became a member of the party's main organization. He agitated among sailors and was arrested at Salonika and charged with treason. During this early period of his political career, the future head of the Greek Communist Party was arrested nine times. He managed to escape five times. All in all, he spent two years in prison during this part of his career.

In 1926, the Communist Party paper *Rizopastis* was attacked by a group of anti-Communists. Zachariadis was accused of killing one of the attackers (whom the Communists labeled a "Trotskyite provocateur"), but he managed to evade the police. Zachariadis spoke at the Seventh Comintern Congress in 1935. Shortly afterward, on December 4, he officially became secretary-general of his party. In addressing the Fifth Congress of the Communist Party of Greece, Zachariadis stated that the "People's Front," the forerunner of the EAM, had been a successful Communist venture. He gave credit to Comintern leadership when he told his listeners, "We are indebted for our success to the fact that the Communist Party, acting in the spirit of the decision of the Central Committee of the Communist International, has actively pursued the line of the Communist International. We have the broadest possible opportunities before us. Only we, the Communists, by rallying together in a united front with all honest, progressive, democratic forces, can save the country from the danger of a barbarous fascist régime, from a foreign yoke, and bring it onto the broad road of emancipation and well-being of the people."

After his arrest by Metaxas, Zachariadis was hailed in the *Communist International* of January, 1937, as "the initiator, founder and organizer of the anti-fascist front, which has rallied to its banners not only the workers, Communists and members of the revolutionary trade unions, but also working class organizations of all tendencies, peasant organizations, the organized partisans and small traders, and broad sections of the intellectuals."

THE RISE OF EAM

The Communists remained underground throughout the Metaxas regime. Following the end of World War II, and the 1944 disturbances, the Greek Communist Party held an important strategic meeting from April 5 to 10, 1945. This conference evaluated the party's wartime activities and charted its future course. In a statement issued at the conclusion of the meeting, the Communist Party recalled that it had "created the gigantic people's organizations of the resistance—EAM, EPON [a youth organization], and ELAS [armed units of the EAM]" and that its policy had "brought about the great, mass Communist Party, with hundreds of thousands of members, which constitutes the greatest guarantee in the struggle for the democratic regeneration of Greece."

The Communists were a dynamic force during the German occupation. EAM was formed in 1941 along the previously established pattern of the "People's Front." Following German violation of the Nazi-Soviet Pact, EAM engaged in sabotage activities that helped the downfall of the Axis and the victory of the Allied powers. EAM was rivaled by the EDES units under the command of General Napoleon Zervas, whose status paralleled roughly that of Mikhailovitch in Yugoslavia. Clashes between the two groups were frequent. They took a heavy toll in Greek lives. As the war drew to a close, the Allied world became conscious of two developments: that EAM represented a determined anti-monarchist coalition that considered the Greek government in exile as unrepresentative; and that EAM and EDES were storing up arms for the postliberation period.

In March, 1944, EAM created a provisional government in rivalry to the Greek exile government at Cairo. The provisional government was called PEEA, or Political Committee of National Liberation. It looked very much like the civil authority that Tito's partisans had created inside Yugoslavia. And it bore a striking resemblance to the Polish Committee of National Liberation, which later was to move from Lublin to Warsaw. A relatively large number of Greek troops in the Middle East mutinied against the Cairo government. British forces surrounded the mutinous troops, disarmed them, and the British government arranged for a conference of Greek spokesmen at Lebanon. EAM sent representatives to this meeting. A national charter was adopted, which provided for the entry of EAM ministers into the Greek cabinet. The charter also provided for the unification of all guerrilla armies inside Greece, for centralized planning, and for the distribution of military supplies.

But EAM headquarters inside Greece refused to ratify the Lebanon charter and advanced new demands. In September, 1944, British and United States authorities negotiated with EAM representatives at Caserta, Italy. The Allies made further concessions to the EAM. They also agreed to denounce the German-inspired collaborationist Greek Security Battalions. This was something the Cairo government had refused to do, a neglect that was not to its credit.

Both the Lebanon and Caserta agreements were later denounced by the Greek Communist Party as a rightist deviation. Applying strict Communist interpretation and vernacular to these EAM actions, the party announced after its April, 1945, meeting that among EAM's "most serious mistakes of a rightist character" had been "the agreement of Lebanon, which did not correspond to the concrete correlation of forces and consequently, did not advance and ensure to the proper degree the realization of national unity and normal democratic development against the plottings of reaction." The Caserta agreement was also described as "a mistake of a rightist character."

"LEFTIST MISTAKES"

After Greece had been liberated, the stopgap Athens government of Premier George Papandreou ordered EAM to disband and to surrender its arms. EAM countered this request with a demand for demobilization of the government's Mountain Brigade, which had been organized in the Middle East and had fought in North Africa and Italy. The government refused. It stated that the Mountain Brigade was part of the United Nations armies and was needed to form the nucleus of a new nonpolitical national army. On December 1, 1944, the six cabinet members belonging to the EAM resigned. Two days later, Greek police clashed violently with EAM supporters who were holding a protest demonstration in Athens. Twenty-nine persons were killed, 140 injured. EAM proclaimed a general strike throughout Greece. This was the beginning of bloody and tragic warfare, which pitted British troops against armed Greek civilians. It was an ugly business. British tanks and even airplanes were used to quell the Communist-led EAM-ELAS units. The forces of Lieutenant General Ronald M. Scobie required several days to subdue their opponents. No matter what the extenuating over-all political considerations may have been, the whole thing looked very bad to many observers on the scene. EAM gave no quarter, and it received none.

The central committee of the Communist Party later criticized itself and its EAM of a leftist deviation during these December events. It stated that "mistakes of a military and leftist political character" had been "caused by the incorrect estimation of the disposition and the role of the English Government of Churchill." It also spoke of "underestimation of the forces of reaction, in the interior and abroad," and of "overestimation of our own potentialities and, in the main, the lack of the necessary political flexibility." The April, 1945, statement said, "These things prevented the Party leadership from having a clear perspective of the course of the conflict and brought them to miss the opportunity of an agreement with the English military authorities under more favorable terms than those of the Varkiza (armistice) agreement made after a military defeat at Athens." This self-criticism bore a strong resemblance to Zachariadis's analysis of the Communist Party's failure to overthrow the Metaxas regime, nine years earlier.

Especially notable was the central committee's admission that "the arrest of non-combatant persons, although a defense measure against the savage persecution and hostage-taking of Papandreou-Scobie, was a serious political mistake which gave the reaction the opportunity to raise a campaign of slanders for the purposes of covering up its own crimes."

This self-criticism referred to the taking of hostages by EAM forces as a means of pressure against the British and Greek governments. Some of these hostages were returned alive; others were later exhumed from their graves. Rightist bands had acted with equal ruthlessness against the EAM, although the extent of such action on both sides escapes objective evaluation. At any rate, as the central committee noted, the taking of hostages proved to be a serious political boomerang. It must certainly have influenced many persons of basically republican and genuinely democratic sentiment to back the Populists and the monarchy against communism.

GOVERNMENT BY EMERGENCY DECREE

Greek governments, from the time of liberation until after the plebiscite, moved farther and farther to the right. Finally, Constantine Tsaldaris, leader of the Populist Party, emerged as premier of a completely Royalist-dominated cabinet. The government's 1946 emergency decrees gave the police power to enter premises without a warrant and to hold persons in jail indefinitely, without bond or trial. Summary courts were authorized to deal with offenders using arms against the authorities. Death sentences could be carried out immediately, even against persons sentenced as moral authors of crimes against the state. The government used its extraordinary powers to purge a great number of non-Communist educators and senior civil servants from civil-service pay rolls. Among those purged was the distinguished resistance leader Alexander Svolos, a Socialist, who could hardly be accused of Communist affiliation. Svolos's views can be discerned from an interview that he gave Ernest O. Hauser, a correspondent of *The Saturday Evening Post*, during which he said, "Numerically, the Communists were a minority in the EAM. But the party maintained actual leadership everywhere. The terroristic acts perpetrated by the Communists finally turned many people against EAM. EAM is merely a front for the Communist Party."

The Greek Communist Party had not yet overcome public revulsion against EAM excesses, when it faced the accusation of backing territorial claims of the Communist-dominated nations to the north. Throughout the summer and fall of 1946, reports of serious unrest in the northern border regions were released by the Greek government. Premier Tsaldaris came to New York to present his government's case against Bulgaria, Yugoslavia, and Albania to the General Assembly of the United Nations. General Spiros Georgoulis, head of the Second Army Corps at Larissa, asserted that "a network of Communist bands, directed from abroad, is attempting to cut off northern Greece and form an autonomous state." The British Foreign Office, commenting on official Greek charges that the northern countries were supplying guerrilla bands with military material, stated that it saw "no reason to doubt" these allegations. The Bulgarian, Yugoslav, and Albanian governments consistently denied these and similar charges.

Nicholas Zachariadis denied that the Communist Party was working hand in hand with the guerrilla units in the north, but added, "We are standing calmly, waiting for an understanding, but with guns at our feet." The Communist Party repeated its stand that it, and the EAM, did not favor any territorial changes in the north. It did, however, press Greek territorial aspirations in regions outside the Soviet sphere of influence. On September 1, 1945, the EAM sent a memorandum to the Greek government, demanding annexation of eastern Thrace, which is part of Turkey and includes the European coast of the Dardanelles. This memorandum, which also asked that Great Britain transfer the island of Cyprus to Greek sovereignty, came shortly before unofficial Soviet spokesmen demanded the annexation of the Turkish provinces of Kars and Ardahan to the Soviet Union.

Outside pressures gave the Royalist government the opportunity to strengthen its hand by appealing to nationalist sentiment. Unable to succeed in genuine internal pacification and economic reconstruction, the monarchist regime moved closer to a dictatorial pattern of government. An Associated Press report from Athens noted on September 17, 1946, that "rightist bands, apparently unmolested by the authorities, were reported active throughout Greece." The report quoted an unnamed Liberal Party member as saying that "Royalist extremists were driving many into the camp of the extreme Leftists by terror and intimidation." The Greek government asked the Paris Peace Conference for 4,150 square miles of Bulgarian territory. It lagged behind the proclaimed Communist policy practiced in other Balkan nations, which extended suffrage to women. It did not hesitate to revive anti-Slav sentiment by combining it with Greek fears of a Communist wave that might sweep down from the hills of Macedonia and Thrace toward the Mediterranean.

AMERICA STEPS IN

Early in 1947, the British government advised the United States that it was no longer able to support Greece. America decided to take over where Britain left off. President Truman made the Greek issue a turning point in United States foreign policy when he indicated that Greece must be supported against the tide of communism that engulfed it. Committing the United States to a general policy of preventing the extension of Communist influence, he said:

"We shall not realize our objectives unless we are willing to help free people to maintain their free institutions and their national integrity against aggressive movements that seek to impose upon them totalitarian regimes. This is no more than a frank recognition that totalitarian regimes imposed on free peoples by direct or indirect aggression undermine the foundations of international peace and hence the security of the United States."

President Truman also said, "We have condemned in the past, and we condemn now, extremist measures of the Right or the Left. We have in the past advised tolerance and we advise tolerance now." And so the United States, reluctantly and without optimistic illusions, made Greece its problem child.

How successful would the United States be in bringing civil peace to Greece, in stemming communism, which approached that nation from four fronts? Would the ultra-right use American support to continue its excesses? Would communism and ultra-nationalism, like two knives that have been sharpened on each other, dismember the body of Greece? Would the United States, by backing the Athens regime, become in the eyes of the opposition coresponsible for any extremist actions by the government?

These questions were asked by Americans and by Greeks. In Washington, it was realized that more was needed than arms for the Greek government against the Communist-controlled guerrillas. Paul Porter, on his return to Washington from a special economic mission to Greece, announced that Greek Premier Demetrios Maximos had followed American suggestions in formulating economic measures. Maximos, who had succeeded Tsaldaris, developed a nine-point program directed mostly against inflation. Porter emphasized, however, that America's job in Greece would require "aggressive administration" of funds.

TOWARD A "FREE GOVERNMENT"

Truman's plan of American aid was announced while a Balkan Commission of the United Nations investigated guerrilla activities in northern Greece. The commission reported to the United Nations Security Council on June 25, 1947, that Yugoslavia, Bulgaria, and Albania had lent their support to the anti-government guerrillas. The commission voted 9 to 2 in recommending a semi-permanent group which was to keep an eye on northern Greece from Salonika. The Soviet Union strongly blocked the creation of such a commission through a series of vetoes.

Meanwhile, large-scale warfare developed on Greek soil. A Communist conference at Strasbourg, France, heard Greek Communists proclaim their intention to establish a "Free Greek Government" in the guerrilla-controlled regions. Nicholas Zachariadis wrote in *Rizopastis* that "creation of a free democratic government in the free democratic areas of Greece" had become a necessity. Zachariadis himself had been living underground ever since the Greek government on May 17 ordered his arrest on charges of criminal libel; he had accused the government of conspiring in the assassination of a high-ranking Communist leader.

On July 9 the Athens government announced that it had intercepted secret instructions from Communist guerrilla leader Markos Vafthiadis, also known as "General Markos." The government asserted that Vafthiadis, a veteran of more than two decades of service in the Greek Communist Party, had instructed party members under "Plan F" to begin uprisings in urban centers. The government subsequently arrested more than 10,000 Communists and others whom it accused of Communist sympathies.

Simultaneously, a force of several thousand guerrillas entered Greece from Albania. The guerrillas managed to entrench themselves in the Mount Gammos area of northern Greece. The establishment of a Communist-controlled "free government" was announced by Vafthiadis on August 16. The guerrilla regime demanded the deposition of King Paul I —who had succeeded King George upon his death in the summer of 1947 —and established a "popular National Assembly." The Athens government prepared a ban on the Communist Party. A guerrilla radio station began broadcasts. Greek intelligence reports stated that an International

Brigade had been assembled by Communists abroad for action inside Greece. Radio Moscow said that recruits for such a brigade were coming even from the Latvian Republic of the USSR. American representatives in France noted that recruits for an International Brigade were being selected from Spanish émigrés residing in southern France. It was under these conditions that Dwight P. Griswold, director of American aid to Greece, began his work in Athens.

American intervention was sure to make the Communist position in Greece more difficult. The Communist Party had alienated many people during the 1944 civil war. It had been unable to clear itself of the suspicion that it favored seizure of Greek Macedonia by Yugoslavia's Macedonian Republic and annexation of western Thrace by Bulgaria. For more than two years, communism had been ruthlessly persecuted by the Royalist government. Adherence to the party demanded sacrifices that few individuals could be expected to make. Although the number of Communist-backed guerrillas rose from 3,500 in November, 1946, to 14,000 in the early spring of 1947, membership in the Communist Party itself was declining rather than rising. Following the 1944 civil war, membership was reduced from 400,000 to 250,000. Greek Communists attributed this to a "purge" of unreliable members from party ranks. But even a "purge," rather than voluntary withdrawal, pointed to disagreement within the party itself.

Although 1947 began as a year of supreme crisis for communism in Greece, there was no evidence that it would weaken in its attempt to gain control of the nation from the inside. After all, not only the concept of democracy but also the Trojan Horse technique originated on the ancient, blood-drenched soil of Greece.

III
WESTERN EUROPE

CHAPTER 14

Germany: Enemy into Ally

OF ALL THE prizes of war, the allegiance of seventy million Germans is the greatest. The fate of Europe cannot be decided without Germany, and it is not being decided without Germany. When Hitlerism crashed into the abyss of history, it left a political vacuum. German Communists, who had spent years of exile in the Soviet Union, reentered the Reich with the Red Army. Other Communists went to the Russian-occupied zone from their overseas refuges, notably Mexico and the United States. As a result, Soviet occupation authorities commanded a group of men and women familiar with German conditions and acceptable to Russia. German Communists had a chance to fill quickly the political vacuum left by Nazism.

The western Allies, above all the United States, emphasized the negative needs of Germany: denazification, demilitarization, deindustrialization. They were careful not to permit political organization at an early stage of the occupation. Only slowly did the political life of Germany, which had been dormant since the rise of Nazism, unfold itself. But meanwhile Communist activity in the Soviet zone had gained enough impetus to extend its ideological influence into the western zones.

What was the political allegiance of Germans shortly after the Allied victory? Throughout 1946, elections were held in various parts of the Reich. One factor made evaluation difficult: the merger, on April 21, of the Social Democratic and Communist parties in the Soviet-occupied zone. At the time of the merger, the Communists claimed a membership of 395,000 in the Russian zone. After the Soviet-sponsored merger with the Social Democrats, from which resulted the Socialist Unity Party, public support of communism in the Soviet-controlled areas became obscured. The Socialist Unity Party was not permitted to organize in the western zones, although its representatives were eager to strengthen their influence among the Social Democrats of the west.

153

Elections in all four zones, including the ballots of some thirty million Germans, gave 10,600,000 votes to the Christian Democrats (a dominantly Catholic party), 7,800,000 to the Social Democrats (in Berlin and the west), 5,000,000 to the Socialist Unity Party (in Berlin and the Russian zone), and 1,250,000 to the Communists (in the west). All through the Russian zone, however, the Communist-sponsored Socialist Unity Party obtained a favorite position.

"A JUMPING-OFF PLACE"

With the Communist Party nonexistent in the east, the Socialist Unity Party must be considered as an amplified Communist organization, which succeeded in gaining the cooperation of several Socialist leaders. Hans Berger (identified by the United States Federal Bureau of Investigation as the Communist agent Gerhart Eisler) wrote in the New York Communist monthly *Political Affairs* that the Socialist Unity Party considered Socialism its "final goal" but was content to press for merely "an antifascist, militant parliamentary democracy."

The "united front" policy, adopted at the Seventh Comintern Congress, is today in effect in Germany. This can best be seen from an indoctrination pamphlet that the Communist Party circulated among its leaders in the summer of 1945. Issued two years after the official dissolution of the Communist International, it was nevertheless entitled *Strategy and Tactics after the Seventh World Congress*. The pamphlet, designed particularly for the United States-occupied zone, said in part:

"It is a fact that the proletariat in Germany does not at this moment represent a power factor. To accomplish that remains our task. The Social Democratic party machinery has been less fully destroyed than ours, as it did not fight Hitler with equal strength. The American occupation force represents the only power factor against which opposition would be a senseless undertaking. Consequently, the proletarian revolution, the dictatorship of the proletariat is not a current matter. We must first create a jumping-off place, our path must be covered step-by-step. (Compare with Russia, 1917: At first with the peasants and bourgeoisie against feudalism and Czarism, then with the middle-peasant against the large estates and the bourgeoisie, and finally with the poor peasants and the peasant workers in the battle for socialization of agriculture.)

"What are the powers we may be able to utilize? There is the still unorganized, heavily suffering labor movement which instinctively yearns for unity. There is part of the middle-class and of youth, concerned about the national continuity of Germany, who are looking for a force which will represent them. There is part of the bourgeoisie which did not achieve its aims under the Nazi régime, and which today fears that it will be swallowed by American imperialism. . . .

"What do Strategy and Tactics mean? Strategy is the forever immovable outlined battle plan toward the final goal: destruction of the capitalist suppression state, dictatorship of the proletariat, Socialism and a class-less society. Tactics means the operation of single battles and skirmishes, necessary in order to reach a strategic goal. These are not all necessarily steps forward; often we must retreat, engage in flank side operations, or remain static. . . .

"Today's tactics require mobilization of all anti-fascist forces in the battle for the nearest momentary goal, which is understandable to all and common to all. In this movement it is quite proper to have Social Democrats or bourgeois in leading positions. If we succeed in keeping this movement going, then we Communists as the most active, determined and adaptable, will in due course succeed in obtaining the lead."

ENTER WILHELM PIECK

The Nazis imprisoned and killed Ernst Thälmann, the Hamburg dock-worker who was Germany's leading Communist at the time of Hitler's coup d'état. So, when the Red Army entered Germany, it brought along a substitute: the aged, wily, sure-footed Wilhelm Pieck, who took Thälmann's place in 1933 as secretary-general of the illegal German Communist Party.

Pieck was born at Guben, in a part of Brandenburg that is now under Polish administration, on January 3, 1876. After going to elementary school, he worked as a carpenter's apprentice. He became an active trade-union worker at an early age and entered the Social Democratic Party when he was seventeen. From 1906 to 1910, he lived in the Atlantic port of Bremen, where he served as a member of the city council. Bremen was at that time one of the few places where there was a Lenin type of oppo-sition to the moderate policies of the Social Democratic Party. The Polish-born Karl Radek, later one of the top Comintern officials, edited a Social Democratic paper in Bremen. Pieck was impressed by Radek's brilliance and became one of the founders of the antiwar "Spartakusbund," which left the Social Democratic Party in 1915. He served as liaison man, smuggling revolutionary literature from the Netherlands into Germany.

The Communist Party of Germany was founded on January 1, 1919 at a Berlin meeting of the Spartacists, over which Pieck presided. The commanding personalities of the meeting were Rosa Luxemburg and Karl Liebknecht. The meeting discussed the Communist policy toward the forthcoming parliamentary elections. The Social Democratic government of Friedrich Ebert, having overthrown the Kaiser's regime, wanted to rule on a basis of democratic representation. That, to the Communists, was mere "bourgeois democracy," and they wanted no truck with it. Why should they not be able to do in 1919 what Lenin had done two years earlier in Russia? Rosa Luxemburg argued in vain for longer preparation and for participation in the elections. She managed to persuade the wavering, hotheaded Liebknecht, but they were voted down by the delegates.

The people closest to the Communists in the German cabinet were the Independent Socialists. The Independents, in protest against the careful and slow policy of the Social Democrats, left the government. Ebert tried to remove the chief of the Berlin police, a left-wing Independent, from his post. The Independents and the Communists made common cause. They issued a manifesto that accused the Ebert government of "seeking to uphold its power with the bayonet, and to secure for itself the favor of the capitalist bourgeoisie whose interests it has always secretly supported." The manifesto called for "a mighty demonstration." The appeal succeeded. Several thousand people, many of them armed, demonstrated in the German capital. They moved into the building of the Social Democratic paper, the *Vorwärts;* an odd revolutionary target, to say the least. In the afternoon of January 5, and over the objections of Luxemburg, the Communists declared the overthrow of the Ebert government. The Social Democrats answered that they would no longer be "terrorized by lunatics," and struck back. The rest was tragedy.

THE MURDER OF LUXEMBURG AND LIEBKNECHT

In order to quell the uprising, the Social Democratic War Minister Gustav Noske called on the regular army and the rightist Free Corps to help dislodge the Communists from the *Vorwärts* building. They forced the revolutionaries to hoist a white flag and to leave the building with heir hands up. Several were killed, others brutally manhandled. Days afterward, Luxemburg and Liebknecht were routed out of their hiding place and murdered in cold blood by cavalry officers. All in all, one thousand people were killed during the week. And the name of Noske became synonymous with death and ruthlessness not only to the Communists but to many in his own party. Wilhelm Pieck was captured together with Luxemburg and Liebknecht. He managed to save his life by a ruse, pretending that he was willing to supply "important information." Thinking they had captured a willing stool pigeon, the officers took him along for questioning. He managed to escape.

Meanwhile, Bavaria had a Communist government. As revolutionary regimes go, it was relatively mild. Its leaders were for the most part idealistic intellectuals. The Communist premier of Bavaria, Kurt Eisner, was democratic enough to permit an election on January 12, 1919, which went overwhelmingly against him. He yielded to popular pressure. But just as he was about to resign, he was assassinated by a nationalist student. The revolutionary government collapsed. About the same time, Béla Kun set up a Soviet dictatorship in Hungary. This inspired a group of Bavarian intellectuals to press for reestablishment of a Communist regime at Munich on April 16, 1919. Among the leaders was the poet and playwright Ernst Toller, who committed suicide in New York in 1938. Behind him and his friends stood several determined Communists. After five days of a government that proclaimed the Kantian ideal of permanent peace, the trained Communists ousted Toller.

The Bavarian Soviet Republic was crushed by Noske, the army, and the Free Corps. This suppression was considerably more ruthless than the Communist government had been. But the whole specter of a Bolshevist regime had inflamed the imagination of many Bavarians. They seemed willing to do anything, follow anyone, to prevent its recurrence. There was an atmosphere of hate. It was in the soil of Bavaria, and in the city of Munich, that the seed of Nazism was planted.

Meanwhile, at Weimar, the democratic German Republic was born. A coalition of Social Democrats, progressive middle-class Democrats, and the adaptable Catholic Center Party created the Republic. Then came the rightist Kapp Putsch. Its leader was the American-born Wolfgang Kapp, whose father, a German liberal, had come to the United States in 1848. On March 13, 1920, he marched the Ehrhardt naval brigade into Berlin. The Social Democratic government discovered that the rightist generals, who were always able to scrape up enough troops to crush a Communist uprising, found themselves unable to oppose Kapp. Ebert and his cabinet left Berlin and asked the workers to "strike, stop working, strangle this military dictatorship." The Communists of Berlin at first would have nothing to do with that. But they had no control over the workers, who struck so effectively that the Putsch was strangled before it started to breathe.

In the Ruhr, the general strike played into the hands of the Communists. They refused to take orders from their own party headquarters. The local command of the German army was out to teach the Communists a lesson. The armed workers were afraid to turn their guns over to the army, fearing that they would then be at the mercy of their opponents. In the end, there was confusion. Some of the Communists turned over their arms; others didn't. Bloodshed followed. When the French occupied the Ruhr in January, 1923, and the German currency went sky-high, communism saw a chance to further its aims. The French occupation inflamed the German nationalists, and it came to serious clashes in the Ruhr. One nationalist, Albert Leo Schlageter, attempted to blow up a French-controlled railroad. He was court-martialed and shot. The Communists sought to use his death as a point of agitation among the nationalist masses. Karl Radek extolled Schlageter as a martyr, as the symbol of a German generation that was seeking its place in the sun. It is one of the diabolical ironies of recent history that a decade later the same Schlageter became one of the greatest martyr-heroes ever to be exploited by Nazi emotionalist propaganda, the same Nazis to whom the name of Radek was identical with everything they hated.

WANTED: ONE INSURRECTION

And then the Communist International decided on an insurrection in Germany. Heinrich Brandler, then head of the German party, had the thankless task of executing this order. Germany was still in ferment, but, as Franz Borkenau puts it in his book *The Communist International,* "the Comintern as a whole mistook the approach of Fascism for the approach of communism." On October 5, 1923, the Communists entered the provincial governments of Thuringia and Saxony. They hoped to gain control of the police in both states and to arm the workers. But the army was not going to let that happen, and the Social Democrats were in no mood for

ivil war. While provincial Communist headquarters were waiting for the
ignal of revolt, one courier reached the Hamburg Communists by mis-
ake. So Hamburg had its insurrection. But only a few hundred rugged
Communists shot it out with the police. They were suppressed. The government of Saxony fell. Berlin was in confusion. Using the Communist
insurrection efforts as his cue, Adolf Hitler declared one month later
in a Munich beer cellar that the "nationalist revolution" had begun. Like
he Communists, the Nazis, too, were stopped by the army. Hitler was
condemned to imprisonment, but not before he could tell the judges that
"the goddess of the eternal court of history will smile and tear to tatters
the brief of the state's attorney and the sentence of the court." In spite
of this picturesque statement, the Nazis got off much easier than had
the Communists four years earlier. S. William Halperin of the University
of Chicago comments in his book *Germany Tried Democracy* that "never
was dual standard of justice, so long prevalent in Bavaria and in other
sections of the Reich, more flagrantly on display."

The Communist defeats in Germany gave support to the Second Strategy
of the Comintern: agitation instead of armed revolt. The ill-fated Brandler
was forced out, and an energetic woman in her twenties became the leading Communist figure. We have already encountered her as Elfriede Friedländer in our chapter on Austria. In Germany, she worked under the name
of Ruth Fischer. In later years, her career was to lead to a death sentence
in absentia at Moscow and into the Washington witness chamber of the
Congressional Committee on Un-American Activities, where she denounced
her brother, Gerhart Eisler, as "the perfect terrorist type, most dangerous
for the people of both America and Germany." But in the 1920's in Germany, she was the advocate of a policy more radical than that prescribed
by Moscow. At that time, the battle of the century, the Stalin-Trotsky bout,
was shaping up in Russia. In the fall of 1924, Stalin's "socialism in one
country" principle was on the offensive against leftist radicalism within
the Comintern. Moscow ordered the members of the German central committee to choose between the Fischer group and the Comintern. Led by
Ernst Thälmann, the committee assured Moscow of its continued allegiance. Now the Thälmann group had the inside track, and the supporters
of Fischer were slowly eased out. The star of Wilhelm Pieck was rising.
Ruth Fischer wrote in the *American Mercury* that Ossip Pyatnitsky, the
Comintern treasurer, was worried about the new, "unreliable" German
leadership. "To whom shall we give the money now?" he asked. But, when

he heard that Wilhelm Pieck had been reelected to the central committee he sighed with relief. Mrs. Fischer says that "with Pieck to handle the money, he could be sure that it would always be spent as the Comintern desired."

The following years of world prosperity brought relative tranquillity to the German political scene. But Social Democrats and Communists increased their support. The May 20, 1928, elections raised the Social Democratic vote from 7,900,000 in 1924 to 9,150,000. The Communists gained half a million votes, increasing their supporters to 3,600,000. The number of their parliamentary seats was 54, as compared with 152 for the Social Democrats and 78 for the Nazis. The Nazis had, in fact, suffered a drop of four million votes. They were able to muster only 4,700,000 supporters. Wilhelm Pieck was one of the nine new Communist deputies in the Parliament. Listing his personal data for the *Reichstag Handbuch,* he described himself as "without religion; profession, carpenter." It was another step forward and upward. The anti-Communist campaign of the Nazis had gained momentum, ever since Hitler's release from the Landsberg fortress in 1924. The Nazi left wing, led by Gregor and Otto Strasser, felt a kinship with the Communists. Even Joseph Goebbels, who later became the propaganda minister of Nazi Germany, sided with Strasser's "brown bolsheviks" for a while. "We are not really enemies," Goebbels wrote to a Communist antagonist; "with our forces split, we can never reach our aim." But Hitler realized the need of support by the propertied and middle classes. He advocated support for private property by the Nazi Party. It was this avowed aim of the Nazis that gained them supporters among business and industrial leaders.

In one major respect, Communist and Nazi goals were truly identical: overthrow of the German Republic in its parliamentary democratic form. This became clear after the Third Strategy of communism was inaugurated, in 1928, implementing the view that defense of the Soviet Union as the fatherland of socialism could best be achieved through a revolutionary offensive. Both Nazis and Communists gained support from the millions of unemployed created by the depression that began in 1929. During these years, the Communists created the label "Social Fascists" for their Social Democratic opponents. Hatred of the Social Democrats carried the Communist Party into a tactical alliance with the Nazis. In the spring of 1931, the Nazis pushed a referendum designed to force the Social Democrats out of the government of Prussia. The Communists joined in this campaign.

"IT WAS A MISTAKE . . ."

Germany was disintegrating economically. The masses were increasingly attracted to the extremes of left and right. In 1932, the Communists polled six million votes, the Nazis fourteen million. Much of this was a negative, protest vote. But both parties took it for an endorsement of their policies and tactics. A parliamentary alliance between Communists and Socialists might have stabilized the government. Instead, the Socialists and the middle-class parties were unable to withstand the destructive onslaught from the extremist groups. The 1945 pamphlet of the German Communists in the American-occupied zone, quoted earlier in this chapter, contains realistic self-criticism. The pamphlet, basing its conclusions on speeches made by Pieck and others at the Seventh Comintern Congress, said, "It was a mistake to thrust our main strength against the Social Democracy, as that merely aided the Nazis, who were the new main support of the bourgeoisie. It was a mistake to rant against the left Social Democrats and to reject them. With skillful treatment, they might have become a bridge which the radicalized mass of workers could have crossed to the Communist Party. It was a mistake to split the trade unions, because it was of decisive importance not to have revolutionary unions, but mass unions, and to come close to the total of organized labor masses. It was a mistake to ask for a united front from below, because the Social Democratic masses are still too closely attached to their leadership, having not yet recognized its reactionary character as clearly as the Communists."

Here we have authoritative Communist self-criticism that supports the view that Nazism found a convenient propaganda target in middle-class hate of Bolshevism, and that the Third Strategy of communism actually facilitated the Hitler coup d'état of 1933. The Nazis cemented their power by engineering the Reichstag fire and blaming it on the Communists. Within a few hours of the fire, they passed the Law for the Defense of People and State, rounded up their opponents of all political shades, and began a terror regime that was to last for twelve years. Only a few top Communist leaders escaped the Nazi wrath. Among them was Wilhelm Pieck, who went to Moscow and joined the staff of the Comintern.

The hero of the Reichstag trial was Georgi Dimitrov, whose courageous opposition to Hermann Göring won him international fame. His performance and the ruthless murder of Communists by the Nazis heightened the standing of communism and the Soviet Union among German anti-Nazis. Moreover, the continuous denunciation of communism by the Nazi tyrants won at least a certain inverse prestige for the illegal Communist Party. Many anti-Nazi Germans could not escape the conclusion that the worst enemies of their enemies were their best friends. After the first shock of Nazism had worn off, the world in general was loth to admit that Hitler and his supporters were a menace to civilization. But the Communists throughout the world were vociferous in their denunciation of the Nazi danger, particularly after the Comintern's Seventh Congress. Communist-led Free Germany committees sprang up in various émigré centers. Among the most intelligently led was the Mexico committee, under Paul Merker. No such committee was ever successful in the United States because of the refusal of prominent non-Communist anti-Nazis to associate with a group that did not fully support genuine democratic principles.

NO SPIES FOR A FRIENDLY ALLY

Leading German Communists, among them Pieck, participated in the National Committee Free Germany, which was founded in Moscow in 1943. At the same time, a union of German officers was founded on Russian soil. Both groups discontinued their public work when civil administrations were set up on German soil. The two Moscow groups had propagandistic value, in that they urged German soldiers to surrender. They also served as an indoctrination center for captured Germans. In November, 1946, a Military Committee for the Revival of Germany was founded under the leadership of Field Marshal Friedrich von Paulus, who had commanded the German Sixth Army until his capture by the Russians at Stalingrad.

A startling new postwar function of Germans indoctrinated at these Communist-inspired bodies was revealed on August 30, 1946, in a report issued by United States Army intelligence officers at Frankfurt am Main. The American officers reported that fifteen former members of the Free Germany Committee had been arrested at Stuttgart on charges of espionage work for the Soviet Union. The report suggested that part of the one million officers and men indoctrinated in Russia had returned to the three western zones of Germany, after they were "converted to communism." The army officers stated that one Russian officer connected with the spy ring had been permitted to return to Soviet-occupied territory.

The Frankfurt report gave further details. A Soviet secret police agent, identified as Major Droshin, who was associated with the founding of the Moscow Free Germany Committee, was in charge of espionage operations in the Stuttgart area. Acting under instructions from Droshin, a former Free Germany Committee member, Walther Kazmarek, obtained a position with the United States Military Government at Stuttgart. He also posed as an informer of the United States Army's counterintelligence corps. In these capacities, he collected information on American troop movements and other secret matters in September, October, and November of 1945. Kazmarek developed a ring of spies, one of whom had been planted by American counterintelligence.

The American Army thus kept informed of Kazmarek's activities. When he was finally arrested, he confessed that he had turned American military secrets over to officials of the Soviet repatriation mission at Stuttgart. This mission was ostensibly charged with arranging the return of displaced Soviet nationals to the USSR. But at least one of its additional functions was the collection of secret information from the western zones. Espionage by former German prisoners of war, who had received Communist indoctrination, showed the many uses to which the men who formed the Free Germany Committee and the Union of German Officers might be put.

The Frankfurt report was immediately followed by an announcement from United States army legal officials at Stuttgart, saying that the American counterintelligence corps had dropped the charges against the fifteen Germans. Colonel Juan Padillo, chief of the United States legal division for Württemberg-Baden, said that he "could not have charged the Germans with espionage," since they were dealing with the Soviet Union, "one of our friendly allies."

REPENTANT NAZIS ACCEPTED

In June, 1945, Wilhelm Pieck arrived in Berlin to lead the reactivated Communist Party of Germany. The German capital, still under the impact of excesses by Russian soldiers, was cool toward Communist advances; Soviet troops had not been able to distinguish between capitalist and working-class quarters in the German capital. The early policy of the USSR of dismantling German industrial installations and shipping them to the Soviet Union created much resentment, which was coupled with concern over the fate of German prisoners of war in Russian labor camps.

Pieck was, however, aided by a change in the Soviet policy from wholesale denunciation of the German people to a conciliatory line. This was heralded by G. Alexándrov in a *Pravda* article, which sharply criticized the Soviet writer Ilya Ehrenburg for referring to Germany as "one huge gang." Alexandrov said that "the Soviet people never did identify the German population with the criminal Fascist clique who are ruling Germany." The Soviet-occupied zone of the Reich was quickly covered with huge portraits of Stalin, which carried the Soviet premier's phrase, "Hitlers come and go, but the German people and the German state remain." Wilhelm Pieck went even further than this. On January 30, 1946, he urged "penitent, nominal Nazis, who have seen the error of their way and are willing to help in reassuring a democratic, anti-fascist Germany" to join the Communist Party. Later, when he was touring the British-occupied zone, Pieck told an audience of 20,000 at Brunswick that the ranks of the Communist movement were open to all young people. He was applauded when he declared that "German youth is free of all political guilt."

After the Communist Party was replaced by the Socialist Unity Party, Pieck's cochairman, the former Social Democrat Otto Grotewohl, said, "Compared to election regulations in other zones, our regulations are so generous as to admit former Nazi members as equal citizens." This policy boomeranged early in 1947, when the Socialist Unity Party was urged by the Russian occupation authorities to reduce the number of former Nazi Party members in its ranks. It was noted at that time that about one third of the Unity Party's membership was made up of ex-Nazis.

"FREE GERMAN YOUTH"

German youths, many of whom had been attracted by the pageants and the aggressive atmosphere of Nazism, found a new political home in the Free German Youth movement initiated by the Communists. Early in 1947, this movement had more than 300,000 members in the Soviet-occupied zone. During a Berlin meeting, leaders of the movement were addressed by Colonel Sergei Tulpanov, representing the Soviet military government, who emphasized the "necessity of unity of the youth movement." Free German Youth groups were also established in the western zones of the Reich. The Department of State *Bulletin* reported that in the British and American zones "Communist leadership may not always be firmly established, nor may Communist sponsorship be apparent to outsiders or even to members of the group." The report added that demands for "unity" pressed by this movement were "strongly suspected" in all zones "as efforts by Communist elements to proselytize German youth by means of neutral labels and nationalistic slogans."

That efforts at political education were also directed toward German children of school age became clear from Communist plans in German schools in the Russian zone. A three-volume set of directives was published for public-school teachers engaged in primary history instructions. According to these directions, the Bolshevik revolution showed "for the first time in any country" a way "toward peace and democracy." The instructions also referred to "powerful democratic liberation movements in a series of countries in which reactionary forces of a monopoly capital were subdued, their power shattered, and new democratic state forms created." The United States army newspaper *Stars and Stripes* reported that Winston Churchill's 1946 speech at Fulton, Missouri, was the subject of a question-and-answer period at a Communist-controlled school in Gera. Pupil and teacher were quoted as follows:

"QUESTION: What does Churchill want?

"ANSWER: A western bloc with the aim of stabbing the East in the back.

"QUESTION: How can you characterize the speech?

"ANSWER: It sabotages the unity of the nations of the world and international peace.

"QUESTION: What is the threat that Churchill utters?"

When the child was unable to answer the question, the teacher supplied the explanation himself: "Another war. If it comes, it will be because capitalistic systems will always bring about another war when they find themselves threatened."

One of the most popular Communist decisions in eastern Germany has been the division of large estates. Wilhelm Pieck said at a party conference in Berlin, late in 1945, that "the feudal Junkers are being expropriated and the land which they took from the peasants is now being restored to them." He reported that "all feudal estates of 100 hectares, the estates of all war criminals, Nazi leaders, and active proponents of Nazism" were being confiscated, pooled, and then redistributed. No system of collective farms was instituted, which would have alienated the political allegiance of property-conscious peasants. All told, some 6,700,000 acres in Saxony, Brandenburg, Mecklenburg, and Thuringia were expropriated.

"FREE GERMAN TRADE UNION FEDERATION"

In the trade-union movement, Communists and Socialists clashed head-on. The Communists, following their world-wide slogan of "trade union unity," favored a single over-all workers' organization, the Free German Trade Union Federation. Pieck stated that "anyone who intrigues against such a union is an enemy of the German people and of Germany." To reorganize Communist trade-union activities, Paul Merker was brought to the Soviet zone from Mexico City. He had been an official of the so-called Red Trade Union Opposition during the late 1920's in Germany. When Hitler came to power, Merker tried vainly to take up residence in the United States. He went to Mexico, where he headed the Free Germany Committee. When the Socialist Unity Party was established, Merker was elected to its central committee while he was still abroad. In the summer, he left on a Russian ship that took him via Vladivostok to Moscow. After a brief stay in the Soviet capital, he came to the Russian-occupied zone of Germany.

The trade-union movement was organized by the Soviet authorities immediately after Germany's surrender. Its center, in Berlin, was responsible for some 140,000 workers and also controlled another 500,000 union members in the Russian zone. When, in the fall of 1946, elections were scheduled for a democratic replacement of the Soviet-appointed trade-union leadership, American and Russian representatives in the Allied Control Council at Berlin found themselves in violent disagreement. American officials accused the Communists of rigging the elections. General Alexander G. Kotikov, the Russian representative on the Control Council, sharply criticized the American attitude and suggested that it had been inspired by the anti-Communist American Federation of Labor. (On January 4, the AFL denounced plans to affiliate the German unions with the World Federation of Trade Unions "as harmful to the best interests of the American people, to world democracy and peace, because the WFTU is nothing else but the Kremlin's world-wide fifth column.") General Kotikov's charges were rejected by the American representative, Major General Frank A. Keating, as "without basis in fact, presumptuous and in fact quite false."

The Free German Trade Union Federation represents an avenue over which Communist influence from the Soviet zone can penetrate to the west, just as it does in the case of the Free German Youth.

BERLIN VOTES

A strong indication of political trends inside Germany was furnished by the Berlin municipal elections on October 20, 1946. The Communist-controlled Socialist Unity Party, the Social Democrats, the Christian Democrats, and the Liberal Democrats were rivals for the votes of some 1,500,000 Berliners. But the Unity Party received less than half the support piled up by the Social Democrats, and the final returns looked like this:

Social Democrats—999,200 votes (48.7 per cent)
Christian Democrats—454,200 votes (22.1 per cent)
Socialist Unity Party—406,000 votes (19.8 per cent)
Liberal Democrats—193,000 votes (9.4 per cent)

Pravda, the Moscow Communist Party organ, commented on these results by saying that "the Social Democrats, headed by socialism-hating Dr. Kurt Schumacher did not attract voters with slogans of peace, democracy, and the road to socialism." Instead, the paper said, "they fascinated the voters with the theory that blame for the hardships and ill-fortune which war-shattered Germany is now enduring belongs not to Hitler and fascism but to members of the Socialist Unity Party."

SCHUMACHER VERSUS PIECK

This comment illustrates well the extreme criticism that German and non-German Communists have expressed regarding Dr. Schumacher. This leader of the Social Democrats in Germany, who spent ten years in a Nazi concentration camp, visited Great Britain late in 1946. He clearly enjoyed the support of the British Labour government, just as Pieck could count on the backing of the Soviet government. *Pravda*, on December 9, 1946, even compared Schumacher with Gustav Noske and accused him of having "successfully divided the working class and undermined German democracy to please nationalist elements among the Germans." The article called Schumacher a British-made "Führer," whose "base methods from the Goebbels arsenal" included "the persecution of Communists."

Dr. Schumacher has indeed been very outspoken in his opposition to communism. The United States Social Democratic weekly, *The New Leader*, printed a letter from Dr. Schumacher on November 23, 1946, in which he accused the Communists of kowtowing to nationalist emotions. The letter said in part:

"The Communists, who, with the Social Democratic carpet-baggers, form the Central Committee of the Socialist Unity Party, preach a new doctrine of Germany First. To be sure, nationalists of this type prattle of a unified and centralized Reich as we used to hear it described by Goebbels—but with their eyes belligerently and exclusively turned toward the West. With regard to our eastern borders, these gentry are strangely silent. . . .

"During the years of the Weimar Republic, the Communist Party frequently changed its tactics and its leadership. Now it has altered both its program and its name. . . .

"A whole series of basic concepts divide us from the Communists. No matter how much of the thought of Karl Marx and Friedrich Engels survives in Social Democracy, the spirit of German classical philosophy, of the English and French revolutions, of the American War of Independence, are equally present in our movement. All that is human and humane is inextricably woven into the pattern of democratic socialism. The notion of unity as it is propagated by the Communists is nothing but an effort on behalf of a foreign power to subdue all Europe and to rob us all of our part in the concert of Europe."

THE COMING BATTLE FOR GERMANY

It is easy to dramatize the battle for power in tomorrow's Germany into a fight between a Soviet-backed Wilhelm Pieck and a British-backed (and cautiously American-favored) Kurt Schumacher. Pieck is an old man. Schumacher has suffered much. Neither of them may see his career crowned by leadership in an economically and politically united Germany. But rivalry between communism and socialism will color Germany's political scene for many years. The Christian Democratic Party is large and made up of many divergent elements. Its leader, Joseph Kaiser, would like to see his party achieve the prestige of the MRP in France. However, Soviet support of the Communists has created in Germany a picture very different from that in France or Italy, where a Communist, Socialist, and Catholic party is the most powerful.

More than anywhere else in the world, the future role of communism in Germany depends on the relations of the USSR, Great Britain, and the United States. The American attitude has been described as "aggressive neutrality." The Republican victory in the 1946 elections has slowed support for any one political group in Germany. Great Britain, weakened by economic bloodletting, finds her political influence lacking in dynamism. Russia, on the other hand, has been clear-cut in its support for the Communists and their Socialist Unity Party. Barring complete and utter economic collapse, Germany is not likely to go Communist of itself. But a Soviet-supported Communist propaganda machine is bound to be successful throughout Germany, particularly among young people.

In the final analysis, the problem of communism in Germany is military. The withdrawal of American and British troops prior to a consolidation of political and economic life in the western zone would create a vacuum that Communist agitation could fill easily. As long as it has the support of Soviet prestige and Soviet arms, the Socialist Unity Party will not falter in its attempt to achieve complete and irrevocable domination.

CHAPTER 15

France: Key to the West

Moscow HAS no right to permit or forbid anything to the French Communists."

These are the words of Maurice Thorez, the miner's son and former member of the Comintern's executive committee, who today is secretary-general of the Communist Party of France. If his statement is correct, a Communist-controlled cabinet would merely be a red pearl on the long string of ever-changing Paris governments. If his statement is inaccurate, a Communist regime in France might provide communism with a key to the western world: to French territories in Africa, in Asia, and in the Western Hemisphere. As French premier, Maurice Thorez could easily achieve permanent control over the metropolitan and dependent areas of the French Union.

The French Communist Party has made enormous strides. Its leadership is intelligent, alert, patient, and militant. At the height of its popularity during the interwar years, the party received a million and a half votes; after World War II, it could count five million ballots and well over one million party members. Neither nearness of Russia nor the proximity of Soviet forces that influenced political conditions in eastern Europe played a role in France.

Communism in the French Republic won victories through its own powers of persuasion. It had to fight an uphill battle. Nowhere has memory of the Nazi-Soviet Pact been more persistent than in France. Nowhere has the role of communism in late 1939, in 1940, and in early 1941 been more severely criticized than inside the French nation. True, French Communists achieved a reputation for patriotic gallantry and courage by active participation in the underground resistance forces. But the old doubts returned, once the war was over: What is the Communists' dominating allegiance, to France or to Russia? Thorez tried to answer this question when he said that Moscow had "no right" to tell French Communists how to run their affairs. And yet, Thorez was unable to erase all doubts.

It is a tribute to the intellectual capacities of the French Communists that they have overcome memories of their own past to a very high degree. After the end of World War II, they were able to apply the Seventh Strategy of world communism in a particularly convincing manner. While they were a government party, their influence tended to reduce postwar labor-management friction in France to a minimum. When Thorez addressed the Tenth Congress of the French Communist Party on June 26, 1945, he defined its three immediate principal tasks as follows: "(1) To speed reconstruction and develop production; (2) to elect a sovereign national assembly which will give to France her new Constitution; (3) to found, with our Socialist brothers, the great French Working Class Party."

The Communists gained respect in 1945 and 1946 by cooperating in French reconstruction. The party applied the same technique that was used by Communist-controlled governments in eastern Europe: it ruled out strikes. The Communists were able to do this through control of the powerful French union organization, the Confédération Générale du Travail (CGT). The executive committee of the CGT consists of six Communists, six Socialists, and one member of the Radical Socialist Party (a moderate, non-Marxist, non-Catholic party that dominated French political life during the interwar years). According to Konni Zilliacus, British Labour Party advocate of close cooperation with the Communists, "the real control of the CGT is about eighty-five per cent Communist." Zilliacus, writing in *The New Statesman and Nation* on October 12, 1946, said, "Working through the CGT, the Communists from the morrow of liberation onwards preached the doctrine of maximum production. They first held back, then co-ordinated and disciplined wage demands."

At the end of the war, French economy faced its major bottleneck in the coal industry. French Communists, by appealing to the miners for early maximum production, earned the gratitude of Frenchmen in the cities and in the country, in industry and among the peasants. This helped break down anti-Communist sentiment among French farmers, a traditionally conservative group. Jacques Duclos, second in command to Thorez and the party's leading theoretician (his criticism of Earl Browder caused the 1945 reorganization of the United States Communist Party), feels that

French peasants are increasingly attracted by communism. Interviewed by a correspondent of the New York *Daily Worker*, Duclos said on November 6, 1946, "The peasants are losing their fear that the Communists will confiscate their land." Pointing to a huge poster alleging that it is "the trusts" which actually confiscate land, he stated that "this poster has been very effective in ridding the peasants of their fear of Communists." Communist showmanship has included the rushing of coal shipments to fuel-less areas, publicity for their appeals to miners, and emphasis on the use of parliamentary methods by their representatives. Communist-imposed antistrike discipline was hardly broken. Veteran Socialist Léon Jouhaux shares the secretary-generalship of the CGT with a Communist, Benoît Frachon. But it is Frachon who carries the burden of policy making.

What is the French Communist Party's secret of success, a success that has opened the road to lasting control of the French nation? Communist influence in France shows the practical character of post-Comintern strategy. Without professing a strictly national character, French Communists could never have created the largest party in their nation. Without moderation, relative dignity of performance, and a high degree of constructive participation in the affairs of the state, the Communists would have perpetuated popular memories of 1940. Today, French communism has achieved, through patience and skill, what it attempted with impatient violence after World War I.

INDIVIDUALISTIC BEGINNING

The vibration of Russia's October Revolution shook the political atmosphere of France in 1917. It was an atmosphere still charged with memories of the great French revolutions of 1789 and 1848, of the Paris Commune of 1871. Rebellion was in the air. André Marty, founder of the French Communist Party and today his party's specialist in colonial affairs, led the mutiny of the French Black Sea fleet in April, 1919. France itself, moving from the sacrifices and fears of war to the chaos and discontent of readjustment, was crisscrossed by strikes. The Socialist Party increased its membership from 34,000 in 1918 to 150,000 in 1920. The CGT, which the Socialists then dominated, had two and one-half million members. French labor was in ferment. At the Socialist Congress in Tours in 1920, a large group split off to join the Third International.

The Communists also broke with the CGT and created a rival union federation, the Confédération Générale du Travail Unitaire or CGTU. (This federation remained separate until the Comintern's "united front" policy opened the way to Communist participation and dominance in the CGT.)

The spirit of Zinoviev hung over the French Communists. They were impatient. French individualism placed its unmistakable stamp on the Communist Party. For many years, it proved to be the most rebellious, critical, and self-critical section of the Comintern. French Communists were violently opposed to the conciliatory line adopted by the Comintern Congress of 1921. Lenin and Radek, they felt, had betrayed the idea of world revolution. French delegates were unable to win their point at the Moscow Congress. And, when the French party held its own national Congress in October, a great number of delegates refused to ratify the Comintern decisions. It was the first open break within the French party. The party was further weakened when it opposed French occupation of the Ruhr. It spread the slogan, "The German workers are our brothers. Fraternize with them," among French occupation troops. Thirty-seven Communist leaders were charged with incitement to sedition and sentenced to imprisonment.

But that was not all. In 1923, three years after the Tours Congress, the honeymoon of French communism was coming to an end. Illusions were withering like daffodils in May. French individualism resented the dominating Russian influence on the party's policies. Frossard, then secretary of the Communist Party, broke with Moscow and rejoined the Socialists. An influential group of leaders followed him. The party, which had counted 150,000 members immediately after the Tours Congress, was reduced one-third in strength.

In 1925, after two years of crisis, the Communists unleashed a nationwide agitation campaign against French suppression of native uprisings in Morocco. They blamed the powerful financial institutions, particularly the nearly omnipotent Banque de France and the Banque des Pays Bas, for "imperialist intervention" in North Africa. Demonstrations were held in Lille, Lyons, Marseilles, Beziers, Strasbourg, and Bordeaux. On October 12, the party called a general strike. This was the first political strike in the French Communist Party's history. It was a show of strength, announced as a protest demonstration not only in opposition to the Moroccan expedition, but also to French action against unrest in Syria, the government's tax policy, and wage limitations. The party claimed that 900,000 workers went on strike. Several instances of violence occurred when police clashed with demonstrators in the Paris area.

The Stalin-Trotsky rivalry had repercussions in France much earlier than in most other countries. In June, 1926, the party's Congress at Lille faced strong and outspoken opposition, headed by the Russian-born Boris Souvarine. He was later forced to leave the movement. Several Communist parties were able to survive the break between Trotsky and Stalin fairly well. Not so the French. Several of the most able and most persuasive men broke with the Comintern. Some threw in their lot with Trotsky; others became politically homeless. The Comintern's Third Strategy, revolutionary extremism as protection for Russia, made the task of the French central committee exceedingly difficult. The party lost influence rapidly. The number of Communist deputies at the 1928 elections was only 14, as compared with 24 four years earlier. (It must be added in fairness that the electoral law acted as a temporary brake on Communist representation.)

"WE DON'T WANT DUMMIES. . . ."

The 1928 to 1936 period was the most trying in the development of the French Communist Party. Communist parties show a rather high percentage of membership turnover. In France, this trend was particularly marked. Official Comintern statistics show that membership in the French party from 1925 to 1928 was cut to less than half: from 83,000 to 46,000. The depression did not bolster membership. On the contrary, only 35,000 were registered as members in 1931, and the *Communist International* quoted Ossip Pyatnitsky as stating that "the French party continues to register new members, while total membership figures are steadily going down."

Comintern impatience with lack of success among individual parties reached a climax during the depression. The extremist Third Strategy resulted in erratic and foolhardy actions on the part of many national leaders. The Comintern struck at some of the most active executors of its own policies. Communist leaders in France, China, Poland, Estonia, and elsewhere suddenly found themselves accused of collusion with the police, of provoking actions that led to suppression of party activities. During this period, the colorful phrase "conspiratorial wreckers" was born. In France, the group around Barbé and Célor experienced the wrath of the Comintern. Célor was labeled "agent of the bourgeoisie," a "master of hypocrisy." In the light of consistent enforcement of Communist discipline then and later (which recently in the United States led to the ouster of Browder), it is worth recalling what Maurice Thorez said about "the Barbé-Célor group, which had managed to secure all the key positions" in the party: "They interpreted the democratic centralism laid down by Lenin in terms of arbitrary decisions from above, passive obedience from all ranks, stifling of all free discussion, suspicion, timid acquiescence or else silence, sealed lips, no fruitful criticism and, in short, a barrack-like atmosphere. The Party sank to a caricature of itself, reduced to impotence and condemned to vegetate hopelessly instead of being, as it should be, the conscious spearhead of the working class."

In October, 1931, Thorez wrote an article in the party daily *L'Humanité*, which he is still very fond of citing. It was entitled, "We Don't Want Dummies in the Party!" (He reinterpreted this slogan in 1945, saying, "The internal discipline of Communists is not a blind discipline; it is a discipline freely granted, the understanding discipline of each one of us. Once discussion is exhausted, the decision is obligatory for all, for the possible minority as well as the majority.") Thus, under the banner of democratic criticism, the campaign against Barbé and Célor removed yet another group of leaders from the party.

THE RISE OF MAURICE THOREZ

The downfall of Barbé and Célor resulted in the rise of Maurice Thorez, who today is the most important Communist leader outside the Soviet sphere of influence. The Communist movement outside the Soviet Union has shown itself relatively independent of personalities. In France, the frequent replacement of top leaders is hardly remembered at all. Still, Thorez, who became his party's secretary-general in 1932, today symbolizes French communism more than any other man. His personality is decisive in determining popular opinion of Communist qualifications and patriotism.

Thorez is one of the youngest leaders of the world Communist movement today. He was born at the turn of the century, on July 20, 1900, in the Pas-de-Calais region near the English Channel. His father and grandfather were miners. Young Maurice's earliest memories are of a mine disaster. He describes this graphically in his autobiography, *Son of the People:*

"One day, like any other, I was playing with the other village kids when suddenly our attention was attracted by a low rumbling, a distant trampling of feet, and the noise of clogs on the cobbled street. Everyone was hurrying in the same direction and I joined with them. It was fun galloping along, overtaking the old people who were out of breath, and the women with their babies in their arms. People were shouting: 'It's at Courrières! The Méricourt pit! Thirteen hundred have been killed.'" He was six years old then.

Misery, conflict over wages, talk about rising prices were part of Thorez's early home atmosphere. But all was not gray, or self-consciously proletarian. There was also a small garden for little Maurice and a dozen rabbits, all his own. There were village fairs with merry-go-rounds, and the sound of the Lucky Wheel as it went click-clicking round and round.

Thorez helped farmers weed their fields, sang in the village choir (although, he says, his parents "scarcely believed in God"); and, when he was twelve years old, he started to work as a sorter in the mine. Two years later came the war. The mines closed. Thorez and his grandfather left their native village, joining the refugees who streamed away from the battle lines. Maurice entered school again at the village of Clugnat and helped on a farm in the neighboring hamlet of Forges.

Maurice lived in an attic on the Forges farm. He borrowed copies of *L'Humanité* from his boss. And from his teacher he obtained Jules Verne's *Twenty Thousand Leagues under the Sea*, Alexandre Dumas's *Count of Monte Cristo*, and other books. In 1917, his grandfather took him to Paris, then to Dreuil-des-Amiens. They found work on a barge that transported timber. They ate and slept on board. A year later, during the Somme offensive, Thorez was called up to dig trenches for a month. Then came six months of apprenticeship at a vermin-infested baker's shop.

When the armistice was signed, Maurice Thorez returned to the village of his parents. The ruddy-cheeked boy of nineteen found work building a railroad line and later returned to his old job in the mine. The Socialist Party of his village voted for affiliation with the Third International. Thorez joined. He had become a Communist. A year later, he was called up for service in the Seventy-second Infantry Regiment. Home on leave, and still wearing his uniform, he hailed the cause of the Communist International before a Socialist audience. People recognized him: "It's that kid Thorez . . ."

When he returned from military service, he did not get his job back at the mine. He became a bricklayer, then a house painter, was active in the Young Communist League and did Communist union work. He helped in organizing several strikes in the Pas-de-Calais area. Opposition to the Third Comintern Congress decision on agitation was strong in the district. Thorez tried hard to defend Moscow's view, but the Pas-de-Calais delegates voted 146 to 40 against the Comintern's policy. In 1923, Thorez quit his work as a house painter and became a paid Communist Party functionary —as he says, "a professional revolutionary." A year later, he joined the party's central committee and was made regional secretary for the Pas-de-Calais, Le Nord, and Somme departments.

In 1925, Thorez made his first trip to Russia. On his return, he went to Paris, and big-time party work. At the 1926 Congress in Lille, he opposed the Socialist endorsement of war-debt payments, saying, "It is the Communists who strive to prevent the produce of many generations of workers from being turned over to Anglo-American bankers." Shortly afterward, he had to defend himself before the Court of Appeals on charges of "incitement of the armed forces to disobedience." Twice he was sentenced to six months' imprisonment and a fine, but he avoided arrest. For two years, he eluded the police, changing his address, living with other Communists, but continuing to attend party meetings.

In June, 1929, the police finally caught up with Thorez. He received two prison sentences and remained imprisoned for more than two years. He did a lot of reading in the Saint Charles Prison. Thorez decided to improve his knowledge of German. His literary diet contained not only goodly portions of Marx and Engels, but also the poetry of Goethe and Heine, novels by Romain Rolland and Anatole France. These prison years widened Thorez's intellectual outlook and influenced his style and oratorical vernacular. Maurice Thorez, who never lost his sense of humor (humorlessness is almost the professional disease of Communist leaders), even found time to enjoy the mischievous pranks of Till Eulenspiegel, the legendary Flanders jester. When his prison sentence ended, a fine had to be paid to assure his freedom. Thorez states that the French Communist Party under Barbé and Célor refused to pay this fine. So he appealed directly to the Comintern. Moscow paid, Barbé-Célor et al. were kicked out of the party, and Maurice Thorez was moved from his prison cell into the secretary-generalship.

Thorez inherited a weak party. The rise of Hitlerism found the French Communists a noisy, politically ineffectual minority. Ernst Thälmann, head of the German Communists, had spoken at the Paris Salle Bullier in October, 1932. Thorez returned this visit, speaking at the graves of Karl Liebknecht and Rosa Luxemburg at Berlin's Friedrichsfelde cemetery on January 12, 1933. Two weeks later, Hitler came to power. Thälmann was arrested, never to be released. Events in Germany came as a terrifying shock to French Communists. Many of their German comrades had fled to Paris. They brought firsthand accounts of Nazi cruelty. The weak French party feared that Hitlerism, or its French counterparts, might reach out to destroy it, too. But, while the French Socialists tried to stem the rising tide of extreme rightism through cooperation with other parties, the Communists were not ready. The Comintern's Third Strategy was still in force. The Socialist Party was still regarded as a "tool of the bourgeoisie," to be fought tooth and nail. The Communists were not ready until the 1935 Comintern Congress announced the "united front" strategy of world communism.

By then the Socialists and Radical Socialists had grown suspicious. They were put off by the sudden Communist change of heart. It took nearly a year before the new policy was put into effect. But then it became more successful in France than anywhere else in the world.

FRANCE IN FERMENT

While the French Communist Party passed through its first decade and a half of organized existence, the French Republic was beset by anxieties at home and abroad. After World War I, the spirit of victory beclouded the economic realities of France. The National Bloc coalition, which dominated French politics from 1919 to 1924, was born during the immediate post-armistice period, strengthened by fear of a Communist revolution following the Russian example. The National Bloc hoped to use German reparations to rebuild French economy. When German payments did not materialize, the franc went into a tailspin. The government neither imposed sufficient taxation nor checked the printing of currency. In 1914, the franc had been worth 19.30 cents; in 1926, it was worth only about 2 cents. During the late 1920's, and particularly during the two-year administration under Premier Raymond Poincaré, France recovered financially. It entered the 1930's facing a double threat: world-wide depression, and the resurrection of a German nationalism that threw a gigantic shadow over French security. Italian fascism and German Nazism found their counterparts in the ultra-rightist L'Action Française and in the Croix de Feu, headed by Colonel Casimir de la Rocque.

The 1934 Stavisky scandal, with lurid revelations of corruption in high places, was munitions for the guns of the ultra-right. Popular revulsion against parliamentary and administrative corruption came to a climax on February 6, when a vast crowd attempted to storm the Chamber of Deputies building. The Communists later took credit for having halted, somehow or other, this wave of antiparliamentary reaction. But police spokesmen insisted that it was a mixed crowd of leftist and rightist radicals who tried to storm the Parliament building. The whole event provides a fascinating study of mass action, spurred by extremist sentiment of different political complexions, which merge in a wild destructive effort. Perhaps neither the leadership of L'Action Française nor that of the Communist Party had planned the demonstration. But it developed into a serious attack. Two days later, a joint Socialist-Communist-Radical Socialist demonstration took place in one part of Paris while the Croix de Feu marched through the streets in another part of the capital city. On February 9, fighting broke out between police and Communist demonstrators. Six Communists were killed. As Thorez described it, "while the fascist hooligans broke into cafés and set fires to busses, the workers steadfastly carried out their duty as the defenders of liberty." Three days later, a general strike was declared.

The Communist Party pushed the new "united front" policy of the Comintern with all its might. The first step was consolidation of the CGT and the CGTU. During its January, 1936, Congress at Villeurbanne, the Communist Party formulated its new policy more clearly. In the domestic field, it emphasized an issue that had sufficient validity to receive the backing of Socialists and Radical Socialists. Its program revived the phrase used originally by the Radical Socialist leader Edouard Daladier that "two hundred families" dominated the political-economic life of France. For the next few years, control of the Banque de France by a limited group of old French families was the target of the leftist political parties. By naming the twelve regents of the Banque de France, which could give or withhold credits to the government, the parties stated, these "two hundred families" exercised control detrimental to the French nation. By emphasizing issues such as these and pointing to the danger of fascism at home and abroad, the Communist Party was able to raise its membership to 100,000. On the eve of the 1936 elections, Thorez spoke over Radio Paris. It was the first time that the Communists had been given such important broadcasting facilities. He said, "The fate of our people will not be decided in Rome or Berlin, nor in any foreign capital, not even in Moscow, for which we openly express our deep regard, but in Paris itself." The April 26 elections almost doubled the popular vote for the Communists: from 790,000 in 1932, to 1,500,000. Together, the Communist-Socialist-Radical Socialist coalition controlled the majority through 375 Assembly seats, 73 of which were Communists. The Popular Front had won.

But the Communists declined to participate in the government. They preferred to leave executive action to the Socialists and Radical Socialists. This gave them a parliamentary veto over the cabinet, without their being directly responsible for possible failures. Thorez and Duclos told the press on May 6 that the "presence of Communists in the government might be exploited by the enemies of the people and used as a pretext for scare campaigns, which would mean a weakening of the Popular Front."

The first thing that happened to the Popular Front government under the premiership of Socialist leader Léon Blum was a wave of strikes. The sit-down strike technique was born on May 26, when eight hundred workers occupied the Usines aircraft works at Issy-les-Moulineaux. These strikes had a genuine enough basis in the wage and working conditions of French workers generally. The Communists who inspired them were backing a cause that was extremely popular among industrial workers. Nevertheless, the sudden wave of labor unrest weakened the prestige of the Blum regime. Blum tried hard to act as a conciliator between labor and management, without crushing the strike movement. Blum's opponents asserted that he was merely the spearhead of a Communist dictatorship, just as the Russian government of Alexander Kerensky had preceded Lenin's Bolshevik regime. On May 30, Blum suggested to the Socialist Congress that fascism was much more likely to follow a downfall of his cabinet, when he said, "I am spoken of as a Kerensky who is preparing the way for a Lenin. I can assure you that this is not going to be a Kerensky government, and it is equally certain that, if we fail, we shall not be succeeded by a Lenin."

When the strike wave continued to threaten the stability of the Popular Front government, the Communists took their foot off the gas pedal. On June 10, Thorez said that "it is important to know when to stop a strike,

for otherwise you are playing directly into the hands of the reactionaries."
The strikes subsided. And four days later, the Communists held a beauti-
fully stage-managed "Fête de la Victoire" celebration at Montrouge. The
flag of the hoped-for Soviet France stood out against the summer sky:
hammer and sickle against a red background, with the tricolor semi-
conspicuous at one side of the design. And the youthful, excited demonstrators cried, *"Les Soviets partout!"*—"We want Soviets!"

"DES AVIONS POUR L'ESPAGNE!"

One month later, civil war broke out in Spain. The issue of intervention brought the first open break between Blum and the Communists. The
slogan *"Les Soviets partout!"* gave way to the cry, *"Des avions pour
l'Espagne!"*—"Planes for Spain!" But France was afraid of war, afraid
of a European-wide conflagration. And Blum knew it. Two meetings
illustrated the cleavage between the heart and mind of France, between
the heart and mind of the scholarly, soft-spoken French premier. On
September 3, 30,000 Parisians listened to Dolores Ibarruri at the Vélo-
drome d'Hiver. Known to them as "La Passionaria," the handsome and
dignified Spanish Communist leader aroused the masses. She spoke in
Spanish, but the emotional appeal for help against the Nazi-backed forces
of General Francisco Franco was not lost. Three days later, Blum addressed the Socialists at the Luna Park. His speech cut through the sphere
of genuine compassion to the hard reality that was the possibility of war,
and the immediate fear of war. The Socialists applauded, sick at heart.
But the rift between the Communists and Blum had widened.

Months of outward tranquillity and underlying apprehension followed.
On March 16, 1937, Blum was attending a concert under the direction of
Sir Thomas Beecham when he was hurriedly called to the suburb of
Clichy. Communists had attacked a Croix de Feu meeting. The meeting,
in which Croix de Feu adherents took part with their families, had taken
place in a motion-picture house. It had received proper police permission.
The Communists considered it provocation. During a subsequent clash
between police and Communists at the Place de la Mairie, six people
were killed and several hundred injured. Thorez denounced the police
and spoke of "governments of the Left, which pursue a policy of the
Right." A few months later, Blum dissolved the Croix de Feu.

In June, the stock market took a nose dive. Strikes halted the Paris

International Exhibition. The public debt, inherited by the Popular Front from previous administrations, endangered the artificially high international standard of the franc. On June 15, Blum asked the Assembly to grant him emergency powers "for the recovery of public finance, as well as for the protection of savings, money, and the public credit." He received the last-minute endorsement of the Communists, but a group of Radical Socialists voted against him in the Chamber. He was defeated in the Senate, and his government resigned on June 21, after nearly thirteen months in office.

Blum was succeeded by Camille Chautemps, a conservative member of the Radical Socialist party. The right was again in the ascendence, and with it fear of an ultra-nationalist coup d'état. Colonel de la Rocque had reorganized his followers in the French Social Party. A new extreme rightist force, the hooded Cagoulards, entered the political scene. Early in 1937, the Communists had been able to list 305,000 members. Now, their sand was running out again. A pre-New Year's Eve wildcat strike of the Paris busses and subways annoyed the capital's public no end. It was quickly settled, and denounced by the Communists.

The Socialist Vincent Auriol, who became president of France in 1947, was replaced as finance minister by the conservative Georges Bonnet. Bonnet, whose later actions as foreign minister brought him the label of an appeaser of Nazi Germany, decreed that the franc was to "seek its own level." But he put a ceiling on prices. His measures to balance the budget were violently denounced by the left, but hailed in business circles. There was mounting anti-Communist sentiment within the Radical Socialist Party. Blum tried to counter it on March 12, 1938, shortly after the German invasion of Austria, when he said:

"In case of war, you will mobilize Communists just as much as anybody else. After all, the Communists represent 1,500,000 workers, peasants and small tradesmen. You have no right to throw them out. You will need them when you want to speed up armament production. You will need their help as you will need the help of the CGT. What are you afraid of? Are you afraid that they will be a liability in our foreign relations? But remember that, when I was head of the government, I preserved my complete independence on the question of Spain. Some of you have said that inclusion of the Communists will have a bad effect abroad. That is an undignified and abominable argument; France cannot bow to the veto of a foreign power." But the Blum government of 1938 lasted only three weeks. Numerous strikes disrupted aircraft production. War was in the air. Nazi demands on Czechoslovakia grew more and more threatening.

"REPULSIVE REPTILE . . . CHAINED DOG"

The governments of Edouard Daladier and Paul Reynaud, which followed Blum, were at serious odds with the Communists. On November 24, 1938, Daladier suppressed the sit-down strike at the Renault works. He sent Gardes Mobiles to force the plant's 33,000 workers to return to their tools. He succeeded, and achieved the prestige of a strong executive.

When the Nazi-Soviet Pact resulted in the invasion of Poland, the French Communist Party reflected the Comintern's policy of denouncing the British and French declarations of war on Nazi Germany as "imperialist." On November 21, 1938, Thorez had told his party's central committee that "the dictators of Rome and Berlin" sought to "isolate France in order to destroy it." Now, a year later, France was isolated, except for British aid that led to the miracle in defeat at Dunkirk. The thirty-nine-year-old Thorez was drafted into the French army. He received a twenty-four-hour pass, and disappeared. The official Communist version of this incident is that he received party orders to save himself from arrest. The Daladier government had banned the French Communist Party and was rounding up its leaders. In November, 1939, Thorez was court-martialed in absentia. He was found guilty of desertion, sentenced to six years in prison, and deprived of his French citizenship.

The French Communist Party opposed the war against Nazi Germany not merely passively, but actively. It attempted to swing at least part of the Socialist Party behind this effort. But it failed, largely because of Blum's backing of the nation's war action. Among the documents that haunt French communism to this day is Thorez's extraordinary denunciation of Léon Blum, which appeared in the February, 1940, issue of the *Communist International*:

"For a political canaille of Blum's complexion, there is no uniform standard by which to measure what he said and did yesterday and he says and does today. Blum, like the repulsive reptile that he is, has given up twisting and hissing like a snake. Now he gives free rein to his savage instincts of a bourgeois exploiter who for a moment trembled for his privileges. He no longer tries to conceal the real content of his policy: protection of the interests of capital. Like a chained dog, he barks at the working class, the Soviet Union, and communism." Thorez continued by describing the head of the French Socialist Party as inhuman, savage, and a cowardly bloodhound filled with hatred of the Soviet Union.

France fell to the invading Nazi forces. The Communist Party denounced this event as an invasion by "foreign imperialism." Its manifesto never once mentioned the name of Hitler. Blum wrote later, during his imprisonment, that "Stalin had betrayed peace, and the Communist Party, remaining obstinately loyal to him, was betraying France." He also noted that "something of a disgust aroused by this treachery" was felt, "with varying degrees of confusion, toward the Socialist Party too, which everyone thought of as closely related to the Communist Party, as its sponsor and guarantor, first in the Popular Front and then in the parliamentary majority of 1936."

The fall of France brought chaos and despair. The Communists had gone underground. They did not join the scattered nuclei of resistance groups, which retained some of the organizational cohesion of the CGT. There were dissident Communists who joined the resistance late in 1940 and early in 1941. But disciplined Communist participation did not occur before the German attack on the Soviet Union. Then, however, Communist activity became very useful to the Allied cause. From 1941 to 1944, communism in France not only was able to build up an effective resistance force, but also gained adherents for postwar political activity. In many areas, where there existed no non-Communist resistance groups, the Communists attracted all militant anti-Nazi Frenchmen.

At the time of the successful Soviet defense of Stalingrad, Allied intelligence officers reported that the Communists had become the most important single resistance force on French territory. The landing of American forces in North Africa and the fall of the Fascist regime in Italy spurred French resistance still further. The relative strength of non-Communists in the resistance was growing. In May, 1943, the National Council of the Resistance met clandestinely in Paris. Communists and pro-Communists received the vice-presidency of the council and three out of fourteen seats in its leading committee. This distribution recognized the fact that the Communists then formed about a quarter of French resistance forces.

It has not been sufficiently appreciated that the problem of disarming resistance forces in France carried with it the danger of civil war. General Charles de Gaulle, head of the French Committee of National Liberation and later of the provisional government of the French republic, recognized the strength of the underground forces. He was also aware of their unwillingness to give up arms. France avoided the harrowing experience of Greece. But that does not mean that the resistance groups were really and effectively disarmed. Token disarmament took place. The Communists were not alone in their reluctance to give up arms. Distrust among the various groups suggested to each that it retain as many guns and as much material as possible. (An understandable human trait of keeping war souvenirs doubtless played a part; guns were kept, even if only to tell a coming generation, "This is the gun with which grandpa fought Hitler.")

The resistance movement created the influential new postwar party, the Mouvement Républicain Populaire (MRP), a left of center grouping under Catholic leadership. Headed by Georges Bidault, an underground leader, the party provided De Gaulle's main support. France was lucky. By agreeing on De Gaulle as a common denominator for all anti-Nazi Frenchmen, the rival underground groups merged in May, 1943, into the French Forces of the Interior (FFI), part of the regular French forces.

Meanwhile, Maurice Thorez was ready in Moscow to return to France. Had he stayed on French soil, as the Communists asserted, until 1943? Had he really helped to organize underground resistance? How did he get to Russia? We only know that he arrived in the Soviet Union sometime during the war. He was accompanied by Jeanette Vermeersch, who bore him two sons and whom he married in 1946.

De Gaulle was not enthusiastic about the prospect of Thorez's return. But the Communists put him on their party's ballot. The general amnesty wiped out the prison sentence and the loss of French citizenship. Thorez again stepped on French soil at Paris' Le Bourget airport. At the time of his arrival, De Gaulle had won wide support for his policies. There was much argument about the treatment of prominent collaborationists. But the trial and imprisonment of General Henri-Philippe Pétain and the trial and execution of Pierre Laval corresponded to public views of justice.

DE GAULLE AND THOREZ

The clash between De Gaulle and the Communists did not come until after the national elections of October 21, 1945. The Communists secured

152 seats in the Assembly, the Socialists 142, the young MRP 141. The Communists had become the strongest party in France. As elsewhere in Europe, they desired the interior ministry, or at least the portfolios of war or foreign affairs. De Gaulle refused. The Communists asserted that their negotiations had broken down because of De Gaulle's insulting attitude. De Gaulle was said to have stated that he could not offer key cabinet posts to a party that he considered as being influenced by a foreign government. This, Maurice Thorez wrote in a letter to De Gaulle, was an insult to the 75,000 Communists who died during the German occupation of France. De Gaulle threatened to resign. The Assembly did not accept his resignation, and he was able to form a government two days later. The cabinet was a shrewd compromise. The Communists received the war ministry, but De Gaulle himself retained the ministry of defense, a major policy-making post. The Communists were given large responsibilities when they obtained the ministries of national economy, industrial production, and labor.

But the break between De Gaulle and the Communists had only been delayed. De Gaulle resigned on January 21, 1946, after pressure from the left to reduce military expenditure. His real reasons were a matter of speculation, but doubtless related to his fear of a French constitution that might open the way for government by a Communist-dominated assembly. Through their control of cabinet portfolios connected with the national economy, the Communists were able to aid in reconstruction and increased production, which Thorez had described as their first aim. Their second self-proclaimed task of preparing a new constitution was put to its first test on May 5, 1946. Among the most important features of this first draft, which they had prepared together with the Socialists, was substitution of a single-chamber assembly for the bicameral system of the Third Republic.

This draft also specified that the unicameral assembly would elect the president of the French Republic, the premier, and the chief magistrates. The assembly would also share legislative initiative with the premier. The opponents of the draft, following General De Gaulle's leadership, believed that it tended to turn the executive branch of the government into a rubber stamp of the assembly. The MRP also opposed the first draft of the constitution. Its spokesmen maintained that the government would be jeopardized by putting the fate of the nation at the mercy of parliamentary maneuvers. The draft, it was said, eliminated proper checks and bal-

ances. When the constitution was put before the public, it was strongly
supported by the Communists. The Socialists were less enthusiastic. They
would have preferred a more moderate version, which would not have
alienated MRP support. As it was, MRP considered the constitution an
opening for rule by a possibly accidental and temporary majority. In
other words, fear of a Communist parliamentary coup d'état formed the
basis of opposition. The constitution was rejected by a margin of one
million votes.

This defeat of the Communists was quickly followed by the June 2
elections, which brought the MRP into a leading position. The Socialists
lost substantially, and the Radical Socialists increased their support
slightly. The Communists elected 149 delegates, MRP 162, the Socialists
122, and the Radical Socialists 40. Georges Bidault replaced the Socialist
Félix Gouin as premier of a three-party coalition regime, and work on a
revised draft of the constitution was begun.

The new draft constitution satisfied MRP. It did not satisfy De Gaulle.
He asserted in one of his rare speeches, on October 9, 1946, that the
planned constitution would lead "first to impotence, then anarchy, and
finally dictatorship." This statement threw the MRP into confusion, but
De Gaulle refused to revise his stand. When the voters accepted the constitution on October 13, De Gaulle renounced his candidacy for the
presidency of the republic. He told France-Press, the French news agency,
that he was unwilling "to preside, powerless, over the powerlessness of
the State." He was promptly accused by the Communists of favoring dictatorial methods. Florimond Bonté said that De Gaulle had "gradually
become the standard-bearer of the reactionary elements and the leader
around whom the adversaries of all democratic progress have assembled."

But there had been real changes in the constitution, as adopted by
referendum. MRP had achieved a change in Article VI, which provided
that the premier is chosen by the president and approved by the assembly
through a vote of confidence. Ministers were made responsible to both
the assembly and the council of the republic; the two houses of the
French Parliament were restored to the constitution, replacing the unicameral setup favored by the Communists in the first draft.

Adoption of the constitution was followed by the national elections of
November 10, which were expected to dictate the appearance of the French
political scene until 1951. The Communists again became the country's

largest political party, winning 173 seats. MRP followed with 161, the Socialists with only 95, and the Radical Socialists (Leftist Rally) with 61. The line-up was similar to January, 1946, just after De Gaulle had resigned. MRP-Communist rivalry was out in the open. The assembly could not agree on either Bidault or Thorez as premier. Blum was finally asked to form a coalition government. But the Communists repeated their demands for either the interior, defense, or foreign ministries. MRP refused to enter a cabinet in which Communists would fill such key posts. Blum was finally forced to form an all-Socialist cabinet, which could serve as a stopgap.

Blum was replaced by a government under Socialist Premier Paul Ramadier, whose first cabinet included Thorez as vice premier and three other Communists. Throughout the spring of 1947, Ramadier was plagued by the Communist technique of voting with the government in cabinet councils, while opposing its measures in the Assembly and by agitation. Ramadier and the Communists clashed openly early in May. The premier decided that the Communists should no longer be able to eat their cake and have it, too: they should not retain the defense ministry while opposing military operations in Indo-China and on the rebellion-ridden island of Madagascar; and they should not control the labor ministry while simultaneously fighting the government's anti-inflationary wage-control policy.

On May 3, the Assembly expressed its confidence in Ramadier by a vote of 360 to 186. The next day Ramadier ousted the Communists from his government. The Communists had been isolated by use of the new French constitution which they themselves had pushed so vigorously; as long as Ramadier had the Assembly's confidence and opposed Communist government participation, the men around Thorez had no legal chance for a comeback. No sooner had the Communists been removed from the cabinet, when they reversed their earlier moderate anti-strike policy. Through their control of Confederation of Labor, the Communists opened the flood gates of labor dissatisfaction. A wave of strikes endangered the Ramadier cabinet. Labor unrest had become a Communist weapon, used to press for their return into the government.

SOCIALISTS RESIST FUSION

Although they were successful in aiding reconstruction and achieving acceptance of the constitution, the Communists found it difficult to reach he third aim listed by Thorez: fusion of the Communist and Socialist parties. When Léon Blum returned to France from German imprisonment, he had not forgotten the events of 1939 and 1940. Lacking the dynamism of an emotional orator, he had only the weapon of intellectual persuasion to express his views of the question of fusion. The war years had moved the French nation to the left. Relatively, the Catholic left represented by MRP was a rightist group. The Socialists, caught between the militant anti-Communism of the MRP and the militant anti-MRP attitude of the Communists, had become a center force. (Even in the Paris Assembly building itself, the Socialists had actually as well as figuratively taken over the center benches.) The postwar period had brought to France the world-wide trend against centrist parties and political moderation. Each succeeding election showed that Socialist strength was waning.

Still, the Communists remained unable to convince the Socialists that fusion would be desirable. This was a difficult and crucial decision for the Socialists. When, in August, 1946, the Socialist Party Congress met in Paris, the old leadership was strongly attacked by the left wing of its own party. Daniel Mayer resigned as party secretary in favor of Guy Mollet, head of the left-wing opposition. But even Mollet did not advocate fusion. He told the Congress that "as long as the French Communists are directed by Moscow, we cannot join them, but must work separately." The Socialist Congress finally resolved that "as long as the different Communist parties are not liberated from political and intellectual domination by the Russian state, there can be no true workers' democracy." The Communist Party remained as undaunted as a persistent suitor.

OPPOSITION TO MOSCOW

The French Communists have ostensibly opposed Russian views on the Ruhr question. Ever since separation of the Rhineland from Germany and internationalization of the Ruhr became major points of French foreign policy, the Communists had expressed an out-and-out nationalist view on these matters. They were decidedly more nationalist than the Socialists. When, during the Paris meeting of the Council of Foreign Ministers, in July, 1946, Soviet Foreign Minister Molotov came out against detachment of the Ruhr from Germany (whereby he greatly strengthened the position of the German Communist Party), it seemed impossible for the French Communists to change their line without enormous loss in prestige. They were able to continue their nationalist policy within the Seventh Strategy of world communism. *L'Humanité* could state with candor, "It is correct that French policy on the Ruhr diverges from the attitude of Soviet Russia. Nobody wants to deny this divergence. Our security is our own business. Frenchmen must express the needs of France. French Communists proclaim once more the salutary truth: there must be an international régime for the Ruhr."

Nevertheless, the belief that French communism is closely tied to Moscow did not die. It was newly documented by Edouard Daladier in the Assembly. Following the June, 1946, elections, the Communists attempted to bar Daladier and Paul Reynaud from taking their Assembly seats. They charged that the two former premiers were "politically and morally unfit" to represent the people of France, because of their role during the early war period. The Assembly voted the Communist objection down, and Daladier used the occasion to recall the Communists' own record. He angered them by talking of their party consistently as if it were Russian. He spoke of the Soviet ambassador to Paris in 1939 as "your Ambassador Suritz," of "your Russo-German alliance which was cemented with French blood," and of "your great country which was already engaged in secret negotiations with Germany."

Can the Communist Party secure lasting control of France—in spite of the many factors that combine against them? Yes, they can. They have achieved the largest parliamentary representation of any single party. They have developed a tight and highly maneuverable political machinery. And, above all, their control over the CGT puts them into a position to use their most decisive political economic weapon: the general strike. Anti-Communist sentiment among other parties was not clearly outlined until the 1946 election campaigns. Anticommunism was responsible for the renewed popularity of General De Gaulle, whose newly formed French People's Rally swept the November, 1947, municipal election, reducing MRP to minor-party status.

Behind it all was fear. The Communists had become powerful. Through control of the CGT, they could halt the production and flow of goods. Through control of the miners, they could close down the mines. Communist influence on the peasantry might influence the flow of food to urban centers. A coordinated coup d'état, much more extensive than

Lenin's seizure of Petrograd in 1917, had become a possibility. Only Communist moderation, and reluctance to face a possibly successful counterrevolution, might prevent such a course.

The Communist Party of France is fighting tenaciously and shrewdly for lasting power and control.

CHAPTER 16

Switzerland: Murder and Illegality

THE DEAD MAN whom the police found on a road outside Lausanne on September 4, 1937, carried a Czechoslovak passport. His papers identified him as one Hans Eberhardt. He had been severely beaten and then shot to death.

His name was not Eberhardt but Ignaz Reiss. His wife who, with her child, lived in a near-by village, identified Reiss as a member of the Communist Party of the Soviet Union and a high official of Moscow's secret service who had been decorated with the Order of the Red Flag. The Swiss police unearthed more details. Reiss had, during a period of two years, used between seven and eight different names. He traveled on forged passports. After executing a series of tasks for the Russian Communist Party and the Comintern, he had decided in Paris to leave the Soviet secret service. But you can't quit that kind of job. Reiss wrote a letter of resignation to the Russian party. His letter was intercepted by a high official of the People's Commissariat who resided at Paris on a diplomatic passport. This man, named Spiegelglass, organized the assassination of Reiss.

Reiss knew that his life was in danger. He took his family from Paris to the outskirts of Lausanne, in Switzerland. Soon afterward, he was visited by an old friend, a lady from Strasbourg by the name of Gertrud Schildbach. They had dinner one night at a restaurant in the village of Chamblandes. As they were walking home in the dark, a car stopped in their path. A man, identified later as Charles Etienne Martignat, got out of the car and hit Reiss over the head. Miss Schildbach and Martignat dragged the unconscious Reiss into the car and killed him with several bullets. The body was hurled out of the car near the Cornavin railroad station. Schildbach, Martignat, and the driver of the car, whose name was said to be Roland Jacques Abbiate, managed to cross the border into France.

Further police investigation revealed that Martignat, who had worked at the Clichy gasworks, eventually reached Mexico. He was sentenced to death in absentia. Abbiate, a Soviet secret agent trailing Reiss, had at various times lived in the United States, Cuba, Mexico, India, France, Great Britain, and Yugoslavia. He, too, was said to have gone to Mexico after the Reiss murder.

Gertrud Schildbach, a German Communist, had lived in Rome in 1934 to "study philosophy and languages." She went to Lausanne from Italy. After the Reiss murder, Miss Schildbach went to Spain, where she is said to have been arrested. She had rented the murder car with the help of a Zurich schoolteacher, Renate Steiner. Miss Steiner had entered the Soviet secret service at Paris in 1934. She was told to watch Reiss. She stated during an interrogation that she had been forced to turn her Swiss passport over to a Soviet agent in Paris. She was sentenced to eight months in prison. Another Swiss citizen serving the Soviet espionage system was Helene Hesse, who was sentenced to two months' imprisonment.

The Swiss police were never quite able to define the role that Serge Efron, chief of a Paris office, played in the Reiss murder. The Efron office ran under different labels, such as "Commercial Delegation of the Soviet Embassy" or "Union of Friends of the Soviet Union." A Report on Communist activities in Switzerland, issued on May 21, 1946, by the Swiss government, stated that the Efron office, "which was linked to the [Paris] Embassy of the Soviet Union, was apparently merely an agency of the GPU." (GPU was at that time the label of the Soviet secret service, which later became the NKVD and, in 1946, the MVD.)

Among the employees of the Efron office were Mr. and Mrs. Groszowsky. Both were connected with Helene Hesse. After the Reiss murder, Mr. Groszowsky left immediately for the Soviet Union, while his wife Lydia remained in Paris. She was arrested at the request of the Swiss police, but later released on bail. The Swiss government asked the French government to rearrest Lydia Groszowsky, but she was taken in the car of the Soviet press attaché to the Russian Embassy in Paris and could not be extradited by the French police.

LENIN LEFT INSTRUCTIONS

Events such as the Reiss case have colored the attitude of the Swiss government toward the Communists in Switzerland. The Swiss Communists have never been numerous, but the strategic position of Switzerland has added to their importance. When Lenin left his Swiss exile in 1917 to prepare the Bolshevik Revolution in Russia, he urged his friends in the Social Democratic Party of Switzerland to prepare themselves for the dictatorship of the proletariat. The Communist Party of Switzerland was organized shortly after the foundation of the Comintern. Made up of the extreme left wing of the Social Democratic Party, it nevertheless retained some of the characteristics of trade-union Socialism. In 1925, while the Comintern was fighting the Socialists tooth and nail, Communists in Zurich offered the Socialists a coalition during the municipal election. They were reprimanded by the Comintern. In a letter signed by Otto Kuusinen, who today is president of the Karelo-Finnish Republic of the USSR, the Swiss Communists were ordered "not to extend such coalition offers in the future" and to refrain from supporting the Social Democratic Party.

The Communist Party of Switzerland served as an efficient outlet of anti-Nazi propaganda. It was able to produce camouflaged German-language literature skillfully. Among pamphlets smuggled into Germany were issues made up to look like Nazi reading matter. One was entitled *Germanic Race Principles*. Others were printed on special thin paper, with very fine print, to facilitate clandestine distribution. Although such help proved useful to the illegal German Communist Party, the Swiss Communists were not able to pursue their "united front" policy in Switzerland itself with much success. Under the leadership of Léon Nicole, the Swiss Communist Party made repeated and persistent efforts to enter anti-Nazi coalitions.

In the fall of 1936, the Swiss Trade Union Confederation adopted a platform of "directives regarding economic restoration and the defense of democracy." This platform, designed to strengthen Switzerland particularly against Nazi Germany, was approved by a number of groups outside the Trade Union Confederation. But, when the Communists tried to enter this coalition, their application was rejected. The platform specifically denounced "all connections with any anti-democratic organization or movement whatever," and it was on this basis that the Communist offer was turned down. However, elsewhere Communist activities proved more successful. The *Communist International* was able to report in its August, 1936, issue that the "development of the united front" was facilitated through "organizations such as the Friends of the Soviet Union, the organizations of the unemployed, the anti-fascist front, etc." Nevertheless, and at a time when the Social Democrats had 40,000 party members and 200,000 in their unions, the Communist Party had only 2,000 members and 4,000 in its trade-union affiliate.

Several Swiss cantons banned the Communist Party and its organizations in 1937. The federal government rejected appeals against these cantonal decisions. After the outbreak of the European war, the Swiss army banned the Communist paper *Freiheit* as the vehicle of "foreign, un-Swiss ideologies." Meanwhile, Léon Nicole had founded the Swiss Socialist Federation (Fédération Socialiste Suisse). The Swiss government banned Nicole's papers *Le Travail* and *Droit du Peuple* on July 5, 1940. It stated later that "both papers were spiritually in the service of the Soviet Union" and read like "a translated Russian paper." The Federation itself was banned later.

To implement the over-all Comintern line of the Fifth Strategy against "imperialist war," the Communists began considerable agitation inside the Swiss Army. The army reported several attempts at the development of Communist cells. Switzerland, hemmed in by Nazi Germany, Nazi-occupied Austria, Fascist Italy, and Vichy France, tried to maintain a policy of armed neutrality. It was touchy about anything that might have weakened its armed forces, which would possibly have to defy a German invasion. The Swiss government report of 1946 defines this condition as follows:

"All agitation designed to foster internal disorder, regardless by whom and on what basis it was undertaken, represented not only a danger to the internal but also to the external security of the nation. All parties based on democratic principles recognized this emergency. But neither the right extremists nor the left extremists cooperated. Since the outbreak of war in Europe, the Communists extended their well-known agitation against our democratic state order, and their related propaganda for the foundation of Soviets after the Russian example was strengthened.

"The Communists of all nations hoped that a long war, with growing need and poverty, would open the path to Communists. They hoped that the Soviet Union might stay out of the war, so that this state might exert the unweakened weight of its political and military might in favor of an international proletarian revolution. The complete ideological and organizational dependence of the Communist parties revealed itself through the surprising change of Russian views, contradicting earlier policies directly prior and during the first months of war. The Communists supported Russia's policy without reservations."

BANNED IN 1940

It was on the basis of such observations and conclusions that the Swiss Federal Council agreed on November 26, 1940, to dissolve the Communist Party of Switzerland and to arrest Communist leaders. But Nicole's Swiss Socialist Federation continued legal Communist activities for a while, and the party itself began to function illegally. (Jean Vincent, a Communist speaker, said on April 5, 1945, at La Chaux-de-Fonds, "The steps which the Federal Council took in 1940 were not important to us, as the Communist Party began immediately after the ban to publish illegal papers and to organize illegal meetings.")

Still following the antiwar line, the illegal party violently attacked the Social Democrats. One pamphlet said, "It illustrates the political bankruptcy of Social Democracy that, at a time when the capitalist system proves its rottenness and impotence by hurling peoples into death and destruction, the leadership of this party united ever more closely with representatives of the collapsing capitalist system." The Communist-sponsored Social Democratic opposition group ("Social Democratic Party—Opposition") addressed a manifesto to Swiss workers, which said, "We believe in the socialist Soviet Union, in the strength of the Red Army, in the wisdom of its political leadership, in its readiness to help the militant workers of Europe, when the time comes, with all the means at its command!"

The Swiss police discovered in Geneva that the Coopérative d'Imprimerie produced and distributed illegal Communist propaganda material. The government dissolved the printing cooperative on April 9, 1941. Similar discoveries were made in Berne, Zurich, and Basel. At Winterthur, Swiss police found quantities of a pamphlet, entitled *They Have Lied to You!*, which concluded, "Victory belongs to the revolutionary Red Army and to the international working class, led by the illegal Communist parties." After the German attack on Russia, illegal Communist literature changed its approach. In November, 1941, a leaflet urged, "Alone we are nothing, together we are everything." Two years later, the Supreme Court of Zurich canton reviewed evidence that an illegal network of Communist cells had existed in that city. In Basel, police unearthed a Communist printing establishment on April, 1943. (From 1939 to 1945, 447 cases of Communist activity were tried by Swiss authorities.)

After the dissolution of the Comintern in May, 1943, the central committee of the Communist Party announced that it was entering the Swiss Socialist Federation, praising the "consistent socialist policy of unity" pursued by the organization. From then on, the two parties acted as one. (Nicole, speaking in Geneva on May Day, 1944, said, "Our organization has changed with the dissolution of the Comintern, but our idea has not changed, but has on the contrary been fortified.")

300,000 FRANCS FOR ESPIONAGE

In September, 1943, Swiss police located a secret radio station at 192 Route de Florissant in Geneva, operated by Edmond Hamel. A similar transmitter was operated at 8 Rue Henri Mussard in the same city by Margareta Bolli. The Swiss police described Hamel and Miss Bolli as "convinced Communists." Both were acting under instructions from Alexander Rado, a Hungarian national described in the government report of 1946 as "beyond doubt" the "chief of a Soviet Russian espionage organization in Switzerland" and "an important Comintern agent." From April, 1941, to September, 1943, Rado spent more than 300,000 Swiss francs for the espionage organization.

Although illegal Communist activities, particularly the distribution of literature, continued throughout 1944, they subsided in 1945. At the same time, Communist activity was channeled into the newly founded Swiss Labor Party. The Swiss government lifted all bans on parties in February, 1945, but the Communists decided to maintain the legal Labor Party. On October 14 and 15, 1944, the Labor Party held its first party congress at Zurich. During the following year, it doubled its membership to 20,000. Léon Nicole and Karl Hofmaier are today the leading figures of the Labor Party. Nicole is Swiss correspondent of *Pravda*, the Moscow organ of the Communist Party of the Soviet Union. He has also functioned as correspondent of the Soviet press agency TASS. In both capacities he receives funds from the Soviet Union. Eduard von Steiger, then president of Switzerland, discussed the position of Swiss Communists in a press conference on October 9, 1945. Steiger said that "so long as the Labor Party has Swiss financial means" the federal authorities had no business to investigate their origin. He added that the state must make sure that "no authorized

Swiss political party receives funds from abroad, openly or otherwise."
Steiger told the press that the government was investigating Nicole's income and that, should a party receive funds from abroad, it would be
"not only dangerous but illegal."

The Swiss Communists, through the Labor Party, are actively pursuing
the "united front" policy encouraged by the Seventh Strategy of world
communism. They succeeded in forming a coalition with the Social Democrats during the Zurich elections on March 24, 1946. But in the Berne
canton, the Socialists two months later rejected such an alliance in unmistakable terms.

The status and allegiance of the Labor Party were further clarified
when a competitive party, calling itself the International Communist
Party of Switzerland, was founded in 1945. Clarification came from
Moscow. On April 13, 1946, *Pravda* and the Moscow radio violently denounced the new party as "a bunch of crooks," trying to "exploit the
confidence of the public" in the name "Communist Party." *Pravda* stated
that the Communists were now in the Labor Party and that its competitors
were merely "political provocateurs, useful to those who hate the Labor
Party and true democracy." Although Premier Stalin denied later that
the Communist parties of western Europe follow instructions from
Moscow, it may be assumed that it is the Swiss Labor Party which,
regardless of names, represents world communism in Switzerland today.
That the Labor Party is thoroughly in line with the world-wide policies
of communism was demonstrated on August 4, 1947, in its organ *Voix
d'Ouvrier;* the paper described American suggestions for coordinated
economic reconstruction as an "effort to create a European bloc which
must do what the Americans dictate."

CHAPTER 17

The Lowlands: Royal Dilemma

WHEN THE Lowlands were crushed under the heel of Nazi Germany, the Communist parties of Belgium and the Netherlands were insignificant. They had gained supporters since the "united front" policy was instituted at the Seventh Comintern Congress, but their influence was not decisive.

The closing years of the war brought much prestige for communism in the Lowlands. The Communists were among the most daring and devoted anti-Nazi underground fighters. Their losses were serious. Impressed by such devotion and singleness of purpose, Netherlanders and Belgians joined the ranks of the Communist parties as never before. After the end of the war, the Netherlands party came out in support of Queen Wilhelmina, while the Belgian Communists bitterly opposed the return of King Leopold III. Both parties pressed the leading Socialist groups for quicker and more revolutionary domestic action.

But it was in the field of world affairs that the Communists of the Lowlands attracted greatest attention: they favored closer commercial and cultural relations with the Soviet Union and opposed vehemently any suggestion of a "bloc" among the nations of western Europe.

NETHERLANDS: COMMUNISTS WHO LIKE A QUEEN

The majority of Europe's monarchies disappeared during or after World War II, but not in the Netherlands, where even the Communists complimented Queen Wilhelmina of the House of Orange on her contribution to the nation's anti-German resistance struggle. That does not mean that Holland's Communists approve of monarchy in principle. They do not. But they feel that the members of the House of Orange have acted well during the war. And, anyway, popular affection and respect for the Netherlands royal family is so profound that any party that opposed it would automatically reduce its own chances of success. The Seventh Strategy of world communism permits such regional and national variations in tactics as the endorsement of a popular royal house.

Paul de Groot, secretary-general of the Communist Party of the Netherlands, said shortly after the end of the war in Europe that his party's "attitude toward the monarchy is unchanged." He stated on August 24, 1945, "We consider monarchies a thing of the past. But when a monarchy plays an important role—then things are different. We must remember that Hitler was not a monarch. We are inclined to regard Queen Wilhelmina in a friendly light because she has played an important and active role in the fight against Germany."

When, two months later, the Communists officially reestablished their party, they looked back on an underground struggle that had cost them dearly. Many of their prominent leaders had been killed by the Nazis. Looking farther back into the history of their party, they could observe the development of small sectarian groups into a mass organization, which contributed materially to the successful underground struggle of their nation. Left-wing socialism in the Netherlands goes back to 1909, when a section of the Social Democratic Labor Party affiliated with the Second International. At that time Lenin voted in favor of admission of the Netherlanders to the International. The party was strongly antiwar and anticolonial in its policies. Its slogan, "Indonesia loose from the Netherlands!" (in translation, "Lepas dari Nederland!"), soon became the watchword of the early Indonesian nationalist movements. During World War I, the party stated, "We prefer civil war above a blood bath with our brothers in Germany, Belgium, France, England, and elsewhere."

In 1917, the Dutch party declared its solidarity with Lenin's Bolsheviks. A year later, it adopted the name "Communist Party, Holland," and joined the Third International in March, 1919. Two eminent Socialists founded a rival Communist group. Herman Gorter, one of the great poets of the Dutch literary movement of the late nineteenth century, and the eminent astronomer, Anton Pannekoek, organized the Communist Labor Party in 1921. But it was the "Communist Party, Holland" which represented the Moscow-led movement in the Netherlands.

This party lost much support during the years of prosperity in the mid-twenties. It received 54,000 votes and two parliamentary seats in 1922. But by 1929, it had only one seat and 37,000 votes. The depression brought many unemployed into the Communist movement. In 1933, it polled 118,000 votes and sent four deputies into Parliament. In the last prewar elections of 1937, 136,000 Communist votes elected three members of Parliament.

The war years and the eminent role of the Communists in the resistance movement quadrupled the number of their supporters. The first postwar elections of May 17, 1946, brought them more than half a million votes and ten seats in a Parliament with a total membership of one hundred deputies. The underground paper *De Waarheid* had become so popular during the occupation that its name (which stands for "The Truth") was adopted as part of the party's name, which now reads, "Communist Party of the Netherlands (De Waarheid)."

The loyalties of the Dutch Communists to the cause of world communism cannot be called in doubt. Secretary-General Paul de Groot said during the party's conference at Amsterdam's Concertgebouw on January 7, 1946, "We want to be a party of Stalinists, not merely as followers of a great leader, but as a party, supple and hard as steel." ("Staal" means steel in the Dutch language; just as Stalin in Russian was adopted as a nom de révolution, because it means "the steel one.") The Communist program of 1946 to 1947 stated that the party "propagates scientific socialism, founded on the lesson of dialectic materialism of Marx and Engels, enriched and further developed by Lenin and Stalin." The program also states that the party "makes the people familiar with the great victory of socialism accomplished by the Communist Party of the Soviet Union (Bolsheviks)." It notes that "the Soviet Union is the first country where Socialism has gained power; it is the friend and ally of all democratic and progressive forces of the world." The program concludes with a variation on the closing words of the Communist Manifesto of Marx and Engels, which were "Workers of the world, unite!" In accordance with the nationalist slogans which the Seventh Strategy of world communism permits, the Dutch party urges, "Workers of the Netherlands, unite!"

Hardly had the guns of war been silenced, when the Dutch Communists approached the new postwar Labor Party with offers of fusion. In the trade-union field, the Communists desire fusion between the Workers Unity Conference (a federation they control, although it contains a variety of unions, including Catholic groups), and the dominant Socialist Netherlands Federation of Trade Unions. During the interwar years, the powerful Socialist trade-union federation had a strictly enforced Communist-exclusion clause.

The issue of Indonesia has been the center of Communist postwar agitation. Paul de Groot, the pipe-smoking Communist leader, said in 1945 that "the ties between the Netherlands East Indies and Holland must remain intact, although the colonial relationship should be altered." He expressed himself in favor of a plan whereby Indonesia would be "linked to Holland by a common allegiance to the Crown but would possess its own parliamentary political status." It was, indeed, a plan following this general pattern that was finally agreed upon by the royal Netherlands government and the Republic of Indonesia late in 1946. The plan carried by a majority of the Netherlands Parliament, with the Communists voting in its favor.

The Communists agitated very strongly for the withdrawal of Dutch troops from Indonesia. Twenty people were injured on September 24, 1946, when the Communists staged a protest strike of transport workers in Amsterdam, in order to halt the transport of 3,000 troops to Indonesia. In a campaign similar to the "bring-the-boys-home" policy adopted by the Communists in the United States immediately after the end of the war, the Politbureau of the Dutch Communists developed the slogan "Bring our soldiers back!" during its meeting of December 8 and 9, 1946. A. J. Koejemans, a member of the party's Politbureau, wrote in the January 11, 1947, issue of *De Waarheid,* of which he is editor, that without "the immediate military exodus from Indonesia" there "can be no peace for Indonesia, no progress for Netherlands democracy."

BELGIUM: COMMUNISTS WHO DO NOT LIKE A KING

Belgium is split in half on the issue of King Leopold's possible return to the throne. The king, who surrendered to Germany in 1940, is violently opposed not only by Belgium's Communists, but by the strong Socialist Party as well. His return is supported by the nation's largest party, the Catholic Christian Socialists. The Communists maintain that Belgium's decision on King Leopold does not in principle reflect on the nation's monarchic form of government. But they and the Socialists consider Leopold a collaborator, and they want him to stay in exile.

The Catholics, on the other hand, feel that the Socialist dog is being wagged by a Communist tail. There is a fairly influential left wing in the Socialist Party that is friendly with the Communists. The first postwar national elections of February, 1946, made the Christian Socialists the largest party but did not give them an absolute majority. The Socialists, on the other hand, needed the support not only of the Communists but also of the small, conservative, and anti-clerical Liberal Party in order to form a government.

The government that finally developed under the premiership of Camille Huysmans, the veteran Socialist who served as secretary of the Second International before World War I, included four Communist ministers. Edgar Lalmand, secretary-general of the Communist Party, became minister of food supply. The election gave the Communists 23 out of 202 deputies and 17 out of 165 senators. They received 300,000 votes and more than doubled the support they received in the last prewar elections of 1939. Party enrollment during the immediate postwar period increased the prewar figure of 9,000 tenfold—to 95,000 early in 1947.

The Huysmans cabinet of 1946 to 1947 included not only Lalmand, but also three other Communists: Jean Terfve, head of the newly formed ministry of reconstruction; Dr. Albert Marteaux, minister of public health and family; and Jean Borremans, minister of public works. Julien Lahaut, the Communist Party's president, became vice-president of the Chamber of Deputies in November, 1946.

Not until the spring of 1947 was a government formed which included the nation's largest party, the Christian Socialists. When the Catholic party decided to refrain from pressing for the return of King Leopold, a Socialist-Catholic coalition cabinet was formed under the premiership of Paul Henri Spaak. The four Communist ministers had created a cabinet crisis when they resigned in March, after serious divergencies among the coalition parties had taxed the delicate framework of the cabinet. The new Spaak government, by bridging the chasm between the Socialists and Catholics, isolated the Communists and could command 162 of 202 seats in the Chamber of Deputies and 86 of 101 seats in the Senate. Belgium had assured itself of a stable government which did not contain Communist ministers.

Secretary-General Edgar Lalmand, born at Antwerp in 1895, is the only prominent Communist leader in the West who is not a veteran party official. The Socialists had a near monopoly on Belgium's labor movement during the interwar years. The peculiar weakness of communism in Belgium goes back to World War I, which Lenin and the Bolsheviks opposed as "imperialist." Belgium, which had been occupied by the Germans while they were still neutral, was fiercely opposed to Germany and would not listen to preachings that might be interpreted as giving in to Berlin.

Although a Communist Party of Belgium was organized in 1919, the bulk of Belgian labor remained loyal to the Socialists, who had played an important part in the leadership of the Second International. The "united front" policy of the 1930's increased Communist membership from 2,500 in 1935 to 8,000 in 1936. Lalmand came to the Communists in 1932 while he was still director of a grain-trading company, a position that he finally left in 1937.

On the domestic scene, communism in Belgium is opposed to the return of King Leopold and accuses the Socialists of slowness in executing internal reforms; in foreign affairs, it concentrates on agitation against a "western bloc." Lalmand told a *New York Times* correspondent on February 27, 1947, that "a series of exclusively western alliances would resemble a bloc group around Britain and directed against the Soviet Union." He also denied any direct link between his party and Moscow. "We do not get and do not want any instructions from Moscow," Lalmand said, "and I do not think Moscow feels it necessary to give them." Belgian's Communists tried in vain to turn their government against United States Secretary of State Marshall's plan for European reconstruction.

It is interesting to note how much more closely the Belgian Communist Party resembles the French Communists in its internal position, than it does communism in the Scandinavian countries. In the Netherlands, the Socialist refusal to accept fusion offers and a merger of labor unions follows the Scandinavian pattern. In Belgium, however, the Communists have achieved a trade-union setup similar to that of the Communist-dominated French Confederation. On April 29, 1945, the Communists and Socialists joined in a General Federation of Labor, which proved to be a powerful weapon in the battle over the proposed return of King Leopold. The Labor Federation more than once intimated that it would call a general strike if the king returned. But various Communist-sponsored strikes failed when they were denounced by non-Communist Labor Federation officials. On August 18, 1947, only half the miners and metal workers in the industrial region of Hainault responded to a Communist call for a twenty-four-hour work stoppage.

Belgium's Communists are trying to make up for the frustrations they suffered during the interwar years. Only control of the Labor Federation and a new split between Socialists and Catholics could assure Communist success.

LUXEMBOURG: NOT TOO SMALL

As nations go in size, the Grand Duchy of Luxembourg is merely a tiny spot on the map. But it is not too small to have a Communist Party, which managed to elect about 10 per cent of the members of the Chamber of Deputies—five out of fifty-one.

After Luxembourg's liberation from Nazi Germany's occupation, its government returned from exile in Canada and arranged for elections on October 21, 1945. Corresponding to its size, Luxembourg had an active and effective underground resistance movement. Communists were strongly represented in it. Their newly won prestige helped to strengthen the support they received from the voters.

Although the Catholic Christian Social Party emerged as the strongest single bloc from the election, a five-party coalition cabinet was formed. The Communist Party of Luxembourg is represented in this cabinet by the Minister of Public Health, Dr. Dominique Urbany, who, together with Arthur Useldinzer, runs the party. Luxembourg's Communists publish a newspaper, called *D'Zeitung*.

CHAPTER 18

Scandinavia: Revolution by Consent

THE COMMUNISTS HAVE multiplied their votes in Sweden three times over, in Denmark twenty-five times, in Norway forty times. These remarkable gains were achieved during World War II and the immediate postwar period. In Norway and Denmark, the Communists enjoyed public admiration because of their outstanding role in the anti-Nazi underground. In Sweden, they absorbed those labor votes which were cast in protest against the Socialist's cooperation with nonlabor parties.

But in all three countries the Communists are opposed by well-established Socialist parties. The Communist parties of Scandinavia have been unable to fuse with the Socialists. This major aim in the Seventh Strategy of world communism has, however, been reached in Iceland. There the Communists were able to merge with the majority of the Socialist Labor Party to form a new Socialist-Communist Party—Socialist Unity Party—which played an important part in preventing the United States from obtaining a ninety-nine-year lease on an Icelandic airfield.

A postwar ebb tide has succeeded the wartime flood of pro-Communist sentiment in Scandinavia. The pendulum of political allegiance is slowly swinging away from the Communists, as their resistance record is overshadowed by their new policies. But recent gains have given them new blood and new brains for a more militant struggle.

SWEDEN: RED SPURS

Compared with Communist progress in other Scandinavian countries, the Swedish party has made very little headway. It works in the shadow of the powerful Social Democratic Party, which in 1944 won half of the 230 seats in Sweden's Parliament for a four-year period. Still, the Communists, led by ex-glass blower Sven Linderot, gained 15 seats and more than tripled their popular support from 100,000 votes in 1940, to 318,000 in 1944.

The Communists find it difficult to make headway in a nation where key public utilities and some industries have been government-owned for decades. Although only 5 per cent of the industrial workers are government-employed, Sweden has known state-owned railroads, telephone and telegraph, as well as municipally owned power plants, for more than half a century. State monopolies on tobacco and liquor date from World War I.

The Social Democrats are carrying out their socialization program slowly, but with determination. The Conservatives (who have 39 parliamentary seats), the Agrarians (with 35 seats), and the Liberals (with 26 seats) view the advance of socialization with misgivings. The Communists, on the other hand, feel that things are not going fast enough. From time to time they sink their red spurs into the Social Democratic horse.

Even before the Communist International was born, Swedish Communists tried to spur the Social Democrats into a gallop of socialization. In February, 1917, Communists started to pull away from the Social Democratic Party Congress. Lenin wrote to Alexandra Kollontai, the "grand old lady" of world communism who later became Soviet ambassador to Stockholm, that the opposition Socialists "must be helped at all cost." Three months later, they emerged as a separate group, joined the Comintern in 1919, and promptly called themselves the Communist Party of Sweden.

The Swedes became one of the most restless sections of the Communist International. Zeth Höglund, one of the earliest party leaders, split away from the Communists when Soviet influence became paramount. In 1926, his group rejoined the Social Democrats. Since 1940, Höglund has been Sweden's finance minister, and he would not think of becoming a Communist again. In 1929, there was another split in Communist ranks. Nils Flyg, who died in 1943, left the party and took a majority of the members with him. The Communists labeled him "a right opportunist who later became a Trotskyite." In point of fact, Flyg's later pro-Nazi sympathies lost him nearly all influence over his temporary followers.

After this double split, the Moscow-led Communists of Sweden commanded a membership of only about 4,000. The "united front" strategy infused new blood into the party, and it listed 20,000 members in 1936, when it polled 96,000 votes. A year later, Georgi Dimitrov told the Swedish party on its twentieth anniversary that it was destined to "play an extremely important and honorable role in establishing complete and militant unity among the Swedish proletariat in the interests of all the working people of Sweden and the struggle for unity in the ranks of the international working class movement." The Communist Party of Sweden found it difficult to live up to this optimistic prognosis. Just before World War II, the party's membership sank to 18,000. It hit rock bottom at 11,000 during the 1940 Russo-Finnish war. After the war, however, it achieved an all-time high of 35,000 members.

Today, under the leadership of Sven Linderot, the party is less concerned with extending its membership (although it wants that, too) than with offers of a Communist-Social Democrat "united front." Linderot has sought to make the most of the Communist key position in Sweden's Parliament. The Social Democrats know that their 50 per cent of the parliamentary seats are headed for a deadlock whenever the Communists decide to vote with the other three parties. Linderot, who has been a member of the Swedish Parliament's Upper Chamber (where the Social Democrats have a clear majority) since 1938, has developed from glass worker and commercial traveler into an experienced parliamentarian. Born in 1889, he became a trade-union secretary at twenty-six and a journalist at thirty-four. From 1925 to 1927, he edited the Communist paper *Norrskensflamman* and from 1935 to 1943, he served on the executive committee of the Comintern.

Linderot told C. L. Sulzberger of the *New York Times* in the fall of 1945 that the Communists disapprove of the Social Democratic Party's willingness "to cooperate with the bourgeois parties and make concessions." The Communists, he said, did not believe in such compromising and favored "an independent labor policy." He regarded the question of Sweden's monarchy as "unimportant" but said that "if a majority of the people should ever demand that the Communists lead the country, we could not let the King stay." Linderot also described the platform of the Swedish Communists as "the same as that in the Soviet Union," but added, "Our methods are obviously different, because we work in a bourgeois state, whereas they work in a Socialist state."

Wartime Communists gained followers who were dissatisfied with Sweden's comfortable neutrality. Today, they lack such help, for in a fear-ridden world, Swedes can appreciate their political-economic equilibrium.

NORWAY: REMEMBER GRINI!

The name Grini is synonymous with Norway's heroic resistance to Nazi oppression. At the Grini concentration camp, Norwegian patriots of all political complexions prepared grimly for the day of liberation. You cannot forget common suffering, or a common fight against a common enemy. Among Allied resistance fighters, the members of the Norwegian underground represented a high degree of daring and efficiency. Communists stood out within their ranks.

In 1944, while Norway was still under German rule, Communist and Socialist inmates of the Grini camp signed an informal agreement of future cooperation. After Norway's liberation, the Socialist Labor Party and the Communists continued their discussion of complete fusion. On December 28, 1945, the Labor Party prepared a nine-point program aimed at organizational union of the two parties. Two delegations were appointed after the Communists had made counterproposals. Through the winter and early spring that followed, discussions continued. In the end, the fusion that had been outlined at Grini did not materialize. Why did the fusion talks collapse?

There were two reasons. First, the problem of publications could not be solved. It was agreed that the two Oslo papers, the Communist daily *Friheten* and the Labor publication *Arbeiderbladet* would be preserved as joint morning and evening papers (both papers are now printed in Labor Party presses, after the Nazis destroyed the Communist plant). But there were difficulties as to which papers should be preserved in cities outside Oslo, where only one publication was planned for the fusion party. The delegations could not agree whether the Communist or Labor mastheads should be preserved. But the second problem was even more crucial. It was agreed that a central body of 400 delegates should run the fusion party. The discussions finally bogged down when the Communists asked for 200, or half the total number of delegates. This was completely out of proportion to the voting strength of the two parties (Labor has a clear majority over all other parties in Norway's Parliament), and it would have put the Communists in a position of being able to run the new fusion party with the aid of left-wingers within the Labor Party.

When the fusion talks ran aground, the veteran Communist Secretary-General Peder Furubotn addressed an open letter to the Labor Party in

Friheten's issue of May 11, 1946. He accused "reactionary elements" among the Labor leaders of having sabotaged the fusion discussions. It was a rambling and angry address, packed with invective, which caused some bewildered shoulder shrugging in Labor ranks. The fusion dream was over.

Furubotn, head of the Norwegian Communist Party since 1925, had always enjoyed a reputation for doing the unexpected in an aura of mystery. Born in 1890, he became chairman of the Communist Youth League of Norway when he was thirty-three years old. During the following two years, the Norwegian Communist Party was nearly obliterated by internal dissensions. Its leader, the old-time labor pacifist Martin Tranmael, simply would not accept orders from Moscow. He got out of the Communist movement, taking most of the party membership with him.

When Furubotn was made secretary-general, he became captain of a sinking ship. From 1925 until the last prewar elections of 1936, Norway's Communists were hanging onto the life rafts. In 1924, they had been able to poll 59,000 votes at the national elections. But, while the moderate Socialists gained supporters, the Communists lost popular appeal. In 1927, their votes were down to 40,000, or to 4 per cent of the total ballot. Three years later, their 20,000 supporters represented only 1.7 per cent of all votes cast. The depression helped them little. By 1933, they received only 23,000 votes, or a 1.8 per cent slice of the electoral cake. Moscow was growing impatient. The magazine *Communist International* noted in its issue of February 1, 1934, that there "still remain many social democratic traditions" in the Norwegian party.

Finally, in 1936, the Communist Party could count exactly 4,376 votes, or a mere 0.3 per cent of the total ballot. While the Communists were unable to elect even a single member to Parliament, the Labor Party rolled up a clear parliamentary majority. When the war came, all of Norway's parties pulled together into a coalition government. King Haakon and his cabinet ran the underground movement from their exile in London. In 1941, the Communists entered the clandestine resistance with the discipline and reckless courage for which they became known in all enemy-occupied countries. In fact, just as elsewhere, they disregarded the cautious policy temporarily advocated by the western powers. During the early stage of the resistance war, western military advisers to the underground movements favored consolidation of clandestine units and single, effective sabotage acts that did not expose the undercover network. The Communists, in their determined effort to pull troops away from the hard-pressed Russians, often entered into open warfare in defiance of advice from the west.

Norwegian underground warfare also provided a good example of the difference between Communist and non-Communist concepts of guerrilla leadership. The resistance movement of non-Communist parties arrived at military-strategic decisions through conference and vote. The Communists were following strict orders that Peder Furubotn gave from his secret hiding place, and without recourse to the opinion of individual guerrilla leaders. Furubotn, who is believed to have attended Moscow's International Lenin School (which includes instructions in clandestine civil warfare in its courses), ordered many a skirmish that cost Norway's Communists dearly. But they knew that they were expendable, and their courage and devotion brought them many supporters and cofighters.

Emil Løvlien, who heads the Communist delegation in Norway's Parliament, was also active in the Norwegian underground and spent several war years in Sweden. He has a reputation for parliamentary competence and for a levelheadedness that contrasts with Furubotn's self-styled "man-of-mystery" personality. Løvlien is the most prominent of the eleven Communist deputies who were elected during Norway's first postliberation election of 1945. The Communist vote skyrocketed from its all-time low in 1936 to 167,000 after the war: the number of Communist supporters had multiplied more than forty times! But the Labor Party retained its clear majority by rolling up a vote of about 600,000, just as it had nine years earlier.

All of Norway's parties, continuing their wartime coalition, agreed on a postwar program of reconstruction and increased production. Norway overcame the Nazi-caused inflation, continued rationing, and avoided strikes through an ingenious arbitration system. Communist union officials have been quick to seek alleviation of inequalities in pay; they have needled labor-management courts into adjustments; and they have been critical of the government-fixed wage-price index which has been used as a measuring stick for pay adjustments. Through their influence in shipping and transport unions, the Communists were able to put pressure on the Labor Party, while continuing to push their fusion offers. In Oslo, the capital, the Communist Party has been active in calling for improved municipal administration. From February 21 to 23, the party held a special community conference that discussed such problems as city finances, schools, cultural work, and recreation facilities.

Following their phenomenal gains in the 1945 elections, the Communists are losing ground in Norway. Their agitation against Great Britain and the United States has estranged some supporters who were impressed by the courage and patriotism displayed by Communists in the underground movement; trade relations between England and Norway have always been close, and Americans of Norwegian descent form a natural link between the United States and Norway. On the other hand, Norwegian Communists have not materially suffered from their avowedly high regard for the Soviet Union. Russian troops withdrew from northern Norway very quickly, and trade between the two countries is growing as the USSR recovers from the ordeal of war.

DENMARK: NO CLEAVAGE

Communism prospers where there is a wide cleavage between a large low-income group and a small high-income group. A prosperous middle class acts as a brake on extremes of exploitation and rebellion. Denmark is a nation of middle-class people. It governs itself through a constitutional monarchy that pursues moderate socialism. Its farmers, who are rugged enough as individuals, have discovered the advantages of co-operative action. Literacy is high, and so is everybody's political boiling point.

That is not an environment in which a Communist Party can make much headway. Still, party membership has increased twenty-four times: from 2,500 before the war, to 60,000 in 1947. But, no matter how great the increase of Communist followers may be on a percentage basis, it is overshadowed by the Social Democratic Party. No one knows the limitations of Denmark's Communist Party more clearly than its Secretary-General Aksel Larsen. Born August 5, 1897, he switched from the Social Democratic Party to the Communists in 1920, when Denmark's ultra-left affiliated with the Communist International. He was a candidate for Parliament for the first time at the age of twenty-seven and was elected deputy from Copenhagen in 1932.

When the Germans invaded Denmark in 1940, they did a very strange thing. In a big show of political tolerance, they permitted the continued existence of all parties—including the Communists. Of course, that was merely a temporary expedient, but it certainly was one of the most inconsistent things the Nazis ever did. After the German attack on Russia, the Nazis swooped down on the Communists. In November, 1942, Larsen was arrested. He spent three years in the notorious concentration camps of Neuengamme and Sachsenhausen and was thus unable to work in the remarkably efficient Danish all-party underground movement. Other Communists, however, were prominent in the resistance, which in the summer of 1944 even engineered an anti-Nazi general strike in Copenhagen and forced important concessions from the German occupation authorities.

Hardly had the Germans surrendered in 1945, when the Danish Parliament cleared away all Nazi-imposed decrees and put the country back on its 1940 basis of democratic government. Larsen returned from Germany. His followers state with admiration that he took only a one-day vacation and immediately plunged into the task of reviving the Communist Party. In the coalition government that was set up after the German surrender, Aksel Larsen became a minister without portfolio. Another Communist, Alfred Jensen, took over the communications ministry. In the parliamentary elections of October 30, 1945, the Communists received 255,000 votes and eighteen parliamentary seats (they had balloted 41,000 in 1939, winning three seats; after the 1932 and 1935 elections, they had only two delegates in Parliament). These Communist votes came mostly from the ranks of former Social Democratic supporters. There was much bitterness during the election campaign; the Communists accused the Social Democratic leaders of having played ball with the Nazi occupation authorities. At any rate, the Social Democrats were able to elect only 48 of the 149 parliamentary delegates and found it impossible to set up a coalition government.

Hostility between Communists and Social Democrats erased any chance of the "united front" of which Larsen spoke so much, and which *Land og Folk*, Copenhagen's Communist daily, lauded in its editorials. In the end, the Liberals, Denmark's farmer party, formed a minority government. It seemed as if all other parties were content to let the farmers tackle the country's difficult economic problems. During the German occupation, Denmark's farmers were able to get considerably higher prices for their produce than the hungry Allied countries were able to pay after the end of the war. After the war, feed for Denmark's cattle and raw material for its industries became expensive and hard to procure. Behind these economic problems looms the political question mark of south Schleswig, a German territory before the war. South Schleswig was under the Danish crown until 1864. The Danes look askance at the tens of thousands of German refugees from Polish-controlled territories in the east, whom the British occupation authorities have settled in Schleswig.

When this issue becomes an international political football, Denmark's Communists may have to take a view opposed to that of the German Communists who favor retention of all Reich territory in the west. Together with this, the internationalization of the Kiel Canal, which links the Baltic Sea with the North Sea and the Atlantic, is bound to create a diplomatic puzzle. A strongly nationalist Danish government might even claim all of Schleswig-Holstein (between the present German-Danish frontier and the Kiel Canal), should internationalization of the canal become a reality.

Soviet occupation of the Danish island of Bornholm at the time of Germany's surrender was temporarily a serious political liability for the Danish Communists. But, when the Soviet garrison withdrew from this Baltic island in March, 1946, the liability turned into an asset. The Soviet Union has received assurances that Denmark would not permit occupation of Bornholm by any other power, such as Great Britain. During the talks that led to Russian evacuation of Bornholm, the question of the Kiel Canal was apparently raised by the Soviet Union, which would welcome it, if another power—such as Denmark—were to raise the issue on an international level. At any rate, withdrawal of Russian troops from Bornholm ended a situation that had embarrassed Danish Communists.

Denmark's Communists are persistent in urging the Social Democrats toward a "united workers' party." But the Social Democrats have been consistently opposed to such a merger. Consequently, Communist denunciations of Social Democratic leaders has been particularly bitter. The Moscow trade-union paper *Trud* reflected the Communist view on April 3, 1946, when it asserted that "the leaders of the middle class parties and of the Social Democratic Party" had led "a life of leisure and luxury under the occupation." The Moscow paper said that "Danish workers enthusiastically supported the Communist suggestion for creation of a united workers' party," while the Social Democrats "declined to form an electoral bloc with the Communists, thus undermining the forces of the working class."

The 1946 municipal elections showed that the Social Democrats were gaining back some of the support they had lost to the Communists during the war. In Copenhagen, where Communist strength has been considerable, the 105,000 votes which the party amassed in 1945 shrank to 63,000 in 1946. In other communities, the same trend could be observed.

LEAKS IN THE RESERVOIR

Any party that can multiply three times, twenty-five times, or forty times its previous voting strength is a political phenomenon of importance. That applies to the Communist Party in Sweden, Denmark, and Norway today. The vast reservoir of good will which the Communists accumulated in the Scandinavian countries during the war years has given them a strength they never knew before. But there are leaks in this reservoir which became apparent when world communism changed from its Sixth to its Seventh Strategy, from wartime cooperation to aggressive opposition against the "imperialism" of Great Britain and the United States.

The tradition of parliamentary democracy, on which the governments in London and Washington are founded, corresponds with dominant political thinking in Stockholm, Oslo, and Copenhagen. The history of the Communist parties in the Scandinavian countries shows that this parliamentary tradition has influenced a great number of men and women even inside the Communist movement. During the existence of the Communist International, the Scandinavian parties were almost continually warned against "rightist opportunism" and the influence of "social democratic traditions." On the other hand, the relative moderation of Scandinavian Communists—relative in comparison with Communist parties in many other countries—has attracted into their ranks people of high public prestige, who sought to find a place from which they could act as a spur on the large and dominant Socialist parties of Sweden, Denmark, and Norway.

The Scandinavian Communist parties are destined to experience a slow decline from the peak of strength they reached immediately after World War II. It is unlikely that they will, in the near future, suffer any strong setbacks. But their influence on the affairs of the Scandinavian countries can only be marginal, as long as the three governments succeed in steering clear of the clashing rivalries of the big powers. In one country, however, which owes its recent historic identity to Scandinavian ambition and initiative, rival power interests do clash. That country is Iceland.

ICELAND: BETWEEN NEW YORK AND MOSCOW

Iceland, which voted itself independent of Denmark on June 17, 1944, has a very militant Communist Party. This party became a factor in world affairs, when it violently opposed a peacetime United States air base on Icelandic territory. The Communist Party of Iceland was not founded until November, 1930, and it did not become a noticeable political factor until the "united front" strategy of world communism took effect. The magazine *Communist International* stated in September, 1937, "Of tremendous importance for the development of the Party were the decisions of the Seventh Congress of the Comintern, which seemed to stimulate the Party to undertake the bold development of the formation of a united proletarian and people's anti-fascist front, and to give concrete form to this policy, correspondent with the actual situation in the country."

Under the leadership of Brynjólfur Bjarnason, who later became a cabinet minister, the party participated in municipal governments during the 1930's. It also gained representation in the directorate of the powerful Cooperative Association of Reykjavik, the nation's capital. The Communists' first large-scale economic-political action was the Reykjavik chauffeur's strike in December, 1935. The party attracted support by pressing for higher wage scales for fishermen and by presenting more radical measures to the peasant cooperatives than did any of the other parties. The Communists also founded a daily paper, *Thjodviljinn*, in the city of Reykjavik, which contains one-third of Iceland's 115,000 inhabitants.

During the elections of June 20, 1937, the Communist Party raised the number of its votes from 3,000 to 5,000 throughout the country. It more than doubled its support in Reykjavik: from 1,014 to 2,742. As a result, the Communists received three out of the forty-three seats in Iceland's Parliament. The 1937 elections were followed by fusion negotiations between the Communists and the Labor Party (although, a year earlier, the Labor Party and the Trade Union Congress had rejected "once and for all, every offer of united front and joint action submitted by the Communist Party"). The fusion talks broke down when the Labor Party suggested united action "on the basis of legality and parliamentarism." This definition did not strike the Communists as revolutionary enough. They proposed that a fusion party should regard the prevailing bourgeois democracy as very inadequate and stated that it "does not merely want to improve and perfect it."

This blunt statement of intentions was followed by a split in the Labor Party. A left wing joined the Communists, who from then on adopted the name Socialist Unity Party, and the right wing established the Social Democratic Party, which from then on consistently opposed any contact with the Communists. The elections of October, 1942, showed that the Communists had made considerable gains at the expense of the Social Democrats. Among the seventeen members of Parliament's Upper Chamber were three Communists, but only two Social Democrats. In the Lower Chamber, five Social Democrats faced seven Communists.

During the war years, on October 21, 1944, the powerful Conservative Party, which has the support of influential commercial and fishing interests, joined with the Communists and Social Democrats in a coalition cabinet. Each party received two ministries. Communist Party Secretary Bjarnason obtained the portfolio of education. Another Communist, Aki Jakobsson, became minister of fisheries and trade. This three-party coalition outvoted the Progressive Party, a dominantly agricultural organization that favors the interests of farmers' cooperatives. Olafur Thors, a Conservative, became premier.

This coalition met a severe test two years later, when the Communists split with their fellow cabinet member in the course of Icelandic-United States negotiations over the future of the American-built airfield at Keflavik. These bases had been established during the war, and the United States desired to continue to use and maintain them with civilian personnel. On September 22, 1946, Communist speakers at a Reykjavik outdoor meeting called the proposed agreement "a surrender of Icelandic sovereignty" and a grant of "unwarranted" rights to the United States. When, later in the day, Conservative leaders spoke in favor of the agreement, Communist demonstrators stormed Conservative Party headquarters and broke up the meeting. Premier Thors tried to halt the demonstration by warning against "fist-rule." Communist opposition to the air-base agreement gained in importance, when it was noted that the Keflavik field lies on the air route from New York to Moscow, or Moscow to New York.

Five months later, on February 24, 1947, a representative of the Icelandic party was able to tell the Empire Conference of the Communist Party of Great Britain that his country's Communists had been successful in "preventing an agreement ceding military bases to the United States

for ninety-nine years." Speaking in London, Einar Algierson, a member
of the Icelandic Parliament, said that the Communists had "mobilized the
whole nation in a fight against United States imperialists seeking to transform Iceland into a military base for the next war." He added that
"despite the greatest mobilization of the Icelandic people we could not
hinder another agreement being signed last Autumn, entitling the U. S.
to use our biggest airfield for six and one-half years."

CHAPTER 19

Great Britain: America's Forty-ninth State?

WILL BRITAIN become "the forty-ninth state of American imperialism"?
Britain's Communist Secretary-General Harry Pollitt believes that only
"closest cooperation with the Soviet Union and the new democratic Europe" can prevent such tutelage and save England from "being drawn into
the consequences of a trade depression in America." Pollitt, one of the
founders of the Communist Party in Great Britain, expressed these views
in London's *Communist Review* early in 1947. He called for a "mass
movement which can reverse the present disastrous course of Labour
Government policy."

The Labour Party, which has governed Britain since 1945 and will
probably retain control until 1950, has found in the Communist Party a
vocal and skilled opponent. While the Conservative Party accuses the
government of rashly dissolving the empire, the Communists believe that
the cabinet is following a "Tory policy" abroad. Weakened by war,
heavily dependent on enlarged exports to maintain its life line of imports, Britain is fighting a desperate battle for survival. The nation's
parties differ greatly in the prescriptions for prosperity they have to
offer. The Communists, according to Pollitt, believe that Britain is paying
"the price of the policy of the Anglo-American Bloc." Warning that
England "may be drawn into the vortex of an American economic depression," he has stated, "Britain's complete isolation from any important
new trade agreements with the Soviet Union and other important European nations, such as would have prevented our future being prejudiced by a breakdown in American economy—which no serious person
now doubts is inevitably bound to take place—is causing widespread
apprehension among the workers."

Communist apprehensions are shared by an important segment within
the Labour Party itself. Indeed, the relatively small membership of Britain's Communist Party (which decreased to 43,000 in 1947) is no clear

indication of Communist influence in Great Britain today. In accordance with the Seventh Strategy of world communism, Britain's Communists have pressed again and again for fusion with the Labour Party. Throughout its organized existence, the Communist Party has made these offers, and they have always been voted down by the Labour Party. But there are influential men within the Labour Party who regret this schism, deplore the foreign policy of the government of Prime Minister Clement R. Attlee, and favor united action of the two parties. Konni Zilliacus and Richard H. S. Crossman, two men whose writings appear regularly in Communist Party publications, represent in Britain practically the same point of view as that favored by Italy's Pietro Nenni, or Germany's Otto Grotewohl.

In the powerful Trades Union Congress, which is an organizational part of the Labour Party, Communist influence is not to be underestimated. Generally speaking, individual unions adhere to the principles represented by the Labour Party's leadership. But there is hardly a miner's pit, a workers' canteen, or a working-class city block that does not have its tightly organized Communist cell. On August 22, 1945, Arthur Lewis Horner, member of the Communist Party's central committee, became secretary-general of the important National Union of Mine Workers. Other Communists have union posts of less prominence, but considerable influence. When the *Daily Worker* sponsored a conference at London's Kingsway Hall in June, 1947, 829 delegates with Communist sympathies represented some 2,600,000 organized British workers.

During the immediate postwar period, Great Britain did not experience as many strikes as took place in the United States. The Labour cabinet, a government of trade unionists, enjoyed sufficient confidence among the workers to assure acquiescence to its policy of keeping wages and prices on an even keel. But Communist agitation might have caused strikes if the Communist Party had not pledged support to the main policies of the government. This Communist policy contributed to the stability of England's domestic scene, which was nevertheless shaken by such outside events as the disastrous cold wave of February, 1947. British communism had not wasted a quarter of a century of political education. It had learned to pull its punches. Nevertheless, Communist leadership of the miners' union is like a knife that might cut off the very life blood of Britain's delicate economy.

INFANTILE DISORDER

That veteran British rebel, Sylvia Pankhurst (daughter of an energetic and colorful suffragette mother) was the first to decide that Britain needed a Communist Party. In 1919, she wrote to Lenin and asked his advice. Lenin was wary. He seemed to think that Miss Pankhurst might find herself held back by nineteenth century liberal traditions. On August 28, he answered with a letter of warning against un-Bolshevik waverings. To get Britain's would-be Communists together called for diplomacy and toughness. Lenin revealed that he had both. First there were four, later two, parties that contested for the true Communist label. The Scottish shop stewards, an angry lot, would have nothing to do with Pankhurst's Parliament-minded London group. While the Londoners met to constitute a party (as Lenin had told them, "on the basis of the Third International and of obligatory participation in Parliament"), the Scottish Communists sent their favorite son, William Gallacher, to Moscow's Second Comintern Congress.

Gallacher, a raw-knuckled young man of twenty-nine who had already been imprisoned twice, went to the Soviet capital with ideas of his own. Born at Paisley in 1881, he had left school at twelve and delivered milk for two years. He was still a lad when he joined the Social Democratic Federation, became an apprentice engineer, and then looked in vain for a job. Finally, at eighteen, taken on as a ship's steward, he was shipwrecked, and even lost his first hard-earned pay as a seaman. He went to sea again. When the boat docked in the United States, he spent a brief period ashore. In 1914, he returned to Glasgow, worked at the Albion Motor Works, and became an organizer in the Brassfounders Association. He was involved in a strike on the Clydeside during World War I and was sentenced to eighteen months in prison. That was in 1916 and 1917. Two years later, during strike riots at Glasgow that went down in the city's history as "The Battle of George Square," he was arrested and again imprisoned.

Young Gallacher got out of jail in time to leave for Moscow and attend the Second Comintern Congress in 1921. He could not get a passport, so he made part of the trip secretly on a Norwegian ship. A fishing vessel took him from Norway to Murmansk. At Moscow, he was overawed by Lenin. Gallacher had gone to Russia a convinced antiparliamentarian. But a few weeks earlier, Lenin had written his famous and scathing attack on super-revolutionism, *Leftist Communism; An Infantile Disorder*. In Lenin's view, the delegate from Scotland was suffering from just such an "infantile disorder." Lenin had said in his book, "In England, the Communists should uninterruptedly, unfalteringly, and undeviatingly utilize the parliamentary struggle and all the perturbations of the Irish, colonial, and world imperialist policy of the British government." Lenin was nice enough to tell Gallacher, "I didn't know you when I wrote my little book," but he told him nevertheless to go back to England and help in making the new parliamentary Communist Party a success.

The Communist Party of Great Britain was founded in London during a conference held on July 31 and August 1, 1920. A few months later, in January, 1921, it made its first offer to affiliate with the Labour Party. From then on, interrupted only by the periods of extreme revolutionism that hit the Communist International from time to time, Britain's Communist Party has extended these offers throughout the decades, like an aging but determined suitor.

At its foundation, the party claimed some 10,000 members. Within two years, it had experienced a serious purge. Sylvia Pankhurst and others (including Ellen Wilkinson, who became a member of the Labour Cabinet in 1945 and died early in 1947) were expelled for their refusal to go along with the changing Comintern line and with Russian dominance in the affairs of the International.

In 1921, Harry Pollitt began his career in the Communist movement as head of the British section of the Red International of Labor Unions. Pollitt, who was to develop from a fast-talking Lancashire lad to be secretary-general of Britain's Communist Party, was born on November 22, 1890. His father, a blacksmith's helper at Droylsden, Lancashire, was fond of drink and the horses. The family was poor, and it was not happy.

Little Harry, only twelve years old, had to work half time in a weaving mill. While still in his early teens, he helped around a boiler shop and the near-by shipyard. The family was seriously considering making him into a butcher boy, when he came crying into the room, "Mother! Mother! I can't be a butcher. I couldn't bear to kill a little lamb." And so Harry Pollitt became a boilermaker, while attending night school up to the age of twenty-one.

The imaginative boy, with a flair for fast and furious oratory, stood on his first speaker's platform when he was only seventeen. He liked to talk, and he did a lot of talking after he came to London. After World War I, he fell in with the pro-Bolshevik crowd. Previously he had been active in the Socialist Party at Openshaw. He did not very much like what he saw of the radicals in London. As he put it later, too many of them went in for sandals and flowing hair. When the question of Communist affiliation with the Labour Party was discussed, Pollitt was against it. But his first trip to Moscow, to attend the Third Comintern Congress, changed all that.

In 1924, Moscow discovered that the name Red International of Labor Unions failed to attract followers in Great Britain. Pollitt was instructed by RILU chief Lozovsky, "You must give the movement a national name." This was done. The Communist labor organization adopted the name National Minority Movement (because it represented a minority within the Trades Union Congress), and Pollitt became its secretary-general.

Britain's Communist Party accelerated its agitation after the fall of the Labour government in 1925. Publication of what purported to be a letter from Zinoviev, urging Britain's Communists to overthrow the Conservative government by force, prompted the police to raid Communist Party offices and to arrest the party's leaders. Pollitt, who had been married on October 10, 1925, was arrested after a four-day honeymoon. Together with other prominent Communists, he was tried, judged guilty of conspiracy, and sent to Wandsworth prison. Of the many accounts of imprisonment written by Communist leaders, Pollitt's is probably the least querulous. But he did dislike washing greasy plates with cold water! And he recalls the grim fashion in which the Communist top leadership at Wandsworth prison argued grimly and violently over a tract that William Gallacher had written on toilet paper and which he planned to circulate as an expression of party policy.

Meanwhile, the police had collected a large number of documents at Communist headquarters. There were accounts of the arrival and dispersal of Moscow funds, detailed strategy instructions written by Otto Kuusinen, and some touching attempts by Nikolai Bukharin at writing letters in English.

In May, 1926, Britain was rocked by the general strike, which affected the mining regions most deeply. But the general strike had not come as a result of orders from Moscow. True, Pollitt's National Minority Movement had gained considerable influence. But even if they had planned the strike—and they did endorse it!—they certainly had no decisive control over it. It had started with wage renegotiations in the coal mines. Arthur

L. Horner was even then a member of the Communist Party and chairman of the South Wales Miners, whom he had led previously in successful strikes. (Horner once fought for the Irish Republicans, but he refused to wear the King's uniform and went to jail during World War I.) The general strike collapsed fairly quickly, although the miners held out for several months. Communist support rose sharply and temporarily, particularly in the mine regions. The party had about 10,000 members in 1926. But finally the miners, too, had to give in. Their secretary-general, then A. J. Cook, was replaced.

From then on, and until the mid-thirties, Communist membership fluctuated between 5,000 and 10,000. Turnover in membership was rapid. The extreme-revolutionary period of world communism was ill suited for British conditions. All kinds of colorful anti-Labour Party statements were made or recalled. Had not Lenin, speaking of Arthur Henderson, once said, "I am prepared to support Henderson by my vote, just as a rope supports the man who has hanged himself"? And wasn't it a memorable phrase that T. A. Jackson used, when he followed the temporary anti-"social fascist" and anti-affiliation line, "I would take them by the hand, as a preliminary to taking them by the throat"? It was a difficult period for communism in Great Britain. Nevertheless, the Communist Party's leadership remained remarkably cohesive. It was hardly touched by the Stalin-Trotsky break.

The "united front" policy adopted by the Seventh Comintern Congress was as well suited to England as the extremist-revolutionary line had been ill-advised. Gallacher, who in 1929 had been roundly beaten when he ran for Parliament from the West Fife district, became the first Communist member of the House of Commons on December 4, 1935. He remained a one-man vanguard in Parliament for ten years, until the 1945 election, which put the Labour Party into power and doubled the number of Communist M.P.'s to two.

But all Communist gains in popular favor were wiped out by the reversal of the party's war policy in 1939. Nowhere else in the world could this sudden switch be observed with more clarity than in Britain. The Nazi-Soviet Pact of August 23 took the British Communists unaware. Instructions had apparently been slow in reaching them. On September 2, 1939, London's *Daily Worker* published an official party manifesto, which said, "We are in support of all measures to secure the victory of democracy over Fascism." Pollitt, in a pamphlet entitled *How to Win the War,* stated that the Communist Party "supports the war, believing it to be a just war, which should be supported by the whole working class and all friends of democracy in Britain." And then the Fifth Strategy of world communism reached the British Isles. The party's *Labour Monthly* said in its November issue, "The Soviet-German agreement of September, 1939, established the Soviet frontiers on an unassailable basis in relation to the principle of national self-determination, while the call for peace to Western Europe placed squarely on the shoulders of British imperialism the responsibility for continuing the war." Pollitt, who had gone overboard in favor of the war, was forced to resign as secretary-general. On October 7, the party issued a manifesto, which said, "This war is not a war for democracy against fascism. It is not a war for the liberties of small nations. It is not a war for the defense of peace against aggression. . . . The responsibility for the present imperialist war lies equally on all warring powers. This war is a fight by imperialist powers over profits, colonies and world domination."

Britain's Communists had been told that the war was no longer "just," and they proceeded to urge the working people do do something about it. Gallacher wrote an innuendo-filled pamphlet on *The War and the Workers,* in which he said that it was "time to prove we are not pawns in a deathly game of chess." He told his readers, "We have the power. It is in the trade unions. It is in the factories." Gallacher urged the workers in Britain's hard-pressed war industries, the young men who were being called up for armed service, to "banish the spectre of war and open the road toward a new, free socialist life."

Soon afterward, the *Daily Worker* was banned. But the party continued to function. It published leaflets and the *Labour Monthly,* which contained testimony by such eminent Britons as George Bernard Shaw and H. G. Wells against the ban of the *Daily Worker.* In the March, 1940, issue of the *Labour Monthly,* its American contributing editor, George Seldes, attacked President Franklin D. Roosevelt's policy of supplying Britain with war materials. Seldes, who today edits a monthly newsletter called *In Fact,* devoted to criticism of the United States publishing industry, told his British readers that Roosevelt had passed within one year "from labour's greatest friend to one of its greatest enemies." He sharply criticized the United States government's war-preparedness budget as "diverting national funds for culture to battleships."

But, in 1941, Britain's Communists—as did all Communists everywhere

—saw that the war had again become a just one. They changed from opposition to undeviating support of the coalition cabinet headed by Prime Minister, Winston Churchill. In May, 1942, the *Labour Monthly* assured its readers that a "weakening of the Churchill Government would mean the weakening of national unity." The Communists were behind the United Nations war effort, and they aided it energetically until the Seventh Strategy of world communism began functioning.

After the end of the war, the Communist Party of Great Britain revived its efforts to achieve fusion with the Labour Party. Their offers and moves were strongly opposed by Labour leaders. On January 21, 1946, Pollitt officially petitioned Morgan Philips, secretary of the Labour Party, pointing out that the Communists desired affiliation without special privileges and were ready to "work wholeheartedly for the success of the Labour Government and the development of the Labour Party."

Two months later, the national executive committee of the Labour Party denounced this offer as "temporary Communist talk of working-class unity behind the Labour Party" which merely served as "clumsy camouflage for their real aim of breaking up the Labour Movement, so as to increase their own chances of establishing a party dictatorship." The executive committee added that the Communists, if they "really believe in unity" should "abolish their own party organization" and "join the overwhelming mass of the British workers as loyal and individual members of the Labour Party."

A few weeks later, no less an authority than Professor Harold J. Laski, chairman of the Labour Party, reviewed the fundamental differences of the two parties in a special study *The Secret Battalion*. He examined the development of Communist doctrine, based on Lenin's experiences in the Bolshevik Revolution. This doctrine, he said, calls for a difference in their behavior "while they are working towards the seizure of power in a capitalist society, and their behaviour after they have seized it." He explained, "In the first phase, they are half an agitation and half a conspiracy. It is difficult to exaggerate the tribute that Communists deserve for the courage and devotion and tireless energy they bring to their work of agitation." But, Laski added, "the conspiratorial side of their work" is designed to "destroy the very parties with which they seek alliance in order to command their own ends."

Answering Pollitt's offer of wholehearted cooperation, Labour's chairman stated that Communist efforts toward destruction of their allies call for declarations "that they are at one with them, loyal to their principles, ready to accept their rules, prepared to serve under their leaders. But since none of these declarations are true, they must also, at the same time, deny these principles, manoeuvre round the rules and do all in their power both to discredit the leaders they agree to serve, and, if possible, secure their places when they are discredited."

Professor Laski, who, particularly in the United States, is sometimes accused of undue sympathy for communism, added to his analysis by saying, "They act like a secret battalion of paratroopers within the brigade whose discipline they have accepted. They meet secretly to propose their own line of action; they have one set of rules to regulate their conduct to one another, and a different set of rules to be observed towards those who are not in the battalion. Organised as a conspiracy, their major desire is not to select the best possible leadership in ability and character for the end socialism desires; it is to get those upon whom they can count for uncritical and devoted obedience to their orders into key positions of a movement or party they enter to use for their own purposes." Laski rejected the idea of Communist affiliation, expressing the belief that "they would wreck the Labour Party by undermining its morale and directing the energy of its members to contesting with all their strength the effort of a secret minority within the greater movement from turning it into one more instrument, not of working-class power in Great Britain, but of subservient devotion to the dictatorship of the Communist Party in Moscow." (Ernie Adamson, when acting as Counsel for the United States Congressional Committee on Un-American Activities, revealed the limits of his own knowledge when, on November 8, 1945, he said, "Mr. Laski is, I believe, one of the leaders in England of the Communist movement.")

When the affiliation offer was voted on, at the Bournemouth conference of the British Labour Party, it was defeated 2,678,000 to 468,000. The meeting was highlighted by a speech delivered by Herbert Morrison, Labour leader in the House of Commons, which was critical of "crypto-Communists" within his own party and linked the Communists with the Soviet intelligence service. Morrison said that during the war there had been "more than one case of espionage against the security of this country in which the Communists were involved." MI 5, a section of Britain's

Military Intelligence, is known to have carried out special investigations of personnel engaged in atomic research and related fields.

The Canadian espionage trials, which linked Soviet military intelligence agents with Communist Party members or Communist sympathizers in Canada, the United States, and Great Britain, did not receive wide publicity in England. But their impact on leaders of the Labour government may have stiffened their attitude toward Communist fusion offers. Top Labour leaders take international links of the Communist parties for granted. Prime Minister Attlee said in an address to the Trades Union Congress on October 24, 1946, that communism had abused the word democracy "to mean the achievement of power, by hook or by crook, by the Communist Party," while Communist use of the word freedom "means the denial of liberty to all those who refuse to accept the Communist philosophy." Attlee added, "If in any part of the world the Communist Party, by no matter what means, is in power, that is democracy. If anywhere the Communists fail, then, however fair the conditions, it is regarded as fascism."

HIGH-CALIBER LEADERSHIP

On the whole, such militant anticommunism on the part of Labour's leaders has not prevented the growth of sympathy with the Communist Party among prominent Labour Party members. This is at least in part due to the fact that Britain's Communists are led by a group of men who compare very favorably with Communist leaders in other parts of the world. The British Communists have attracted a number of persons of high intellectual caliber and undisputed professional excellence. Rajani Palme Dutt, son of a Hindu father and a Swedish mother, vice-chairman of the party and editor of the *Labour Monthly*, has maintained strict adherence to prevailing Communist tactics in his speeches and writings, while preserving a lucid and eminently persuasive presentation. Professor J. B. S. Haldane, who teaches biology at London's University College, is chairman of the *Daily Worker*. The *Daily Worker*'s editor, William Charles Rust, who has achieved the record of never committing left or right "deviations," has contributed much to the growth of this paper, which sells 100,000 copies on weekdays and 150,000 of its week-end edition. R. Palme Dutt's *Labour Monthly* has printed contributions by such non-Communists as Professor Laski, Sir Norman Angell, Jawaharlal

Nehru, and Aneurin Bevan, as well as articles by such Labour left-wingers as Zilliacus and Crossman.

The British Communist Party is a home-grown thing. A large group of Labour Party members and Labour M.P.'s regard it with affection, as if it were a younger brother whose adolescent enthusiasm sometimes results in startlingly bright ideas. Such incidents as Pollitt's official apology for his initial support of World War II have, of course, hurt Britain's Communist movement at least temporarily. To force an antiwar policy on the Communist Party of Britain was most certainly extremely shortsighted on the Comintern's part. However, today's Seventh Strategy of world communism recognizes the need for greater leeway on the part of national parties.

Britain's Communists take great care not to let long-range aims penetrate the realm of immediate policies. At one time, a book providing an *Elementary Course of Communist Party Training* contained the phrase, "The immediate demands of the C.P., unlike those of the Reformist Parties, are merely a means to our end, and not an end in themselves." But this passage was eliminated in a later edition of the indoctrination manual.

The British Communist Party has suffered a marked decline in membership from its wartime peak of over 62,000. After the dissolution of the Comintern, the party changed the name of its central committee to National Executive Committee. While thus abandoning a label used by Communist parties on a world-wide basis, it nevertheless benefited from the popularity that the Soviet Union's war effort had created in the British Isles. The rapid decline in membership during the immediate postwar period to two-thirds of its wartime peak was ahead of over-all global trends in Communist membership. This was probably due to the particular sensitivity of the British public to international events. During the war, the blitzed and V-bombed Britons were on the front line of the war against Nazi Germany. Thus, they were particularly grateful to any alleviation of their plight that might have been due to Russian military action. Communist membership figures reflected this feeling. When, after the war, the belief gained ground that Russia had become Britain's rival on the European continent and throughout the world, the seismograph of British public opinion also registered this trend with particular sensitivity.

From the point of view of Britain's Communist Party, its postwar loss in membership is not necessarily a bad omen. Lenin's principle of the party as a vanguard of the revolution, formed by devoted and fanatical rebels, might well be applicable to the Communist Party of Great Britain. Its work inside the Trades Union Congress calls for fanatical devotion and energy. And it is there that future Communist efforts are likely to be concentrated.

CHAPTER 20

Italy: Black into Red

For TWO DECADES, the fascism of Benito Mussolini filled the Italian political balloon to the bursting point. There was no room for anything else. Fascism was ruthless in suppressing opposition. It was particularly determined not to let communism reenter Italy. The Fascists recognized the strong economic-emotional appeal that communism might have for the Italian people. When the Fascist balloon burst, many Italians turned toward the political faith that had been most fiercely denounced by Mussolini: communism. Nearly everyone active in public life during the 1920's and 1930's had been the member of one or another Fascist organization. And in newly found enthusiasm for antifascism, there was a tendency to embrace the other extreme.

Italy provides the world with the best example of basic similarities in political extremism. Benito Mussolini himself illustrated this well. Prior to World War I, Mussolini was a leading member of the Socialist Party of Italy. More than that, he belonged to its radical left wing. He took a line akin to that of Lenin. At the 1910 Congress of the Italian Socialist Party, he argued brilliantly against "reformism." His actions and career during the next few years prompted the philosopher Benedetto Croce to write that "on the left wing of the Socialists there developed a man of revolutionary temperament, unlike most Italians, and with consequent shrewdness." Mussolini expressed this revolutionary temperament in his criticism of trends that Lenin labeled "social chauvinism." He stuck to the antiwar policy later expressed by Lenin's group at Zimmerwald, when he wrote that the Socialists were falling for outworn patriotic slogans. "This old cliché of the threatened fatherland," Mussolini said shortly before World War I, "is the ideological cliché of all bourgeois democracies, a cliché used for thirty years to drain the blood of the proletariat." But, when he flouted the official Socialist line by writing an editorial favor-

231

ing "armed neutrality," the party gave him his walking papers. Mussolini's attitude toward the war changed quickly afterward. He could tell which way the wind of public sentiment was blowing. And, while the Socialists pursued a tortuous neutral road, Benito Mussolini prepared the rise of fascism.

When the war was over, two small groups within the Socialist Party favored affiliation with the Third International. One was led by Amedeo Bordiga, an antiparliamentarian intellectual extremist. The other centered around the paper *Ordine Nuovo* (New Order), published in Turin by Antonio Gramsci. A young man by the name of Palmiro Togliatti belonged to Gransci's vanguard.

The Second Comintern Congress, committed to immediate world revolution, laid down twenty-one points. Any party that wished to affiliate with the Communist International had to endorse these points. Serrati, then leader of the Socialists, had participated in the Moscow Congress. When he returned to Italy, his enthusiasm for the Comintern had cooled off. He felt that the Russian pattern could not be applied to Italy's moderate trade-union Socialists.

The die of Italy's future Communist Party was cast at the Leghorn Socialist Congress of January, 1921. The Comintern was represented by Matyas Rákosi, who today is a member of the Hungarian government, and by the experienced Bulgarian Communist Christo Kabaktchiev. Kabaktchiev urged the Italians that "not a day, not half an hour" should delay "the victory of world revolution." Lenin called on them to show "greatest fanaticism, greatest devotion to the cause of revolution." The Leghorn Congress led to a split of the Socialist Party, with only Bordiga and the Turin group backing the establishment of a Communist Party of Italy.

EX-SOCIALIST MUSSOLINI TAKES OVER

The Comintern was never grateful to Bordiga. He defied Lenin on the first "united front" policy by playing a lone-wolf game. But all Communist aspirations faded into oblivion when Mussolini's Fascists marched on Rome in October, 1922. As time went on and fascism grew more and more entrenched, more and more efficient, the infant Communist Party disappeared. In 1925, Bordiga was replaced by Gramsci. As leader of an illegal party, Gramsci was imprisoned. He died in 1927. It is not known just when Palmiro Togliatti started to run the clandestine Communist

Party of Italy from Moscow. Using the pseudonym of "Ercoli," he visited Spain during the civil war.

Mussolini's organizational machinery penetrated all phases of Italian life. His secret police was efficient. The Fascist Party entrenched itself deeply during the prosperous 1920's. The Communists organized a number of "cells" in urban streets and in villages, which served almost exclusively for the distribution of illegal literature. But this was not enough for the Twelfth Plenum of the Comintern's executive committee. The Italian Communist Party was urged to "come out from underground by developing the mass struggle against the Fascist dictatorship on the basis of the defense of the everyday interests of the toilers, taking advantage of Fascist meetings, organizing impromptu meetings in the factories, penetrating into the Fascist trade unions, cultural and cooperative organizations, preparing and carrying on strikes and demonstrations." The Comintern concluded its order by stating that "mass illegal work must be increased to the maximum extent." The Italian Communists, who included many sincere and courageous people, tried to carry out this order. As a result, the Communist Party of Italy stuck its neck out and promptly had it chopped off. Communists now describe 1928 and 1929 as "the years of Fascist police terror." The Italian Communists exposed their underground network by trying to comply with the Comintern instructions dictated by the extremist-revolutionary Third Strategy.

In the early 1930's, the illegal Communist Party of Italy was as completely shattered as it had ever been since Mussolini boasted in 1923 that he had "broken the back of the Communist Party." The "united front" policy at least helped to bring Socialists and Communists a little closer together. Pietro Nenni, as Socialist leader then in exile, had been approached by the Communists in 1934. He agreed to help in their program of "united action" against fascism.

During World War II, the "united front" aided the Allied war effort in Italy considerably. Although the melodramatic aspects of underground warfare were often exaggerated (as was the picture of partisans who merely lacked a halo to make them saints), there can be no doubt that partisan activity in Italy contributed substantially to United Nations victory. Italy's Communists, using the clandestine machinery that they were able to restore slowly during the late 1930's, played an important part in the underground armies, and their losses were severe.

The major Allied powers agreed at the Moscow Conference of 1943 on a coalition of Italian anti-Nazi parties. Thus, after the fall of Mussolini and the occupation of Italy by German troops, local interparty Committees of National Liberation were organized in various parts of northern Italy. About two-fifths of the patriot fighters north of the Apennines were organized in the Communist "Garibaldi" brigades. All other important anti-Fascist parties had similar military units, which cooperated with each other, more or less. Followers of the Catholic Christian Democratic Party and of the Socialist Party also excelled in the patriot movement, as did members of the smaller parties. (Today, the National Association of Italian Partisans has some 220,000 members and follows Communist leadership on all major domestic and international issues.)

Palmiro Togliatti arrived from Moscow by airplane at Naples, shortly after United States troops had landed in southern Italy. Soon, a deadlock developed over the question of the monarchy. Several of the leftist groups were in favor of an immediate resignation of King Victor Emmanuel, who had been instrumental in legalizing Mussolini's 1922 coup d'état. The controversy threatened to hamper the political and military progress of the Allies in Italy. Following the general "all-for-the-war-effort" policy of the Communist Party at that time, Togliatti surprised everyone by agreeing to a delay on the monarchy question. Thus a dangerous political gap was bridged, and Italy rid itself peacefully of the monarchy in 1946.

WELCOME TO EX-FASCISTS

Similar realism was displayed in the Communist Party's attitude toward former Fascists. Sixteen Communist party leaders met secretly at Bologna on April 20, 1945, where general policy was phrased as follows:

"Comrades, while fighting Fascism you will seek out every former Fascist and offer him membership in our party with a guarantee of amnesty if he joins us. You will attack any Fascist who enters any other party. Give verbal allegiance to the Catholic Church and its priests. It is of prime importance to show the people that our party is not anti-religious. Make friends with disgruntled priests and help organize Catholic branches of the party with them.

"Reveal the Anglo-Americans as greedy capitalists and imperialists ready to enslave our people. Enroll as members of other parties to create discord in their ranks. Our party will thus prove itself the only strong and united force in the nation."

Now, such a policy is sure to be called cynical by political sentimentalists. But it revealed the shrewd realism that has contributed so much to the growth and influence of the Communist Party in Italy. The fall of fascism, like the collapse of Nazism in Germany, created a political vacuum. A large part of the population missed the bread as well as the circuses that the dictators had supplied. Gone were the pageants, the rousing meetings and parades. Gone was the vitality and enthusiasm, and the chance for the insecure individual to identify himself with a strong and uncompromising cause. For all these lacks, communism in Italy has found substitutes. Particularly former members of the Fascist youth organizations have turned to the Communist Party for new inspiration, new songs, new slogans. Black turned into red. But the emotional oratory, the banners, and the mass meetings were there. Above all, Italy's Communists have convinced their more than two million party members that they know exactly where they are going.

The Socialists lost ground to the Communists until they finally split, early in 1947. It was inevitable. The oratory of Socialist leaders, well-truffled with Marxian vernacular, had tried to compete with the speeches of the Communists. In their heart of hearts, Italy's Socialists knew the political dilemma of speaking big and carrying a soft stick. They were unable to arouse their followers to the high pitch of emotion that fascism had created. It was a battle that the Communists were sure to win. Representing the older generation of Italian workers, the Socialists under Nenni followed the leadership of younger Communists under Togliatti. Within the Socialist Party, Giuseppe Saragat opposed Nenni's policy of favoring Communist-Socialist fusion. In October, 1945, the Socialists' central committee had confirmed at Rome that fusion was not opportune but that unity of action with the Communists should be reinforced. In May, 1946, at Florence, the antifusionists again voted against Nenni. But on January 11, 1947, the right wing of the party, led by Saragat, seceded as a minority to form the anti-Communist Socialist Workers' Party.

The move was variously interpreted as a success and as a setback for the Communists. But all sides agreed that the lines had been clearly drawn. Certainly, the Socialist majority's acceptance of the Communist fusion offer implemented the Seventh Strategy of world communism. Rid of its antifusionist wing, the Socialist Party became more maneuverable in the hands of Communist policy makers.

RELIGIOUS PEACE, ECONOMIC WAR

Italy's postwar elections emphasized the rivalry between the two Marx-its parties and the Catholic Christian Democrats, led by Alcide DeGasperi. The world-wide extremist trend expressed itself in Socialist losses to the Communists, and Christian Democrat losses to the ultra-rightist Uomo Qualunque (Common Man) Party. Neither the Communists nor the Socialists emphasized opposition to the role of the Catholic Church during the immediate postwar period. The Communists followed a line that made it possible not only for only nominal Catholics, but also for practicing Catholics to become party members. Roman Catholic religious symbols and pictures could be found in Communist offices. In December, 1946, the Communists supported retention of the Lateran Pact between the Catholic Church and the Italian state, which had been negotiated in 1929 by the Mussolini government. Togliatti, supporting the pact in the Constitutional Assembly, expressed his party's view that it did not wish to disturb the religious peace of the Italian nation. He said, "The only essential problem would be to change the Fascist signature on the Lateran Pacts with the signature of the Italian Republic, which will achieve and defend religious peace in Italy."

The Vatican has viewed this conciliatory Communist policy with suspicion. Several statements by Pope Pius XII have been interpreted as directed against communism in Italy, a nation whose fate is particularly close to the Holy See. On June 1, 1946, on the eve of elections in both Italy and France, the pontiff said to the College of Cardinals that the voters were deciding between the Christian "belief in the spiritual dignity and the eternal destiny of man" and "the unfeeling omnipotence of a materialistic state without any ideal beyond this world, without religion and without God."

In the political-economic field, organized Catholicism clashed with Communist efforts more and more frequently. Throughout 1946 and into 1947, strikes and other unrest rocked Italy from north to south. Continued coal and food shortages, the price of a lost war, contributed to the embitterment of workers and peasants. Italy's General Confederation of Labor, meeting at Florence in June, 1947, revealed that 57.2 per cent of the delegates representing the organization's 6,000,000 members were Communists. This made Communist control of the Italian labor complete;

it even eliminated the need for a Socialist-Communist coalition. Giuseppe DiVittorio, the southern peasant boy who edited a Communist publication in Paris under the pseudonym "Nicoletti," became secretary-general of the Confederation and thus the super-boss of Italian labor.

In the summer of 1946, general strikes hit Milan and Turin. Armed workers took possession of several plants. DeGasperi, as premier, called on the army, navy, and police to help end the strikes. In this, he was supported by the Socialists. DeGasperi aimed at increased production without strikes, which would automatically reduce inflationary prices. Such a policy had been adopted not only by Communist-controlled governments in eastern Europe but also by the Communist Party of France. In Italy, however, the Communists demanded decrees guaranteeing immediate substantial pay increases. Because of its inflationary implications, this was refused by the DeGasperi group.

Later in the year, and early in 1947, riots broke out in the southern provinces of Calabria, Basilicata, Apulia, and Sicily. In the port of Bari, crowds of men, women, and children stormed through the main thoroughfares. They looted shops, wrecked businesses, attacked police stations and government buildings, and threatened to lynch city officials. Anti-Communist political elements throughout Italy attributed these excesses to Communist agitation. The party's central committee countered these allegations with an official statement, saying:

"The young Italian Republic, generous and indulgent to an unbelievable degree towards its enemies of the people, towards those answerable for the catastrophe of the motherland, towards persecutors of patriots, toward black market 'big shots,' shows its greatest severity towards the popular masses which suffer most heavily from the consequences of the war, in other words, towards returned prisoners of war, unemployed and starving. The event in Bari was not an isolated incident, but rather a link in the long chain which persists in grinding down the working masses of Southern Italy."

The statement also said that "throughout all Southern Italy, power is in the hands of Monarchists and Fascists, many of whom do not even feel the need to disguise themselves. In all Southern Italy, traditionally reactionary cliques wield absolute and unhindered overlordship." Those reading the Communist statement could judge for themselves that it contained propagandistically well-presented facts.

The food-supply problem, which had taxed Italy since the end of the war, continued as the main responsibility of the government. With supplies of the United Nations Relief and Rehabilitation Administration (UNRRA) coming to an end, DeGasperi succeeded in negotiating a substantial loan from the United States. But Communist leader Togliatti disapproved of the loan and suggested that it would lead to American interference in Italian affairs. The peace treaty for Italy, approved at the Paris Conference, gave the Communist press an opportunity to express criticism of the United States, Great Britain, and the Christian Democratic Party. The Rome Communist daily *L'Unità* wrote on August 17, 1946, that the treaty was an Anglo-American draft "reviewed by the USSR," thus suggesting that Soviet participation had been passive. Russian reparation demands on Italy were played down by Communist spokesmen.

Events during the spring of 1947 taxed the DeGasperi coalition government to the breaking point. The final break occurred late in May, when the premier decided on a cabinet in which neither Togliatti's Communists nor Nenni's Socialists would be represented. It was a desperate and daring step, which brought the wrath of the Communists down on DeGasperi. The wave of strikes which had preceded the premier's decision grew higher and higher. DeGasperi, backed by a strange mixture of rightist and middle-of-the-road parties, faced the growing unrest of Italy's Communist-led labor movement.

But these were passing events, which merely illustrated long-range problems of communism in Italy. Domestically, Italy's position seemed beyond an immediate solution. Its soil has for decades been unable to feed the large and growing population. The end of World War II corresponded to conditions that brought fascism to power, two decades earlier. Coal shipments from Germany and Great Britain were reduced to a trickle. Italian industry, which relies on imported raw materials to a large extent, was unable to function fully during the immediate postwar period. These economic conditions fed the flame of political extremism of the right and left. By pointing to inequalities at home and the limited help coming from the western nations, the Communists were able to reflect popular resentment and economic frustration. The American plan for European reconstruction was labeled by Italy's Communists as another expression of United States "imperialism" which would result in political interference rather than in genuine economic betterment.

TOGLIATTI'S TRIESTE TROUBLE

Italy's foreign relations created great difficulties for Communist policy makers. They were faced with a choice between popular Italian desire to retain Trieste and the Venezia Giulia region, and the demand of the Communist government of Yugoslavia that these territories be ceded to it. When it became clear that the Communist Party of Italy would weaken its appeal if it backed the Yugoslav demand, Palmiro Togliatti came out in favor of Italian control of Trieste. Indeed, the French Communist leader Jacques Duclos criticized Togliatti on April 20, 1946; *Cahiers du Communisme* accused the Italian party of "political and theoretical deviations" and "erroneous conceptions."

Togliatti modified his stand late in 1946, with the help of Premier Broz-Tito of Yugoslavia. Togliatti visited Belgrade for three days in November. On his return, he reported through *L'Unità* that Tito had agreed to an autonomous status for Trieste, provided that the Gorizia region were ceded by Italy to Yugoslavia. The Italian Communist leader echoed Tito's criticism of the western nations, when he said that the Yugoslav premier had a full understanding "of the fight which the Italian people must conduct in defense of their economic and political independence against those who would like to reduce them to the rank of more or less colonial people." Opposition against the Communist proposal was expressed by the independent Rome daily *Il Messagero*, which said, "Tito suggested that we cede him a very Italian city, such as Gorizia, which already has been assigned to Italy by the terms of the peace treaty draft, in exchange for another city equally very Italian (Trieste), which the same treaty has not given to Yugoslavia. In other words, Tito would give us what is not his and would take what is already ours."

Three weeks after the original Tito offer, it became known that Yugoslavia also wanted control of the port city of Monfalcone. This information had been withheld from the public. Since this would have cut off Trieste from Italian territory, surrounding it by Yugoslav-controlled regions, the Communist proposal encountered growing opposition. Opponents of the Tito-Togliatti plan expressed the fear that Yugoslavia would eventually seize Trieste by force. Meanwhile, negotiations among the foreign ministers of the United States, Great Britain, France, and the Soviet Union were going on in New York. A compromise on the Trieste problem was being worked out by the Big Four. Togliatti then shifted emphasis away from Trieste, by expressing Italian territorial demands on Austria. Writing in *L'Unità,* he said that the question of Italy's frontier with Austria was far more serious than its disagreement with Yugoslavia in the east. Togliatti formulated the official Italian Communist view as follows:

"There was never any attempt to attack or invade our country from the east, if one excepts the period of the great barbarian migrations. From the north, on the other hand, the menace of Germanic invasion has been permanent. The people of Yugoslavia were direct victims of Fascist imperialism and criminality and are therefore among those who with greatest justice present reparation demands on Italy and seek guarantees from Europe. . . . The Italian people must be friends and close collaborators of the Adriatic Slavic peoples if they want to guarantee not only their defense against the danger of a renascent Germanic expansionism but also achieve their economic development and future in Europe generally.

"For these reasons we Communists have been against the stolid nationalist campaign on the international scene about Trieste. That is why we condemn as criminal the campaigns of lies and hatred conducted against Yugoslavia and its new regime of democratic progress. That is why we declare it was a mistake not to express from the first that we ourselves regard the Rapallo frontier as unjust and on this basis seek to make a direct agreement with the new Yugoslavia."

Togliatti, by denouncing the frontier that had been fixed under the Treaty of Rapallo following World War I, did not clearly back either Yugoslav or Italian nationalist views. This enabled the Italian Communist Party to play the role of a reasonable mediator, while sponsoring the cause of closer Yugoslav-Italian relations. In Trieste itself, a separate Guilian Communist Party functioned under the secretaryship of George Jaksetitch. Leaning heavily on the Slavic part of the Trieste population, this party made no bones about favoring annexation by Yugoslavia. Through the media of its Italian-language paper *Lavoratore,* and its Slovene-language *Primorski Devnik,* the party denounced the role played by the United States and Great Britain and agitated for complete union with Yugoslavia.

Generally speaking, Communist policy in Italy has been strikingly successful. Early in 1947, the party claimed to have registered 2,300,000 members—or more than any other Communist Party outside the Soviet Union. This was largely accomplished by ingenious moderation in policy. The Communists offered a political home for the rootless Italian masses. But they also took great care not to affect traditional sensibility too much. By favoring "religious peace" and refraining from pushing for early or widespread nationalization, the Communist Party put its shoulder to the wheel of undisturbed reconstruction. Palmiro Togliatti's moderate-sounding speeches in the National Assembly were a source of wonderment and worry to Rome's political sophisticates, who had seen Communist tactics change from day to day and who waited apprehensively for what might happen next.

CHAPTER 21

Spain, Portugal, Eire: Underground

IN 1937, the Communists gained control of the anti-Franco forces in Spain, because they had support and military aid from abroad. Today, the anti-Franco underground again sees the Communists as the best equipped, most strongly supported clandestine force opposing the government of Generalissimo Francisco Franco. Will history repeat itself? Will communism again win decisive leadership when Franco's successors battle among themselves for control over Spain's destiny?

To answer these questions, we need to unearth the facts about communism in Spain, which lie buried under a layer of propagandistic rubble. *Rojos*—Reds—that is the nom de propaganda which the Franco regime applies to all its militant opponents. The Franco government presented its attack on the government of Republican Spain on July 18, 1936, as a move to forestall a Communist uprising. This claim had a familiar ring. It sounded like the Nazi story about a Communist-set Reichstag fire. And when Franco received the aid of Nazi Germany and Fascist Italy, men of good will throughout the world came to disregard the vague and emotion-laden talk about a Communist conspiracy in Spain, or the sickening adulation of the Generalissimo as a savior of Christian culture and virtues.

Emotions on both sides reached so high a pitch that oversimplification, generalization, and distortion soon triumphed over intelligent analysis. There were more than two sides to the Spanish story in the mid-thirties, there are more today, and there will be more tomorrow. It so happened that Spain's Communists were not planning a coup d'état in 1936. It so happened that they were one of the strongest moderating forces of the left at that time (an attitude for which they were violently denounced by some of their extremist partners). It so happened that they had to resort to ruthless measures in order to suppress the dominant anticommunism inside Republican Spain.

All this may have been confusing to the average subway rider, lecturer, editorial writer, clergyman, doctor, or lawyer in the United States—and to their equivalents throughout the world. But that cannot excuse the continued prevalence of political illiteracy on the subject of Spanish communism. The Communist Party of Spain was formed in 1919 by adolescent hotheads of the Socialist youth organization who were fed up with the moderate policies pursued by their elders. When the Socialist Party itself considered affiliation with the Communist International two years later, it voted 8,000 to 6,000 against it. The party was split, and the minority formed a group of its own. So there were two Communist parties in Spain, which bickered over such questions as the transfer of party headquarters from Madrid to Barcelona, and which caused the Comintern much trouble and disappointment. Enrique Matorras, former head of the Communist youth movement in Spain, has reported in his book, *El Comunismo en España*, that the party was in continual hot water with Moscow. From 1923 until the depression, Spain was governed by a military dictatorship headed by José Primo de Rivera. The Spanish Communists felt that they could do nothing while Primo de Rivera was in power. The Comintern urged them into action during the period of revolutionary strategy, which began in 1928. According to Matorras, the Spanish party used all the paraphernalia of underground revolt, including "illegal membership administration, the obtaining of false passports, administration of funds obtained from the International, relations with Moscow by correspondence, distribution of manifestos and clandestine bulletins, preparation of false documents," and so forth.

ANARCHISTS AREN'T COMMUNISTS

When Spain's left and center groups overthrew the depression-weakened dictatorship and established a republic in 1931, the Communist Party had —according to Comintern records—only 150 members. It gained full legality and several thousand supporters, but it was overshadowed by two giants, the Anarchists and the Socialists. It is impossible to talk or write intelligently about Spanish communism, as long as the label "Reds" is pasted all over these three distinct groups on the Spanish left. There is nothing like Spanish anarchism anywhere on earth (it has lost its identity in most Latin-American countries). Through a quirk of political history, Spanish workers allied themselves overwhelmingly with the disciples of that colorful antagonist of Karl Marx: the revolutionary par excellence Michael Bakunin.

The Anarchists, who led the powerful Spanish National Confederation of Labor, had no need for imported radicalism after the establishment of the Republic. They had cut the throats of landowners, murdered priests, and burned churches when the Comintern was only a gleam in Lenin's eye. They needed no lessons from Moscow. Spanish anarchism had been responsible for burning churches as far back as 1823, 1835, 1868, 1873, and 1909. In the minds of these antistate rebels, the church of Spain was a symbol of suppression, of moribund feudalism. The Anarchist credo called for the destruction of the state machine, individualism of the greatest extreme, and for the elimination of Spain's ignorant, arrogant, and fabulously wealthy landed society.

After the establishment of the Republic, the Communists adhered to the extremist-revolutionary strategy adopted by the Comintern in 1928. They regarded the new republic as an illusion, concocted by the bourgeoisie to fool the proletariat. The Socialists, headed by Francisco Largo Caballero and Indalecio Prieto, were regarded by the Communists as traitors to the working class. In 1933 the Communist paper *Mundo Obrero* published a party statement that characterized Prieto as "a bloody social fascist lackey of imperialism." In 1934, the party said that the belief that Hitler's ascension to power had opened a "new era of fascist terrorism" was "a fraud" designed to "kill the confidence of the masses in their class party."

While the Communists opposed the newly installed government, the republic fought desperately against the effects of the depression on Spain's economy. It attempted to institute land reforms, to extend social-security measures, and to adapt the nation's educational system to a republican form of government. But it was unable to satisfy the electorate. The political pendulum swung to the right again. In 1934 and 1935, a rightist government ruled Spain. The left feared a monarchist revival. Meanwhile the Communists had begun to implement the "united front" policy adopted at the Seventh Comintern Congress. They were even willing to make common cause with the former followers of Leon Trotsky, the Workers Party of Marxist Unification. (All in all, there were then four different groups labeled "Reds" by the oversimplifiers.) The Socialists, afraid that the republic might be overthrown, grew more radical. Within the Socialist Party, Largo Caballero was accused of "bolshevizing" his movement through one-man rule.

In October, 1934, the Socialists tried to achieve by revolt what they had been unable to accomplish at the polls. The Communists cooperated in this "united action." For a few days, the two groups gained complete control in the Asturias, in Spain's northern mountain region. The magazine *Communist International* asserted on November 5 that "the workers of the Asturias fought for Soviet power under the leadership of the Communists." Atrocities were committed during these uprisings, in accordance with Spain's revolutionary traditions. The rebels murdered and mishandled priests and civil guardsmen. In smashing the revolt, the Spanish Foreign Legion and Moorish troops killed and tortured civilians. It was a tryout for the civil war that was to start two years later. More than 1,300 people were killed; 30,000 were imprisoned, and many of them were treated brutally.

The unsuccessful insurrection united the forces of the right. The rightist parties formed a coalition. The left established a Popular Front on January 16, 1936, one month before the national elections. The Communists, who by then had about 50,000 party members, were instrumental in drawing up the Popular Front program, although they did not control the coalition at that time. The program was attractive to the Anarchists, because it called for the liberation of the 30,000 prisoners, many of whom were Anarchists. So even the Anarchists, who usually looked with disdain upon political action, went along. The political pendulum swung once more to the left. The Popular Front elected 158 deputies to the Spanish Parliament, as compared with 62 for the center parties, and 152 for the parties of the right.

AVALANCHE OF REBELLION

The returns were hardly in, when extremists in the leftist parties went completely haywire. Agitation for amnesty was so strong that the middle-of-the-road Republican government gave way. Prison doors were flung open. The amnesty snowball turned into an avalanche of rebellion. Again the traditional burning of churches, and even convents, swept the country. Offices of rightist parties were attacked and pillaged. Peasants seized large estates. The Anarchists had a field day. Unrest continued for months. Gil Robles, head of the Catholic Action Party, told the Parliament on

June 16 that in four months of nation-wide lawlessness 269 persons had been killed, 1,500 wounded, and 251 churches fully or partly destroyed. (Today, Gil Robles is a refugee from Franco dictatorship.)

On July 17, 1936, Spain's twentieth century tragedy began. The extreme left had taken advantage of popular support for the republic to indulge in excesses. Now the extreme right used these excesses as an excuse for ruthlessness and violence of its own. Franco wanted to assure the traditional privileges of a highly corrupt officer class and of a landed gentry of some 20,000 who held about half the territory in a nation of twenty-five million. He also sought the favor of a clergy whose interests coincided with protection of the status of pre-Republican days.

It was a militarist revolt. Its avowed reason was protection of Spain against a Communist rebellion. But where was the Communist rebellion? Where were its strategists and arms? There cannot be any doubt that the Communists hoped, and worked, for eventual control in Spain. The Franco attack, backed by Hitler and Mussolini, needed a convenient propagandistic reason. From the Fascist point of view, it was probably realistic to launch a preventive civil war. But the Communists were still a dwarf party hemmed in by the Anarchist and Socialist giants. If there is any merit at all in fixing the guilt of aggression in the Spanish civil war, that guilt lies with Franco.

The civil war threw the world into frenzy and bewilderment. The Republicans called for arms, particularly for airplanes that might defend the populace against German bombers. It took Moscow a little over a month to decide on a course of action. But, once the decision had been made, Soviet-Communist support was the only substantial help the anti-Franco forces received. The rest of the world, although it had a fearful hunch that Spain was the testing ground for World War II, adopted a policy of nonintervention.

STALIN SENDS HELP

Russia acted fast. The Soviet secret police and Communist parties all over the world cooperated, just as they did in Spain itself. Spanish officers, offering gold for war material, landed in Odessa, the Soviet Black Sea port. Russian advisers arrived at the Spanish war ministry in September. All over the world, buying offices for Republican arms were set up. Franco's troops were marching on Madrid. The Republican capital was in danger. Today, more than a decade after the event, it is clear that the International Brigade that was then recruited for Republican Spain owed its existence to Communist initiative. The world had become incensed over the aggression of Nazism and fascism in Spain. Many men who rejected communism as a political doctrine considered it their duty to join the International Brigade. In the United States, about 4,000 men signed up for service with the Abraham Lincoln Brigade. Communist leaders everywhere, from Canada to Bulgaria, from Mexico to Switzerland, from Czechoslovakia to Australia, organized an efficient recruiting system.

While Franco's troops paused outside Madrid, 3,500 men of the International Brigade entered the city. The attack was halted. Italy was forced to send 100,000 troops. German airplanes were shuttled to Franco territory. The Republicans knew that the Communists had used their efficient world-wide machinery to recruit the International Brigades. They also knew who had helped to get arms into Spain. The rest of the world had chosen nonintervention in the dress rehearsal for World War II. Only the Communists had come through with tangible help. Only the Communists were able to say, "We've got the guns, we've got the men, we've got the money, too." Soon they had won some 300,000 party members in Republican territory, and their prestige was high.

On October 16, 1936, Premier Stalin cabled José Díaz, then secretary-general of the Communist Party of Spain, "The toilers of the Soviet Union are only doing their duty when they give all aid within their power to the revolutionary masses of Spain. The Spanish struggle is not a private affair of Spaniards. It is the common cause of all advanced and progressive mankind." Backed by the Soviet Union, and strengthened by material and men from abroad, Spain's Communists then sought to gain complete leadership within the Republican camp. They were aided by two Soviet representatives on Republican territory: Arthur Stashevsk, who officially acted as Russian trade representative but who was concerned with political matters; and General Ian Berzin, in charge of military affairs.

PURGES BEHIND THE LINES

The Communists were anxious to neutralize the political power of the Anarchists, the Socialists, and the Trotskyite followers of the Workers Party group. And so the purges began. They were particularly fierce in the independence-minded state of Catalonia. On December 17, 1936,

Pravda, the Moscow Communist party organ, wrote, "As for Catalonia, the purging of Trotskyists and Anarcho-Syndicalists has begun. It will be undertaken with the same energy with which it was conducted in the USSR."

While eliminating politically suspect members of their own party with deportation and purges, and Anarchists and Trotskyists with guns and bullets, the Communists advocated fusion with the Socialists. This fusion policy, which is still pursued today by Communist parties throughout the world, was not successful with the party of the then Spanish premier, Francisco Largo Caballero, or with Indalecio Prieto. But a merger of the Communist and Socialist youth organizations was achieved, through the cooperation of the Socialist leader Julio Alvárez del Vayo. Communist spokesmen praised Alvárez del Vayo, who today is political editor of the New York weekly magazine *The Nation.* Dolores Ibarruri, now secretary-general of the Spanish Communist Party, hailed his efforts in the magazine *Frente Rojo* of June 21, 1937, when she said, "Comrade Alvárez del Vayo is fighting untiringly for the union of the Communist and Socialist parties."

Later, José Díaz wrote in the *Communist International* that suppression of "Trotskyists" should proceed with new vigor. He said, "No mercy must be shown such criminals. They must be wiped out as mercilessly as the fascists." Andrés Nin, the ex-Communist leader of the Trotskyists, was imprisoned and finally killed. Many others disappeared. At the same time, while purges continued inside Russia itself, the Soviet representatives General Berzin and Arthur Stashevsk also vanished into oblivion. Communist political indoctrination was emphasized in the Republican army. Díaz described the political commissar as "the soul of our army" who "maintains ideological consciousness."

In May, 1937, not quite a year after Franco's attack, an uprising of anti-Communist Anarchists took place in Catalonia. Bands stormed the telephone exchange. Walter G. Krivitzky, a key agent of the Soviet secret service in western Europe, suggested later that the Communists had inspired this uprising to have a reason for breaking the Anarchist hold on Catalonia. Krivitzky, who died at Washington under mysterious circumstances in 1941, said in his book, *In Stalin's Secret Service,* that the Communists had asked Largo Caballero to suppress the Anarchist movement. He refused and was replaced by Dr. Juán Negrín. Julio Alvárez del Vayo joined the Negrín cabinet as foreign minister.

Anarchist-Communist antagonism continued while the Negrín cabinet was in power, and until the collapse of Republican resistance in March, 1939. Harry Gannes, writing on *Soviets in Spain* for the United States Communist Party, said that "anarchist leaders fought against the Soviet Union and the proletarian dictatorship more vigorously than against the capitalist state, considered by them freer than proletarian rule, which they call 'red imperialism.' " The Anarchists themselves defined their differences with the Communists after the end of the civil war in a manifesto published at London in April, 1939. This manifesto, bearing the title *Three Years of Struggle in Spain*, said in part:

"To get the arms of which we were in need, we both gave away our national wealth, and had to tolerate the control of our political and military activities by the foreign and Spanish agents of the USSR. This nobody wanted, but in view of the indifference of the world to our wretched situation, all anti-fascist parties acquiesced in it, in order that the people should not be crushed. It was then that the real danger of the Communist Party became evident. Forestalling the bourgeoisie, it set up the cry that it was not the revolution for which we were fighting, but a new kind of democratic republic; that our politics should circulate in the orbit of the western democratic tradition of England and France; that the small proprietors should be respected; that free commercial activities should be permitted—that is to say, that the people should be at the mercy of the speculators; that the churches should be opened, as if we had never been fired at from them, or we could allow centres of treason in the rearguard."

In the eyes of the Anarchists, the Communists thus appeared as compromisers, intent on preserving private enterprise and freedom of religious worship. If nothing else, this view should help to dispel the hypnosis of Franco propaganda that somehow he is opposed by a vast flood of "reds," all of whom do Moscow's bidding. From a western point of view, the relative moderation of which the Anarchists accuse the Communists was probably the only possible answer to the atrocities that had been so widely and authoritatively reported. The Communists, with a vastly greater revolutionary experience, knew much better how to adjust their policies to prevailing conditions than did the Anarchists. Anarchism is an anachronism in our time. Without support from abroad, orthodox Spanish Anarchists are being replaced by a younger generation that can be attracted by another, stronger, political magnet. Today, that magnet is communism. And the Spanish underground is experiencing 1937 all over again.

HEADQUARTERS: TOULOUSE

When France was liberated, the Communist Party of Spain set up its headquarters at Toulouse, not far from the Spanish frontier. A training center of guerrillas was established under Communist supervision "somewhere in France." The central committee of the Spanish Communists, under Dolores Ibarruri, was represented inside Spain through a special operational delegation. In Madrid, *Mundo Obrero* was published as a weekly underground paper. A clandestine radio station, identifying itself as "Independent Spain," advocated "united action" of all anti-Franco forces.

Until the end of 1945, the Communists controlled a resistance coalition under the name of National Union. Anarchists, Socialists, and Left Republicans were united in the Democratic Alliance. On January 8, 1947, *Mundo Obrero* published a statement by the Communist Party's central committee that the National Union group would seek to combine forces with the Democratic Alliance. The National Union was dissolved, the underground weekly stated, "to disprove the Franco statement that Spain's future is either with the Falange or in chaos." The National Union's dissolution was represented as a step toward "a completely unified position in the fight against Franco and the Falange on the premise of the recovery of the Republic."

After the end of the European war, Communist organizers were able to make their way back into Spain. Well trained, equipped with funds, and fired by the same determination that had made Communists prominent and successful in anti-Axis underground movements throughout the world, these organizers supplied anti-Franco resistance forces with the leadership it lacked. The Anarchist-led National Confederation of Labor had retained much of its identity. The immediate postwar period brought a strengthening of Communist influence inside the Confederation, such as it had never experienced before. The Franco regime countered this heightened underground activity with police measures of considerable effectiveness. On November 4, 1945, the Madrid police announced that several representatives of the Toulouse central committee had been arrested. The police identified the arrested persons as Agustín Zoroa Sánchez, Teodora Carrascal, and Fernando Bernal, a radio operator. Two radio transmitters, equipped for sending and receiving, were seized. The police stated that this equipment had been used for radio contact with Toulouse headquarters. A printing press and 5,000 copies of *Mundo Obrero* were also confiscated.

Although the Spanish police were able to arrest a number of Communists or alleged Communists, *Mundo Obrero* did not stop publishing. It appeared to shift its printing premises often, and its circulation seemed to gain in late 1946 and early 1947. Much of the growing Communist prestige among the Anarchist rank and file could be attributed to the regularity and efficiency with which *Mundo Obrero* appeared.

Other anti-Franco groups lacked such support. They could also observe that the arrest or trial of Communist leaders resulted in considerable publicity and pressure from abroad. This, too, illustrated Communist connections outside Spain. To the isolated, weak forces of the anti-Franco underground, communism thus grew in stature. In their hatred of Franco, they could appreciate the interpretation that the Communists applied to the United Nations discussions of Spain in 1946. When it became clear that the British Foreign Office was attempting to unify anti-Franco forces among monarchists and in army circles, *Mundo Obrero* considered this a "compromise with Franco," engineered by "reactionary foreign financial and industrial groups." In June, 1946, the paper compared "foreign intervention in Spain which favors the continuance of the Franco regime" with "foreign intervention in Greece." *Mundo Obrero* added that "foreign interventionists are aiding reactionaries under the mask of peaceful change, thus encouraging pro-Fascist elements and trying behind the backs of the masses to force a compromise of the Greek type upon the Spanish people."

While opposing negotiations for a constitutional monarchy, the Communists nevertheless offered their cooperation to the monarchists in a common endeavor to unseat Franco. Dolores Ibarruri said on December 27, 1945, that a "government of national coalition" should include not only the "Republicans, Socialists, Syndicalists of the National Confederation of Labor (Anarchists), Communists, and representatives of Catalonia and the Basque provinces" but also "the monarchists and anti-Franco military elements." Encountering opposition to such a broad let-bygones-be-bygones policy, Miss Ibarruri had told a national conference of the Spanish Communist Party a few weeks earlier (on December 6, 1945), that it was better to fight with the monarchists and the anti-Franco elements in the army than against them. "Either we have them as allies," she told the Communist delegates, "—uncertain and wavering allies, if you like—in the fight to end the present regime, or we have them as enemies, re-grouped around some figurehead or other, trying to prevent the democratic development of our country."

GOVERNMENT IN EXILE

While strengthening their influence in the Spanish underground, the Communists pursued a very cautious policy with regard to establishment of a recognized Spanish government in exile. In the fall of 1945, such a group was established in Mexico City. It quickly received the recognition of the Mexican government, but not that of Great Britain, the United States, or the Soviet Union. The first cabinet did not contain Communist members. But the Communists were careful not to press their reservations too strongly, lest they might destroy the delicate construction of the regime. A few months later, the Communists were included in the cabinet.

The Communists thus participated in two successive cabinets: that of Dr. José Giral, and the government of his successor early in 1947, Rodolfo Llopis. The Communists were willing to have the Monarchists support the exile government, but they did not want them to have any decisive influence.. Dolores Ibarruri said, "We cannot facilitate the liberation of our people by renouncing the Republic, just to get the approval of the Monarchists." The Monarchists, in turn, were unwilling to join a cabinet which included Communists.

In the summer of 1947, at a meeting at Toulouse, the right-wing Socialists around Indalecio Prieto decided to ally themselves with the Monarchists, even if it meant dropping the Communists. Inside Spain, the Monarchists had been able to retain influential followers. The Communists were forced out of the Llopis cabinet, and the way was open for a government which would include the Monarchists, but not the Communists. Prieto could be sure that London and Washington would like it better that way.

PORTUGAL: DEEP UNDERGROUND

The Communist Party of Portugal had hardly been established when, in 1926, a military coup d'état suppressed all parties. Subsequently, Antonio de Oliveira Salazar became premier and authoritarian leader of the Portuguese people. After sixteen years with sixteen revolutions—from 1910 to 1926—Portugal entered a period of outward calm.

The Salazar regime, which adheres to social concepts of the Roman Catholic Church, is strongly anti-Communist. It resembles the Austrian government of Dr. Kurt von Schuschnigg, which ruled in Vienna before the Nazi invasion. Salazar has been able to govern Portugal without interference from any organized opposition, although there are circles inside the army and among the politically conscious Lisbon population who desire a government of parties with free elections and unfettered vote. On November 18, 1945, Portugal had its first general election in twenty years. An opposition coalition operated under the name United Democratic Movement. The government won the election.

The illegal Communist Party, which supported the movement, has restricted its observable activity to publication of a monthly clandestine paper, *Avante*. This paper, which bears hammer and sickle and the legend "Workers of the world, unite!" on its masthead, seeks to crystallize diverse opposition trends among the Portuguese people. As central organ of the Portuguese Communist Party, it seeks to shake the opposition out of its lethargy and favors such demonstrations as hunger marches and group actions by women against hoarders of food.

The Portuguese Communists were not outwardly prominent in the United Democratic Movement, but they endorsed its demands. On December 1, 1946, the movement held its first authorized meeting since the 1945 elections. The resolutions, approved in *Avante*, called for restoration of constitutional rights, freedom of assembly, and uncensored domestic mail, total amnesty for political prisoners, authorization for the establishment of papers and parties, and an electoral law based on new census figures.

Through the medium of *Avante*, the Communists have expressed their opposition not only to the domestic policies of the Salazar regime but also to its conduct of foreign relations. In its October, 1946, issue, the paper described Salazar's international policy as "anti-national" and as favoring "the monopolies" and "foreign imperialism." *Avante* said that oil concessions granted by the Portuguese government in Timor and Cabo Verde were tying Portuguese industries to American capital. The same issue carried a front-page appeal, entitled "The Hour of Offensive," in which the Communist Party asked for broad support of the United Democratic Movement.

On February 2, 1947, the headquarters of the United Democratic Movement were closed by the Lisbon police, who referred to the movement as "illegal." Thus robbed of any outlet through a legally functioning political organization, the Communists were forced to continue their activities exclusively on a clandestine basis.

EIRE: ALMOST HOPELESS

There's little hope for communism in Ireland. The inherent conservatism of the farming population and the dominant influence of the Roman Catholic Church have made the political soil of Eire unreceptive for the seeds of Marxist-Leninist-Stalinist thought. Consequently, the Communist Party of Eire is deep underground. And, though the word "Communist" is sometimes flung about as an epithet useful against political opponents, it is only rarely used with accuracy.

But we would underestimate the determination and thoroughness of world communism if we thought that it had given up Ireland as a country lost to its efforts. During the early 1930's, the period of extremist-revolutionary strategy, the Revolutionary Workers' Groups of Belfast, in Northern Ireland, were used as a base for Communist operations not only in the north, but also within the Irish Free State. Agitation among miners and among the unemployed was undertaken. The Irish Trades Union Congress was considered by the *Communist International* to offer a base for class-war propaganda. In 1932, Irish Communists were told by the Comintern's Moscow bureau that in southern Ireland "it is possible to utilize the legal reformist trades union branches for our work."

Communists had been active within the revolutionary Irish Republican Army until, in 1933, the IRA resolved at its convention to expel all Communists. During this extremist-revolutionary period of world communism's Third Strategy, Ireland's Communist movement appears to have received instructions to emerge somewhat from its deep underground position. Consequently, the Communists held their First Congress in June, 1933, during which they resolved to "establish the Communist Party as the class leadership of the workers at the head of the only class which can lead the struggle for the liberation of Ireland from British imperialism and destroy the role of the Irish capitalists." The party proclaimed the following manifesto:

"The Irish working class will carry on the national struggle to the end, attaching itself to the masses of the peasant farmers, so as to crush the power of resistance of the British imperialists and paralyze the unreliability of the Irish capitalist class. The Irish proletariat will bring about a Socialist revolution, attaching to itself the masses of the semi-proletarian elements of the population, so as to break the power of resistance of the capitalists, and paralyze the unreliability of the peasants and the petty bourgeois."

A workers' study circle was formed in Dublin, and an attempt was made to agitate among small farmers against the owners of large estates. The success of these efforts must have remained very small. If Communists in Eire and Northern Ireland ever got beyond the passing of revolutionary resolutions, this phase was closed by the beginning of the "united front" strategy. Eire is probably the only spot on the globe where the "united front" techniques proved ineffective. This was largely due to the nation's spiritual remoteness from the world's concern with the rise of Nazi Germany. Nearly everywhere else, the dangers of Hitlerism were recognized sooner or later, and fear of Nazi domination caused many to ally themselves even with communism to stem the tide of totalitarianism from the right.

Eire lived in a self-made atmosphere of splendid isolation, a fairyland of neutrality that seemed quite callous and selfish to a world that suffered from Nazi tyranny. But Eire went serenely about its own affairs, and—quite incidentally, to be sure—remained immune from Communist influence. Aside from the period of the Nazi-Soviet Pact, communism contributed much to the world's understanding of Nazism. Eire did not understand Nazism, and it has apparently not understood it to this day. It is a weird illustration of emotional isolationism, and lack of political imagination, to observe Irish reaction to such monstrous Nazi doings as the conditions in the Belsen concentration camp. The word Belsen has, throughout the civilized world, become synonymous with unspeakable atrocities against helpless humans. It is only in Eire that one could find people who had understood so little of what Belsen meant, that letters to editors would compare conditions in some Irish prison, or the mistreatment of passengers at the hands of impolite bus drivers, to the Belsen horrors.

All this is said merely to illustrate the peculiar emotional conditions that made Eire practically immune not only to much of the feeling of Allied solidarity during the war years, but quite accidentally also to Communist appeals. This should be viewed as neither good nor bad. It is quite conceivable that a prolongation of the Nazi-Soviet Pact might have opened the door to communism in Ireland. The view that World War II was "imperialist," something to be kept away from at all cost, paralleled Eire's own position of stubborn neutrality. But the Nazi-Soviet Pact period was too short for full exploitation on Irish soil, and Communist wartime policy after that had little appeal in Eire.

Today, communism in Eire is again deep underground. The Irish-Soviet Friendship Society is active, particularly in Dublin. Although it doubtless attracts many people who seek in it an expression of their own protest against the dominant conservative political beliefs, it also forms the only openly established forum for pro-Soviet and consequently pro-Communist sentiments. The society has sought to broaden its appeal by such events as the visit of the Dean of Canterbury, the Reverend Dr. Hewlett Johnson. The Reverend Johnson, who is a member of the board of London's Communist *Daily Worker*, spoke on November 25, 1946, in Dublin's Mansion House.

The most important mouthpiece of Marxist-Leninist-Stalinist ideas in Eire is the monthly magazine *Irish Review*, published at Dublin under the editorship of Sean Nolan. This magazine has been recommended highly in the New York *Daily Worker*. Nolan's article on Soviet-Irish relations, published in the November, 1946, issue of his magazine, was reprinted in the New York Communist paper on January 19, 1947. Communist literature is sold at the "New Books" shop, 16a Pearse Street, Dublin, but care is taken not to give prominence to the fact that books and pamphlets originate in the affiliates of the Communist Party of Great Britain.

It can hardly be doubted that efforts continue to extend Communist influence into the Irish Labour Party and the Irish Trades Union Congress. Generally, Communist policy in Eire is similar to that applied in India, now that its political independence is achieved. "British imperialism" is still presented as economically dominant, and the slogan of "American imperialism" has been introduced. The *Irish Review*, for instance, interpreted the United States-Chinese Trade Treaty of 1947 in a manner identical with that expressed by Chinese Communists. The Dublin magazine said in its issue of February, 1947, that this trade agreement "means, in practice, the complete control of one of the potentially richest countries in the world by the greediest and most powerful ruling class in the world—of Wall Street: hence the existing civil unrest in China."

SUPERFICIAL SIMILARITIES

We have grouped Spain, Portugal, and Eire together in one chapter, because there are basic similarities in the three countries' relations to communism. The governments of these nations are strongly opposed to Communist thought, and Communist parties do not operate except underground. But these, we wish to emphasize, are rather superficial similarities. The Communist Party of Ireland could open offices tomorrow on Dublin's Sanford Road, if it wanted to and thought it useful. Spain's Communists, in contrast, face an utterly ruthless dictatorship, which thinks nothing of imprisoning or executing the various groups of political opponents that it lumps together as "reds." Portugal, where suppression of all opposition is severe, is far from the violence practiced in Spain.

All three countries are dominantly Roman Catholic. But this, too, though it contributes to anti-Communist sentiment, is only a superficial similarity. There are many other Catholic nations outside the Soviet sphere of influence—notably Italy, France, Brazil, and Chile—where communism has achieved important or even decisive positions. Communism in Spain, Portugal, and Eire today is underground. It is preparing, with the astounding tenacity that characterizes this movement, for the day when conditions will be more favorable for its activities and influence.

IV
WESTERN HEMISPHERE

CHAPTER 22

Canada: Atomic Espionage

On the night of September 5, 1945, Igor Gouzenko, cipher clerk in the Soviet Embassy at Ottawa, collected a number of documents from the files. These papers included confidential notes on Soviet military espionage, data on Communists in the employ of Russian agents, and many deciphered cables. Gouzenko took the documents to the office of the *Ottawa Journal*. He was unable to convince the editors that the Embassy papers were newsworthy. Discouraged, Gouzenko went to his home on 511 Somerset Street, Apartment 4. Next day, he tried again to persuade editors and officials to take him seriously. He was unsuccessful.

After returning to his apartment, Gouzenko noticed that two men were watching the house from across the street. A few minutes later, someone knocked at the door of his apartment. Gouzenko was getting worried. He persuaded his neighbors to take him and Mrs. Gouzenko and their child into the adjoining apartment. One of the neighbors, Harold W. Main, a noncommissioned officer of the Royal Canadian Air Force, left on his bicycle to call the police. They agreed to keep the building under observation.

Between 11 p.m. and midnight, four men broke into Gouzenko's apartment. Police, summoned by neighbors, were able to identify the men as Vitali G. Pavlov, second secretary of the Soviet Embassy and chief of the Soviet secret service in Canada; Lieutenant Pavel Angelov, assistant military attaché of the Embassy; Lieutenant Colonel Rogov, military attaché, Russian Air Force; and Alexandre Farantov, a cipher clerk at the Embassy. A police inspector asked the four men to wait while he made inquiries. When he returned, they had left.

On the next day, September 7, Igor Gouzenko was escorted to the offices of the Royal Canadian Mounted Police. His testimony and the documents that he had brought with him led to the appointment of an investigative royal commission on February 5, 1946. Headed by Justices Robert Taschereau and R. L. Kellock, this commission issued a report on its findings some five months later. The commission revealed that the Soviet government had used its Ottawa Embassy as a clearinghouse and headquarters for espionage in Canadian territories. Gouzenko's papers and statements, backed by testimony of people in the employ of the Soviet espionage system, outlined the existence of military intelligence service with headquarters in Moscow and directed in Ottawa by Colonel Nikolai Zabotin of the Soviet army.

The inquiry showed that the Canadian Communist movement was the principal base of this espionage network. According to the royal commission's report, the Communist movement supplied personnel with adequately developed motivation and "provided the organizational framework wherein recruiting could be and was carried out safely and efficiently." In every instance but one, Canadian espionage agents turned out to be Communist Party members or Communist sympathizers. The exception was one Emma Woikin, who was sympathetic to Russia because of "what I have read." She was sentenced to three years in prison.

When Colonel Zabotin arrived in Canada in the summer of 1943, he found already in existence in Ottawa, Montreal, and Toronto numerous groups that studied communism and Marxist writings. To outsiders, these groups were presented as social gatherings, music-listening circles, and meetings for the study of international affairs. These study groups served as recruiting units for agents. They developed the frame of mind necessary for later espionage work. Occasionally, these groups were visited by leading Communist Party officials who reported to Colonel Zabotin on the ability of candidates to become full-fledged espionage agents. When it was found that a candidate fulfilled all requirements, he was definitely recruited as an agent, and specific tasks were assigned to him.

HOW AGENTS WERE RECRUITED

The technique of selecting agents fell into three steps:

1. A senior member of the Canadian Communist Party (such as Sam Carr, the party's national organizer; or Fred Rose, the Quebec organizer) would propose a Communist to be a member of Zabotin's staff.

2. Colonel Zabotin would collect details about the candidate, including

his place of work and the information to which he had access, and send them to Moscow.

3. Moscow would then telegraph Zabotin either permission or refusal to use the particular person as an agent.

According to Gouzenko, Moscow checked all candidates through one of several parallel intelligence networks. Sometimes Moscow would take the initiative in suggesting to Zabotin some Communist to be enlisted for espionage work. Moscow made these suggestions on the basis of personnel dossiers on file in the Soviet capital.

A good illustration of the ease with which Moscow was able to obtain espionage agents from the secret membership of the Canadian Communist Party in selected Canadian organizations was provided by a "research group" consisting of Israel Halperin, Durnford Smith, and E. W. Mazerall, under the leadership of David Gordon Lunan. These men were scientists, engaged in work of interest to the Soviet espionage system. Two of them were members of a Communist cell of scientists, most of whom were employed by the National Research Council in Ottawa.

The royal commission's report and Gouzenko's testimony suggest that the Communist International continued to exist even after its official dissolution in 1943. Gouzenko stated on October 10, 1945, that "the announcement of the dissolution of the Comintern was probably the greatest farce of the Communists in recent years." He asserted that "only the name was liquidated, with the object of reassuring public opinion in the democratic countries; actually, the Comintern exists and continues its work."

Documents supplied by Gouzenko tend to corroborate this testimony. A registration card in the Soviet Embassy's dossier kept on Sam Carr, national organizer of the party, contained the following entry, in Russian: "Detailed biographical information is available in the Center in the Comintern." Evidence showed that this document, referring to the Comintern in the present tense, was prepared by Lieutenant Colonel Rogov in 1945. When Gouzenko was questioned by the royal commission's investigators on this entry, the following conversation developed:

QUESTION: "I just want to come back to that last subject for a moment, to make it perfectly clear to myself. I am looking at Exhibit 19, the first sheet, which is headed 'Registration Card' dealing with Sam Carr. The last two lines read, 'Detailed biographical information.' Apparently that is the form before it was filled in; after that it says '. . . the Comintern. Knows Russian perfectly. Finished the Lenin School in Moscow.' If the

Comintern means the staff in Moscow which runs the Communist Party, as I understand it, in Russia and abroad, does that reference on Carr's registration card mean that he is a member of that staff?"

GOUZENKO: "No."

QUESTION: "All right; then what is the explanation?"

GOUZENKO: "On every Communist there is a file at the Comintern in Moscow; for every Communist in the whole world there is a file at the Comintern at Moscow. More detailed information is on the files at the Comintern."

QUESTION: "So this reference on the registration card means that if anybody is looking at this registration card and wants more information on Carr than it contains, there is more information on file at Moscow?"

GOUZENKO: "That is right."

QUESTION: "And am I correct in understanding that the word 'Comintern' is also used in Russia to refer to the secretariat in Moscow of the foreign Communist parties? Is that correct?"

GOUZENKO: "No. The Comintern or Communist International is like a headquarters that directs the activities of the Communist parties in the whole world."

QUESTION: "That is approximately what I said; a headquarters staff?"

GOUZENKO: "Yes. . . ."

QUESTION: "The first sheet in Exhibit 19-A was not typed out until early in 1945, but it contains a reference to the Comintern, does it not?"

GOUZENKO: "Yes."

QUESTION: "The Comintern was supposed to have been abolished before 1945?"

GOUZENKO: "Supposed to be abolished in 1943; but it is not so."

QUESTION: "It is not abolished?"

GOUZENKO: "That is right."

QUESTION: "In 1945 Rogov typed or had typed the statement that they had Comintern records still available to refer to?"

GOUZENKO: "He knew very well the Comintern existed in Moscow."

QUESTION: "Rogov knew the Comintern had not been abolished and that all the records were complete there?"

GOUZENKO: "That is right."

QUESTION: "It would have been possible—I am not saying that it is so —for the Comintern to have been abolished as an organization and all the records still kept?"

GOUZENKO: "That is right, and all the personnel is still kept in Moscow; it is just the name that is abolished."

The royal commission report also states, "Gouzenko, in his evidence on the Comintern, spoke generally of it as a headquarters staff controlling the activities of Communist parties in other countries in various aspects, including political aspects. His detailed evidence dealt however with the role of the Comintern specifically in espionage activities, since it was in one of the espionage branches that Gouzenko himself had direct personal experience."

Prior to coming to Canada in 1943, Gouzenko had worked a little over a year in the Moscow center of the Soviet military intelligence organization. The center was usually referred to—and signed its cables as—"The Director." Gouzenko testified that, while in Moscow, he had enciphered and deciphered telegrams to and from many other countries. He assured the commission that throughout the world Communist parties served espionage purposes, in networks similar to Colonel Zabotin's staff in Canada.

FORGED PASSPORTS

Comintern use of forged passports was illustrated by the "Witczak passport" case. Sam Carr, national organizer of the Communist ("Labor-Progressive") Party, undertook in 1944 to obtain illegally a Canadian passport for a Soviet agent in California. Acting on instructions from Moscow to Colonel Zabotin, Carr managed in August, 1945, to obtain such a passport through forgery and bribery. The royal commission found evidence that "The Director" in Moscow intended to develop further the practice of planting agents, under cover of false documentation, not only in other countries as pseudo Canadians, but in Canada also. Sam Carr, as a veteran Canadian Communist, was enlisted in this work. The Russian dossier on Carr, under the heading of "Task No. 3 of 1.8.45," specified that he was to supply information on the following subjects:

"1. Requirements which a person living as 'illegal' must meet (nationality, citizenship, occupation, knowledge of languages, family and financial conditions, etc.).

"2. Ways of legalization (organization of a commercial undertaking, joining a business firm as a partner, kind of firm, joining as a member any office, joining the army as a volunteer, accepting employment).

"3. Documents which an 'illegal' must possess (passports, different kinds of certificates, references, recommendation letters, etc.).

"4. More expedient methods to slip into the country.

"5. To provide for secure living quarters and financial means during the period when the 'illegal' gets acquainted with the local set-up and conditions. [The words, "The possibilities of attracting . . ." were found crossed out in the dossier at this point.]

"6. To reveal the channels of influence of the English government on the foreign policy of Canada.

"7. Conditions of entry into the country and of moving about in the country.

"8. Conditions of adaptation and living in the country.

"9. Methods of work of the counter-espionage. The organization of the Federal and provincial counter-espionage services."

In recruiting personnel for the espionage services of the Soviet Union in Canada, emphasis was placed on enlisting people sympathetic to communism, rather than men or women who were primarily interested in making money as agents of a foreign power. The royal commission noted that "there is no evidence that monetary incentive played an important part in the original motivation of the persons whose ideology was sympathetic to the Communist cause, who agreed to act as espionage agents." On the contrary, evidence from documents and testimony showed that motivation was a product of political indoctrination.

Care was taken by the espionage recruiting agents not to mention the possibility of monetary rewards when the first assignment was put to the selected recruit. Senior members of the network felt that the mention of money would act as a deterrent rather than as an inducement to secret Communists facing consciously for the first time the critical issue of entering an illegal conspiracy directed against Canada. This was illustrated by the testimony of Captain David G. Lunan, the Scottish-born staff member of the Canadian Information Service and editor of the military journal *Canadian Affairs*, who organized a cell of scientists for espionage purposes.

Lunan told investigators that "Jan" (cover name for Lieutenant Colonel Rogov) was always "bringing up the question of expenses and he did mention this question of taxi rides, but it was from our point of view a preposterous suggestion and I simply ignored it." The testimony continued as follows:

QUESTION: "When you say 'from our point of view,' whose point of view do you refer to?"

LUNAN: "Mine and Smith's and Mazerall's." [Durnford Smith, assistant research engineer in the Canadian National Research Council, obtained information on secret radio equipment for the Russian espionage services. Edward W. Mazerall, engineer with the National Research Council, obtained data on radar equipment.]

QUESTION: "Did you discuss it with them?"

LUNAN: "Yes, I did."

QUESTION: "With the three of them?" [Another member of Lunan's group was Israel Halperin, mathematics professor and army major, who was accused of obtaining military information, but later acquitted.]

LUNAN: "No."

QUESTION: "With whom?"

LUNAN: "With each one at one time or another, and I discussed the question of expenses."

QUESTION: "Tell us what you said to them."

LUNAN: "I told them that if they were involved in any expenses, there was an offer for those expenses to be covered. Each one of them, however, said there was no such possibility, the question did not arise for them."

QUESTION: "From what you say I take it that they did not want to take any money."

LUNAN: "Correct."

QUESTION: "Either as a disbursement to cover expenses, or otherwise?"

LUNAN: "That is correct."

QUESTION: "What was their motive for what they did?"

LUNAN: "Their motives would be idealistic or political."

QUESTION: "What do you mean by political?"

LUNAN: "That they felt they were serving a valid political motive in doing this."

QUESTION: "What do you mean by political?"

LUNAN: "I cannot describe for them their motives."

QUESTION: "What do you understand they meant by political?"

LUNAN: "I used the word myself."

QUESTION: "What did you use the word for?"

LUNAN: "That certainly there would be some motivation for doing this type of work, and it would have to be one involving ideals."

QUESTION: "Party sympathy?"

LUNAN: "Yes, that would be fair."

QUESTION: "When we say 'party' there is only one party that is meant, the Communist Party?"

LUNAN: "That is correct."

Nevertheless, Lunan testified, Lieutenant Colonel Rogov was quite insistent in offering money. Lunan said that Rogov "would try to persuade me to take it." The royal commission commented on this and similar testimony by saying, "One purpose of the directors of the network in insisting on paying money, even relatively small sums, to recruits, would be to further the moral corruption of the Canadians caught 'in the net' and thus to assist in their further 'development.'" Lunan, Mazerall, and Smith received prison sentences.

CANADA'S COMMUNIST RESERVOIR

The reservoir of Communists and Communist sympathizers that the Soviet espionage system could tap in Canada originated in 1921, when the Pan-American Department of the Communist International took the initiative in founding the Communist Party of Canada. For three years the Canadian party operated underground. In April, 1924, it came to the foreground when it published a four-point program calling for the "overthrow of the dictatorship of capitalism and establishment of the dictatorship of the working class and the republic of labor." The party at first concentrated on agitation among the foreign-born, notably inside the fraternal organizations of immigrants from the Ukraine and Finland. Although some success was achieved in this direction, the Communists were unable to gain decisive control in the ranks of organized Canadian labor. In fact, the turnover of party membership and the extreme-revolutionary platform of the Communists kept the number of members very nearly stagnant for a decade. In 1922, the party had 4,810 members, and in 1935, it claimed only 6,500 members. But the evidence unearthed by the royal commission in 1946 certainly showed that Lenin's principle of a small and devoted party membership was successful in Canada.

After the Comintern changed to the "united front" strategy, membership in the Canadian Communist Party reached 15,000 in 1937. A pamphlet, issued by its central committee, *What the Communist Party Stands For*, stated openly that it "is active directly as an organization, and indirectly through its members within other organizations." The pamphlet, with remarkable frankness, admitted that the party "got to the law-making institutions" not to aid the nation's progress through parliamentary bodies but "to be a monkey-wrench in their machinery."

The Canadian government kept a rather close eye on the Communist Party's activities. As early as 1921, the Royal Canadian Mounted Police planted an agent in the Communist Party under the name of "Comrade Esselwein." This man, Sergeant John Leopold, remained inside the party until 1928. It was not until August, 1931, that the Canadian police decided to take action on the data collected by Sergeant Leopold. This was the period of Communist extremist-revolutionary activity, which the Canadian party practiced in a particularly undisguised form. On August 11, police entered Communist headquarters at Toronto, the office of the party's trade-union body, the Workers' Unity League, and the plant of the party paper *The Worker*. Tim Buck, secretary-general, was arrested, as was John Boychuk, a Ukrainian organizer. Sam Carr, who later figured prominently in the 1945-1946 espionage investigation, and the writer Malcolm Bruce were brought to Toronto from Vancouver.

In all, six Communists were arrested and tried under Section 98 of the Canadian Criminal Code, which considers "unlawful" any organization that teaches governmental or economic change by violence. The party was declared illegal, and the accused—with one exception—sentenced to ten years' imprisonment. S. A. Clark, speaking several years later before the Seventh Comintern Congress, said that the 1931 illegality had prompted the party to change itself "into a party of the native working class," in an attempt to gain mass support outside of Canada's foreign-born population.

SAM CARR

The career of Sam Carr reflects the changing fortunes of the party. Carr, born July 7, 1906, at Tomachpol in the Russian Ukraine, came to Canada in August, 1924. He worked as a harvester and laborer in the Regina region and later stated that he had been badly treated and exploited there. Carr said that he had no particular feeling about Russia. His memories of that country are bitter. His father was killed before the eyes of his family during the 1917 revolution.

One can only assume that his experience as a nineteen-year-old in the harvesting fields of western Canada was strong enough to turn him against the prevailing economic system. In 1925, he went from Winnipeg to Montreal, where he joined the Young Communist League as an organizer. Two years later, he moved to Toronto and joined the Communist Party itself. According to Canadian government records, "it is alleged that in 1929 he went to Russia for a course of study at the Lenin Institute." Carr denies this. In 1931, he was appointed organizing secretary of the Communist Party. He became a naturalized citizen on June 23 of that year.

After the November trial, he was sent to the Kingston Penitentiary on February 19, 1932. His naturalization was revoked. He served less than three years of his sentence and was freed when the party's legality was restored. After his release, Carr immediately returned to party work. He conducted a national training school for young Communists at Toronto, and it has been alleged that he visited Russia and Spain in 1937. Carr denies having made these visits abroad but has testified that, in his capacity as national organizing secretary of the Communist Party, he recruited Canadians for the International Brigade of Spain. In 1938, Carr briefly worked in the reorganization of the party's paper *The Clarion*. The party had pledged at the time of the Comintern's Seventh Congress to develop *The Clarion* into a mass paper.

In 1940, after the outbreak of the war, the Communist Party was banned under the Defense of Canada Regulation. The party went underground, and its prominent members did their best to elude the police. (In 1943, the Communists founded the Labor-Progressive Party. On June 13, 1943, Secretary-General Tim Buck said in Toronto, "Our first loyalty has been, is and will always be to the true national interests of our country—Canada." Commenting on the announced dissolution of the Comintern, Buck said that "The Communists in Canada, as in other countries, now stand without any international affiliations whatsoever." The Canadian government refrained from extending the ban of the Communist Party to the new Labor-Progressive Party. Using their considerable experience in illegal activity, the Communists would doubtless have been able to form parties more quickly than they could have been banned.)

Canadian government authorities believe that Carr went to the United States and took up residence in Philadelphia, while contributing to Communist publications in the United States, Canada, and Great Britain. In February, 1940, he wrote in the *Ukrainian Daily News* of New York, "Ignoring its losses brought about by terrorizing actions and internments, the Communist Party (of Canada) is improving its methods of activities and expansion of contacts with the masses of the people, fighting hard in order to draw away these masses from under the influence of the war machine of the Canadian bourgeoisie." About the same time, he appealed to Canadian youth in the British magazine *World News and Views* to "defeat the bloody conspiracy of the rich, demand that the country withdraw from the imperialist war." The Advisory Committee of the Defense of Canada Regulations showed these and other samples of his writings to Carr after the Soviet Union had entered the war against Germany. He then considered these articles "rather sharp" and "extravagant." The war's progress in 1941 proved to Carr that it had become "just" and "a people's war." He was set free in October, 1942, under the condition that he refrain from "activities of the Communist Party of Canada or of any organization over which the Communist Party exercises control." In spite of this pledge, it appears that Carr quickly got in contact with Soviet espionage representatives. Colonel Zabotin's notebook listed Carr as having met a Soviet agent "at a meeting in October 1942." This same notation stated that he "studied with us in 1924-26 in the Soviet Party School." When the Canadian espionage affair was investigated, Carr went into hiding and could not be located.

Carr was later used extensively by the Soviet espionage system under the pseudonym "Frank." His case parallels that of Fred Rose, who was elected a Member of Parliament in 1943 and 1945. Rose was active under the cover names of "Fred" and later as "Debouz." He, too, pledged himself to refrain from Communist activities after his release in 1942. The Advisory Commitee's report contains the following paragraph:

"He joined the Young Communist Party when only seventeen years of age and appeared to be proud of the progress he had made in that organization, and in the Communist Party of Canada, having attained almost all of the top-ranking positions, of both. He boasted that he was the only Canadian ever appointed to the International Committee of the Young Communist League, and described his duties as Chief of the Central Control Commission of the Communist Party of Canada as those of counter-espionage within the Party, i.e. the duty of 'ferreting out traitors, spies, and fascists' who might have become members for ulterior purposes." Among the documents that Gouzenko turned over to the Canadian government was a dossier on Rose which stated that he had "previously worked at the neighbors, up to 1924." "Neighbors" was the cover word used for the Soviet secret service (which has functioned under various names, abbreviated successively as OGPU, NKVD, and MVD). In 1924, Rose, who was born in the Polish Ukraine in 1907, was only seventeen years old. On June 20, 1946, he was sentenced to six years' imprisonment.

It may be useful to stress that the Gouzenko papers not only revealed Soviet espionage in Canada with the use of recruits furnished by the Communist Party but also pointed to the existence of parallel-functioning intelligence services of the USSR. Colonel Zabotin represented the intelligence service of the Red (Soviet) Army. According to Gouzenko's testimony, a five-man intelligence committee in Moscow is made up of representatives of the NKVD (MVD), the military intelligence, the naval service, the commercial service, and the diplomatic service. It may be assumed that any intelligence service operated by the Soviet Union would prefer to recruit its foreign personnel among Communists and Communist sympathizers, whose ideological loyalty to the USSR can be regarded as high.

SAMPLES OF U 233

The most sensational revelation of the Ottawa investigation was connected with the activities of Dr. Allan Nunn May, a temporary British civil servant. May was part of a research group that came to Canada in connection with experiments in atomic energy. He was, according to the royal commission's report, "an ardent but secret Communist and already known to the authorities at Moscow." May participated in the Atomic Energy Project at Montreal and Chalk River. Zabotin, whose cover name was "Grant," received direct instructions from "The Director" in Moscow to get in contact with May. Zabotin's organization gave May the pseudonym "Alek." "The Director," on July 28, 1945, sent a telegram to Zabotin, which follows in part:

NO. 10458
30.7.45

TO GRANT

REFERENCE NO. 218

. . . TRY TO GET FROM HIM BEFORE DEPARTURE DETAILED INFORMATION ON THE PROGRESS OF THE WORK ON URANIUM. DISCUSS WITH HIM: DOES HE THINK IT EXPEDIENT FOR OUR UNDERTAKING TO STAY ON THE SPOT; WILL HE BE ABLE TO DO THAT OR IS IT MORE USEFUL FOR HIM AND NECESSARY TO DEPART FOR LONDON? . . .

DIRECTOR.   28.7.45

Zabotin apparently acted quickly on the basis of these instructions. He not only was able to give some information about the atomic bomb but also received a uranium sample. He sent the following telegram to Moscow on August 9, 1945:

241

TO THE DIRECTOR

FACTS GIVEN BY ALEK: (1) THE TEST OF THE ATOMIC BOMB WAS CONDUCTED IN NEW MEXICO (WITH "49," "94-239"). THE BOMB DROPPED ON JAPAN WAS MADE OF URANIUM 235. IT IS KNOWN THAT THE OUTPUT OF URANIUM 235 AMOUNTS TO 400 GRAMS DAILY AT THE MAGNETIC SEPARATION PLANT AT CLINTON. THE OUTPUT OF "49" IS LIKELY TWO TIMES GREATER (SOME GRAPHIC UNITS ARE PLANNED FOR 250 MEGA WATTS, I.E. 250 GRAMS EACH DAY). THE SCIENTIFIC RESEARCH WORK IN THIS FIELD IS SCHEDULED TO BE PUBLISHED, BUT WITHOUT TECHNICAL DETAILS. THE AMERICANS ALREADY HAVE PUBLISHED A BOOK ON THIS SUBJECT. (2) ALEK HANDED OVER TO US A PLATINUM WITH 162 MICROGRAMS OF URANIUM 233 IN THE FORM OF OXIDE IN A THIN LAMINA. . . .

GRANT.

9.7.45

Dr. May furnished other information and additional uranium samples to the Soviet military intelligence service. He gave them to Lieutenant Angelov. In February, 1946, May was arrested in London. He confessed his guilt. In a detailed written statement, he gave as his motivation the desire to make sure that "development of atomic energy was not confined to U.S.A." He did not receive very substantial financial return from this. Documents show that he was given at least $700 and two bottles of whisky. He wrote, "I accepted these against my will." May was sentenced to ten years' penal servitude.

"FOR PEACE AND HUMANITY"

The report of the "Royal Commission to investigate the facts relating to and the circumstances surrounding the communication, by public officials and other persons in position of trust of secret and confidential information to agents of a foreign power" was published in Ottawa on June 27, 1946. It is the most thorough official document relating to Communist activities to appear since the announcement of the Comintern's dissolution. The report and the testimony of Igor Gouzenko suggest that Communist parties elsewhere may be employed for similar purposes.

Official reaction to the Ottawa trials was militant and brief. The Moscow radio on April 23, 1946, quoted the newspaper *Trud* as referring to Igor Gouzenko as "an embezzler and traitor" in the service of "the dark political forces which are thinking of a third world war, who fear their own people, and who hide their own plans with allegations that the Soviet Union is threatening war." The article concluded on an optimistic note: "Fortunately for peace and humanity, these dark forces do not have the final say. That depends on the people who are firmly determined to preserve peace, and whose will to peace cannot be broken by the dark forces of reaction."

The espionage affair apparently has not seriously affected Communist activity in Canada. Early in 1947, the Communist Labor-Progressive Party claimed a membership of 25,000, twice the number it had ten years earlier. The *Canadian Tribune,* the Labor-Progressive weekly organ, was transformed into the *Daily Tribune.* Agitation and propaganda were accelerated.

CHAPTER 23

U.S.A.: Target Number One

THE UNITED STATES has become the main target of Communist agitation throughout the globe. According to William Z. Foster, national chairman of the United States Communist Party, this country hopes "to establish American imperialist hegemony over the other peoples and areas of the world." Foster wrote in the monthly magazine *Political Affairs* in August, 1946, "The major objectives of American imperialism are to reduce the British Empire to a subordinate position, to cow or smash the USSR; to subjugate China to the status of a satellite country to reduce Latin America to a semi-colonial system of the United States; to take charge of the internal economies of Germany, Japan, and various other countries; to dominate the Atlantic and Pacific Oceans with its big navy and air force."

Communism is determined to halt this trend, which, it asserts, dominates the foreign policy of the United States. To accomplish this, it not only arouses peoples everywhere to the danger it sees in American imperialism, but it also seeks to influence men and women in every stratum of American society to accept its views and to act accordingly. In Canada, according to the report of the Royal Commission which we examined in the preceding chapter, many citizens became so completely convinced of their country's errors that they willingly and gladly served the military espionage system of the Soviet Union. The United States, ten times more populous than Canada and formed by many diverse population groups, is a vastly more important target for Communist activities of all kinds.

Does there then exist inside the United States a Communist-controlled espionage system paralleling the machinery that was partly uncovered in Canada in 1945 and 1946?

Unquestionably. All Communist practices in use anywhere on the globe are being applied and perfected inside the United States. This country

275

is so large, so highly industrialized and complex, that Communist organizational machineries in America are more widely expanded and carefully perfected than anywhere else. The Communist Party of the United States is the Communist Party in a capitalist nation par excellence. Whatever Communist apparatus exists anywhere abroad can be found on a larger scale on American soil.

The historical development of American social life does not, in our time, permit the emergence of a Communist Party as a mass party—such as it has become in the Soviet Union, in China, Italy, France, and Czechoslovakia. Lenin's concept of the party as a devoted and fanatical vanguard can be applied to communism in America. Members of this vanguard exercise influence through leadership or as part of the rank and file in other organizations. Communists are active through two different organizational mediums: by working within an association that has been created by non-Communists (such as the American Veterans Committee); or by building an organization themselves, into which they draw non-Communists for indoctrination and political action (such as American Youth for Democracy). Unions fall into both categories.

Before the Communist Party of the United States could achieve this complexity of organization and such perfection of operation following World War II, it had passed through years of frustrating, marginal existence, which tried and seasoned the hard core of its membership and its leaders.

AMERICA'S BABEL

After Russia's Bolshevik Revolution, not one but two Communist parties in the United States endorsed the cause of world communism. Rival Chicago conventions in September, 1919, created the Communist Labor Party (representing American-born men and women who had seceded from the once influential Socialist Party), and the Communist Party (which represented the federations of the foreign-born). It was a situation peculiar to the American scene. The federations of the foreign-born overshadowed the native-born element in number of members and resources.

It was not a good time to introduce Bolshevism to America. The country was on edge after a wave of strikes, notably the Seattle general strike. America's Communists were for the most part a wild-eyed, romantic lot, who implicitly believed Zinoviev's forecast of an early world revolution. In the federations, the Ukrainians, Lithuanians, and Russians were dominant. The cartoonist's cliché of the Communist as an exotic-looking, oddly dressed character goes back to this period. It is a highly misleading symbol today.

Hardly had the two rival parties set up shop in Chicago, when they were hit by the nation-wide "red scare" of late 1919 and early 1920. Under instructions from Attorney General A. Mitchell Palmer, leaders and headquarters of radical groups all over the United States were seized. The raids began on November 7, and the Communists found their parties banned on January 20, 1920. They remained illegal for nearly two years, until December 16, 1921. But meanwhile, efforts to merge the two rival groups under Comintern control were successful. This was a far from easy task. Moscow sent as its representative Joseph Pogány, a Hungarian who had been among Béla Kun's aides during the short-lived Budapest Bolshevik regime. Pogány operated in the United States under the name John Pepper. On May 26, 1923, Pepper unburdened himself in *The Worker* as to the difficulties of keeping "this modern Babel together in a party," made up of no less than sixteen foreign-language federations, each complete with leaders, committees, and newspapers.

For about two years, the Communist Party continued its existence illegally. It maintained affiliation with the Comintern, while its legal counterpart, the quickly organized Workers Party, did not officially belong to the Communist International. When the ban was lifted, the Workers Party became the official United States section of the Comintern, and it continued to exist under that label. The Communist International had been cold-shouldered by the Socialist Party, whose leader, Eugene V. Debs, characterized Moscow's twenty-one-point program as "ridiculous, arbitrary and autocratic." He said, "They want to commit us to a policy of armed insurrection." When the Communists broke away from the Socialists, they took the majority of the membership with them. But, like Communist parties everywhere, the American party suffered a serious decline during the 1920's.

In 1921, William Z. Foster secretly became a Communist. He had become prominent in the revolutionary trade-union movement. The Communists saw an asset in his background and experience, and he seemed to believe that Communist backing might help him in his fight against Samuel Gompers, head of the American Federation of Labor.

William Zebulon Foster, the ex-hobo who three times ran for United States President on the Communist Party ticket, was born on February

25, 1881, at Taunton, Massachusetts. When he was seven years old, his family moved to Philadelphia. There he earned his first pennies as a paper boy; and, when he was eleven, he took care of a studio and ran errands for a down-at-the-heels sculptor.

No one can accuse Foster of being a labor theoretician. He came to be a professional revolutionary the hard way. After three years in the lead-filled air of a type foundry, he took a job in a factory that produced fertilizer. The dead carcasses of horses and other animals were boiled and their bones ground to dust, and the workers were constantly exposed to disease and pulverized bone. After three years of this work, Foster developed tuberculosis.

Three years of sea air cleared up his lungs. These were adventure-filled years that took Foster as a seaman to the four corners of the globe, to nearly every major port of Europe, Asia, and Africa. This period in Foster's life and his subsequent odyssey as a transient laborer on the American mainland might have inspired a Jack London to write a shelfful of adventure stories. After a brief and unsatisfactory stay as an agricultural worker in Florida, William Foster became a streetcar motor-man on New York's Third Avenue Line in 1901. He was, as he recalls it, fired because of his union activity. He joined the Socialist Party but was expelled in 1909 because he advocated violence.

We find him next in Echo, Texas, as cook in a tough railroad yard. In 1904, he claimed a homestead in the beautiful and rugged mountain country of Oregon. While working the homestead, the twenty-five-year-old Foster still did odd jobs around logging camps and railroad lines.

After three years of futile attempts to make a living from the barren mountain soil, he sold his claim. Then he became a shepherd. He had little taste for the loneliness of a shepherd on a remote mountain range. But he picked the 1907 lambing season, when the sheep had been driven back to their home ranches. When the spring season was over, he joined a railroad grading team on the northern bank of the Columbia River in the state of Washington. Two years later, he was digging sewers in Spokane, and it was there that he became an organizer for the International Workers of the World, the IWW.

Foster never had much of a taste for mining work. But, in the spring of 1909, the IWW asked him to try to organize the Coeur d'Alene Mines in Idaho. He was a miner for four weeks, that is, until the company forced him to leave. Union work, syndicalism, had taken hold of his imagination. He had seen too much barefaced exploitation, too much callousness on the part of employers, to be able to quit organizing work. In 1910, he participated in a Budapest Anarchist Conference. In the summer of 1912, he became a canvasman with a tent show of actors who were playing Indiana and Idaho. While traveling with the troupe, he wrote a pamphlet on syndicalism.

Foster finally settled down in Chicago and founded the Syndicalist League of North America. While continuing syndicalist agitation, he worked as a brakeman on railroads running west out of Chicago. He was connected with railroads, in one way or another, for ten years. His observations of the independent spirit that marks railroad workers are based on close and long study. He continued to read and write a lot, while working during the day as a railroad-car inspector. It was minute work, and finally his eyes gave way. For nearly three years he lived in constant fear that he might go blind. At last, an operation restored his eyesight completely.

As a transient worker and IWW organizer, he traveled for sixteen years, hobo-fashion, on trains all over the United States. He still recalls his numerous encounters with brakemen who hunted hoboes off the trains. And he believes that organized American labor owes much to the aggressive spirit of the floating laborers who traveled the rails and who formed the nucleus of the old IWW. As a former packinghouse worker, Foster organized an AFL union in this field during the war. He transformed the Syndicalist League into the Trade Union Educational League when he joined the Communist Party. He led an unsuccessful, widely publicized steel strike in 1919, and his league had been weakened by the general wave of antilabor, antiradical sentiment in the nation.

In 1921, William Z. Foster went to Moscow, where he attended a conference of the newly founded Red Labor International. His first important contact among the Russian leaders was A. Lozovsky, who then headed the Labor International and who today is prominent in the Soviet Foreign Ministry. While in Moscow, Foster became a Communist. He kept this affiliation secret, so that his Trade Union Educational League would not be compromised. In August, 1922, the underground Communist Party held a secret meeting in the woods near Bridgeman, Michigan. Foster came from Chicago to address the meeting on its second day and to outline plans for Communist infiltration into the trade-union movement.

His extensive trade-union background was the basis of Foster's later prominence in the party. The Red Labor International was at that time establishing branches in all parts of the world. Foster's Trade Union Educational League was chosen to function as the International's American branch and subsequently had Russian-furnished funds at its disposal. Foster's prominence in Communist Party affairs soon brought him into serious and long conflict with its official leader, the ambitious and single-minded Charles E. Ruthenberg. For six years, until Ruthenberg's death in 1927, the Communist Party was torn by intrigues between the Foster and Ruthenberg factions. An interminable seesawing went on, which caused Moscow and successive Comintern representatives to the American party no end of trouble. Woven into real or artificial theoretical differences between the two groups, the Foster-Ruthenberg struggle for power provided for endless debates, recriminations, manifestoes, convention strategies, and cables to Moscow.

The parallels between American Communist policies during the early 1920's and the period following World War II are striking. In both instances, the postwar economic readjustments spurred Communist activities. Particularly after world communism began to apply its Second Strategy (the first time the "united front" slogan was used on a globe-wide scale), its activities developed along lines that are in use today. Prior to the 1924 presidential election, the Communists followed Comintern instructions to create a Labor Party in the United States. This slogan was again introduced prior to the 1948 elections, when the atmosphere for a third party was also regarded as favorable.

In 1923 and 1924, the Communist Party sought to affiliate with the Farmer-Labor Party of Robert La Follette. Shortly before the St. Paul Convention in June of 1924, which was to nominate a presidential candidate, the Farmer-Labor organ, the *Minnesota Union Advocate*, said in an editorial on May 24 that the Communists, "closely organized, and highly disciplined as a political party" were "carrying on their intrigues and plots to control." The Communists did, in fact, control the St. Paul Convention by means of a highly ingenious strategy on the selection of delegates and the organization of committees, and through preparation of motions. But La Follette did not ally himself with the St. Paul meeting. Instead, he accepted the support of a Cleveland Conference for Progressive Political Action. The Communists, urged by Moscow, had decided, in any case, that La Follette was not a good choice after all. They speedily dissolved the newly born National Farmer-Labor Party

and selected their own campaign ticket, with Foster as presidential
candidate.

The 1924 election brought La Follette five million votes. Foster polled
33,361. According to Benjamin Gitlow, who ran for vice-president and
who later broke with the Communist Party, Moscow furnished a special
$50,000 fund for the campaign.

FOSTER'S "UNDERGROUND ORGANIZATION"

William Z. Foster, the defeated presidential candidate, not only faced
the internal party obstacle represented by Secretary-General Charles E.
Ruthenberg, but also growing anti-Communist sentiment inside the labor
unions. This, too, is in striking parallel to conditions that developed after
World War II, when the Congress of Industrial Organizations (CIO)
went through an upsurge of opposition to Communist activities. In 1925,
the position of Foster's Trade Union Educational League had become so
precarious that its members no longer dared to reveal their Communist
loyalties. Foster wrote in the June, 1925, issue of the *Workers' Monthly*
that his League had become "an underground organization in nearly
every trade union in the country." Shortly afterward, the *Daily Worker*
took cognizance of the weakening of Communist influence in the unions.
Communists were being expelled at a mounting rate, and the party's
organ said, "Our fight against expulsion must be a flexible attitude." It
told Communists that they "must be prepared to deny" their party loyalties, "rather than be expelled from the unions."

In spite of these and other ingenious stratagems, Communist popularity
was declining seriously. This was due only partly to the Foster-Ruthenberg
feud, which had a demoralizing influence in those strata of the rank and
file which were aware of it. The years of prosperity were marked by an
ebbing of Communist influence throughout the world. In the United States,
whence prosperity seemed to spring, this trend was particularly marked.
At the time of the Workers Party's official affiliation with the Comintern
in 1923, it boasted a membership of 6,500. Its election propaganda
boosted this figure to 8,500 a year later. The mid-twenties slump brought
membership down to 4,000 in 1925 and 2,300 in 1926. It climbed slowly
during the following years and jumped considerably during the depression period.

The Comintern's Sixth World Congress, which inaugurated the extremist-revolutionary strategy, was of decisive importance to the American Communists. After Ruthenberg's death in 1927, Jay Lovestone took up the anti-Foster gantlet. At the 1928 Comintern Congress, Foster finally won out. He ran for president again the same year. The Comintern appointed a special commission, headed by Vyacheslav M. Molotov, to settle once and for all the rift in the Communist Party of the United States. Lovestone and his group were eventually expelled, but it was Earl Browder, not Foster, whom Moscow made head of the party. The Comintern gave very specific instructions as to the future line the United States party should take. Years later, Alexander Bittelman, the party's historian and Foster's outstanding adviser on theoretical matters, said, in a pamphlet entitled *Milestones in the History of the Communist Party,* that, during the party's internal crisis of the late 1920's, "the Comintern did interfere; there can be no doubt of that. And it is fortunate that it did."

But the Comintern's decisions not only cut the Gordian knot of the intraparty rivalries; it also created the extremist-revolutionary pattern that made the Communists into vociferous opponents of President Roosevelt's initial New Deal policies.

INSTRUCTIONS FROM STALIN

In May, 1929, American Communist delegates to the Comintern received detailed instructions from Joseph Stalin himself. With the authority that undivided control in the Russian government and the Communist International had given him, Stalin said:

"I consider the Communist Party of the United States one of the Communist parties to which history has given decisive tasks from the point of view of the world revolutionary movement. The revolutionary crisis has not yet reached the United States, but we already have knowledge of numerous facts which suggest that it is approaching. It is necessary that the American Communist Party should be capable of meeting the moment of crisis fully equipped to take the direction of future class wars in the United States. You must prepare for that, comrades, with all your strength and with every means; you must constantly improve and bolshevize the American Communist Party. You must forge real revolutionary cadres and leaders of the proletariat who will be capable of leading the millions of American workers toward the revolutionary class wars."

These instructions opened a period that, from the point of view of America's Communists, was filled with both success and excitement. The "united front" efforts abandoned. Foster's American branch of the Red Labor International was re-formed in 1929 into the Trade Union Unity League (just as there developed the Workers' Unity League in Canada, and corresponding organizations wherever Communists were active in the labor movement). The economic depression was reaching its peak. Unemployment figures mounted. On March 6, 1930, Communist parties throughout the world organized their dramatic "hunger marches."

The American Communist Party demonstrated violently on New York's Union Square. Foster, Robert Minor, and Israel Amter were sentenced to six months' imprisonment, which they spent in the New York penitentiaries on Welfare Island, Riker's Island, and Hart's Island. The United States Communist Party organized the unemployed councils throughout the nation. "Hunger marches" to Washington were staged in 1931 and 1932.

Membership figures mounted. The party had some 9,000 members when the depression began in 1929. By 1933, as Roosevelt entered the White House, this figure had nearly doubled. The party was becoming more and more radical in its approach, in accordance with the resolutions of the Comintern's American Commission. Molotov, speaking for this commission, had told the Tenth Conference of the Comintern's executive committee that United States Communists had been urged to create "conditions of real Bolshevik development of the party and a reinforcement of its authority among the working masses."

The extremist-revolutionary Third Strategy was expressed with frankness and clarity in William Z. Foster's book *Toward a Soviet America*. There, in 1932, he outlined a blueprint for a Communist government of the United States, as follows:

"The American Soviet government will be organized along the lines of the Russian Soviets. The American Soviet government will join with the other Soviet governments in a world Soviet Union. The American Soviet government will be the dictatorship of the proletariat."

Foster specified that "in the early stages of the revolution, even before the seizure of power, the workers will organize Red Guards." He also said that "under the dictatorship of the proletariat, all the capitalist parties— Republicans, Democrats, Progressives, Socialists, etc.—will be liquidated,

the Communist Party alone functioning as the Party of the toiling masses."
According to Foster, "the establishment of an American Soviet government will mark the birth of real democracy in the United States." He
characterized "the right to vote and all the current talk about democracy"
as "only so many screens to hide the capitalist autocracy and make it more
palatable to the masses."

Foster had hardly finished his book, when he stumped the country on
a series of several hundred speeches. He was running for president on
the Communist ticket, just as he had done in 1924 and 1928. On September 8, two months before the elections, he suffered a heart attack. He had
to rest for five months. But he recovered well, although he remained
conscious of his weak heart from then on.

FOR AN AMERICAN LABOR PARTY

The Seventh Comintern Congress enabled the American Communists
after 1934 to offer their "united front" efforts to liberals and labor
groups backing President Roosevelt's New Deal. Above all, the idea of an
American Labor Party, which had been dead since the abortive Farmer-
Labor Party experiment, was revived. The extremist period had been used
for militant efforts in trade unions and among unemployed. In January,
1935, the Communists decided to merge these efforts into a new channel.
Stalin had proposed in 1928 that the American party should "concentrate its attention on the work in the trade unions, on organizing the
unorganized, etc., and in this way lay the basis for the practical realization of the slogan of a broad Labor Party organized from below."

Earl Browder told the American party early in 1935 that the time had
come to do something about the Labor Party project. It had, of course,
been impossible to push the idea during the extremist-revolutionary
period. The "united front" strategy opened new vistas. But Browder
expressed official Communist caution, "In this early stage of the development (toward a Labor Party), our attitude is to be directed towards
helping to determine in advance what kind of form this movement will
take, so that we become an active factor in determining what will be the
result." The Communist Party, according to Browder, was nevertheless
not going "to take the initiative in the organization of a Labor Party on a
national scale." Instead, it closely observed trends throughout the United

States, ready to help organize a new party wherever it emerged on a regional basis.

A year later, prior to the 1936 elections, the Communists extended their project to include not only labor but farm elements. They were particularly anxious to weld the Farmer-Labor Party in the state of Washington into a nation-wide organization. But, when Browder talked to the Communist central committee on June 17, 1937, he had to admit that their hopes had been premature. He said, nevertheless that "the Farmer-Labor Party, conceived as the American equivalent of the People's Front in France, is taking shape and growing in the womb of the disintegrating two old parties." This complex metaphor was followed by another: "The wavelets of the relatively small Farmer-Labor Party movement are only apparently falling, are in reality merging with a great tidal wave of complete reconstruction of American politics."

All this was wishful thinking. It had reality only in the strongly Communist-supported American Labor Party in New York. There, Congressman Vito Marcantonio emerged as the outstanding political figure. Although not associated with the Communist Party, he had previously achieved prominence as head of the International Labor Defense, an American expression of the legal aid societies organized by Communists throughout the world, following the pattern established by the International Red Aid.

The whole program of establishing a third party—or of influencing the Democratic Party with the threat of a third party—was interrupted with the outbreak of the war, and the Nazi-Soviet Pact of 1939. The loss in prestige and backing that the Communist Party experienced in America were, on a relative scale, second only to that which it suffered in Great Britain; conditions in France did not permit a measuring of the change.

Earl Browder had, ever since he had become Communist secretary-general, displayed a personal quality for extreme expressions of Comintern policy. During the "hunger marches," his orders to Communist-led unemployed brigades created friction with non-Communist groups of unemployed. When the Russian-German Pact forced Communist parties throughout the world into a painful somersault, Browder used extreme phrases in expressing the official Comintern view. Foster, in his pamphlet *What's What about the War?*, published in 1940, said merely, "This is an imperialist war. It originates in the very structure of the capitalist system." That was the official argument used by all spokesmen of the Communist International. But Browder, in May, 1941, went so far as to say, "The new Roosevelt course is essentially for America the same direction which Hitler gave for Germany in 1933."

Consequently, the American Communists alienated many sincere anti-Nazi supporters. Throughout the United States, the party organized "The Yanks Are Not Coming!" demonstrations. "I did not raise my boy to be a soldier for Wall Street" was the title of one propaganda tract against the anti-Nazi war. Communist pickets marched in front of the White House, denouncing President Roosevelt's policy of aid for isolated Britain. The draft, Lend-Lease arrangements, and appropriations for national defense were denounced by the Communists just as vigorously as by the ultra-right, which found its expression in the America First movement.

THE ROAD TO TEHERAN

After Germany's invasion of Russia, American Communists added two words to their earlier slogan. It now read, "The Yanks are not coming too late!" The Communists completely endorsed the "no-strike" pledge of American labor. In due course, the slogan in favor of a second front was launched. The Communist Party officially cut its ties with the Communist International in November, 1940, so that its members, no longer directly linked to Moscow, would not have to register as agents of a foreign power. Internal United States affairs found the Communists affable and co-operative. Browder became the exponent of a super-"united front" effort. The height of this ideological climb was reached after the Teheran Conference of President Roosevelt, Premier Stalin, and Prime Minister Churchill in December, 1943. There, it appeared, spheres of influence were agreed upon which fitted the interests of the Soviet Union.

Browder, in his book *Teheran*, added further emphasis to the need of cooperation among Americans of all political and economic backgrounds. A month after the Teheran Conference, Browder said, "We must be prepared to give the hand of cooperation and fellowship to everyone who fights for the realization of this coalition. If J. P. Morgan supports this coalition and goes down the line for it, I, as a Communist, am prepared to clasp his hand on that and join with him to realize it." Not only had Browder thus committed himself to shake hands with the corpse of a Wall Street banker of international renown (Morgan had died shortly before Browder's speech), but he had also gone to an extreme that was to cost him dearly.

Throughout this tense love affair between the Communist Party and American capitalism, William Z. Foster had bided his time and spoken softly. If he thought that Earl Browder had become too big for his breeches, he certainly did not let the public know it. There may also have been a remnant of fondness for Browder in Foster. Had he not shown Browder the ropes of the revolutionary labor movement? And had Browder not consistently and self-effacingly stuck to Foster throughout the trying years of battle against Ruthenberg and Lovestone? Indeed, he had. But Moscow's endorsement of Browder for the American party's highest post had been a disappointment to Foster. And the rules of the political jungle, which apply to political organization everywhere and of every ideological hue, are stronger than sentimental memories. This is not written here in facetious speculation. It is based on the testimony of people who were part of the Foster-Browder controversy and who had occasion to hear Foster's often quite unguarded comments on the attitude of his one-time protégé.

EXIT BROWDER

Browder had stuck his neck out, and Foster was looking for a handy ax. Such an instrument of political execution came in the May, 1945, issue of *Les Cahiers du Communisme,* theoretical monthly of the French Communist Party. Jacques Duclos, who had just returned from a visit to Moscow, sharply criticized the temporary replacement of the United States Communist Party with a Communist Political Association. But Duclos did more than criticize the dissolution of the party. He lashed into Browder's forecast of "long-term class peace in the United States." It appeared from the Duclos article that Browder had indeed gone beyond the official strategy of world communism. What was meant to apply only throughout the period of the Sixth Strategy of win-the-war unity had been projected into the future by Browder's speeches and writings. He had no business to anticipate strategy. It was embarrassing and confusing all around.

The Browder affair was vitally important because it affected not only the United States. The statements of the American party leader had been widely translated by Communist parties throughout the world and had been particularly influential in Latin America and the English-speaking countries. Browder tried in vain to take the sting out of Duclos's criticism. When the *Daily Worker* of New York reprinted the Paris article,

Browder introduced it with contrite remarks. He noted that it had been "clear at all times that the end of the war in Europe would require a fundamental review of all problems of American Marxists." The Duclos criticism was a very helpful thing, Browder said, since it reflected the "opinion of European Marxists in relation to America, and thus demands our most respectful consideration."

All this respectfulness got Browder nowhere. Foster had his ax ready, and he was using it. Later events, particularly Browder's trip to Moscow in 1946 and his position as official United States representative of Soviet publishing houses, suggest that Foster pushed the "affaire Browder" beyond the line of a severe reprimand which the top leadership of world communism may have had in mind. The phrase "Browderism" was created and was linked with such vituperation as is usually used to describe "Trotskyism" and similar heresies. The Communist national committee resolved to expel Browder from the party for "gross violation of Party discipline and decisions, for active opposition to the political line and leadership of our Party, for developing factional activity and for betraying the principles of Marxism-Leninism and deserting to the side of the class enemy—American monopoly capital."

Those were harsh words. But they were hardly as violent as comment from Communist leaders in other parts of the world. Blas Roca, secretary-general of the Cuban Popular Socialist Party, told his party that its North American counterpart had discovered "a malignant tumor, which calls itself Browder." The worst that Foster ever found to say about Browder was that he had been guilty of "idiocy" in advocating a postwar "no-strike" policy, that he had committed "a monstrous crime against the working class and the democratic forces of the world" in considering American foreign policy progressive, that he displayed "lickspittle servility towards American Big Business" and "tailism" (a new word, meaning that he was tailing after the policy of the Truman administration).

CLASS WAR IN THE UNITED STATES

The American Communist Party had cleared the decks of Browder's "right opportunism." It reverted to the principle of class war in the United States. The ousting of Browder had been a symbol of a change in world Communist strategy, and now the ground was laid for a new Communist offensive in the United States. Browder's exit did not weaken the party. He carried with him no substantial part of the membership. True, there were some later expulsions. In 1946, a number of prominent and veteran party members were expelled, because of their "semi-Trotskyism and unprincipled Leftist adventurism." The party stated that it was entering the battle for decisive influence in American domestic affairs while fighting internally against "Left deviations, but also against Right opportunism and all remnants of Browder revisionism."

Party activity increased enormously, using the channels it had developed during more than a decade. Foster's Trade Union Unity League had been disbanded after the Seventh Comintern Congress decided on the "united front" policy of infiltration. Communist trade unionists entered the AFL. And, when John L. Lewis launched the CIO in 1935 by breaking with the AFL's William Green, he had the support of trained and energetic Communist organizers and agitators. These skillful and devoted party representatives in the CIO unions played a leading role in extending the influence of the CIO. They were also active in the CIO's aggressive Political Action Committee, which proved successful in the 1944 elections but was unable to stem the tide to the right in 1946.

In 1946, an anti-Communist rebellion inside the CIO tested the adaptability of Foster's representatives. The veterans among them could have recalled Foster's 1925 instructions to deny their Communist affiliations. At a Conference of Progressives in Chicago, CIO President Philip Murray charged that a "well-organized and financed conspiracy" was trying "to undermine and even actually destroy the labor movement." In November, the CIO resolved at its eighth annual convention at Atlantic City to "resent and reject efforts of the Communist Party or any other parties and their adherents to interfere in the affairs of the CIO." Throughout the CIO unions, people known by their actions as Communists endorsed this resolution. They were leaning with the trend, like palms in the wind, while seeking to hold their ground. The fight between Communists and anti-Communists for control of American labor had begun.

At the same time, Communist activity among racial and religious minorities was increased. Henry Winston, who had been the leader of the Young Communist League before it was replaced by an organization known as American Youth for Democracy, told the Communist national committee in February, 1946, that its National Negro Congress could look back on ten years of sustained effort. He was particularly pleased to report that Communist efforts to operate inside the respectable National

Association for the Advancement of Colored People had borne fruit. But American Negro Communists were continuing their decade-long disagreement over a policy favoring the right of Negro self-determination in the Black Belt (which has often been interpreted as an application of the Soviet system of autonomous Republics, hardly suited to American conditions). Doxey A. Wilkerson regarded a revival of the self-determination slogan as "theoretically incorrect and therefore disastrous." Others maintained, with more or less caution, that what was good enough for the Uzbeks in their self-determined Soviet Republic of Uzbekistan ought to be agreeable to American Negroes in the Black Belt. Francis Franklin, writing in *Political Affairs* in May, 1946, foresaw "total reorganization of Southern county and state governments in such forms as to guarantee majority representation to Negroes in all departments of government, including police and militia, in all areas of Negro majority, a reorganization which will require redrawing of electoral and county lines."

Communist work among American Jews was outlined by a special commission of the United States Communist Party in October, 1946. Conscious of the double resistance against communism among Jews—from Zionists because of Communist opposition to Palestine as a Jewish homeland, from orthodox as well as reform-liberal leaders because of communism's atheist traditions—the commission outlined a fight against "bourgeois-nationalist pressures" and "bourgeois assimilationism," which it considered a "reflection of Anglo-Saxon race supremacy 'theories' of American imperialism."

The Communist opening gun for the 1948 elections was fired by William Z. Foster in an article in the February, 1947, issue of *Political Affairs*. He reviewed Communist experiences with Senator La Follette in the Farmer-Labor Party in 1924. His penetrating and highly interesting analysis was followed by an endorsement of the work done in the late 1930's and early 1940's by such organizations as the CIO's Political Action Committee, the National Citizens Political Action Committee, and the American Labor Party of New York State. (Communists had been urged to vote for the ALP's Vito Marcantonio during the 1946 elections.)

All these activities, Foster noted, should be regarded merely as the groundwork for the creation of a third party. He said that the Communist Party "must play a much more important one in the 1948 political struggle and in the building of the third party. Our Communist party must understand that the formation of such a labor party will represent a gigantic political advance for the American working class. We must, therefore, make the question of building the new party our major task and leave no stone unturned for its realization." Foster noted that "the only possible chance (a faint one at best) to get a progressive candidate from the Democratic Party leaders will be precisely by holding over their heads the threat of a new party."

SPIES

Canada had its red spy scare in late 1945 and early 1946. The United States heard revelations regarding Communist underground activities in late 1946 and in 1947. It was discovered that a German-born Austrian, Gerhart Eisler, had been Comintern representative to the American Communist Party for many years. Witnesses before the Committee on Un-American Activities stated that Eisler had run the American Communist Party on instructions from Moscow. This was, of course, not news to anyone who knew that Moscow had practiced this technique of liaison with the faraway American party ever since John Pepper, alias Joseph Pogány (who was shot in Russia in 1936), made the trip across the Atlantic back in 1923.

Pepper had been succeeded by a Russian representative known as S. Gusev, P. Green, or Drabkin. Gusev took part in a conference of American Communists in 1925. He has been identified as a former Red Army general. From 1926 to 1927, the Comintern was represented by a former chairman of the Finnish Communist Party, Y. Sirola, who used the name of Miller. A sincere and fanatical German Communist, Arthur Ewert, came to the United States in 1927. He operated under the names of Brown, Braun, and Berger. In 1935, he was arrested and imprisoned by Brazilian police in Rio de Janeiro. His mind broke under the years of strain which conspiracy and imprisonment had imposed on him. In 1929, British Communist leader Harry Pollitt participated in the American Party's March conference. Philip Dengel, a German, was in the United States at the same time.

In 1929 and 1930, a prominent member of the Russian Communist Party, B. Mikhailov, operated in the United States under the name of George Williams. He was presumably succeeded by Gerhart Eisler (a brother of Ruth Fischer, alias Elfriede Friedländer, nee Eisler). The United States Federal Bureau of Investigation advised the Congressional committee on October 16, 1946, that Eisler had been known as "Edwards" when he served as Comintern representative in the United States from about 1933 to about 1938. During this period, the FBI explained, "He was responsible for and instrumental in the determination of American Communist policy, and the control and direction of American Communist operations."

Eisler had arrived in the United States in 1941 by way of France and Trinidad, ostensibly as a refugee. In the United States, he wrote under the name of Hans Berger for the *Daily Worker* and *Political Affairs*. The FBI statement added that Eisler's "primary contacts in the United States have been important Communist functionaries, many of whom are strongly suspected of involvement in Soviet espionage operations." On June 27, 1947, Eisler was sentenced to a year in jail and $1,000 for contempt of Congress. On August 15, he was found guilty of passport fraud. "It was a fair trial," Eisler commented, "on a very unfair indictment."

The United States Department of Justice, through the Federal Bureau of Investigation, is charged with safeguarding of American security. When William Z. Foster spoke at a clandestine Communist meeting in the Michigan woods, back in 1922, Justice Department agents were among the audience. A particularly mysterious affair was the disappearance early in June, 1937, of Juliet Stuart Poyntz. Miss Poyntz, a good-looking college-bred American woman, had once been known as American communism's Joan of Arc. She broke with Foster and is said to have entered the Soviet secret service in 1935. Eisler's sister has written that Miss Poyntz was Eisler's "ex-girl friend."

When Juliet Stuart Poyntz left her home at 353 West 57th Street back in 1937, she never returned. No trace of her was ever found. Carlo Tresca, a prominent Italian anarchist, who named a Soviet agent allegedly connected with the disappearance of Miss Poyntz, was shot to death on Fifth Avenue in 1943. His murder was never solved. There is a possibility that Miss Poyntz furnished information to the FBI, but this cannot be confirmed.

One of the most colorful stories of an American in the service of Soviet military espionage is the episode of Nicholas Dozenberg, who for eight years worked as a railroad mechanic before he was discovered by espionage talent scouts. Dozenberg was sent to Romania, ostensibly as representative of an American photographic equipment firm. His real task was to photograph Romanian military and other strategic installations. He succeeded so amazingly well that high Romanian officials cooperated with him in his various operations. On one occasion, he had the use of King Carol's private airplane to take pictures of Bucharest and its environs.

While Gerhart Eisler was prevented from leaving the United States for Germany, another reputed Comintern agent, Alfred Kantorowicz, was able to return to Germany. He had been granted an immigration visa by a special Washington board of appeals on April 17, 1945. This had been done, the United States Department of State announced on February 13, 1947, "over the repeated objections of the visa division and the unanimously unfavorable recommendation of the inter-departmental visa committee on which the State Department and the FBI were represented."

Kantorowicz, whose writing appeared not only in the weekly magazine, *German-American* (where Eisler's articles were also printed), but also in such a respectable weekly as *The Nation,* had originally been on the editorial staff of the *Vossische Zeitung,* a Berlin daily. He went to Paris after the rise of Hitlerism and was instrumental in founding the League of German Writers in Exile. Kantorowicz received funds to establish a library in Paris and became best known for his forceful dramatization of the book burnings of the Nazi government. After his arrival in the United States, he found employment with the Columbia Broadcasting System. From April, 1942, to April, 1943, he was a foreign news reporter in the Public Affairs division of CBS. He left temporarily, presumably to legalize his immigration by reentering the United States from Canada. He returned to CBS in October, 1943, and left its employ in September, 1946, shortly before he returned to Germany. In 1947, he was in Berlin, where he helped to organize the Aufbau-Verlag, which specializes in publishing Communist and pro-Communist authors.

The report of the Canadian Royal Commission specified that the documents removed by Igor Gouzenko from the Soviet Embassy in Ottawa indicated the presence of Soviet secret agents in the United States. Lieutenant Colonel Peter S. Motinov noted the following in his personal notebook under the date of June 12, 1945:

"Debouz is to tie up with Berger and depending on the circumstances is to make a proposal about work for us or for the corporation. Contact in Washington with Debouz's person. To work out arrangements for a meeting and to telegraph. To give out 600 dollars. If Debouz should be unable to go to U.S.A. then there should be a letter from Debouz to Berger containing a request to assist the person delivering the letter to Berger."

"Debouz" was the cover name for Fred Rose, the Communist member of the Canadian Parliament, who was sentenced to six years' imprisonment on June 20, 1946, having been found guilty of conspiring to give secret information to Soviet secret agents. "Berger" was the cover name of Arthur Steinberg, a United States scientist who did not cooperate with Soviet agents. "Corporation" was the cover name of the Communist Party.

THE TWO WITCZAKS

The Canadian report also refers to the presence in the United States of a Soviet agent whose passport was running out, and for whom the Canadian Communist leader Sam Carr apparently managed to get a new passport. The Soviet agent entered the United States in 1938 under the name of Ignacy Samuel Witczak. He was using a passport that had been collected by Communist agents during the Spanish civil war from a Polish-born Canadian volunteer whose name really was Witczak. The real Ignacy Witczak had been told in Spain that his passport had been destroyed during a bombing attack. He returned to Canada in 1939.

The phony Witczak went to Los Angeles, attended the University of Southern California, and later became an instructor there. Apparently through bribery in the Canadian passport office, records for Witczak's passport were changed and photographs of the Soviet agent substituted. The agent was placed under surveillance by the United States Federal Bureau of Investigation, and he and his family soon afterward left Los Angeles.

Another link to the United States that was uncovered during the Canadian affair came in the case of Hermina Rabinowitch, an employee of the International Labor Office in Montreal who had previously worked in Switzerland, at the Geneva International Labor Office. The records of the Canadian Commission indicated that a group of persons in Geneva was in the employ of the Soviet military intelligence service, whose Moscow headquarters address, Znamensky 19, was somewhat carelessly mentioned in letters written to Miss Rabinowitch in Canada.

These events, which took place in the summer of 1944, were apparently prompted by the difficulty experienced by the Soviet secret service in supplying its Swiss agents with funds. Switzerland was surrounded by German- and Italian-controlled territory, and even transfers from the United States had to be made under cover. Miss Rabinowitch, who somewhat vaguely thought that her actions might help her aged parents in Soviet-occupied Lithuania, was used by the Soviet Embassy to transfer $10,000 to Switzerland. Difficulties were envisaged by the Soviet agents, if money had to be transferred from Canada to the United States through regular channels. Documents furnished by Gouzenko suggested liaison between Soviet military intelligence officers in Ottawa and Washington. One such document stated, "We consider if there is to be a transfer of money, then the money must be transferred Washington and hand it over to Hermina in New York, as it is dangerous to cross the border with such sum. For one thing our banks are not releasing American dollars."

It was then arranged that Hermina Rabinowitch was to meet an unidentified man, presumably a person in the employ of Soviet military intelligence in the United States, at a New York hotel. This was done. Ten thousand dollars were turned over to Miss Rabinowitch, who arranged for transfer of the money to Switzerland.

Lieutenant Colonel Peter S. Motinov, whose notebook furnished the Canadian authorities with much material and who had flown to Moscow with uranium samples, arrived in the United States in November, 1945. He went to Washington to join the staff of the Soviet Embassy as military attaché. It was shortly after Igor Gouzenko left the Ottawa Embassy and approached Canadian authorities, that Motinov transferred his residence from Ottawa to Washington. On March 2, 1946, the Canadian Commission made its first interim report, which stated that Lieutenant Colonel Motinov had been one of Colonel Zabotin's "active assistants in this work" of "obtaining secret and confidential information." And it was in March, 1946, that Motinov suddenly left his Washington post, which he had entered only about four months earlier. The Soviet Embassy in Washington declined late in 1946 to discuss Lieutenant Colonel Motinov's whereabouts.

The United States Civil Service Commission announced on July 17, 1947, that some 811 federal employees had been found disloyal within a nine-month period beginning July 1, 1946. Shortly before this announcement, the Department of State discharged ten employees for reasons of security, including members of its Intelligence Division. A federal court jury in Washington found Carlo Aldo Marzani guilty of defrauding the government by concealing his Communist Party affiliations. Eugene Dennis, general secretary of the United States Communist Party, was convicted by a Washington district court of contempt of the Congressional Committee on Un-American Activities. Dennis chose a year in jail and a $100 fine rather than answer the committee's questions.

Louis Budenz, who left the Communist Party of the United States in 1945 after ten years' membership and editorial work on the *Daily Worker*, told the House committee investigating Un-American Activities on April 3, 1946, that each member of the American Communist Party was "a potential spy against the United States." Major General William J. Donovan, wartime head of the Office of Strategic Services, stated on February 25, 1946, that the Soviet Union had "the biggest stockpile of information in the world." This, he said, was "due to the wide dispersion of Russian agents and to the strong fifth column which Russia maintains in foreign countries, including the United States, through the Communist parties."

TARGET FOR TOMORROW

The Soviet Union and the United States of America are the two strongest nations in the world today. It is no more than natural that Communists who look to Moscow for guidance should see in the United States the most serious adversary of the country they consider the first nation to have achieved socialism. Certainly, Communist propaganda and agitation throughout the world presents the United States, or "American imperialism," as the most serious obstacle to the progress of Communist ideas.

When world communism adopted its Seventh Strategy after the end of World War II, it made the United States its target for tomorrow. American Communists are in a vital and strategic position, which enables them to contribute substantially to the realization of Communist aspirations.

CHAPTER 24

Central America: U. S. Back Yard

DURING THE immediate postwar period, the most influential Communist parties in Latin America were those of Cuba, Brazil, and Chile. In these three countries, the Communists achieved representation in national, provincial, or municipal government. Their militant and well-organized political associations became an important factor in the domestic and foreign affairs of these three nations. Although the Brazilian and Chilean parties suffered considerable setbacks in 1947, their influence, particularly in the labor movement, remained profound.

CUBA: SPECTACULAR PROGRESS

The Cuban Communist Party has particular importance because it has served as a Central American headquarters in the past and because it offers theoretical and practical guidance to other parties south of the Rio Grande even after the official dissolution of the Communist International.

Progress made by Cuba's Communists in recent years has been spectacular. Now known as the Popular Socialist Party, the Communists doubled their voting strength during the war years: from 81,255 in 1942, to 124,619 in 1944, and 197,000 in 1946. The party's membership of some 200,000 only partly illustrates its true influence, although, if the United States Communist Party corresponded in size to its Cuban counterpart, it would have 6,000,000 members. Cuba's Communists exercise tight control over the Cuban Confederation of Labor, which is affiliated with the Latin-American Confederation of Labor, in which Communists hold many key positions.

During the years of President Machado's tight and ruthless dictatorship, from 1924 to 1933, Cuba's Communists did not stand a ghost of a chance. When Machado fell, the Communists helped to push him. He was finally forced out by a military revolt of the rank and file, headed by Sergeant

Fulgencio Batista. On September 10, 1933, Dr. Ramón Grau San Martín, professor of physiology at Havana University, became provisional president of Cuba. This was no victory for the Communists. The Grau government sought to quash its opponents on the left as well as on the right. The Communists' most ambitious attempt at unseating Grau came early in March, 1934. The Confederation of Labor announced a general strike, designed to force the government into submission. Grau had resigned.

But there was no peace. In the struggle against Machado, his opponents had learned how to handle bombs and to assassinate political antagonists. They now turned their bombs and guns against the government of Grau's successor, Mendieta. Grau and the Communists were temporarily in the same boat. In March, 1935, there was another general strike. Nearly half a million workers participated. Mendieta's retaliation was fierce. It looked as if another military dictatorship had gained control of Cuba.

Behind six successive Cuban governments stood Colonel Fulgencio Batista, the sergeant who had promoted himself to the rank of colonel. He finally was elected president in October, 1940. Juan Marinello, who today is titular head of the Communist Party, served in Batista's cabinet as minister without portfolio. Marinello, a handsome gray-haired man, is a professor at Havana University. The 1944 elections gave the presidency to Grau San Martín but did not provide him with a clear-cut parliamentary majority. Remembering the strikes and violence that previous administrations had faced, Grau made a deal with the Communists. It was a realistic, even cynical, deal. Both sides gained much from it. Grau had relative labor peace, and the Communists had a chance to strengthen their position as members of the governing coalition.

While Marinello serves in Grau's cabinet as vice-president of the Senate, the Communist Party is headed by Blas Roca. Lázaro Peña represents the party's interests in the Confederation of Labor, of which he is secretary-general. The Cuban party's policy is representative of Communist views and aims throughout Latin America. Thus it is worth close analysis. Communist appeals to nationalist sentiment are combined with violent opposition to the influence of the United States. At the same time, communism throughout Latin America has become the most vocal champion of economic betterment for workers and peasants. The unbalanced postwar economy of most Latin American nations has heightened the appeal of communism to the masses. Among the economic demands expressed by Communists are many genuinely sound and desirable reforms.

The party's third conference evaluated its relations with other organizations and with the government. It "noted with satisfaction" that "the Cuban Labor Confederation, with the orientation and aid given by our party, succeeded in achieving such notable triumphs as the successive general and specific increases in wages, the widening of social legislation to cover the agricultural workers, the subsidy for the harbor workers displaced by the war, etc." The party also expressed its approval of various domestic measures taken by the Grau administration, but was severely critical of its cordial relations with the United States.

Another representative Communist viewpoint was expressed on January 10, 1947, by Anibal Escalante, editor of the lively Havana Communist daily, *Hoy*. Escalante, who assured his readers that he was reflecting "the viewpoint of all the Communists of each of the Latin American countries," said in part:

"The Popular Socialist Party does not follow or serve the foreign policy of the Soviet Union or any other state. It is based on the activities, necessities, and interests of our people, our nation. If we applaud the international politics of the USSR it is because it coincides with the Cuban interest— for a long peace, for the liquidation of fascism to the roots, because the USSR does not recognize superior races or countries, because it has broken with the Franco regime, the foundation of the Falangist conspiracies against our liberties. And the same can be said of each of the other parties of Latin America."

Escalante also wrote that Latin American Communists do not ask for more than what has "already been won in other countries under the leadership of the bourgeoisie . . . no more than has been achieved in other lands, including the United States." If orthodox Marxists should question a Communist policy that ostensibly merely presses toward "bourgeois" aims, the emphasis put by Latin American Communists on nationalist beliefs is even more striking. The third conference of Cuba's Communists in fact went so far as to speak of "the lofty ends imposed by the present needs of our fatherland."

MEXICO: CROSSING THE RUBICON

The Communist International was assured in a report on Mexico before World War II that "the influence of the Communist Party and the Communists is far in excess of the impression one might get." That holds true today. The Mexican Communist Party is a puny group under the leadership of Secretary-General Dionisio Encina, an uninspiring, wide-mouthed man whose deep-set eyes lack the spark of brilliance. The party claims some 25,000 members (a figure that is probably compiled with more optimism than accuracy), and during the 1946 national elections it polled about 40,000 votes.

Founded in 1919, the Mexican Communist Party had a slow beginning. Encina, who was born in 1908 in the state of Zacatecas, worked as a carpenter before he became active as a young Communist. In the 1920's, the party was poor and feeble. In 1925, the Comintern was told by scouts it had sent down from New York that the Mexican Communists had begun to infiltrate into the railway, textile, and oil unions but needed outside help. Although immediate prospects were bleak, Moscow heard that "once the Communist International establishes a strong foothold in Mexico, it shall have, as it were, crossed the Rubicon in the establishment of a mighty Pan American Communist movement."

A Pan American office was subsequently installed at Mexico City, subsidized by Moscow via New York. Still progress was slow. Mexico had gone through a sweeping revolution, back in 1910. The Comintern executive advised Mexican Communists that during the "period of preparation and organization for the proletarian dictatorship," it was advisable to know that "the penetration and entrenchment of North American capitalism in the countries of Central America and South America means the consolidation of the entire capitalist system throughout the American continent." Moscow wrote in 1923, "The workers and peasants government means civil war. But only the proletarian dictatorship can guarantee the victory of the workers and peasants."

This was a large order. The Mexican party could not fill it right away. It had to fight three major obstacles. First, it lacked leaders with mass appeal. Mexico has a tradition of *caudillismo,* of political movements clustering around a colorful chief. It needed a *caudillo.* Second, it could not effectively battle "North American capitalism" and "Yankee imperialism," when its brains in Mexico City were Yankees imported from New York's Communist headquarters. Third, its tactical acrobatics bewildered many potential followers but remained constant in one respect: atheism and anti-Catholicism. Taken all together, these obstacles were too much for the small group of Mexican Communists to overcome.

There was some improvement after the Comintern adopted the "united front" policy in 1935. Two years later, during the presidential elections, an attempt was made to form a Popular Front coalition. The Communist Party hoped to line up the dominant National Revolutionary Party, the Confederation of Mexican Workers, and the Confederation of Mexican Peasants. It had managed to win a number of adherents in these organizations, but in the end its attempt fizzled out.

And then, overnight, Mexican leftist labor got itself a *caudillo*. His name, Vicente Lombardo Toledano, soon became synonymous with that of the Mexican labor movement in particular and with most of Latin-American labor in general. Early in 1936, he became head of the Confederation of Mexican Labor. The very first sentence of its principles and aims, published March 13, 1936, specified, "The Confederation of Mexican Workers is not Communist." The confederation did not "propose to abolish private property in defiance of historic reality." The manifesto continued, "The Confederation of Mexican Workers looks forward, naturally, to a society without exploiters or exploited; but it does not try to play at social revolution, nor to anticipate historic destiny in an absurd and unjustified manner. In the present state of our country's development, the Confederation of Mexican Workers sets itself the task of bettering the economic and moral conditions of the working class, of defending the political, moral and economic independence of the Mexican nation, and of preventing the enthronement of a dictatorial or tyrannical government, which would deprive the people of their social and civil liberties."

The Mexican Confederation could not affiliate with Moscow's Red Labor International, which—in accordance with the "united front" policy—had been dissolved in 1935. It joined the Socialist International Federation of Trade Unions at Amsterdam. In 1938, at a meeting of thirteen Latin American trade unions, Lombardo Toledano became head of the powerful Latin American Labor Confederation, known as CTAL. John L. Lewis, representing the Congress of Industrial Organizations of the United States, attended the meeting. William Green of the American Federation of Labor had turned down the invitation. Lombardo Toledano today is violently opposed to the AFL. In 1946, he went to Moscow and became vice-chairman of the newly created World Federation of Trade Unions, which the AFL shortly afterward described as "a new Red labor union international."

During the 1946 Mexican presidential campaign, Lombardo Toledano told a press conference that the AFL was in partnership with the American business and church groups in an attempt to "sabotage" the Latin American Labor Confederation. Later in the year, the Moscow trade-union publication *Trud* echoed these ideas when it hailed Lombardo Toledano's union organization for its efforts to remove the "yoke of foreign monopolies striving to convert Latin America into one huge colony." *Trud* accused the AFL of defending "the policy of imperialist penetration into the Latin-American countries." For all this agreement on principles between Moscow and Lombardo Toledano, the Mexican labor leader has emphasized that "it would be impossible to have a strong labor movement if labor were affiliated with the Communist Party, or were open only to Communists."

What is the solution to the Lombardo enigma? He is not a Communist; he never attended the Lenin School in Moscow or was in any way officially connected with the Communist International. And yet his policies have certainly coincided with those pursued by the Communist parties throughout Latin America. It seems fair to assume that his loyalties are less to Moscow than they are to himself. But he may well realize that the services of Communist agitators and labor organizers throughout the southern half of the Western Hemisphere are an important part of his federation's machinery. If he were to oppose Communist policies, as the Chilean Socialists have suggested, the Latin American Confederation of Labor would be torn by internal controversy. But the issue of communism is bound to become more important throughout the Latin-American labor movement. Vicente Lombardo Toledano is useful to the Communists. They are useful to him. As long as their interests coincide, it is safe to assume that they will stick together.

The Communist Party of Mexico has followed the over-all policy changes of world communism faithfully. During its First Extraordinary Party Congress, held from March 19 to 24, 1940, at Mexico City, it warned against "extension of the imperialist war into an anti-Soviet war." Earl Browder came down from New York to replace the recalcitrant and inefficient secretary-general, Hernan Laborde, with Enciñas. And only after the Soviet Union was invaded did Mexico's Communists back their country's contribution to the United Nations fight against Nazi Germany and militarist Japan. Less than four months before the German attack on Russia, on March 10, 1941, the central committee of the Mexican

Party stated that it was "only beneficial to the interests of the Yankee bankers that the war be prolonged."

Communist activity in Mexico moved into the international limelight after Leon Trotsky, having been exiled by Stalin, took up residence outside Mexico City. A complex international conspiracy led to the killing of Trotsky in 1943 by a man who identified himself as Frank Jacson. Earlier, an unidentified band had assaulted Trotsky's residence and killed his secretary-bodyguard Robert Sheldon Harte.

Although the details leading up to Trotsky's assassination will probably never become fully public, it is doubtless a fact that "Jacson" was infiltrated into Trotsky's entourage through the machinations of a highly secret international Communist machine. One link in this chain was an American Trotskyist, Sylvia Angelov, who introduced Jacson to a group of French followers of Trotsky. Jacson obtained credentials from this French group, which opened Trotsky's house to him in Mexico.

Jacson became a welcome and trusted member of Trotsky's circle. He used this trust one day by entering Trotsky's home with various weapons hidden under the overcoat he had slung over his arm. When he was alone with Trotsky, he killed him with a pickax. Jacson did not succeed in doing this silently, because Trotsky struggled and cried for help. Jacson was arrested and sent to prison. At the time of his arrest, he was carrying a Canadian passport. It has been asserted that his true identity was Jacques Mornard, a Belgian national, or that he was Salvador Torkov, native of a Slavic eastern European country.

HAITI: UNEXPECTED LUCK

The Communists of Haiti, together with their three million countrymen, had some unexpected luck on August 16, 1946. On that day, the National Constituent Assembly of the all-Negro Caribbean republic voted Dumarsais Estime into office as president. Haiti hadn't had much luck for a century and a half of self-rule, after overthrowing the French colonial government. But the Estime regime went off to a good start. Long-suppressed opposition groups, including the Communists, were permitted to function freely.

Haiti's so-called "Socialist movement," a vain protest against the ultra-autocratic methods used by successive dictatorial regimes, was inspired by the poet Jacques Roumain. After his death, Socialists and Communists tried to operate clandestinely. During its underground period, the Haitian Communist Party was headed by Félix Dorléans Just Constant, a priest of the Episcopal Church, United States Diocese. He was inspired in his work by a desire to reduce the dominant influence of the Roman Catholic Church in Haiti. Louis Budenz, former editor of the New York *Daily Worker*, said in his book, *This Is My Story*, that a member of the United States Communist Party's top leadership had characterized the Haitian minister as "both a zealous Episcopalian and a hardworking Communist."

But, when the Communist Party assumed legality, early in 1946, it seemed to have lost touch with international Communist policies. Félix Dorléans Just Constant began publication of a paper, *Combat*, complete with hammer and sickle on its masthead, and written in the most revolutionary language imaginable. On February 8, the paper said that "the people of Haiti understand at last that communism is the only possible solution." The party violated the cautious policy applied by world communism in predominantly Catholic countries when it asked for "rupture of the concordate with Vatican, and separation of Church and State."

Meanwhile, a left-wing Haitian politician, Max L. Hudicourt, arrived in Haiti from New York. He founded the Popular Socialist Party (which is also the name under which the Communist Party goes in Cuba) and published a program that was in striking contrast to the guillotine language used in *Combat*. The two parties competed for the endorsement of the Cuban Communists. A decision was not long delayed. On February 22, 1946, the Havana Communist paper *Hoy* handed down the judgment, "The Popular Socialist Party of Haiti is based on the principles of Marxism and an immediate program which is conscious of the pressing needs of the Haitian people. The Communist Party of Haiti is filled with infantile concepts, which tend to make it sectarian, and which separate it from the masses."

Consequently, it was the Popular Socialist Party, and not the Communist Party, which got the green light from Havana. Hudicourt died in the spring of 1947 and was succeeded by Etienne D. Charlier as secretary-general. The original Communist Party gave up the struggle and dissolved. The whole thing was so confusing that even veteran Communist leader Jacques Duclos, writing in far-off France, seemed somewhat bewildered; in the May issue of *Démocratie Nouvelle* he criticized Haiti's Communist Party and called its dissolution an "error."

DOMINICAN REPUBLIC: TRUJILLO'S DISLOYAL OPPOSITION

Even people in a tight little dictatorship must let off steam from time to time. A safety valve is needed to keep political tempers from exploding. This principle of elementary diplomatic physics applies to the Dominican Republic, which shares the Caribbean island of Hispaniola with Haiti. President Generalissimo Rafael Trujillo, who rules the Dominican Republic as if it were his private estate, must have thought so, too, when he decided in 1946 that what his country needed was a good, five-cent opposition. Communism would not only lend a strikingly red tinge to his nation's drab political hue; it would also show some people inside and outside the Dominican Republic how much Trujillo was needed as an anti-Communist bulwark in Central America.

And so a party of Communists was permitted to organize in the summer of 1946. There had been in existence, clandestinely, a so-called Democratic Front of National Liberation. This group had been created by the Democratic Revolutionary Party (Communists), which operated underground until Trujillo permitted it to emerge into the bright Caribbean sunlight. The legal Communist Party took its name from its Cuban counterpart and called itself Popular Socialist Party. It also set about to organize a young people's movement, the Democratic Youth.

Under the leadership of Secretary-General Machado Fuenmayor Arrieta, the party soon claimed 2,000 members. Trujillo had let a red genie out of a bottle, and he was having difficulty putting it back in again. The Communists imported leaflets from Cuba. They organized meetings even in the more remote parts of the island. Trujillo's administration did its best to discredit the Communists. As a result, Dominican businessmen one day received a mysterious and disquieting letter, allegedly written by the "Central Committee of the Communist Party," which threatened them with expropriation. The mimeographed letter, which was doubtless a forgery, violated all current Communist policies. It asked recipients to "prepare an inventory of your immovable property," so that the party might "decide the manner in which your property will be distributed." The fake letter ended with blood-curdling phrases: "The hour of social justice has struck. No more rich, and no more poor. All equal, or death and destruction!!!"

Anyone who had studied Trujillo's earlier machinations could sympathize with the Communists. They would never have been guilty of so clumsy a bit of agitation. A month later, in October, a demonstration in the country's capital (the former Santo Domingo, renamed by Trujillo as "Trujillo City"), brought the Communist affair to a climax. Some 6,000 Communists, or may-be Communists, listened to a series of speakers. Then somebody sabotaged the loudspeaker system. Someone built a fire underneath the speakers' stand. Groups of alleged Communists marched through the streets and stoned the stores. People shouted, "Down with the U.S.A.! Viva el Partido Comunista!" Someone entered the Cuban, Mexican, and United States consulates. And then Trujillo's police struck at the demonstrators. Communist headquarters were raided. A number of leaders were arrested.

In a cable to the world press, Trujillo's office presented the events as follows: "Last night the Communists tried a coup d'état. They notified the authorities of their intention to hold a meeting. In the early afternoon they distributed knives, machetes and clubs, and at 10 P.M. attacked foreigners and unarmed citizens. They have created a disturbance throughout the city. The Mexican Embassy was violated."

That was the official version. The Communist leaders were later released from prison. The Dominican Republic had let off red steam. Trujillo was back on the job of "El Benefactor" in his domain. The Communists continued their agitation, although in a somewhat more sedate manner.

A year later, Trujillo made the sensational charge that "an army of Communist revolutionaries" was plotting in Cuba to invade and conquer the Dominican Republic. There were quite a number of exiled Dominicans on Cuban soil—not all of them Communists, by any means—who would have liked to oust Trujillo. But the picture conjured up by Trujillo, with thousands of Guatemalan, Venezuelan, and Cuban Communists poised to land on his island's soil, looked too much like the nightmare of a guilty fantasy. Perhaps the Communists were really plotting against Trujillo. But, like the legendary shepherd, he had cried "Wolf!" once too often.

PUERTO RICO: FOR INDEPENDENCE

Puerto Rico, the United States island possession in the Caribbean Sea, has faithfully followed the flip-flops of Communist Party affairs on the

American mainland. When Earl Browder, as head of the United States Communists, favored cooperation between all groups of the population and dissolved the party to create a Communist Political Association, the Puerto Rican Communist Party followed suit. It dissolved and promptly created the Puerto Rican Congress of Independence. In 1946, the party denounced "Browderism" and reconstituted itself along old lines.

Puerto Rico's two million people are hemmed in by the Caribbean and by the limited agricultural land that is available to them. The island doggedly seeks to gain its own identity. But its problems are less political than economic. Without the aid of the United States, Puerto Rico would be worse off than it is under Washington's control. There are no disagreements on that point. That is why Puerto Rico's most dynamic leader, Luís Muñóz Marín, president of the Senate, rejects the ideas of some members within his own overwhelmingly dominant Popular Democratic Party.

The Communists, however, favor complete independence for Puerto Rico. They are violently opposed to the possible development of the island into one of the states of the United States. Many reasons have been advanced against the granting of statehood for Puerto Rico. Muñóz Marín favors a high degree of self-government within the economic orbit of the United States. Puerto Rico has enjoyed certain privileges as a United States possession, which it does not want to lose.

During the war, Puerto Rican Communists refrained from pressing the independence issue. The New York Communist monthly *Political Affairs* wrote in October, 1945, that the then existing Congress for Independence had "broken and isolated a handful of its members who tried to use the independence issue as a partisan weapon and to destroy the democratic coalition presented by [Muñóz Marín's] Popular party."

When Browder was replaced by Foster in the United States, and when the Seventh Strategy of world communism took effect, the Puerto Rican Communists became more militant. On March 10, 1946, the Communist Party of Puerto Rico was reconstituted in the capital city, San Juan. The party's secretary-general, Juan Santos Rivera, said on that occasion that "the independence of Puerto Rico deserves first consideration." He joined in the anti-Browder chorus when he blamed the conciliatory policy pursued by Puerto Rican Communists during the war years on "insufficient comprehension of Marxism-Leninism-Stalinism and the influence of the revisionist policies of Earl Browder."

The party furnishes the top leadership of the Confederation of Puerto Rican Labor. Juan Santos Rivera is a member of the Confederation's central committee. It is violently opposed by the Free Federation, an affiliate of the American Federation of Labor. Caribbean Communists have expressed approval of a bill (H.R. 2781) introduced in the United States Congress by Vito Marcantonio of New York's American Labor Party. Marcantonio's congressional districts include a large percentage of immigrants from Puerto Rico. The Marcantonio bill, in contrast to a measure introduced by Senator Millard Tydings, Democrat from Maryland, would make it possible for Puerto Rico to export sugar duty-free to the United States, even after achieving complete independence. The Marcantonio bill would enable Puerto Rico to impose a tariff on imports from the United States, in order to protect its own infant industries. The veteran New York Communist Israel Amter supported the Marcantonio proposal, when he wrote in the *Daily Worker* of February 16, 1947, that they would create "independence with economic and political guarantees."

Luís Muñóz Marín's popularity in Puerto Rico is not endangered by Communist efforts. In 1940, the United States Supreme Court supported the Puerto Rican government in its enforcement of the so-called "Foreaker Act." This act provides that landholdings should be limited to 500 acres. The Supreme Court thus forestalled agitation that might have accused the United States of perpetuating large feudal estates, which go back to the period of Spanish rule. When President Harry S. Truman in 1946 for the first time named a native Puerto Rican, Jesus T. Piñero, governor of the island, another step toward self-government was taken. Communist reaction to such measures had been mixed. The *Daily Worker* conceded that Piñero was a "leader of the popular masses of Puerto Rico," but it warned that he also represented "the United States government and hence American imperialism in Puerto Rico."

Puerto Rican state initiative in the creation of various industries has also broken the pattern of economic life as it exists elsewhere in the Caribbean and throughout Latin America generally. Muñóz Marín, who favors state enterprise where private capital fears to tread, managed to escape a "reformist" label from the Communists. His enormous prestige makes it advisable for would-be opponents to join him, rather than to fight him.

What happens to Puerto Rico is important to United States-Latin American relations, because the island is a symbol of American efforts to deal constructively with a Spanish-speaking Western Hemisphere dependency. Chances of Communist influence on Puerto Rican affairs were further limited when the United States, in August, 1947, announced that the island will in the future be able to elect its own Governor, rather than merely accept the choice of the President of the United States.

NICARAGUA, COSTA RICA, PANAMA

Southward from Mexico to the Panama Canal, the traveler passes through three countries in which no legal Communist parties exist: Guatemala, Honduras, and El Salvador. But then come two countries of strong contrast: Nicaragua and Costa Rica.

After ten years of dictatorial powers, President Anastasio Somoza of Nicaragua arranged on Feb. 1, 1947, for the election of a substitute, Dr. Leonard Arguello. Somoza, however, remained as commander of the National Guard, a post that guaranteed him a decisive voice in the affairs of Nicaragua. But on May 26, Somoza decided that Arguello had become too independent and ousted him by force. Somoza apparently believes only in ineffective opposition to his rule. It is for that reason that a party of Communists, operating under the name of the Socialist Party of Nicaragua, has managed to continue a frustrated existence. W. H. Lawrence, a *New York Times* correspondent, reported on December 30, 1946, that this party had about 1,500 members, but he quoted government supporters as admitting that it "might have as many as 75,000 votes (in a nation of 22,000 votes), if it were not repressed by the Government." Lawrence added that the Communists had "influence in the labor movement" but that they lacked formal control of it, "because of the activities of the Somoza administration."

Things are very different in the democratic and relatively tranquil Costa Rica. There the Republican and Democratic parties (which hardly differ in their policies) take turns in governing the country. Candidates, rather than issues, decide elections. The Communist Party of Costa Rica was organized in 1930. Its supporters come from intellectuals in San José, the capital, from students and workers. It has had little success among the peasantry. Governments, whether Republican or Democratic, have shown disapproval of the Communists but have not interfered with their activities. In the 1944 elections for a four-year period, the Communists won 4 out of 45 seats in Costa Rica's Parliament. Manuel Mora Valverde, the party's secretary-general, has pushed labor legislation and social-security measures in parliamentary sessions.

When the Comintern was dissolved in 1943, the Communist Party ceased its existence under that name. It was immediately reconstituted under its old leadership as the Popular Vanguard Party. Under this label, it has emphasized such aims as redistribution of land and nationalization of industries. John and Mavis Biesanz wrote in their book *Costa Rican Life* that, during World War II and after the German attack on Russia, the Communists "urged, unsuccessfully, greater national unity and participation in the war effort."

After the end of the war, their denunciation of "Yankee imperialism" paralleled those of ultra-conservative political circles in Costa Rica. Although strongly opposed by the Roman Catholic Church, the Communists agreed with some members of the clergy when it came to criticism of the United States, but on the basis of different concepts. As in most predominantly Catholic countries, communism in Costa Rica refrains from attacks on the church as such. Communists and the Catholic Church fought side by side, a few years ago, for a liberal labor code. The new code permitted more extensive union activities on the part of the Communists.

Lack of Communist success among Costa Rica's agricultural population must be attributed to the fact that about 80 per cent of the land is owned by small farmers. An agricultural middle class exists, which is lacking elsewhere in Latin America. There is no contrast between enormously wealthy *hacendados* and underprivileged peons which would call for land reform. Communist control of Costa Rica's Confederation of Labor is exercised through Rodolfo Guzman, who is also a member of the executive committee of the Latin American Confederation of Labor. Both Guzman and Mora Valverde were trained in Moscow. Guzman's labor group is opposed by the Catholic-sponsored union "Rerum Novarum."

Panama, which gets nearly 40 per cent of its national income through the United States-owned Panama Canal, has a very difficult labor problem. Disparity between the payments received by white and by colored workers in the Canal Zone has tended to strain relations between Panamanian labor and the canal administration. The personnel management of the Canal Zone maintains that wage differences are due to varying skill, but the Panamanian Confederation of Labor contends that it is caused by discrimination. The confederation has militantly fought for

Panamanian labor, and it has had the advice of Mexican and Cuban labor officials in this battle. It is opposed by the National Association of Labor Unions, which seeks to mobilize Panamanian workers against communism.

The top leadership of the Panamanian Labor Confederation is made up of Communists, who also function as officials in the People's Party, which is Panama's party of Communists. This party is very weak. It claims a membership of only 500. This weakness, however, is more than made up for by Communist control over important sections of labor in a region that is of strategic importance to the United States, and where the slogan of "Yankee imperialism" has perhaps more meaning than anywhere else in Latin America. Panama's top Communist is Cristóbal L. Segundo, president of the People's Party.

CHAPTER 25

Brazil: A "Knight of Hope" Returns

LATIN-AMERICA'S Number One Communist once led a column of revolutionaries through 15,000 miles of Brazil's jungle hinterland, joined the Comintern's executive committee during a three-year stay in Moscow, was jailed for nine years by President Getúlio Vargas, and finally formed a political alliance with the same Senhor Vargas.

The name of this colorful and dynamic rebel-politician, secretary-general of Brazil's Communist Party, is Luíz Carlos Prestes. His followers call him "The Knight of Hope," *O Cavalheiro da Esperança*. Prestes emerged from his prison cell in May, 1945. His newly legalized party quickly enlisted some 4,000 supporters. Within a year, it had gained 130,000 members, stood accused of revolutionary plotting, was engaged in violent anti-"Yanqui" agitation, and faced the repression measures of Vargas's much-plagued successor, President Eurico Gaspar Dutra. In the spring of 1947, Brazil's Communist Party was banned once more.

The tall, dark, and gaunt Prestes personifies communism in Brazil. His career is almost identical with the varying fortunes of the party he leads. Prestes's courage and buoyancy create admiration. He is a rebel in the tradition of Robin Hood, a politician after the heart of Tammany Hall, a political martyr in the great revolutionary pattern, and an orator with Latin fire in his eyes. Prestes, one of Moscow's prime assets in Latin America, has been one of Washington's top antagonists south of the Rio Grande. How did he get that way?

Luíz Carlos Prestes comes from a military family and is a trained soldier. Born in January, 1899, he entered an army school at Rio de Janeiro when he was eleven years old. His family was far from well to do. Military training involved little expense. Young Luíz Carlos went to the military academy when he was eighteen. In 1920, he graduated as a lieutenant in the engineering corps. His record at the academy appears

:o have been excellent, particularly in mathematics. On July 5, 1922, military schools and army garrisons in the Rio de Janeiro district revolted against the administration of President Arturo Bernardes. Prestes was among the revolutionary officers in the Copocabana garrison. The rebellion was crushed. The Bernardes government dispersed the revolutionaries. Prestes was sent to San Angelo, a small garrison in the extreme southern state of Rio Grande do Sul. He was in command of 300 engineer troops, who were to build a railroad. In sending him to such an isolated spot, the Bernardes government made it difficult for Prestes to keep in touch with revolutionary elements in the capital. But he was able to propagandize his own troops and discontented elements in near-by military units. While at San Angelo, Prestes advanced to the rank of captain.

In July, 1924, there were new anti-Bernardes uprisings in São Paulo, as well as minor revolts elsewhere. When Prestes heard about the São Paulo rebellion, he decided to join the antigovernment forces. His first plan was to capture Porto Alegre, capital of Rio Grande do Sul province. But he was repulsed, almost surrounded, and began his trek through the Brazilian hinterland. This march began late in October, 1924. It lasted well over two years, until February, 1927.

Prestes later stated that his unit fought fifty-two engagements with government troops. The number of troops that made up *La Columna Prestes*, "The Prestes column," has variously been given as 300, 500, 1,500, and even 2,000. It seems safe to assume that the guerrilla unit lost and gained supporters as it continued its march through the mountains, jungles, and highlands of Brazil. There are several touching anecdotes, not without propagandistic overtones, as to the sacrifices made by individuals and whole villages in support of the "Prestes column." There even exists a folk song, immortalizing a real or legendary Negro peasant named Joel. The song described how Joel brought Prestes all his worldly goods, a sack of flour and a horse ("Please, take it, General!"). And, finally, Joel himself joined the ranks of the revolutionaries. The song ends by saying that, weeks later, Joel was taken prisoner and shot by government troops.

The continuing march of the "Prestes column" aroused the imagination of many Brazilians who despised the Bernardes regime. Prestes's skill as a guerrilla leader was demonstrated in encounters with, or evasions of, government troops. The Prestes march continued in loops and semicircles all across Brazil's hinterland. His trek, which started at a point roughly halfway between the borders of Uruguay and Paraguay, led almost to the tip of the Brazilian bulge around Natal. The column was forced to turn back at Ico and then attempted to move in the direction of Rio de Janeiro.

But stubbornness was not enough. Although Prestes's march has now become a legend, carefully nurtured by the Communists, impatience with his efforts developed during the last part of the trek. Peasants who had to feed and clothe Prestes's guerrillas began to anticipate their arrival with anxiety. Of course, they could hardly expect a group of soldiers, jungle fighters for more than two years, to have retained all the manners and inhibitions of civilization. But Prestes ended his Odyssey after twenty-eight months, and before his popularity had been seriously reduced. His column crossed into Bolivia, on February 3, 1927, where it was disarmed and interned.

Shortly afterward, the British-owned Bolivian Concession Company hired the members of the "Prestes column," who had formed a cooperative under Prestes's leadership. In 1929, when things inside Brazil had cooled off, most ex-members of the "Prestes column" returned to their homeland. "The Knight of Hope" himself, *persona non grata* to Bernardes's successor, President Washington Luiz, went to Argentina. In Buenos Aires, he met Rodolfo Ghioldi, secretary-general of the Argentine Communist Party, member of the Comintern's executive committee and—at least in the case of Prestes—a Moscow talent scout. Ghioldi and Prestes exchanged experiences and ideologies. An anonymous Brazilian Communist, writing in a pamphlet entitled *Luíz Carlos Prestes: The Struggle for Liberation in Brazil,* said that Prestes at that time "developed from a national rebel into a conscious revolutionary with clear aims." While in Buenos Aires, "The Knight of Hope" became a member of the Communist Party.

Prestes remained in Argentina until he was incautious enough to call the newly installed government of President José Felix Uriburu an "imperialist dictatorship." He was forced to move to Uruguay. Meanwhile, the revolutionary caldron inside Brazil was sending up new bubbles. The Brazilian Communist Party had been almost completely inactive since its formal establishment in 1921. Now it began new activities. Prestes kept in touch with Rio de Janeiro political affairs from Montevideo. In 1929 and early 1930 Getúlio Vargas heightened his efforts to take control of the Brazilian government. It is entertaining to recall that Vargas charged Washington Luiz with suppression of democratic liberties and favoritism toward the São Paulo coffee interests, and that Luiz called Vargas a

"Moscow agent." At any rate, Vargas talked a good democratic revolution. Prestes gave him a long-distance endorsement, at least until Vargas had actually overthrown the Luiz regime.

Communist spokesmen have since glossed over this endorsement. Bryan Green, writing in *Brazil*, asserted that Vargas "offered Prestes complete amnesty and a high post in the government." This, Green writes, Prestes "indignantly refused and thus won Vargas's hatred." That may have been the case after Vargas came to power. But Prestes appears definitely to have endorsed Vargas during an earlier period. Samuel Putnam, writing in the quarterly *Science and Society* (spring, 1942), states that Prestes "supported Vargas in 1930, but was speedily disillusioned."

PRESTES GOES TO MOSCOW

Soon afterward, and without returning to Brazil, Luíz Carlos Prestes went to Moscow. This was the period of the Comintern's Third Strategy, that of revolutionary expansion. Prestes, an army captain and the idol of many Brazilians who were weary of opportunists and corrupt governments, would definitely be an asset to the Communist International. But, before the gallant leader of jungle guerrillas could safely run the Brazilian Communist Party after the hard-and-fast pattern of the Comintern, he had to receive ideological indoctrination and learn to conform with party discipline. During his three years in Moscow, Prestes acquired not only proficiency in the use of Marxist nomenclature but also a handsome blond wife, the German-born Olga Benario.

His return to Brazil on a false Portuguese passport, early in 1935, followed the "united front" policy announcements of the Seventh Comintern Congress. Prestes immediately organized a National Liberation Alliance, which Vargas denounced as "the work of Moscow agents," allegedly "financed by the Soviet Union." On July 13, 1935, the National Liberation Front was declared illegal. The Communists went underground.

When, on May 20, 1935, the magazine *Communist International* reported the results of the third party conference of the South American and Caribbean Communist parties, which had taken place in Uruguay in 1934, it singled out the Brazilian Communists in its tribute, saying, "Of all the parties in South and Caribbean America, the Communist Party of Brazil is the one which has actually succeeded in energetically setting about the application of the decisions of the (Uruguay) Conference, by becoming the initiator in establishing the National Liberation Alliance. In the short period of its existence, the NLA has succeeded in drawing into its ranks very wide masses of the working-class organization, of office employees, students, important sections of the army and navy, various peasant organizations, the petty-bourgeois 'travaillists' and 'tenientists' parties, some national reformist groups, numerous socialist 'parties,' big trade unions, and mass young people's organizations."

Before Vargas banned the NLA, the Communists were, according to reports in *Communist International*, at least partly responsible for a wave of strikes that hit Brazil. Genuine grievances were numerous. This was the period of world depression. But these months of unrest were only an overture. In November, 1935, the army garrisons at Natal and Pernambuco revolted. They were joined by the Third Regiment at Rio de Janeiro. Troops in the two northeast provinces resisted for more than three days, before the Vargas regime was able to quell the revolt. The Communists later asserted that this uprising had been engineered by Vargas's *agents provocateurs*, so that the opposition would reveal itself. But in 1946 they celebrated the anniversary of the uprising. Vargas was undoubtedly extremely ruthless in suppressing the November revolt. His police made wholesale arrests among peoples from all walks of life and of varying political views.

Prestes and his wife Olga succeeded in evading the Vargas police until March 5, 1936. They were finally arrested in a Rio de Janeiro apartment, where they had lived in hiding. Senhora Prestes is said to have clung to her husband all the way to the police station, thus preventing police officers from shooting him down "while trying to escape." Many revolutionaries or suspected revolutionaries were killed during this period. Her action may indeed have saved Prestes's life.

NINE YEARS IN PRISON

On May 20, Luíz Carlos Prestes appeared before a military tribunal, charged with "desertion from the army." This charge went back to 1924, when he took his San Angelo company into the Brazilian hinterland. Now he asserted that he had properly resigned his captaincy before turning against the government in power. The tribunal considered his case as outside its jurisdiction and referred it to the personnel department of the army. A sixteen years' prison sentence followed. In December, 1940,

Prestes was given an additional prison sentence: thirty years, on a charge of "sedition."

Shortly after Prestes's arrest, an incident occurred that makes his post-war political liaison with Vargas appear in a weird light. In the fall of 1936, police arrived at the jail in which Olga Prestes was held, claiming that they were going to take her "to the hospital." Senhora Prestes was about to have a child. But, after her removal from prison, she was taken aboard a German freighter bound for Hamburg. A daughter was born on November 27, 1936, while Olga Prestes was in a Nazi prison as a German-born Communist. After a brief period in a German orphanage, the child, Anita, was permitted to join Prestes's mother, Doña Leocadia Felizardo Prestes, in France. Olga Benario-Prestes appears to have died in a Nazi concentration camp. Anita, now in her teens, joined her widowed father in Rio in 1946.

It has long been argued whether the November, 1935, revolt had really been instigated by the Communists. Certainly, the Prestes-led National Liberation Alliance, although robbed of its legality, continued its activities clandestinely. The NLA may have had support within the three garrisons that led the rebellion. But such support could not have been very substantial. The NLA was too young to have achieved very far-reaching influence. Although Rodolfo Ghioldi, Argentina's veteran Communist leader, chose the time of the November coup to arrive in Brazil "to extend his best wishes to the Brazilian working masses" (Vargas arrested him, too), there had been very little time for the organization of a full-fledged Communist-led revolution. The Comintern agent Arthur Ewert, who had previously been active in the United States as "Braun," was arrested by Brazilian police. Several branches of the Brazilian Communist Party were later named after him.

The November revolt enabled Vargas to enforce martial law throughout Brazil. This included suspension of the right of assembly and of freedom of speech and the press, and it formed the basis for news censorship. Martial law, which, of course, affected not only Communists but anti-Vargas forces in Brazil, helped tighten Vargas's grip. It was not revoked until two years afterward, on June 18, 1937. A few months later, on October 2, and conveniently right in the midst of an election campaign, the Vargas regime discovered another "Communist plot." Martial law was restored. A month later, on November 10, Vargas abolished the

National Assembly and instituted government by decree. The pseudo-legal basis for this was a constitution that created the so-called *Estado Novo*, a "New State" somewhat along European totalitarian lines. The 1937 constitution enabled Vargas to suppress all opposition very effectively. Prestes remained closely guarded.

Vargas changed his tactics markedly during the period that brought the end of World War II. In February 28, 1945, the Brazilian constitution was amended, to provide for elections. A few days later, almost exactly nine years after his arrest, Prestes was permitted to have visitors. And finally, in May, he was released from prison. The Communist Party was legalized together with other opposition parties. An electoral code was established on May 28, and elections were scheduled for December 2, 1945.

Immediately following his release, Prestes began energetic political activities. It was generally expected that he would add his prestige and personality to the forces trying to overthrow the Vargas regime. But "The Knight of Hope" was pulling his punches. His speeches were cautious. There were repeated references to the "need for slow transition toward democracy." What had happened to Prestes? Where was Brazil's Communist Party going? Who was holding Prestes back? Why didn't he take revenge on Vargas?

Prestes was playing for time. He faced the problem of organizing a mass party, with elections only a few months away. The Communists could not possibly do all they wanted to do in so short a time. They faced a formidable political phalanx. The Vargas machine, while fostering the *Queremistas* (derived from *Queremos Getúlio*—"We want Getúlio"), also backed the candidacy of ex-War Minister General Eurico Gaspar Dutra. The anti-Vargas, anti-Dutra forces had nominated Major General Eduardo Gomes of the Air Force.

TWO ENEMIES MAKE A DEAL

But Prestes did not turn against Vargas. Instead, he attacked both Dutra and Gomes. He said, in effect, that it was useless to choose between tweedledee and tweedledum. Both Dutra and Gomes were army men, the Communists insisted, who would use the Vargas-dictated constitution of 1937 to run the country along dictatorial lines. Prestes therefore emphasized constitutional reform, rather than presidential elections. He said on one occasion, "The Communists take a realistic position by supporting Vargas in his moves toward democracy, his permitting the re-establishment of the freedom of the press and assembly and his legalization of party activities." Vargas, according to Prestes, would be "able to consolidate pro-democratic forces within the Constituent Assembly and so promote a democratic and progressive solution of the nation's problems."

Statements such as this confirmed reports that Vargas and Prestes had agreed on political cooperation. Prestes desired to remain politically active and to gain time. Vargas was using the Communists to help perpetuate his rule. On August 16, 1945, the Communists urged Vargas in a telegram to call a national constituent assembly. The assembly was to prepare the draft of a new constitution. This would have postponed the presidential elections until a new constitution had been discussed, drafted, and adopted. Meanwhile, Vargas would have remained in power.

But Dutra and Gomes, although rivals in the presidential race, did not like this smooth teamwork between Prestes and Vargas. Two weeks after the Communist telegram to Vargas, top political circles in the Brazilian capital heard the rumor that the president had decided to "accept" the Communist's "suggestion." Dutra and Gomes, together with other officers, decided to remove Vargas from his post. Although Dutra was nominally the candidate of the Vargas machine, he showed that he had a mind of his own.

The coup d'état was brief and bloodless. Vargas made a trip to the country, under pressure but in good health. Troops occupied Communist party headquarters and the offices of *Tribuna Popular,* the party's daily newspaper in Rio. Prestes went into hiding in order to, as he put it, "await developments." The team-up between Prestes and Vargas had not brought the ex-president any luck. The Communists had to change their short-range policy.

Prestes split the Gomes-backing opposition by naming an alleged non-Communist, Yeddo Fiuza. Fiuza, mayor of the town of Petropolis, and later road commissioner under Vargas, was a political nonentity. But, as a civilian, he appealed to voters who were tired of military administrations. Dutra won the election as candidate for the Conservatives, who called their party "Social Democratic Party." The Communists received

650,000 votes, 10 per cent of the popular vote. They also gained fourteen seats in the National Assembly. Prestes himself was elected Senator.

On the Senate floor, Prestes could greet as a senatorial colleague ex-president Vargas, who had returned from his brief rest in the country. Vargas had been elected to the Senate on the ticket of his Labor Party, which also had been part of the group that backed Dutra. To add to the confusion, Vargas soon became the spearhead of a wing within the Labor Party that opposed Dutra on a great number of issues. Again, Prestes and Vargas found much on which they could see eye to eye.

A new constitution was approved by the National Assembly on September 17, 1946. It was a substantial modification of the 1937 constitution but remained elastic enough to reflect the political color of the government in power. The Communists vigorously opposed an article of the new constitution that gave the government power to declare illegal any party or political association whose program "is contrary to a democratic regime based on the plurality of parties and on the guarantee of fundamental human rights." Their fears turned out to be well-founded when this very phrase was later used to ban the Communist Party.

INFLATION AND UNREST

Throughout 1946, the Dutra regime encountered mounting Communist-inspired unrest. Strikes and demonstrations made matters difficult for Dutra and the chief of the Brazilian Federal Police, José Pereira Lira. The Communists were on the forefront of strikes, designed to raise wages to correspond with skyrocketing living costs and to improve working conditions as they prevailed, for instance, in the harbor of Santos. On May 23, 1946, Lira sent mounted troops against Communist crowds that came to celebrate the first anniversary of their party's legality. The police chief, a tough and not very diplomatic official, had banned the meeting at which Prestes was scheduled to speak. But thousands defied his ban and streamed into Carioca Square. Lira sent cavalry and mechanized units to stop the meeting and disperse the crowd. The police lost control of the situation. They shot and clubbed wildly. Three persons were killed, thirty-two wounded.

On the same day, the Brazilian Army announced that it considered Prestes "unworthy" of returning to the armed forces, which he left (or from which he deserted, or from which he resigned, or from which he was expelled—this remained a much debated issue) at the beginning of the revolt of 1924. When, on June 2, 1946, three Rio labor unions struck against a Canadian-owned traction company, police seized Communist Party headquarters on Flamengo Beach. Police Chief Lira charged that the projected walkout of 26,000 union members had been called "for political and not economic gains."

On August 31, Lira conferred with parliamentary leaders at the presidential Guanabará Palace. Afterward, the police chief told the press that he had been able to make a "sensational revelation" to the Assembly representatives. He added, "The evidence we have available proves, in my opinion without a doubt, the double-character and existence of the Communist Party: on the one hand, it is ostensibly legal; on the other hand, it is devoted to systematic preparation for civil war. Schools of sabotage, as well as courses for the preparation of civil war have been opened here by the Communists, who attempt, by means of strikes, to reduce the productiveness of the nation's labor." He also charged the Communists with indoctrination of minority groups and singled out the Pan-Slavic Union of Brazil as "a society devoted to illegal activities" along Communist lines.

Coinciding with the growth of the Communist Party, Soviet influence was strengthened when Brazil established diplomatic relations with the USSR in 1946. Soviet Ambassador Jacob Surits arrived in Rio de Janeiro early in May. Two months earlier, on March 18, Prestes had stated that his followers would "form guerrillas" to fight their own government, if Brazil "should become involved in an imperialist war against Russia." This created an uproar in the National Assembly. Prestes was asked to clarify his stand within a five-day period. Answering the challenge, "The Knight of Hope" took the Assembly's floor and violently attacked "a reactionary section of United States capitalism," which, he asserted, "wants and is provoking" a war against the Soviet Union.

Prestes later gave a rather complex explanation of his remarks on a possible future war. The Soviet Union, he pointed out, was a completely peace-loving nation. Therefore, his deduction continued, any possible war between America and Russia could only be the result of "imperialist" pressures on the part of the United States. "Our party," Prestes said on this occasion, "is profoundly Brazilian, but naturally we look to Russia as the first Socialist country."

DUTRA BANS THE COMMUNISTS

Brazil's elections of January 19, 1947, increased Communist votes to 800,000. The Communist-supported Adehmar de Barros won the governorship of the state of São Paulo. In the capital of Rio de Janeiro, the Communists became the largest party and elected eighteen out of fifty members to the city council. Shortly after the elections, the Brazilian government, through Attorney General Alceu Barbedo, accused the Communist Party of violating the 1946 constitution and designated it as an organization "whose program of action is contrary to the democratic regime." Acting on the government's initiative, the Supreme Electoral Tribunal ruled on May 7 that the party was illegal. The largely Communist-controlled Brazilian Confederation of Labor was banned for six months by President Dutra, who charged that it had "provoked friction among the workers and had agitated in a manner harmful to production."

There was no doubt that this was not the end of Brazil's Communist movement. It had worked for two years to establish a well-organized party, with 445 local clubs throughout the nation. It was sure to continue agitation among labor, and to reorganize its more militant followers in ostensibly non-political associations. Prestes, who had shown his patience during nine prison years and his organizational ability in two years of party-building, could apply three decades of Communist experience in illegality to a nation in fear of economic chaos. He quickly began to reorganize the Communist movement under a new label: Popular Progressive Party of Brazil.

CHAPTER 26

South American Roundup: Anti-Yanqui

Y ou know," Brazil's delegate to the United Nations, Dr. Oswaldo Aranha, told New York reporters, "communism is a very old idea for improving economic, political and social ways of living. What we are afraid of is not communism itself, but Russianism. The idea we respect, but foreign intervention is something else." These words, spoken early in 1947 on La Guardia airfield, were transmitted a few hours later on the Latin-American cable circuits of the world-wide news services. They provided food for thought for many a Chilean, Venezuelan, Colombian, Peruvian, Uruguayan, and Argentinian.

Are South American Communists really representatives of Russian interests? Do they not favor the national interests of the countries in which they operate? Have they not adjusted their aims to cooperation with members of the Roman Catholic Church? And do they not push legislation and reforms that have long been adopted in the United States, in Canada, and in many countries of western Europe?

The countries of South America, with their predominant high-profit and low-wage economies, have provided fertile ground for the growth of communism. In some of these nations, where communism is ruthlessly discouraged by dominant economic interests, liberal democrats have often sympathized with militant Communist pressure against an unenlightened feudal aristocracy. Communism on the South American continent has allied itself with nationalism in fighting "Yanqui imperialism." Drawing support from liberals, nationalists, and underprivileged alike, it has made great strides during the postwar years.

VENEZUELA · 50,000 VOTES

President Romulo Betancourt, who gained power in Venezuela by revolution and free vote, is a former Communist. He overthrew the regime of

General Isaias Medina Angarita, whom the Communist Party supported. Betancourt brought a relative measure of reform and democracy to a nation that had known little but political despotism for decades. The calm elections of October 25, 1946, which endorsed the Betancourt revolution, gave the Communists 50,000 votes, or about 4 per cent of the total ballots cast.

When Betancourt came to power, the Communists were split into three different groups. Not until after the arrival of Soviet Ambassador Foma Trebin, several months later, did a unified Communist Party emerge under the leadership of Secretary-General Juan Bautista Fuenmayor. Prior to that, two major Communist factions had appealed to Betancourt for permission to use the name Communist Party of Venezuela. Bautista Fuenmayor attempted to ally himself with the successful Betancourt. But the president made it clear on December 11, 1945, that he would not include Communists in his government. He did not infringe upon the Communist Party, but he promised that he would crack down if they tried to infiltrate into the army.

In August, 1946, Venezuela heard that fifty American businessmen had written a detailed letter to United States Ambassador Dr. Frank P. Corrigan, expressing alarm at "indications that connections exist and that financial aid is being given" to Venezuelan Communists by the Soviet Embassy at Caracas. The businessmen urged reintroduction of a United States government information service, along the lines adopted during World War II. The letter, after being published in the United States, was interpreted by the Communist press of Venezuela as an expression of "Yankee imperialists" bent on "intervention." The Communist paper *El Nacional* and the Caracas tabloid *Ultimas Noticias* kept the story alive, long after the full text of the letter had shown that the only intervention suggested was that of the spoken or written word.

The Communists, however, continued to demand that Ambassador Corrigan be discredited and the fifty American businessmen expelled. When one hundred Communists attempted to demonstrate before the United States Embassy, they were arrested by the government because their meeting had "not been authorized." Three leaders were imprisoned for two days. The Communist press referred to them as "Mr. Corrigan's prisoners." The excitement prompted President Betancourt to reiterate, on August 13, 1946, that "the political forces supporting this government have signed no pact with the Communists."

Oil-rich Venezuela, which has to import most of her food, suffered a postwar inflation that struck the lower classes heavily. The Betancourt program of introducing modern farming methods, road building, and port improvements, seems well designed to alleviate conditions at least to a degree. Betancourt and the Communists clashed head-on in their attitude toward the oil industries, which are largely American-owned. Communist agitation in the oil and transport unions pressed for a strike to obtain concessions. Betancourt intervened and arranged for settlement of grievances without interruption in work.

The Communist election platform in 1946 included demands for changes in the petroleum law, as a basis for "future nationalization." The party demands also specified that all Venezuelan oil should be refined inside the country and that producing companies should reinvest 50 per cent of their net profits in Venezuela. The October 27, 1946, elections gave Betancourt's Democratic Action Party a four-fifths majority in the Assembly. This removed the possibility that Betancourt might have to accept Communist coalition offers after all, if only to retain a leftist majority over the rightist parties.

That rightist ambitions had not been downed completely became clear two months after the elections, when parts of the army attempted a coup d'état against the government. Bautista Fuenmayor, speaking for the Communists, described the uprising as "a movement with reactionary tendencies" and pledged support for Betancourt against the ultra-right. The rightist parties generally, whether connected with the futile revolt or not, are violently opposed to the Communists. The Copei (Comité de Organización Política Electoral Independiente), which ran a poor second behind Betancourt in 1946, at various times clashed with Communists in open battles. Betancourt knew that the extreme right, as well as the extreme left, might sooner or later endanger his regime, which had given Venezuelans the rare taste of democratic freedom.

COLOMBIA, ECUADOR: ON THE DEFENSIVE

The political affairs of Colombia bear a superficial resemblance to those of the United States. In 1946, the Liberals were defeated by the Conservatives for the first time since 1930. Mariano Ospina Pérez became president for a four-year term. The Liberals and the Conservatives are the two dominating parties, with the Communists way behind in third place. Nevertheless, the Communists—who call themselves Social Democrats in Colombia—elected one Senator and one member of the Chamber of Deputies with their 25,000 votes in 1946. But the parliamentary elections of May 16, 1947, wiped out these gains.

The 1947 elections reduced the Communist vote to 16,000, and left the party without parliamentary representation. Augusto Durán, the secretary-general, faced a revolt within the Communist movement after the disastrous election results became known. He is a long-time Communist leader who adhered to the Fifth Strategy of world communism when he said in 1941 that the "imperialist" war placed an unbearable "burden on the back of the workers."

Colombia's Communists had vacillated between the rival factions within the Liberal Party. In 1946, they supported the right wing Liberal candidate Gabriel Turbay. They did not think the left wing Liberal Jorge Eliécer Gaitán had much of a chance. They changed their mind after the presidential elections. In January, 1947, Communists and "Gaitánistas" came to a coalition agreement within the Colombian Federation of Labor. But after the parliamentary elections revealed the Communists as weak, Gaitán saw little reason to tolerate Communist competition for labor support.

The Communist defeat in the March elections created a serious crisis inside the Communist Party. Finally, at the party's national convention of July 24, Colombia's Communist movement split in two. Augusto Durán decided to organize the Communist Workers' Party. Gilberto Vieira, who had been president of the old party, founded his own Colombian Communist Party.

While clearly on the defensive in Colombia, communism has suffered even more serious reverses in Ecuador. Dr. José María Velasco Ibarra, who was put into power by a combination of leftist parties in 1944, two years later bit the hands that wrote his ballot slips. Communists, Socialists, and Liberals were among the original supporters of Velasco Ibarra. The Communists, who had been semi-underground during the dictatorial regime of his predecessor, Dr. Carlos Alberto Arroyo del Rio, saw in Velasco a champion of parliamentary government.

But Velasco Ibarra shocked his supporters when he suspended the Ecuadorean constitution on March 20, 1946, and went dictatorial himself. His former friends had become his enemies. Talk of revolt was followed by the expulsion of leading political figures. Velasco's opponents, the Conservatives, made such headway during the June 30 elections to the National Assembly, that the Communists felt impelled to go to the support of their ex-friend, if only to avoid an all-Conservative government. The Conservatives, strongly backed by the Roman Catholic Church, were relentless in their opposition to the Communists. Facing the repressive measures of Velasco and the pressure of their old-time antagonists on the right, the Communists lost supporters and prestige heavily.

They joined the Liberals and Socialists in abstaining from the high-pressure elections of May 5, 1946, on the basis of which a new Constitutional Assembly was selected. The Assembly, overwhelmingly composed of Velasco supporters, dutifully confirmed his powers until 1948 and made such constitutional changes as were necessary to permit government by sweeping executive action.

Some Communist propaganda during the first period of the Velasco regime was rambunctious and shortsighted. By painting hammers and sickles on houses in Quito and Guayaquil, the Communists managed to frighten not only property owners but right-wingers generally. In August, 1947, the regime was overthrown in a series of revolts and counter-revolts, but the outlook for communism in Ecuador remained as dark as ever.

PERU: STOLEN THUNDER

On June 10, 1945, Peru voted itself a new deal for at least six years. After fifteen years of fierce opposition and suppression at the hand of Conservative governments, Peru's Apra (Alianza Popular Revolucionaria Americana) achieved a dominant position in the nation's Parliament. It was a great day for the Apristas, rechristened the People's Party, when Dr. José Luís Bustamente became president as head of a leftist coalition. It was also a great day for the Communists, although they received only four seats in Peru's Chamber of Deputies, while Apra had sixty-five.

Apra, headed by the legendary radical and champion of Peru's under-privileged Indians, Victor Raul Haya de la Torre, soon began to take part in the nation's policies. He had stolen the Communists' thunder for decades, and he planned to continue to do so on a strictly Peruvian basis. His program included irrigation, land reform, public works, and alleviation of Peru's inflation. To be able to do all this speedily, and with up-to-date machinery, Haya de la Torre invited the participation of capital and machinery from the United States.

The Apristas and the Communists have never been friends in Peru. The Communists, handicapped by remote and un-Peruvian directives from Moscow, for years had to look on as Aprista knowledge of Indian needs and hopes helped to win supporters for Haya de la Torre. Then, too, the Communists were never able to match in color and vigor the figure of Haya de la Torre. One of the first Communist leaders, Carlos Mariateguí, had a way with a colorful phrase. When he spoke at the Leghorn Congress, which originated the Italian Communist Party in 1921, he said that "just as the monkeys shed their tails, when they became men, so the intelligentsia on reaching maturity sheds any trace of religion." But that was in the days of Comintern atheism, and, anyway, Mariateguí was soon considered a "racial chauvinist"; like Haya de la Torre, he was forever talking about Indians, rather than about the dictatorship of the proletariat.

The Communist Party of Peru was not officially founded until 1930, when the Apristas had already done a lot of political spadework. From 1931 to 1945, the Communists shared the space of Peru's political underground with the Apristas. The two parties saw eye to eye in their opposition to the successive Conservative governments, which were backed by Peru's thirty or forty leading families, but in nothing else. In 1946, when Apra was fully committed to participation in the government and cooperation with the United States, the Communists found themselves again in the opposition. There, they discovered strange allies—the Conservatives. When it came to talk about "Yankee imperialism," the Conservatives and the Communists were quite able to give each other a run for the money.

Apra, for the first time in its existence, was handicapped in 1946 by government participation. With Apra ministers in the cabinet and large representation in Parliament, the people were beginning to hold Haya de la Torre's party responsible for Peru's woes as well as joys. There were more woes than joys, to be sure—above all, the enormous postwar inflation, which Conservatives and Communists tended to blame on the United States. The Communists, using the inflation issue and Apra cooperation with the United States as their major arguments, began agitation among Haya de la Torre's followers in the shipping, transport, and communication unions. Emerged from underground existence, during which they had scarcely more than 1,000 or 2,000 members, the Communist Party claimed in 1947 that it controlled a membership of 35,000. They are led by secretary-general Jorge Acosta. When the party was legalized in 1945, it adopted the name Socialist Vanguard Party.

CHILE: THIRD ROUND

The Communist Party of Chile won the first round of its battle for political influence in 1936, when it entered the Popular Front coalition. It emerged victorious and with three cabinet ministers, from the second round, the 1946 elections. It has now entered the third round, trying to get back the power which it lost by being maneuvered out of the government in 1947.

The Communist Party succeeded the Socialist Party, founded in 1906 by Luís Emilio Recabarren. On January 1, 1922, the Socialists joined the Communist International. Recabarren, a typesetter who pioneered in the field of trade unionism, visited the Soviet Union for six months. Two years later, he committed suicide. But the party continued on its hard upward road. In 1926, during the dictatorial rule of Carlos Ibáñez, it was banned as "against the constitutional and social order." It promptly became the National Democratic Party. Under this name, it played a major role in Chilean politics for twenty years.

Chilean rebellion against Ibáñez rule and the moribund rule of the landed aristocracy found its expression in unrest during the 1925 to 1932 period. The Communist Party was split into Elias Lafferte's Stalinists and former Communist Senator and Manuel Hidalgo's Trotskyists. Chile has been one of the few countries in which Trotskyists managed to retain their party identity at least for a few years. But Lafferte managed to reorganize the Communist Party in 1931, and ran for president in 1932.

The 1932 election was won by Arturo Alessandri, whose roaring anti-Ibáñez oratory had brought him the nickname "The Lion of Tarapacá." Alessandri received 184,000 votes, Lafferte 4,621. The Socialist candidate, Marmaduque Grove, polled 60,261 votes. Alessandri had been elected because of his persistent and courageous opposition to Ibáñez. But his regime soon went autocratic, mainly because of the almost totalitarian-minded Gustavo Ross, Alessandri's finance minister. Ross, a brilliant economist and poor politician, was to the leftists what a red rag is to a bull. He did not hide his disdain for the masses. He alienated the Radical Party, a left-of-center middle-class group. Alessandri managed to keep the Radicals in line until 1936. But, when the railroad workers struck in protest against Ross, the government declared a state of siege, dissolved the Parliament, and banned the opposition press. Leftist leaders were arrested or neutralized in other ways. Oscar Schnake, an outstanding Socialist leader, was banished from the country.

Ross had done what the Communists had tried in vain to accomplish. He had driven the left into a solid alliance. Following the Comintern "united front" strategy, the Communist Party's central committee had issued a manifesto in August, 1935, calling for "the constitution of a Popular Front for labor, democracy and national independence." But it was not until six months later that their appeal was echoed by the Radicals. When, on February 22, the Radicals assembled at Santiago, their deputy Justiano Sotomayor submitted a Popular Front resolution that was enthusiastically adopted. Carlos Contreras Labarca, Communist secretary-general and a deputy from Tarapacá, later spoke of his party as the "creator and champion of the Popular Front." There are other indications that the Communists planted the coalition idea in the Radical camp, by way of Sotomayor. The declaration stated that "the enslaving of Chile to the foreign conquerors has only been made possible because of the treachery of a reactionary oligarchy, sold out to the gold of London and New York." (Santiago's La Hora, on May 22, promptly blamed the Popular Front on "the red gold of Moscow.")

Just who started the Popular Front ball rolling has never been satisfactorily proved. John Reese Stevenson, in his book The Chilean Popular Front, writes, "Having a Radical propose the ideal of a Popular Front in Chile was but one instance of the clever Communist political strategy." At any rate, the proposal was superbly timed. The parties of the left banded together and prepared for the 1938 elections. Alessandri might still have been able to appease the Radicals. But Ross was instrumental in forcing the Radical ministers out of the Chilean cabinet in September, 1937. That did it. The Radicals, Communists, and Socialists nominated Pedro Aguirre Cerde, a right-wing Radical, to the presidency.

The election was an exceedingly curious and confusing affair. In the end, even the Chilean Nazi party, the Nacistas, backed Aguirre—out of sheer hatred for the Alessandri-Ross regime. Aguirre got 222,700 votes, Ross 218,609. The Popular Front rubbed its collective eyes, and it was in power. But the Communists left governing to others. They did exactly what the French Communists had done during the Popular Front regime.

They coyly refused to enter the cabinet, since this might give people abroad the idea that Communists were running Chile, which would handicap the Popular Front.

Things went fairly well for a year, and then the Socialists and Communists were at each other's throats. The Socialists, led by Schnake, were in favor of beating Nazi Germany, while the Communists were talking about "imperialist war" and generally took an anti-United States line. By mid-1940, Communist-controlled unions within the Chilean Confederation of Labor kept the country on edge with demonstrations and agitation. And, when the Washington-sponsored Havana Conference for Western Hemisphere Solidarity took place, Communist howls could be heard from Antofagasta to the Magellan Straits. When Schnake, then Minister of Industrial Development, went to Havana and Washington (where he negotiated a loan for Chile), Communist fury knew no bounds. Schnake was called "a tool of Wall Street." When the Socialist leader came back, he asked ten thousand party members at Santiago's Teatro Caupolican to "revive our independent line of action, as we cannot remain tied to a party which has betrayed us." A few days later, the Socialists proclaimed that they would no longer support "the Popular Front, as it is inspired by the Communist Party, whose national and international policy is contrary to the interest of the country." The Confederation of Labor, its membership divided about evenly between Socialists and Communists, also pulled away from the Popular Front. And, when the Radicals came out in favor of "freedom of action," the show was over. The Popular Front ended six months before the German attack on Russia.

When the Communists started to support the United Nations war efforts, broken political bones began to heal slowly. Ibáñez, like an old circus horse hearing the sound of trumpets, entered the electoral arena in 1941 with the support of the ultra-right. The Radicals had nominated anti-Communist Juan Antonio Rios, who barely defeated the leftist Gabriel González Videla for the nomination. The Communists didn't like Rios. They supported him grudgingly and grouchily.

The Communists, ably led by Contreras Labarca, used the war years to strengthen their position within the Confederation of Labor. They managed to gain ground at the expense of the Socialists. Communist control of the coal mining unions became complete, and their hold on the nitrate, copper, and communications unions was strengthened considerably. During the war years—after the invasion of Russia—they advocated the antistrike policy favored by Communists everywhere. But, early in 1946, 8,000 nitrate workers in Tarapacá province went on strike.

On January 30, 1946, the confederation announced a twenty-four-hour general protest strike. Two days earlier, police clashed with demonstrators on Santiago's Plaza Bulnedz. Ten workers were killed, several hundred demonstrators and policemen injured.

On February 2, the Socialists denounced the general strike as a Communist attempt to force a shake-up in the government, while President Rios lay ill. Two days later, the Communists answered with another call for a general strike. Communist strength was demonstrated convincingly. The nitrate and copper plants of the north were shut down, although the cities of Valparaiso and Santiago managed to get along. But the political aim of the strike had not been reached. The Communists called it off without achieving a cabinet change. Socialist-Communist antagonism did not recede. On June 12, members of the two parties clashed during union elections at the Sauzal electric plant in Rancagua. A few days later, Rios died.

Fear of a rightist victory created a temporary leftist truce during the September 4 elections. With Rios dead, Gabriel González Videla easily obtained the Radical nomination. As an old friend of the Communists, he quickly received their backing. The rightist parties had been unable to agree on any one candidate. With rightist votes split, the left gained a 50,000 majority over the second candidate—a majority that corresponded almost exactly to the Communist vote. In all, González Videla owed the Communists about one-fourth of his support.

Following his victory, the new president declared that "it is an error to maintain that the Communists will bring destruction" to the community of the Western Hemisphere. He also denied that his government was "coupled to the coach of Soviet imperialism" or that "Chile is being transformed into a Communist bridgehead." Having achieved new standing and prestige, the Communists shed the name National Democratic Party, to call themselves again the Communist Party of Chile.

Carlos Contreras Labarca, the party's secretary-general, became minister of communications and public works. Two other Communists, Miguel Concha and Victor Contreras, received the ministries of agriculture, and of land and colonization, respectively.

González Videla's aims were linked to Chile's battle against inflation. Industrialization, extended housing, and land reform were on his program. In foreign affairs, his government committed itself to a middle course. Frank L. Kluckhohn, reporting to the *New York Times* on September 5, 1946, quoted Chilean Communist leaders as having stated that "in the event of war between the United States and Russia, we will be on the side of Russia." During the early postwar period, Chile's Communists opposed not only "Yankee imperialism" according to the pattern adopted by all Latin-American Communist parties, but also the regime of Premier Juan Perón of Argentina. However, when Perón permitted the activity of a Communist Party in Argentina and arranged for a 150 million dollar credit to Chile, the Santiago Communist paper *El Siglo* stated editorially, "The agreement will allow both sister countries to break away from the imperialistic predomination of Wall Street and conquer their independence."

But in the spring of 1947, González Videla suddenly turned against the Communists. In order to gain Liberal Party support for the pact with Argentina and to warm up the somewhat chilled relationship with the United States, the president ousted the Communists from his cabinet. When this action was followed by strikes and unrest among transport and nitrate workers, González Videla blamed the Communists. He accused them of responsibility for four deaths resulting from riots in mid-June. And when Chile's president visited Brazil a few days later, he said, "I asked the Communists to share the government with me; but once they became merely Communists and not democrats, I asked them to leave the cabinet." He added that the Communists would have to respect the nation's constitution, or "the Communists in Chile will cease to be."

The Communists were quick to hit back. Strikes and unrest plunged the copper and nitrate industries into near-chaos, transport and agriculture grew disorganized. On August 19, González Videla ousted all Communists from high government office. He asked for, and the Chamber of Deputies approved, powers to declare a state of siege during a six-month period. The president had nearly come full-circle in his attitude toward the Communists. It looked as if he might even ban the party which had helped him to power.

BOLIVIA, PARAGUAY: LAMPPOST SHADOWS

On June 21, 1946, members of a revolutionary coalition hanged Bolivia's ruthless, pro-Nazi President Gualberto Villaroel to a lamppost in the city of La Paz. The rebellion that overthrew his government was long and bloody, and for a while there was danger that it might lead to chaos. But Bolivians entered the road to democratic government clearly and simply on January 7, 1947, when they followed their revolution with a sober and fair election. Among the groups that had supported the revolt was the Party of the Revolutionary Left (PIR), whose leader José Antonio Arze identified himself as "not Communist, but pure Marxist." His party backed Dr. Luis F. Guachalla, the candidate of the Liberals who was narrowly defeated in the race for the presidency by Dr. Enrique Hertzog of the Radical Socialist Union (which is neither radical nor Socialist, but a conservative party).

President Hertzog began his government with a program that included workers' insurance, progressive education, votes for women, and full religious freedom. José Antonio Arze's PIR avoids direct or open association with Communist parties elsewhere, but has consistently followed Communist policy.

The Bolivian revolution had a deafening echo across the border, in neighboring Paraguay. President General Higinio Moríñigo, who had ruled Paraguay's 1,500,000 people with a dictatorial hand for three years, suddenly experienced a democratic change of heart. A few days after the lamppost affair in La Paz, Moríñigo legalized opposition parties. The Communists were specifically recognized on August 1. During its years of illegality, the Communist Party had managed to retain about 500 devoted members. Its control of the Paraguayan Council of Labor, an affiliate of the Latin American Labor Confederation, was never doubted.

In the fall of 1946, Paraguayan Communists quickly gained several thousand new adherents and adjusted their party machinery to legal agitation. This frightened conservative Paraguayans. On October 13, Catholic groups demonstrated in the downtown section of Asunción, the capital. They demanded that the Communist Party be dissolved in a "great national anti-Communist crusade." Archbishop Sinforiano Bogarín of Asunción stated, however, that no Catholic institution was backing the demonstration. The Communists were worried, particularly since the Catholic demonstration took place during the one-month period in which the party had been temporarily suspended. Moríñigo's interior ministry banned the Communists from September 25 to October 25, accusing them of "not having collaborated as a legitimate opposition." In order to ease pressure on the government, Communist leaders Dr. Oscar Creydt and

Obdulio Barthe assured Auxiliary Archbishop Mena Porta that Paraguay's Communists had no intention of interfering with Church activities.

It was no use. All through the late summer and fall, General Moríñigo showed that he could have more than one change of heart within a six-month period. Members of opposition parties were in and out of grace, and in and out of jails. The Asunción ministry of the interior arrested and then freed leaders of the Colorado and Febrerista opposition parties.

On January 15, 1947, after less than six months of jack-in-the-box legality, the Communist Party found itself banned once again. Creydt managed to dive underground, or flee the country, while other Communists were rounded up by Moríñigo's police. Two days earlier, the president had imposed a thirty-day state of siege in an effort to forestall an alleged Communist-inspired revolt. Moríñigo reinstated the decree of April 7, 1936, which makes Communist activities punishable by law. The Communists were back where they had been for a decade: deep underground. Shortly afterward anti-Moríñigo forces of all political shades tried to overthrow the government; long, bitter civil war began to rage in Paraguay.

URUGUAY: TIPPING THE SCALES OF PARLIAMENT

During the elections that determined Uruguay's political fate from 1947 to, presumably, 1951, the Communists doubled their votes. In 1942, they had received not quite 15,000 votes; in 1946, nearly 30,000. They also elected one Senator, where they had none before, and elected five members of the Chamber of Deputies, where they had only two previously. They claim 15,000 members.

The big battle had been between Uruguay's ultra-nationalist Herrerista Party and the liberal Colorados. The world-wide postwar trend toward extremism benefited not only the Communists but also the followers of Luis Alberto de Herrera, who were accused of undue affinity to the militarist nationalist Argentine regime of General Juan Perón. Herrera's opponent, Tomas Berreta, won the election, but his party lost the absolute majority it had enjoyed in the Parliament. That is where the importance of the Communist deputies comes in: the Colorados need them for an effective majority, among the 100 deputies.

The Communists emerged as the second largest party left of center. The Herreristas, who have thirty deputies, can rally fifteen supporters from the smaller rightist parties. The Democrats and Socialists, natural allies of the Colorados, have only one deputy each. With its 46 deputies, the Colorado Party is at the mercy of its parliamentary allies. In fact, the Communists can stop any Colorado measure, whenever they consider it opportune to ally themselves with the right in a parliamentary vote.

This key position in the Parliament has not escaped the astute Communist politicians of Uruguay, and it has caused no little concern to the Colorado government, which opposes extremism of the left and right with equal determination. When Uruguay's Foreign Minister Eduardo Rodríguez Larreta visited New York early in 1947, he stated that his government was aware of the progress that communism has made in postwar Latin America but warned that "care must be taken not to provoke the opposite reaction." Larreta added, "Both communism and Fascism join in common cause to fight the democracies. Communism will thrive where social differences are deep. It has no chance where they do not exist. That phenomenon may be observed in certain Latin American countries."

ARGENTINA: MARRIAGE OF INCONVENIENCE

Relations between Argentina's Communists and the government of President General Juan D. Perón reflect aims and problems of the Buenos Aires regime with particular clarity. From 1943, when the men around General Perón first seized control, until after the 1945 election, the government and the Communists opposed each other bitterly. But, once Perón had been elected, the Communists not only ceased most of their attacks on him but even hailed many of his measures.

This switch in political attitude gains in importance if we consider four basic factors in Western Hemisphere affairs:

1. Disagreement between the United States and Argentina has been the most important inter-American issue for decades. It came to a head when, during the war, Argentina harbored a number of prominent Nazi agents. But Argentine resentment of the United States and its dominance in the Western Hemisphere goes farther back and much deeper than the war years. Cultural and economic reasons are mixed with emotional antagonism. During the war years, and operating under the Sixth Strategy of world communism, Communist parties throughout Latin America favored a unified war effort, hemisphere solidarity, and cooperation with the United States. The illegal Communist Party of Argentina was opposed

to the aggressively neutral line taken by Perón. But, when the war ended, and the Seventh Strategy of communism emphasized "imperialism" on the part of the United States, a major objective—the weakening of United States influence in Latin America—was shared by Communists and Perónistas alike.

2. In order to bolster his country's position in relation to the United States and other nations in the Western Hemisphere, Perón combined recognition of the Communist Party in 1945 with the establishment of diplomatic relation between his country and the Soviet Union. General Perón said at that time, "I have nothing against Russian communism inside Russia. No nation should concern itself with the internal affairs of another."

3. Communist parties in various parts of Latin America exercise political and propagandistic influence. While Argentina's Communists may battle Perón within the labor unions at home, Communist newspapers and speakers back this policy of pushing trade and financial relations with other Latin-American nations. This is much more agreeable to Perón than having to face Communist-organized resistance in Chile, Peru, or in any other country to which he extends Argentina's economic-political influence.

4. The Latin American Confederation of Labor and its affiliates throughout the southern half of the Western Hemisphere are a political and economic power to reckon with. It is true, as we have seen in discussing Communist influence in Mexico, that the Latin American Labor Confederation denies the dominance of Communist policies in its affairs. But it cannot be ignored that the Confederation's leaders opposed Perón until the time of the Argentine-Russian and Perónista-Communist *rapprochement*. Vicente Lombardo Toledano said after the 1945 elections that his organization's policy had to be adjusted because "the situation has changed." He added, "The former dictator is now the head of a legal government. We welcome the change and support the new régime."

On an external basis, the policies of the Perón government and world communism did coincide. But at home relations were not quite so serene. During his exile in Uruguay, Argentina's veteran Communist leader Rodolfo Ghioldi signed a declaration that was sent to Chapultepec, which said that Perón's "dictatorship arms itself, intrigues and conspires to install Nazis in neighboring state governments, seeks to divide the nations of the continent by disrupting the unity of foreign policy."

Ghioldi, who discovered the political talents of Brazil's Luíz Carlos Prestes, was a member of the extreme left Argentine Socialist group that associated itself with Lenin's Bolsheviks and the Third International. He visited the Soviet Union shortly after the Bolshevik Revolution and now has the prestige of an elder statesman of communism in Latin America. Ghioldi edits the party's daily, *La Hora*. Although he guides the affairs of Argentina's Communist Party through his intellectual ability and tactical experience, he leaves details of party affairs to others.

Gerónimo Arnedo Alvarez is the party's secretary-general; Victorio Codovilla, a persuasive speaker, has been instrumental in increasing membership to about 30,000. During the 1945 elections, the Communists polled nearly 100,000 votes in the anti-Perón coalition. One of the most difficult jobs of the party is held by José Peter, who leads the drive for control of the labor unions. Perón is well aware that his appeal to the *descamisados*, the "shirtless ones"—which is his affectionate oratorical phrase to describe the underprivileged workers—helped him win the presidency. Through his Labor Party and the Ministry of Labor, Perón (who was labor minister in earlier cabinets) exerts a powerful organizational and propagandistic influence on the labor movement. The Communists have nevertheless gained some control over organized labor in the building industries, the railroads, and the meat-packing trade.

On the surface, much of Perón's economic and labor program corresponds with socialization demands pushed by the Communists. His Five-Year Plan, which covers the 1946 to 1950 period, calls for "a reform of agriculture, industry and society." Specifically, it seeks to "restore the land to those who work it, even though it means taking it from those who regard themselves as owners." The plan includes a reorganization of industries, designed to "produce one hundred per cent of Argentina's needs and pave the way for competition in the world markets." Perón did not disguise the fact that his plan was an imitation of the famous Five-Year Plans that have characterized Premier Stalin's Soviet regime. Late in 1945, he said that he had chosen "the Russian victory pattern," because he considered it "obvious that they planned better than any other country." The Communists approved Perón's Five-Year Plan.

By the summer of 1946, when Perón could feel firmly entrenched, he began to take a more aggressive line toward the Communists. They, in turn, seemed less eager to see in Perón a champion in the fight against United States influence. These attitudes sharpened as time went on.

Speaking before a gathering of Argentina's leading businessmen, Perón said on November 27, 1946, that "capitalism remains only in two countries" and that "you must either accept a system of state intervention and controls, or lose everything by way of communism." Thus his antidote for communism seemed to be a kind of state capitalism on a national basis; that is, national "socialism" linked with military strength and a militant foreign economic policy. On March 8, 1947, Perón lashed out at Argentina's Communists, saying, "I will not discuss Russian Communists, because we have friendly relations with them. But we cannot allow a party, which we ourselves have recognized, to disturb our land by sabotage." This speech was made one day after the Soviet trade mission left Argentina, following more than a year of inconclusive negotiations for a treaty of trade and navigation.

The Communists began to cool towards Perón. The Communist-Perónista marriage of convenience had become quite inconvenient. For purely tactical reasons, the Communists had found themselves forced to defend Perón's labor policies against the criticism of the American Federation of Labor. Indignation towards Perón's domestic attacks on communism did not, however, weaken the collaboration of Latin-American Communists with Perón's foreign policy. At home, too, the Communists did not dare to oppose Perón aggressively. They knew him to be quite capable of condemning the party to illegality once more.

V
THE ORIENT AND AFRICA

CHAPTER 27

Japan: Rival Leaders

THE UNITED STATES does not favor communism, either in the United States or in Japan." This comment was made by George Atcheson, Jr., the late chairman of the Allied Council of Japan, on May 15, 1945. It has been a cornerstone of United States occupation policy, as expressed and executed by General Douglas MacArthur's military government.

Communism in Japan faces two imposing hurdles: MacArthur's desire to stem Soviet influence, which he considers detrimental to American interests in the Far East; and the traditionally conservative, anti-Communist, anti-Soviet, and anti-Russian attitude of large parts of Japan's populace and political leadership. In addition, the Communist Party lacks trained organizers and agitators. Successive Japanese militarist governments have arrested, maltreated, or executed Communists and those accused of Communist sympathies or other "dangerous thoughts." Shortage of trained leaders has brought impetuous, half-indoctrinated men into positions of authority within the Japanese Communist Party.

After more than two decades of illegality, the Communists are obviously too weak for extremist action. A conciliatory policy, in accordance with the Seventh Strategy of world communism, would be most likely to bring mass support. Instead, many Communists are naïvely impatient, hotheaded, and eager to do political battle.

The Communist Party of Japan has never been a mass party. Russia's October Revolution found an ideological echo in urban Japanese intellectual circles. At the same time, large sections of Japan's labor became conscious of their economic power. After World War I, a labor shortage coincided with high prices, particularly in food. Rice riots and strikes in arsenals and even among civil-service employees were the result. There were four hundred walkouts in 1918 alone.

A general trend toward Marxism developed in Japan. *The Story of*

Poverty, a popular analysis of Marxist thinking, sold more than half a million copies. This sudden interest in a revolutionary economic-political belief alarmed the conservative government. But democratic freedoms were still being respected, at least outwardly. Organization of the Communist Party in 1922 was tolerated.

The first of several violent anti-Communist, anti-labor, anti-opposition drives was undertaken by the Japanese police at the time of the Tokyo earthquake in September, 1923. Arrests and even executions were made during the confusion created by the quake. Two years later, the so-called "Peace Preservation Law" banned all "organizing of, joining or inducing others to join, any society which aims at altering the national constitution or at repudiating the system of private property." Originally, this drastic law imposed a maximum penalty of ten years in prison. Three years later, the death penalty was decreed.

VIOLENT SUPPRESSION

In March and April, 1928, the government of General Giichi Tanaka, who became notorious for his imperialistic "Tanaka Memorial," arrested some thousand persons accused of communism or Communist sympathies. This drive particularly affected social-study groups at universities and other educational institutions. A few weeks later, Japanese troops landed on Chinese soil. The following year brought further large-scale roundups, but the Communist Party continued to function underground; it reported a membership of three thousand. But the character of its membership was changing, and, according to contemporary non-Communist accounts, it was losing the support of trade unionists. The magazine *Kaizo* asserted in its December, 1929, issue that "few students and no women at all took part in the original Communist party, whereas many students and quite a number of women could be found in the reorganized party." The article added that "veteran Socialist agitators" no longer played a decisive part in Communist activity, which had become "more and more formalized and idealistic." *Kaizo* concluded that "the sphere of action is passing from factories, mines and rural villages to the schools and colleges," with the tenor of agitation growing "too abstract for the proletarian mass to follow its lead."

The early 1930's brought the Communists isolated successes, as well as a serious crisis inside the party. A new police drive in 1931 almost ended

.s existence. The Comintern apparently realized the gravity of the situation in which its Japanese supporters found themselves. In 1933, Yamamoto Masami left Moscow secretly for Japan. He managed to pull the demoralized party together, at least temporarily. But he was arrested shortly afterward. During this period, the magazine *Nippon* reported that "Communists carried on propaganda in the First Aviation School in Tokyo, issued a propaganda publication, *The Soldier's Friend*, organized a special unit which carried on activities during last year's (1932) maneuvers in Kansai, organized cells in certain army units, while in the navy section they nearly succeed in forming a nucleus right inside the headquarters of the Admiralty itself."

In spite of such attempts to build up underground activity, police methods were successful in curbing Communist advances. The technique of the "thought police" included torture and threat of death. Apparently as the result of such police efforts, two former members of the Communist Party's central committee denounced the Comintern in 1933. They were Professor Sanu Gaku, who had been arrested in 1929 after serving at Waseda University, and Sadakichi Nabeyama. The police also produced a startlingly high number of "converted" Communists who were permitted to return to freedom after denouncing their beliefs. Some 60,000 persons were arrested by the political police between 1928 and 1936, the majority non-Communists who had been accused of sympathizing with the party.

This continuous police drive discouraged Social Democrats and other labor-peasant groups from associating with Communists, who continued to distribute illegal propaganda and were active in political strikes. The Tokyo ministry of justice maintained that Communist Party headquarters had been transferred to the west coast of the United States. In spite of police vigilance, numerous centers for the distribution of underground propaganda existed throughout the Japanese home islands. Communist booklets appeared under such innocent covers as *A Key to Chess*, or in the guise of Biblical literature under the imprint of "The Beacon Society" of New York City.

In the spring of 1934, the Japanese Christian Council reported to the London office of the International Missionary Council on the development of Communist sentiment inside Japan. The council gave the following reasons for the influence of Communist ideas: "Antipathy against capitalism and narrow nationalism; the stimulus furnished by labor and tenant problems; the effect of the economic depression on small shopkeepers and owners of small factories; the desperate straits of the farming class; corruption of the political world and dissatisfaction with the existing political parties; a deficient consciousness regarding constitutional self-government; and the extreme-materialistic tendency of our times."

"FAKUMOTOISM" AND "YAMAKAWAISM"

This period of public discontent and violent police measures coincided with factionalism inside the Communist Party. During its first period of illegality, the party had experienced two purges. It had rejected the ideas of Kazuo Fakumoto, who advocated continued and violent Marxist class struggle, and it had expelled Hitoshi Yamakawa, who favored cooperation with Social Democratic or nonparty labor and peasant groups. In the international Communist vernacular, "Fakumotoism," as it was called represented a "leftist deviation" and "Yamakawaism" was labeled a "rightist deviation." (After World War II, Hitoshi Yamakawa became the spokesman of the Social Democratic Party's left wing, which favored coalition with the Communists.)

On November 5, 1933, Sen Katayama, one of the founders of Japan's Communist Party, died in exile of tuberculosis. Katayama, an ardent Marxist pacifist, had attended the Amsterdam Conference of the Second International in 1904 and denounced nationalist tendencies within the Socialist parties. He split with the Second International on the war issue and helped develop the Communist Party of Japan together with like-minded Socialists. One of these cofounders was Sanzo Nozaka, who succeeded Katayama as Comintern representative after the latter's death.

Nozaka, who later used the name of Susumu Okano, was born in 1892, attended Keio University, and visited the London School of Economics in 1918. He became interested in Marxism while still a student, was imprisoned in Japan during the 1928 raids, but managed to escape to the Soviet Union eighteen months later. He attended the Comintern Conference of 1931. He may later have returned to Japan illegally, but this cannot be confirmed.

Nozaka, writing under the name of Okano, revealed in the September 5, 1934, issue of the *Communist International* that conditions inside the Japanese party had become chaotic. Frightened by police suppression and extremist action on the part of the central committee, an opposition group had accused the party leaders of acting as *agents provocateurs*. The opposition charged that the central committee had surrounded itself by a super-bodyguard that was killing innocent Communists accused of being police spies. Spear-headed by the district committee at the town of Kansai, these opposition groups demanded a change in leadership.

Nozaka-Okano expressed Moscow's confidence in the central committee. By comparing the tactics used by the party in Japan with the world-wide strategy of communism during that period, it would indeed seem that the central committee was loyally following over-all policies, even though these may have been ill adapted to conditions inside Japan. Nozaka-Okano wrote, "The Communist Party of Japan is now threatened with a split and the disorganization of all its party work, a position which is being egged on by the agents of the police, which is artfully using the situation inside the party." Although the central committee managed to survive this crisis, the party had been weakened. The Tokyo ministry of justice nevertheless admitted shortly afterward that it had been unable to stamp out communism entirely. Justice Minister Chara said on March 8, 1935, in a speech before the Diet:

"Notwithstanding all the measures taken by the government since 1928 to cut the roots of the Communist movement, this movement has taken such deep hold that even after repeated arrests of the entire leadership of the movement and after suppression of the Communist organization, those Communists who remain at liberty continue their activities. The government is unable to achieve the final destruction of communism."

The Comintern urged the Japanese Communists to gain control of the legal labor and peasant organizations. Ossip Pyatnitsky, reporting on a decade and a half of the Communist movement, accused the Japanese party of being "weak" when it came to infiltration of legal organizations; he urged that "the Communist Party not only work in these organizations, but also carry on a furious campaign against the leaders of these organizations." A summing up of the party's accomplishments was published in the *Communist International* on July 5, 1935. The article recalled that the central committee had succeeded in "crushing liquidationism from the right (Yamakawaism) and from the left (Fakumotoism)" in "Bolshevik fashion" and was continuing its advance against "the fever of chauvinism, bourgeois nationalism and social chauvinism." Thus, the article continued, the party had "developed the illegal revolution against the war-making monarchy" in "a situation of unprecedented terror." In spite of these reported successes, Japanese Communists were accused of having failed to infiltrate the Social Democratic groups and of having "not yet learned to utilize every manifestation of dissatisfaction, or to grasp and develop even the smallest manifestation of protest against the vileness of the monarchist regime."

PREPARATIONS IN YENAN

This anti-monarchist, anti-emperor policy was pursued throughout the period of Japanese aggression against China and during World War II. Sanzo Nozaka made his headquarters in the Chinese Communist capital at Yenan in 1943, where he took over the leadership of the Japanese People's Emancipation League. This group, whose activities served as a model for the Korean People's Emancipation League, conducted a three-fold campaign: (1) indoctrination of Japanese prisoners or deserters who had come into the hands of the Chinese Communist Eighth Route Army; (2) psychological warfare among Japanese troops by means of broadcasts, leaflets, loudspeakers, and other propaganda devices; and (3) resistance and sabotage inside the Japanese-controlled areas of China, in cooperation with Chinese guerrillas.

By 1944, some 325 Japanese had joined the Yenan Communist-led Emancipation League. This figure was comparatively low. Considering the fact that the Communist Party of Japan had been nearly destroyed during the war period, Nozaka's desire to create a larger nucleus of politically indoctrinated Japanese is understandable. To this end, recruiting among prisoners was accelerated late in 1944 and early in 1945. Political reeducation was undertaken in the so-called "Japanese Peasants' and Workers' School." Marxist ideas were presented in simple terms. A booklet entitled *An Appeal to the Japanese People,* written by Nozaka, was used as a basic text for new prisoners. The next step was a class in "Political Common Sense," which included an analysis and criticism of the emperor. In this class, Nozaka experienced the same psychologic-political difficulties that he was later to encounter in Japan itself. Emperor worship was so deeply rooted in the Japanese soldiery that even those willing to be indoctrinated on other subjects were horrified by Communist criticism of the emperor system. Andrew Roth writes in his book, *Dilemma in Japan,* that reverence for the emperor was "the last portion of the military ideology to give way; and then, in most cases, only after many months of indoctrination."

The nucleus of the Emancipation League was the Communist League, whose one hundred members were the most promising propagandists and agitators. This core had, at least superficially, come to look upon the emperor as the symbol of a monarchic system that would have to be eliminated. But Nozaka was aware of the difficulties that a hard-and-fast anti-emperor policy would create for the Communists. He told *New York Herald Tribune* correspondent Harrison Forman, "The Emperor is still too much of a god-like figure to a good many Japanese, for us to shout 'Down with the Emperor!' at this moment."

TOKUDA, IMPATIENT FIREBRAND

But inside Japan, those Communists who were freed after Tokyo's surrender had retained the radical ideas that their party advanced during the 1920's and 1930's. Kyuichi Tokuda, who spent eighteen years in jail, quickly gained the reputation of a sharp-tongued firebrand. Both he and Yoshio Shiga, who became editor of the party paper *Red Flag*, had received permanent injuries during their imprisonment. Shiga, imprisoned during the 1928 drive, had hardly left the Fuchu prison on October 2, 1945, when he told Japanese reporters, "In order for Japan to organize herself on a democratic basis, it is necessary for her to abolish her present system of Emperor rule. The reason for this is that, as long as Emperor rule remains, the vestiges of the military caste and the clan of vassals might use the Emperor to regain power."

Only two weeks after his release, Shiga approached the Social Democratic Party with suggestions on future united action of the two Marxist parties. He seemed incredulous regarding reports that Sanzo Nozaka and his Yenan Japanese Communists were coming around to a go-easy-on-the-Emperor policy. On October 18, the Tokyo radio was quoting Shiga as saying, "There have been reports that Japanese Communists in Yenan are advocating Communistic principles within the framework of Emperor rule and that they are making this the aim of their activities inside Japan. I believe that these reports are false. There is no reason for comrades in Yenan to advocate such a thing."

Shiga was wrong. The "comrades in Yenan" knew much better how the mass of the Japanese people felt about the emperor than either Shiga or Tokuda had been able to perceive from their prison cells. As soon as Nozaka arrived on Japanese soil in January, 1946, he stated that the

Communists would favor retention of the emperor, provided that he was stripped of most of his power. While Shiga was beginning to see the wisdom of such a strategy, Nozaka had a hard time persuading the excitable, wild-eyed Kyuichi Tokuda. As a politician returned from relatively comfortable exile, Nozaka also encountered Tokuda's idea that his years of suffering in prison entitled him to a decisive voice in party affairs. Yoshio Shiga thus found himself more than once in the role of mediator between the realistic Nozaka and the "leftist deviationist" Tokuda.

Just how these rivalries affected Communist statements of policy can be seen from two party resolutions, issued within little more than a month of each other. On January 14, 1946, the Communists declared with Nozaka-like moderation that "as a prelude to the firm establishment of democracy in Japan the Emperor must be completely separated from political power, and whether a politically isolated Emperor would be allowed to exist, will depend on the people's judgment." After thus tacitly agreeing to continuation of the emperor system in principle, the party made a Tokuda-like announcement on February 28, which referred to "the Emperor and all other war criminals," a phrase that could hardly endear the Communists to the overwhelming number of Japanese.

This confusion prompted the Social Democrats to steer away from repeated Communist offers of a coalition. In the May, 1946, elections, the Social Democrats had received nine million votes, the Communists two million. In many ways, the policies of the Socialists reflected or paralleled the thinking of American occupation authorities. Both had favored the enforcement of far-reaching domestic reforms immediately following Japan's surrender. As the Communists became more and more active and extended their agitation to the large National Congress of Industrial Unions, United States occupation authorities and the Social Democrats adopted a more conservative policy.

The initial governments of Japan after World War II represented coalitions of the Liberal and Progressive parties, which were largely composed of elements prominent during Tokyo's nationalist-militaristic regimes of the prewar and war periods. There can be little doubt that the conservative elements in these two parties used the issue of communism to swing the support of the military government and of the nation to their side. The sweeping reforms that General MacArthur initiated required implementation by the conservative cabinets. The Communists were quick to say that the Progressive-Liberal administrations gave little more than lip service to these changes of Japan's political and economic scene. Non-American members on the Allied Council in several instances supported charges that the conservative regimes were skillfully sabotaging the avowed policies of the military government. The representative of the Soviet Union on the Allied Council was outspoken in this respect, but the delegates of the United Kingdom and Australia also voiced doubt as to the sincerity of the Japanese government's efforts.

As the post-surrender period faded farther into the background, American occupation authorities became more and more Communist-conscious. This was in part due to the overzealous elements within the Communist Party which, for the sake of a label, might be called the Tokuda wing. General MacArthur reported on November 18, 1946, that the wave of strikes called by the National Congress of Industrial Unions with the backing of the Communist Party earlier that year had been staged in spite of a warning by Sanzo Nozaka. Apparently, Nozaka's objections had been ignored by his own party as well as by radical elements within the NCIU.

The strike wave extended into early 1947. Economic conditions became more and more critical, and demands for higher wages were pushed vigorously by the unions. In the planning and execution of strikes, Kyuichi Tokuda and Yoshio Shiga were prominent. When, in January, government workers and public utility unions planned a general strike, Tokuda and Shiga led negotiations that aimed at 100 to 300 per cent wage increases. General MacArthur intervened at the last moment and banned the general strike. He said that he had acted "with the greatest reluctance," because a strike of such proportion might have become "a deadly social weapon in the present impoverished and emaciated condition of Japan."

Shortly afterward, MacArthur announced that a second postwar election would take place in the spring of 1947. The Communists asked the Social Democrats for a "united action" election campaign. They were rebuffed. The Social Democrats answered, "Your party has been insisting on a general strike as the key to economic recovery, but our party is absolutely opposed to political general strikes. Your party declares joint Communist and Socialist efforts are the people's passionate desire, but our party is confident that the opposite is the case."

The election of April 25 brought victory to the moderate Social Democrats and premiership to the party's leader, Tetsu Katayama. The Social

Democrats elected 143 of the 466 parliamentary delegates. The Communists barely managed to get their two top leaders, Nozaka and Tokuda, into Parliament. Shiga was defeated. So was Nozaka's wife, who had arrived from the Soviet Union shortly before the election. The Democrats (mostly former members of the Progressive Party) elected 122 delegates, the Liberals 132. General MacArthur commented that the Japanese people had "firmly and decisively defeated" communism and chosen "a moderate course."

IMPROVED AGITATION TECHNIQUE

Since it emerged from its underground position on October 1, 1945, Japan's Communist Party has overcome some of its shortcomings. The party had a long record of idealistic naïveté, hardly in keeping with the realistic policies practiced by world communism today. Violations of world-wide Communist tactics during the immediate postwar period were doubtless due to inexperienced leadership and lack of discipline within the party.

There are a number of striking similarities between the Communist parties of Japan and of Italy. Both parties gained influence in a political vacuum, created by the disappearance of a dictatorial-militaristic state machine. Each party is led by a shrewd, carefully restraining leader. The small, dapper, smoothly speaking Sanzo Nozaka has followed a policy similar to that of Palmiro Togliatti in Italy; just as Togliatti put the issue of the monarchy aside, when that seemed useful, so has Nozaka influenced Japanese communism to tone down its attitude toward the emperor. Nozaka might have preferred a more restrained labor policy, but the Tokuda wing and the rank and file of the NCIU were impatient with subtle techniques.

A curious role has been played by the Youth Action Groups, the Japanese equivalent of Communist youth leagues elsewhere. These young men have displayed many of the characteristics of Fascist youth elsewhere. That is not surprising. They include former "Kamikaze" suicide fighters and other militaristically inclined ambitious young men. During the January, 1947, strike movement, these Youth Action Groups at times invaded the rooms in which labor councils were held and forced the acceptance of extremist decisions.

Communist extremism strengthened the hand of the ultra-conservative elements of the Tokyo government. It has at times prompted the Mac-Arthur administration to back conservative and often discredited politicians. Although the moderate Social Democrats and the National Federation of Labor resist Communist advances, the Communist Party was able to win control not only of the National Congress of Industrial Unions, but also of the powerful Farmers' Union.

Sanzo Nozaka is one of the few nonconservative Japanese politicians who achieved prominence after the war. His personality has done much to overcome the hotheadedness of other Communist leaders. But he had to begin indoctrination and agitation completely anew, after he landed in Japan. Late in 1945, the Japanese Communist Party had 10,000 members. Eighteen months later, its membership had increased by 50,000 and continued to mount. Its Tokyo daily paper, *Red Flag*, reached a circulation of 300,000. The party's pamphlets and leaflets overshadowed the propaganda material of other groups in quantity as well as in skill of preparation.

Although the Allied Supreme Command, under General MacArthur, is acutely aware of Communist activities and aspirations (military government specialists even prepared a pamphlet for labor leaders, showing the technique of Communist infiltration), the Japanese Communist Party can be expected to make a come back, should the country's critical economic situation grow chaotic.

CHAPTER 28

Korea: Test Tube of Power

$\mathbf{K}$OREA IS the prime example of a nation on the periphery of rival power interests. In Korea, the United States and the Soviet Union met head-on. There was no buffer territory to cushion the shock.

A year after Korea's liberation, rioting endangered the American-occupied southern zone. Pak Huen Yung, secretary-general of the Communist Party of south Korea, was in hiding. Lieutenant General John R. Hodge, commander of United States forces in the southern region, accused the Communists of becoming ever "bolder and more fanatical in their blatant perversion of the truth, their falsehoods and their lies." Meanwhile, in northern Korea, Soviet occupation forces were backing a Communist-dominated government. The two zones were divided by the thirty-eighth parallel. Soviet-American negotiations aimed at unified administration, rather than partition, had broken down. American military spokesmen charged that the Communists, already undisputed masters in the north, were trying to gain total power in the southern zone as well.

The conflict faced by United States occupation authorities had its root in the development of the Korean nationalist movement. Leaders of the Korean Independence Party, which spear-headed the abortive anti-Japanese rebellion of 1919, had been active in exile for decades. Led by Syngman Rhee and Kim Koo, the Independence Party founded a provisional government in Shanghai, while pro-Soviet Koreans sought refuge in Siberia. On April 17, 1925, a Communist Party was organized secretly inside Japanese-occupied Korea. It drew most of its support from the Siberian exiles. Koreans who adhered to this movement were, in many ways, nationalists first and Communists second. The rising power of the Soviet state gave them a concrete chance of liberation from Japanese rule. For several years, the Korean Communist Party was torn by factionalism. When the Kuomintang broke with the Chinese Communists, this rift deepened the division between the leaders of the Independence Party and the Communists, who had never recognized the provisional government at Shanghai.

In 1928, the Comintern dissolved the Communist Party of Korea, accusing it of irresponsible factionalism. It was not until 1935 that the Communist International permitted the formation of an "initiatory Group of Korean Communists." This group denounced the "fierce factional struggle going on among the Communists, which has assumed absolutely unheard-of and monstrous forms." The Communists later formed the Korean National Revolutionary Party.

After the Japanese invasion of China, the provisional government followed the geographical movements of the Chinese government of General Chiang Kai-shek, on whose financial support it depended. During World War II, the Korean provisional government made its headquarters in Chungking, where Kim Koo lived as chairman. Syngman Rhee, president of the provisional regime, took up residence in Washington. He served as chairman of the Korean Commission and as unofficial ambassador to the United States.

In December, 1941, the Communist Korean National Revolutionary Party expressed its support of the provisional government in a special manifesto. This document stated that Communist support had been withheld because the provisional body could not "exercise real authority, until the national territory had been recovered," had not won the recognition of other countries, did not contain "representatives of the various revolutionary bodies," and had "not been lawfully elected by the Korean people." But, the manifesto continued, "the democratic countries of the world have now formed an anti-Fascist bloc and gone to war against the Fascist powers, and in Europe refugee governments have . . . been recognized by the democratic countries." The Communists concluded that, therefore, "a similar Korean government may now hope to also gain their recognition and assistance."

TWO COALITIONS

The Independence Party and the Communists, together with some smaller parties, established a Korean Party Congress in October, 1943, at Chungking. This coalition did not last. Korean Communists left Chungking for Yenan, capital of Communist-controlled regions of northern

China. At Yenan, they worked hand in hand with the Chinese Communist Party and with the Communist group forming the Japanese People's Emancipation League. Late in 1944, the Korean Communists formed their own Korean People's Emancipation League. They also founded a workers' and peasants' school. Yenan became the center of Korean Communist activities in 1945. The Korean People's Emancipation League, reporting a membership of two thousand, undertook anti-Japanese guerrilla activities inside Korea. Following Moscow's denunciation of the Soviet-Japanese neutrality pact in the spring of 1945, the Yenan Koreans urged Koreans everywhere to form a "united front of all parties" against the Japanese.

While the Communists were active in Yenan and the provisional government in Chungking, a coalition of several groups prepared for the day of liberation inside Korea itself. This coalition, headed by Lyuh Woon Heung, stood ideologically between the Syngman Rhee and the Yenan Communists. While the United States negotiated with the Tokyo government on the technicalities of Japan's surrender, Lyuh Woon Heung entered into discussions with General Noburo Abe, Japanese commander in Korea. Abe turned his authority over to Lyuh; and, when American troops entered Korea, the nationalist leader had already proclaimed a "People's Republic." American occupation authorities in Korea had originally been scheduled for participation in the occupation of Japan. They had little knowledge of Korean internal affairs and found it difficult to distinguish between Lyuh Woon Heung's People's Party and the Yenan Communists. The People's Party was ignored. Instead, Kim Koo and Syngman Rhee were brought to Seoul, much to the chagrin of Lyuh and his followers.

A pattern that could be noted in nearly all liberated nations also became visible in Korea: underground leaders felt that they were better suited to head a government than those who had been in exile. Cold-shouldered by the occupation authorities, Lyuh Woon Heung turned toward the Communists. Pak Huen Yung, the Communist leader who had been a Japanese prisoner from 1919 to 1929, was willing to cooperate with Lyuh in opposing the provisional government. (Incidentally, American occupation authorities insisted that men like Syngman Rhee had come to Seoul only as private persons. They stated that Rhee had no authority to sign his statements as the official of a "provisional government." United States officers said that Rhee was merely aiding the American occupation authorities as a member of the "Korean Advisory Council.") Pak Huen Yung stated on October 7, 1945, that the Communists of southern Korea favored a coalition government in which "all political parties, excepting the pro-Japanese reactionaries, can work together in a united front for progressive democracy." Pak told a United Press reporter that the demarcation point at the thirty-eighth parallel should be "abolished immediately." He said that, in his opinion, the Soviet zone was being administered properly, while the Americans were too soft on pro-Japanese collaborationists. The Communist leader, at that time, placed membership of his party at 11,000, although American observers believed this figure to be somewhat exaggerated. (The total alleged membership of Korea's many parties was approximately three times the number of its twenty-five million inhabitants.)

THE MOSCOW DECISION

Only one issue united all Korean parties: they bitterly opposed division of their nation. Partition had thrown the economy of Korea out of balance. Right after Japan's surrender, President Truman had stated that "the assumption by the Koreans themselves of the responsibilities and functions of a free and independent nation" would "of necessity require time and patience." As 1945 drew to a close, Korean patience had worn quite thin. This mood was not enhanced when the Moscow Conference of Foreign Ministers announced on December 27 that Korea was to be united under a trusteeship. This trusteeship, with Russia and the United States in charge, was to last not longer than five years. During the trusteeship period, the Moscow decision said, the Koreans were to develop a "provisional government, which shall take all the necessary steps for developing the industry, transport, and agriculture of Korea, and the national culture of the Korean people." A joint Soviet-American commission was to prepare a provisional Korean government after consulting "the Korean democratic parties and social organizations."

All Korean parties immediately opposed the Moscow decision. They wanted independence right away and no foreign-controlled administration. All parties, including the Communists, agitated violently against the trusteeship proposals. The Communists scheduled a protest meeting for January 3, 1946. But, when it became clear that the Soviet government favored the trusteeship decision, the Communist party line in Korea made a complete turnabout. The meeting came out for rather than against the Moscow plan.

Negotiations between American and Soviet representatives on the joint commission took place in the spring of 1946. They failed completely. According to American sources, Soviet Colonel General Terenty Shtykov made it clear that his government considered only those parties as "democratic" which had agreed to the Moscow decision on trusteeship for Korea. But only the Communists had come out in favor of trusteeship. All other parties considered support of the Moscow decision unpatriotic. The American delegation, headed by Major General Archibald V. Arnold, took the view that it was neither unreasonable nor subversive for Korean nationalists to want their independence right away. General Hodge clarified the American position on March 11, stating that the United States delegation did not intend to "bring about a government by any particular group or wing." He also said that only unification of the two zones would make it possible "to form a genuinely representative, democratic government."

On April 13, the Soviet delegation agreed to consultation with those Korean parties which pledged themselves to support the Moscow decisions. By that time, most of the parties realized that the Moscow plan provided the only available road toward eventual self-government. Consequently, they signed the required pledge. But, on May 8, the Russians reversed their previous stand. They insisted that only parties that actively supported the Moscow blueprint should be consulted. This, again, would have left only the Communists. The American delegation did not agree. The negotiations broke down.

The above account is an informal summary of the negotiations as they were reported by American authorities. Soviet sources did not provide a similarly detailed version of the joint talks. The Moscow paper *Izvestia* expressed the official Soviet view on May 15. The paper accused the American command in Korea of seeking to "justify the actions of reactionary parties and organizations against the Moscow decisions" and of encouraging them "in their struggle against the Moscow decisions." These tactics, the editorial stated, were designed to "mislead the Korean people and break up the ranks of genuine democratic parties and organizations."

The chips were down. From then on, the Communist Party in southern Korea and the American command at Seoul were at sword's points. The Communists engaged in violent opposition against the military government and against those Korean parties which cooperated with the American command. General Hodge's office, in turn, cracked down on the Communists with exasperated fury. The Communist Party used the economic crisis to undermine the prestige of the United States occupation forces. The Communists compared distribution of rice and other grains under the American regime unfavorably with conditions during Japanese occupation. This was an issue Korean peasants and laborers could fully appreciate. The results were unrest, strikes, and finally a series of riots in the Taegu region. Early in October, 1946, these incidents had become so serious that Korean national police and civilians were clashing nearly every day. Losses in dead and wounded were suffered by both sides. General Hodge appealed to Korean workers on October 5 not to be persuaded by "vicious agitators from outside."

Following the breakdown of Soviet-American negotiations, the American command in Seoul prepared the ground for a Southern Korean Legislative Assembly, to be partly elected and partly appointed by the United States military government. Pak Huen Yung declared July 4 that the Communists considered such a body merely as "a way of prolonging the military government and a strengthening of American control." He said that his party would not participate in the formation of the Legislative Assembly, since there was "no need of creating or entering such a body." Richard J. H. Johnston, *New York Times* correspondent in Seoul, commented on Pak's statement by saying that "the Communists have dedicated themselves unequivocally to the contention that American motives are heinous, dishonest, and selfish, while the salvation of Korea lies chiefly in the hands of the Soviet Union."

Whether the majority of Koreans had accepted this view could, of course, not be determined. But Lyuh Woon Heung broke with the Communists when he signed a coalition agreement aimed at participation in the Legislative Assembly. On July 17, Lyuh was attacked by three armed Koreans. He was blindfolded, taken to a deserted spot, maltreated, and forced to sign a letter in which he withdrew his support for the projected legislative body. The three men then attempted to throw the People's Party leader over a cliff. They had removed the blindfold before forcing Lyuh to sign the letter. He screamed and battled his attackers. They finally fled, taking the letter with them. After returning to Seoul, frightened and dazed, Lyuh said that the letter had apparently been a phony suicide note, in which he was to have labeled himself as a traitor unworthy to live. Lyuh evaded his enemies for another year; on July 19, 1947, he was killed by two bullets fired by an unknown assassin who had jumped on a car that carried Lyuh through the streets of Seoul.

NINE MILLION COUNTERFEIT YEN

Communist prestige was further weakened by the discovery of a counterfeiting establishment in the party's building at Seoul. Seventeen accused members of the counterfeiting ring were brought to trial on July 29, 1946. Among the accused was Song Un Pil, financial director of the Communist Party of south Korea. The defendants were accused of having printed nine million yen in counterfeit money. The Communists attempted to prove that the alleged counterfeiters were merely victims of political persecution. The whole thing, they asserted, was a frame-up.

On the day of the trial, the party organized a violent protest meeting outside the court house. The trial had to be postponed. The Communists then sent a petition to General Hodge asking, among several other things, that the American-Soviet commission be reconvened to supervise the trial. Hodge, in turning the document over to military government officials, observed that "the Korean Communist party has apparently the mistaken concept that it is intended to make the trial of the defendants in this large counterfeiting plot a trial of the Communist party." He added that "The fact that several of the accused happen to be members of the Communist party has no bearing on the dispensation of justice" and that it would be handled "exactly as any other trial against alleged criminals." But the Communists went all out in defending the counterfeiters. The party's weekly paper *Kun Kuk* even issued a special edition, demanding the release of the defendants and asking that the trial court be "smashed." Song Un Pil and three other Communists were later sentenced to life imprisonment.

While pressing its campaign of nonparticipation in the American-backed Legislative Assembly, the Communist Party faced two obstacles: cleavage within its own ranks, and growing opposition from Lyuh Woon Hueng's People's Party. Pak Huen Yung made a trip to the northern, Soviet-occupied zone and returned with instructions for an amalgamation of the Communists with the People's Party and the small Democratic Party into a "Labor Party of South Korea." This southern combination was later to fuse with the already existing "Labor Party of North Korea" (backbone of the Soviet-inspired north Korean government) into an "All-Korea Labor Party." Seoul's Communist paper *Inmin Po* said on August 6 that such a combination of parties would "develop democracy in Korea and overcome the reactionary elements that have been hampering both unification and the progress of democracy." Pak's plan was opposed by the vice-chairman and cofounder of the Korean Communist Party, Lee Yung Yung, and by five other members of the party's executive committee. The People's Party also proved recalcitrant. The project was nevertheless carried out.

Meanwhile, the Allied Command tried to stem Communist propaganda, designed to discredit the United States in the eyes of southern Koreans. This campaign asserted that American "imperialism" was exploiting the people of Korea, while the Soviet Union had decisively beaten Japan and greatly desired the uplifting of small nations, such as Korea. This propaganda barrage became so heavy that General Hodge decided to contradict it point by point. On August 31, he released a message to the Korean people, saying that "the United States is not interested in any exploitation of Korea, but is interested in helping the nation in every way." He denounced "vicious propaganda coming from speakers, the press, pamphlets and posters of some political groups in southern Korea." Hodge also emphasized that the United States fought Japan for four years and that "crushing blows by the United States in the Pacific" spurred the Japanese into "making peace overtures as early as June, 1945."

His message was backed by a statement of Dean Acheson, Acting Secretary of State, who emphasized that the United States had no imperialist aims in Korea. A few days later, on September 8, General Hodge again spoke out against "croaking voices and venomous pens." He said, "We have not brought liberty across bloody seas to see it abruptly discarded or lightly suspended." The Communist papers countered by carrying a news story that asserted that "American troops have been ordered to bayonet Korean laborers." Hodge temporarily suspended the Communist or pro-Communist papers *Inmin Po, Hyern Dai Albo,* and *Choong Ang Sin Moon.*

As unrest spread, the arrest of agitators was ordered by military government authorities. Pak Huen Yung went into hiding. The Soviet *Tass* news agency accused the American command of "brutal repression" by "purely Fascist methods." The Communist Party, for all practical purposes, became an anti-American underground movement in southern Korea, receiving support from the northern zone. The conflict had begun in earnest.

COALITION WITHIN COALITION

The South Korea Labor Party was finally formed while Pak Huen Yung remained underground. He was listed as one of the party's vice-chairmen. The official chairmanship was given to Ho Hun. Although the South Korea Labor Party was supposed to be a coalition of various leftist groups, it was itself part of another coalition: the Democratic Front, with which Lyuh Woon Heung affiliated, in spite of his difficulties with the Communists. Lyuh's difficult position was illustrated by a memorandum that he published in the *Christian Science Monitor*. He accused the United States and the Soviet Union of playing power politics, saying, "Soviet Russia openly favors the Communists in the North, while the American Military Government backs the Rightists in the South." How tragic-grotesque the Korean situation had become was made clear on January 23, 1947, when the disappointed Syngman Rhee accused General Hodge of "efforts to build up and foster the Korean Communist Party," and said, "Fifteen months ago, Korea had a few Communists infiltrated from the north. It has only a small number of them today, despite the active encouragement given by the American Military Government. Communists in Korea have been allowed every possible resource for anti-American propaganda and organization."

A month later, on February 13, Korean police raided the South Korea Labor Party's headquarters at Seoul and seized a letter from Major Nikolai Gusunov, education officer of the Soviet army in north Korea, addressed to Ho Hun. The clumsy and unreliable translation published by the police asserted that Ho had been instructed to organize demonstrations at the time of the Moscow Conference of Foreign Ministers. According to the police, the letter stated in part:

"Through reliable information we discovered that at the conference on March 10, consisting of the four powers, the Soviet Army would strengthen the situation in Korea. To accomplish this object, the South Korea Labor Party should raise a great revolution all over South Korea. The purpose of this revolution is to wipe away the legislative body established by the United States Army Military Government in Korea and to maintain closer connection in the coming battle of destruction in Southern Korea. . . .

"Hence, do I order you, Ho Hun: To agitate all students in South Korea to fight against their schools and the United States Army Military

Government according to the form attached to this letter. This revolutionary movement is to organize students to strike."

In 1947 the pattern of United States-Soviet negotiations was repeated. After an elaborate exchange of notes between Secretary Marshall and Foreign Minister Molotov, a new series of consultations between American and Russian officials began in Korea. In a somewhat artificial atmosphere of new optimism, talks between the two delegations began late in May. As the conversations continued, it became clear that the Soviet determination to eliminate all but Communist or pro-Communist southern Koreans from effective participation in self-government had not changed during the year which had elapsed since the breakdown of the first conversations.

NORTH KOREA: 99.6 PER CENT

Ever since Pak Huen Yung returned from his visit to northern Korea, carrying orders to organize the South Korea Labor Party, it had become clear that Communist and Communist-inspired activities follow instructions from the Soviet-occupied zone. In the north, the Communist Party also functioned as the "Labor Party." Its leader, Kim Il Sung, became president of the governing Provisional People's Committee at the time of its organization on February 8, 1946. Kim Il Sung aspires to govern all of Korea, and his speeches and statements foresee a period when north and south are united under Communist leadership.

The North Korea Labor Party operates through a Democratic Front, which has its equivalent not only in the coalition by the same name in southern Korea, but also in Bulgaria's Fatherland Front, Yugoslavia's People's Front, Romania's National Democratic Front, etc. The Korean Democratic Front gathered 99.6 per cent of the vote when it held elections. Like its counterparts in eastern Europe, this government is highly security-conscious and has created groups of armed troops that total well over 100,000 men. Syngman Rhee asserted early in 1947 that this figure was closer to half a million, but neither of the two occupation authorities has ever published an official estimate.

Kim Il Sung's administration, guided by Soviet occupation authorities, has stated that it "thoroughly purged" all "pro-Japanese as well as anti-democratic reactionaries." It also decided that Korean people "should be taught in a truly democratic spirit, and the cultural enlightenment of all classes of people should be extensively instituted." The Communist-controlled government has also advanced extensive land reforms, using a carefully worked out system of confiscation and redistribution. North Korean broadcasts have claimed that these reforms have been very popular and have contributed greatly to the prestige of the regime.

"WHEN THE WHALES FIGHT . . ."

Korea is a danger zone in big power relations. Next to Greece, it is probably the most explosive spot on earth. Infiltration of trained troops from the northern into the southern zone might be accomplished in a fashion that would render the American occupation forces helpless. Communism can conquer Korea from the inside. By remaining north of the thirty-eighth parallel, the Soviet army can avoid a warlike international incident. But Communist-trained Korean guerrilla fighters could become equally or even more effective than Yugoslav-trained guerrillas have been inside Greece.

Although initial political mistakes made by the American authorities have been partly corrected, south Koreans still chafe under the occupation. Koreans want their independence, and to many of them the Soviet Union is Tweedledee and the United States is Tweedledum. Consequently, Korean nationalists have made life quite miserable for American occupation authorities. It would be wrong to blame all of southern Korea's unrest on communism. Rightist extremists have shown just as little inclination to accept American authority. Of course, no liberal-minded and world-conscious persons can tolerate the idea of a permanently divided Korea, condemned to suffer the hardships of dual occupation. It is difficult for patriotic Koreans, who have passed through nearly three decades of suppression by Japanese occupants, to display the patience and political sophistication that the current situation requires. But Koreans have a long revolutionary history. They have a saying, "When the whales fight, the shrimps are killed." It matters little to them whether a whale is red or whether it is red, white, and blue.

CHAPTER 29

China: Fight to the Finish

THE BATTLE FOR China is a fight to the finish. Conciliation is a mirage of men who thirst for peace in the desert of civil war. For more than two decades, this fratricidal struggle has continued. Having freed itself from foreign domination, China today decides its own fate.

Can we permit communism to gain control of China? Is it true that the Communists have given new dignity and democratic rights to China's peasants?

Is Russia backing the Communists, and must America support Chiang Kai-shek in a battle of big-power rivalry?

These questions can be answered only after we examine the development of today's violent rivalries inside China. After World War I, the revolutionary government of Russia was the only great power to denounce its imperialist privileges on Chinese soil. Lenin's generous gesture was appreciated by Dr. Sun Yat-sen, whose *Three Principles of the People* has remained the Bible of Chinese nationalism to this day. Sun Yat-sen's principles called, first of all, for China's full independence. His second principle demands popular democracy, or sovereignty of the people. Both Generalissimo Chiang Kai-shek and China's most outstanding Communist leader, Mao Tse-tung, have expressed support of it. And the third principle, that of a socialist-like "promotion of general welfare," remains foremost among the goals toward which China strives.

SUN YAT-SEN GOES BOLSHEVIK

Sun Yat-sen had sought for decades to find support abroad, which would enable China to free herself from foreign control. In the end, during the last two years of his life, he allied himself with Lenin's Russia. Impressed by the successful Bolshevik Revolution, Sun Yat-sen reorganized his Kuomintang (People's Party) along the pattern of the Communist Party of the Soviet Union. The first emissary of the Communist International to China was George Vitinsky, who organized Marxist study groups and published a monthly magazine devoted to communism. On July 1, 1921, the Communist Party of China was formally founded in Shanghai. Two Soviet specialists, Litnovsky and Malin, established local Communist Party groups.

After the initial period of world revolutionary policy, the Comintern Second Strategy of the "united front" was applied to China. Dr. Alfred Joffe negotiated with Sun Yat-sen in January, 1923. In June, the third congress of the Chinese Communist Party met at Canton. Wang Ming, the official Chinese historian of the Communist International, said in his pamphlet *Fifteen Years of Struggle in China* that, at Canton, "The Communist Party of China, under guidance and with the aid of the Comintern, succeeded in drafting a concrete political and tactical line" for the "organization of a national united front." The Communists were still weak. They had fewer than one thousand members when they asked their members to join the Kuomintang.

But the Chinese revolutionary movement gained impetus through the assimilation of Bolshevik tactics. Michael Borodin came from the Soviet Union in August as political adviser. Russia's Civil War General Bluecher-Galen became the Kuomintang's military specialist. Chen Tu-hsiu, secretary-general of the Communist Party (or Kuangchantang), remained opposed to fusion with the Kuomintang, but he was overshadowed by the more experienced Comintern representatives, who also supervised the use of Moscow's monthly subsidy of 12,000 American dollars.

The fusion Kuomintang party waged a successful military campaign in northern China, defeating the war lords and foreign interests, and capturing Shanghai. After Sun Yat-sen's death, Chiang Kai-shek became the most prominent leader of the Kuomintang, of which the Communists were part. (He ousted Wang Chin-wei, who later became a Japanese puppet ruler.) Chiang Kai-shek was able to increase his power at the expense of the Communists. He needed their military advice but limited their influence in the army and demanded adherence to Sun Yat-sen's program in Communist agitation among workers and peasants. The Communists agreed to these restrictions in May, 1926, although they were far from happy about this watering down of their revolutionary slogans. Their greatest accomplishment was the Chinese Trade Union Congress, with headquarters at Shanghai, which claimed two million members and served as a branch of the Red Labor International.

MUTUAL DISTRUST

As Chiang Kai-shek marched on Shanghai, the Communist-led workers of the city rose against the war lord in command of the city. They battled fiercely and opened Shanghai for Chiang Kai-shek's army. He occupied the city and immediately demanded that the workers deliver all arms to him. On orders from Moscow, the Communists buried their arms. Both Chiang Kai-shek's demand and Moscow's advice indicated mutual distrust. By burying the arms, the Communists neutralized their own fighting power and were helpless when Chiang Kai-shek on April 12, 1927, arrested their leaders. An anti-Chiang rebellion was quickly crushed. Chiang Kai-shek installed his government at Nanking and announced his break with the Communists in April. He rejected "a super-government under Borodin" and stated, "Dr. Sun admitted the Communists into the (Kuomintang) Party as collaborators and the Russians as friends. If the Communists wish to dominate, and if the Russians desire to mistreat us, that means the end of their activity." Shortly afterward, because of a combination of intricate political-strategic factors, the Communists suffered a staggering defeat in Wu-han province. Borodin was forced to leave Hankow for Moscow in July, 1927. Chen Tu-hsiu, the party's secretary-general, refused to sign a statement testifying that the defeat of China's Communists had been due to faulty execution of Comintern orders. He had to resign from the executive committee of the Communist International.

The Comintern, under Stalin's personal supervision, then decided to dispatch a number of European specialists to China. This group, which included Heinz Neumann, Gerhart Eisler, and John Pepper, alias Joseph Pogány, were to apply the insurrection methods taught at the Lenin Institute with Vitinsky's military experience. For three days, from December 11 to 14, 1927, this group installed a "commune" in Canton. It was a bloody rebellion. The commune gave and received no quarter. This event became a turning point in China's modern history. It symbolized rivalry between Chiang Kai-shek and his former Communist fellow revolutionaries, stripped of all pretenses.

During the years that followed, Chiang Kai-shek and the Communists fought each other mercilessly. The Communist Party, which had some 60,000 members at the time of the Canton massacre, was ruthlessly suppressed by Chiang. Mao Tse-tung emerged as China's most outstanding Communist leader. Born in 1893 at the village of Shao Shan, Hunan Province, Mao comes from a well-to-do peasant family. The most striking characteristic of this revolutionary's early life is fanatical rebellion against his father. He finally overcame the handicap that his father represented in his youth, but he remained a rebel all his life.

MAO TSE-TUNG, BOY REBEL

When Mao was six years old, he started doing small chores on the parental farm. From the age of eight to thirteen he visited the local primary school. His teacher was a most severe man. Caught between the strict regime at home and the stern instructor at school, little Mao decided to run away. For three days, he wandered about the countryside, until he was finally found by members of his family. To his surprise, he got away without a beating. In fact, both father and teacher became more understanding toward the rebellious little boy. As Mao recalled this incident to Edgar Snow later on, he said with a wry smile, "It was a successful 'strike'."

He received an old-fashioned education that heavily emphasized the Chinese classics. When he was thirteen, he used this newly won knowledge to argue with his father, quoting ancient sayings about parental tenderness. On one occasion, when his father accused him of laziness, Mao ran to a near-by lake and threatened to jump into it. From this, he concluded, "When I defended my rights by open rebellion, my father relented, but when I remained meek and submissive, he only cursed and beat me more." In later years, he was to apply this lesson of father-versus-son antagonism in terms of the class struggle.

After a few years of helping the hired hands around the farm, Mao entered a school in a neighboring county at the age of sixteen. Mao joined in the growing agitation against Manchu rule from Imperial Peking and approved of such outward symbols of rebellion as the removal of pigtails. Caught in revolutionary sentiment, he joined the rebel army for six months. Afterward, he was at loose ends. He considered the attractions of a police school, a soapmaking school, a school of law, and an economic school before he finally entered a commercial high school. He stayed there only one month, because all instructions were given in English. He changed to the First Provincial Middle School but grew tired of it after six months. He preferred self-education at the Hunan Public Library.

He settled down after that, entered the Hunan First Normal School at Changsha, and graduated after five years. For a while, he thought of himself as a wandering scholar and explored the countryside by walking through several counties. Back in Changsha, he placed an advertisement in a paper, asking young men to join him in "patriotic work." The response was meager. One youth, named Li Li-san (he later became Mao's antagonist in the Chinese Communist movement, spent fifteen years in Moscow, and returned to China in 1946), visited Mao Tse-tung after reading the advertisement. Mao tried to convince him of the excellent things he intended to do for China. But Li only listened, remained noncommittal, and finally walked away. Mao did, however, succeed in building up a New People's Study Society, made up of earnest, talkative, and ambitious young men with vague ideas about world improvement.

In 1918, Mao became assistant librarian at Peiping University. There he came into contact with the men who later were to found the Communist Party of China. He became editor of a Hunan student paper and was active in organizing the League for Reconstruction of Hunan, which favored autonomy for that province. In 1920, disillusioned with bickering inside the Hunan autonomy movement, he began to study Marxist writings. It was during this year that he married Yang Kai-hui. His parents had married him to a twenty-year-old woman when he was still fourteen, but this marriage was never consummated, nor did Mao consider it binding. Mao's wife Yang is said to have been killed during fighting in the early 1930's.

Together with Chen Tu-hsiu and others, Mao Tse-tung founded the Communist Party in Shanghai in 1921. When the Communists entered the Kuomintang, Mao belonged simultaneously to the Communist central committee and to the Kuomintang's executive committee at Shanghai. In 1925, he became editor of a weekly Canton Kuomintang paper and took charge of the party's propaganda department.

Mao Tse-tung entered more critical battles for China's future when he returned to his native Hunan province as a Communist peasant organizer. He was president of the All-China Peasants Union, which boasted of more than nine million members, when Chen Tu-hsiu fell into disgrace with Moscow. Mao became leader of China's Communists at the most difficult period of his party's career. His later relations with Chiang Kai-shek were doubtless influenced by the depth of antagonism that existed between the Communists and the Kuomintang at that time.

Mao's power was strengthened in 1930, when Li Li-san, formerly one of the deposed Chen Tu-hsiu's right-hand men, tried some daring local rebellions on his own. His Changsha insurrection defied Mao's more cautious policy. He failed, and Moscow backed Mao against Li, who was accused of deviating dangerously from the established policy of careful mass education. Li Li-san was removed from his post and ordered to Russia.

THE CHINESE SOVIET REPUBLIC

During this extremist-revolutionary period, the Third Strategy of world communism excluded any rapprochement with the Kuomintang, even if Chiang Kai-shek, whose anticommunism yields in intensity to no one, had been favorable to it. The most definite illustration of the cleavage between Chiang Kai-shek and the Communists came on November 7, 1931. In celebration of the anniversary of Russia's Bolshevik Revolution, a "Provisional Government of the Chinese Soviet Republic" was set up, with Mao Tse-tung as president. Throughout the remaining years of the Third Strategy of world communism, this Soviet government continued its existence.

Japan created the puppet state in Manchuria in 1931 and attacked the Chinese east coast a year later. China's rival parties were threatened by an outside enemy. Both Mao Tse-tung and Chiang Kai-shek, weakened by continuing warfare against each other, had to face Japanese invasion forces. But, inasmuch as Comintern policy was not changed until the mid-thirties, there could be no immediate rapprochement. About the fact that Mao's later conciliation offers to Chiang originated in Moscow there can be no doubt. Wang Ming writes in his historical account: "As is well known, the Communist Party on the basis of the political line of the Seventh Congress of the Communist International drew up its new political line, which was expressed in the appeal of the Central Committee of the Party and of the Central (Chinese) Soviet government, dated August 1, 1935." This Comintern policy of a "united front" between Communists and Kuomintang against the Japanese encountered opposition in Chinese Communist circles. Wang Ming refers to this but notes that these reservations were overcome when it was made clear that the Communists intended to retain "full political and organizational independence." It was Wang Ming himself (his real name is Chen Shao-yü) who arrived at Chinese Communist headquarters from Moscow, carrying instructions for the implementation of the new "united front" with Chiang Kai-shek.

Chiang did not accept this offer right away. It was repeated several times. Finally, on September 22, 1937, the Communists issued a manifesto in which they pledged that "the policy of insurrection which aims at the overthrow of the Kuomintang's political power, the policy of land confiscation, and the policy of Communist propaganda shall all be disowned and discontinued." The manifesto also expressed Communist willingness "to fight for the realization of Dr. Sun Yat-sen's revolutionary principles." This document was welcomed by Chiang Kai-shek in a message of acknowledgment the following day. Chiang expressed the hope that the Communists would "sincerely carry out what is contained in the statement" and would "work in unison with the rest of the nation to accomplish national salvation." It was a shotgun marriage. The Japanese army was pointing its guns at Chiang and Mao.

After a decade of violent antagonism and nearly continuous warfare, it would have been a miracle if the two groups had become convinced of each other's sincerity. Both sides knew that. No such miracle had happened. In their pamphlet entitled *Present Strategy and Tactics of the Chinese Communist Party*, published at Yenan in 1937, the Communists stated that "it is the present strategy of the Chinese Communist Party to establish a democratic republic and its tactics are to cease civil war and to cooperate with the Kuomintang." This, the document explained, was done because "present circumstances require a temporary compromise," although "to give up temporarily the revolutionary regime is merely a change of name and a preparation for greater victory in the future." The pamphlet added that "our compromise is designed to weaken the Kuomintang and to overthrow the National Government," but "in reality, the Red Army will continue its independent existence."

Although it is unusual for Communist tactics to be explained as candidly as this, the document was prompted by considerable resistance to the "united front" policy in Yenan itself. The pamphlet on strategy and tactics was, moreover, designed for distribution to only a limited circle of leaders. Nevertheless, criticism of the newly found support for Chiang

Kai-shek continued. In order to strengthen his own position, Mao Tse-tung found it necessary as late as October 12, 1938, to assure the Communist central committee that "the Communist International is in complete agreement with the new policy line of the Communist Party of China."

The Yenan opposition had good cause to be bitter about a policy that forced Chinese Communists to whoop it up for Chiang Kai-shek. They remembered his series of ruthless anti-Communist campaigns, and they witnessed the tightening of a virtual Kuomintang blockade against areas in which organized Communist armies or Communist guerrillas operated.

THE "FAVORABLE" WAR

The outbreak of the war in Europe did not affect conditions inside China itself. But it has generally been overlooked that Mao Tse-tung quickly adhered to the suddenly imposed Fifth Strategy of world communism, following the Nazi-Soviet Pact. On September 1, 1939 (while Harry Pollitt in Britain was still off the beam), Mao told a correspondent of the Eighth Route Army newspaper that China's Communists were against the "imperialist war" that had broken out in Europe, as "Communists oppose predatory wars, but support those which are waged for freedom and emancipation." Thus assuming that the people of Poland, Czechoslovakia, Great Britain, Denmark, Norway, France, and Belgium—who had been, or were about to be attacked—were not concerned with a war for freedom, Mao said, "We cannot doubt that the great masses of the world will arise in a great anti-war movement." He urged the men of the Eighth Route Army not to concern themselves unduly with the war in which the capitalist states were engaged, because "beyond the capitalist world, there is another, brilliant world—that of Soviet Russia."

Two weeks later, during a Yenan staff conference, Mao Tse-tung gave a picture of the brighter side of the war, when he said, "War and crises weaken and cripple the imperialists. This is favorable for the people's national liberation and freedom movements, for China's resistance and for the construction of a Communist order by the Soviet Union." Throughout World War II, friction between Chiang and Mao continued, often to the detriment of the over-all United Nations war effort. American officials attached to Chiang Kai-shek's headquarters were often extremely nettled by the government's apparent desire to preserve strength for later use against the Communists. Brooks Atkinson, the *New York Times* correspondent who is quite free from pro-Communist bias, cabled on October 31, 1944, that "no diplomatic genius could have overcome the Generalissimo's basic unwillingness to risk his armies in battles with the Japanese." Atkinson added, "The Chinese government hedges and hesitates over anything involving the use of its armies. Foreigners can only conclude that the Chinese government wants to save its armies to secure its political power after the war."

Exaggerated claims of military exploits against the Japanese were made at Chiang's and Mao's headquarters. Still, Communist guerrillas were without doubt extremely active in certain Japanese rear areas, and Communist armies fought many encounters against Japanese troops. Perhaps Chiang's reluctance was particularly apparent, because a large number of American army and diplomatic officials, and many newspapermen, were stationed at Chungking. Visits to Yenan headquarters were difficult to arrange. This condition was not eased by Chungking's desire to keep the Communists isolated or by Yenan's reluctance to have a lot of foreigners nosing about the countryside.

That Mao Tse-tung did not waver in his ideological allegiance after the outbreak of World War II was made clear in his book *China's New Democracy*, which was published by the United States Communist Party in 1944. In it, Mao said, "The world now depends on communism for its salvation, and so does China." Although this book was later withdrawn from sale in the United States, it served to answer the question that had been asked with sincere bewilderment by many Americans: Are China's Communists really Communists?

Raymond Swing, one of America's best informed radio commentators, said on August 11, 1943, that the Yenan group "should not be called Communists, whatever their origin may be." On the other hand, Edgar Snow, whose *Red Star over China* did so much to popularize the spirit and devotion of China's Communists, said in *The Pattern of Soviet Power*, "It is misleading to contend that Chinese Communists are not Marxists, or that they do not hope, ultimately, to build up a classless socialist state in China, or that they are not very close to the Soviet Union in their sympathies. People who try to persuade Americans to accept them on the ground that they are not 'real Communists'—in the foregoing sense—are either misinformed or deliberately dishonest." Snow also said of China's Communists, "It is wrong to suppose that these people do not aspire to ultimate complete power. It is also wrong to suppose that they, any more than the Kuomintang, would establish a liberal democracy in China in the American sense, although they would probably bring about a kind of democratic equalitarianism, such as is now realized in areas they control."

FAILURE OF THE KUOMINTANG

It must be recognized that the Kuomintang government, under the presidency of Generalissimo Chiang Kai-shek, has made itself highly unpopular in the United States. This can be attributed only in small part to Communist propaganda efforts. Few serious students of Chinese affairs in the United States do not feel that the Kuomintang has failed disastrously to alleviate China's pressing economic problems. It is impossible to divorce a report on Chinese communism from the failures of Kuomintang administration. From 1927 to 1937, the Chiang Kai-shek government carried out five organized and planned anti-Communist campaigns. But it did not halt the progress made by the Communist Party, which today numbers two million members.

Particularly those scholars and political analysts who specialize in Chinese affairs emphasize the reforms accomplished by China's Communists. This appreciation of Communist methods is often caused by sheer disgust with Kuomintang corruption, narrowness, ineptitude, and a growing ultra-nationalism combined with badly disguised anti-foreignerism. However, the over-all problem of world communism cannot be grasped from an isolated review of the Chinese scene (or from an analysis of conditions in Greece alone, where another ultra-nationalist clique drove genuine democratic elements into the Communist camp). But Kuomintang shortcomings have certainly contributed most substantially to the growth of Chinese Communist prestige abroad.

There is only half an acre of land per person under cultivation in China. By contrast, there are four acres per person in the United States. About three-fourths of China's farm land is worked by owners themselves, and one-fourth by tenant farmers. In Kuomintang territories, the tenant pays the landlord usually with 50 per cent of the crop. In Communist territory, efforts have been made to alter this percentage to the advantage of the tenant. Among small landowners, the Communists have gained popularity by reducing taxes.

Generally speaking, the masses in Communist territory have gained more political consciousness. Communist agitation efforts have aroused the interests of many who previously had led a life of indifference to communal affairs. This sense of new importance, of recognized identity, has contributed to Communist popularity. Both in economic alleviation and in education, the Kuomintang has been passed by the Communists.

Although both sides are determined on a fight to the finish, democratically minded men and women outside China find it difficult to side with either the Communists or the Kuomintang. Professor Nathaniel Peffer of New York's Columbia University, said in February, 1947, that he opposed any aid to Chiang Kai-shek, because he regarded his government as "just as insincere as the Communists." Secretary George C. Marshall stated on January 7, 1947, after more than a year of efforts to bring Kuomintang and Communists together, that the Chinese Communists had "indicated an unwillingness to compromise," while a "dominant reactionary group" of the Kuomintang believed that "only a policy of force could definitely settle the issue." Secretary Marshall placed his hope in moderate, liberal elements in both camps. But it is well to recognize that these elements enjoy control neither in the Kuomintang nor among the Communists.

WANTED: CHINESE LIBERALS

The Marshall report added that "a very harmful and immensely provocative phase of the Chinese Communist procedure had been the character of its propaganda." The report stated, "In the deliberate misrepresentation and abuse of the action, policy and purposes of our [U. S.] Government, this propaganda has been without regard for the truth, without any regard whatsoever for the facts, and has given plain evidence of a determined purpose to mislead the Chinese people and the world and to arouse a bitter hatred of Americans."

One unquestionable fact arises from the maneuvering, charges, and countercharges that have characterized China's internal affairs since the "united front" policy was put into effect in 1937: both parties seek complete dominance. The Kuomintang does not trust the Communists. The Communists do not trust the Kuomintang. And both are undoubtedly right. They have known each other since 1923, when Dr. Sun Yat-sen invited Michael Borodin to China. And they have hated each other since

1927, when Chiang Kai-shek achieved dominance through a ruthless coup.

When the "united front" policy was adopted at the Seventh Comintern Congress of 1935, Dmitri Z. Manuilsky said that "the first place among the Communist parties of the world, right after the Bolsheviks of the USSR, belongs to that of China." He assured his listeners that "in the end there must be the defeat of Chiang Kai-shek, because the Chinese Communist party and the red armies of China possess what its enemy does not possess; namely, the ever-victorious idea of communism and the enthusiastic support of the masses, ready for boundless sacrifices."

Doubtless, relations between the Chinese Communists and Moscow have remained cordial during the war years. But only the end of the war made close contact again possible. The return of Li Li-san to China late in 1946 was perhaps the most striking example of tightened liaison between Moscow and Yenan. Li Li-san accompanied the Soviet army into Manchuria. In May, 1946, he was named chairman of the Far Eastern Bureau of the International Revolutionary Action Committee. This bureau appears to have replaced the Communist International's East Asia Department.

Thus Li Li-san, whom the Fourth Plenum of China's Communist Party had once labeled an "adventurist, counter-revolutionary and liquidator," and who had also been called a "Trotskyite" on more than one occasion, was reinstated. After his forced exit from the Chinese Communist Party in 1930, he had gone to Moscow's Sun Yat-sen University for an ideological overhauling. Later, he married a Russian woman and for two years worked on the staff of the Red Labor International in the Soviet capital. After a brief spell as editor of the Soviet publication *National Salvation Times,* he was for seven years associated with the Foreign-Language Publishing Company in Moscow.

After his arrival in Harbin, Manchuria, Li Li-san immediately resolved all speculation about his future relations with Mao Tse-tung. They had, after all, been rivals sixteen years earlier. On August 28, 1946, he told *New York Herald Tribune* correspondent A. T. Steele, "The facts of history show that Mao was right and I was wrong. I am happy to be back under Comrade Mao's leadership." The ex-firebrand showed his adherence to the Seventh Strategy of world communism when he said, "All the countries of the world are advancing toward socialism and communism. But the forms will vary from country to country. In China we are in the stage of new democracy—a necessary step toward socialism. It is difficult to say how long this stage will last." (In his book *China's New*

emocracy, Mao Tse-tung had said that "proletarian revolution" would
ɔrm the second stage of Communist evolution in China and that this
second stage must follow the first closely, not permitting a capitalist
ictatorship to be inserted between them.")

NO END IN SIGHT

Communist policy in China today is designed to eliminate any Ameri-
an support for the Chiang Kai-shek government. A document purporting
o contain confidential views of the Chinese Communist Party's political
*ureau was circulated in Washington in 1946. This document, entitled
Votice No. 16 *of the Central Political Bureau*, was said to have been
vritten while General George C. Marshall was attempting to achieve a
:ompromise between Chiang Kai-shek and the Communists. The alleged
Politbureau memorandum stated that "the Far Eastern Bureau" (presumably the Far Eastern Bureau of the International Revolutionary
Action Committee, successor to the defunct Comintern's East Asia Department), had approved the following three-point program adopted by the
seventh conference of the Politbureau:

"(1) Use of the appeal for democracy to unite people of all parties
and all factions and of no party and no faction, in order to solidify and
strengthen the anti-Kuomintang front;

"(2) To convince and absorb the progressive elements within the Kuomintang, so as to disintegrate its organization and to bring about its dissolution;

"(3) Continue to expand propaganda against the C.C. elements
(reactionary wing) within the Kuomintang and the special service (secret
police), in order to turn the Chinese people and all toiling masses against
them."

Even after the United States, on January 29, 1947, decided to withdraw
its troops from Chinese soil (with the exception of some 750 instructors),
the Chinese Communists were far from satisfied with the American position. This was stated clearly by General Chou En-lai, whose position
among Chinese Communist leaders corresponds to that of a foreign minister. Chou said on March 8, 1947, that "only the support of the United
States is keeping Chiang and his dictatorship government from complete
collapse." A week later, Chiang Kai-shek declared "hopes for settlement
by political means" had been shattered. Shortly afterward, government

troops occupied Yenan, which had been the Communist capital for te
years. But even this symbolic victory for Chiang did not change the fac
that the fight to the finish in China's civil war is likely to continue fo
years.

MONGOLIAN REGIONS, SINKIANG, TANNU TUVA

Outer Mongolia in central Asia was separated from China in 1912 and
became a protectorate of Czarist Russia. In 1924, a "Mongolian People'
Republic" was set up which isolated itself from the rest of the world
except the Soviet Union. The country is governed by Marshal Kharloi
Choibalsan. After Japan's collapse in 1945, a Soviet-sponsored plebiscit
in Outer Mongolia resulted in 487,409 votes favoring independence from
China.

To the south, Inner Mongolia, an outlying dependency of China, an
nounced its independence on April 23, 1947. Characteristically, the an
nouncement of this event came from the Chinese Communist radio; the
"People's Representative Assembly" of Inner Mongolia met inside Com
munist-controlled territory of Manchuria. The People's Revolutionary
Party is the party of Communists in both Mongolian regions.

The Chinese government believes that the Soviet Union aspires to set
up a Communist-controlled region in at least part of Sinkiang (Chinese
Turkestan). Clashes at the Sinkiang-Outer Mongolian border occurred
during the summer of 1947. Another central Asiatic region, Tannu Tuva,
was absorbed by the Soviet Union on October 11, 1944. It became the
"Tuva Autonomous Region" of the Russian Soviet Federative Socialist
Republic and is governed by the local Communist Party's secretary-
general, S. K. Toka.

CHAPTER 30

Southeast Pacific: Sudden Awakening

THE DAWN OF independence is casting its light over southeast Asia. Here and there, the sky is tinted red. The young Philippine Republic seeks economic as well as political independence, while its underprivileged peasants turn to the extreme left for want of other militant leaders. The blood of gallant French soldiers and courageous Annamite nationalists has drenched the soil of Indo-China, which seeks to establish unhampered self-rule under the presidency of a veteran Communist organizer. Siam draws the scorn of Asiatic Communists, for its persistent and sometimes ruthless suppression of ultra-left agitation. In Malaya, Communists seek to unite opposing Chinese, Malay, and Indian elements on a basis of revolutionary nationalism.

The new Indonesian Republic, conceived during Japanese occupation and born as Tokyo's hold weakened, contains divergent Communist elements that are anxious to retain their limited influence in the young regime. The Communist Party of India advocates Moslem-Hindu unity and seeks to strengthen its influence in the two opposing religious camps. In Burma, a revolutionary independence movement has ousted Communist leaders who now represent a well-organized and undaunted opposition. Across India's gateway to the Soviet Union and the Near East, Afghanistan registers the weakening of British influence and the rising power of Russia in the colonial world. And "down under," in Australia and New Zealand, where Labour governments reject Communist "united front" offers, the red-tinted sky of dawn over southeast Asia fills the horizon.

PHILIPPINES: POST-INDEPENDENCE PROBLEMS

On July 4, 1946, the Philippine Republic was born. After forty years of control by the United States, it was finally on its own. But its problems seemed to have just begun. There was, first of all, the terrible devastatio brought upon by the war. And then, after the enormous task of reconstru tion was finished, the Philippines would seek to cease being an economi dependency of the United States. Like many a dependent nation, th Philippines had looked forward to the day of liberation with great hopes Somehow, nothing seemed much different on July 4 from the way it ha been the day before. Basically, the economic-political problems of th nation were the same as they had been decades earlier.

President Manuel Roxas, addressing his countrymen on Independenc Day, said, "We must perform near-miracles to bring prosperity to thi our land." None of his countrymen knew this better than the peasants o the plains in central Luzon, who had been battling for agrarian reforn for decades. In 1931, there were uprisings among the farmers in Tayug Pangasinan Province. Land titles were burned, debt records and tenancy contracts destroyed. The government quelled the riots that ensued. It arrested leaders of the Communist-led National Peasants' Confederation. Juan Feleo, secretary-general of the confederation, was charged with sedition and imprisoned. So was Cresanto Evangelista, the head of the Communist Party of the Philippines, who had spent a period of training in the Soviet Union. The Communist Party was declared illegal and went underground.

But the Peasants' Confederation was able to continue its functions. Late in 1938, it claimed a membership of 60,000. The Communist Party was again legalized and held its third congress from October 29 to 31. President Manuel Quezón told the National Assembly shortly afterward, "There is growing unrest and discontentment, especially among the farm laborers. This is not entirely due to the activities of professional agitators and irresponsible so-called labor leaders. Our laborers cannot be easily led astray by agitators when they have no real grievances." Amnesty was extended to political prisoners, among them a number of Communists. The Communist Party absorbed the Socialist Party. The former Socialist and Communist vice-chairman, Pedro Abad Santos, asked that peasant laborers be permitted to carry arms, because the landlords were "hiring thugs and ex-convicts to kill tenants and laborers."

On May 11, 1939, the Philippine secretariat of labor called a conference of the three major trade-union organizations. The conference created a national commission of labor. The Communist-controlled unions were represented side by side with the moderate organizations. Guillermo Capaocia, secretary-general of the Communist Party, was among the members f the commission. He was supported by Luís Taruc, who after World War II became prominent in the Hukbalahap movement of armed peasants nd was elected to the Philippine Congress from the turbulent Pampanga rovince.

The Communist Party advocated collective bargaining, the eight-hour lay, slum clearance, and a minimum wage. It later included demands for he confiscation of large estates in its program.

Creation of the labor commission was followed by formation of a national commission of peasants. In the New York quarterly, *Science and Society*, Harlan R. Crippen said in December, 1946, that "among the organized rural populace the Communist influence was clearly dominant." The Communist Juan Feleo, who had been arrested in 1932 and who in 1945 became one of the leading figures of the Democratic Alliance of the Philippines, was elected secretary of the Peasant Commission. He was aided by another Communist, Mateo del Castillo, with whom he later shared the leadership of the Congress of Labor Organization.

The Labor Commission, which represented varying views, was frequently split on major issues. The Peasant Commission, with Communists predominant, was able to steer a clear course. This may have prompted President Quezón to intervene in 1940. As a result, the department of labor withdrew its sponsorship from commissions. Its members had, however, gained in prestige through the period of government cooperation. The provincial and municipal elections that took place the same year saw the creation of a Popular Front coalition, in accordance with the "united front" principles adopted by the Comintern five years earlier. The Communist-inspired coalition elected eight out of twenty-one mayors in Pampanga province, traditional stronghold of the revolutionary peasants.

On December 26, 1941, after the Japanese invasion, Pedro Abad Santos instructed Luís Taruc to prepare for a resistance movement. Taruc sent Casto Alejandrino, who had been one of the Communist members of the Peasant Commission and who was then a mayor, to establish contact with General Douglas MacArthur's Bataan headquarters. Alejandrino was advised by a member of the general's staff, Lieutenant Colonel C. A. Thorpe, and given a letter of authority. On March 29, 1942, the Philippine resistance movement Hukbalahap (abbreviation for Hukbong Bayan Laban sa Hapon, People's Anti-Japanese Army) was founded at a hide-out in the woods near Mount Arayat. Any doubt as to the initiative taken by the Communists in creating Hukbalahap would be a detraction from their courageous role in this guerrilla movement. Luís Taruc and Casto Alejandrino, who, as we have seen, were veteran Communist organizers, became commander-in-chief and deputy commander-in-chief, respectively.

From then on, and until the end of the war in the Philippines, the Hukbalahaps are credited with 1,100 skirmishes with the enemy and with having killed an estimated 20,000 Japanese soldiers. They played a courageous part in the rescue of American fliers. Taruc was in touch with Lieutenant Colonel Thorpe, who remained as liaison man after the fall of Bataan. Thorpe was killed by Japanese. Cresanto Evangelista, the veteran Moscow-trained Communist, was tortured and murdered by the enemy. Lieutenant Richard Otis Ulin, writing in the *Christian Science Monitor* for December 11, 1945, gave a sympathetic account of the heroism displayed by the Hukbalahap and said that much misunderstanding of its activities stems from the fact that it "did not restrict itself to destroying Japanese." He added:

"It dealt just as severely with government officials who turned puppet as with the propertied compradores and feudal landlords who preferred to do business with the invaders. In the welter of confusion the Huks must have made mistakes. Their tempers raised by the agonies of occupation, some of them must have been guilty of excesses. These errors and excesses the present political opponents of the Huks have magnified or invented to discredit the organization."

The Hukbalahaps were incensed when, at the end of the war, Taruc and Alejandrino were imprisoned. They were freed, after several months in prison, following a cable from Harold L. Ickes, then United States Secretary of the Interior, to the Philippine government. During their imprisonment, Taruc and Alejandrino were replaced by Tony Collantes, acting commander-in-chief of the Hukbalahap. The *New Masses*, United States Communist weekly, in its issue of October 30, 1945, published an interview with Collantes, whose real name is Mariano P. Balgos. George P. Hitchok, author of the *New Masses* article, commented that he "could not help but think of comparisons with Mao Tse-tung and Marshal Tito, both of whom he greatly admires." The interview revealed that the Chinese of Manila had formed a special Huk resistance section, "led by the Manila section of the Communist Party of China." Among the organizations mentioned in the article as pursuing a policy agreeable to Hukbala-

ιap leaders were the Democratic Alliance, the Committee on Labor Or-
ζanizations, and the Conference of Civic Liberties.

President Manuel Roxas, who was elected in 1946, faced a most mili-
ant opposition from the Democratic Alliance. This group of organiza-
ions, which was formed in July, 1945, included the Hukbalahap, the
Communist Party, the National Peasants' Union, the Conference on Civic
Liberties, and the Committee on Labor Organizations. Its platform was
strongly anti-collaborationist. Although General MacArthur had testified
that President Roxas served the Allied nations while ostensibly cooperating with the Japanese occupation authorities, Democratic Alliance statements continued to refer to Roxas as a collaborator. Banners with the
inscription, "Give Roxas back to the Japs" have been carried in Democratic Alliance demonstrations.

Many of the names mentioned among the supporters of the Alliance are
known to the student of communism in the Philippines. Guillermo Capa-
docia, former Communist secretary-general, backs the Democratic Alliance in his capacity of deputy president of the Committee on Labor
Organizations. Mateo del Castillo and Juan Feleo represent the Peasants.
Pedro Casto, then secretary-general of the Communist Party, and Luís
Taruc, as Hukbalahap leader, are also represented on the central committee of the alliance. Clashes between Hukbalahaps and rival guerrilla
organizations continued throughout 1946 and early 1947 in central
Luzon. The Huks were asked to surrender their arms by September 1.
When this date passed, the government, according to President Roxas,
used "implacable force" to disarm them. Shortly afterward, 4,000 Manila
city workers struck for sixteen days under sponsorship of the Congress
of Labor Organization. Roxas used strikebreakers to continue essential
services, such as garbage collection, street cleaning, and burial.

The program of the Democratic Alliance is moderate. It does not correspond to popular conceptions of "communistic" demands. According
to the New York Communist monthly *Political Affairs* of June, 1946, the
Alliance favors "meaningful democratic advances within the new Republic." The magazine expressed the belief that United States granting
of independence to the Philippines was "neither contradictory nor in-
explicable in any fundamental sense from the viewpoint of the basic
characteristics and direction of American imperialist expansion." The
article contrasted "American imperialist policy" with "the great prestige
already enjoyed by the Soviet Union among the colonial people" which

"is increased by the unequivocal Soviet advocacy of independence and self-determination." James S. Allen, author of the article, concluded his findings by saying that "the decisive thing is to expose and block the imperialist policy, and to aid the Filipino people to establish a republic based on anti-imperialist and democratic forces which will safeguard the sovereignty of the nation and undertake its development, without the military and political interference of the United States."

Moderation also was the keynote of the Philippine Communist Party's conference of January, 1947. Jorge Frianeza replaced Pedro Casto as secretary-general. He immediately denied vigorously that the Communists intended "to establish Socialism in our country at the present time." Instead, he said, the Philippine Communists are working for a "People's Democratic Republic." That, it should be remembered, is the same formula under which eastern European nations such as Bulgaria are governed by Communist regimes. Frianeza went so far as to state that his party "wants to create opportunities for the broad development of capitalism." That was indeed a startling aim to be advocated by a Communist leader. But Frianeza assured his listeners that "liquidation of feudalism and imperialism" would ultimately lead to the "establishment of socialism." He concluded, "The Communist Party does not and will not struggle for the immediate establishment of a Socialist society. Basing itself on this policy, the Communist Party extends its hand of unity to all democratic groupings and political parties in the struggle against imperialist intervention in our economy and politics, for a truly independent democratic and industrialized Philippines." Thus, the Democratic Alliance remained the most important forum of the Communists.

Casto remained a member of the party's Politbureau. Other members included Mateo del Castillo, president of the National Peasants' Union, Mariano P. Balgos, president of the Printers' Union, and G. G. Lacuesta, editor of the Communist paper *Katubusan*.

MALAYA: IN A THREE-CORNERED FIGHT

Communism in Malaya isn't Malay. It is Chinese. There are nearly as many Chinese in the Malayan Union and Singapore as there are Malays, or about 2,500,000. There is strong antipathy toward the Chinese (and the three-quarters of a million Indians) among the Malay population. Roughly speaking, the Malays oppose the Chinese on the same grounds on which Arabs in Palestine differ with the Jewish population. Will Malaya become another Palestine? This question is often asked in Singapore.

The best answer probably is: not for a while, anyway. The Chinese are not trying to make Malaya their homeland. But their leftist as well as their rightist leaders urge them to pay more attention to Malay affairs, to fight for civil rights, to oppose Malay domination. There is a strange partial truce between Kuomintang supporters and Communists among Malaya's Chinese population. In November, 1946, the predominantly Chinese "Communist Party of Malay" stated that it was not a branch of the Chinese Communist Party. According to this statement, it was "created to launch a movement in Malaya and it deals chiefly with matters concerning Malay." The Malayan Kuomintang, the Communists said, was by contrast a branch of the Chinese Kuomintang and devoted to Chinese problems. Thus, the statement concluded with an air of friendly rivalry, "each has its own aims and spheres of influence."

But, to many nationalist Malays, particularly those represented by United Malays National Organization, a Chinese is a Chinese. With Chinese taking the initiative in Communist and Communist-sponsored organizations, there is an increasing and erroneous tendency to identify Chinese political activity with communism. Thus, the excitable editors of the Malay daily *Majlis*, of Kuala Lumpur, declared on November 11, 1946, that Malays who participate in Chinese-run movements were "tools" and "renegades." The paper accused the Chinese of trying to bribe Malays into doing their bidding. It specifically warned its readers not to be lured into the Democratic Youth Corps.

On a small scale, the Malay organizations in which the Communist Party is interested correspond to associations that developed at the end of the war throughout southeast Asia and, indeed, throughout the world. In December, 1945, a Malayan Democratic Federation was formed. It has the support of the Malayan Communist Party, of the Democratic Youth Corps, and of the Indian Democratic League. In the city of Singapore, there exists the Singapore Chinese Federation for Peace and Democracy. Its leading officials are Communists.

The Malayan Communist Party, founded in 1925, was illegal until the war. Its top leaders were released from a Singapore prison late in 1941, shortly before Japanese troops marched down the Malay Peninsula toward Singapore. Skilled organizers, these Communists quickly gathered units of militant Chinese and Malays into the ranks of their anti-Japanese resistance groups. They utilized their previously established intelligence and hide-out network.

The Communists displayed a courage that contrasted strongly to the apathy shown by nearly everyone else throughout the Malay Peninsula. At first, they formed the so-called "Dal" force, named after its British commander, Colonel John Dalley. With one thousand rifles of all kinds, they battled the Japanese valiantly among the mango swamps in the northwest corner of Singapore Island. But resistance was useless. The Japanese pressed on and captured Singapore. The Communist resistance fighters dispersed, rid themselves of their uniforms, and reverted to civilian status.

The resistance group spread throughout the Malay Peninsula. It corresponded closely to the guerrilla movement in the Philippines. In fact, its name, the Malayan People's Anti-Japanese Army, is almost identical with that of the Philippine People's Anti-Japanese Army. According to a report that the Malay Communists sent to the Communist Party of Australia in 1946, their guerrillas were subjected to tortures when captured by the Japanese. Following the pattern of vicious cruelty practiced by Japanese troops against American, Chinese, and other soldiers, the Communists in Malaya had long needles forced under their nails, red-hot irons run over their bodies, burning cigarettes pressed against tender parts, fingers, tongues, ears, and noses chopped off, and eyeballs dug out.

The daring Malayan Communist Army developed its own civilian basis of support. It grew into an efficient guerrilla force of 5,000 Chinese, who received air-borne material support from the British Army in India. Two commando-trained British officers were landed by submarine into guerrilla territory to act as liaison personnel and to guide operations. For nearly two years, these two officers, Colonel John Davis and Colonel R. N. Broom, helped to organize resistance units throughout the Malay Peninsula.

The British also imported, by submarine, the Chinese Communist resistance organizer Lim Boh Seng, who managed to raise a labor force of 10,000 men for defense work in Singapore. He was high on the Japanese black list. To avoid his falling into enemy hands, the British finally arranged for his escape.

It was never necessary to use this carefully prepared underground network. The Japanese home islands fell, and with them the troops in Malaya quit without a fight. After Japan's surrender, the Malayan Communist Party retained its legality. It had gained much prestige because of its intelligent and courageous clandestine work. But the honeymoon did not last long. The Communists, who had created local people's committees, desired political influence which the British considered out of proportion to their popular support. Some of the Communists, particularly a few hundred young men who had taken a liking to the life of an outlaw, began to use the power of their newly obtained arms to put the squeeze on shopkeepers and to sell "protection" in gangster style. A number of arrests were made.

Communist influence was also blamed for the wave of strikes and unrest that culminated in the general strike at Singapore on January 29, 1946. The strike was suppressed, but it left a permanent scar on the political face of Malaya. While the Communists seek to extend their influence among Malaya's laborers of all races and religions (they supported the twenty-day strike of 6,000 Singapore dockworkers in November, 1946), they also seek to influence the future status of Malaya generally. The British were working, just after World War II, for a new constitution, aimed at self-government. They were warned by an editorial in the Communist Singapore Chinese-language daily *Min Sheng* that "it would be a serious mistake for the British to draw up a new Constitution for this country, without respecting the political status and the financial interest of the Chinese, who no longer are as uninterested as they were in pre-war days." On the other hand, the Communists have to work hard to whip up interest in Malayan affairs among the resident Chinese, who for the most part have retained strong ties to China. This attitude is not limited to Malaya itself. Throughout southeast Asia, Chinese have in the past cared little for citizenship rights and participation in local government.

Wartime single-mindedness has given way to peacetime concern with many issues. This can be seen by the programs that the Malayan Communist Party has published during the past few years. During the war, it urged its followers simply to "turn each street, lane, mine, and village and rubber plantation into a bulwark for the defense of the land." Today, on the basis of a statement issued on the first anniversary of Japan's surrender, it is concerned with many issues. It has taken a strong stand against continued United States aid to the Chinese government of

Generalissimo Chiang Kai-shek. The Malayan Chinese Communist leader Ta Kah Kee even went so far as to send a message to President Truman, which created wide discussion among Malaya's Chinese colony. The Malayan Communist Party urged in its V-J Day anniversary statement that constitutional discussions between the government and Malay leaders should be public. It accused the government of having dealt with only "a minority of the Malays," instead of putting these discussions "on a broad base, including all shades of opinion." The Communists also accused the British of "insincerity" in carrying out the White Paper for Malayan self-government.

Malaya's Communists are having a difficult time, trying to overcome the basically conservative attitude of the Chinese colony. They have been relatively successful in organizing the Pan-Malayan Labor Union and the Malayan Democratic Alliance. They have shown militancy and leadership qualities in pressing for efficient and fair distribution of rice, one of Malaya's most pressing postwar problems. And they are seeking to create a mold for Malaya's still young nationalist independence movement.

INDO-CHINA: "ENLIGHTENED PERSISTENCE"

The independence movement of Indo-China tested the usefulness of communism's new strategy. After World War II, the Communist parties of France and Indo-China were committed to separate nationalist policies. The French party endorsed the principle of a "French Union," a federative scheme favored by the Assembly, which would give various degrees of autonomy to colonial regions. The policy was put to a severe test when open, bloody, and cruel fighting started on Indo-Chinese soil. The Indo-Chinese independence troops were led by a Soviet-trained professional revolutionary, Ho Chi Minh. The French party gave less than half-hearted support to its government's effort to put down the rebellion.

The Communist Party of Indo-China was founded in 1930, in the wake of a peasant revolt. Tran Phu, secretary-general of the Indo-Chinese Communist Party, who had declared war on "the imperialists, the feudal lords, the big landowners, the clique of mandarins, thieves, and oppressors," was arrested. He died later at a Saigon jail. During World War II, nationalist resentment was kindled by Japanese occupation and French weakness. In 1941, the Communists joined with the Association of Young Revolutionists, the Indo-Chinese Section of the International

Anti-Invasion Association, the New Annam Party, and dissident leftist members of the Annamite Nationalist Party (the Indo-Chinese equivalent of China's Kuomintang), in creating the Independence League of Indo-China.

On August 28, 1945, as Japan surrendered to the United Nations, the league proclaimed a Viet Nam (Annam) Republic, with Hanoi as capital. The Communist Party dissolved officially. Three Communists (Tran Van Giau, Duong Bach Mai, Nguyen Van Tao) became cabinet ministers. Thus men who had been leaders of the Communist Party became key figures of the Viet Nam administration, but the party itself no longer existed. On October 12, 1945, a so-called "parliamentary election" gave Ho Chi Minh 330 out of 400 seats. France did not accept the Viet Nam Republic. Months of fighting followed. On March 7, 1946, the French government recognized Viet Nam as "a free state within the Indo-Chinese Federation and the French Union." The rice-rich province of Cochin-China was not included in this arrangement. The French had already sponsored a degree of internal autonomy in the easily governed Cambodia province of Indo-China. However, Ho Chi Minh, President of Viet Nam Republic, desired not only the union of Tonkin and Annam, which he had achieved, but also the incorporation of Cochin-China.

Ho's views coincided with those expressed in the influential Soviet magazine *New Times*, which asserted on July 15 that French proclamation of a Cochin-Chinese Republic was "an unquestionable violation of the provisional agreement" made at the time of Paris' recognition of Viet Nam. The Moscow magazine accused the French government of attempting to "sever Cochin-China from the Viet Nam Republic and to disrupt the unity of the new state which has reunited the three parts of the former state of Annam on democratic, republican principles."

In the summer of 1946, President Ho Chi Minh arrived in Paris for further negotiations with the French government. This unassuming, soft-spoken, philosophical, and charming man proved to be a tough low-pressure bargainer. The French Communist press commented on his visit and personality in affectionate terms. But was he a Communist? Ho tried to avoid questions about his career. He merely said, "I entered on my revolutionary career at a very early age. I went into clandestinity. I have stayed in clandestinity for the last forty years of my life." Sidney Keller, *New York Herald Tribune* correspondent, noted that Ho was "so clandestine that not even his personal secretary knows whether Ho Chi Minh is his real name." Very likely it isn't. Even in Tonkin, where he was born, they don't call their babies "Enlightened Perseverance"—which is what his name means. Ho has had many aliases in his life, as have most well-traveled Comintern agents. For a while, he called himself Nguyen Aï Quôc, which may be translated simply as "Man of the People."

Ho has, however, admitted his conviction that Marxism is the best answer to the world's woes. He told American correspondent George Weller, "Everyone has a right to his own doctrine. I chose Marx. Jesus said two thousand years ago that one should love one's enemies. That dogma has not been realized. When will Marxism be realized? I cannot answer. Heavy industry is necessary, and so is more extensive agriculture and a chance for everyone to develop his possibilities. In Viet Nam we are not yet in a position to meet such conditions." That is mighty soft talk to come from a revolutionary who spent several years of study in the Soviet Union and who was one of the original Soviet liaison men with the Chinese Communists.

Ho Chi Minh was born in Tonkin in 1890, where his father was on the staff of the Annamite emperor's regional administration. In 1911, when his father was jailed for political activity, Ho worked his way to France as cabin boy on a French ship. In Paris, he edited a small magazine called *The Pariah*, studied during the day, and worked in a photographic laboratory at night. His rebellious Tonkinese spirit brought him in touch with the French Socialist Party, which consistently criticized the government's colonial policy. Ho made a rousing, highly emotional speech at the historical Socialist Congress at Tours, which split the Communists from the Socialists. He joined the Communists. He went to Moscow. Years later, he turned up as one of Michael Borodin's assistants, operating in China.

Ho Chi Minh has been a prominent member of the Far Eastern Bureau of the Communist International. He helped to organize a Moscow training center for Asiatic Communists. He initiated the 1930 Annamite rebellion and was imprisoned at Hong Kong from 1931 to 1933. Later he worked at the Soviet consulate in Canton, China.

Ho talks softly, and his followers swing a mighty big stick. Just what does this small, bearded, wiry, and wily revolutionary believe in? Why does he hide his background so carefully? What is his real allegiance? He denies Communist Party membership, but then, the Indo-Chinese Communist Party has been dissolved. Did he ever break with communism?

And how did it happen that one of the Comintern's Far Eastern agents emerged as president of an Annamite Republic? Ho has a characteristically evasive, mellow, and amusing answer to this question. He became president, he says, because he had no earthly possessions: no family, no house, no fortune, and only one suit of clothes, the one he was wearing. On October 30, 1946, the French government and Ho signed an agreement at Fontainebleau. Viet Nam was recognized as a "democratic republic" within the Indo-Chinese Federation of the French Union.

The French then prepared for a plebiscite in Cochin-China, which they hoped would choose independence within the Indo-Chinese Federation itself, rather than incorporation by Viet Nam. But, late in December, all hell broke loose in Annam and Cochin-China. The French assert that 11,000 Viet Nam soldiers infiltrated into the southwestern province, in violation of previous understandings. According to the French Foreign Office, Ho had expressed his willingness to settle everything in a "friendly fashion" as late as December 18. The very next day, Viet Nam forces struck against the French. It was a tricky attack. The French even charged that Viet Nam soldiers disguised as sick civilians had entered the Yersin Hospital at Hanoi.

The Communists of France faced a dilemma. Their central committee had earlier spoken of a "campaign of reactionary circles against the Viet Nam government." When, on December 24, members of the French Council of the Republic were urged to rise in honor of the French troops in Indo-China, a number of Communists remained in their seats. Only when urged by the leader of their delegation did they reluctantly stand up. A few days later, the Communists joined with the rest of the council in calling for maintenance of French power in Indo-China, to assure the "civilizing mission of France in respecting the legitimate liberties of native populations." As a red endorsement of the white man's burden, it did not make good reading in Viet Nam. But later on the Communists tried to block funds for military operations in Indo-China; such opposition to French government policy caused premier Ramadier to oust them from his cabinet. The battle for Indo-China was on, one of the most disheartening and confusing struggles after World War II. Fighting was ferocious. The French used tanks, artillery, and airplanes. Ho's troops were at times forced to fight with spears, bows, and arrows. Atrocities were committed on both sides. French and Viet Namese censorship made the campaign one of the worst reported in recent history. German members of the Foreign Legion were fighting Japanese among the Viet Nam troops. The world remained generally in the dark about the extent and character of the fighting.

INDONESIA: JUNGLE EXILES RETURN

For twenty years, several hundred Indonesian rebels lived as political exiles in the wilderness of southeastern New Guinea. Surrounded by jungle and swamps, they built the settlement of Tanamerah in the upper region of the crocodile-infested Digoel River. The upper Digoel is more escape-proof than Alcatraz. To fight your way from hilly Tanamerah to the New Guinea coast, you'd have to cross through miles and miles of head-hunter territory. Even the most determined rebel preferred Boven Digoel to the certain death that would follow escape.

The Communists in Tanamerah, exiled after the bloody rebellion in Java and Sumatra in 1926, listened daily to the short-wave broadcasts of the powerful Moscow radio. They were able to obtain books and magazines; they had the company of their wives and children. On occasion, they could even see a motion picture. But it was not freedom. Head-hunters are just as effective barriers as prison bars, and you can't saw your way through a crocodile.

Indonesia's Communists kept their faith in Moscow. And when, after the Nazi attack on Russia and the Japanese assault on Pearl Harbor, the troops of Nippon landed on Indonesian soil, the Communists were eager to help oust the totalitarian invaders. One of their leaders, Sardjano, told them that Indonesia would have to be freed from Japanese rule before the fight against control by the Netherlands could be continued.

And then, one day, an Allied plane made a daring landing just outside Tanamerah. Charles O. Vanderplas, Netherlands member of the Allied Political Warfare Council, had come all the way from General MacArthur's Headquarters at Canberra, Australia. He talked to Sardjano and the other exiled Communists. It was a difficult task. He wanted their help against the Japanese. And he had a great prize to offer: freedom. Vanderplas knew what he was doing. Japan was propagandizing the people of the Indonesian islands, trying to convert them to the doctrine of the Greater East Asia Co-Prosperity Sphere. If they were successful in gaining the genuine collaboration of the native population, few Japanese troops would be needed to hold the island, and the assault on Australia could be undertaken.

The Allies needed help. They needed espionage agents, men who were daring enough to operate clandestine radio stations or to distribute anti-Japanese leaflets. A nucleus of militant underground workers was essential to the dual flow of information from Indonesia and of Allied propaganda into the islands. American seaplanes ferried dazed Communists out of their jungle prison. For several years, Indonesian Communists fought alongside the Allied powers, including the Netherlands. But, as soon as Japan's surrender was assured, they joined in the battle of Indonesian nationalists against continuing Netherlands control.

At the turn of the century, after three centuries of colonial rule by the Kingdom of the Netherlands, the spark of independence had been struck. But not until the 1920's did nationalist thought turn into open, fierce, and bloody rebellion. The Communist Party was founded in 1919 and immediately sought "Soviet power." Alimin Prawirodirdjo, one of its leaders, visited Moscow in 1921. For a brief period, he opposed the Comintern policy of a "united front." In August, 1924, he left the party, but he rejoined it when the nationalists of Indonesia rose against the Dutch.

In 1924, the Communist Party in Indonesia adopted the slogan of "work and agitation among the working class through the trade unions." A year later, under Sardjano's leadership, the Communists were able to claim that 70 per cent of the trade-union members were under their influence. One outstanding Communist leader was Tan Malakka, who represented the Communists in the Moslem society Sarekat Raya. On March 25, 1925, the *Communist International* reported that "other nationalist organizations are progressing, that is, they are being revolutionized and their membership is growing, although not as rapidly as our party and the Sarekat Raya, which is under Communist influence."

A year later, nationalist agitation bore fruit. Netherlands authorities managed only with difficulty to extinguish the flame of rebellion. From then on, and until the surrender of Japan in 1945, the Communist Party was banned. The Dutch had known that an uprising was coming. On the eve of the 1926 rebellion, they ordered the arrest of Alimin, who had then made his peace with the Comintern. Alimin went underground. He arrived in Singapore by way of Palembang when the uprising began. Arrested and questioned by British authorities at Singapore, he nevertheless managed to escape.

Alimin made his way to China. After a difficult and daring journey, he arrived at Kwantung, where he helped to prepare the Pacific Labor Conference of the Red Labor International. After Chiang Kai-shek's break with the Communists, Alimin had to flee again. He stepped on Soviet soil from a boat that docked at Vladivostok, in time to represent the Indonesian Communists at the Fourth Comintern Congress in 1928. The Indonesian Communist paper, *Bintang Merah,* stated late in 1946 that Alimin was among the prominent attendants of the International Lenin School at Moscow. Quoted by the paper, Alimin said that he had shared these instructions in Marxist theories and Communist underground techniques with other leading Communists. He specifically, and in this order, mentioned Chou En-lai of China, Harry Pollitt of Great Britain, L. L. Sharkey of Australia, Susumu Okano (alias Sanzo Nozaka) of Japan, Ernst Thälmann of Germany, and Maurice Thorez of France.

Like most other members of the Lenin School's class of 1929, Alimin reached the peak of his career after World War II, when he was able to return to his homeland. But, before that, he widened his knowledge and ability as a professional revolutionary by visits to Paris, Brussels, Berlin, London, and the Near East. In the company of many other Asiatic Communist leaders, Alimin spent the war years in China. Although he stayed mostly in Yenan, it was in Kuomintang-controlled Chungking that he heard the news of the creation of the Indonesian Republic. Alimin was grateful to the Chungking bureau of the United States Information Service (a branch of the Office of War Information), which transmitted the startling report. He was thrilled, Alimin said later, when on August 7, 1945, at 9 P.M., he heard that Indonesia was the first Asiatic nation to declare its independence. His first reaction was surprise. This feeling was shared by the Chinese Communist Chou En-lai, whom Alimin quoted as saying that collaboration of Indonesian nationalists with the Japanese had been "clearly a tactical matter."

Meanwhile, Sardjano had been able to rebuild the machinery of Indonesia's Communist Party. As an Allied underground agent, he was able to reestablish old contacts and to create new ones. He was successful, particularly in the Federation of Trade Unions (which claims 750,000 members), but he encountered rivalry from other Indonesians who claimed to follow the banner of Marx and Lenin. Prominent among them was Tan Malakka, once an Oriental pillar of the Comintern, but now dubbed "Trotskyite" by his former comrades. Another ex-Communist,

Mohammed Hatta, obtained a cabinet post in the government of President Achmed Soekarno, the fiery ex-collaborator, and the Socialist-minded, clearly and cleanly anticollaborationist, Premier Sutan Sjahrir.

For fourteen months, the troops of the young Indonesian Republic fought British and Dutch troops. Finally, on November 15, 1946, the Netherlands and the Indonesian Republic agreed on a compromise. Recognizing the Republic's authority over Java, Madura, and Sumatra (about 86 per cent of Indonesia), the agreement foresaw "rapid formation of a democratic state on a federal basis, to be called the United States of Indonesia." In the end, the compromise stated, there would be a "Netherlands-Indonesian Union," under an over-all loyalty to the Netherlands royal house.

In the Netherlands itself, the agreement was opposed by the conservative parties, approved by the dominant Labor Party, and hailed by the Communists. According to the Amsterdam Communist daily *De Waarheid*, of January 16, 1947, Alimin "duly recognized the influence which Great Britain and the United States have had on the decision, and the party realizes that under the prevailing circumstances no better arrangement could have been devised." But, in Indonesia itself, some people looked upon Sardjano, Alimin, and Soekarno as traitors. Tan Malakka was one of them, and he exerted influence on the utmost outer fringes of Indonesian revolutionism. There were even allegations that Tan Malakka had a hand in a brief kidnaping of Sjahrir, in June, 1946.

The Communist Party, with Sardjano as chairman and Alimin as secretary-general, pledged its cooperation to the Republic's government. The Communists had a long and difficult road ahead of them. Their thunder had been stolen by the inspired oratory of Soekarno. Followers and potential followers, many of whom had difficulty distinguishing between Stalinism and Trotskyism (or between socialism, as represented by Sjahrir, and communism of the Moscow school), were slow and vacillating in their support. Yes, the so-called National Concentration of Revolutionary Nationalists, which had been founded in May, 1946, was a coalition of various parties, including Communists. But it was not a Communist-led combination. The Netherlands military attack on nationalist-held areas, which began in July, 1947, did not alter the Communist position. The cabinet which Sjahrir formed on July 3 contained one Communist member. The Dutch Parliament defeated a Communist motion denouncing the use of force in Indonesia by a vote of 79 to 9.

Indonesia's Communist Party must bide its time, organize and agitate, indoctrinate and propagandize, if it wants to gain power. Compared with the youthful Soekarno and Sjahrir, Sardjano and Alimin looked to the adolescent activists of the young Republic like washed-up old-timers. But the Republic government must show its administrative ability. Once warfare in Indonesia ends for good, it will have to govern, and govern well. If it runs into serious economic or domestic political trouble, according to the postwar pattern noticeable elsewhere in the south Pacific, the Communist Party of Indonesia might well get its second wind.

BURMA: FROZEN OUT

Britain's Number One spy in Japanese-occupied Burma was a Communist. His name is Maung Thein Pei. He escaped to India, wrote a book, *What Happened in Burma*, and later made several clandestine trips into Burmese territories controlled by anti-Japanese underground forces. When the Indian troops of the Fourteenth Army entered Burma to oust the Japanese in 1945, Maung Thein Pei had set up radio connection between the resistance groups and British army headquarters.

But he was only one small figure before a vast and intricate background dominated by misguided nationalism and tightrope-walking opportunism. Educated Burmese had been uncompromisingly anti-British for decades before World War II. This attitude was little changed by the new constitution of 1935, which was to prepare Burma for eventual independence within the British Commonwealth. The constitution was adopted in 1937, a year after the elections that gave the national-revolutionary Dobama Asiayon (Our Burma National League) three seats in the national representation. This party, under the leadership of Than Tun, who later emerged as head of the Communist Party of Burma, drew most of its support from students and younger elements in the cities.

Than Tun's party had the hammer and sickle as its emblem, and there is little doubt that it took its ideological gunpowder from the arsenals of the Communist International. But, as in most other colonial areas, nationalism was its main driving force. In 1938, the All-Burma Student's Union, which was close to Than Tun, organized a brief school strike. A year later, there were more serious disturbances. Burmese nationalism contains a strongly anti-Indian element. It is mainly directed against the *cheyars*, immigrants from India who have become prominent in Burmese commercial and financial life and whose business practices have aroused the ire of a large part of the population. When the Japanese occupied Burma, 400,000 *cheyars* who feared excesses fled to India. In 1939, after further student strikes and work stoppages in several Burmese oil fields for which Than Tun's party was believed responsible, serious anti-Indian riots broke out. A British Riot Inquiry Committee judged later that the riots had been "a deliberate and determined attempt to create social disorder."

So strong was anti-British sentiment among Burma's political leaders at the outbreak of the war that collaboration with the Japanese became the rule rather than the exception. Than Tun himself found it possible to accept high offices under the Japanese. In this, he personified a trend in the nationalist movement that partly explains previous and possible future Communist successes in Burma. From the middle twenties to the middle thirties, anti-imperialist statements made by Communist leaders abroad inspired agreement by the group around Than Tun. The rise of Nazism and the growing power of militarist Japan created an appreciation of the totalitarian powers among nationalist Burmese.

Than Tun is still a young man. He was born in 1911 and educated at the Rangoon Teachers' Training College. Under the Japanese occupation, he became executive for agriculture and member of the Burma Independence Preparatory Committee. On August 1, 1943, he was appointed minister for agriculture in the Japanese-controlled Burmese puppet government. Aung San, who later became Burma's outstanding leader, was made a major general by the Japanese and placed in command of the Burmese Independence Army.

While Than Tun served the Japanese, another leading Communist kept himself free from the taint of collaboration. He was Thakin Soe, who used the underground Communist Party to form an anti-Fascist organization in 1943. Following the pattern of similar groups elsewhere, it became a catchall for resistance-independence parties of various political complexions. By that time, Burma had come to realize the true intentions of the Japanese: domination rather than liberation. Within Aung San's Burmese Independence Army, and within the puppet cabinet itself, there was mounting secret opposition to the Japanese. The Independence Army was slowly transformed into an anti-Japanese resistance group. Arms were being smuggled into Burma through British intelligence channels. It was early in 1945 that Maung Thein Pei executed his dangerous and daring missions from India into Burma and back again. An estimated 50,000 guerrillas began to operate against the Japanese occupying armies.

At the time of liberation, Aung San's army and the Communist-led anti-Fascist organization merged into one nationalist coalition, the Anti-Fascist People's Freedom League. Than Tun became secretary-general of the league, Aung San its president. Thakin Soe also occupied a leading position. The Anti-Fascist League sought to establish a nation-wide administration. This, under immediate postwar conditions, was a difficult undertaking. The country had been ravaged by war. Agriculture had been disorganized. There were a lot of arms around, some of which had been supplied to the guerrillas by the British. Others had been abandoned by the Japanese. Peasant banditry was not a new thing in Burma. Armed gangs are called *dacoitists,* and *dacoitism* had a field day after the liberation. Tens of thousands of Burmese were charged with banditry and imprisoned in 1946 and early 1947.

These critical economic and security conditions faced the Anti-Fascist League, and, on their return, British authorities. The character of the league itself was questioned in Great Britain. On February 4, 1946, Arthur Henderson, Britain's Undersecretary for India and Burma, was asked in the House of Commons at London, "Is the Anti-Fascist League of Burma also anti-Communist?" Henderson said, "I would prefer them to answer for themselves on that point." As a matter of fact, only a nucleus of some 3,000 party members in the league were definitely Communists. Hundreds of thousands of others were affiliated with it. The league included Socialists, the Communist-created Peasant Union (which claimed half a million members, mostly in lower Burma), the Rangoon Trade Union, the All-Burma Trade Union Congress (which has an influential Communist leadership), the Students' Union, the Women's League, and the Youth League. The former anti-Japanese guerrilla group, known as the Patriotic Volunteers Organization, was also at least partly under Communist control. It was clear at the time that these groups represented much of the politically active part among Burma's seventeen million inhabitants.

Disagreements within the Communist camp caused a split in the summer of 1946. Thakin Soe was expelled. On July 13, his group was declared illegal, and he was arrested three months later. But he escaped the Burmese police, which searched for him without success. On one occasion, when the police entered a Buddhist monastery, they ran into an elaborately garbed mute nun. The nun was finally arrested. She turned out to be Thakin Soe. Than Tun denounced "Soe-ism" as indulging in extremist and sectarian notions.

While independence negotiations with the British continued in 1946, the Communist-led organizations pressed for political and economic concessions. In September, 3,500 policemen went on strike. Civil-service workers, railroad employees, and postal workers also walked out. They were followed by the employees of the Burma Oil Company, the Burma Trade Company, and of a large steel corporation. On September 23, the central committee of the All-Burma Trade Union Congress announced a general strike. Simultaneously, the Communists inside the Anti-Fascist League pressed for an immediate reorganization of the government.

Three days later, Sir Hubert Rance, governor of Burma, offered the league six of the eleven seats in the executive council. The council was to function as an interim government under the provisions of the 1935 constitution, with the governor retaining a veto. The offer was accepted. Among the league members nominated to enter the council was the Communist Maung Thein Pei, who had previously served as head of the department of agriculture and who belonged to the Than Tun Communists. When the Than Tun group continued its demands within the Anti-Fascist League, it was expelled late in October. Aung San said on November 3, 1946, "The Communists have dug their own grave. They have made serious blunders, and British imperialism is taking advantage of that." Than Tun, commenting on the rift between his party and the Anti-Fascist League, said, "It is immaterial." The Communist slogan, he added, would remain, "On with the revolution!" He then began to create a rival organization, the United National Front.

This move robbed Aung San of some of his most militant supporters. After all, the Anti-Fascist League had begun its growth on the initiative of the very Communists who were now opposing it. Warfare between supporters of Aung San and Than Tun began soon afterward. While Aung San visited London in January, 1947, pressing for immediate acknowledgment of Burma's independence, Communists and members of the Anti-Fascist League clashed in Yamethin, 250 miles north of Rangoon. Than Tun's red-shirted followers were said to be using trench mortars during the engagement. Later, clashes in Rangoon itself symbolized the high pitch to which the disagreement between Communists and league supporters had developed. When the London talks ended with an agreement on Burmese elections in April, 1947, the All-Burma Trade Union Congress tied up Rangoon in a general strike. The elections were nevertheless an overwhelming success for Aung San.

Than Tun issued a statement which denounced the British-Burmese agreement and the elections as a "shameful compromise." He hailed the "armed risings by the People's Volunteer Organization, glorious actions of the peasantry in taking over the rice stocked by monopolist projects throughout Lower Burma and the armed resistance of the peasantry against the outrages of the British troops." Than Tun asserted that "only the Communist policy will lead to independence" and stated that Aung San had described the Communist Party "as the main enemy."

On July 19, 1947, Aung San and five other members of the Burma Interim Government were killed by unknown assassins with machine guns in the offices of the Executive Council. Somewhat hastily, London Foreign Office observers suspected the Communists. But subsequent arrests indicated that rightist extremists close to the ultra-nationalist leader U Saw had been involved in the assassination plot. Aung San was immediately replaced by his loyal follower, Thakin Nu. But the death of the Burmese nation's most colorful leader automatically strengthened the relative status of Than Tun and the Communist Party. Forgetting his own earlier violent attacks on the murdered Aung San, Than Tun proclaimed, "It is time the Burmese people recognized their real enemy—British bureaucrats and their hirelings—whose machinations cost them the lives of Aung San and other Burmese patriots."

INDIA: AGAINST PARTITION

The Communist Party of India, under the leadership of Puran Chand Joshi, faces religious and social conditions that make its task appear mountainous. The Comintern realized the possibility for revolutionary agitation in India in 1922. But British governmental authorities immediately banned the party. Manabendra Nath Roy, who led the Indian party, was expelled from the Communist International in 1929 because of his "rightist deviations." He had allegedly taken the side of Bukharin against Stalin and so had sealed his fate as a Communist. In 1940, he became head of the Indian Federation of Labor, which has some 115,000 members.

Roy's Labor Federation is opposed to the All-India Trade Union Congress, which he himself helped to create on October 31, 1920. During the period of Communist illegality in India, the Trade Union Congress was the main center of Communist influence. The party nevertheless continued to lead a precarious illegal existence of its own. Its action program, published April 25, 1924, asked Communists and their sympathizers to enter the local councils "with the object of wrecking them" and to prepare the country for "mass civil disobedience (general strike)." India's Communists have railed against the dominating influence of Mahatma Gandhi for a quarter of a century. The party's newspaper, *The Vanguard*, then published by Roy and his American wife Evelyn, nee Trent, at Zurich, Switzerland, accused Gandhi as long ago as 1924 of "patriarchal despotism." Joshi no longer permits himself such personal laboring, but he, too, has little use for Gandhi and his policy of nonviolence. India's Communists feel that violence and strikes are their most powerful weapon.

Through their control of the All-India Trade Union Congress (which has about 700,000 members), they are expanding their influence in the labor movement generally. Mulhar Narayan Joshi, a veteran of the defunct Red Labor International, is TUC secretary. The Communist Party represents a small island in the swirling, turbulent sea that is India today. It is pulled hither and thither by the religious-social peculiarities of the vast Indian nation. Not being quite able to absorb its relatively rapid increase in membership, it has a particularly difficult job of Communist education to perform. Even back in 1927, the party's magazine, *The Masses of India*, had to warn its followers that "it is absurd to seek for a special Indian variety of communism; an Indian who calls himself a Communist must be a Communist like the others in the rest of the world."

P. C. Joshi is one of the youngest Communist leaders in the world. He was born in 1907, the son of a school principal at Almora, in the United Provinces. He studied law at Allahabad University. In 1929, during the extremist-revolutionary phase of Comintern policy, Joshi was arrested and accused of conspiracy. The United Provinces Student Movement, which he led, showed influences of Communist agitation. Together with 28 others, he was sentenced to five years' imprisonment.

But Joshi spent only three and a half years in prison. Following an appeal to the High Court, he was released on August 6, 1934. He immediately returned to illegal Communist activity. For nine years, until the party achieved legality during World War II, he organized the Communist Party as a small underground nucleus. Prior to Nazi Germany's attack on Russia, Joshi's party represented the war effort as just another phase of British imperialism; but, after 1941, it was nearly the only strong prowar force in India. Consequently, the party was permitted in January, 1942, to organize legally.

In the beginning, party activity was restricted to such communities as Bombay (where the party has its headquarters and publishes the paper *People's Age*), Calcutta, and Cawnpore. It soon extended its agitation to the peasant workers and small industrial laborers. These are sections of the population in which the predominantly Hindu Congress Party (under the leadership of Pandit Jawaharlal Nehru) and the Moslem League (under Mohammed Ali Jinnah) have grown less influential during the postwar years. Consequently, the Communists—who claimed 12,000 members in 1943—gave their membership figure as 60,000 in 1947. The *Daily Worker* of New York reported on November 10, 1946, that "another 150,000 workers are close sympathizers and they actively support the party." India has seventeen Communist publications, printed in various languages, with a combined circulation of about 70,000.

The policy of the party underwent the changes characteristic to Communist parties everywhere. In 1940, it agitated among Bombay textile workers against even indirect support of the war. Later, widespread anti-war sentiment in India gave the Communists a particularly difficult task of supporting unity behind the war effort. To this end, its central committee pressed for unity between Nehru's Congress and Jinnah's League in a manifesto on September 19, 1942. It said, "To the Hindu masses we must explain that what is just in the Pakistan demand, namely the right to autonomous state existence, including the right of separation, must be conceded. . . . Similarly, we must get the Congress-minded people to recognize the urgency of the Congress conceding the right of self-determination of the Moslem nationalities and thus hasten the achievement of Congress-League unity."

After the end of the war, the Communists moved into opposition to the larger parties' leadership. However, Joshi said on October 12, 1945, that "in spite of differences with Congress and Moslem League, we recognize them as major patriotic organizations." This seemed like the cautious beginning of a "united front from below" policy. The Communists consider the policy makers of both the Congress and the League as bourgeois or capitalist supported. They violently attacked Nehru and Jinnah for their acceptance of the 1947 British proposal for self-government of a Congress-controlled Hindu India and a League-controlled Pakistan. Joshi accused the Hindu and Moslem leaders of making common cause with "British imperialism" in the "partition" and "Balkanization" of India.

There can be no doubt that the young independent governments of India will face Communist opposition. Communist tactics during the immediate postwar years are designed to split both Hindu India and Pakistan into left and right wings. Then, the Communists seem to hope, the two left wings might coalesce with the Communist Party. Such a coalition would seek to sever even the thinnest remaining ties with Great Britain and to gain control of India.

In the minds of some leading Indians, the Communist Party and its aspirations are linked very closely with the foreign policy of the Soviet Union. On September 16, 1945, Dr. Pattabhi Sitaramayya, former member of the Congress Working Committee, told a meeting at Muslipatam that "Russia is knocking at our doors and is hardly forty miles from our frontier." He asked, "If the Russians should invade the country—and this is not a fantastic proposition—on whose side will these Communists in India fight? Will they side with their mother country of their birth, or with their father country of their ideal? This eccentric party, whose center of gravity is in Leningrad, whose head is, however, in the Himalayas, is a dangerous party to be reckoned with."

AFGHANISTAN: POOR GOAT

Dr. Sitaramayya's fears made him look north to the Himalayas, just as he might have looked to India's North West Province, which borders on Russia's gateway to India: Afghanistan. Emir Abdur Rhaman, who ruled Afghanistan before the turn of the century, called his country "this poor goat, a victim which is being eyed by a lion on one side and a terrible bear on the other, both ready to swallow it at the first opportunity." But today, the British lion is being pushed and pulled out of India. In 1946, when the question of Afghanistan's admission to membership in the United Nations was considered, the application was approved without delay. Both Great Britain and the Soviet Union supported it. Britain seemed to hope it could continue to exercise a decisive influence on Afghanistan, while Russia believed that the Kabul government could hardly refuse pointed suggestions coming from its great northern neighbor. The Turkmen, Uzbek, and Tadzhik Soviet Republics border on Afghanistan to the north. Early in 1946, the Soviet and Afghan governments agreed that the USSR should enjoy permanent territorial control over the Kushka province, close to the Iranian frontier.

Communist efforts to line up Afghanistan go back to 1921, when the Soviet government instructed a trade delegation to Kabul that "commercial relations must first of all serve the interest of the Communist propaganda of the Third International." Lavish entertainment in the most colorful Oriental manner was suggested to the delegates, who were to form an "organization of Communist cells, which should develop into a Communist Party." Nevertheless, organized communism today is nonexistent in Afghanistan, although the proximity of the Soviet Union has left an imprint on the small Moslem nation.

It is difficult to imagine a more barren soil for the seed of communism than the Afghan people. They are fiercely nationalist, tough, and fanatically religious Moslems. When the westernized King Amanullah tried to follow the example of Turkey's Kemal Ataturk of moderate social reforms, he was deposed by the mullahs, the Moslem priests of which there are some 20,000. The mullahs control much of Afghanistan's life, and any power intending to gain influence in Afghanistan does well to have the mullahs' support and the mullahs don't like communism, unless it permits them to maintain their tight control on the nation.

AUSTRALIA: LABOUR'S LOVE LOST

The Australian Communist Party, which quadrupled its membership during the war years, knows what it means to be opposed by a dominant Labour Party. In this, the Communists of Australia share the experience of their Scandinavian comrades. Australia's Communist boom coincided with the party's earnest support of the Allied war effort and of the Australian Labour Party's candidates during the 1943 elections. When the war had ended, bringing in its wake a wave of Communist-supported strikes, the Labour Party ended this alliance. Australian Labour proved during the postwar elections that it could win, just as well or even better, without Communist backing. So the government of Premier Joseph B. Chifley, which received a public mandate on September 28, 1946, faced angry Communist opposition for another three years.

It had not always been thus. Following the Seven Strategies of world communism faithfully (although not without some very serious rebellion within their party), the Australian Communists have blown hot and cold toward the Labourites for more than a quarter of a century. The Communist Party of Australia was formed on October 30, 1920. Three years later it received the support of groups of dissident members of the Australian Socialist Party and of the Australian affiliate of the International Workers of the World (IWW). It was during that year, 1923, that Australia's Communists first approached the Labour Party in their efforts toward affiliation. This was the period of Lenin's "To the masses!" policy, following the Third Comintern Congress. But the Labourites were cool to the proposal.

Hardly had the Communists planted their feet on Australian soil, when the controversies inside the Russian party and the Comintern sent waves of tremors to Sydney. Between 1924 and 1929, Australia's Communist Party dwindled into obscurity. The leaders of the Australian party hit the ceiling when Moscow, in 1928, embarked on its extremist-revolutionary strategy. Kavanagh, secretary-general of the Australian Communist Party, told the Comintern that Australia was not ready for out-and-out class warfare. He had liked the united front policy much better. But Moscow knew better. The Comintern, in a message to the Australian party, accused it of "virtual isolation of the Communist Party from the masses." Moscow told Sydney that it "gravely underestimates the intensity of the class struggle in Australia." In fact, "the decision of the majority of your Central Committee to support the Labour Party in the last elections (of 1928) is a glaring example of grave right deviation, deserving the severest condemnation." The Moscow message concluded, "If you really have the cause of communism at heart, you will alter your course and henceforth pursue the line of the Communist International." Kavanagh was thrown out of the party, and with him most of the other members of the central committee.

For all practical purposes, Australia's Communists had to start all over again. They were particularly handicapped by the government's ban on import of publications from the Soviet Union. The Foreign-Language Publishing House in Moscow used to print books and pamphlets for distribution by Comintern sections abroad. But the Australian party had to produce its own propaganda material, which was a much more expensive process than letting Moscow foot the printing bill. In 1929, the Communists followed Comintern instructions by sponsoring the Workers Defence Corps, which was active during the coal strike in New South Wales. But the strike ended with a defeat of the strikers. The Communists also created the Unemployed Workers Movement, organized protest demonstrations, and agitated among seamen, textile, and sugar workers. The party's membership turned over so fast that much of its agitation was useless. In 1932, it had only 2,058 members. Even the Comintern's new "united front" policy did not help the Australian party. From 1936 to 1938, it gained no more than 317 members: from 3,252 to 3,569.

Then came the war, and the Australian Communist Party found itself denouncing the "imperialist war." The government banned the party, which nevertheless continued its activity underground. The Nazi attack on Russia opened the way for Communist support of the war effort, in Australia as everywhere else. The party's thirteenth congress, in 1943, was a joyous occasion for its leaders. Membership had jumped, from 7,200 in May, 1942, to 16,000 by the end of that year, and 20,000 at the time of the party congress. Public prestige of the party had risen, in proportion to admiration for the Soviet Union's war effort. The Australian Labour Party in New South Wales agreed to united action with the Communists, but the federal Labour leaders still would have none of it. (The Labourites in New South Wales expressed their disillusionment three years later, when they rejected "without hesitation or qualifications any pact or working agreement or association with the Communist Party." Voting 450 to 40, the Labourites resolved on June 16, 1946, that the Communists were a danger to Australian democracy and a permanent enemy of the Australian Labour Party.)

The 1943 support of Labour by the Communists did not come up to the Communists' hope. The *Communist Review* noted that, except for isolated districts in Queensland and South Australia, the Communist vote "was below expectation." However, the magazine stated that "the main aim of the Communist Party in the elections, of course, was the defeat of the reactionary parties" and the retention of the Labour government. This aim, Communists read, "was thoroughly achieved." All in all, the party's seventeen candidates received 80,000 votes.

The Australian public has been particularly elephant-minded in refusing to forget the Communists' policy during the early part of the war. J. B. Miles, who today heads the Australian Communist Party as secretary-general, had to explain over and over again just what had prompted the party to oppose the war in its beginning. On June 8, 1943, the *Sydney Morning Herald* stated editorially, "It suits the Communists to forget that Britain also put up a splendid—and a solitary—fight at the time when they were opposing the so-called 'imperialist' war. Their concern then was not for Australian welfare, but for dutiful adherence to the Moscow Line." The *Communist Review* countered this argument by comparing the war aims of Great Britain with those of Nazi Germany, saying, "To fight splendidly does not make a cause just, otherwise the cause of the Nazis would be just."

Australia's Communists have strongly opposed the government's experiments with transcontinental rockets and supersonic aircraft in the vast empty inland territories. This led R. A. King, secretary of the New South Wales Labour Council, to say, "Communists in Australia would sabotage the rocket venture if they thought it was in Russia's interest to do so." After the return of the Australian delegate to the Empire Communist Conference in London, early in 1947, the party strongly accelerated its agitation against the foreign policy of the United States and began to soft-pedal somewhat its anti-British propaganda.

The final die for postwar relations between the Australian Labour Party and the Communists was cast back in 1946, when a Labour convention rejected a motion for a joint election campaign. The Communist Party of Australia has doubtless been able to improve its position considerably during the past decade. Dissolution of the Comintern has enabled it to emphasize concern with strictly Australian interests. But the Labour Party's moderate socialism, which has favored government authority in the field of child endowment, widow's pensions, and socialized medicine (an issue on which it is opposed by the relatively conservative Liberal Party), has taken much wind out of the Communist sails. In fact, Labour also favors control over investments, prices, aviation, appropriations, and other fields. The Communists consider such changes halfway measures but cannot of course oppose them with consistency.

NEW ZEALAND: IT'S NO USE

New Zealand's Communists might as well forget their dreams of power and influence. It's no use. Although their party claims 2,000 members, it polled only 1,000 out of 1,000,000 votes in the 1946 national elections. Most New Zealanders are satisfied with the choice they have between the socialist Labour Party and the conservative Nationalist Party.

Since 1936, Labour has run New Zealand and created one of the purest socialized democratic countries in the world. It did this mainly by taxing the landowning sheep growers (there are twenty sheep for each of the

1,600,000 New Zealanders) and distributing this wealth through an advanced, cradle-to-grave social-security system. As a result, New Zealand knows little ostentatious wealth and no real poverty.

This is not a setup that lends itself to Communist agitation. What little economic-political rebellion there is can be found in the state-owned mines and on the waterfronts. Communist National Chairman Alexander Brennan is president of the Auckland Trade Council and vice-president of the New Zealand Waterside Workers, and he belongs to the National Council of the Federation of Labour.

Communist strength is concentrated among the wharf workers, and there again in the nation's largest city, Auckland. It is no secret that Communist agitation among dock workers' has accounted for most of the strikes that occurred before and after World War II. Brennan himself did not become a Communist until 1931 and did not join the party's national committee until 1935. Born in Greenock, Scotland, in 1900, he was active in the New Zealand Labour Party in the late 1920's. During the depression, he organized unemployed councils in Auckland.

New Zealand's Communist Party was founded in December, 1920, in the Socialist Hall at Wellington, the nation's capital. Its founders came for the most part from the old New Zealand Marxian Association. Far removed from Moscow, New Zealand's Communists have sometimes been slow in following party-line changes. They did not properly catch on to the extremist-revolutionary Third Strategy of world communism until it was almost over. In September, 1933, the Moscow bureau of the Comintern admonished its New Zealand section for continuing dealings with the "social reformists" of the Labour Party and demanded that more be done to make Communists out of the native Maoris.

When the line changed two years later, New Zealand's Communists did not react fast enough to make something of the "united front" policy during the 1935 elections, which put the Labour government into power. Moscow promptly accused the party of shortsighted "sectarianism." The 1939 policy flip-flop caused by the Nazi-Soviet Pact caught the party's General Secretary Leo Sim asleep at the switch. For a while, Sidney W. Scott, the ambitious and bright editor of the party's publications (the weekly *People's Voice* and the *New Zealand Labour Monthly*), was the brains of New Zealand's Communist movement. After Brennan had been properly indoctrinated, he was officially named party chairman in February, 1946.

The party's activity has been limited by the narrow framework of New Zealand's undramatic political life. The nation's delegate to the 1945 conference of the World Federation of Trade Unions was a Communist, Roy Stanley, national secretary of the Carpenters' Union. Ever since 1922, the party has made the usual "united front" offers to the Labour Party, which have been declined with polite monotony. The Comintern's idea about agitation among the Maoris has borne only shriveled fruit. However, efforts to gain adherents among these 5 per cent of New Zealand's inhabitants are continuing. At its 1946 conference, the party saw to it that it received a message from a real Maori princess, Te Puea Herang, who said, "May your work in the ensuing year be productive." In its May 1, 1946, issue, the party's *People's Voice* took editorial notice of a native movement to set up King Koroki as king of the Maoris. This, the paper said was "a symbol of Maori unity," and the Labour government would do well to recognize it as a "manifestation of Maori national feeling." The party's publications find a limited audience among Indians in Samoa.

New Zealand's Communist Party follows the Seventh Strategy of world communism faithfully. The *Labour Monthly* said in December, 1946, that the government (which had been confirmed in power by the November elections) had formed a "junior partnership with British imperialism." The magazine also criticized an "increasing tendency on the part of some sections of the New Zealand and Australian bourgeoisie to look toward the U.S.A. for 'protection'." Such protection, the publication warned, "means being swallowed by the U.S.A."

The government looks with disfavor on Communist attempts to break through the delicately adjusted price- and wage-control system. Contradicting the arguments that Communists have made in eastern Europe, and with particular emphasis in Czechoslovakia, the New Zealand party insists that wage rises have nothing to do with inflation. Scott, writing in February, 1947, denounced the "irrelevancies and confusions of the reformist trade union leaders" and said that "people who talk about wage rises causing inflation are putting the cart before the horse."

RED-TINTED DAWN

From the foothills of the Himalayas to the humid villages of Java, from the docks of Singapore to the still ancient bazaars of Kabul, the red-tinted dawn of southeast Asia's independence is clearly visible. Empires that have existed for centuries are crumbling faster than cabinet councils in London, Paris, and The Hague can desire.

The seeds of empire were planted by private business organizations, by missionaries and educators. Will tomorrow's allegiances be prepared by professional revolutionaries, some of whom were trained in the Soviet Union? Revolutionary nationalism in southeast Asia is more than merely native rebellion against imperfect rule by foreign overlords. It is also revolt against social privilege, moribund feudalism, against sultans and princes. The underprivileged peasants of the Philippines, of Burma, of everywhere in southeast Asia, were looking for a creed that would lift them out of their misery. They were hungry for leaders.

And then leaders came. Some of them were Communists, or ex-Communists, or Communist-influenced emotionalists. Those who, in Indo-China, for instance, had professional revolutionary training, went farthest most quickly. Men make revolutions. Trained men. Intelligent men. In our century of specialization, rebellion has become a science. What is more natural than that professional revolutionaries should lend their experience and ability to eager and untrained rebels. The Seventh Strategy of world communism has made cooperation between Communist parties and nationalist groups a desirable union of forces.

Men who suffer under a rule that is obnoxious to them are glad of all possible encouragement. Among those who in the past have been critical of British, French, and Dutch colonial rule were many enlightened and patriotic Englishmen, Frenchmen, and Netherlanders. They knew that every fault, every shortsighted measure administered by an unthinking and impersonal bureaucracy, can start an avalanche of resentment. Today, the wave of nationalism, that has hit the world as an aftermath of war, has risen higher in colonial areas than anywhere else. In communism, nationalist rebellion has found a new and vigorous ally.

CHAPTER 31

Near East and Africa: Political Quicksand

Marx CANNOT compete with Allah, nor Stalin with Mohammed. World communism does not attempt to replace the Koran with the Communist Manifesto. It would never work. Islam, one of the world's most militant religious forces, defies orthodox Communist atheism. But the still feudal society of the Near East offers communism an opportunity in the political-economic field. Communist planners have found it difficult to make maximum use of this opportunity. There are many reasons for that. The Near East, crossroads of four continents, key to the Moslem world, and center of vast oil reserves, is a labyrinth of power aspirations. These are the things Communist agitation in the Near East has to deal with: dictatorial control by tribal chieftains, beys, pashas, and kings, which effectively discourages any and all rebellion; Islamic fatalism, which, though easily exaggerated by western observers, has nevertheless conditioned political thinking among the Moslem masses; a relatively clear-cut and determined policy on the part of the western powers; and, finally, Palestine, always Palestine.

For very complex political-emotional reasons, Palestine has become the focal point of Arab-Moslem thinking. It has unified the rival interests of Arab heads of state on a religious-nationalistic level. Palestine is the alpha and omega of Moslem aspirations in the Near East. Any power or political ideology that seeks allegiance in the Arab world must take a stand on Palestine. But, when it comes to Arab-Zionist claims to control of the Holy Land, communism grows vaguely righteous. And that doesn't mean very much to strongly nationalist Arabs or Zionists.

PALESTINE. ANY STRAW?

If it were merely a question of applying orthodox Communist tenets to the Near East, communism might come out in clear-cut opposition to

411

Zionist claims for "a Jewish homeland in Palestine." Back in 1923, when the Comintern's executive committee recommended recognition of Palestine's Communist Party, it urged that Palestinian Communists "support the nationalist movement for freedom of the Arab population against the British-Zionist occupation." The fight against "British-Zionist occupation" might have been revived after World War II. But it would seem that Near Eastern Communist policy today is more concerned with weakening the hold of western interests than with ideological purity. And it is the warfare waged by ultra-nationalist Zionist groups that causes most of the British difficulties in Palestine today.

Although it certainly does not endorse Zionist policy in Palestine, communism also does not oppose it with the strength it could muster. Communist policy has been much more consistent where Arab aspirations are concerned. The Communist International defined its Near Eastern activity as follows: "The international imperialists, to further their policy of robbery, have split up the Arab countries and raised artificial frontiers between them. Yet, the Arab Communists, though under the rule of various imperialist powers, must strive to build an anti-imperialist popular front that extends to all Arab lands, founding it on a program containing demands that will unite all anti-imperialist forces in the Arab countries." To this day, cooperation with Arab nationalism against the influence of the western powers (Great Britain, the United States, France) remains a cornerstone of Communist efforts in the Near East.

Even these efforts, realistic as they are, have met with only limited success. Power in the Near East is built on political quicksand. Arab nationalism, opportunist in character, has made a wavering ally for communism. The Mufti of Jerusalem sought and received the support of Nazi Germany and Fascist Italy in ousting British rule from the Near East. He aided Germany by creating an all-Moslem troop unit in Yugoslavia, and he was originally listed by the Yugoslav government as a war criminal. But the Communist-led government of Yugoslavia later removed the name of the Mufti, whose prestige among Arab nationalists was unimpaired by his cooperation with Nazism, from its war-criminal list. Although Communist spokesmen have never defended the Mufti's actions, they have also avoided criticism of his career in their statements addressed to the Near East. Jamal al Husseini, a close relative of the Mufti (whose name is Amin al Husseini), is a member of the Arab Higher Committee for Palestine. When the findings of the Anglo-American Committee of

Inquiry on Palestine were published in 1946, Jamal al Husseini foresaw a "general trend to the Left, all over the Middle East." He said, "We will grab at any straw—Russia, or any one else who will aid us." But other members of the Higher Committee did not agree with him. Together with many Arab leaders outside Palestine, they feel that the influence of communism and the Soviet Union would ultimately weaken their own interests.

Communist policy among the Jews of Palestine was expressed by Meir Vilner before the Anglo-American Committee on March 25, 1946. Testifying for the Communist Party of Palestine, he accused the committee of "presenting the problem of our country as a question of antagonism between Jews and Arabs, instead of regarding it as a problem of oppression by British imperialism of Arabs and Jews alike." He denounced the "chauvinistic evidence submitted by the official Jewish and Arab leadership" and characterized the "plan for partition of Palestine" as an "imperialist program designed to find a new form for the continuation of the old British rule and for the increase of tension between Jews and Arabs." Vilner expressed the official Communist formula for a solution of the Palestine problem as follows: "An independent and democratic Arab-Jewish state."

Although the slogan of "Arab-Jewish unity" is used frequently by Communist spokesmen, the deep schism that divides Arabs and Jews in Palestine forced the Communists in 1944 to create a group that would operate exclusively among Arabs. Palestine's weak Communist Party claims 1,500 members, mostly among Tel Aviv's Jewish community. It publishes the Hebrew-language daily *Kol Ha'am* and the Yiddish-language weekly *Volksstimme*. Its Arab counterpart is the Palestine National Liberation League, under the copresidency of Emil Touma, who edits the League's organ *Al Ittahad* in Haifa, and of Fead Nassar, who organized the Arab Trade Union Congress in 1945. This union group claims 20,000 members.

The policy of the two groups is identical in all main points. On February 7, 1947, the Palestine Communists appealed to the United Nations for the evacuation of British troops and the "setting up of a democratic Arab-Jewish state." These aims have also been expressed by the Arab group. Touma told the Empire Communist Conference at London on February 26 that "American monopoly capitalism is preparing for a new war and is infiltrating the Middle East." He also said, "Zionism is trying, by promoting immigration, to keep its hold on the masses in Palestine and thereby to promote imperialism, especially American imperialism." British policy, he said, was designed to keep Palestine as a military base "against the Soviet Union and the Arab freedom movement."

Communism continues to find it difficult to break the hold of Arab nationalist leaders on the Moslem population of Palestine. The powerful Socialist Jewish trade-union body, the Histadruth, is anti-Communist. It corresponds to the non-Communist labor organizations of western Europe, rather than to the Communist-led unions in eastern European countries.

IRAN: FAILURE OF AN EXPERIMENT

In 1941, the Soviet Union began its experiment of establishing a Communist-led government in the Azerbaijan province of northern Iran. In 1946, this experiment failed completely. What had happened?

This had not been the first time a Soviet-inspired regime had been created in northern Iran. Both after World War I and World War II, a man who today is known as Jaafar Pishevari was associated with Moscow-directed attempts to establish autonomous governments in the Azerbaijan region. Pishevari is a Comintern veteran. He was born at Harau in northwestern Iran in 1888 and migrated to Baku in 1904, where his parents worked in the oil fields. In 1918, he entered northern Iran with the Red Army under the name of Sayid Jaafar Badku Bayi (the last two words of his name mean "of Baku Bay").

He participated in the so-called "jungle revolution" at Gilan, by the Caspian Sea. In 1919, he became Minister of the Interior of the Revolutionary Jungle Government, whose militants proudly called themselves The Jungleers. This regime adopted the Hammer and Sickle for its flag. When the jungle government collapsed, he fled to Russia and became one of the many exotic occupants of Moscow's Hotel Lux, where Comintern representatives from abroad used to stay. Under the name of Sultan-Zade he headed the Communist International's Iranian Section and was prominent in its Near Eastern Committee.

In 1936, Pishevari returned to his native Iran after sixteen years of absence. He claimed to have fled from the Russian purges of Comintern personnel. He was given police protection by the Iranian government. A year later, however, the Iranian government changed its mind. It had become suspicious of Pishevari. He was sent to the village of Kashan, where he stayed from 1937 to 1941 under strict police control.

After the British-Russian occupation of Iran in 1941, he was released from Kashan and went to Teheran, where he founded the daily paper *Ajhir*. He made several trips to the Azerbaijan provincial capital of Tabriz and in July, 1944, was elected as a candidate from Azerbaijan to the Iranian Parliament. The Fourteenth Parliament, however, refused to admit him, charging that his connection with earlier military insurrections and his long residence and political activity in Russia disqualified him as a representative of the Iranian people.

In July, 1945, Pishevari founded the Democratic Party of Azerbaijan at Tabriz. On December 12, 1945, he was proclaimed president of the Azerbaijan government. This period is of great importance not only to the affairs of Iran, but also in recent world history generally. The months which followed Pishevari's ascendance to the Azerbaijan presidency changed the course of United States foreign policy. They led to the Truman doctrine which in 1947 made energetic opposition to communism a cornerstone of America's position in the world.

The importance of the Iranian events in early 1945 can hardly be exaggerated. Here was a clear case of Soviet intervention in favor of a government led by a veteran of the Communist International. Here also was a clear violation of international contracts. When the foreign ministers of the major powers met at Moscow in December, 1945, the Soviet government refused to discuss the question of Iran. It is a matter of historical record that both Premier Stalin and Foreign Minister Molotov told United States Secretary of State Byrnes and British Foreign Minister Bevin that there was no need to settle the Iranian matter, because both Britain and Russia were pledged by their 1941 agreement to evacuate Iran on or before March 2, 1946. Stalin and Molotov were indignant that the pledge of the Soviet government should be doubted.

But even while the foreign ministers met in Moscow, Pishevari officially took control over the Azerbaijan province. And when March 2, 1946, came around, Soviet occupation troops did not withdraw from Azerbaijan. On the contrary, two Soviet armored corps of fifty heavy tanks were moved all the way from Lake Balaton in Hungary to northern Iran, to strengthen the hold of the Pishevari regime. The case was discussed before the United Nations Security Council, over the spirited objection of Soviet delegate Andrei Gromyko. On one occasion, Gromyko walked out of the Council chamber in a gesture of protest.

Soviet troops were finally withdrawn in the late spring of 1946. But the United States government noted the reluctance and bad grace with which this was done. Recalling the assurances which Stalin and Molotov had given verbally in Moscow, the U. S. government reappraised the policies of the Soviet government in regard to Communist and Communist-controlled movements throughout the world.

The Iranian government was, at that time, headed by Premier Ahmad Ghavam Sultaneh. While Pishevari led the Democratic Party of Azerbaijan, another Communist party in Iranian dress existed in central and southern Iran: the Tudeh (Masses) Party, which occupied several posts in Ghavam's Teheran government. Azerbaijan was cut off from the non-Soviet world. The aggressive, propagandistic news reports of the Tabriz radio assured listeners that Pishevari enjoyed the support of the Azerbaijan masses. Liberals in many parts of the globe were encouraged by reports that Tabriz had embarked on a sweeping program of land reform and a campaign of improving general living conditions. Withdrawal of the United States Persian Gulf Command had contributed to unemployment at a time when Iran's economy was highly inflationary. If Pishevari could have lightened the economic burden borne by the people of northern Iran, he might have gained genuine and lasting popular support.

Pishevari's Tabriz regime had created or inspired a so-called Kurdish People's Republic. Headed by Ghazi Mohammed, even the name of this regime—corresponding to "people's republics" from Outer Mongolia to Albania—suggested that it had the endorsement of Soviet communism. This Kurdish nationalist regime was the potential spearhead of a Communist-led offensive against the governments of Turkey and Iraq. The Kurds are in the Near East what the Macedonians are in the Balkans; they have independence aspirations within at least three countries—Iran, Iraq, and Turkey.

At the same time, the Tudeh Party was extremely active in central and southern Iran. Tudeh-led strikes broke out on plants of the Anglo-Iranian Oil Company. Tudeh sponsored a trade union, named "The Workers and Toilers of Iran." Again, the vernacular was familiar. On May Day, union members paraded with their families through the town of Abadan. Later, they presented a series of demands to the oil company. Walter Lucas, reporting to the *Christian Science Monitor* from Ahwaz, asserted that the strikes that followed the demonstration "had little to do with industrial disputes or conditions of pay and labor." He wrote, "They were of a political nature. Most of the leaders were not genuine representatives of the company's employees. They were young men of the Tudeh Party who had been insinuated into the company's service. Some were Russian-trained and some were from the Russian-supported semi-autonomous state of Azerbaijan." But a British government representative admitted that there was a basis for unrest and genuine grievances in Iranian history, which "has been one of exploitation by landowners and moneylenders and extensive corrupt practices." This British representative, J. H. Jones, a member of Parliament, visited southern Iran on a special mission for the British Foreign Office. He wrote in *The Times* of London that there exists in southern Iran "a great immature labor force, lacking in understanding of trade unionism and constitutional procedure."

This was the situation when the central government announced that national elections would be held late in 1946: Azerbaijan and Kurdish regions were in the hands of Communist-inspired regimes, and the Communist-type Tudeh Party agitated extensively in central and southern Iran. Then Premier Ghavam sent troops into Azerbaijan to "assure law and order" during election time. Pishevari defied him. But Ghavam's troops moved on, and the autonomous regime collapsed. Pishevari could not rally the mass support that his government had claimed. Even though he told his followers over the Tabriz radio on December 10, 1946, that the central government intended to "make us the slaves of the British and Americans," such last-minute appeals did not strengthen support for the government. He sought refuge in the Soviet Union. Ghazi Mohammed, head of the Kurdish People's Republic, was less fortunate. He was captured by Ghavam's troops, convicted of treason, and executed.

On January 11 to 17, elections were held in Teheran. They continued in the provinces for several weeks. Premier Ghavam's newly formed National Democratic Party gained a victory that surprised no one. The Tudeh Party prudently chose not to present candidates for elections. Other opposition parties, whose leaders belonged to the same aristocratic stratum of Iranian society as Premier Ghavum, charged that the elections had not been free.

The failure in Azerbaijan nearly wrecked the Tudeh Party throughout Iran. On January 7, 1947, a revolt within the party's central committee took place, probably engineered by the Iranian government. Those associated with extremist policies were ousted, among them Secretary-General Iraj Iskandari. Tudeh then set up an executive board consisting of Ehsan Tabari, editor of the party's Teheran paper; Khalil Maleki, Dr. Fereidun Keshavarz, Dr. Yazdi; the professors Ferouten and Radmanesh; and an artist by the name of Neushin. The party established new publications: *Mardom* and *Aras,* both dailies.

At the same time, the government inspired a change of leadership in the trade union movement affiliated with Tudeh. The central committees of Tudeh and of the Iranian Trades Union were identical. On February 13, 1947, a meeting of the union's central committee was called. The more prominent committee members were afraid to appear. The labor union was then captured by government agents. Shortly afterwards, a delegation of the World Federation of Trade Unions arrived in Iran to investigate labor conditions. The majority of the delegation was Communist (it included Mustafa Al Ariss, secretary-general of the Lebanese Communist Party), and it denounced the Iranian government in sharp terms.

The Iranian chapter of world communism is not closed. Communism has suffered many defeats in its history. But it has always come back to fight again.

EGYPT: IN WAFD'S CLOTHING?

Egypt, negotiating with Great Britain for a new treaty to govern relations between the two countries, was hit by a violent red scare in the summer of 1946. The government of Premier Sidky Pasha faced continuous fire from the ultra-nationalist opposition party, the Wafd. It did not like that, and it stated that Wafd was honeycombed with Communists. The pro-government Egyptian press, which tends toward emotionalism rather than factual reporting, gave contradictory outlines of an alleged Communist plot.

Sidky Pasha himself sounded less fantastic than the government press revelations. He expressed the belief that Egyptian Communists had received instructions "from abroad" to interfere with the Anglo-Egyptian negotiations. Automatic mutual help in case of armed conflict was under discussion, a clause not necessarily agreeable to certain non-British governments.

The Norwegian Communist paper *Friheten* published a report of the Egyptian Students' Union in its issue of February 6, 1947. According to this report, government troops raided universities from October 5 to

November 16, 1946. Mechanized units were said to have been used in rounding up student demonstrators at Fouad, Farouk, and Azhar universities. The report alleged that ten tanks had been used against demonstrators at Cairo's Medical College. The Students' Union reported that 174 demonstrators were arrested in the Technical High School at Cairo on November 26. The following day, another large-scale demonstration occurred outside Fouad University.

It was not immediately clear whether the Egyptian government was justified in labeling a great number of its opponents as "Communists." The fact that Communist policy elsewhere favors an alliance with nationalist elements made the government's allegations feasible, but it did not prove them conclusively.

The government charged that a young Italian bookseller in Cairo, Henri Curiel, organized Communist activities in Egypt. Curiel was accused of using funds at his command to subsidize pro-Communist, ultra-nationalist weeklies and to send young men and women to Communist-governed European countries for study. The bookseller was arrested. Together with nineteen others (including six newspapermen, two lawyers, and five students), he was officially charged with "Communist activities" on January 12, 1947.

Sidky Pasha also accused Dr. Mohammed Mandour, editor of the nationalist paper *Wafd al Misri*, of being a "notorious Communist." The paper was banned. The pro-government Cairo paper *Akhbar el Yom*, accusing Curiel of being the "link between the Communists and the Third International," asserted that the Lebanon newspaper *El Chaab* had served as headquarters of Communist activities inside Egypt.

SYRIA, LEBANON: AFTER INDEPENDENCE

The aftermath of World War II brought independence to Syria and Lebanon, the two Levant states that had formed part of the French Empire. French-Arab friction dated back to 1920, when the Allied powers transferred Syria from Turkish to French mandate. The French government promised independence to the Levant states on and off throughout the 1920's and 1930's. During this period, Communist activity in Syria and Lebanon was hardly distinguishable from that of the nationalist groups. It followed the Comintern policy of backing the independence aspirations of the Arab nations against western control.

The Communists faced quadruple opposition: from the French administration, which looked askance at independence agitation; from the Syrian and Lebanese upper classes; from orthodox Moslems; and from the Christian Maronites of Lebanon, who leaned on the French for support against the Moslems. Levant Communist existence, far removed from the Moscow Comintern headquarters and from the French Communist Party, was precarious. The selection and training of Syrian and Lebanese Communist leaders appears to have been difficult and often unsatisfactory in its results.

When Syria and Lebanon achieved their independence after World War II, Communist agitation changed from attack on French and British colonial influences to pressure against the governing groups at home. In Syria, the "National Bloc," which ruled the country after the withdrawal of the French administration and the evacuation of British and French troop units, came increasingly under Communist fire. Khalid Bagdash, secretary-general of the Communist Party of Syria, after his return from a visit to the Soviet Union, boosted party membership to 8,000 early in 1947.

Bagdash had been accompanied on his trip to Russia by Mustafa Al Ariss, secretary-general of the Communist Party of Lebanon. Al Ariss was even more successful than his Syrian colleague. He reported a 15,000 membership, and his Beirut offices became a center of Communist activities in the Near East. The Egyptian government asserted repeatedly that Communist underground work in Egypt had been directed and planned from Beirut.

Soviet policy toward Armenians did much to boost communism in the two Levant states. Looking toward the Armenian Soviet Republic for strength and national identity, Armenian exiles in Syria and Lebanon became the strongest single group of Communist supporters. However, Russian appeals to Armenians abroad, urging them to migrate to Soviet Armenia, indirectly weakened communism in Syria and Lebanon. Armenians who obtained immigration visas at the Soviet consulates in Baghdad and Beirut and subsequently left the Levant region were a total loss to the Communist parties of Syria and Lebanon.

The Communist press, particularly *El Chaab* of Beirut, followed the Seventh Strategy of world communism in sharpening its attacks on United States policy in the Near East. It backed the temporary refusal of the Syrian government, late in 1946, to negotiate with the United States regarding oil rights and air traffic. The Syrian and Lebanese Communist press denounced the American decision to give aid to the governments of Greece and Turkey with particular vehemence. Traditional Turkish-Syrian animosity responded to this presentation, and the phrase "American imperialism" was quickly echoed in the non-Communist press.

TURKEY: WHERE COMMUNISTS WERE DROWNED

Communism is illegal in Turkey. There is no Communist Party. It was suppressed after World War I. Founded July 25, 1918, by the Moscow-born Mustafa Sübhi, the Turkish Communist Party had headquarters in Baku until 1920. It recruited followers among Turkish prisoners of war in the Soviet Union. Sübhi and fourteen other Communists represented Turkey at the Far Eastern Communist conference at Baku in 1920. When they sought to spread their newly found doctrine inside Turkey in 1921, they were arrested and ordered out of the country.

They never reached the Soviet border. Village mobs stoned, tortured, and finally drowned the Communists. Nevertheless, the Soviet government signed treaties of friendship with Turkey in 1921 and 1923. The Soviet government, which had provided Kemal Pasha with arms to fight for Turkish independence, favored cooperation between the two countries at a time when both were almost completely isolated. It was therefore deeply disappointed when the Turks turned against communism. Moscow notified Kemal Pasha that "the Communist International has followed with special sympathy the heroic struggle of the Turkish people against the whole gang of Entente thugs." The Communists reminded Ankara that, without Soviet support, "the attacks of the imperialist pirates would long ago have ended in the doom of little Turkey," and "without the support of the international proletariat, you will not be able to hold your own."

It is interesting to recall today that the Fifth Congress of the Comintern in 1924 was advised that the Soviet delegation at the Lausanne Conference "in supporting the closing of the (Dardanelles) Straits to warships" had "firmly supported the interests of the Turkish people against the imperialist powers of Europe."

But, as soon as he had consolidated his power, Kemal Pasha went his own way. After his death, successive Turkish regimes followed a nationalist and anti-Communist policy. Relations with the Soviet Union were generally good, until March, 1945. It was then that the Soviet Foreign

Ministry advised Ankara that it wished to renegotiate the Turkish-Soviet Treaty of Friendship. This opened the way for strong official and semi-official Soviet pressure on Turkey. Among Soviet aims were a bilateral arrangement regarding the Dardanelles Straits and possible Turkish territorial concessions to the Soviet Union. The eastern regions of Kars and Ardahan have frequently been mentioned by Soviet spokesmen as properly part of the Armenian Soviet Socialist Republic.

The Armenian question is Turkey's weakest spot. Almost simultaneously with its denunciation of the friendship pact, the Soviet Union appealed to Armenians abroad to emigrate to the Armenian Republic. Armenian nationalists, united in disaffection for Turkish rule, see no other hope of achieving at least partial self-government, except within the USSR. As a result, a most remarkable migration of émigré Armenians has taken place since 1945. From all parts of the world, including Turkey, Armenians have entered the Soviet Union. It is in the name of the Armenian people that future Soviet claims against Turkey are likely to be pushed. A substantial increase in its Armenian population could enable the Soviet government to advance its claims for Turkey's eastern territories with particular vigor.

Turkish persecution of Armenians in the recent past, and anti-foreign legislation supported by nationalist Turks, have made it easy for the Soviet government to win the affection of Armenians. Consequently, pro-Soviet and pro-Communist sentiment inside Turkey is most prominent among Armenians.

In May, 1946, the Turkish government abolished the "Law on Societies" which had limited the establishment of political parties and labor unions. Labor groups and political organizations developed throughout the nation. Among these was the Turkish Proletarian and Peasant Party. It was headed by Dr. Safik Husni Deymer, who had been active in Communist movements ever since 1918. The party, whose membership in 1946 was estimated at 5,000, published the weekly paper *Sendika* and the biweekly *Ligin*.

In the fall of 1946, Turkey was hit by a wave of fear. High government officials believed at that time that Soviet-inspired revolt or an attack on Turkey's eastern provinces was imminent. They felt that political and labor agitation inside the country might weaken Turkey and make outside pressure more successful. The government therefore began to repress the newly organized opposition and labor groups on December 16.

In its efforts to avoid Communist infiltration, the Turkish government has apparently not always exercised full discretion. Persons who in other parts of the world might be classified as rather mild liberals are likely to find a "Communist" label pasted across their careers and social standing. The Turkish police is not known to be able to distinguish any better between Communists and democratic Socialists than are some violent and ignorant anti-Communists in other parts of the world.

When the United States decided in 1947 to support Turkey with 100 million dollars in order to strengthen its stand against communism, this was done with few illusions regarding the political alertness of the Turkish ruling groups.

CYPRUS: AIRCRAFT CARRIER

The majority of inhabitants on Cyprus, the eastern Mediterranean island, are Greeks. They would like Cyprus to become part of Greece, just as the Dodecanese Islands were placed under Greek sovereignty after World War II. The Dodecanese had been under Italian rule in violation of international agreement, whereas Cyprus is under British rule in accordance with arrangements that were again confirmed by the Treaty of Lausanne in 1924.

Britain's Premier Benjamin Disraeli obtained Cyprus from the Sultan of Turkey in 1878. Today it is a British crown colony. But three very different forces favor Greek sovereignty over Cyprus: Communists, Greek-Cypriote nationalists, and the United States government. The Communist point of view was authoritatively stated by R. Palme Dutt of the British party at the Communist Empire Conference in January, 1947. (He also expressed the Communist belief that the island of Malta, another British-held Mediterranean island, should go to Italy.) In Cyprus itself, there is no official Communist Party, because Cypriote law does not permit one to be formed. There is a party of Communists, however, which states clearly that it "follows the teachings of Marx, Engels, Lenin, and Stalin."

Communist efforts to organize Cypriotes were largely unsuccessful during the 1920's. During the extremist-revolutionary period of world communism, a serious rebellion took place in Cyprus in 1931. The main sentiment of this uprising was Greek nationalism, spurred on by the island's desperate economic conditions during the depression years. The Cypriote party of Communists was founded in 1934 under the name

Reform Party of the Working People (Authortikon Komma Ergazomenou Laou, or Akel for short). It grew out of suppressed Communist organizations, and during the Nazi-Soviet Pact Communist agitation was blamed for the twenty-four-hour general strike in February, 1940.

After Germany's attack on Russia, Akel held its first conference on September 28, 1941. Akel followed the Sixth Strategy of world communism, supporting the Allied war effort, until 1945. It managed to draw much support from labor, particularly from the Pan-Cyprian Trade Union Committee. This labor body, which includes eighteen unions, was formed in 1944. It sent a representative to the 1945 congress of the World Federation of Trade Unions. In May of that year, police raided the headquarters of the Pan-Cyprian labor union, seized books, documents, and files, and arrested the committee's leadership. The leaders were tried, found guilty of illegal activities, and sentenced to prison terms.

In 1947, Akel claimed 4,000 members. It is organized in cells of twenty members and is said to control 285 clubs which have a total membership of 22,500. Akel also influences veterans' organizations, which have some 24,000 members. The party is represented in London, where it publishes the paper *Vema*. Akel is headed by Ploutis Servas, who in May, 1946, was elected mayor of the town of Lemosol. At that time, all four of Cyprus's major towns—Nicosia, Lemosol, Famagusta, and Lenarca—elected Akel members as mayors. All told, Akel members now head eight out of eighteen municipalities in Cyprus.

Akel political activity resembles closely that of the Greek Communist Party. Akel's National Cooperation Front is the counterpart of Greece's National Liberation Front (EAM). Communist activity in Cyprus is of strategic importance to Great Britain. The island replaces some of the air bases that Britain is losing by withdrawal from Egypt. Cyprus is also used to retain Jewish displaced persons seized by British troops during attempts to enter Palestine in violation of immigration laws.

NORTH AFRICA: THE TRAVELS OF ANDRÉ MARTY

In May, 1945, as the world watched the collapse of Nazi Germany, French troops battled Arab nationalists in North Africa. Riots occurred in Guelma and Setif, Algeria. French censorship completely obscured this sensational event. Private reports, which possibly exaggerated unrest and suppression, asserted that several hundred Frenchmen were killed and that airplanes and tanks were used to quell the rebellion. The number of Algerians killed was estimated in thousands and tens of thousands (from 7,000 to 40,000). Ever since that time, Arab nationalists in North Africa have not lacked emotional ammunition for their aspirations.

A year after the Algerian outbreaks, André Marty, veteran French Communist and leader of a Black Sea rebellion in 1919, visited North Africa. He traveled through Algeria and Tunisia, conferring with party officials and planning future activities. His visit coincided with that of a Russian representative, Nikolai Kalnikov. Shortly afterward, Communist parties in the two areas organized "united front" groups with the aid of nationalist leaders. Known as the United National Front, these bodies began to publish magazines, organize meetings, and distribute leaflets.

The Algerian Communist secretary-general, Amar Ouzegane, has attempted to form alliances with the two nationalist factions. The more moderate of these two, the Democratic Union of the Algerian Manifesto, favors autonomy but not immediate independence. The Union did not officially ally itself with the Communists, but its delegates in the Assembly at Paris followed the Communist lead with marked consistency. Algeria's Communists publish the newspaper *Liberté*. Communist influence among European residents of Algeria is larger than among Moslems. During elections to the Non-Citizens Assembly, which is made up almost entirely of Moslems, Communists received a vote of about 80,000, or 17 per cent. The Citizens College, which is largely European, received 84,500 Communist votes, or 23.8 per cent of the total. Both the Communists and the Democratic Union demand Algerian autonomy "within the French Union." The nationalist extremists, who are distinctly anti-Communists, seek complete independence.

In Tunisia, the Communist Party was restored to legal status in 1943, after the American troop landings in North Africa. The Tunisian Communists are led by Secretary-General Ali Djerad. Party members and sympathizers are estimated at 45,000. The party's organ, *L'Avenir de la Tunisie*, is a weekly newspaper. The nationalist Destour Party is believed to have received Communist encouragement and possibly funds. In September, 1946, the local Federation of Trade Unions broke with the CGT of France and reorganized itself with Communists in leading positions. This illustrated Communist desire to cater to nationalist sentiments, even if it meant a break with Communist-led bodies in metropolitan France itself.

Morocco's Communists differ with the dominant nationalist Independence Party only slightly. The extremist Independence wing seeks complete sovereignty, while the Communists insist that Morocco must remain within the French Union. In spite of their persistent efforts to gain public support on the independence issue, the Communists are far less influential in Tunisia and Morocco than they are in Algeria.

The island of Madagascar, off the east coast of Africa, has a strong and energetic Malagasy Independence Party. In the spring of 1947, a long smoldering rebellion broke out on this island, which somewhat resembled fighting in another French colonial possession, Indo-China. However, this parallel was not complete. While there could be no doubt that Communist veterans played a major role in the Indo-Chinese fighting, the Madagascar revolt appeared to be largely spontaneous. Independence Party agitation technique showed Communist influence, but American officials suggested that the revolt could be described as "ten per cent Communist-inspired and ninety per cent spontaneous."

ERITREA: YOUNGEST AND SMALLEST

Eritrea, Italy's oldest colony, has the youngest Communist Party in the world. It was founded in 1944, four years after British troops occupied this East African territory. Under the British Military Administration, light industries have developed that are for the most part in the hands of Italians. The membership of the Communist Party of Eritrea stems from workers in these new industries.

Originally, Eritrea's Communists were exclusively Italians. In 1946 and 1947, an effort was made to include some natives in this party, which favors self-determination for Eritreans. As a result, a few Eritreans and half-castes are today among the 200 party members. In addition to being the youngest Communist Party, the Eritrean party is also the smallest.

SOUTH AFRICA: COLOR SCHEME

Fewer than three million Europeans (whites) and about eight million non-Europeans (native Negroes) live in the Union of South Africa. Consequently the race question dominates South African politics more clearly than the affairs of the state of Mississippi. Native grievances are numerous. Above all, government control of the colored population through the "pass system" and lack of native representation in legislative bodies are sharply criticized by Negro leaders. Few South African whites favor abolition of the color bar and full equality. Dr. D. F. Malan's Nationalist Party (which followed an isolationist line during the war and has a minority in the Assembly) favors strictest segregation. Jan Christiaan Smuts's United Party takes a more conciliatory line. But this is just a question of degree. A segregation policy is also in force against South Africa's 300,000 Indians, which has strained relations between South Africa and the government of India and led to deliberations before the United Nations Security Council.

It is against this background that the Communist Party of the Union of South Africa operates. It is a young party, which recruits support mainly among natives. Its secretary-general, Moses Monai Kotane, is a lean, sharp-featured Negro. The party maintains offices in several South African cities, sponsors literacy courses, and publishes magazines and pamphlets. To assure maximum distribution of its propaganda material, it is not restricted to the English and Afrikaans languages, but also appears in native dialects, such as Sechuana, Sesuto, Zulu, Xhosa, Venda, and Shangaan. The Communists have promoted the Council of Non-European Trade Unions, and their candidates have received as many as 200,000 votes in the 1942 elections for Native Representation Council, an advisory parliamentary body.

The party has reflected the world-wide policy pattern of communism, gaining relative importance after the Seventh Comintern Congress decided on its "united front" policy. The South African party had difficulties in clarifying this swift change of strategy to the rank and file of its members. On January 11, the Communist Party organ *Umsebenzi* explained the changed policy by writing, "We cannot organize all the workers and other toilers into the Communist Party, as the latter consists only of the most fearless, energetic and advanced fighters of the toiling masses." The paper added, "The workers may sooner strike for one penny per hour more or against the reduction of one penny from their wages, but it may be difficult to get them to strike for the abolition of the Riotous Assembly Act or for the abolition of the imperialist rule of oppression and exploitation. Hence the necessity to have mass organizations, which the Communist Party should organize, support and endeavour to lead." As organizations that the Communists could lead, *Umsebenzi* listed trade unions, the Labour Defence League, the National Liberty League, the

League against Fascism and War, and the Friends of the Soviet Union.
Even the Communists of South Africa have to face the almost unani-
mous pro-segregation attitude among the European population. In order
not to forego agitation among the whites, the Communists were thus forced
to practice segregation themselves. Meetings and discussion groups in
several districts carefully separated whites and Negroes. A party statement explained this as follows: "Where the whites have not yet reached
the high political consciousness as to allow themselves to be organized
side by side with the natives, they must be organized along parallel lines
and both sections be taught the necessity of unity."

While South Africa's Communists concentrate their agitation on domestic racial and labor issues, world affairs are not ignored. Reports of racial
discrimination against Negroes in the United States, lynchings, and race
riots are carried in the party press and discussed at meetings. The Soviet
Union is looked upon as the only great nation practicing racial equality,
and its performance in peace and war is presented reverently. The Communist Party's monthly paper *Inkululeko* concluded an editorial in March,
1942, by saying, "There is only one country which is beating back the
Fascist murderers. That country is Soviet Russia, the land of Socialism,
the home of the working class." The South African Communists had
opposed the war in its early stages, characterizing the British and South
African war effort as "imperialist." As a rule, international events are
presented to native Communists on a basis that makes self-identification
easy. One party paper, for instance, commented on the Palestine problem
by saying, "The Zionist scheme and Jewish immigration in Palestine are
undoubtedly a pure imperialist adventure, just as the early immigration
of whites into South Africa."

Communist efforts to organize native workers received world-wide
prominence in August, 1946, when classes developed at the Witwaters
Rand gold mines. Some 50,000 workers went on strike to achieve quadrupled wages, in addition to food and lodging. Police were called in and
required five days to quash the strike movement. Nine strikers were killed
and 1,248 injured. The Chamber of Mines announced that native workers
were "not yet sufficiently advanced" to organize labor unions. The African
Mine Workers Union was referred to as "self-styled" and as being "connected with and has the support of communistic influences." Premier
Smuts blamed the strike movement on "agitators," and police raided various offices in eight cities. Eight Communist leaders, including Secretary-

General Kotane, were arrested at Capetown on charges of sedition. Their trial took place early in 1947, shortly after the visit to the Union of South Africa of King George and the British royal family. The visit was opposed in the London Parliament by its Communist member William Gallacher, in protest against discrimination practices in South Africa.

The program of the South African Communist Party has been formulated as follows:

"1. To raise the workers as a class to establish working class rule and a Socialist Republic.

"2. To prepare the way for a Socialist Republic and to defend and promote the interests of the workers and oppressed nationalities by organizing and leading them in political and industrial struggle for: (a) the abolition of imperialism and the establishment of an independent republic of the people; (b) the extension to all adults, regardless of race, color or sex, of the right to vote for and be elected to parliamentary, provincial, municipal and other representative institutions; (c) the removal of all political, social, economic and cultural color bars that hold up the progress and development of any national group and divide the working class; (d) the raising of wages, distribution of land, and improvement of social living conditions for all persons."

The South African Communist Party is young but, as the program shows, conscious of the political-social position that it might occupy among the native population. It has the support of a group of Europeans who disagree with the policies pursued by the leading parties, notably on the race issue. It is also extending its agitation to the Indian population, which, however, is politically close to the Congress Party of India rather than to the South African political scene.

VI
THE CHALLENGE

CHAPTER 32

What Is the Strength of Communism?

WORLD COMMUNISM has grown strong in defiance of violent opposition. Its followers have overcome social ostracism, unnerving isolation, ruthless suppression. The large turnover in Communist Party membership shows that thousands and tens of thousands abandon communism every year. They are disillusioned and disappointed. But new members join. New Communist-sponsored organizations successfully enroll supporters. Rallies overflow.[Prominent men and women join with Communists in manifestos and on speakers' platforms.

What is the secret of this success? Where are the sources of Communist strength? Just what makes a Communist? How does communism attract mass following? What is its appeal to different people all over the world?

WHAT MAKES A COMMUNIST?

The millennium-old struggle for human security forms the economic-emotional basis of Communist appeal. Germany's first Communists called themselves "Spartacists." They consciously emphasized their kinship with Spartacus, who led the revolt of Greek slaves in ancient Rome. In modern times, the French revolution inspired politically and economically dependent men and women everywhere. During the last century, before Marx and Engels wrote the Communist Manifesto, workers were hopefully listening to the humanitarian appeals of the so-called Utopian Socialists. Europe's growing labor movement, the freeing of Russia's serfs, the breakdown of feudal societies, the Anarchist movement that inspired the International Workers of the World (IWW)—all these were modern expressions of the ancient desire for security, prosperity, and self-respect.

But modern society has not fulfilled the promise of nineteenth century humanitarianism. It failed to develop and perfect the promises of liberal tradition. Instead, it created the super-state and its total dictatorship in the name of the people. In the economic field, society has failed to provide a high measure of individual security. The cycles of prosperity and depression that Marx saw as the ever-more destructive death throes of capitalism are still with us. The second half of the twentieth century opens in an atmosphere of fear. Another critical world depression is likely to develop in the early 1950's.

It is this anxiety that spurs the growth of communism. Fear of a new economic cataclysm is not limited to any one stratum of society. It affects most strongly the economically weak. But it also seems to charge the very atmosphere of daily living with insecurity, with dread of chaos, with mounting disillusionment and despair. This fear affects the thinking and actions of men and women in all parts of society. And it is from all these strata of society that communism today draws supporters.

The end of World War II brought a sharpening of political extremes. The parliamentarian tradition of Europe's labor movement is on the defensive. It continues today in Scandinavia, the Lowlands, Canada, Australia, and New Zealand, in the British Trades Union Congress, in the American Federation of Labor and in many CIO and Latin-American unions. But it is fighting for its very existence in France, Italy, and in a number of Latin-American nations. It must fear further radicalization during a period of continuing economic crisis. In the past, communism has been able to mobilize the unemployed effectively, and it is ready to apply these lessons of the past with new vigor and determination.

COMMUNISM, A MODERN CULT

Communist strength is based on fear of economic insecurity, on the inability of our society to halt the disastrous cycles of boom and bust. But it would be false to speak of Communist success and appeal in economic terms only. Certainly, it is a modern counterpart of the rebellion of slaves and serfs. Certainly, it draws major support from men and women who are economically insecure or destitute. It is open to question whether Russian communism today has really overcome the economic limitations that plague the rest of the world. The Soviet government discourages independent investigation by foreign scholars and correspondents. It thus leaves itself open to criticism by its antagonists, which is often as badly documented as the adulation of its enthusiastic supporters at home and abroad. But Russian communism has given its adherents more than the hope of economic emancipation. Its psychological effect appears greater than its economic achievements.

Communism today is less an economic school of thought than a modern cult. It has the characteristics of a religious movement. The strength of established religions today is much less than at any time in recent centuries. To a high degree, communism has filled this vacuum of faith. It has replaced religious beliefs and patterns with counterbeliefs and counterpatterns. Even outwardly, the resemblance between communism and traditional religious practices is striking. There are scriptures that the initiated study. There are speeches and writings of prophets. There is a hierarchy, and there are missionaries. There is excommunication for heresy. There is public confession of sin, nearly identical with self-castigation at revival meetings. There is a center of strength which inspires and demands devotion. And there is final salvation that will reward the sacrifices of the present.

Like any transcendent religious faith, communism helps to heal—outwardly, at least—the soul pains of human insecurity. It provides its adherents with a Great Purpose. It gives their lives a meaning. It reveals a path for the lost or bewildered. It has an answer to every question. It seeks to destroy all doubt and demands full allegiance. The burden of individual decision does not strain the shoulders of its followers.

Among many reasons that have caused men and women to embrace communism, the need for a meaningful life is probably the most powerful. This motivation may be conscious or unconscious. Human idealism seeks a direct outlet. Communism claims to be such an outlet of particular efficiency. Few world-conscious men and women in our time deny that political-economic realities fall short of perfection. Many of them feel frustrated, helpless, unable to right the wrongs of modern life.

This frustration exists even in a parliamentary democracy. Checks and balances that seek to guard against overcentralization of power slow down constructive action. Many of us feel remote from the scene of political events. There must be something more weighty to do, we are tempted to believe, than to argue with our friends about the day's news or to vote for a candidate on election day. Communism tells us that it can free the individual from this frustration. It opens the door to direct action.

Such action takes many forms. Its attraction lies in the fact that it is concrete. Its effect seems immediate. There is, first of all, the inspiring mass meeting, which gives the individual the feeling that he "belongs." There are others like him, he believes, and in such unity lies strength. What such strength will be used for may be ignored in an atmosphere of mass intoxication through oratory and slogans. Something is being done. It may be the collection of funds, the drafting of a resolution, the organization of a strike, the sending of a delegation, or an outdoor demonstration of strength. Such need for action to fill otherwise drab and politically frustrated lives motivated many Canadian Communists and their sympathizers to enter the Soviet military espionage system. They felt that they were doing something concrete, as indeed they were. This feeling of accomplishment appears to have blinded them to the actual consequences of their actions.

A basic human trait, that of opposition for the sake of opposition, has also brought supporters to the Communist movement. We have all experienced that one is easily tempted to choose sides merely "for the sake of an argument." The French have a word for it: *esprit de contradiction.* This spirit of contradiction often drives people into political or philosophical camps that are off the beaten path. The attraction is heightened when a group is subject to extreme criticism. It is somehow glamorous to be a Communist, just as it is daring to smuggle perfume past the customs control.

PATTERNS OF THINKING

Other human factors that affect the choice of communism as a politicaleconomic doctrine have been little explored. The question "What makes a Communist?" has not as yet provoked detailed answers from the scientists who probe into the depths of man's mind and soul. Psychiatry would be the field from which such research might logically be expected. However, Communist writings and actions follow extremist-religious patterns to a startlingly high degree. Psychiatrists have therefore speculated on similarities between Communist reasoning and religious paranoid thinking.

Aurel Kolnai, in his book, *Psychoanalysis and Sociology,* found in communism many factors that are "common in religious paranoia." Paranoia in an individual is usually shown through the need to dominate, suspiciousness, an exaggerated opinion of one's own importance, reinterpretation of the past to rationalize current ideas, and the thought of being persecuted.

We have seen that the concept of the dictatorship of the proletariat, that is, dominance by one group, is part of the Communist doctrine. Communism, from Marx onward, has sharpened suspicion of capitalist-bourgeois trickery (Kolnai sees in communism "delusions of persecution," because it teaches that "all the institutions of the state, religious and moral systems, and even dominant scientific trends are lumped together as methods of exploitation."). Communism shares with religious extremism the idea of its own transcendent importance, of its exclusive mission to bring salvation to suffering mankind. Finally, during every one of the Seven Strategies of world communism, we have observed an immense effort of reinterpretation of events, tactics, and conclusion. Every new policy line creates a global flood of speeches, editorials, pamphlets, and books that furnish an understructure of rearranged facts and interpretation.

It would, of course, be false to conclude from this that all Communists can be regarded as paranoid in their thinking. Paranoid trends are noticeable in nearly every organized group. They are certainly very marked among ultra-right groups that specialize in hating something or somebody. But Communist writing and talking have a particularly noticeable paranoid aura. The flood of words used in justification of Communist policies closely resembles paranoid self-justification. Communist spokesmen who argue in extreme terms of black and white, negative and positive, show paranoid characteristics. Communism is outstanding among political groups through its established practice of rearranging past events to suit its changing policies; it practices what psychiatry knows in individuals as "retrospective falsification."

The lives of outstanding Communist leaders also lend themselves to study and research in this field. Speaking only in general terms, it is interesting to observe that nearly all of them were attracted to political extremism while still in adolescent rebellion against family and society. This tendency continued without making room for full mature adjustment. Doubtless, the life of the Chinese Communist leader Mao Tse-tung can supply a psychiatric research worker with much material. As we have seen, Mao's self-confessed hate of his father led in a straight line to rebellion against established society and to leadership in world communism. Among other prominent Communists who adopted extreme revolutionary ideas in their early youth and retained them rigidly to this day are Georgi Dimitrov of Bulgaria, Klement Gottwald of Czechoslovakia, Harry Pollitt of Great Britain, Anna Pauker of Romania, Maurice Thorez of France, Peder Furubotn of Norway, Palmiro Togliatti of Italy, and many leaders of the Bolshevik Revolution, including Leon Trotsky. Few Communist leaders entered the movement as the result of mature considerations.

But the appeal of communism to wide masses of so-called "fellow travelers" or "crypto-Communists" is quite another matter. It is the result of an efficient and astute propaganda method.

THE "UNITED FRONT" TECHNIQUE

Are you in favor of low rents, better housing, higher wages, abundant and low-priced food? Are you against racial and religious discrimination, fascism, ruthless exploitation of labor, profiteers, corruption, and inflation? If the answer is yes, the Communists will tell you, you are one of them—at least, they say, you should fight shoulder to shoulder with the Communist movement.

That is the essence of the "united front" technique which has been developed since 1935. This technique has created a large variety of openings through which the average person can enter Communist-backed activities without being aware of it. When the extremist-revolutionary strategy was abandoned, the Communist movement recognized that it is a drawback to be known as a Communist or for an organization to be clearly labeled Communist. The Communist parties were retained as a basis for other activities. But a large part of the agitation and propaganda was turned over to groups that did not reveal their Communist links or even denied their relationship to the Communist movement.

To develop a policy that would attract mass support, world communism had to analyze and evaluate popular needs and desires. It began by gauging the world's revulsion against the excesses and expansionism of Nazi Germany and Fascist Italy. It is useful to recall that, once the Soviet Union had become convinced of Nazism as a threat to its own existence, Communists throughout the world became the most insistent in their warnings against the Nazi menace. Democratic Germans who left Germany during the mid-thirties were shocked to find that, aside from a minority of alert liberals, only the Communists and their front organizations seemed to have fully grasped the dangers of Nazism. Tales of concentration camps and Nazi torture were met by public officials and the press with a shrug of the shoulder and an unbelieving smile. This was the period when President Roosevelt's historical quarantine speech in 1937 fell on deaf ears. Thus the Communists attracted many sincere anti-Nazi and anti-Fascist democrats who had nowhere else to turn.

World War II widened the circle of those who were willing to join with anyone determined to defeat the Axis power. Winston Churchill recalled in April, 1947, that the western powers armed Greek Communist-led guerrillas, because they were giving "arms and such help as we could spare to anyone who would kill a Hun." Today, world communism is denouncing "American imperialism," while pressing for such popular aims as high wages and low prices. Where a battle against "American imperialism" can count on little support, the fight against inflation or for better housing is as safe as a crusade against man-eating sharks.

Through propagandistic juxtaposition, communism succeeds in gaining support for its primary aims by linking them with problems that are of immediate interest to the individual. A housing rally may come out against American policy in Greece and China. An anti-inflation demonstration may support "German unity" on terms favored by the Soviet government. An anti-discrimination meeting may issue a protest against the investigation of secret Communist activities. As a result, we find a man or woman who has been attracted by a secondary tactical aim of the Communist Party backing primary aims about which he knows little or nothing. To a metalworker concerned over rising food prices, the question of German reparations may seem quite unimportant. But, as Communist agitation links them in slogans or speeches, he feels vaguely that both matters are part of the same fight. And so it goes: you're against low wages, therefore you must also be against world-wide and enforced inspection of atomic-energy plants; you're for nondiscriminatory employment practices, therefore you must consider the government of Bulgaria as free and democratic; you hate lynchings, therefore you must also favor a maritime strike, or "workers' unity," or the election of Paul B. (the Communist-backed candidate) for the delegation of your labor union. . . .

Often, then, a Communist's first interest is in a facet of Communist activity with which he can identify himself directly. In due course, propagandistic juxtaposition prompts him to identify his interest with all other Communist aims. (A similar pattern of extended identification is practiced by the ultra-right, which is likely to say: you're against communism, therefore you must be against extended social-security regulation, or corporation taxes, or religious-racial equality. . . .) A Communist—similar to the adherent of any other extremist belief—ceases to examine each issue on its merits. He judges merely on the basis of party-dictated patterns. He substitutes a highly emotional reaction for cool reasoning.

It is far from easy for the average person to examine each issue of daily life independently, for himself. He is almost bound to accept somebody's say-so more often than not. This dilemma is solved for the Communist, just as it is solved for the adherent of many another extremist political-religious belief. The Communist has found a framework of organization and ideology that promises and often provides peace of mind.

THE INTELLECTUAL'S DILEMMA

All this applies to the general run of rank-and-file followers of Communist or Communist-controlled movements. It does not fully cover the phenomenon of the well-educated urban intellectual who either adopts communism completely or follows its policies on all important points. We are dealing here with a very small and very influential group which today is concentrated in Rome, Paris, New York, London, and Rio de Janeiro. It is, first of all, necessary to distinguish between intellectuals who are professionally concerned with world affairs and those who are engaged in the arts and sciences and in writing that is remote from political realities. It is from this second category of urban intellectuals that much support for communism or Communist-sponsored activities comes. We are all familiar with the singer, painter or sculptor, actor or novelist, who seeks to influence direct political action through channels opened by Communist organizers.

The creative artist is nearly always extrovert. He must be, in order to give his work quality and power. He is also often conscious of the rift between his own rather comfortable existence and that of the mass of low-paid workers throughout the world. He can be expected to feel, with a pang of insecurity in his heart, that "there, but for the grace of God, go I. . . ." Doubtless, he feels that his support of good social causes may take the place of atonement for his own secure position in a world that knows so much pain and misery. It will not do at all to sneer at the sincerity, the eminent good will, and the sacrifice in time and effort that such creative artists are making every day for causes that they believe to be just. One can only wish that they would examine more closely the organizations with which they ally themselves. And one must hope that their artistic work may leave them time to study more closely the complex and skillfully administered mechanism of which they have become a part.

Among those intellectuals who are professionally concerned with current affairs—educators, political writers, and editors—we also find men and women of good will, whose concern with the limitations of our political-economic system has driven them to endorse direct political action after the Communist pattern. Often these men and women feel that the choice between the ultra-right and the ultra-left demands cooperation with Communists. There are not many outstanding intellectuals inside the Communist movement itself, although it would be a great mistake to underestimate the qualities and skill of Communist leaders generally. Much more often do we find intellectuals in a sort of no-man's-land into which they have been frightened by a perfectly legitimate fear of ultra-right excesses. Sometimes, in this no-man's-land, we hear denunciations of the more obvious crudities that mark the Communist movement. But more often do we find endorsement of Communist-backed policies that are represented as a defense against the ultra-right. It is in this sphere that the "united front" policy has been most successful.

A few prominent opinion makers have yielded personal integrity to the applause and good fellowship offered by Communists and Communist-led groups. We might take the hypothetical case of a radio commentator whose wartime broadcasts gained the appreciation of wide circles, including Communists. He appeared as speaker at rallies, wrote for Communist-backed publications, and found that his speeches received much favorable publicity. In due course, he became a big fish in the medium-sized pond of Communist-led activities. Personal vanity and the desire for continued appreciation then prompted that commentator to express himself along lines which were sure to be approved by the circle of which he had become a part. After the war, he refrained from criticism of the Soviet Union, attacked American foreign policy, and generally reflected Communist policy in broad outlines. His commentaries were distributed by Communist-run news agencies throughout the world, they appeared on Soviet overseas broadcasts as the expression of American progressive sentiment. And thus the commentator became a figure of world importance.

There have been other cases, paralleling such a career: artists who feel the need for publicity or appreciation by a sympathetic crowd;

writers who find it agreeable to substitute ideological generalities for sustained professional excellence; educators who have the strong desire to be part of a lively pulsating group of energetic people—all these may be classified as opportunists who delight in the warmth of Communist-inspired appreciation or who do not have the strength to face the vilification that is the price of a break with Communist movements.

Nevertheless, such cases of opportunism, or fear of adverse criticism, are probably few. In the Soviet Union and elsewhere, Communist organizations practice a stern and ascetic mode of life that contrasts with corruption or opportunism. The Soviet state apparatus is staffed by men who for the most part work devotedly and energetically to strengthen the USSR. Opportunism doubtless has played a role in the development of Communist mass parties in Romania, Czechoslovakia, Hungary, Italy, and Germany. In many cases, the closeness of the Soviet Union made it opportune to obtain a Communist membership card as insurance against criticism. In countries where large ultra-rightist parties existed, members of Fascist organizations have embraced the Communist faith. One of the most spectacular cases has been that of Curzio Malaparte, the former Italian Fascist propagandist.

Communism's attraction to youth is linked with its colorful meetings and disciplined organizations. Its rousing slogans and calls for action appeal particularly to the impatient adolescent. On the European continent, the Communists have been able to dramatize their aims in the colorful manner that was the trade-mark of German Nazism and Italian fascism. Banners, and crowds, slogans and loudspeakers—the whole ecstatic cheering-section atmosphere that Americans know from football fields—are part and parcel of Communist mass appeal in many parts of the world. In the Soviet Union itself, this demonstration technique is brought to quantitative perfection at the annual May Day celebration on Moscow's Red Square, where millions of men, women, and children, and the machinery of war, pass in day-long parade.

GUNS AND MONEY ARE NOT ENOUGH

However, all mass appeals and all cooperation of prominent men and women would be of little use if Lenin's concept of the party as a group of devoted fanatics had not served the Communist movement well. Although Communist parties experience a continuous large turnover in membership, a hard core of devoted followers remains. This group adheres faithfully to all changes in party policies, all "retrospective falsification." It is adamant in emphasizing the party's mission of salvation, its labeling of opponents as "Fascists" in black-and-white terms. The men and women who form this core furnish the leadership of nominally independent organizations that follow Communist policy.]

[Joseph and Stewart Alsop analyzed Communist control in the Congress of Industrial Organizations in *The Saturday Evening Post* of February 22, 1947. They asked a number of CIO leaders how Communists had managed to gain control of several unions. One answer was repeated over and over: "They work like hell." The Alsops added, "While another trade union leader will naturally expect to see his family from time to time, to have a night off with the boys, to relax every now and then with his feet up on the desk, a Communist will devote every minute of his waking hours and every ounce of his energy to a mission given him by the party. . . . Every member is as much a fanatic participating in a holy war as any whirling dervish, and is furthermore completely indoctrinated in the belief that the ends justify the means. And where it is the objective of the party to capture the major industrial unions, this fanaticism and religious energy can make a Communist an exceedingly valuable union servant."]

[Those who wish to combat communism need to reflect seriously on just what it is that they are fighting. Former United States Vice-President Henry A. Wallace told a British audience on April 12, 1947, "As long as workers live in slums, as long as farmers struggle for a bare existence, as long as all classes live in fear of unemployment and war, the idea of communism will endure. It will be overcome only when free societies demonstrate in action that through democratic planning they can offer better opportunities for all their citizens." He recognized that there is more to communism than merely economic fear when he said that "no powerful idea—and communism is a powerful idea—can be countered by guns and money."

This realization doubtless also played a part in the adjustment of United States foreign policy in 1947, which moved from the largely negative so-called "Truman Doctrine" of opposition to communism to the positive emphasis of Secretary Marshall's proposals for American-aided European reconstruction. Secretary Marshall said on June 5, 1947, that "the United States should do whatever it is able to do to assist in the return of normal economic health in the world without which there can be no political stability and no assured peace." He added, "Our policy is directed not against any country or doctrine but against hunger, poverty, desperation, and chaos. . . . Governments, political parties, or groups which seek to perpetuate human misery in order to profit therefrom politically or otherwise will encounter the opposition of the United States."

COMMUNISM IN OUR TIME

What, then, makes a Communist in our time?

It is the need to find a way out of the labyrinth of conflicting human needs. It is the hope to discover a short cut to salvation from misery and want. It is the fear of being alone, of being crushed by the impersonal juggernaut of events beyond individual control. It is the hope of gaining control of this juggernaut, of shaping events through direct action. Or it is the desire to atone for well-being; the need for companionship; the desire for power; or the desperate wish to find a purpose in what seems confusion and emptiness.

What makes a Communist may be adolescent rebellion that failed to mature; or merely the wish to become the recognized and appreciated member of a group; or the hope to find at last a full and convincing answer to the questions of our time. The whole of human revolt against misery and imperfection in our society has found an expression in communism today. Arms and loans alone cannot answer this basic challenge. More is needed. That is why the most powerful global antagonists of Communists are those forces which compete with it in their offers of economic or spiritual salvation, those forces which have recognized that its challenge is to be met not on national or regional levels but on all continents of this globe.

CHAPTER 33

Global Antagonists

THE COMMUNIST INTERNATIONAL was dissolved in 1943. The Socialist International has not been revived. A Catholic International never took political-organizational form. The Moslem International is limited to the Arab League. Allied victory crushed the Fascist International, which linked the ultra-nationalists of many lands. And business interests, although exercising some international control through cartels, have been too competitive to permit development of a Capitalist International.

And yet, in the perpetual shifting of global political and economic forces, the patterns of Internationals in all but name are too clear to be denied. Are not the Communist parties of the world united in their support by and of the Soviet Union? Are not Socialist, Social Democratic, and Labor parties linked by identical ideas and dilemmas? Can we ignore the basic moral concepts that provide a common ground for the Catholic parties? Is it impossible that the strength which the Arab states have found in their young alliance may be extended to Moslems everywhere? Surely, the battered links between ultra-nationalist groups are being rebuilt through the exchange of literature, the visits of leaders. And is it unlikely that businessmen, recognizing the interdependence of their economic interests, may attempt to act politically on international levels, as some of them have done on a national or regional basis?

The battle for allegiance is shifting. Its skirmishes are fought between forces that transcend national boundaries and hemispheric limitations.

In Europe, political Catholicism competes with Communism and Socialism for dominance in national affairs.

In the Near East, the communism of the Soviet Union and the interests of a Socialist-governed United Kingdom are clashing in an area of Moslem religious-nationalistic control.

In Latin America, Communist parties have allied themselves with ultra-nationalism to fight the influence of the United States, which itself is torn between the heritage of a moderately socialist New Deal and the supporters of unhampered private enterprise.

In Asia, the layers of feudalism, imperialism, religious and nationalist fanaticism, and of Soviet-inspired communism shift and mingle; human frustrations have heated them into a bubbling political lava.

The battles for nations, for regional empires, for the allegiance of thousands, hundreds of thousands, and of millions, have been fought, and won or lost. They are over and done with. The battle for the globe has not as yet begun. But it is well to think in hemispheres, in rivalries of Internationals that count their followers in hundreds of millions, and their aspirations into billions.

The Internationals are not clear-cut. They do without the formal framework of organization. The Communist and Socialist Internationals formerly existed as definite organizations. The religious work of the Roman Catholic Church proceeds within a world-wide framework. And even unification of the Catholic parties has been considered. At the time of the 1946 consistorial ceremonies at the Vatican, the organ of the Italian Catholic Action group quoted a Catholic official as urging that a "Christian Social International, linking all Christian parties everywhere, might take its place alongside the Communist and Socialist Internationals." This demand, published in the Rome daily *Il Quotidieno*, recognized the threat of isolation that political Catholicism faces from existing and potential Communist-Socialist coalitions.

INTERNATIONAL CATHOLICISM

In a number of countries, Communist, Socialist, and Catholic parties are the most powerful. Union of any two of these groups automatically isolates the third. Ideological cleavages rule out the possibility of Communist-Catholic coalitions. Both Communists and Catholics have therefore tried to win over the Socialists. Generally, communism has been more successful in creating unity of action, or even complete fusion, with the Socialist parties. When communism abandoned the rigid international policy practiced during the Comintern era, it became able to compromise for the sake of ultimate gains. By comparison, political Catholicism has often shown itself less able to adjust techniques and demands to postwar political realities.

The Catholic Church is the best organized and most spiritually determined foe of modern communism. It has tried to fight its battle alone. And, more than once, it has thus isolated itself. Most striking was the case of Belgium, where even combined Socialist-Communist strength in 1946 did not match that of the Roman Catholic Christian Socialist Party. Nevertheless, the Socialists refused to join with the Catholics, preferring an alliance with the Communists and the small Liberal Party. The Christian Socialists, although the strongest party in the Belgian nation, found themselves out in the cold. Only early in 1947 was this anomalous situation changed. It is exactly that sort of Communist-Socialist coalition which endangers Catholic parties in France, Italy, Germany, Austria. It is exactly that sort of coalition which has made Communist-dominated governments in eastern Europe possible.

Socialist leaders, while fearing alliance with the Communists, have often shied away from alliance with the Catholic parties. This is a Europe-wide state of affairs. It has found an echo in several Latin-American nations. Socialist leaders everywhere are afraid of alienating their supporters. They know that the Communists are quick to exploit apparent weaknesses of other parties. Europe's Socialist leaders, including the men who run Britain's Labour Party, are constantly under fire from the left wings of their own parties, which keep up close liaison with the Communists. Socialist leadership finds itself in a strategically precarious position. It does not dare to run the risk of being too closely linked with Catholic parties that, in the minds of many rank-and-file leftists, show what are called "reactionary" strains.

But to paste a "Fascist" label on the Catholic parties is downright falsification and primitive-partisan political thinking. European Catholicism contains many strongly liberal elements. They are to be found in France (whose envoy to the Vatican is that outstanding Catholic liberal, Jacques Maritain), in Italy, in Belgium, and elsewhere. These groups, and a good part of Catholic political leadership, are much closer in their political-economic ideology to, let us say, the British Labour Party, than to some of the rightist factions within their own parties. These men and women do not like it one bit that their parties have become the cloak for ex-Vichyites, former Italian Fascists, or one-time Austrian Nazis. At any rate, no European political party has been immune to infiltration from the ultra-right, certainly not the Communist parties.

Again and again, Socialist Party leaders in France have faced overtures from the predominantly Catholic Mouvement Républicain Populaire (MRP), as well as from the Communists. But the rift between Socialists and Catholics in France is deeper than the cleavage between Socialists and Communists. Strong elements within the weakened Socialist parties of Europe favor close cooperation or even fusion with the Communists. The Catholics have few spokesmen within the Socialist parties. In Czechoslovakia, the Catholic People's Party is completely overshadowed by the Communist-Socialist coalition government. Even in Hungary, where the important Small Landholders Party has unofficial Catholic support, the Communists have managed by various means to make the Socialists the tail of their party meteor.

RUSSIA'S RELIGIOUS OFFENSIVE

Catholicism and Soviet-backed communism have met head-on in eastern Europe and in the Near East. The Polish government denounced its Concordat with the Vatican on September 16, 1945. Nowhere have Communist and Catholic interests collided with more vehemence than in Yugoslavia, where Archbishop Stepinac was tried and convicted of treason. Communist atheism, of the old Comintern brand, was probably less deadly to Catholic influence than the new Communist policy of seeking the allegiance of religious bodies. When the Uniate Church, the Catholic denomination of the western Ukraine, denounced its 350-year-old affiliation with the Vatican in March, 1946, to join the Russian Orthodox Church, the Vatican asserted that such action could only have been taken under Communist pressure.

In the Near East, Russian Orthodox dignitaries have established contact in a number of Catholic communities. During the 1946 consistorial ceremonies at the Vatican, Pope Pius XII singled out Peter XV Cardinal Agagianian of Armenia for special honors during and after the ceremonies. The Soviet Union, through the Armenian Soviet Socialist Republic, has a strong appeal to Armenian nationals everywhere, a large number of whom are Roman Catholics.

The global friction between communism and Catholicism can be felt with particular intensity in the Latin nations. Fear of communism must be considered the dominant factor in consistent Vatican backing of the Spanish regime of General Francisco Franco. Throughout Latin America, Catholic laymen and clergymen are trying to counter the progress made by Communist parties. Whatever happens to communism's bid for allegiance in Europe's two strongest Catholic nations, France and Italy, is bound to influence political trends in the southern half of the Western Hemisphere. Italy, as seat of the Vatican, has symbolic importance in this conflict.

Communist policy toward Roman Catholicism is now much more supple and subtle than it was in the days of the Comintern. Communism seeks to win individual Catholics to its cause by a sort of "united front from below"—a slogan that was used often during the years of the extremist-revolutionary Third Strategy of world communism. Maurice Thorez, the French Communist leader, has advocated "unity among Communists, Catholics, and Protestants of all denominations," thus putting the creed of communism on the same level as that of religious faiths. He then added, in his book on *France of the People's Front:*

"Our goal is not a mysterious, unacceptable collusion with the leaders of the Church. Our aim is the unity of the masses of the people for their well-being, for liberty and peace. This means that it is not merely a question of the Communists carrying on propaganda for the 'outstretched hand.' Their actions above all must win over the Catholics and draw them into joint activity. There is no other way of winning over all the workers to the cause of the people, except through action, actions of solidarity and kindness, and through multiplying the gains all around us. We will win over to the People's Front and communism those who are kept away from us by prejudices, to just the extent that we prove to them that communism, our noble ideal, is inspiration for selfless and good deeds; to the extent that we prove that nowhere else is to be found such a spring of purity of generous feelings."

When Karl Marx published the Communist Manifesto, it was condemned by Pope Pius IX. Ever since, Catholic spokesmen have denounced "atheistic communism" and "godless Bolshevism." But the current strategy of world communism has robbed these phrases of their old accuracy. No longer does official communism reject religion as an "opiate for the people." In the Soviet Union itself, the Orthodox Church and Islam are tolerated within the framework of Communist society. Rather than suppress religion, modern communism seeks to replace it, while retaining its structure of worship and belief.

If communism had not been able to persuade a relatively large number of Roman Catholics in countries such as Poland, Yugoslavia,

Slovakia, France, Italy, and Brazil that it had broken with some of its old tenets, it could hardly have achieved the startlingly high support that it secured. Among the 385,000,000 Catholics of the world, there are a great number of Communists. Some of them are leaders such as Thorez of France, or Broz-Tito of Yugoslavia, just as there are Protestants, Jews, Moslems, and members of many other religious denominations among the leaders and the rank and file of communism. But Catholicism has not used its spiritual weapons very widely against Communist members of its church. Excommunication has remained rare.

CAN SOCIALISM AND CATHOLICISM AGREE?

Nevertheless, the basic attitude of the Roman Catholic Church on the question of communism has never been in doubt. In fact, it has been so strong that part of the laity and even the clergy have opposed communism by allying themselves with the totalitarian ultra-right before, during, and after World War II. Father Joseph Tiso, the Nazi puppet premier of Slovakia, was a Catholic priest. On the other hand, Cardinal Schuster of Milan and Cardinal Faulhaber of Munich have been courageous critics of fascism and Nazism. When Pope Pius told the Italian clergy on March 16, 1946, that it had the "right and duty" to participate in public life and should instruct Catholics in their "moral duties arising from the electoral right," he encouraged political as well as religious instructions. He added, in fact, "It should not be forgotten that it was exactly with the pretext to fight so-called 'political Catholicism' that National Socialism aimed at the destruction of the Church. The Catholic Church will never permit herself to be shut within the four walls of the temple. The separation of religion and life, the Church and the world, is contrary to the Christian and Catholic idea."

In spite of these strong efforts, Catholicism continues to face the danger of isolation and impotence through Communist-Socialist coalitions. Can Catholicism overcome its tendency to go its political road alone? The political realities of the postwar world have prompted some Catholic leaders to emphasize that socialism and Catholicism can, after all, work hand in hand. They cite the papal encyclical *Quadragesimo Anno* of 1931, which noted that Socialist programs "often strikingly approach the just demands of Christian social reform."

Specifically, the Catholic attitude toward nationalization has been the subject of analysis. Pope Pius XII said on March 11, 1945, that nationalization is desirable "where it appears to be truly required by the common good, that is, as a means of effectively remedying an abuse, of squandering of a country's productive forces, and of directing these forces to the development of the material prosperity of all—a prosperity which also provides a sound foundation for the cultural and religious life." Father DeMarco, S.J., commented on that statement in the Vatican newspaper *Osservatore Romano* on November 12, 1946, saying that "in accordance with the social thinking of the Church, it is well to emphasize that nationalization of enterprises is in special cases, not only licit but also opportune."

Although he wrote that "excessive nationalization, with the economic power which it places in the hands of the State, does not solve complex social problems," Father DeMarco said that nationalization of such enterprises as large banks, transportation, war industries, and certain chemical industries might well be advantageous. He also said, "Excessive nationalization rather displaces, and like any other excess, aggravates the problem by strengthening a weapon that can be used for oppression and shifting such a weapon from the hands of the private capitalists to the hands of those who hold the fate of the country."

Father John LaFarge, S.J., editor of the United States Catholic weekly *America,* said early in 1947, "Of all contemporary political facts, I know none more significant than the recent developments in the way of collaboration between Christian Democrats and Socialists." He specifically cited the Netherlands, "where Catholics and Socialists are working together in order to promote social and economic reforms." Father LaFarge added that the church finds itself unable to collaborate with a Socialist system "that adheres to a purely materialistic scale of political values." He noted "a steady increase in those elements in the various Socialist parties who do acknowledge Christian values, in society or in politics, and are deeply concerned about their activation. Such Socialists as Ignazio Silone of Italy or Willem Schermerhorn in the Netherlands, are striking examples. The inmost phenomenon in this matter is the struggle within Socialism: between those who would rather surrender to totalitarianism than give up their cherished anti-clerical or anti-Christian prejudices, and those who are so animated by the love of the good of society that they learned to realize that even temporal welfare cannot be achieved unless man's supreme spiritual welfare is given due place."

Another American Catholic leader, the Reverend George H. Dunne, S.J., member of the faculty of Loyola University, Los Angeles, has stated in the Catholic weekly, *The Commonweal*, that "there is no insurmountable obstacle in the way of establishing peaceful relation between Catholicism and Socialism. It is of paramount importance to the interest of each and to the interest of the people of Europe that they do establish peaceful relations with each other. Only if these two forces are able to collaborate in a spirit of mutual understanding is there hope in Europe finding a middle path between equally intolerable extremes of violence and tyranny. . . . The issue that faces Europe is not between capitalism and socialism. That issue has been decided. The issue is between freedom and slavery, between democracy and tyranny. It will be resolved in favor of slavery and tyranny unless Socialism and Catholicism can work together."

However, not even the ranks of the Socialists themselves are sufficiently closed to permit a coordinated policy of the moderate Socialist parties of Europe and the world. In eastern Europe, large sections of the Socialist parties work under the guidance of the Communists. In central Europe and in the west, opposition against cooperation with the Catholic parties is stronger, or at least more vocal, than opposition against alliance with the Communists.

Socialists from eighteen countries met from November 8 to 10, 1946, at Bournemouth, England. The rift between the moderate Socialist parties of northern and western Europe, on the one hand, and the Communist-influenced parties of the east, proved too great to be surmounted. The participants merely agreed on loose liaison for consultation, on exchange of facts and views. The desire not to offend the Soviet Union, not to embarrass the Socialist parties of eastern Europe, influenced the conference's decision against official revival of the Second International. A year later, the Socialists met again, at Zurich. There, another trend was revealed: Communist hope to dominate a new International through the medium of Socialist parties—such as Nenni's Italian group—who follow Communist leadership. The Moscow magazine *New Times* noted with approval on June 27, 1947, that "the Italian Socialist Party is in favor of a united international organization which would embrace all working-class parties—Socialist and Communist."

The difficulties that stand between common rejection of communism and coordinated cooperation in opposing it, are realized not only by Socialists and Catholics. They have also been emphasized by a leading American Protestant, Bishop G. Bromley Oxnam, past president of the Federal Council of Churches of Christ in America. Bishop Oxnam has stated that "men who summon us to a holy war against communism" were "diverting our attention from the primary obligation to democratize our own economic, political, ecclesiastical and social life." According to Bishop Oxnam, opposition to communism is consistent only if it is "understood as a struggle against totalitarianism in all its forms."

"PETRIFIED PREJUDICES"

Similarly, informed businessmen have expressed the view that a negative approach to the political-economic problems of our time cannot be sufficient. When Eric A. Johnston resigned his post as president of the Chamber of Commerce of the United States, he called for a new "competitive economic system designed for the enrichment of the many and not to make a few men rich." He warned against a capitalist system "loaded down with petrified prejudices" which considers people merely the "inert tools of the system." Capitalism cannot run away from destiny, he said, and "we in business must liberalize or have the threat of economic liquidation."

Of the Internationals in all but name, communism is today the most successful. Its ability to combine single-mindedness and extreme militancy with opportunist adaptability is the basis of this success. This was particularly noticeable in Spain, where Communists were willing to ally themselves with Monarchists in overthrowing the Franco government. In this, they split with the left-wing Socialists, who refused to compromise their anti-monarchist principles to gain a temporary advantage. But the Communists felt that monarchists would play an important part in any coup d'état or revolt against Franco, and they were willing to ignore other considerations for the time being.

By taking the long view, displaying patience and tenacity, Communists in many parts of the world have placed themselves in advantageous positions. Catholicism and socialism have moved slowly toward regional cooperation. When, in Belgium, the Catholic Christian Socialists put the issue of King Leopold's return temporarily aside, a coalition with the

Socialists could be achieved early in 1947. But businessmen, the representatives of capitalist ideas, have apparently found it most difficult to think beyond immediate economic advantages. Even the consideration of ultimate economic developments has often escaped the understanding of business leaders. Much less, then, could they see beyond economic matters to understand the intricate political picture of the world today. When Peru's Aprista Party came to power in 1946, owners of large estates and of industrial enterprises were dismayed. They proved unable to see beyond immediate advantages. To many of them, the Apristas were about the same as Communists. Peruvian and foreign business interests lacked the political sophistication to understand the schism that separated communism from the Aprista movement.

COMMUNISM HAS A HEAD START

Communism, by thinking in world-wide terms and adapting its tactics within the regional pattern of the Seventh Strategy, outmaneuvered the other Internationals. Next in efficiency, the Socialists have grown more conscious of the need to retain their identity in the areas inside and outside the Soviet sphere of influence. They have not been more than moderately successful. The British Labour Party, harassed by the burdens of government, has been unable to furnish effective leadership. And the United States, with Republican influence strengthened, has not been able to appreciate fully the importance of democratic socialism.

While the Socialists have become conscious of the shortcomings resulting from too rigid a policy, several Catholic groups have often failed to rectify mistakes of the past. Thus they have more than once played straight into the hands of their most determined antagonists, the Communist parties. This was strikingly illustrated in Argentina, early in 1947, when the Perón government decreed compulsory religious instructions. In this, he was backed by the Catholic Church. The Communist Buenos Aires daily La Hora used this issue quickly to point to collaboration between the church and the militarist-nationalist regime of General Perón. Elsewhere, political Catholicism was able to adjust itself to postwar conditions with more insight.

Last on the ladder of political adroitness must come the attitude of leading businessmen and business organizations. Eric A. Johnston's analysis, cited above, remains nearly isolated. Generally speaking, however, representatives of industry have shown more political astuteness than agricultural interests, particularly in Latin America. Oblivious of anything but retention of their privileged status, landowners in underdeveloped areas throughout the world have indirectly fed the fires of revolt.

In the race of the Internationals in all but name, the Communists have a head start. Although there is some evidence that their global antagonists begin to realize the carefully worked out methods with which the Communists avoid obstacles, they remain far behind in world-wide efficiency. With the Communists out in front, and the Socialists and Catholic parties competing for second place, international business interests seem to be promenading along the track, earnestly discussing yesterday's stock-market fluctuations.

★

CHAPTER 34

The Comintern Goes Underground

Has the Communist International really been dissolved?

The official Communist view, expressed by so high an authority as Joseph Stalin himself, is that it ceased to exist in 1943. But the striking similarities in policy, activities, and organizational methods that Communist parties display in every part of the world point to the existence of an international synchronization machinery.

When the Comintern was still functioning officially, it managed worldwide contacts through an International Liaison Section, the OMS (Otydel Mezhdunarodnoi Svyazi). The OMS, with headquarters in Moscow, arranged for financial support of parties abroad, transmitted instructions, prepared papers, took care of visiting Communist leaders quartered in Moscow's Hotel Lux, and generally handled all the large and small matters that are the business of an international political bureau. OMS, staffed by specialists from many countries, followed the directions that the central committee of the Russian Communist Party gave the Comintern. It is reasonable to suppose that OMS today functions as an adjunct to the Communist Party of the Soviet Union and that its carefully compiled files and its trained personnel were not discarded in 1943. The precision with which the Seventh Strategy of world communism is being carried out permits the conclusion that the Comintern has ceased official existence while going underground.

HOW INTERNATIONALS ARE DISSOLVED

Dissolution of the Comintern was not the beginning of a striking new phase in Communist policy. It was rather the final touch applied to the "united front" policy. One by one, world communism has discarded its various Internationals. The Communist International itself was one of

456

the last to go. But, before it disappeared from the surface of world affairs, Communists had already gathered much experience in operating in the absence of a clear-cut, rigid International.

As far back as 1925, the Red International of Labor Unions replaced some of its branches with associations bearing different national names. We have already seen how the British Communist Party received instructions to "give the movement a national name." When the "united front" policy was introduced a decade later, the Red Labor International was officially dissolved. After 1935, Communist unions joined larger federations. In France, they fused with the General Confederation of Labor; in Britain, with the Trades Union Congress; in the United States, with the AFL (until the CIO was born). Throughout the world, from Iceland to India, from Australia to Chile, this process was repeated.

Another decade passed, and, eventually, in 1945, the World Federation of Trade Unions was founded in London. Today, the WFTU has some seventy million workers in its affiliates. This figure includes twenty-seven million USSR trade-union members, seven million members of the CIO, and five million workers belonging to the Latin American Confederation of Labor. The American Federation of Labor has refused to participate in the WFTU, regarding it as "a Moscow fifth column." It is worth noting, however, that the WFTU is a rather precariously organized body, in which a high degree of autonomy exists. The Paris headquarters of the WFTU appears to follow a Communist policy in all its actions. But the rank and file of the affiliated labor organizations is for the most part completely unaware of the subtle guidance that it follows. The WFTU, loosely organized, seeks to influence its membership to follow Communist policies only in matters of major importance.

Another international Communist body that has been dissolved is the Young Communist International. Throughout the world, a network of youth organizations existed. As a rule, its local branches were known as Young Communist Leagues. Many of today's leading statesmen entered the Communist movement through these organizations. When the Young Communist International was dissolved, it was found useful to organize substitute bodies in several parts of the world. In some countries, for instance in the Union of South Africa, the label Young Communist League was retained.

The United States Young Communist League dissolved itself on October 16, 1943, during a New York meeting. It resolved immediately to organize a new association that would "broaden the base of leadership" and include non-Communist youth. On the following day, this plan was carried out, and the American Youth for Democracy was formed. The leaders of the dissolved Young Communist League were made permanent officers of the AYD. On April 3, 1943, the *Daily Worker* of New York described the AYD as "a mass, advanced anti-fascist youth organization in which the Communists play a leading role."

A World Federation of Democratic Youth was founded in 1945 at Prague. A year later, student organizations from forty-three countries met at Prague and organized an International Union of Students. This new youth international is even less homogeneous than the World Federation of Trade Unions. The Prague meeting appeared so devoid of Communist influence that twenty-eight United States youth organizations sent representatives. Most of these organizations were completely non-Communist. Again, as in the case of the WFTU, rigid ideological principles were sacrificed for an appearance of neutrality. Nevertheless, there can be no doubt about Communist intentions. The New York Communist monthly *Political Affairs* stated in February, 1947, that "the members of the student clubs of the Communist Party will meet their responsibilities in both the broad student movement and in the advanced, anti-imperialist, anti-fascist student movement. They will loyally carry out the programs of the organizations to which they belong, and at the same time they will contribute their Marxist knowledge and understanding to the work to be done."

The 1947 World Youth Festival which WFDY sponsored in Prague from July 20 to August 17 was attended by thousands of delegates from all parts of the world. Sports, lectures, artistic presentations, dancing, and motion-picture performances were part of the impressively staged event. The festival was followed by the athletic competitions of the World Inter-University Games at Paris from August 24 to 31, organized by the International Union of Students.

The pattern adopted in reorganizing the labor and youth internationals was also used after the dissolution of the Red Women's International. A Women's International Democratic Federation was created in Paris in 1945. Its United States affiliate is the Congress of American Women. Here, again, Communist initiative has been subtle and restrained. The origin of this organization becomes apparent only after careful investigation of its background and a study of its propaganda techniques.

One of the oldest and financially most successful world-wide Communist enterprises was the International Red Aid. This body combined fund raising for avowed medical purposes with legal work. Official dissolution of the International Red Aid did not in any way interrupt the activities throughout the world. In the United States, an International Labor Defense was created under the chairmanship of Congressman Vito Marcantonio. In 1946, this organization was replaced by the Civil Rights Congress. It protested vigorously against the arrest of Gerhart Eisler, whom Justice Department authorities described as the leading Communist agent in the United States. In Canada, the local continuation of the International Red Aid is named Civil Rights Union. On January 18, 1947, this organization demanded suppression of the Royal Commission report on the use of Communists in Soviet espionage.

Throughout the world, organizations devoted to the cause of friendship with the USSR were set up during the 1930's. As a rule, they were called Friends of the Soviet Union. Later, they adopted names in which the country in which they were functioning was also included. In the United States, the organization fulfilling this function is the National Council for American-Soviet Friendship. A few others are the Australian-Russian Society, the Korean-Soviet Culture Association, the Society of Norwegian-Soviet Friendship, the Mexican-Russian Institute for Cultural Relations, the Irish-Soviet Friendship Society, and the Swiss-Russian Association.

A wartime and postwar creation is the All-Slav Congress, with headquarters in Prague. This organization became influential after Communist or Communist-led governments were formed in eastern Europe. Wherever men and women of Slavic descent live throughout the world, local branches of the All-Slav Congress exist. This goes for the Latin-American nations, Australia, New Zealand, and Canada, but most of all for the United States. An American Slav Congress was held in New York in November, 1946. Communist newspapers exist in the United States in all Slavic languages.

In many countries, there are also Communist-led national organizations devoted to over-all world political questions. These have consistently reflected the varying strategies of communism. For the sake of brevity, we cite only the development of one such an organization in the United States. Its equivalents exist wherever political action may have value. After the Seventh Comintern Congress, the American League against War and Fascism was founded. It later became the American League for Peace and Democracy. After the Nazi-Soviet Pact, during the "The Yanks are not coming!" campaign, this organization changed its name to American Peace Mobilization. After the end of the war, a National Committee to Win the Peace was formed, which complies with the Seventh Strategy of world communism.

A GOOD EXECUTIVE DELEGATES AUTHORITY

Decentralization has become a characteristic of Communist organizations since the "united front" policy came into being in 1935. One International after the other was dissolved and replaced by regional organizations. Loosely affiliated and unobtrusive in their agitation, these bodies attracted a large number of people who would not otherwise have placed themselves under Communist influence.

When the Communist International itself was officially dissolved, the "united front" policy had been fully translated into organizational terms. Decentralization was the key word. Ability to delegate authority marks a good executive. The Comintern had become such an executive during the quarter of a century of its existence. It had trained branch officers who could be relied upon to execute policy with a fair amount of independent discretion. When the Comintern announced its dissolution, it traced the decentralization trend back to the 1935 congress and stated that "greater flexibility and independence" for its regional sections had become necessary.

Nevertheless, even a decentralized organization needs central coordination. The obvious synchronization of Communist efforts throughout the world leaves no doubt that a central authority exists. Observation of Communist activity during the Seventh Strategy period suggests that the following factors play a part in coordinating the work of the various parties.

1. *The Moscow Politbureau.* The Political Bureau of the Communist Party of the Soviet Union (Bolsheviks) remains the highest authority of Communist affairs. Parties abroad look to Russia as the First Socialist Nation. They, in turn, are guided and supported by the Soviet Union. Through the Russian Communist Party and its foreign contacts (most likely the machinery of the old OMS), the decisions of the Politbureau are communicated to Communist parties abroad.

2. *Traveling Representatives.* Throughout its existence, the Communist

International relied on roving representatives to carry confidential instructions and to advise foreign Communist parties on the scene. The
presence of former top officials of the Comintern in high government
posts in Europe (notably in the east, but also in France and Italy) suggests
that it may no longer be necessary to dispatch advisers to these areas.

3. *Regional Bureaus.* To coordinate Communist policy within wider
geographical regions, a number of bureaus appear to be in existence.
During World War II, the Communist capital of Yenan was the center of
Far Eastern activities. Shortly before the fall of Yenan, this center
appears to have been moved to Manchuria, where it began to function
under Li Li-san, who had just come from the Soviet Union. The slowly
growing Communist parties of the Near Eastern nations appear to be
guided from Lebanon, with Beirut as headquarters. North Africa, however, seems to have received its instructions from Paris, the western European center of Communist activity on the continent. The nations of the
Caribbean area are clearly the domain of the Havana Communists. South
American Communist Party work generally seems to be guided from
Spanish-speaking Buenos Aires, where the veteran party leader Rodolfo
Ghioldi is most prominent.

Foundation of a Communist Information Bureau in Belgrade in October 1947, following a conference in which the Eastern European parties
and those of France and Italy participated, served to knit together the
sometimes opposing interests of Europe's Communist parties on a conti-
nent-wide basis. The nine-party conference was mistakenly interpreted
by some observers as an official revival of the Communist International,
whereas it represented little more than a regional rounding-out of the
Seventh Strategy.

It is difficult to escape the impression that some overlapping or shifting of regional authority has occurred. It is known that the New York
headquarters of the United States Communist Party has had the Philippines
under its jurisdiction in the past. With the advent of Philippine independence, these islands may have been placed under the supervision of the
Far Eastern bureau. In the Caribbean area and in Central America generally,
Havana and New York are both active. Puerto Rico follows New York
guidance, while the Dominican Republic, right next door, looks to
Havana. Communist activities in the British Empire are largely under
the supervision of the Communist Party of Great Britain, a fact that was

well illustrated by the London British Empire Conference of the Communists in 1947.

4. *Day-by-day Policy Guidance.* Statements made by Soviet leaders or leading Communists furnish the basic guidance for Communist propaganda throughout the world. *Pravda,* organ of the Russian Communist Party, and the weekly Moscow magazine *New Times* are often cited in the world Communist press. Changes in policy are usually expressed in important speeches by Joseph Stalin or Vyacheslav M. Molotov. Former Comintern officials, such as Dmitri Z. Manuilsky and Otto Kuusinen, are also carefully observed by Communist speakers and editors abroad. In the field of world economics, the Hungarian-born Moscow analyst Eugene Varga has a near monopoly on expressing official Communist policy.

5. *Financial Matters.* Former Communists have reported consistently that the Soviet Union has furnished funds to Communist parties abroad. On occasion, government investigations have borne out such reports. It is impossible to gain an over-all picture of the financial affairs of even a single Communist Party. It should be noted, however, that the postwar period has brought accelerated agitation and propaganda activity, which doubtless is very costly.

Everywhere, from Stockholm to Rio de Janeiro, from Los Angeles to Paris, Communist parties have made enormous promotion efforts. In the United States, papers were started in Chicago and Detroit. In both America and England, literary quarterlies are now being published by the Communists. In Paris, *Humanité* sponsored an international sports meeting. In Brazil, no less than twenty-one publications existed early in 1947; the Brazilian party set a promotional precedent with a samba festival that attracted almost 100,000 participants and onlookers. Throughout the United States, teen-age students attended square dances arranged by American Youth for Democracy. Cuban Communists spent $100,000 to buy the radio station Diez Mil.

Production of books and pamphlets, rental of halls, and the printing and distribution of leaflets constitute a drain on the parties' treasuries. There are few known cases of Communist parties operating on a completely balanced budget. It must be assumed that deficits exist, that the more prosperous parties subsidize those which are smaller or operate underground (funds have definitely been transferred from the United States party to Canadian Communist leaders), and that certain amounts are similarly contributed by the Communist Party of the Soviet Union.

★

CHAPTER 35

Will Communism Win?

Wᴏʀʟᴅ ᴄᴏᴍᴍᴜɴɪsᴍ reached its all-time peak after the end of World War II. In two decades, membership of Communist parties outside Russia increased tenfold. In 1926, world communism had 1,200,000 registered supporters. By 1936, this figure had risen to 3,600,000. And at the Communist British Empire Conference of 1947, sixty-six parties that "follow the teachings of Marx, Engels, Lenin and Stalin" claimed a total of 12,000,000 members.

The question which such increased influence raises in the minds of Communists and anti-Communists alike, is this: *Can communism win the battle for world domination?*

Let us be frank: *Yes, it can.*

The chances of communism today are better than ever. Its center of strength, the Soviet Union, has shown impressive power on battlefields and at conference tables. The antagonists of world communism are weak, or confused, or ignorant.

⌊Above all: communism retains its appeal in a world where economic inequality remains as flagrant as it is today. Inequality between the very poor and the very rich, and the absence of a substantial middle class, are most striking in Latin America, the Near and Far East; they also exist in more regions of the western world than most of us realize.⌋

The decisive test of Communist strength is still to come. During the first two decades of its existence, from 1919 to 1939, world communism tried repeatedly to unfurl the banner of world revolution. It failed. It was defeated in Germany, in China, in Bulgaria, in Spain—wherever it thought that the time for action had come. Instead, fascism and Nazism achieved dominance, until they were crushed through the joint efforts of Communist Russia and the democratic west.

When will the next important test of Communist strength come? Will

463

it be war between the Soviet Union and the west, notably the United
States? Or will it be some other form of conflict, a bloodless political
attack on a weakened non-Communist world?

*The coming test of Communist strength will develop when the next
serious economic crisis spreads across the globe.*

Since the establishment of the Third International, communism has
experienced three boom periods: the years immediately following World
War I; the depression and postdepression era; and the years immediately following World War II. These three periods were years of despair
for many millions. The next depression will parallel these phases of
Communist success. Thus the next world economic crisis will give communism its fourth major chance to achieve world domination.

THE WEAPON OF POVERTY

Communism is organized desperation. It does not need the weapons
of war to achieve its aims, although it may use them as collateral or
alternative tools of revolution. Hunger and despair can be as effective
as the most devastating weapon of war. As President Harry S. Truman
said on March 12, 1947, when he asked the United States Congress
to support Greece against communism, "The seeds of totalitarian regimes
are nurtured by misery and want. They spread and grow in the evil soil
of poverty and strife. They reach their full growth when the hope of
people for a better life has died."

Communist strategists operating under the Seventh Strategy of world
communism—which combines militant representation of Soviet interests
and a "united front" policy of collaboration with liberal-labor elements—
regard the United States as the major obstacle that confronts Communist aspirations throughout the world. America's decision to halt
communism confirmed this belief; the lines were clearly drawn. How,
then, will communism meet this challenge?

We are going to see a lessening of Communist strength in the immediate
future. This will be attributed, at least in part, to Washington's militant
anti-Communist policy. But it will be difficult to assess the true effect of
that policy. A temporary ebbing of Communist influence would merely
follow a pattern noticeable after previous boom periods in world communism. It would parallel developments after World War I. Already, in
1946 and 1947, some Communist parties have experienced a slackening

of support. The Communist Party of Great Britain lost 10,000 members in 1946; its membership was reduced from 53,000 to 43,000. The Communist parties of the United States and Sweden entered ambitious promotion drives to offset a postwar decrease in support. The Greek party reduced its membership from 400,000 to 250,000, officially because of intraparty purges, but also because of opposition within the rank and file. In Japan, where European trends were being experienced after a delay, the 1947 elections reduced Communist parliamentary strength by one-half.

The lessening of Communist strength in terms of membership figures need not reflect a reduced influence of communism as a whole. Lenin's concept of the party as a vanguard of devoted fanatics is still alive. Communist parties have little use for fair-weather friends. They prefer a reliable nucleus of members to an ever-changing mass of supporters. In a world-wide depression, communism will gain millions of new recruits among unemployed, among starving peasants, among a despairing, hopeless and rootless mass of humanity.

COMMUNISM IS READY FOR DEPRESSION

When the next depression comes, communism will be ready for it. As Communists see it, this depression will have its root in the United States. They are already contrasting the American system of free enterprise with the Soviet system of economy. On November 27, 1946, the Moscow *Pravda* carried a detailed analysis by Dr. Eugene Varga, Director of the Soviet Institute for World Economics and World Politics. A former professor of economics at the University at Budapest, Dr. Varga is today the leading political economist of the USSR. He said in *Pravda* that "the fear of a new approaching economic crisis is beginning to be felt in the capitalist world" and contrasted this with the depression-proof economy that he attributed to the Soviet Union. He wrote that such fear was "very well founded" and cited Marx as having "proved that the inner laws of capitalism must inevitably lead to a cyclical course of industrial production and to periodically recurring crises." Varga added:

"The general crisis of the capitalist system, as pointed out by Comrade Stalin, has changed the cyclical process of capitalist production in the sense that the phases of crises and depressions have become longer, and that a depression is followed only by a phase of revival, but not by a phase of full prosperity. He noted that World War II had dislocated global economic life and wrote:

"The coming economic crisis in the United States will inevitably have a tremendous effect upon the situation in other capitalist countries. The crisis in the U. S. will be a grave blow to the process of postwar reconstruction in these countries. The destructive effect of the crisis will hardly allow these countries to reach a state of even moderate prosperity.

"In capitalist countries the transition from war to peace is always bound up with narrowing markets, decline of production, closing down of industrial enterprises, and growth of unemployment. Only the Soviet Union does not know such phenomena. In the Soviet Union there is no anarchy of production, characteristic of capitalism, which leads to the rotation of periods of boom and crisis, which shake the very foundation of the economic system and create a constant uncertainty among the working masses as to their future."

Dr. Varga's statements about the instability of America's economy, in contrast to the Soviet system, coincided with warnings by Communist leaders in Great Britain, western and northern Europe, and Latin America, that close economic-political relationship with the United States might prove disastrous to other nations. To ensure themselves against an expected American depression, these countries were urged to strengthen their ties with the Soviet Union and with the nations of eastern Europe.

ENCIRCLEMENT OF AMERICA?

Further deductions from the international political-economic situation were drawn in January, 1947, by the Chinese Communist Information Director Lu Ting-yi. Writing in Yenan's *Emancipation Daily*, he called for a development that could easily be interpreted as a Communist encirclement of the United States. He called it a "world-wide united front against American imperialism" when he wrote:

"The world anti-democratic forces are the American imperialists and the reactionaries in various countries. These world anti-democratic forces are attacking the American people and the peoples of the other capitalist countries, colonies and semi-colonial countries in unison. Consequently, the peoples of the U. S. and of the various capitalist countries, colonies and semi-colonial countries must also act in unison to form a world-wide united front against American imperialism and the reactionaries in all countries. This world-wide united front, this colossal army comprising well over one billion people, is precisely the world democratic might. This world-wide united front cannot possibly be of any other character than that of a united front, fighting for world peace and democracy and the independence of all nations against American capitalism and its running dogs in various countries.

"This united front on a world scale will undoubtedly have the sympathy and the moral support of the Socialist Soviet Union. This united front on a world scale will characterize a new page in world history, the history of the world from the end of the Second World War down to the day when stable and lasting peace is assured. . . .

"The present time is still a period when world reaction can be cocky, can bare its fangs and extend its talons. This is primarily because the struggles of the peoples in the various countries have not entered the higher stage, and at the same time it is also because the American economic crisis has not yet arrived. But even in this kind of period, the reactionary forces have already revealed that they are hollow within and only outwardly strong. When the struggle of the peoples of all countries has reached a higher level of development and the American economic crisis has broken out, that will be the time when the great arrogance of the reactionaries will collapse. That time is not far distant."

When the next depression comes, how will communism slant its agitation? Will there be a new strategy of world communism?

It seems likely that the depression strategy of communism will be an extension of current methods. There is need to realize that today's Communist strategy has been perfected over a long period of time. It is the result of many trials and many errors. Never before in its history has communism operated within a policy framework that suited so well the interests of the Soviet state, while at the same time gaining the endorsement of non-Communist men and women of good will.

The current Seventh Strategy of world communism combines the most successful features of two previous strategies. During the extremist-revolutionary period from 1928 to 1935, communism tried to put all its cards on the table, sought to make the world safe for the Soviet Union. This strategy proved far too revolutionary to be widely popular, although the depression years gave communism a firm base of agitation.

The 1935 Seventh Congress of the Comintern opened a period of much more successful agitation. Georgi Dimitrov said at that congress that communism should use "Trojan horse" methods, should infiltrate into non-Communist groups and conquer them from inside. His speech was soon forgotten by those who saw in communism a champion of eminently desirable causes: the fight against Nazi Germany, Fascist Italy, and all ultra-nationalism elsewhere; the freedom of labor to organize; racial and religious tolerance; social-security measures, and so forth.

VESSEL FOR HUMAN IDEALISM

At last, communism had managed to gauge the world's basic desires. It had created a vessel into which human idealism could be poured. Nothing illustrates this better than the number of non-Communists who joined the International Brigades, who gave their lives during the Spanish civil war (and who unknowingly furnished passports for the use of Comintern and Soviet secret service agents). This use of mankind's deep and genuine desire to destroy ultra-nationalist tyranny, this exploitation of man's wrath against suppression and government by terror, is a strong moral indictment of Communist methods. But we are not discussing the moral implications of the "united front" or "Trojan horse" strategy. We are judging its effectiveness. And there can be no doubt that it was effective. It is highly effective still, because it is part of current strategy.

Today's Seventh Strategy includes the "united front" technique, in that it seeks the collaboration of sincere (although politically superficial and naïve) men and women of good will, and in that it obscures the ultimate aims of world communism by emphasizing short-range objectives. But, in addition, the Seventh Strategy has also revived the 1928 to 1934 policy of making the world safe for the Soviet Union. That is why Communists in Scandinavia and western Europe agitate against the formation of northern or western blocs. That is why Britain's Communist Party favored the withdrawal of British troops from overseas territories. That is why the American Communist Party favored Soviet policy over United States policy on control of atomic energy. That is why Communists everywhere describe the foreign policy of the United States in terms of an "American imperialism" which threatens international peace and progress and endangers the security of the First Socialist State, the Soviet Union.

Use of the "united front" policy in a militant effort to make the world safe for the Soviet Union has given world communism maximum effectiveness. The resulting strategic framework makes it possible to present pro-Russianism as internationalism and to present Communist-controlled organizations as outlets of mankind's longings for peace, liberty, and progress. Above all, the Seventh Strategy made it possible to combine Communist efforts with native nationalisms. This is particularly marked in Germany, where nationalist sentiment is one of the few basic emotions that have survived defeat. It is also effective in China, where anti-foreign sentiment is shared by the opposing sides of the civil war. Latin-American nationalism, born of a feeling of inferiority in comparison with the mighty "Colossus of the North" also fits well into this pattern. And, in colonial areas, the nationalist desire for liberation from foreign rule is so strong that it even threatens to absorb the communism that collaborates with it.

All this should not create the impression that current Communist strategy lacks shortcomings. For all its astuteness in developing the Seventh Strategy, world communism has been unable to escape the self-isolation that undoubtedly exists among leading Russian Communists. There are overwhelming indications that the men in Moscow who plan Communist progress have at their disposal the greatest information-gathering machinery ever created. But information is not useful until it has been carefully sifted and evaluated. It is sometimes said that the data transmitted to Moscow by the Soviet embassies abroad and by the Tass news agency are selected and slanted in such a way as to supply the Soviet government officials with only the kind of facts and comment they want to hear, rather than with unbiased information. That may well be so, but it is not the whole story. There is hardly a magazine, newspaper, or book dealing with current affairs published anywhere in the world that does not find its way to a policy-making office in the Soviet Union. Many periodicals have on their subscriber lists the Narkomindel, the Soviet Foreign Ministry. Other informational data are purchased abroad. In the United States, it is the Four Continent Book Corporation, of 253 Fifth Avenue in New York, that acts as a purchasing agent. Information reaching the Soviet Union is therefore not restricted to material cabled home by Russian diplomats and foreign correspondents. The question is whether even the original source material that reaches Moscow directly is objectively evaluated.

It is clear that many of the over-all policy decisions of world communism are still made in an ivory tower. Communist policy regarding American Negroes, which reflects the status of USSR minorities rather than United States conditions, is one example of this. Self-isolation has obviously affected the thinking of prominent Russian Communists. Such thinking is inbred. Nevertheless, and this is well to remember, communism has come a long way since 1935, when the "united front" policy began, and since 1943, when the Communist International was officially dissolved. Authority given Communist leaders within their countries has increased vastly. And Communist regional policies are adaptable as they have never been before.

SHOULD COMMUNIST PARTIES BE BANNED?

When the new and aggressive Seventh Strategy was introduced after World War II, it bewildered a great many people who had forgotten the words "class war." Viewing with alarm became the fashion. Undertones of hysteria were audible. Inevitably, the question was asked: Should the Communist Party be banned? In Latin America, where Communists had emerged from an underground existence only recently, this question was answered according to varying conditions in the different countries. When, however, it was also discussed in the United States, it became linked with rights of freedom of speech and of assembly. It was a question worth clarification and discussion. Decisions in all facets of political life should be weighed in accordance with their ultimate effects. Emotional rantings and hysterical urgings are likely to ignore anything but surface appearances. The question is therefore not merely whether the Communist Party should be outlawed but whether such a measure can be effective. Is there, then, any sense in banning the Communist Party in the United States, and in other nations of the west?

The answer is: No. There is no sense to that at all. Only legislators who have never seriously studied the history and tactics of communism can doubt that the Communists would always be three jumps ahead of the slow-moving legislative and judicial government machinery.

Look at Canada! There, the Communist Party was banned in 1940. Nevertheless, its most prominent members engaged in espionage for the Soviet Union. In 1945, they organized a party of Communists, the Labour-Progressive Party. The Canadian government did not bother to ban that party. It knew full well that the Communists would reappear, chameleon-like, under another color the following day.

Or take Switzerland, a small country that is much easier to police than the United States or any of the larger western nations. The Swiss government banned the Communists in 1940. A so-called Labor Party developed. It was so clearly Communist that its leaders did not even reestablish the original Communist Party, once the ban was lifted. Only an out-and-out police state can outlaw the Communist Party and even hope to enforce such a ban.

Even police states have not done so well at enforcing a ban on the Communist Party. Mussolini's Italy was perhaps most successful; even more so than Hitler's Germany. But then, Mussolini had a head start of ten years. Varga's Brazil did not effectively eliminate the Communists; they continued as an underground nucleus of some 4,000 devoted fanatics. The methods of Franco's Spain have been as ruthless as those of most other dictatorships, but the Communist underground movement in Spain continues to function in spite of repeated setbacks.

Suppression of communism does one other thing: it opens the gate for the excesses of the ultra-right. Nazism seized power while shouting "Thief, thief!" after the Communists. Today, in Madrid, enormous posters bear the slogan "Franco Sí! Comunismo No!" They suggest, of course, that anyone who is against communism must be for Franco. The ultra-right throws a red cloak over anyone who opposes it and pastes over it the label "communism." In identical fashion, communism has come to use the label "fascism" for anyone or any group that is militantly anti-Communist. And communism does something else, which makes things even more convenient for the ultra-right: it seeks to identify itself with the men of good will who feel that our world can still stand quite a lot of improvement. The results are two nets of confusion. In these nets, the emotional, the politically primitive, the overenthusiastic, and the ideologically frustrated are caught by either the ultra-right or the ultra-left. Greece is perhaps the most tragic example of this trend toward radicalization.

RECIPE FOR A CONFUSION STEW

Of course, such confusion is deliberately fostered by professional propagandists on both extremes. The recipe is simple. One needs only to mix superficially related political issues, add platitudes liberally, spice well with emotional oratory or vituperative writing, stir quickly, and serve it hot. In the United States, this was well illustrated when two otherwise unrelated events occurred early in 1947: Gerhart Eisler was named as a long-time agent of the Communist International; and David Lilienthal, chairman of the Atomic Energy Commission, was linked by his political opponents with communism. The accusations against Eisler were well founded and convincingly documented. The innuendoes against Lilienthal were wicked and malicious.

As a result, the spokesman of the ultra-right, Lilienthal's opponent Senator Kenneth McKellar of Tennessee, and the spokesman of the ultra-left, the Communist *Daily Worker*, joined in creating a vast amount of confusion. By trying to pin a Communist label on Lilienthal, McKellar enabled the *Daily Worker* to claim that all accusations against alleged Communists were lies. The attack on Lilienthal collapsed of its own weakness. Consequently, argued the *Daily Worker*, the arrest of Eisler was also merely part of a "stupid, lying, disruptive 'red menace' hysteria." The confusion ball was thus tossed back to Senator McKellar, who could claim that the Communists were making common cause with Lilienthal.

The political stew in which Eisler and Lilienthal were cooked together was merely a particularly striking example of a widely practiced confusion technique. On the Communist side, its use would not have been possible before the "united front" strategy was perfected. Under the old extremist-revolutionary strategy, communism would have viewed the McKellar-Lilienthal affairs as merely another tussle between different exponents of bourgeois capitalism. Today, communism uses the we're-in-this-with-you and let's-stick-together-or-we'll-all-be-licked approach with the ease of a decade's practice.

The slogan, "The enemies of my enemies are my friends" has a dangerously attractive ring. Its appeal to primitive political thinking is enormous. And it is well to remember that political naïveté is not limited to the illiterate peasantry of exotic regions. Political sophistication is a rare flower. It does not always thrive in metropolitan sitting rooms. It has more of a chance to bloom in union offices, where the use of legitimate grievances for hidden political ends can be easily observed. The best way to tell a genuine thing from a fake is still to look at it closely.

The confusion technique shows one facet of the similarity between the ultra-left and the ultra-right, between communism and fascism. It would be much easier to show the close relationship between these two ideologies if the development of Europe's parliamentary seating arrangements had not etched the concepts of "Left" and "Right" as distinctly opposed into our minds. We think of communism as standing on the left, and of fascism as standing far on the right. They seem poles apart. That is a fallacy. Today, German Nazis, Italian Fascists, and Brazilian Integralists have found their way into the Communist camp. One of the reasons for communism's success after World War II is the way in which it filled the vacuum left by the collapse of Nazism and fascism.

Let us forget for a moment about the way in which European parliaments are set up. Instead, let us view the political scene as if it were an oval: with moderate forces meeting on one end, and with extreme political forces meeting at the other end. The contrast between political ideas rests not on slogans and avowed purposes, not on surface appearances of intent. It finds its final test in the willingness or unwillingness to adhere to genuine democratic parliamentary methods—not for a given period, as a matter of tactics and with the aim of overthrowing the very machinery of democratic parliamentarism, but now and forever.

The opponents of both communism and fascism find themselves in a precarious position. They refuse to join the one to fight the other. One Hollywood writer has put it this way, "If they ever want to stand us up against the wall, they'd better make it a glass wall—so they can shoot us from both sides. . . ." To oppose communism without falling into Fascist traps is no easy matter. Fascism, the tempter, stands ready with glittering eyes and a line of persuasive suggestions: "Go ahead," it says, "ban 'em. Slug the Reds. Wipe up the floor with 'em. Lock up the whole bunch of them. And all the fellow-travelers. And everybody else who thinks that the world needs fixing."

THE BATHTUB SCHOOL OF ECONOMY

Can we untangle the mass of propagandist-made confusion? The issues are essentially simple, when divorced from the nomenclature used in diplomatic notes, on speaker's platforms, and in learned newspaper editorials. The future of world communism depends on the answer to two major questions:

Will the majority of people defy propagandist confusion? And: *Will the western world avoid self-destruction in the next economic crisis?*

There is no ground for optimism in answering the first question. We see no evidence that political sophistication is keeping pace with the advance of propagandistic subtlety. And, when the next depression comes, organized desperation will have an even better chance than it does now. Hunger does not make for detached reasoning.

The future of world communism thus depends almost entirely on the character of the next depression. The survival of regulated western capital-ism is likely to depend on the intelligence and insight of the men who represent it today. Here, again, there is no need for optimism on the part of those who wish to halt communism. For more than a century, com-munism has learned to think in world-wide terms. For more than three decades, it has applied these lessons in its global propaganda and agita-tion. But the world-consciousness which such thinking requires has not correspondingly developed among the more vocal spokesmen of capital-ism. A devastating self-indictment of isolationist economic thinking was contained in an advertisement which the Electric Light and Power Companies of the United States placed jointly in American magazines in March, 1947. Written in a facetious vein, the advertisement said:

"America must awaken to the dangers of free enterprise! Do you realize that the United States has less than 7% of the world's population —but it has 54% of the world's telephones, 84% of the world's auto-mobiles, nearly half the radios, 92% of all the bathtubs on this planet, 50,000,000 savings bank accounts and 70,000,000 life insurance policies? Furthermore, Americans spend over $4,000,000 a day just for tickets to the movies alone! This is unfair! We have more than our share of everything. What is to blame for this state of affairs? Free enterprise! It is appalling to think that a mere 7% of the world's population should be in a position to take 92% of the world's tub baths—as the rising younger generation will, I am sure, agree! The way out of this shameful abundance is to scrap the system of free enterprise and adopt com-munism, socialism or some similar plan."

This free-enterprise message not only provides excellent statistical material for Communist propaganda outside the United States (and among men and women inside the United States, who feel that maldis-tribution of wealth weighs on their social conscience); it also shows remarkable callousness concerning the very real suffering of millions who in their despair may tomorrow turn toward communism.

Organized world-wide desperation will not be prevented by people who cannot think beyond their bathtubs. One major reason why communism today has a better chance than ever is exactly the narrow economic-political thinking which still sees the world divided into independent compartments, called nations. As far as the United States is concerned, political isolationism is dead. But economic isolationism is still alive. The policy of the United States, designed to counteract communism, cannot remain standing on one leg—political intervention. It will topple over at the first push of a depression. Without farsighted economic cooperation, the second leg of such a policy, it is in vain to hope for a depression that will avoid extremes of suffering and desperation. This was clearly recognized by the United States when Secretary of State Marshall endorsed coordinated, American-aided European reconstruction efforts. However, the United States Congress did not indicate immediately that it fully understood the urgency of Europe's needs and the importance of unhesitating and constructive American cooperation.

STOP COMMUNISM BY STOPPING POVERTY!

The international trade conference, held at Geneva in the summer of 1947, did show that economic isolation is in retreat. But it is retreating very slowly. Above all, even in a completely tariff-less world (a state of Utopia that probably cannot be reached until another Utopia, world government, has been achieved), the high-profit and low-wage economy of much of Latin America, the Near and Far East, and a great part of the western world would not automatically disappear. The best cushion against economic blows and the victory of political extremism from the left and right would appear to be a prosperous middle class. We see the greatest political-economic tranquillity in the Scandinavian countries, where the middle class is most influential. And we see the greatest unrest in countries like China, where governmental corruption is allied with vested economic interests of the super-rich.

It can reasonably be said, without being the least bit wide-eyed, that the hungry will forever resent the luxuriously well-fed or wasteful. We have it on the authority of Senator Robert A. Taft, the Republican leader from Ohio, that "if the free enterprise system does not do its best to prevent hardship and poverty," it "will find itself superseded by a less progressive system which does." Senator Taft favors "a minimum standard floor under subsistence, education, medical care, and housing," something that would "give to all a minimum standard of decent living, and to all children a fair opportunity to get a start in life."

These are reasonable aims. Doubtless, men and women of good will not only in Ohio but also in Hunan Province, in Azerbaijan, in Normandy, in Saskatchewan, in Pernambuco and New South Wales are in favor of them. Communists feel that such aims are useful as short-range targets, as "reformist" measures that will lead to governments under Communist control. Others believe that such measures, when properly perfected and administered, are ends in themselves that will effectively forestall Communist endeavors.

In line with its political efforts to prevent the spread of communism, the United States in 1947 sought to abandon all remnants of economic isolationism. Even before the Geneva trade conference that opened April 10, President Truman had said that members of the new International Trade Organization, "instead of retaining unlimited freedom to commit acts of economic aggression," would "adopt a code of economic conduct and agree to live according to its rules." This new and truly international economic policy did not unfold without opposition from representatives of the bathtub school of economics in the United States itself. It seemed that some vocal spokesmen of unbridled free enterprise lacked the political-economic long-range vision needed to save their own system. In a world where capitalism found itself weakened by a downpour of ultra-left agitation, some of its representatives, like drenched kittens, did not seem to know enough to come in out of the rain.

But, even if the International Trade Organization perfected a smoothly functioning export-import system, would that be enough? Probably not. It has a chance to eliminate economic isolationism in the western world, but it could do little to offset the appeal of the Soviet-Communist system in countries that are rich in manpower and poor in capital and technique. In the Near and Far East, and in a number of Latin-American countries, communism offers an aggressive alternative to a nineteenth century type of investment and domination. No "Marshall Plan" can be expected to reach these areas directly.

In crystallizing its foreign policy, the United States faces the difficult choice of bolstering a primitive type of capitalism against state-sponsored reforms. This is particularly true of China, but it applies to other areas where communism offers social benefits or at least offers to alleviate extremes of luxury and of degradation. The small educated classes in these countries, attracted perhaps against their will by the magnetism of Communist ideas, cannot be expected to see in a primitive capitalist society a true expression of free enterprise. In fact, the phrase "free enterprise" is frequently used by Communist economists (for instance, in Romania, Bulgaria, and Poland) to describe the system that they seek to develop.

On the other hand, the controlling government circles (with China and Greece as the most striking examples) often appear unable to see that genuine reforms and regulations are required to check communism. This was noticeable in Greece, where American suggestions on taxes and anti-inflation controls at first met with thinly disguised opposition.

It is no more than realism to conclude from the recent progress of communism that some of the very reforms that Communists support need to be adopted in order to take the wind out of Communist sails. That, of course, does not mean the adoption of communism. Certainly, a nation like Norway, which has perfected an efficient system of controls and of labor-management cooperation, is as far removed from communism as any country on earth. But the Communists of Latin America have accurately emphasized that their immediate programs call for no more than the introduction of measures that have been accepted in the United States as a matter of course.

WHAT DOES IT ALL ADD UP TO?

But, before long-range political and economic answers to the challenge of communism can be developed, it is necessary to analyze in forthright terms the realities of world communism today. We have, in previous chapters, examined the leadership, organization, and policies of Communist parties on a country-by-country basis. We have found that it is impossible to evaluate communism on the basis of its performance in only one given country, or one given region, or during one given phase of its Seven Strategies.

What then, to sum it all up, is world communism today?

Let us look at some of the questions that opened the first chapter of this book, and let us examine the answers that have emerged:

1. WHAT ARE THE AIMS OF WORLD COMMUNISM TODAY?

World communism aims at the victory of its ideas everywhere. It aims at world domination.

2. HAS IT ABANDONED THE IDEA OF GLOBAL REVOLUTION?

No. But it has learned many lessons in three decades of existence. Klement Gottwald, the Communist Premier of Czechoslovakia, told the central committee of his party in September, 1946, "Experience and the classical Marxist-Leninist teachings show that the dictatorship of the proletariat and the setting up of Soviets is not the only way leading to socialism. Under certain conditions it can be achieved in a different manner." The London *Communist Review,* commenting on this and other statements by leading Communists, said that "the road to socialism will vary widely," because of "important differences in relations between parties, use and adaptation of historical forms of local and national government, tempo of agricultural and industrial reform." Thus, under the Seventh Strategy of world communism, global revolution is to be carried out by varying methods.

3. DOES MOSCOW STILL CONTROL COMMUNIST PARTIES THROUGHOUT THE WORLD?

Yes. Like an efficient executive, Moscow has delegated authority to trained representatives throughout the world. By delegating authority, efficiency has been improved, but local policies regard the needs and desires of the Soviet Union as uppermost. Statements by Soviet leaders and articles in leading Russian Communist journals provide the directives for party activities in every part of the globe.

4. AND JUST HOW STRONG ARE THE COMMUNISTS?

In 1947, there were about twelve million organized Communists outside the Soviet Union, and six million members of the Russian Communist Party. Through numerous international or national organizations not specifically labeled Communist, world communism exercises a political influence many times greater than that implied by mere membership figures. We can distinguish five stages in Communist progress today:

(a) *Complete Domination.* This has been achieved in the USSR, and in the territories it has incorporated. To the regions that formed the Soviet Union at the outset of World War II were added about 275,000 square miles, with a total population of some twenty-five million. By incorporation, communism extended its complete dominance to the Baltic states of Lithuania, Latvia, and Estonia; to the former Finnish territories of Petsamo and western Karelia, the former Polish regions east of the Curzon Line; the Carpatho-Ukraine, which was ceded by Czechoslovakia; the former German area of Königsberg in East Prussia; to Bessarabia, which Romania had seized from Russia after World War I; to northern Bukovina; and to the Kuril Islands, which, together with southern Sakhalin, were placed in Soviet hands by the Allied heads of state. To these territories, which now form part of the Soviet Union, other states in which Communist regimes have gained effective dominance should be added: Yugoslavia, Bulgaria, Albania, the Mongolian People's Republic (Outer Mongolia), the Communist-held territories of China, and Soviet-occupied north Korea.

(b) *Leadership in Coalitions.* The line between complete dominance and Communist leadership in coalition regimes is thin. Yet it exists. In Czechoslovakia, Communists gained decisive governmental control by democratic means. In Poland and eastern Germany, both under Soviet army control, coalitions exist in little more than name (those of Yugoslavia, Bulgaria, Albania, and so forth, are coalitions in name only). Romania has a coalition government under Communist leadership, and conditions in Hungary are similar.

(c) *Important Influence in National Affairs.* Communist parties have emerged from World War II with prestige and power. Their policies are of importance in the internal and external affairs of France, Italy, Finland, and Chile. They hold a key position in Cuba, and they strongly influenced the affairs of Brazil in 1945 and 1946. In the colonial world, communism is gaining in prestige and power.

(d) *Militant Minority Status.* In the United States, the British Commonwealth of Nations, in the Scandinavian countries, the Lowlands, Switzerland, and several Latin-American nations, Communists form a militant and active minority. They do not decisively influence the internal or external affairs of these states, but they aspire to do so.

(e) *Illegality.* In several Latin-American countries, in Spain, Portugal, Turkey, and elsewhere in the Near East, communism is illegal. Illegality is not necessarily a barrier to successful agitation.

5. How ARE THEY ORGANIZED, WHO ARE THEIR LEADERS, HOW DO THEY WORK?

The pattern of organization still conforms basically to the example offered by the Communist Party of the Soviet Union (Bolsheviks). The majority of top Communist leaders throughout the world are veterans of revolution. Many of them are graduates from Moscow's International Lenin School. The work of Communist parties has been facilitated by the Seventh Strategy, in that it permits them to adapt themselves to local conditions.

6. IS COMMUNIST USE OF PARLIAMENTARY DEMOCRATIC METHODS ONLY A TEMPORARY DEVICE, OR DOES IT REVEAL A SINCERE CHANGE OF CHARACTER?

It is not a sincere change of character. Use of parliamentary methods was favored by Lenin in his book, *Left-wing Communism,* because "it is only from within such institutions as bourgeois parliaments that Communists can, and must, wage a long and persistent struggle" to "prove to the backward masses why such parliaments deserve to be destroyed." This principle has not been altered, although the shell of parliamentary procedure continues to exist in Communist-controlled countries. As we have seen, the Canadian Communist Party considers its parliamentary work a means "to be a monkey-wrench" in the machinery of law-making bodies.

SECURITY WITH LIBERTY

Can our economic system prevent another world-wide breakdown?

The answer to this question cannot wait until a new crisis is upon us. The battle against economic-political disintegration must be prepared in advance. Only then will it be carried out successfully. A depression-weakened America would be unable to carry out the "Marshall Plan," or any other effort to normalize Europe's political-economic scene.

Communism expects a crucial American depression in the very near future. It is warning the world against United States instability. It is preparing for the time when, it expects, America will suck the world into a giant economic whirlpool.

If past economic cycles are an indication, the period from 1948 to 1955 may well put western civilization to its major test. How can the west meet this test? How can it answer the challenge of communism today and tomorrow? Not by shrieking, by wildly waving its arms, by suppression or persecution. Because, in the final analysis, the coming struggle of western civilization is not a fight against communism. It is a battle against human despair. Communism is a danger signal. It is symptom, not cause.

That is why suppression of communism is the counsel of the ignorant and shortsighted. To stifle a coughing spell will not cure pneumonia. And the banning of Communist organizations is no more than a quack remedy.

Communism grows powerful where fabulous wealth clashes with abject poverty. Ultra-left and ultra-right agitation is least successful where there is an alert and substantial middle class. Another depression, however, might easily decimate the middle class and swell the armies of desperation. Then communism will make its political-economic alternative doubly attractive to men and women in despair.

Although it is one of man's most cherished hopes, liberty has a price. Where freedom is the price of security, the frightened will choose security. Where liberty is the price of bread, the starving will choose bread. In times of chaos, liberty, like an old and cherished family possession, may be sold on the black market of despair.

The answer to communism is not the suppression of communism. It will not do to answer its challenge in negative terms and by negative actions. The answer is: security with liberty, rather than at the price of liberty; bread with freedom, rather than at the price of freedom.

No, it can never be enough to make loans for armaments or to bolster governments whose only claim to excellence is their anti-Communist fervor. In various parts of the world, the answer to communism differs. But some of its major points are:

1. The reduction of enormous social gaps through taxation reform.

2. Education and emancipation of the underprivileged. The spread of literacy and hygiene.

3. The strengthening of social-security laws.

4. The extension of private or community systems of insurance in health, unemployment, old age, accident, and other critical fields.

5. The United States must do its utmost to make its own domestic economy depression-proof, by providing safeguards against the effects of economic stagnation.

6. The fight against trade barriers must continue with vigor and persistence. The need for imports on a basis for a continual flow of exports must be fully realized not only in the United States, but in all strong producing nations.

7. Religious leaders need to reexamine their work as it extends beyond worship into the field of social relations, so that true faith may again take the place of emptiness and frustration.

R 8. Education must strive to overcome the shortsighted group interests of business and labor groups, opening the way to fuller understanding of the economic and political interdependence of nations.

R 9. Growing appreciation of interdependence of individuals can help to overcome the remnants of man's herd instincts and tribal traditions, which express themselves in group discrimination.

R 10. The study of world political factors needs to be coordinated, so that national and regional conditions can be evaluated more accurately in their relationship to each other.

WORLD PATRIOTISM

Communism has adapted its Seventh Strategy to the lack of imagination, the provincialism and shortsighted selfishness among its opponents. Its coordinated efforts are well planned to deal with confused and emotional nationalist-regional interests.

But there is a common denominator for the interest of men everywhere. It is not communism. To find this real basis of man's interests, we need to look beyond our civic price, our professional egotisms, our nationalist self-intoxications, our provincialist approaches to economic and political questions.

We have seen that communism cannot be understood as it presents itself in one country or another, in one region or another. It is part of one great movement, which is fully grasped only when viewed as a whole. To confront it, more is needed than the limited scope of individual fear, or of national self-preservation. It certainly cannot be halted under the flag of patriotism, which may easily be snatched away by the ultra-right.

Communism can be effectively confronted only by a newly developed force: World Patriotism, which accepts the challenge of tomorrow with an understanding of the interdependence of people on this small planet.

Western civilization can answer communism only by positive and constructive actions. It cannot fight communism on the battlefields—in mountainous Greek Macedonia, in China's Shensi province, or in Near Eastern deserts—and expect to win lasting victory. The tractor is, in the end, a weapon superior to the tank. The fire in the hearth sheds more warmth than a flame thrower.

Among the weapons in tomorrow's struggle, only security can make fear obsolete.

VII
APPENDIX

INDOCTRINATION TECHNIQUES

*The following analysis of Communist indoctrination techniques which ulti-
mately led to espionage activities in the service of the Soviet Union, has been
excerpted from the Report of the Royal Commission of Canada, issued June
27, 1946 (see Chapter 22, Canada: Atomic Espionage, page 261):*

Perhaps the most startling single aspect of the entire Fifth Column network
is the uncanny success with which the Soviet agents were able to find Canadians who were willing to betray their country and to supply to agents of a
foreign power secret information to which they had access in the course of
their work, despite oaths of allegiance, of office, and of secrecy which they
had taken.

Many of the Canadian public servants implicated in this espionage network were persons with an unusually high degree of education, and many were
well regarded by those who worked with them in agencies and departments
of the public service, as persons of marked ability and intelligence. . . .

The motivation which led persons such as these to take part in an espionage
conspiracy directed against Canada by agents of a foreign power is significant
and seems to us to be of great importance. There is no evidence that monetary
incentive played an important part in the *original* motivation of those persons
whose ideology was sympathetic to the Communist cause, who agreed to act
as espionage agents.

The evidence before us shows that in the great majority of cases the motivation was inextricably linked with courses of psychological development
carried on under the guise of activities of a secret section of what is ostensibly
a Canadian political movement, the Labour-Progressive Party (Communist
Party of Canada); that these secret "development" courses are very much
more widespread than the espionage network itself; and that the Canadian
members of the espionage network themselves took an active part in directing
and furthering such courses for other Canadians, which were calculated to
allow them to draw suitably "developed" persons later into active participation
and thus to expand the network itself. . . . In virtually all cases, as has been
stated, the agents were recruited from among "cells" or study groups of secret
members or adherents of the Communist Party (Labour-Progressive Party).

It seems to be general policy of the Communist Party to discourage certain
selected sympathizers among certain categories of the population from joining
that political Party openly. Instead, these sympathizers are invited to join
secret "cells" or study groups, and to take pains to keep their adherence to the
Party from the knowledge of their acquaintances who are not also members
of the Communist Party. The categories of the population from which secret
members are recruited include students, scientific workers, teachers, office and
business workers, persons engaged in any type of administrative activity, and
any group likely to obtain any type of government employment.

The reason suggested by some of the agents in their evidence for the curious
practice of keeping their political affiliations secret was that by this means

485

they would avoid unfavourable discrimination in obtaining positions. There were enough such cases to justify us in concluding that this practice is a Party technique, the real objectives and results of which seem to be quite different.

One objective, we conclude, is that this technique facilitates the achievement of a basic policy of the Communist Party, viz., to get control, through the election of secret members to the directing committees, of as many types of functionary organizations as possible, including trade unions, professional associations and broad non-party organizations such as youth movements, and civil liberties unions. Similarly, secret members or adherents of the Communist Party may be used to take the lead in organizing new, broad and ostensibly non-political organizations, after which they obtain for themselves and other secret adherents key positions on controlling committees of the organization. By these means the technique of secret membership is calculated to facilitate essentially dishonest but not ineffective methods of propaganda in the interests of a foreign state. . . .

Control by the Communist Party over a broad organization such as the Canadian Association of Scientific Workers could be used in a variety of ways not only for propaganda purposes, but eventually as a base for recruiting adherents to that Party from among scientists, and in due course no doubt for recruiting additional espionage agents in key positions in the national life.

But there would appear to be a further basic object and result of this technique of secret membership of the Communist Party organized in secret "cells" or study-groups. This object is to accustom the young Canadian adherent gradually to an atmosphere and an ethic of conspiracy. The general effect on the young man or woman over a period of time of *secret* meetings, *secret* acquaintances, and *secret* objectives, plans and policies, can easily be imagined. The technique seems calculated to develop the psychology of a double life and double standards.

To judge from much of the evidence, the secret adherent is apparently encouraged never to be honest or frank, outside the secret "cell" meetings, about his real political attitudes or views, and apparently is led to believe that frankness in these matters is the equivalent of dangerous indiscretion and a potential menace to the organization as a whole. . . . An inevitable result of this emphasis on a conspiratorial atmosphere and behaviour even in political discussions, correspondence, and meetings which are in themselves perfectly legal and indeed are the cherished right of everyone in a democratic society, would seem to be the gradual disintegration of normal moral principles such as frankness, honesty, integrity and a respect for the sanctity of oaths.

A reading of the evidence before us, taken as a whole, indicates also that this technique seems calculated to affect gradually and unconsciously the secret adherent's attitude towards Canada. Often some of the agents seem to have begun their Communist associations through a burning desire to reform and improve Canadian society according to their lights. But one effect of prolonged habituation to conspiratorial methods and the conditions of secrecy in which these people work is to isolate them from the great mass of the Canadian people. As the courses of study in the "cells" undermine gradually the loyalty of the young man or woman who joins them, it is necessary to say something as to the content of the courses pursued in them, as that is reflected by the evidence.

The curriculum includes the study of political and philosophic works, some of them far from superficial, selected to develop in the students an essentially critical attitude towards Western democratic society. This phase of the preparation also includes a series of discussions on current affairs, designed to further a critical attitude toward the ideals of democratic society. But this curriculum would appear in reality to be designed not to promote social reform where it might be required, but to weaken the loyalty of the group member towards his or her own society as such.

Linked with these studies at all stages, moreover, goes an organized indoctrination calculated to create in the mind of the study-group member an essentially uncritical acceptance at its face value of the propaganda of a foreign state. Accordingly the study-groups are encouraged to subscribe to Communist books and periodicals. . . .

In some cases the effect of these study courses seems to be a gradual development of a sense of divided loyalties, or in extreme cases of a transferred loyalty. Thus it seems to happen that through these study-groups some adherents, who begin by feeling that Canadian society is not democratic or not equalitarian enough for their taste, are gradually led to transfer a part or most of their loyalties to another country, apparently without reference to whether that other country is in actual fact more or less democratic or equalitarian than Canada.

Indeed, a sense of internationalism seems in many cases to play a definite role in one stage of the courses. In these cases the Canadian sympathiser is first encouraged to develop a sense of loyalty, not directly to a foreign state, but to what he conceives to be an international ideal. This subjective internationalism is then usually linked almost inextricably through the indoctrination courses and the intensive exposure to the propaganda of a particular foreign state, with the current conception of the national interests of that foreign state and with the current doctrines and policies of Communist Parties throughout the world.

A further objective, pursued through the study-group, is gradually to inculcate in the secret membership of the Communist Party a habit of complete obedience to the dictates of senior members and officials of the Party hierarchy. This is apparently accomplished through a constant emphasis, in the indoctrination courses, on the importance of organization as such, and by the gradual creation in the mind of the new adherent or sympathiser, of an over-riding moral sense of "loyalty to the Party." This "loyalty to the Party" in due course takes the place in the member's mind of the earlier loyalty to certain principles professed by the Party propaganda.

In view of the rigidly hierarchic organization of the Communist Party, particularly in its secret sections, the concept of "loyalty to the party" means in practice, rigid obedience of adherents to those party members who are recognized as occupying a senior position in the hierarchy. . . .

The indoctrination courses in the study groups are apparently calculated not only to inculcate a high degree of "loyalty to the Party" and "obedience to the Party," but to instill in the mind of the adherent the view that loyalty and obedience to the leadership of this organization takes precedence over his loyalty to Canada, entitles him to disregard his oaths of allegiance and secrecy, and thus destroys his integrity as a citizen. . . .

In many cases prolonged membership in the Communist Party seems to have resulted in a very high degree of discipline and to have induced a semi-military habit of largely unquestioning obedience to "orders" and "Party policy." Such habits, once developed, naturally made the task of the espionage recruiting agents, who are senior members of the Party, relatively simple. . . . Thus the leaders of the Fifth Column solved what would appear at first sight to be their most difficult problem—that of motivation, or finding capable and well-placed Canadians who would be willing to engage in espionage against Canada for a foreign power—by means of a widespread system of propaganda and in particular by organizing a system of intensive study-groups. This system has been functioning for years, and was already a going concern used for espionage in 1935.

These groups have provided a large base of Canadians in various stages of carefully induced evolution—emotional, mental, and moral—from which base the leaders can recruit those who are considered adequately "developed" into expanding illegal networks for espionage or other purposes.

A further technical advantage, which this system has provided to the leading organizers of the espionage network, has been a surprising degree of security from detection. By concentrating their requests to assist in espionage within the membership of secret sections of the Communist Party, the leaders were apparently able to feel quite confident—and apparently with reason based on an experience in Canada over a period of at least eleven years—that even if the adherent or member should refuse to engage in activities so clearly illegal and which constitute so clear a betrayal of his or her own country—such adherent or member would in any case not consider denouncing the espionage recruiting agent to the Canadian public or to the Canadian authorities.

Not one even of those who have described, in evidence before us, serious hesitation and struggles with their consciences which they underwent before they agreed to act as spies against Canada, ever suggested to us that they contemplated taking the one loyal or legal course of action—i.e. reporting the criminal request to the Canadian authorities. This is a striking illustration of the efficiency of the Communist study-groups in inducing a motivation for clearly illegal Party assignments directed against Canada.

What appears from the evidence to be the real purpose of the study-group or "cell" organization—as a wide and ever expanding base for the recruiting, psychological development and organization of a Fifth Column operating in the interests of a foreign power—would have been frustrated if rank and file members of these groups or junior adherents of the Communist Party of Canada had been aware of the real objectives and policies of . . . senior members of the conspiracy.

The evidence we have heard shows that at each stage of "development" the adherent is kept in ignorance of the wider ramifications and real objectives of the organization, to one of the fringes of which he has allowed himself to be attached. Indeed it appears from the evidence that some at least of the adherents recruited to study-groups are not told that these groups are in reality secret "cells" or units of the Communist Party. . . .

Any small study-group, however called, which will allow more experienced Communists to influence and simultaneously to study the psychological development of potential "recruits" will do so in the early stages of the new recruit's "development." Participation of secret Communists in genuinely informal small discussion groups appears to be one of the methods used to attempt to develop some or all of the other participants and gradually draw them into more specifically Communist groups, if possible by turning the earlier informal body into such a unit without the full, immediate realization by all the other participants of the metamorphosis. Alternatively, persons considered suitable for "development" can be designated to cell leaders and then invited to join the cell instead of continuing with the broader group.

The extent of the secret section of the Communist Party is not normally disclosed at any time to the junior members of the secret group. The leader of each such group, who attends secret meetings of five or more such group leaders, will know them, plus the secret "chairman" of these meetings. . . . However, over a period of time secret members will get to know many others through joint participation in various "front organizations" and otherwise, though they may not know the extent of their "development" unless designated to work with them for some purpose of the Party leaders.

It is, apparently, not the present practice for secret members of the Party to fill out any membership forms, or sign any declaration, or to be given any membership cards. This relatively loose system obviously assists in maintaining the secrecy of the organization. But it appears also to play a role in the expansion of the organization, since at each stage of his "development" the adherent is allowed to feel that he is still politically independent and merely assisting in the general activities of the movement without taking at any time, what he might consider to be a specific and binding step to acquire or ratify definite membership. This technique allows the development courses to proceed and to have their gradual effect on the adherent without raising any unnecessary resistance in the adherent's mind to any specific stage of early development.

Apparently at each stage of "development" the adherent is carefully kept from an appreciation of the nature of tasks likely to be assigned to him when he is considered adequately "developed" for the next stage. Apparently also many even among relative senior and "developed" secret members of the Communist Party are kept unaware of the nature and existence of specifically illegal activities, directed against Canada, which are carried on by a section of the organization which they support. Indeed, most persons actively engaged in such illegal activities are apparently given to understand that their activities are exceptional, and are kept quite unaware of the extent to which they are carried on by top leaders. . . .

Regarding the original attraction of Canadians to the "development" courses or study-group organizations, it is difficult to speak with certainty. The appeal naturally varied greatly with each individual. In some cases it lay apparently in the highly systematized metaphysical concepts used by the Communist

Party in its propaganda directed to certain types of "intellectuals" and students.

A factor which appears to have played a part in first attracting at least one of the Canadian espionage agents whose evidence we have heard, was the belief that through these study groups he could fight against the social evils of anti-semitism and racial intolerance. . . . In some cases a desire for companionship and intellectual discussion may have played its part. With certain persons there is apparently an emotional appeal and glamour, as it were a sense of adventure, inherent in the conspiratorial methods and purposive activity of the groups. With more sophisticated persons, fascination by what may appear to them to be the efficiency of the unusual and essentially totalitarian system of Party organization through pyramiding cells may offer an attractive appeal.

In the vast majority of cases, one important element in the original appeal would seem to have been propaganda carried out by the Communist Party for various measures of "social reform" in Canada. The policy of carrying on propaganda for various domestic measures which in themselves are calculated to appeal to a substantial section of the Canadian people, has obviously served two important objectives of the leaders of the Fifth Column.

In the first place, by associating such domestic propaganda, in the minds of as many people as possible, with the external propaganda of a particular foreign state, this policy serves in itself to "carry," by implication, that foreign state's propaganda. This is a common and very effective non-rational technique of modern advertising. An obvious commercial example is the use of a pretty face in advertisements for cigarettes.

Secondly, such domestic propaganda has unquestionably played an important part in recruiting Canadians for the "development" courses calculated eventually to make these Canadians instruments for more sinister and illegal Fifth Column purposes.

By these means, a number of young Canadians, public servants and others, who begin with a desire to advance causes which they consider worthy, have been induced into joining study groups of the Communist Party. They are persuaded to keep this adherence secret. They have then been led step by step along the ingenious psychological development courses we have outlined, until under the influence of sophisticated and unscrupulous leaders they have been persuaded to engage in illegal activities directed against the safety and interests of their own society.

Essentially what has happened is the transplanting of a conspiratorial technique, which was first developed in less fortunate countries to promote an underground struggle against tyranny, to a democratic society where it is singularly inappropriate.

MEMBERSHIP AND LEADERS

The following table presents the membership and leaders of Communist parties (or parties of Communists under different names) in 1947. Membership figures are based either on claims made by the parties themselves, or on the most reliable estimates available. The names of the most prominent leaders were selected. These did not always coincide with the secretary-general of each party, nor are the persons listed necessarily the most influential in shaping policies on a regional level.

Country	Membership	Prominent Leader
Albania	5,000	Enver Hoxha
Algeria	25,000	Amar Ouzegane
Argentina	30,000	Rodolfo Ghioldi
Australia	25,000	L. L. Sharkey
Austria	150,000	Ernst Fischer
Belgium	95,000	Edgar Lalmand
Brazil	130,000	Luíz Carlos Prestes
Bulgaria	450,000	Georgi Dimitrov
Burma	4,000	Thakin Than Tun
Canada	25,000	Tim Buck
Chile	50,000	Carlos Contreras Labarca
China	2,000,000	Mao Tse-tung
Colombia	5,000	Augusto Durán
Costa Rica	20,000	Manuel Mora Valverde
Cuba	200,000	Blas Roca
Cyprus	4,000	Ploutis Servas
Czechoslovakia	1,250,000	Klement Gottwald
Denmark	60,000	Aksel Larsen
Dominican Republic	2,000	Machado Fuenmayor Arrieta
Ecuador	2,500	Pedro Saad
Finland	25,000	Ville Pessi
France	1,300,000	Maurice Thorez
Germany (east)	1,600,000	Wilhelm Pieck
Germany (west)	350,000	Max Reimann
Great Britain	43,000	Harry Pollitt
Greece	250,000	Nicholas Zachariadis
Haiti	500	Etienne D. Charlier
Hungary	650,000	Matyas Rákosi
Iceland	1,000	Brynjolfur Bjarnason
India	54,000	Puran Chand Joshi
Indonesia	6,000	Alimin Prawirodirdjo
Iran	75,000	Fereidoun Keshavarz
Italy	2,200,000	Palmiro Togliatti
Japan	60,000	Sanzo Nozaka
Korea (north)	40,000	Kim Il Sung
Korea (south)	10,000	Pak Huen Yung
Lebanon	15,000	Mustafa Al Ariss
Luxembourg	5,000	Dominique Urbany
Malaya	10,000	Ta Kah Kee
Mexico	25,000	Dionisio Encina
Netherlands	50,000	Paul de Groot

Country	Membership	Prominent Leader
New Zealand	2,000	Alexander Brennan
Nicaragua	2,000	
Northern Ireland	500	
Norway	33,000	Peder Furubotn
Palestine	1,000	Samuel Mikunis
Panama	500	Cristóbal L. Segundo
Paraguay	(clandestine)	Oscar Creydt
Peru	35,000	Jorge Acosta
Philippines	3,000	Pedro Casto
Poland	600,000	Boleslaw Bierut
Portugal	(clandestine)	
Puerto Rico	1,000	Juan Santos Rivera
Romania	500,000	Georghe Gheorghiu-Dej
Spain	(clandestine)	Dolores Ibarruri
Sweden	46,000	Sven Linderot
Switzerland	20,000	Léon Nicole
Syria	8,000	Khalid Bagdash
Tunisia	20,000	Ali Djerad
Union of South Africa	1,500	Moses Monai Kotane
United States	75,000	William Z. Foster
USSR	6,000,000	Joseph Stalin
Uruguay	15,000	Eugenio Gómez
Venezuela	20,000	Juan Bautista Fuenmayor
Yugoslavia	150,000	Josip Broz

TABLE OF KEY PUBLICATIONS

Following is a tabulation of publications issued by parties of Communists in various parts of the world. Many more Communist newspapers and periodicals are being published, but those listed occupy key positions in Communist propaganda and agitation.

Country	Name of Publication	City	Frequency
Albania	Bashkimi	Tirana	Daily
Algeria	Liberté	Algiers	Weekly
Argentina	La Hora	Buenos Aires	Daily
	Orientación	Buenos Aires	Weekly
Australia	Communist Review	Sydney	Monthly
	The Tribune	Sydney	Bi-weekly
Austria	Oesterreichische Volksstimme	Vienna	Daily
Belgium	Le Drapeau Rouge	Brussels	Daily
Brazil	Tribuna Popular	Rio de Janeiro	Daily
	Hoje	São Paulo	Weekly
Bulgaria	Rabotnichesko Delo	Sofia	Daily
Canada	Daily Tribune	Montreal	Daily
Chile	El Siglo	Santiago	Daily
	Principios	Santiago	Monthly
China	Emancipation Daily	Yenan	Daily
Colombia	Diario Popular	Bogotá	Daily
	Union Popular	Bogotá	Weekly
Costa Rica	Trabajo	San José	Weekly
Cuba	Hoy	Havana	Daily
	Dialectica	Havana	Quarterly
Czechoslovakia	Rude Pravo	Prague	Daily
Denmark	Land og Folk	Copenhagen	Daily
Finland	Vapaa Sana	Helsinki	Daily
	Vapaa Pohjola	Helsinki	Weekly
France	Humanité	Paris	Daily
	Les Cahiers du Communisme	Paris	Monthly
Germany	Der Vorwaerts	Berlin	Daily
	Neuer Weg	Berlin	Monthly
Great Britain	Daily Worker	London	Daily
	Labour Monthly	London	Monthly
	Communist Review	London	Monthly
	World News and Views	London	Weekly
Greece	Rizopastis	Athens	Daily
	Kommounistike Epitheorisi	Athens	Monthly
Haiti	La Nation	Port-au-Prince	Monthly
Hungary	Szabad Nep	Budapest	Daily
	Tarsadalmi Szemle	Budapest	Monthly
Iceland	Tjhodviljinn	Reykjavik	Daily
India	People's Age	Bombay	Weekly
Indonesia	Bintang Merah	Soerakarta	Weekly
Iran	Mardom	Teheran	Daily
	Aras	Teheran	Daily

493

Country	Name of Publication	City	Frequency
Italy	L'Unita	Rome	Daily
	Azione Comunista	Rome	Monthly
Japan	Akahata Shimbun	Tokyo	Daily
Korea (north)	Nodong Sinmun	Pyengyang	Daily
Korea (south)	Dok Lip Sinpo	Seoul	Daily
Lebanon	El Chaab	Beirut	Daily
Luxembourg	D'Zeitung	Luxembourg	Daily
Mexico	La Hora	Mexico City	Daily
	La Voz del México	Mexico City	Weekly
	Orientación	Mexico City	Weekly
Morocco	Espoir	Casablanca	Daily
Netherlands	De Waarheid	Amsterdam	Daily
	Vorwaarts	Amsterdam	Weekly
	Politiek en Cultuur	Amsterdam	Monthly
New Zealand	Communist Review	Wellington	Monthly
Norway	Friheten	Oslo	Daily
	Var Vei	Oslo	Monthly
Palestine	Kol Ha'am	Tel Aviv	Daily
	Volksstimme	Tel Aviv	Weekly
Panama	La Opinión	Panama City	Weekly
Philippines	Katubusan	Manila	Weekly
Poland	Glos Ludu	Warsaw	Daily
Portugal	Avante (clandestine)	Lisbon	Monthly
Puerto Rico	El Boricu	San Juan	Semi-monthly
Romania	Scanteia	Bucharest	Daily
Spain	Mundo Obrero (clandestine)	Madrid	Weekly
Sweden	Ny Dag	Stockholm	Daily
Switzerland	Voix d'Ouvrière	Geneva	Daily
	Socialisme	Geneva	Monthly
	Der Vorwaerts	Basle	Daily
	Sozialismus	Basle	Monthly
	Lavoratore	Tecino	Weekly
USSR	Pravda	Moscow	Daily
	Bolshevik	Moscow	Monthly
United States	Daily Worker	New York	Daily
	People's World	San Francisco	Daily
	New Masses	New York	Weekly
	Political Affairs	New York	Monthly
Syria	Sait al Shaud	Damascus	Daily
Tunisia	L'Avenir	Tunis	Weekly
Union of South Africa	Inkululeko	Johannesburg	Monthly
	Guardian	Cape Town	Weekly
Uruguay	El Diario Popular	Montevideo	Daily
	Justicia	Montevideo	Weekly
Venezuela	El Nacional	Caracas	Daily
Yugoslavia	Borba	Belgrade	Daily

DISSOLUTION OF COMINTERN

*Following is the announcement of the presidium of the executive committee
of the Communist International on the dissolution of the Communist International, as published in Moscow on May 15, 1943.*

The historical role of the Communist International, organized in 1919 as the
result of the political collapse of the overwhelming majority of the old pre-war
workers' parties, consisted in that it preserved the teachings of Marxism from
vulgarization and distortion by opportunist elements of the labor movement.
In a number of countries it helped to unite the vanguard of the advanced
workers into genuine workers' parties, and it helped them to mobilize the
mass of toilers in defense of their economic and political interests for struggle
against fascism and war, which fascism had been preparing, and for the support of the Soviet Union as the main bulwark against fascism.

The Communist International revealed in good time the true significance of
the "Anti-Comintern Pact" as a weapon in the war preparations of the Hitlerites. Long prior to the war the Communist International tirelessly exposed the
base, undermining activities of the Hitlerites in foreign states, who masked
these with outcries about alleged interference of the Communist International
in the internal affairs of these states.

But long before the war it had already become increasingly clear that to
the extent that the internal as well as the international situation of individual
countries became more complicated, the solution of the problems of the labor
movement of each individual country through the medium of some international
center would meet with insuperable obstacles.

The deep difference in the historical roads of development of each country
of the world, the diverse character and even the contradiction in their social
orders, the difference in level and rate of their social and political development, and finally, the difference in the degree of consciousness and organization of the workers, conditioned also the various problems which face the working class of each individual country.

The entire course of events for the past quarter of a century, as well as the
accumulated experiences of the Communist International, have convincingly
proven that the organizational form for uniting the workers as chosen by the
First Congress of the Communist International, and which corresponded to the
needs of the initial period of the rebirth of the labor movement, more and more
outlived itself in proportion to the growth of this movement and to the increasing complexity of problems in each country; and that this form even
became a hindrance to the further strengthening of the national workers'
parties.

The world war unleashed by the Hitlerites still further sharpened the differences in the conditions in various countries, showing the deep line of
demarcation between the countries which became the bearers of Hitlerite
tyranny and the freedom-loving peoples united in the mighty anti-Hitler
coalition.

Whereas in the countries of the Hitlerite bloc the basic task of the workers,
toilers and all honest people is to contribute in every conceivable way toward

the defeat of this bloc by undermining the Hitlerite war machine from within and by helping to overthrow the governments responsible for the war, in countries of the anti-Hitler coalition the sacred duty of the broadest masses of the people and first and foremost of the progressive workers is to support in every way the war efforts of the governments in these countries for the sake of the speediest destruction of the Hitlerite bloc and to secure friendly collaboration between nations on the basis of their equal rights.

At the same time it must not be overlooked that the individual countries which adhere to the anti-Hitler coalition also have their specific tasks. Thus, for instance, in countries occupied by Hitlerites and which have lost their state independence, the basic task of progressive workers and broad masses of people is to develop the armed struggle which is growing into a national war of liberation against Hitlerite Germany.

At the same time, the war of liberation of the freedom-loving peoples against Hitlerite tyranny, which set into motion the broadest masses of people who are uniting in the ranks of the mighty anti-Hitler coalition irrespective of party or religion, made it still more evident that the national upsurge and mobilization of the masses for speediest victory over the enemy can best and most fruitfully be supplied by the vanguard of the labor movement of each country within the framework of its state.

The Seventh Congress of the Communist International, held in 1935, taking into consideration the changes which had come to pass in the international situation as well as in the labor movement—changes which demanded greater flexibility and independence of its sections in solving the problems facing them—already then emphasized the need for the Executive Committee of the Communist International, when deciding upon all the problems of the labor movement, "to proceed in deciding any question from the concrete situation and specific conditions obtaining in each particular country and as a rule to avoid direct intervention in internal organizational matters of the Communist Party."

The Executive Committee of the Communist International was guided by these same considerations when it took note of and approved the decision of the Communist Party of the United States of America in November, 1940, to leave the ranks of the Communist International.

Communists, guided by the teachings of the founders of Marxism-Leninism, have never advocated the preservation of those organizational forms which have become obsolete. They have always subordinated the organizational forms of the labor movement and its methods of work to the basic political interests of the labor movement as a whole, to the peculiarities of given concrete historical conditions, and to those problems which arise directly from these conditions.

They remember the example of the great Marx who united the progressive workers into the ranks of the International Workingmen's Association. And after the First International had fulfilled its historical task, having laid the basis for the development of workers' parties in the countries of Europe and America, Marx, as a result of the growing need to create national workers' mass parties, brought about the dissolution of the First International, inasmuch as this form of organization no longer corresponded to this need.

Proceeding from the above-stated considerations, and taking into account the growth and political maturity of the Communist Parties and their leading cadres in the individual countries, and also in view of the fact that during the present war a number of sections have raised the question of the dissolution of the Communist International as the guiding center of the international labor movement, the Presidium of the Executive Committee of the Communist International, unable owing to the conditions of world war to convene a congress of the Communist International, permits itself to submit for approval by the sections of the Communist International the following proposal:

To dissolve the Communist International as the guiding center of the international labor movement, releasing the sections of the Communist International from obligations ensuing from the constitution and decisions of the congresses of the Communist International.

The Presidium of the Executive Committee of the Communist International calls upon all adherents of the Communist International to concentrate their forces on all-round support and active participation in the liberation war of the peoples and states of the anti-Hitler Coalition in order to hasten the destruction of the moral enemy of the working people—German fascism and its allies and vassals.

Signed by the members of the Presidium of the Executive Committee of the Communist International: Gottwald, Dimitrov, Zhdanov, Kolarov, Koplenig, Kuusinen, Manuilsky, Marty, Pieck, Thorez, Florin, Ercoli.

NINE PARTIES FORM INFORMATION BUREAU

Following are excerpts from a resolution signed by the Communist parties of the Soviet Union, Yugoslavia, Bulgaria, Romania, Hungary, Poland, France, Czechoslovakia, and Italy, as published at Moscow, October 5, 1947.

The conference states that the absence of connections between Communist parties who have taken part in this conference is in the present situation a serious shortcoming. Experience shows that such division between Communist parties is incorrect and harmful. The requirement for an exchange of experience and voluntary coordination of actions of the separate parties has become particularly necessary now in conditions of the complicated post-war international situation and when the disunity of Communist parties may lead to damage for the working class. . . .

The resolution established a Communist Information Bureau in Belgrade, and was followed by a manifesto which stated in part:

The battle of the two opposite camps—capitalistic and anti-capitalistic—is waged amid conditions of a further sharpening of the universal crisis of capitalism, a weakening of the forces of capitalism and a strengthening of the forces of socialism and democracy. Because of the above, the imperialist camp and its directing force, the United States of America, show a growing aggressive activity. This activity evolved at the same time in all spheres in the sphere of military and strategic activities, economic expansion and ideological warfare. . . . The Communist parties should place themselves in the vanguard of the Opposition against the imperialistic plans of expansion and aggression in all its manifestations. . . .

BIBLIOGRAPHY

A NOTE ON SOURCES

Official statements of Communist leaders and the publications of Communist parties have served as the main basis of the research for this book. They have been supplemented with data from other sources, which have served both as background for and contrast to the official Communist Party material.

To obtain a well-rounded picture of Communist activity in a specific country, it is desirable to study material on that country which deals with communism only peripherically or not at all. Readers of *World Communism Today* who seek to collect more material on the role of communism in a specific nation are urged to view Communist activities against the general political-economic development of the country under study. Otherwise, the danger of overemphasis on the role of communism is bound to be considerable. It is for this reason that the bibliography on the following pages contains not only a selection of works that have specific bearing on communism, but also volumes that may be used for background reading.

No study attempting to deal with world communism factually and definitively on a country-by-country basis in a single volume has heretofore been published. There are few exhaustive studies of individual Communist parties, compiled by either Communists or non-Communists. A notable exception is the detailed official *History of the Communist Party of the Soviet Union*, of which more than twenty million copies have been distributed in Russia and which has been translated into many languages; it does, of course, reflect completely the Stalinist point of view. An excellent analysis of trends and countertrends during the 1920's and early 1930's exists in Franz Borkenau's *World Communism* (published in Great Britain as *The Communist International*). The *History of Bolshevism* by Arthur Rosenberg should also be mentioned in this connection.

From the time of its foundation until its dissolution, the Comintern published the magazine the *Communist International* in several languages. The reader will have noticed that we have frequently cited that publication. Together with *Inprecorr* (International Press Correspondence), a newspaper service issued in the German language during the 1920's and early 1930's, the *Communist International* provides the best source material available on the earlier periods of world communism. There is no adequate substitute today for the discontinued *Communist International* and *Inprecorr*. It would be incorrect to assume that the weekly Moscow magazine *New Times*, which is published in several languages, replaces *Communist International*. The magazine of the Belgrade Communist Information Bureau, which began publication in November, 1947, may be regarded as a reliable policy guide for Communist parties.

The theoretical magazines issued by the various parties exchange material, and it is thus possible to get at least a cursory picture of world-wide activities. In the United States, the principal theoretical party publication is the monthly *Political Affairs* (formerly *The Communist*). The British Communist weekly *World News and Views* is concise, the *Labour Monthly* possibly the most ably edited Communist magazine issued anywhere today. *Les Cahiers du Communisme* (formerly *Les Cahiers du Bolshevisme*), published by the Communist Party of France, is important, because of the guiding position that leading

French Communists appear to have in world communism today. Communist key publications and their frequency of appearance are listed on pages 493 and 494 of the Appendix. These and others have been used as sources or for background information in the preparation of this book. All Communist parties issue pamphlets or books. To obtain a rounded view not only current but also earlier publications should be studied.

There does not, at this time, exist a central research depository of literature on modern communism, or of Communist publications. Establishment of such a depository or library would be highly desirable. A collection of manuscripts and documents exists at the Marx-Engels-Lenin Institute in Moscow. In the United States, the Hoover Library of Peace and War at Stanford University has published several exhaustive volumes of documents and analysis pertaining to the development of the Third International and the Bolshevik Revolution in Russia.

CHAPTER 1: A CENTURY OF REVOLUTION

Little Lenin Library, Pamphlet volumes, Nos. 1 to 28, International Publishers, New York, 1929 to 1942.

ANONYMOUS: *Karl Marx: Chronik seines Lebens*, Marx-Engels-Lenin Institute, Moscow, 1934.

ANONYMOUS: *Marx und Bakunin*, Birk, Munich, undated.

BELL, THOMAS: *A Dictionary of Terms and Quotations, Compiled from the Works of V. I. Lenin*, Lawrence and Wishart, London, 1942.

The Collected Works of V. I. Lenin, International Publishers, New York, 1927 to 1932.

EASTMAN, MAX: *Marxism: Is It Science?*, Norton, New York, 1940.

GANKIN, OLGA H., and H. H. FISHER: *The Bolsheviks and the World War: The Crisis of the Third International*, Stanford University Press, 1940.

KAUTSKY, KARL: *Demokratie oder Diktatur?*, Cassirer, Berlin, 1919.

KAUTSKY, KARL: *Die Diktatur des Proletariats*, Vienna, 1918.

KAUTSKY, KARL: *Friedrich Engels*, Kerr, Chicago, 1899.

KAUTSKY, KARL: *Die historische Leistung von Karl Marx*, Dietz, Berlin, 1933.

KAUTSKY, KARL: *Social Democracy versus Communism*, Rand School Press, New York, 1946.

KAUTSKY, KARL: *Wandlungen der Internationale*, in *Der Kampf*, Vienna, September, 1924.

LENIN, V. I.: *Die Diktatur des Proletariats und der Renegat Kautski*, Vulkan-Verlag, Leipzig, 1919.

LENZ, JOSEF: *Beiträge zur Geschichte der Arbeiterbewegung*, Hoym, Hamburg, 1930.

MARX, KARL: *Das Kapital*, Meissner, Hamburg, 1872.

MARX, KARL, and FRIEDRICH ENGELS: *Das Kommunistische Manifest*.

RENNER, KARL: *Karl Kautsky*, Dietz, Berlin, 1929.

SCHWARZSCHILD, LEOPOLD: The Red Prussian: *The Life and Legend of Karl Marx*, Scribner, New York, 1947.

SHADWELL, ARTHUR: *The Socialist Movement, 1824 to 1924*, P. Allen and Co., London, 1926.

CHAPTER 2: THE SEVEN STRATEGIES

BORKENAU, F.: *World Communism*, Norton, New York, 1939.

DIMITROV, GEORGI: *The United Front*, International Publishers, New York, 1938.

FLORINSKY, MICHAEL T.: *World Revolution and the USSR*, Macmillan, New York, 1933.

JAMES, CYRIL L. R.: *World Revolution, 1917-1936*, Secker & Warburg, London, 1937.

KOMOR, I.: *Ten Years of the Communist International*, Workers Library, New York, 1929.

LE ROSSIGNOL, JAMES E.: *From Marx to Stalin*, Crowell, New York, 1940.

YPSILON: *The Pattern of World Revolution*, Ziff-Davis, New York, 1947.

CHAPTER 3: USSR

CHAMBERLIN, WILLIAM HENRY: *Russia's Iron Age*, Little, Boston, 1934.

CHAMBERLIN, WILLIAM HENRY: *The Russian Revolution*, two volumes, Macmillan, New York, 1938.

DALLINN, DAVID J.: *The Real Soviet Russia*, Yale University Press, New Haven, 1944.

DEAN, VERA MICHELES: *Russia: Menace or Promise*, Holt, New York, 1947.

The History of the Civil War in the USSR, edited by M. Gorky, K. Voroshilov, S. Kirov, A. Zhdanov, J. Stalin, translation from the Russian edition of 1936, International Publishers, New York.

History of the Communist Party of the Soviet Union (Bolsheviks), edited by a Commission of the Central Committee of the CPSU, International Publishers, New York, 1939.

KERENSKY, ALEXANDER F.: *The Catastrophe*, Appleton Century, New York, 1927.

KERENSKY. ALEXANDER F.: *The Crucifixion of Liberty*, John Day, New York, 1934.

LEGISLATIVE REFERENCE SERVICE, LIBRARY OF CONGRESS: *Communism in Action. A Documented Study and Analysis of Communism in the Soviet Union*, United States Government Printing Office, Washington, D. C., 1946.

LENIN, V. I.: *The Revolution of 1917*, International Publishers, New York, 1929.

PARES, BERNARD: *A History of Russia*, Knopf, New York, 1944.

REED, JOHN: *Ten Days That Shook the World*, Boni & Liveright, New York, 1919.

ROSENBERG, ARTHUR: *A History of Bolshevism*, Oxford, New York-London, 1934.

SOLOVEYTCHIK, GEORGE: *Russia in Perspective*, Norton, New York, 1947.

STALIN, JOSEPH: *The Road to Power*, International Publishers, New York, 1937.

TROTSKY, LEON: *The History of the Russian Revolution*, three volumes, Simon and Schuster, New York, 1932.

WEBB, SIDNEY, and BEATRICE WEBB: *Soviet Communism*, Scribner, New York, 1938.

CHAPTER 4: FINLAND

KATAJA, S. A.: *Der Terror der Bourgeoisie in Finland*, Bef Verlag, Amsterdam, 1920.

KUUSINEN, OTTO: *Prepare for Power*, Workers Library, New York, 1933.

VON DER GOLTZ, GRAF RÜDIGER: *Als Politischer General im Osten*, K. F. Koehler Verlag, Leipzig, 1936.

CHAPTER 5: POLAND

ANONYMOUS: *Der weisse Terror in Poland,* Neuer Deutscher Verlag, Berlin, 1924.

CIECHANOWSKI, JAN: *Defeat in Victory,* Doubleday, New York, 1947.

LUTOSLAWSKI, WINCENTY: *Bolshevism and Poland,* Flinikowski, Paris, 1919.

MACHRAY, ROBERT: *The Poland of Pilsudski,* Allen & Unwin, London, 1936.

STRONG, ANNA LOUISE: *I Saw the New Poland,* Little, Boston, 1946.

CHAPTER 6: CZECHOSLOVAKIA

BIRLEY, ROBERT: *Czechoslovakia,* Clarendon Press, Oxford, 1939.

GEDYE, G. E. R.: *Betrayal in Central Europe,* Harper, New York, 1939.

HINDUS, MAURICE: *We Shall Live Again,* Doubleday, New York, 1937.

HINDUS, MAURICE: *Bright Passage,* Doubleday, New York, 1947.

KROFTA, KAMIL: *A Short History of Czechoslovakia,* McBride, New York, 1934.

PAPANEK, JAN: *Czechoslovakia,* International Universities Press, New York, 1945.

SETON-WATSON, ROBERT W.: *A History of the Czechs and Slovaks,* Hutchison, London, 1943.

CHAPTER 7: AUSTRIA

ADLER, FRIEDRICH: *Democracy and Revolution,* Rand School Press, New York, 1934.

BAUER, OTTO: *The Austrian Revolution,* Parsons, London, 1925.

BAUER, OTTO: *Bolschewismus und Sozialdemokratie,* Volksbuchhandlung, Vienna, 1921.

BULLOCK, MALCOLM: *Austria, 1918 to 1938,* Macmillan, London, 1939.

KLEIN, ERNST: *The Road to Disaster,* Allen & Unwin, London, 1940.

RATZENHOFER, EMIL: *Die Niederwerfung der Februarrevolte,* Verlag Militärwissenschaftliche Mitteilungen, Vienna, 1934.

SCHUSCHNIGG, KURT VON: *Austrian Requiem,* Putnam, New York, 1947.

CHAPTER 8: HUNGARY

BIZONY, LADISLAUS: *133 Tage Ungarischer Bolschewismus,* Verlag Waldheim-Eberle, Vienna, 1920.

BOEHM, WILHELM: *In Kreuzfeuer zweier Revolutionen,* Verlag für Kulturpolitik, Munich, 1924.

BOVET-GRISEL, RICHARD: *L'Opinion d'un neutre sur le bolshevism magyar,* Librairie Française, Berne, 1919.

KOLOZSVARY, BLASIUS (BELA KUN): *Von Revolution zu Revolution,* Genossenschaftsverlag der "Neuen Erde," Vienna, 1920.

Rakosi, Matyas: *The Guilty Man of Hungary*, Free Hungarians, London, 1944.
Vambery, Rustem: *A Rákosi Fez*, Budapest, 1935.

CHAPTER 9: ROMANIA

Aus den Folterkammern Rumäniens, edited by C. G. Costa-Foru. Published for the Romanian League for Human Rights by Kulturpolitischer Verlag, Vienna, 1925.
Politics and Political Parties in Romania, International Reference Library, London, 1936.
Roucek, Joseph S.: *Contemporary Roumania and Her Problems*, Stanford University Press, 1932.

CHAPTER 10: BULGARIA

La Conspiration Bolcheviste Contre La Bulgarie, no publisher given, printed at Imprimerie de la Cour, Sofia, 1925.
Malone, Colonel C. L.: *Bulgaria, the Bulgarian Social Democratic Party and the Labour and Socialist International*, Plebs League, London, 1925.
Markham, Reuben H.: *Meet Bulgaria*, published by the author, Sofia, 1931.
Swire, J.: *Bulgarian Conspiracy*, R. Hale, London, 1939.
Todorow, Kosta: *Balkan Firebrand*, Alliance-Ziff-Davis, New York-Chicago, 1942.

CHAPTER 11: YUGOSLAVIA

Struggle, translated and with a preface by Louis Adamic, Tomorrow Publishers, New York, 1935.
Fotitch, Constantin A.: *The Political Situation in Yugoslavia*, Washington, D. C., 1945.
Kardelj, Edvard: *Put nove Yugoslavia*, Tanyug, London, 1944.
Martin, David: *Ally Betrayed*, Prentice-Hall, New York, 1946.
Melville, C. F.: *Balkan Racket*, Jarrolds, London, 1941.

CHAPTER 12: ALBANIA

Chekrezi, Constantin A.: *Albania, Past and Present*, Macmillan, New York, 1919.
Lepon, C. A.: *Unconquerable Albania*, Albanian Liberation Committee, Chicago, 1944.
Robinson, Vandeleur: *Albania's Road to Freedom*, Allen & Unwin, London, 1941.

CHAPTER 13: GREECE

ANONYMOUS: *Greece, 1821 to 1941*, American Friends of Greece, New York, 1941.

BIRTLES, BERT: *Exiles in the Aegean*, Gollancz, London, 1938; *The Truth about Greece*, Greek Unity Committee, London, 1944.

CHASE, GEORGE H., editor: *Greece of Tomorrow*, American Friends of Greece, New York, 1943.

METAXAS, IOANNES (GEORGE): *La Grecia contro il Comunismo*, Edizioni C.A.U.R., Rome, 1938.

NOEL-BAKER, FRANCIS E.: *Greece, the Whole Story*, Hutchinson, London, 1946.

PISTOLAKIS, STELIAS W.: *The Truth about Greece*, Greek-American Committee for National Unity, New York, 1944.

CHAPTER 14: GERMANY

ANONYMOUS: *Was will der Spartakusbund?*, Verlag der KPD, Berlin, 1919.

EISLER, GERHART, and ALBERT NORDEN: *The New German Unity*, International Publishers, New York, 1945.

FISCHER, RUTH: *Stalin and the German Communists*, Harvard University Press, Cambridge, Mass., 1947.

LENZ, JOSEF: *Was wollen die Kommunisten?*, Internationale Verlagsanstalten, Berlin, 1927.

MERKER, PAUL: *Deutschland: Sein oder Nicht-Sein*, El Libro Libre, Mexico City, 1944.

MERKER, PAUL: *Revolutionäre Gewerkschaftsstrategie*, Hoym, Hamburg, 1929.

NEUMANN, HEINZ: *Maslows Offensive gegen den Leninismus*, Hoym, Hamburg, 1925.

NOSKE, GUSTAV: *Die Abwehr des Bolschewismus*, in *Zehn Jahre deutscher Geschichte*, Stohlberg, Berlin, 1928.

PIECK, WILHELM: *Der Neue Weg*, Editions Prométhée, Strasbourg, 1935.

PIECK, WILHELM: *Wir kämpfen für ein Räte-Deutschland*, Foreign-Language Publishing House, Moscow, 1934.

Programm der Kommunistischen Arbeiter-Partei Deutschlands, Verlag der KAPD, Berlin, 1920.

PUTZ, HANS: Dokumente Kommunistischer Führer-Korruption, Wildeis, Leipzig, 1931.

RADEK, KARL: *Die Entwicklung der deutschen Revolution*, Hoym, Hamburg, 1920.

RADEK, KARL: *Proletarische Diktatur und Terrorismus*, Hoym, Hamburg, 1919.

THALHEIMER, AUGUST: *1923: Eine verpasste Gelegenheit?*, Junius-Verlag, Berlin, 1931.

WEISKOPF, F. C.: *Die Stärkeren*, Neue Deutsche Blätter, Prague, 1934.

CHAPTER 15: FRANCE

BLUM, LEON: *Bolshevism et Socialism*, Librairie Populaire, Paris, 1928.

BLUM, LEON: *For All Mankind*, Viking, New York, 1946.

Le Communisme; d'après les textes du parti et d'après ses actions, L'Illustration, Paris, 1938.

DUCLOS, JACQUES: *Communism, Science and Culture*, International Publishers, New York, 1939.

FERRAT, A.: *Histoire du Parti Communiste Français*, Bureau d'Editions, Paris, 1931.

Manuel Elémentaire du Communiste, Bureau d'Editions, Paris, 1929.

MARTY, ANDRE: *La Revolt de la mer noire*, Bureau d'Editions, Paris, 1932.

THOREZ, MAURICE: *France, Today and Tomorrow*, Communist Party of Great Britain, 1945.

THOREZ, MAURICE: *Notre Lutte pour la Paix*, with an introduction by Jacques Duclos, Editions Sociales Internationales, Paris, 1938.

THOREZ, MAURICE, and MARCEL CACHIN: *Du Front unique au front populaire*, Bureau d'Editions, Paris, 1935.

THOREZ, MAURICE: *Son of the People*, International Publishers, New York, 1938.

TROTSKY, LEON: *Whither France?*, Pioneer Publishers, New York, 1936.

WERTH, ALEXANDER: *Whither France*, Hamilton, London, 1942.

CHAPTER 16: SWITZERLAND

ANONYMOUS: *Am Werk*, Neue Jugend Verlag, Basel, 1921.

Bericht an die Bundesversammlung über die antidemokratische Tätigkeit von Schweizern und Ausländern, Federal Council of Switzerland, Berne, 1946.

CHAPTER 17: NETHERLANDS

GORTER, H.: *De Organisatie voor den Klassenstrujd van het Proletariat*, Kommunistische Arbeiderspartij, Amsterdam, 1922.

MIGNOT, JOHN: *Het Leninisme*, R. Fonteyn, Leuven, 1931.

Het Opportunisme in de Nederlandsche Communistische Partij, J. J. Bos & Co., Amsterdam, 1921.

STEERINGA, G.: *Wat Willen de Communisten?*, J. J. Bos & Co., Amsterdam, 1920.

CHAPTER 18: SCANDINAVIA

ARNESON, BEN A.: *The Democratic Monarchies of Scandinavia*, Van Nostrand, New York, 1939.

BRAATOY, BJARNE: *The New Sweden*, Nelson, London, 1942.

Den Danske Regering of Rigsdag, 1903-1934, Arthur Jensen Forlag, Copenhagen, 1934.

CHAPTER 19: GREAT BRITAIN

Twenty Years of the Communist Party, anniversary issue of the *Labour Monthly,* London, 1940.

ANGELL, SIR NORMAN: *Must Britain Travel the Moscow Road?,* T. Fisher Unwin, London, 1926.

ANONYMOUS: *Elementary Course of Communist Party Training,* Communist Party of Great Britain, undated.

The Betrayal of the Left, edited by Victor Gollancz, Gollancz, London, 1941.

Class against Class, election program, Communist Party of Great Britain, London, 1929.

Communist Papers, Documents selected from those obtained on the arrest of the Communist leaders on the 14th and 21st October, 1925, H.M. Stationery Office, London, 1926.

DUTT, R. PALME: *Why This War?,* Communist Party of Great Britain, London, 1939.

FYFE, HAMILTON: *What Communism Means Today,* Nisbet, London, 1937.

GALLACHER, WILLIAM: *Marxism and the Working Class,* Lawrence and Wishart, London, 1943.

GALLACHER, WILLIAM: *The War and the Workers,* Communist Party of Great Britain, London, 1939.

LASKI, HAROLD J.: *The Secret Battalion,* Labour Publications, London, 1946.

POLLITT, HARRY: *How to Win the War,* Communist Party of Great Britain, London, 1939.

POLLITT, HARRY: *Serving My Time,* Lawrence and Wishart, London, 1940.

The Reds and the General Strike, Communist Party of Great Britain, 1926.

CHAPTER 20: ITALY

ALAZARD, JEAN: *Communisme et "Fascio" en Italie,* Editions Bossard, Paris, 1922.

ANONYMOUS: *Il Processo ai Comunisti Italiani,* Parti Comunisti, Rome, 1924.

AQUILA, GIULIO: *Der Faschismus in Italien,* Hoym, Hamburg, 1923.

BONOMI, IVANOE: *From Socialism to Fascism,* Martin Hopkinson & Co., London, 1924.

KABAKTCHIEV, CHRISTO: *Die Gründung der Kommunistischen Partei Italiens,* Hoym, Hamburg, 1921.

SAAGE, ADOLF: *Mussolini ohne Mythus,* Hess & Co., Vienna-Leipzig, 1931.

CHAPTER 21: SPAIN, PORTUGAL, EIRE

BORKENAU, FRANZ: *The Spanish Cockpit,* Faber, London, 1937.

BUCKLEY, HENRY W.: *Life and Death of the Spanish Republic,* Hamish Hamilton, London, 1940.

DUFFY, REV. CLARENCE: *It Happened in Ireland.* The Christ Press, New York, 1944.

GANNES, HARRY, and THEODORE REPARD: *Spain in Revolt*, Knopf, New York, 1936.

HOGAN, PROFESSOR J.: *Can Ireland Become Communist?*, University of Cork, 1938.

HUBERTUS PRINCE OF LOEWENSTEIN: *A Catholic in Republican Spain*, Gollancz, London, 1937.

IBARRURI, DOLORES: *Speeches and Articles, 1936 to 1938*, International Publishers, New York, 1938.

KOESTLER, ARTHUR: *Ein Spanisches Testament*, Europa-Verlag, Zurich, 1938.

KRIVITSKY, WALTER G.: *In Stalin's Secret Service*, Harper, New York, 1939.

MATTHEWS, HERBERT L.: *Two Wars and More to Come*, Corck and Evans, New York, 1938.

MORROW, FELIX: *Revolution and Counter-revolution in Spain*, Pioneer Publishers, New York, 1938.

Ireland's Path to Freedom. Manifesto of the Communist Party of Ireland, with an introduction by Sean Murray, Sphinx Publications, Dublin, 1933.

O'NEILL, BRIAN: *The War for the Land in Ireland*, Sphinx Publications, Dublin, 1932.

PRIETO, INDALECIO: *La Tragedia de España*, Editorial Claridad, Buenos Aires, 1939.

SALAZAR, OLIVEIRA: *Portogallo e Comunismo*, Beltrami, Florence, 1938.

SOUCHY, AUGUSTIN: *The Tragic Week in May*, Oficina de Información, Exterior de la C.N.T. y F.A.I., Barcelona, 1937.

TROTSKY, LEON: *Die Spanische Lehre*, Edition de Lee, Antwerp, 1938.

DEL VAYO, J. ALVAREZ: *Freedom's Battles*, Knopf, New York, 1940.

WOLFE, BERTRAM D.: *Civil War in Spain*, Workers Age Publishers, New York, 1937.

CHAPTER 22: CANADA

The Report of the Royal Commission to Investigate the Facts Relating to and the Circumstances Surrounding the Communication, by Public Officials and Other Persons in Positions of Trust of Secret and Confidential Information to Agents of a Foreign Power, Ottawa, 1946.

BUCK, TIM: *An Indictment of Capitalism*, Canadian Labor Defense League, Toronto, 1932.

BUCK, TIM: *What We Propose*, Communist Party of Canada, Toronto, 1936.

CHAMBERLIN, WILLIAM HENRY: *Canada, Today and Tomorrow*, Little, Boston, 1942.

COLDWELL, MAJOR JAMES W.: *Left Turn, Canada*, Duell, New York, 1945.

CHAPTER 23: UNITED STATES

BITTELMAN, ALEXANDER: *Milestones in the History of the Communist Party*, Workers Library, New York, 1937.

BROWDER, EARL: *The Communist Party of the U.S.A.*, International Publishers, New York, 1941.

BROWDER, EARL: *Teheran*, International Publishers, New York, 1944.

BUDENZ, LOUIS: *This Is My Story*, Whittlesey, New York, 1947.
COUNTS, GEORGE S., and JOHN L. CHILDS: *America, Russia and the Communist Party*, Day, New York, 1943.
FOSTER, WILLIAM Z.: *From Bryant to Lenin*, International Publishers, 1929.
FOSTER, WILLIAM Z.: *Pages from a Worker's Life*, International Publishers, 1939.
FOSTER, WILLIAM Z.: *Toward Soviet America*, Coward-McCann, New York, 1932.
GITLOW, BENJAMIN: *I Confess*, Dutton, New York, 1940.
GREEN, WILLIAM: *Communist Propaganda in America*, as submitted to the State Department, United States Government, American Federation of Labor, 1934.
LOVESTONE, JAY: *The People's Front Illusion*, Workers Age, New York, 1937.
LYONS, EUGENE: *The Red Decade*, Bobbs-Merrill, Indianapolis-New York, 1941.
The Path of Browder and Foster, Communist Party, U.S.A., New York, 1940.
WALDMAN, LOUIS: *Labor Lawyer*, Dutton, New York, 1940.

CHAPTER 24: CENTRAL AMERICA

ANONYMOUS: *Los Partidos Comunistas de América del Sur y del Caribe, y el movimiento sindical revolucionaria*, Publicaciones Edeya, Barcelona, 1933.
ANONYMOUS: *Strategy of the Communists; a letter from the Communist International to the Mexican Communist Party*, Workers Party, Chicago, 1923.
BEALS, CARLETON: *America South*, Lippincott, Philadelphia, 1937.
CALDERIO, FRANCISCO (BLAS ROCA): *Al Combate!* Ediciones del Partido Socialista Popular, Havana, 1946.
CALDERIO, FRANCISCO (BLAS ROCA): *Cuba y la guerra imperialista*, Ediciones Sociales, Havana, 1939.
CALDERIO, FRANCISCO (BLAS ROCA): *Estados Unidos, Teheran y la América Latina*, Ediciones Sociales, Havana, 1945.
ENCINA, DIONISIO: *Fuero el Imperialismo sus Agentes*, Editorial Popular, Mexico City, 1940.
LOMBARDO TOLEDANO, VICENTE: *Lenin, el Genio*, Universidad Obrera de Mexico, Mexico City, 1942.
LOMBARDO TOLEDANO, VICENTE: *La Revolución Rusa, la Revolución Mexicana —pasado, presente, porvenir*, Universidad Obrera de Mexico, Mexico City, 1943.
MONTAGUE, LUDWELL LEE: *Haiti and the United States, 1714-1938*, Duke University Press, Durham, N. C., 1940.
PARTIDO COMUNISTA MEXICANA: *Primero Congreso Extraordinario*, Editorial Popular, Mexico City, 1940.
TUGWELL, REXFORD G.: *The Stricken Land; the Story of Puerto Rico*, Doubleday, New York, 1946.

CHAPTER 25: BRAZIL

ANONYMOUS: *Luís Carlos Prestes*, Workers Library, New York, 1936.
LOEWENSTEIN, KARL: *Brazil under Vargas*, Vanguard, New York, 1942.

CHAPTER 26: SOUTH AMERICA

ALLEN, HENRY J.: *Venezuela, a Democracy*, Doubleday, New York, 1940.

CUSANO, ANGEL MARIA: *Sud America bajo la Amenaza Soviética*, Barreiro, Montevideo, 1939.

DE LA GUARDIA, CRISTOBAL: *Nuestra Pequeña Obra; Estudios Sobre el Comunismo*, Fernandez, Havana, 1939.

ESTRADA, JOSE M.: *Problemas Argentinos*, Impr. de la Universidad, Buenos Aires, 1943.

FITTE, RODOLFO: *Génesis de un Sentimiento Democrático*, Buenos Aires, 1944.

GOMEZ, EUGENIO: *¿Qué Pasó el 21 de Febrero?* Editorial "America," Montevideo, 1943.

GOMEZ, EUGENIO: *Por la Unión Nacional*, Partido Comunista, Montevideo, 1944.

JOSEPH, RAY: *Argentine Diary*, Random House, New York, 1944.

PEREZ, RICARDO: *Los Fanatismos Políticos*, Baranquilla, 1934.

PIVEL DEVOTO, JUAN E.: *Historia de los Partidos Políticos en el Uruguay*, Garcia, Montevideo, 1942.

RESTREPO, FELIX: *El Comunismo en Colombia*, Universidad Católica Bolivariana, Medellin, 1938.

SANCHEZ, RODRIGO: *Panorama Político de Nicaragua*, Managua, 1940.

VELASCO IBARRA, JOSE MARIA: *Letter Addressed to President Arroyo del Rio*, Lima, 1941.

WEIL, FELIX J.: *Argentine Riddle*, Day, New York, 1944.

CHAPTER 27: JAPAN

Fortune Magazine, September, 1936.

CHAMBERLIN, WILLIAM HENRY: *Japan over Asia*, Little, Boston, 1939.

Japan's Prospect, School for Overseas Administration, Harvard University Press, Cambridge, Mass., 1946.

KENNEDY, M. D.: *Changing Fabric of Japan*, Constable, London, 1930.

ROTH, ANDREW: *Dilemma in Japan*, Little, Boston, 1945.

CHAPTER 28: KOREA

GRAJDANZEV, ANDREW J.: *Modern Korea*, Institute of Pacific Relations, and John Day, New York, 1944.

OLIVER, ROBERT T.: *Korea: Forgotten Nation*, with an introduction by Syngman Rhee, Public Affairs Press, Washington, D. C., 1944.

CHAPTER 29: CHINA

FORMAN, HARRISON: *Report from Red China*, Holt, New York, 1945.

MAO TSE-TUNG: *China and the Second Imperialist War*, New China Information Committee, Chungking, 1939.

MAO TSE-TUNG: *China's New Democracy*, International Publishers, New York, 1943.

MAO TSE-TUNG: *The Fight for a New China*, New Century Publishers, New York, 1945.

MAO TSE-TUNG: *The New Stage*, New China Information Committee, Chungking, 1938.

MAO TSE-TUNG: *Red China*, International Publishers, New York, 1934.

POWELL, J. B.: *My Twenty-five Years in China*, Macmillan, New York, 1945.

ROSINGER, LAWRENCE K.: *China's Crisis*, Knopf, New York, 1945.

SMEDLEY, AGNES: *China Fights Back*, Vanguard, New York, 1938.

SNOW, EDGAR: *Red Star Over China*, Garden City Publishing Company, Garden City, N. Y., 1939.

STEIN, GUNTHER: *The Challenge of Red China*, Whittlesey, New York, 1945.

STRONG, ANNA LOUISE: *One Fifth of Mankind*, Modern Age, 1938.

THOMAS, JAMES: *Die Kantoner Kommune*, Mopr-Verlag, Zurich, 1933.

WALES, NYM (HELEN FOSTER SNOW): *Inside Red China*, Doubleday, New York, 1939.

WANG MING: *Fifteen Years of Struggle in China*, Workers Library, New York, 1937.

WHITE, THEODORE, and ANNALEE JACOBY: *Thunder out of China*, Sloan, New York, 1946.

World-wide Soviet Plots, documents seized at the USSR Embassy in Peking, Tientsin Press, Tientsin, 1928.

YAKHONTOFF, VICTOR A.: *The Chinese Soviets*, Coward-McCann, New York, 1934.

CHAPTER 30: SOUTHEAST PACIFIC

BEAGLEHOLE, JOHN C.: *New Zealand*, Allen & Unwin, London, 1936.

CHRISTIAN, JOHN L.: *Modern Burma*, University of California, Los Angeles, 1942.

DE HAAS, J. ANTON: *Our Allies: The Netherlands East Indies*, Oxford, New York, 1942.

GRANT, W. J.: *The New Burma*, Allen & Unwin, London, 1940.

JOSHI, P. C.: *The Indian Communist Party*, Communist Party of Great Britain, London, 1942.

JOSHI, P. C.: *Release the Patriots!* People's Publishing House, Bombay, 1942.

MARQUARDT, FREDERIC S.: *Before Bataan and After*, Bobbs-Merrill, Indianapolis, 1943.

MILLS, LENNOX: *British Rule in Eastern Asia*, University of Minnesota Press, Minneapolis, 1942.

MUSSEN, SIR GERALD: *Australia's Tomorrow*, Robertson, Melbourne, 1944.

Rosinger, Lawrence K.: *Restless India*, Holt, New York, 1946.

Sharkey, L. L.: *Australia Marches On*, Communist Party of Australia, Sydney, 1943.

Smith, Robert Aura: *Divided India*, Whittlesey, New York, 1947.

CHAPTER 31: NEAR EAST AND AFRICA

Avalov, M.: *Le Caucase, le Bolchevisme et la Turquie*, Comité National d'Études Sociales, Boulogne, 1920.

Ben-Horin, Eliahu: *The Middle East, Crossroads of History*, Norton, New York, 1943.

Communist Party of South Africa: *The Communists Plan for Victory*, Johannesburg, 1943.

Dennen, Leon: *Trouble Zone*, Ziff-Davis, New York and Chicago, 1945.

Hurwicz, Elias: *Die Orientpolitik der Dritten Internationale*, Deutsche Verlagsgesellschaft, Berlin, 1927.

Ireland, Philip W. (editor): *The Near East, Problems and Prospects*, University of Chicago Press, Chicago, 1942.

Jackh, Ernest: *The Rising Crescent*, Farrar, New York, 1944.

Locker, Berl: *Moskve un Tsyionism*, Jewish Socialist Workers Alliance, Vienna, 1921.

Millspaugh, A. C.: *Americans in Persia*, Brookings, Washington, D. C., 1946.

Radek, Karl: *Liquidation des Versailler Friedens*, Verlag der Kommunistischen Internationale, Hamburg, 1922.

Sherman, Bezalel: *The Communists in Palestine*, League for National Jewish Labor in Palestine, New York, 1939.

Shotwell, James T.: *Turkey at the Straits*, Macmillan, New York, 1940.

Stark, Freya: *The Arab Island*, Knopf, New York, 1945.

CHAPTER 32: WHAT ARE THE SOURCES OF COMMUNIST STRENGTH?

Austin, Frederick B.: *The Red Flag*, Lippincott, Philadelphia, 1934.

Brickner, Richard M.: *Is Germany Incurable?*, Lippincott, Philadelphia, 1943.

Brinton, Crane: *The Anatomy of Revolution*, Norton, New York, 1938.

Freeman, Joseph: *An American Testament: A Narrative of Rebels and Romantics*, Farrar, New York, 1936.

Hobson, John A.: *Poverty and Plenty*, Macmillan, New York, 1932.

Hunter, Robert: *Revolution, Why, How, When?*, Harper, New York and London, 1940.

CHAPTER 33: GLOBAL ANTAGONISTS

Atheism and Communism, Encyclical Letter (Divini Redemptoris) of his Holiness Pope Pius XI, National Catholic Welfare Conference, Washington, D. C., 1937.

CHANDLER, ALBERT R.: *The Clash of Political Ideals*, Appleton-Century, New York, 1940.

FEIBLEMAN, JAMES: *Christianity, Communism and the Ideal Society*, Allen & Unwin, London, 1937.

Christianity and Communism, edited by HENRY W. HARRIS, Oxford University, New York, 1937.

MAURIAC, FRANCOIS, PERE DUCATTILL, and others: *Communism and Christianity*, Paladin Press, London, 1938.

MILLER, ALEXANDER: *The Christian Significance of Marx*, S.C.M. Press, London, 1946.

POPE LEO XIII: *Five Great Encyclicals: Labor, Education, Marriage, Social Order, Atheism, Communism*, Paulist Press, New York, 1939.

CHAPTER 34: THE COMINTERN GOES UNDERGROUND

ANONYMOUS: *The Communist International between the Fifth and Sixth World Congress, 1924 to 1928*, Communist Party of Great Britain, London, 1928.

KOMOR, I.: *Ten Years of the Communist International*, Workers Library Publishers, New York, 1929.

KUUSINEN, OTTO W.: *La Position de l'Internationale Communiste devant la crise, la guerre et le fascisme*, Bureau d'Editions, Paris, 1934.

LOZOVSKI, A.: *The World's Trade Union Movement*, Trade Union Educational League, Chicago, 1924.

MANUILSKY, DMITRI Z.: *The Work of the Seventh Congress of the Communist International*, Workers Library Publishers, New York, 1936.

MOLOTOV, VYACHESLAV M.: *Der Sechste Weltkongress und der Kampf für den Kommunismus*, Hoym, Hamburg, 1928.

PYATNITZKY, OSSIP A.: *The Twenty-one Conditions of Admission into the Communist International*, Workers Library Publishers, New York, 1934.

CHAPTER 35: WILL COMMUNISM WIN?

BLOOM, SOLOMON F.: *The World of Nations*, Columbia University Press, New York, 1941.

BLUM, LEON: *For All Mankind*, Viking, New York, 1946.

DOBB, MAURICE: *Political Economy and Capitalism*, Routledge, London, 1937.

HOOK, SIDNEY: *Reason, Social Myth and Democracy*, Day, New York, 1940.

KEYNES, JOHN MAYNARD: *The Economic Consequences of the Peace*, Harcourt, New York, 1920.

KEYNES, JOHN MAYNARD: *Essays in Persuasion*, Harcourt, New York, 1932.

LASKI, HAROLD J.: *Communism*, Holt, New York, 1927.

LASKI, HAROLD J.: *Faith, Reason and Civilization*, Gollancz, London, 1944.

LASKI, HAROLD J.: *Reflections on the Revolution of our Time*, Viking, New York, 1943.

NATIONAL ASSOCIATION OF MANUFACTURERS: *The American Individual Enterprise System*, McGraw-Hill, New York, 1947.

INDEX

A

Abad Santos, Pedro, 380-381
Abbiate, Roland Jacques, 192-193
Acheson, Dean, 92, 361
Acosta, Jorge, 329
Action Française, 179
Adamic, Louis, 116
Adamson, Ernie, 227
Afghanistan, 379, 403-409
Africa, 15, 424-429
African Mine Workers Union, 428
Agrarian Party of Finland, 49
Agrarian Party of Sweden, 207
Aguirre Cerde, Pedro, 330
Ajhir, Teheran, 415
Akel, Cyprus party, 424
Akhbar el Yom, Cairo, 419
Al Ariss, Mustafa, 418, 420
Al Husseini, Amin (*see* Mufti of Jerusalem)
Al Husseini, Jamal, 412
Al Ittahad, Haifa, 413
Albania, 72, 128, 132-136, 146, 148, 416, 479
Alejandrino, Casto, 381-382
Alessandrino, Arturo, 329-330
Alexander, King of Yugoslavia, 114, 126
Alexandros, King of Greece, 139
Alexandrov, G., 164
Algeria, 422-425
Algierson, Einar, 218
Alimin Prawirodirdjo, 393-396
All-Burma Students Union, 396-398

All-Burma Trade Union Congress, 398, 400
All-Burma Women's League, 398
All-Burma Youth League, 398
All-China Peasants Union, 369
All-India Trade Union Congress, 401
All-Slav Congress, 459
Allen, James S., 384
Allied Council for Austria, 76
Allied Control Commission for Finland, 49
Allied Control Council for Germany, 166
Alsop, Joseph, 443
Alsop, Stewart, 443
Alvárez del Vayo, Julio, 68, 248, 252
Amanullah, King of Afghanistan, 404
America, New York, 451
American Federation of Labor, 166, 277, 279, 289, 301-302, 434, 457
American Labor Party, 276, 284-285, 290
American League for Peace and Democracy, 459-460
American League against War and Fascism, 459
American Mercury, New York, quoted, 159
American Peace Mobilization, 460
American Slav Congress, 97, 459
American Veterans Committee, 276
American Youth for Democracy, 276, 289, 458, 462
Amter, Israel, 283, 308
Anarchist movement of Spain, 243-252

517

L